And when he had opened the fourth seal, I heard the voice of the fourth beast say, Come and see. And I looked, and behold a pale horse: and his name that sat on him was Death, and Hell followed with him. And power was given unto them over the fourth part of the earth, to kill with sword, and with hunger, and with death, and with the beasts of the earth.

Book of Revelation

TO MISTY—
HAPPY HAUNTS!

To Misty
Happy Haunting!

A PALE HORSE WAS DEATH

More American Hauntings & Horrors

BY TROY TAYLOR & RENE KRUSE

- A Whitechapel Press Publication from Dark Haven Entertainment -

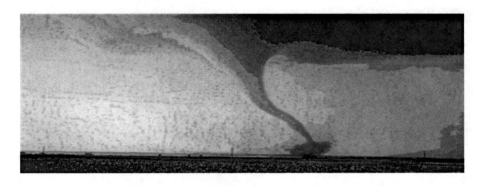

To my girls: Bethany, Elyse and Rachael. They truly are the wind beneath my wings. Special thanks to Troy Taylor for his friendship and his continued faith in me, and to Cindy Stonick for her encouragement, suggestions and keen eye.

And to all those who remind me that life is truly too short. Here's hoping for another trip to the rodeo in one way or another!

Original Cover Artwork Designed by

©Copyright 2012 by Michael Schwab & Troy Taylor (with thanks to April Slaughter)
Visit M & S Graphics at http://www.manyhorses.com/msgraphics.htm

This Book is Published By:

Whitechapel Press
A Division of Dark Haven Entertainment, Inc.
Decatur, Illinois / 1-888-GHOSTLY
Visit us on the internet at http://www.whitechapelpress.com

First Printing -- May 2012
ISBN: 1-892523-79-5

Printed in the United States of America

INTRODUCTION

There will never be an end to the horrors visited on the American landscape.

Just as we were beginning this book – a sequel to our earlier book on American disasters and the hauntings that followed in their wake – calamity struck once more in the southwest Missouri town of Joplin.

On the balmy Sunday afternoon of May 22, 2011, a devastating F-5 tornado blasted through the city. With a maximum width of nearly one mile, it cut a swath of destruction through the southern part of the city before turning eastward and traveling into the rural portions of surrounding counties. Along with the Tri-State Tornado and the 1896 St. Louis Cyclone, it ranks with Missouri's deadliest storms. It was also the first tornado of this magnitude to hit Missouri in more than half a century. Leaving more than 150 dead, it ranks as the seventh deadliest tornado in American history.

The tornado initially touched down just east of the Kansas state line near the end of Joplin's 32nd Street. Damage was minor at first, only tearing up a few trees, but as it tracked southwest near the Twin Hills Country Club, it began to intensify, breaking windows and ripping off roofs. By 5:41 p.m., it had entered more populated parts of the city – and it grew in strength. As it entered the residential subdivisions in southwest Joplin, the damage became catastrophic. As the storm struck St. John's Regional Medical Center, windows were shattered, walls were damaged and upper floors were destroyed. Several people were killed as the building shifted several inches from its foundation. Virtually every house in the area around McClellan Boulevard and 26th Street was wiped out. Trees were ripped out by the roots. Schools, churches and nursing homes were flattened.

The tornado intensified as it tracked eastward, crossing Main Street between 20th and 26th Streets. Every business along that stretch of road was either destroyed or damaged beyond repair. The storm somehow managed to miss the downtown area but it wiped out entire neighborhoods and destroyed two large apartment buildings, as well as the Franklin Technology Center and Joplin High School. It was graduation day, but as luck would have it, no one was at the school. Graduation ceremonies had been held about three miles away at the Missouri Southern State University and had ended before the storm struck.

Bearing down on Range Line Road, Joplin's main commercial strip, the tornado peaked in intensity. It crossed Range Line Road and at this point, was at its greatest size, nearly a mile wide. As the tornado hit the Pizza Hut at 1901 Range Line Road, manager Christopher Lucas thought quickly enough to get four employees and 15 customers into the walk-in freezer. Since the door could not be shut from inside, Lucas wrapped a bungee cable around his arm and the door handle to hold it shut. The force of the storm ripped off the door and Lucas was sucked into the tornado, where he died. A waitress was also pulled from the freezer and killed, but the others inside survived.

The commercial district was destroyed. The storm devoured the Wal-Mart, scores of restaurants and the Home Depot. Seven people in the front of the Home Depot survived when all but two of its walls collapsed in a domino effect. The walls in the back of the building blew outward, saving the lives of 28 people who were huddled there against the force of the storm. Three people died at Wal-Mart when the roof of the building blew off, but 200 more managed to survive. Dozens of others along Range Line Road were not so lucky. Heavy objects, like concrete parking bumpers and large trucks, were carried for significant distances.

The devastation continued in the area of Duquesne Road in southeast Joplin. Homes were wiped out, along with industrial and commercial buildings. The industrial park near the intersection of 20th and Duquesne was flattened. One of the warehouses, made of concrete block and steel, simply vanished in the force of the tornado.

The storm continued on toward Interstate 44, where it weakened, but was still strong enough to wreck and overturn vehicles near U.S. Route 71. The flagging storm then tracked into the rural area of Jasper and Newton counties, where some damage occurred. The tornado's track was at least 22 miles long.

In the aftermath of the storm, people were rescued from the rubble of the more than 7,000 homes. Water, electricity and communications were shut down, but word quickly began to spread of the destruction. Volunteers and emergency workers descended on the city, pulling survivors and lifeless bodies from the ruins. People from the surrounding area and even complete strangers who traveled hundreds of miles to help, worked hard to lend assistance to the shattered community. Within days, power was partially restored, fresh water had arrived and three temporary communication towers had been raised. The Missouri National Guard and a contingent of Missouri State Highway Patrol officers kept order and worked side by side with residents and volunteers during the rescue and recovery efforts.

The days and weeks that followed were a testament to the human spirit and proved what can happen when people come together with a common, unselfish goal. Those days were a sharp contrast to the terrifying minutes of the storm as it wreaked havoc throughout the countryside, forever changing the face of Joplin, Missouri.

Disasters and calamities have been with us since the beginning of recorded time and, as noted in the preceding pages, will always continue. Perhaps this was one of the reasons why we decided to write another book about the way that fires, storms, earthquakes and other assorted disasters have had an effect on American history – and our hauntings. After finishing our previous book on the subject, *And Hell Followed With It*, we found that there were still many stories left to tell. As we searched through old books and newspaper archives, we realized that we had only scratched the surface with the original book. In fact, our list of additional tales was even longer than our first had been. We once again compiled the stories under the categories of the four elements: earth, air, fire and water. This time around, we added one more – "blood," a section that will take a stark and disturbing look at massacres in American history.

The tales of floods, epidemics, fires, explosions, shipwrecks, train wrecks and storms are here, as are numerous stories of ghosts that surround these events. Keep in mind that while not every story in this book will be related to ghosts, you will undoubtedly find them so strange and so horrifying that you will understand why we had to include them. They remind us that disaster can strike anywhere, at any time. This uncomfortable fact will likely cause you some sleepless nights – you can take our word on that.

One side effect of our writings on American disasters and hauntings were a lot of sleepless nights. In the course of writing the stories, both of us had terrifying dreams of death. After a long day of writing about deadly fires, Rene woke up one night convinced that she smelled smoke. Troy had a nightmare about being trapped in a burning theater, fighting to escape the choking smoke and push his way through a crowd of panicked people as the victims of the infamous Iroquois Theater Fire once did. We can both also tell you that the stories in these books were among the most depressing we have ever written -- and yet we never considered *not* writing them. They have also been some of the most compelling and fascinating pieces that we have ever done and they were stories that simply had to be told.

We hope that when you read these tales, you will understand why we had to write them. Among them will be stories that you have never heard before and others that may have taken place almost outside your own back door. Every story in this book has left a bloody mark on the history and landscape of America. They are frightening, disturbing and not for the faint of heart.

Trust us when we tell you because we know it for ourselves....

Troy Taylor
Rene Kruse
Winter 2011-2012

TABLE OF CONTENTS

EARTH

1860: TWO DISASTERS FOR THE PRICE OF ONE
The Pemberton Mill Disaster

All too often, we hear about an accident or event somewhere that resulted in almost unimaginable tragedy and loss of life. This book was built around just such events, and yet there are even more stories where an accident occurs but tragedy is averted by the slimmest chance. In those cases, there remains that haunting codicil: "what if?" What if it had happened 15 minutes earlier, or 15 minutes later? What if it had been a weekday, or what if it had been a weekend? We hear of an elementary school that was struck by a tornado just minutes after the last child had left for the day, or a church that was flattened an hour before it would have been full for Sunday services, or the mine explosion on a holiday that kept many miners at home. There is the train that falls into a ravine shortly after most of the passengers have disembarked. How many times have you heard of a natural gas leak causing an house to explode - but no one was home at the time?

The disaster that took place at the Pemberton Mill on January 10, 1860 was truly such a tragedy that fits into each of these categories – but with a twist. There occurred a terrible disaster that resulted in an impossibly small loss of life, followed by second disaster that left a community, and a nation stunned!

Lawrence, Massachusetts was a city founded to promote the growing textile industry. The land that was to become the site for the new city was purchased in 1845 by a group of Boston industrialists with the intention of bringing in textile mills. The location was perfect for this purpose. It was on the Merrimack River (a great amount of water was required to run the mills), it was just a short train ride from Boston, and it was downriver from Lowell. The city of Lowell had been founded twenty years earlier and was already the largest textile producer in the U.S. The Boston investors were certain that they could capitalize on the growing demand for manufactured textiles and the already established industries in the area.

There was another advantage to the location -- a huge labor force that was ready, willing and able. For years, men had been traveling to Europe, encouraging immigration to the New England states by guaranteeing employment and housing. As ships arrived in New York and Boston harbors, there were wagons waiting to take the immigrants straight to the textile mills. In some cases, these newcomers to America's shores were on a ship one day and operating a loom the next. Their ranks included men, women and children. It was a sad fact that children as young as eight years old were employed in the mills. The new city (to be named Lawrence, after Congressman Abbott Lawrence, one of the initial investors) would simply tap into the already established pipeline of workers. Unbeknownst to the mill owners, they were about to get a great boom in the labor market. The "Great Famine" (better known in America as the Irish Potato Famine) was a time of mass starvation and disease in Ireland. Between 1845 and 1852, over a million Irish people died and another million immigrated - mainly to the U.S. - where jobs awaited them in the textile mills.

The Boston investors were exactly correct in their plans. Lawrence did indeed become a major player in textiles. The city was incorporated in 1853 and within a few years, several very large mills had been built and work was underway. Several tenements had been built along with the mills since the city was brand new and the factory workers would need housing soon as they arrived so they could get right to work.

It all seemed too good to be true. Business was booming and by 1860, only seven years after it was founded, Lawrence had a population of over 17,000. It had been nicknamed "Immigrant City," employing workers from almost every country in Europe and French Canadians as well.

The dreams of the Boston investors had come true in ways they probably hadn't dared to imagine but not so for the immigrants. True, they had received what they had been promised, but it wasn't really what they had expected. Almost anyone who wanted a job could easily get one. The mills needed as many unskilled workers as they did those with specialized training. They worked 65 hours per week and the vast majority of workers (called "operatives") earned about 40 cents a day, for a total about $2.00 per week. At those wages, a head of household couldn't possibly earn enough to support his or her family, so entire families had to work in the mills.

The single largest group in the textile labor force was women, and usually young women. The largest employer in Lawrence was the American Woolen Company. Over half of their operatives were girls between 14 and 18. Many children accompanied their parents and older siblings into the mills, some as young as eight, but most companies shied away from hiring children that young, preferring to wait till they were at least 10. Women and children could do much of the work and it was expected that they would be paid less than the men. It was a sound business practice for increasing profits.

Housing was another one of the promises made to immigrants when they were being enticed to come and work. This promise, too, was kept, though again very

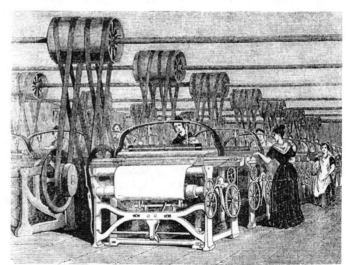

A sketch of a pleasant day for women in the mill, though reality would present a more harsh picture.

likely not as the immigrants envisioned. Lawrence operatives and their families lived in overcrowded and dangerous tenement buildings. Frequently, several families had to share a single apartment as wages were low and rent was high. It was the only way they could afford to keep a roof over their heads. Food was expensive, too. The main staples were bread, molasses and beans. Meat was costly and was usually reserved for holidays.

The working and living conditions did not allow for a healthy work force. The mills were terribly dangerous, especially for the children. It was not unheard of for an operative to be terribly injured, perhaps losing a hand or arm in a loom. The procedure was to escort the injured outside where they would wait, in hopes that they did not bleed to death, until a friend or family member would find them and take them home. Workplace injuries, along with disease and malnutrition, took a very high toll. A child in Lawrence or one of the other mill towns had only a 50 percent chance of surviving past the age of six. Life expectancy wasn't much better for adults. Of those who worked in a textile mill, 36 out of every 100 men and women died before reaching the ripe old age of 25.

In 1853, John Lowell and his brother-in-law, J. Pickering Putnam, decided to go into the textile business. They hired an engineer named Charles H. Bigelow to construct a large building that would house the most modern textile equipment available. Their new Pemberton Mill, a cotton-spinning mill, met their expectations and then some. The building was five stories high with a basement and measured 280 feet long and 84 feet wide, giving them roughly 141,000 square feet of workspace. The building and equipment cost a previously unheard-of amount of $850,000. Several hundred operatives were hired and Lowell and Putnam were in business.

After only four years, Lowell and Putnam lost their nerve during a financial panic in 1857. They sold Pemberton Mill to George Howe and David Nevins, Sr. for a substantial loss. The new owners moved in more equipment and hired more operatives to increase the output. The mill operated with great success and earned the owners an average of $1.5 million each year. The building was so packed with machines and workers that it was said to "vibrate with energy." Based on what was to come, that vibration was more than likely literal rather than figurative, as over 1,000 people toiled there, running 2,700 spindles and 700 looms.

The industrial area where the Pemberton Mill was located had several working textile mills, situated side by side along the Merrimack River. There were thousands of operatives going to and from work at the same times each day. The area was terribly congested with buildings and people and buildings filled with people. Looking back, it was a disaster waiting to happen. And so it was that on Tuesday, January 10, 1860, at a few minutes before 5:00 in the afternoon, there were many people on hand to witness what was to be the single worst industrial accident in Massachusetts, and one of the worst in U.S. history.

People outside and inside the Pemberton Mill building were startled when, as described in *American Heritage* magazine: "Suddenly there was a sharp rattle, and then a prolonged, deafening crash. A section of the building's brick wall seemed to bulge out and explode, and then, literally in seconds, the Pemberton collapsed. Tons of machinery crashed down through crumpling floors, dragging trapped, screaming victims along in their downward path. The factory was a heap of twisted iron, splintered beams, pulverized bricks, and agonized, imprisoned human flesh."

Workers from neighboring mills could do nothing but watch in horror and disbelief as the entire Pemberton building - all five stories - collapsed before their eyes.

The air was rent by the screams of the operatives trapped inside the ruins. Where there was once a huge industrial building was now a pile of rubble under a huge plume of dust. Nothing remained except a section of an exterior rear wall. Everything else was gone, reduced to a massive pile of rubble. Cries for help filled the air as workers in nearby mills rushed to the scene. Somewhere between 800 and 900 people had been in the building when it collapsed.

To the utter amazement of the witnesses, living, breathing people began crawling out of the rubble. A few hundred people were either unhurt or had only minor injuries and were able to pull themselves from the wreckage. With a catastrophic event that should have meant certain death for almost everyone in the building; there were survivors -- many survivors! In fact, other than a few dozen who had died instantly, almost everyone in the building survived the collapse, even after falling several stories as the floors fell from beneath their feet. Iron columns had crumbled, massive beams had had splintered, and many tons of brick and mortar lay in heaps, but somehow many, many people were still alive. Witnesses believed it was nothing short of a miracle.

As the dust began to settle, more than 600 workers were still held captive in the tangled, twisted ruins. Some were merely trapped, some had minor or at least survivable wounds and still others were still breathing but had sustained substantial injuries. George Howe, one of the owners, had escaped as the structure was falling. His partner, David Nevins, was away from the building when it fell.

Apparently, the large and heavy machinery inside the building that had helped cause the collapse also helped protect the workers inside. Those who were able to avoid being crushed by the falling machines were in turn protected by them, as they created safe pockets of space while holding up the timbers and other debris. In some cases, as many as 25 people survived by huddling in the same protected space.

One woman, who was standing near a window along the wall that remained standing, became so frightened that she threw her bonnet and shawl out the window and then jumped out herself. She soon died from injuries sustained from her dramatic leap.

While many people were able to free themselves from the wreckage, it took herculean efforts to free others. Workers from nearby mills and the surrounding community ran to the aid of the victims. Every able- bodied person pitched in, working at a breakneck pace to free trapped people as quickly as they could. Friends and family members arrived on the scene and began a frantic search for their loved ones. A general alarm had gone out to the Lawrence fire department and to those in the surrounding towns. When the firefighters arrived they climbed down and went to work with the rescue effort.

There were many tales of daring escapes, remarkable rescues and unbelievable recoveries. A group of men heard a young girl screaming and crying for help. She was found covered by at least 10 feet of rubble and debris. After working to remove the twisted mass from on top of her, the rescuers were shocked when the girl jumped up unhurt and smiling, thanked them for freeing her, and ran off to find her family. In another part of the ruins, a family of five was released from their tomb unharmed when a large section of floor was lifted from above them. They climbed from the hole, the terrified mother scooped her children to her, and praising their rescuers, cried out a prayer of thanks.

Another miraculous escape was that of Selina Weeks. Miss Weeks had been working in the fifth-floor spool room and dropped with it when the building fell. As she regained her senses, she realized that she was still standing on the spool room floor, but was waist-deep in debris. She was able to dig her way out and made her way home unharmed.

At the same time that Miss Weeks fell from the top floor, Damon Wyhom was working in the basement. He found himself completely buried under a dozen feet of debris. After repeated tries, he was able to tunnel his way to an area where rescuers could reach him and he was pulled to safety.

A small boy who was working on one of the upper floors realized what was happening when he heard the crashes. He jumped into a trashcan and rode down with the floor, becoming buried under several feet of wreckage. When rescuers lifted the material from what contemporary reports described as his "safety capsule," he jumped out and walked away as if nothing had happened.

Three young sisters with the appropriate surname of Luck all survived. Jane Luck was buried for nearly five hours but was released unharmed. Her sister Anna Luck heard the crashing as the building collapsed and dove under her loom. She called to her other sister and friend to do the same. All three of the girls survived. Not all of the Luck family was as lucky. The girls' two uncles who were working in the mill were killed.

Thomas Watson was on the fifth floor when it fell. His jaw was broken in three places, and he sustained three broken ribs and several deep cuts. Despite his injuries, he climbed out from the rubble unaided. He noticed to his surprise that he had not felt any pain until he was walking about free. His wife also worked at the mill, but that day she had stayed home for the first time since she had started work six months before. It so happened that Watson was to leave on a trip the next day and she had stayed home to prepare his traveling clothes and pack his things.

A child was found pinned under a large iron pillar by a rescue team, lying next to a woman. The following is a contemporary description of the dramatic events that followed:

"On Tuesday evening, while two thousand men were exerting every energy in rescuing the survivors from their living sepulchers, and the dead from the rubbish which buried them, a party came upon the body of a little girl. She lay apparently crushed beneath a ponderous block of iron, weighing over a thousand pounds, and which covered her body to her chin. Her back was pressed against a huge timber, one of her arms was thrust to the elbow through a ring in a piece of machinery, and she was completely wedged in by heavy iron gearing.

Intent only on preserving her features and form as little disfigured as possible, the men labored carefully to remove the block of iron without crushing her still further. Four of them tugged upon it and succeeded in loosening it. The other rubbish was then removed, and the body taken out, when, what was the surprise and joy of the men to find that they had rescued a living girl instead of a corpse, and more, that her injuries were not fatal, but comparatively trifling. The heavy iron had met with some more powerful obstruction than her body, and her life was spared as if by a miracle.

The body of the woman lying next to her was extracted from the ruins by her friends and relatives. The bricks and iron had buried her so tightly that there were no hopes of her survival. When her body was at last drawn out, the circle of friends found their worst fears confirmed. Her husband took her carefully in his arms, and bore her toward his home. A number of relatives were there waiting. Suddenly the woman revived, and throwing up her hand cried out: "I'm safe, I'm safe!" She was received as one risen from the dead."

Henry Nice was both victim and hero. He was working in the boiler room when the building fell. As rubble began to fall on him, he rushed for the door and fell out onto the porch, where debris piled onto him. After being nearly suffocated by a cloud of steam and dust, he was able to burrow through to safety, but instead of leaving, he began a search of the area. He found a young girl whose arms and legs were injured, pinned to the floor by a beam across her neck. He found a saw and cut her free, passing her off to a rescue team as he continued to search for survivors. Then, he located a friend of his, lying over a young woman who was pinned under a mass of wreckage. The woman urged Nice to free the man first as she was not as badly injured. After the man was removed, a team worked feverishly, trying to remove a heavy piece of machinery from over her, but they were unable to free her. They planned to come back to later with tools but after the second disaster of

Mr. Adams and his daring self-rescue. Sketch: *Frank Leslie's Magazine*, January 21, 1860.

An unknown woman burns to death, just as she is about to be freed. Sketch: *Frank Leslie's Magazine*, January 21, 1860.

the night befell them, she was killed where she lay.

In another area, a man named Adams was trapped in the basement by several heavy beams. Because of the precarious position of the beams relative to where he was trapped, rescuers were unable to reach him, but instead passed him an axe and a saw. With these tools, he was able to cut and chop his way to freedom.

Dramatic rescue efforts continued throughout the site, with person after person being pulled from the wreckage. The Lawrence City Hall had been prepared for double duty as a makeshift morgue and as a hospital. As the dead were removed, they were carefully carried to the "dead room." When the injured were removed, they were taken to the hospital room in the same building.

It was a cold January day, but the rescuers stayed warm with exertion. Soon it began to grow dark and colder. Large bonfires were built in a circle around the collapsed building to provide light for the rescuers as they continued their search into the darkness. At about 9:30 that night, after four and a half hours and hundreds of people freed from the wreckage, someone either kicked over or dropped an oil lamp. The burning fluid quickly spread to a pile of debris. The flames shot across the splintered wood and wads of cotton, some soaked with oil, and quickly ignited the ruins of the building where many trapped but living people were waiting to be released. The second disaster of the day had begun.

In one area, a man who saw the flames coming toward him cut his throat rather than be burned to death. He was rescued before the fire reached him but he soon died of his injuries. In another section, very near to where the fire started, rescuers had nearly succeeded in freeing a woman when the fire swept through. She had survived the collapse, only to be consumed by the fire.

As the fire spread, rescue volunteers, firemen, friends and family were forced back by the extreme heat. Fire crews poured a steady stream of water on the burning section, seeking to halt the spread of flames while rescues

Ruins of the Pemberton Mill building, after the fire. *Frank Leslie's Magazine,* **January 21, 1860.**

continued on the other side, but it was a losing battle. The fire soon spread across the entire ruin and the terrified screams of those still trapped inside were quickly silenced, with only the sounds of the fire remaining. Fourteen people were known to have burned to death in the sight of their friends and families.

The fire burned long and hot, raging through the night and into the next day, Wednesday, January 11. There was little that anyone could do but stand back and watch. Anyone who had been left alive after the collapse was now dead, ravaged by fire. By evening, the fire had mostly burned itself out but too much heat was radiating from the wreckage for anyone to approach.

During the day on Wednesday, a crowd had begun to form. Flocks of people from other towns and cities, including Boston, began arriving by train. They filled every available inch of space they could find, filling the streets and lining the bridge over the Merrimack. They had come to see the wreckage of the once-thriving factory. They wanted to be a part of history, to be able to say that they had been there to see what was left after the great building had collapsed. As the day drew on, a light rain had begun to fall, later turning to snow. The Pemberton Mill Company took over the ruins. From here on, company men would be directing the efforts, as rescue had become recovery.

By 10:00 o'clock Thursday morning, January 12, the fire was almost completely out but smoke continued to bellow up from deep inside the rubble. The firefighters continued to pour streams of water where they saw smoke. It was still too hot to enter the wreckage so recovery efforts had to be put off another day. The smoke and cold didn't seem to deter the crowds of the morbidly curious. They would have to wait another day to see flesh and bone released from the ashes. As snow continued to fall, it drifted down through the burned-out beams and machinery, falling gently onto the upraised faces of charred corpses who patiently waited to be released from their tomb and taken to their families.

On Friday morning, January 13, the pit had cooled enough for the recovery efforts to continue. Derricks were set up around the ruin to help lift and remove heavy machinery and debris. Victims were once again being removed, but this time, none were among the living. The recovery was now more dangerous, but the 100 men working there were determined that no one would be left in that miserable pit. The crowd continued to look on, but a few of the men left the safety of the road and stepped inside the perimeter, adding themselves to the recovery operation.

At one point, as groups of two and three worked their way through the wreckage, a man remembered where he had seen a young woman named Kate Cooney partially buried. She had been struck by a beam and her legs were pinned under her so she couldn't move. It had been just before the fire found her that he had heard her cries for help. The men dug in the area the man indicated and they soon came upon her body. She had been badly burned about her head and neck and her arms had been burned off up to her elbows, but her lower body was relatively untouched. Her skirt and apron were not even scorched.

Thirteen more bodies were pulled out on Saturday, the 14th. As before, some were only partially burned. Some were completely charred, and others were found with only portions of limbs remaining to indicate that a human body had once lain in that spot. As darkness approached, the men stopped working, as they did not want to further mutilate, by accident, any bodies they might find in the darkness. They made every effort to get everybody identified and returned to the people who loved them.

On Sunday the 15th, over 150 men arrived for work at sunrise and the search continued. They did not wish to cause any more grief than was absolutely necessary for the families that were still waiting for someone to be pulled out of the rubble. They chose to work through their one day of rest.

On January 20, ten days after the building had collapsed, the last bodies were recovered from the debris. These bodies were completely unrecognizable. They were taken to the "dead room" at the city hall, even though no one there would be able to claim them. In the end, 13 bodies had been charred and mutilated beyond any possibility of identification. A little more than two months after the disaster, the city purchased a plot in Lawrence's Bellevue Cemetery and on Sunday, March 4, 1869, funeral services were held and the remains of the unknown workers were laid to rest. Later, a monument was placed at the head of the plot in memory of all who lost their lives in Pemberton Mill.

The crowds remained at the disaster site for many days after the last body had been removed. It was as if they just couldn't move on. Soon, people began to wander onto the site and started sifting through the debris, searching for relics or mementos of the disaster. A man from St. Louis collected a large bundle of gristly souvenirs that included burned clothing from some of the victims. Two New Yorkers collected pieces of broken bricks and splinters of burned beams. The ferocity with which the relic-seekers went about their business was becoming a hazard to the cleanup crews and the intruders alike. Eventually, realizing it had to stop, the mayor and the company gave orders for it to stop, and hired men to guard the ruins. Eventually, the crowds dispersed and went home.

Calls went out across the country for financial assistance. The New England Society of Manufacturers collected a total of $19,000 and handed it over to Mayor Daniel Saunders. Boston clubs and societies brought in another $9,000. Churches, schools, and fraternal organizations collected donations from around the country, raising the total to $65,579.29. Mayor Saunders put together a committee to determine how best to use the money to assist the victims.

Hearings were held to investigate the cause of the collapse and to determine fault. After several days of testimony, the blame was laid at the door of engineer Charles Bigelow. The primary problems with the building lay in faulty, or otherwise substandard materials. The iron pillars that had been put in place to support the heavy machinery were found to be brittle and badly cast. In a moment of stress, they had crumbled. It was also determined that the mortar used with the bricks was extremely poor and was completely ineffective at holding the brick joints together. The committee felt that the use of appropriate materials and construction systems should have been Bigelow's responsibility and that his design must somehow be at fault as well. The committee failed to take into account that most of the other mill buildings in Lawrence had also been designed and built by Bigelow. They also ignored the fact that the mill's second owners had severely overloaded the structure, well beyond its design limits. No blame was assigned to the owners, since they obviously had purchased a faulty building without knowledge of its shortcomings.

Some of the final statistics were startling. Women and girls made up 62 percent of the mill's workforce, but they made up 73 percent of the dead and missing and 67 percent of the injured, leaving questions of how these proportions became so out of balance. After the dead and the living had been counted, and counted again, it was believed that of the 1,003 employees of the Pemberton Mill, between 99 and 145 people lost their lives in the disaster. The best estimate as to those injured is 302.

All of these numbers are horrifying and unfortunate, but the most remarkable thing of all is that while a five-story building suffered a catastrophic collapse into rubble in a matter of seconds, nearly 600 people either climbed out or are pulled free of the wreckage without injury, and were able to walk home on their own.

After all the bodies had been recovered, the company called in those who were unemployed as a result of the disaster and hired them to work on the cleanup crews. When all the wreckage had been removed, the owners rebuilt a new mill on the old foundation and reopened for business.

For a long time after the second Pemberton Mill was opened, workers reported seeing people they didn't recognize walking through a room, or down an aisle. The employee might turn a corner and catch a glimpse of a mysterious person wearing old-fashioned clothes who suddenly vanished. It didn't take long for the living workers to suspect that they were sharing their workspace with people who were long since dead. Over time, fewer and fewer people spoke about seeing these spectral workers in the mill. It is impossible to determine if they were appearing less frequently or if the living had grown so accustomed to their ethereal comrades that they no longer noticed when they were around.

The mill has long been closed down but the

The second mill building today.

building still stands on the bank of the Merrimack River. There is talk of turning it into loft-style condominiums, or possibly a shopping center. It will be interesting to see if any of the future occupants of the old Pemberton Mill building turn a corner one day, and come face to face with a woman in a floor-length skirt and long apron, looking for her machine in order to spin cotton into yet another century.

1867: THE "ANGOLA HORROR" TRAIN WRECK

Death seems to have set his mark on the traveler. Every day the record of mortality is continued. Now it is a collision; now the explosion of a locomotive; and then again the sudden precipitation of an entire train down a steep embankment or perhaps into some river. It is a fact that more lives have been lost by accident this year than in some of the severest battles of the war."
Harper's Weekly, 1865

During the nineteenth century, Americans were frequently horrified by the railroad catastrophes that were featured in their daily and weekly newspapers. As more and more people took to the rails for travel, newspaper editors seemingly delighted in presenting stories of just how dangerous the railroads could be. In many ways, they were not exaggerating. Readers were horrified as boilers exploded, bridges collapsed and engines derailed. Reports of wrecks appeared frequently in national journals like *Harper's Weekly* and *Leslie's*, publicizing the frightful cost in lives and property. The stories were accompanied by blood-curdling illustrations of wrecked locomotives, twisted passenger cars and human debris. It was no wonder that railroad accidents haunted the imagination of the American public – and sent shivers down the spines of many of those who even contemplated buying a ticket to travel by rail.

The names of major railroad disasters became household words: Camp Hill, Revere, Chatsworth, Ashtabula and Angola. Books were published on the topic, laced with outpourings of morbid Victorian sentimentality, and popular songs were written about horrendous deaths of passengers and railroad workers.

Apart from the publicity given to railroad wrecks of the era, the possibility of death when traveling by rail was a very genuine one. Some experienced travelers made it a point to get seats in the middle of the train because they believed this to be the safest place to be if the train was hit from either the front or the rear.

It was not human carelessness that caused the vast majority of wrecks in the middle and late 1800s, it was the railroads themselves. After the Civil War, there had been a slow improvement of some railroad equipment to reduce the number of accidents that occurred. Telegraphs replaced the old signal posts, but the telegraph was not universally adopted by railroads until late in the century. Safety devices were added, but the speed of the trains was also

The bridge where the "Angola Horror" accident occurred

increased. In turn, traffic on the lines increased much more quickly than improvements could be made. With more trains, moving at faster speeds, problems were inevitable. To make matters worse, while the engines had been improved, little had been done to update the railroad cars or – most importantly – the rails they ran on and the roadbeds they crossed. In the majority of cases, competing railroad companies used different size tracks, which could spell disaster.

As author and railroad historian Lucius Beebe observed, "The Grim Reaper has never been altogether outdistanced by progress."

The most notorious railroad accident of the day was dubbed the "Angola Horror" when it occurred on December 18, 1867. Nearly 50 people died and many more were burned and badly injured in the wreck, which stunned a country that was still reeling from the Civil War. Accounts of the tragedy, accompanied by grisly illustrations, filled the pages of newspapers and periodicals for weeks — and prompted calls by the public for safer trains, tracks and improved methods for heating rail cars.

The accident was caused by oversized wheels on a narrow-gauge track, a problem not uncommon at the time. During the 1850s and 1860s, scores of independent railroad lines crossed the country, all with varying track widths. Tracks could be as narrow as four feet, eight inches, or as wide as seven feet. To compensate, some companies used "compromise cars," interchangeable vehicles equipped with extra-wide flanges that could be adapted for different track widths. One of these compromise cars was the last coach on the Lake Shore Railroad's New York Express as it made its way out of Angola, New York, on that cold and fateful day.

December 18 was a good day for traveling, accounts later stated. The New York Express picked up travelers in Cleveland, Erie, Dunkirk and other towns as it skimmed the Great Lakes. By midafternoon, the Lake Shore Express, now a couple of hours behind schedule, reached western New York. It consisted of four passenger cars — three first-class and one second-class, each holding about 50 people — plus three or four baggage cars. It also contained several potbellied stoves to heat the coach cars, and kerosene lamps mounted on the walls for lighting.

The hours of the early afternoon slipped past uneventfully on the train. At Dunkirk, New York, the train stopped for 10 minutes and a few passengers boarded. They were the last to do so. At the small village of Silver Creek, the train stopped again, briefly, to take on wood and water. At 2:49 p.m., Silver Creek telegraph operator George P. Gaston noted the departure of the Lake Shore Express from his station. He messaged ahead to J.M. Newton, the daytime agent and telegraph operator in Angola: The express was on its way.

Ahead was Angola, with its small depot and just beyond that a bridge – a plain wood and stone span – that loomed about 50 feet above Big Sister Creek. Only two and a half years before, this same bridge had been crossed by the funeral train of President Abraham Lincoln, carrying his body to its burial place in Illinois.

On December 18, Newton watched as the express steamed through his village, nearly three hours behind schedule, moving at about 28 miles per hour. Newton later testified this was well within a typical range of speed.

On his routine rounds, Conductor Frank Sherman worked his way through the last car of the train. Sherman, a Buffalo resident, would later recall seeing Stephen W. Stewart, a banker and the president of the Oil Creek Railroad, sitting in his usual spot in the last seat. Stewart was a frequent traveler on the Lake Shore Express.

At 3:11 p.m., Sherman opened the door of the end car, stepped through it, and began making his way forward through the second-to-last car. At the same time, Dr. Frederick F. Hoyer, a country physician, walked from the second-to-last car into the one in front of it, a move that most likely saved his life.

Also at 3:11 p.m., passengers felt the first sensations of something wrong with the train – a "trembling motion," was how a wood dealer named Benjamin Betts, who had been riding in a forward car, later described it. It was followed by a terrific jarring sensation and then a shrill whistle rang out to warn the brakemen to stop the train.

Those not on the train could already see what was happening. As the train passed the Angola depot, a local resident and tin shop proprietor named John Martin noticed that the last car rocked unsteadily as the train picked up speed. Martin ran after the train, waving his hat, but his warning came too late. The whistle alerted the two brakemen on board to stop their individual cars, but there were only brakemen working on the train that day and they did not have enough time to stop all seven cars.

An image from *Leslie's Illustrated* of the scene of terror at the site of the accident.

By the time one of the brakemen began working his way to the end of the train, the last car had already derailed and was being dragged sideways across the bridge. With a great screech of twisting metal, its coupling snapped and the car tipped over the ravine and plunged down onto an ice- and snow-covered slope. The second-to-last car, according to Martin, who was still running after the train, along with a number of Angola residents, "scooted the other way... it rolled off sideways like a sawn log."

The cause of the crash was simple – yet deadly. As the express traveled toward the bridge, the unstable compromise car ran over a "frog" – the crossing point of two rails -- in the track about 600 feet past the depot. One of the wheels of the car hit the frog in such a way that it jarred the wheel loose, making it vibrate back and forth. Still, all might have been well if the train's vibrating, off-center wheels had not hit a metal spike just a short distance down the track, throwing the end car even further off balance. As the train sheared the head off the spike, it jumped the tracks.

Once the last car derailed, it began to rock back and forth, slowly at first and then more quickly, sending the passengers into a panic. Many of them tried to run toward to the front of the train but were thrown off their feet by the rocking motion. The car began to pull heavily on the train. As the Lake Shore Express crossed Big Sister Creek, the end car came loose from the train. It felt like something popping loose, survivors later remembered, after the rattling of the derailment. Once free of the train, the car plummeted down into the creek, flipping over several times before shuddered to a stop on the ice.

Meanwhile, the second-to-last car, pulled off balance, held onto the track for a few moments longer. It managed to shakily cross the railroad bridge and started to climb up the opposite side of the embankment. But the motion of the last car's uncoupling proved to be too much. It came off the tracks and tipped over, and then rolled and tumbled back down the embankment and into the creek.

Two railroad cars – and the passengers inside of them – plunged to their doom.

One passenger escaped certain death that day by uncharacteristically missing the train. John D. Rockefeller had planned to take the Lake Shore Express to New York City that morning to check on business operations there. But he got a late start that morning, which was not like him at all.

He was delayed with packing. Rockefeller planned to squeeze in some holiday visits with friends and family in the city before returning home for Christmas, so he packed his luggage with gifts that he intended to give to his relatives and associates there. He sent his bags ahead to Cleveland's Union Station and then, after saying goodbye to his wife and daughter, headed off to catch the train.

Rockefeller was 28, a successful young businessman already well known in the oil refining industry. A disciplined man, Rockefeller prided himself on working hard and keeping to a demanding schedule. He knew that if he caught the 6:40 a.m. Lake Shore Express, due in Buffalo around 1:30 in the afternoon, he could then take the 6:00 p.m. New York Central Express, which would deliver him into Manhattan by 7:00 the next morning, in plenty of time to make full use of the business day. Although his plans were meticulously arranged, Rockefeller arrived at the Cleveland station just a few minutes too late; his bags made the train but he didn't, and it saved his life. Since he had arrived at the station at the last minute, he would have been seated in the last car of the Lake Shore Express.

Rockefeller came across the scene of the accident when his later train was forced to stop in Angola because of the wreck. He immediately telegraphed his wife from the Angola railroad station. "Thank God I am unharmed," his message read, "the six forty train I missed had bad accident."

Rockefeller, of course, lived a long and productive life after the Angola Horror and went on to change the course of American history.

Many others were not so lucky.

Among them was William Towner, 25, a surveyor from Erie, Pennsylvania, who had decided to treat himself to a pleasure trip before the holidays. He left on the express to New York with two friends, J. Alexander Martin and Edward T. Metcalf, who were also young businessmen from Erie.

Jasper and Eunice Fuller, a young married couple, had recently opened a small general store in Spartansburg, Pennsylvania. They were taking the express to Buffalo to buy new stock for their store.

Also on board were Charles Lobdell of La Crosse, Wisconsin, an editor at the *Daily Republican* newspaper; Eliakim B. Forbush of Buffalo, an attorney returning home from a case he had won in Cincinnati, and Isadore Mayer, a New York theatrical agent. There was also a honeymooning couple on board and two men who were traveling to their weddings. The honeymooners were Mr. and Mrs. Granger D. Kent of Grand Island, New York. They were on their way home from their wedding trip.

As the next-to-last train car plunged into the creek gorge, the passengers were thrown about and most were injured — many seriously. Robert M. Russell, a Confederate veteran from Tennessee who had severed under General Nathan Bedford Forrest, was battered so badly that it wasn't clear whether he would live or die. In the end, he survived but the passengers in the last car were not as fortunate. The ones that lived through the derailment and the fall into the creek found themselves in a railroad car that had begun to burn.

The stoves had come loose during the fall, emptying fire and red-hot coals all over the inside of the car. Kerosene spilled from the gas lamps fed the flames, which quickly consumed the wood and upholstery inside the car. "I saw the coals of fire from the stove scattered all over the car," reported Josiah Southwick, an Angola farmer and justice of the peace, who witnessed the disaster from his nearby house. He ran to help, but was stopped by the intense heat. "Inhaling the flames," Southwick later said, "I was obliged to go back."

He wasn't the only one driven back by the fire. Many villagers who ran to the scene of the wreck would report the smell of burning flesh in the air, and the screams of the dying as the car burned. "The car was all in flames," said John Martin, who himself pulled five people from the inferno. "I could not see them," Martin said, "I could hear them."

From inside the car, several gunshots were heard. A reporter later speculated that someone had been carrying a pistol and the intense heat from the fire had ignited the bullets. Another person insisted that some merciful soul had dispatched those helplessly pinned in the wreckage rather than see them roasted alive. There was little anyone could do but stand by in anguish as the trapped passengers died.

The *Erie Observer* reported the tragedy: "The hideous, remorseless flames crackled on; the shrieks died into moans, and moans into silence more terrible, as the pall of death drew over the scene." Eyewitnesses said the screams of the dying lingered for close to five minutes before silence fell over the snow.

Stewart, the railroad president, was among the victims who burned to death in the end car, along with Lobdell, the newspaper editor, and the Fullers of Spartansburg, Pennsylvania. The honeymooning Kents died together. The gold wedding band that Granger had presented his bride — inscribed with her initials — survived the flames. The couple were identified more than a week later by the luggage claim tickets found on their remains.

As for the three friends from Erie — Towner, Martin and Metcalf — they had taken seats together, and all three were burned so badly that their bodies they were almost unrecognizable. Towner was identified and claimed by his brother, brother-in-law and a doctor who came from Erie to recover his remains. Metcalf's body was returned to his family and friends in Erie on Christmas Day. Martin, on the other hand, was so badly burned that

Victims from the accident were taken to the Angola depot but most of them were so badly burned that they could not be identified (*Leslie's Illustrated*, 1867)

he was placed into a wooden case at the scene, along with other remains, for sorting and identification. Weeks later, at the Soldiers' Rest Home in Buffalo, some of Martin's friends eventually identified what they hoped was his body and they took it away with them.

Darkness soon fell over the smoking wreckage. The people of Angola tended to the victims as best they could. Supervising the effort was Dr. Romaine J. Curtiss, Angola's local physician and, until teams of backup doctors arrived later that night from Buffalo, the chief caretaker of the train's wounded. Curtiss, 27, had served as a Union hospital ship surgeon during the Civil War. He checked over the bodies of the burnt and dispatched the badly wounded to nearby homes. He treated those suffering from shock and lesser injuries in the snow at the edge of the creek.

At the residence of Josiah Southwick, "persons were lying in beds and upon the floor, in almost every room in the house, and not only Mr. Southwick's family, but a number of the neighbors...were kindly and most patiently doing all in their power to assuage their pain and make them comfortable," reported *The New York Times*. It would be one of the scores of newspapers around the country that praised the people of Angola for their quick and unselfish response to the disaster.

The bodies of the dead were carried to the Angola depot. There they were boxed, sometimes two or three to a casket, and sent by funeral train to Buffalo. The Soldiers' Rest Home, the Tifft House and the National Hotel all served as temporary morgues where relatives and authorities could view the corpses. A memorial service for the victims took place inside Buffalo's Exchange Street depot on December 22. Afterwards, the boxes were buried in Forest Lawn, a cemetery on the edge of Buffalo. Railroad officials claimed 19 people lay in the boxes; passenger lists, had they been kept, would have indicated that far more unidentified and unclaimed victims presumably lay in the coffins as well. For this reason, no one knows exactly how many victims of the Angola Horror were laid to rest that day. The simple marker that designated the burial spot no longer exists. It fell down, or was taken down, decades ago and has never been replaced.

The disaster had repercussions for American history – often in unexpected ways. The "Angola Horror" shocked the nation and prompted the railroads to make sweeping changes. Compromise cars were no longer used and track gauges finally began to be standardized.

John D. Rockefeller went on to form the Standard Oil Company within three years of the Angola tragedy. By the early 1880s, Rockefeller — perhaps influenced by his brush with disaster — was selling oil products specifically designed to make rail travel safer. An 1883 advertisement for his Mineral Seal 300 Fire Test Burning Oil claimed to be superior "to all other burning oils in this respect, withstanding a heat of 300 degrees before igniting, for which reason it is especially adapted for use in Railway Coaches and Passenger Steam Boats."

Another American businessman, George Westinghouse, was also shocked by the disaster. He became determined to find a quicker and safer way of stopping rail cars in an emergency. The result was an invention that revolutionized train travel: the air brake. By 1893, the federal government made air brakes and automatic couplers mandatory on trains in the United States, a change that cut the accident rate on the nation's rails by 60 percent. The brakes became known as the single most important safety device in railroad history.

It took the deaths of nearly 50 people at Angola to save the lives of countless others in the future.

Drive over Big Sister Creek in Angola today, and you'd never know that it had been the scene of anything important. No marker identifies the spot of the "Angola Horror" train wreck – but locals know what happened and many of them believe that the area where the wreck occurred is haunted.

According to reports, those who travel down a weather-beaten road outside of Angola, a one-way, barely paved street that passes through a dark stretch of thick forest, often have bizarre encounters with a ghostly train. A silent steam train seems to come from nowhere, roaring through the woods and then suddenly coming to a dead halt, without a warning or slowing down in any way. Then suddenly, it speeds away and vanishes into the distance.

The roadway, Holland Road, is located off New York Route 5 between Angola and the Evangola State Park and has been a part of western New York folklore for decades. Scores of teenagers, ghost hunters and local residents have all visited this place and many of them have tales of wandering spirits, photographic and audiotape anomalies and weird legends about the mile-long roadway.

Not surprisingly, the "Angola Horror" is the root of most of the bizarre stories about Holland Road – but strangely, not all of them. To many locals, the wooded drive is known simply as "Pigman Road," named for a man who allegedly lived in a house between two bridges on the road and who had a penchant for blood. There are a couple of variations to the story, dating back 50 or 60 years. Each describes a dangerous killer who supposedly lurked along the road. Some say he might have been a butcher, others say he was a local farmer. He is said to have received the name "Pigman" because he routinely placed the heads of pigs on stakes in front of his house to frighten trespassers away. It didn't always work. One night, three teenagers decided to sneak onto his property and spy on him. The story goes that when the Pigman caught them in the act, he snapped. He decided that he would keep away intruders once and for all. He murdered the three boys, chopped off their heads and then placed them on stakes in his yard. After that night, the Pigman disappeared and was never seen again, although many believe that his ghost still lurks along Holland Road, watching for unsuspecting teenagers whose lives he can take.

Unlike the tale of the murderous Pigman, the "Angola Horror" however, is not merely an urban legend. The 1867 disaster, in which 50 people lost their lives, still stands as the deadliest in Erie County history. Area teenagers are familiar with the witnesses' descriptions of the cries that came from the last car as the passengers burned to death. Only three people survived being trapped in the car, the stories say, and they were left scarred for life, both physically and emotionally.

To this day, personal accounts claim that the ghosts of the doomed passengers still wander the area around the site of the old bridge. They are frequently reported by those brave enough to travel along Holland Road at night, hoping for a brush with the supernatural. Will they ever rest in peace? No one knows. But one thing is sure: As long as the chilling tales of their deaths are told, they will live on in our history.

1887: THE LOSS OF "HUMAN FREIGHT"
The Bussey Bridge Collapse

Bridges were always a problem for the railroad companies. They fell down; flash floods washed them away; derailments caused calamities; and drawbridges were sometimes left open in front of approaching trains. But perhaps most problematic were the simple collapses – events that were always deadly.

Bridge collapses were primarily a matter of engineering and construction. An amazing number of railroad bridges fell down under trains in the nineteenth century. In 1887 alone, there were 21 bridge collapses. Up until about the 1870s, railroad bridges were built from wood. Timber was cheap, and high, rickety trestles were built in place of those made of more substantial metal or stone. The wooden bridges swayed and groaned under the weight of the trains. The early railroad companies cared more for money than safety and so the majority of bridges were constructed using shoddy patterns that were cheap and easy to build.

From 1840 until about 1870, the standard railroad bridge was the Howe Truss, a rectangular trussed frame of wooden diagonals and vertical iron tie rods. The design was invented by William Howe, a farmer and amateur inventor. The Howe Truss was believed to be responsible for more railroad deaths than any other bridge design in history. Although the design and construction of these bridges was probably not always the cause for their failure, there is no doubt that they were particularly vulnerable to floods, fire and decay. They required constant inspection and repair – which was frequently not carried out as it should have been.

Around 1870, the weight of locomotives and other rolling stock began to increase. This change, together with the manufacture of iron beams, spurred the building of metal bridges. Even though iron bridges were designed to carry much heavier loads than wooden ones, they still collapsed quite often. The horrible Ashtabula bridge disaster in 1876 claimed 80 lives and was due to the failure of an all-iron Howe Truss bridge.

In 1887, another Howe Truss design collapsed near Forest Hills, Massachusetts, shocking the entire nation. The disaster killed 24 and injured another 125, all of whom suffered dreadfully. The reports of the accident were horrendous – people were crushed, dismembered and mangled and some were pinned to their seats by huge splinters driven through their bodies. The first body taken from the wreck was that of a headless woman.

It was a tragedy that could have been prevented. Although the bridge was iron, it was poorly designed and never built to withstand the weight that passed over it. A few weeks before the tragedy, local residents discovered loose nuts and bolts beneath it. A report was made to the railroad, but it never bothered to have it inspected.

In the late 1800s, commuters began traveling from small towns into the cities to work. By 1887, there were thousands of workers who made the daily trip into Boston. The vast majority did so by rail. The Boston & Providence Railroad, as well as many other lines, scheduled frequent commuter service from suburbs like Dedham to downtown Boston.

Traveling by rail was safe, or so it was thought. Since the creation of the Board of Railroad Commissioners, the Boston & Providence Railroad had not had a fatal accident, or even a serious injury. But that record of safety came to an abrupt end on the morning of March 14, 1887.

As was usual on a Monday morning, conductor William H. Alden ordered brakemen to put together a train of nine cars at Dedham for the morning commute. With eight years of experience on the Dedham to Boston route, Alden knew that one extra car would be necessary on a busy Monday morning. Behind the locomotive, Alden instructed the men to add eight red-varnished passenger coaches and a final "smoker car," a combination baggage car and smoking car.

The train left Dedham and at 7:00 a.m. reached Roslindale, where it took on a heavy load of passengers – mostly businessmen, workingmen and young female store clerks -- or as the railroad company referred to them, "human freight." The train continued to make stops to take on passengers until nearly 300 people were aboard. They selected their seats and settled in for what, for some of them, turned out to be the last journey of their lives.

The train left the Roslindale station at 7:18 a.m. with engineer Walter E. White at the controls. White, 52, had spent 31 years on the Dedham to Boston run. As he eased the thirty-two-ton steam locomotive away from the station, there was nothing to indicate that Match 14 was not a day like any other.

The journey from Roslindale to the next station at Forest Hills was a little over a mile and usually took about four minutes. About halfway between the two stations, trains on the route passed over the Bussey Bridge, named for the old Bussey family farm. The bridge carried the tracks at an oblique angle across South Street, rising about 40 feet above street level and spanning 120 feet between two granite abutments set into high embankments that extended beyond the bridge at both ends.

The Bussey Bridge was originally made of wood in the Howe Truss style. It became known locally as the "Tin Bridge," when parts of it were later covered with tin to prevent fires caused by the belching smokestacks of crossing locomotives. In 1870, the wooden truss on the west side was replaced by one of rectangular iron. In

1876, the railroad hired Edwin Hewins, a representative of the Metropolitan Bridge Company, to move the newer truss from the west to the east side of the bridge and to build a new iron truss (actually a copy of the Howe Truss, but what he dubbed a new "Hewins Truss") on the west side.

All was not as it appeared to be with Edwin Hewins. He was, in fact, a fraud. The Metropolitan Bridge Company never existed. It was a figment of Hewins' imagination, just like his engineering credentials were. The tracks that were attached to the bridge by hangers were merely welded straps rather than forged iron. The hangers were off-center, cracked, and couldn't been seen during an inspection. The bridge had been designed to hold two tracks but only one was ever used – the west side, where Hewins' new truss was built. As later investigation discovered, at a time when trains were getting longer and locomotives heavier, the so-called "Hewins Truss" alone carried 80 percent of the weight of the trains that crossed the bridge. Disaster was inevitable.

Running about five minutes behind schedule, engineer White reached the Bussey Bridge with his train traveling (by his estimation) at about 12 to 15 miles per hour. Others later stated that they thought the train was traveling much faster on the downhill grade from Roslindale, perhaps as fast as 30 miles per hour. White testified later that things were normal when the train entered the south end of the bridge. He felt no swaying or settling. The crossing was routine until he reached the north end. At that point, a sudden jerk grabbed White's attention as the front of his engine lifted slightly on the track. As the massive rear wheels made it to the edge of the span, White felt a sudden shock and he turned to see what the problem was. He quickly realized that it was a horrible disaster. He later recounted:

I looked around as the forward car went off the track and the coupling broke. I reversed the engine and was about to stop, when I looked back and saw the first and second cars off the track... saw a cloud of smoke rise, then I knew they had gone through the bridge.

The train stopped before I did, so that it didn't strike me after it broke away... it flashed across me that help more than we could give was needed, so and I threw the running-gear forward and went for Forest Hills as fast as I could, blowing the whistle and both the fireman and I waving our hands toward the wreck to let people know that something had happened. I told the station agent to telegraph for doctors and ambulances. I backed up to the bridge again and started in to help, but couldn't do much, for my strength and courage were gone.

In the matter of moments before the engineer turned to see a cloud of dust where the bridge had been, horror had occurred. The hangers had snapped when the drive wheels of the engine had passed over them, leaving the track and ties unsupported. The strength of the rails themselves had allowed for the track to sag for a few seconds before the entire structure twisted and crashed down onto the street below. That brief pause saved the lives of the passengers in the first three cars behind the locomotive.

In the first seconds of

A *Leslie's Illustrated* sketch of the collapsing of the bridge.

the bridge's collapse, the slow sag of the rails made the first car rise up when it reached the abutment on the north end. Its wheels jumped the track and the rear wheels tore away. As the sag increased, the second car clipped the abutment with a hard jolt but was pushed beyond the bridge when the rest of the train smashed into it from behind.

The passengers in the third car may have been the luckiest. Their coach car collided with the second so hard that the twisted and crumpled steel stuck together, locking the two cars into place. All of its wheels were torn off, the floor ripped away and both sidewalls were sheared open but the third car was pulled over the abutment to safety by the weight of the second car.

Of the 23 people who died that morning, most were in the fourth car and they were killed instantly. The bottom half of the car struck the bridge's abutment with such force that the roof tore loose and landed on the tracks behind the bridge. The car itself slammed into the stone and shattered into pieces, falling to the street 40 feet below. According to the *Boston Post*, "The body of the car was literally ground to pieces against the abutment, and the bits of iron, wood, upholstery and human beings were strewn on the road beneath."

The crash and the fall were devastating enough, but even more unfortunate was when the front of the fifth car smashed into the remains of the fourth car, further adding to the damage. The fifth car crumpled in the impact, telescoping to half its length. Car six fell on its side diagonally across the street, landing on top of the fourth and fifth cars. Cars seven and eight also fell down into the wreckage below the bridge. Car seven protected its passengers by somehow handling upright on the street, nearly unscathed. Car eight fell heavily onto its side, shattering windows and smashing its walls. The most terrifying fall was experienced by the men in the smoking car at the rear of the train – it flipped over on its way down and landed on its roof.

A man named Pike from Roslindale was inside the smoker car and survived. He later recounted:

Just as we reached the bridge, I felt a tremor, which swayed the car from side to side… All at once I was aware that the car was tipping over to the left, actually going into the great deep hole below… I had the presence of mind to catch hold of the wooden cleats which are nailed to the studding of the baggage car, and then over we went. Baggage rolling and skipping around the car, men jumping and holding on… others making for the door, and still others rolling and jumping around as best they could to keep away from the trunks and boxes that were everywhere at once. The impact jarred me terribly, but I managed to keep my grip and still held my balance until the car ceased to crash and sway.

Survivors told harrowing tales of their near-death experiences. W.E. Whittemore of Boston was injured but managed to survive in the obliterated fourth car. He said, "The first sensation was one of suffocation, and it appeared to me that the sides of the car were coming together, while the top of the car was sinking… I found myself on my right side with my hand pinioned between the side of the car and the stone-work on which the bridge had rested."

Another man, John Murphy, was also in the fourth car, accompanied by his daughter who was badly crushed, but survived. "I felt the bridge sink under me," he reported. "We grabbed hold of the seats and in an instant, all of the people and the seats in the car came tumbling down on us. I had one leg pinned down under me… My body was under a pile of seats, and directly in front of me was a young man who appeared to be dead."

As the dust began to clear, survivors and locals who rushed to the scene surveyed the terrible wreckage of the train. Metal and wood were piled in confusion and the bleeding and crushed bodies of the passengers were thrown about among the steel and glass, At first glance, it looked as though everyone had been killed. Soon, however, the injured and wounded began to crawl – and be carried out – of the horrible debris.

P.W.A. Pickard, a firefighter from Roslindale, was among the first emergency workers to reach the scene. He later said that the wreck resembled a "giant kindling-wood factory blown to pieces." Several witnesses stated that the entire span of the bridge was gone. The iron trestle was all mixed up with the wreck of the cars and one iron rail arched above the ruins, bent into a curve. The witnesses described the entire scene as being eerily quiet, the stillness broken only by the moans of the wounded and dying.

Engineer White's split-second decision to speed to the next station for help proved to be a fortunate one.

Firefighters from Forest Hills quickly arrived and put out a small fire that had started in the wreckage near one of the stoves that were used to heat every car. A special train carrying doctors arrived from Boston, but for the most part, aid and comfort was largely provided by local citizens, who hurried to help. Wagons, carts and horse-drawn buggies descended on the scene. Laborers and workmen from nearby factories and stores dropped what they were doing to assist in the rescue effort. Because many of the dead and injured lived within a mile of the wreck, locals knew that they might be coming to the aid of family members, neighbors and friends.

Men set to work with whatever tools they could find -- hammers, saws, crowbars and jackscrews -- hurrying to pry loose the wood and metal and extract the injured from the crash. The living and the dead were pulled from the ruins. At one point, a man was discovered alive at the bottom of a pile of three dead bodies. Although the rescuers worked as quickly as possible, the man died soon after being pulled from the wreckage.

Amazingly, the dead and injured were all removed from the massive wreck in less than 40 minutes. In fact, the local recovery efforts were so

The bodies of the dead being removed from the wreckage of the train. *Leslie's Illustrated*; 1887

quick that a final tally of the injured could not be accurately made. Initial estimates placed the number of injured at around 150, but many of the injured passengers were simply taken to their nearby homes and were never counted. Others were taken away in wagons or to shops or the homes of those who lived close to the scene. Some of the most seriously injured were carried to a local fire station rather than to a hospital. Doctors feared that they would not survive the trip into Boston.

The official inquiry into the accident began the following afternoon and it lasted for the next 13 days. Railroad commissioners reported their findings to the state legislature within the month and faulty work by Hewins and lax inspections by the railroad received most of the blame.

On March 15, a crew of 100 men was brought in and set to work cleaning up the wreck. With axes and crowbars, and assisted by a massive block and tackle that was hoisted by a locomotive on the track above, the scene was cleared within 48 hours. A squad of policeman kept back the crowds of people who had gathered to watch.

Two days, later the Boston & Providence Railroad replaced the fallen structure with a temporary wooden bridge so that the trains could start running again. The bridge was eventually replaced and the Bussey Bridge Collapse became just another forgotten – but deadly -- footnote in history.

But it was one with an eerie story still left to tell.

According to local stories, the "Fog Man" lurks near the bridge, which was the scene of disaster so many years before. He has been seen roaming the neighborhood around the bridge almost since the time of the disaster. He lurks, they say, around open yards and stretches of lonely street, looking out in the distance, as if waiting for someone. He is always described the same way -- wearing old-fashioned overalls, the kind that railroad men used to wear. If anyone approaches him, he always disappears, leaving a mystery in his wake.

Who is he? No one knows, but most believe he is a lingering spirit from the Bussey disaster -- just another piece of "human freight" that never made it to its destination.

1887: THE EXCURSION TRAIN DISASTER
Death in Chatsworth, Illinois

The late nineteenth century was the era of the robber baron. Notorious men like Jim Fisk, Jay Cooke, J.P. Morgan and Jay Gould were held responsible for bilking the public, swindling the government and amassing untold fortunes through often-nefarious means. In the case of the horrific railroad disaster that occurred on August 10, 1887 in Chatsworth, Illinois, which claimed 81 lives and crippled 140 more, the blame could be squarely placed at Jay Gould's door.

Gould had eliminated the Toledo, Peoria and Western line as a competitor to his Wabash Railroad by leasing the rail line for 50 years, draining it of all of its assets and then dumping it into bankruptcy so that it fell into the laps of the trustees holding the first mortgage. In a desperate attempt to bolster the finances of the Peoria line and to fill its 247 miles of track with trains carrying paying customers, the railroad began offering extensive excursions at cut-rate prices.

Although the railroad realized some immediate profit, its tracks and trestles were allowed to fall into disrepair. The employees were overworked and underpaid and became unconcerned and irresponsible about their duties and passenger safety.

In the summer of 1887, Illinois was in the grasp of a severe drought. By August, the newspapers were reporting that stream beds were dry, wells were running out of water and that cornfields were scorched beyond recovery. It was so bad that even sporadic showers and thunderstorms became newsworthy events.

After a few brush fires were started by sparks from passing locomotives, section hands on the Toledo, Peoria & Western Railroad were sent to work burning out weeds that grew along the tracks. But as it turned out, their safety efforts were much more dangerous than chance sparks from a locomotive's smokestack.

On August 10, a group of workers headed by foreman Tim Coughlan were burning the high prairie grass along a section of the Toledo, Peoria & Western Railroad line between Chatsworth and Piper City in eastern Illinois. They quit work around 5:00 p.m. and Coughlan stayed about a half-hour longer to ensure that none of the burned patches of grass were still smoldering. He later stated that he was sure that all of the fires had gone out by the time he left.

Three hours later and seventy miles to the west, more than 600 happy tourists, cheap tickets in hand, boarded 15 cars pulled by two engines. It was one of the longest trains ever to be pulled on the Toledo, Peoria & Western line. Engineer Edward McClintock and Conductor J.W. Stilwell had both protested to no avail that the train was too long and too heavy to be safe. Behind the two engines were a baggage car, a passenger coach that held railroad officials, five more coaches, two parlor cars and six Pullman sleeper cars.

The passengers were a mixed lot, their ranks swollen with poor families who were excited to be able to afford a vacation. In the late nineteenth century, excursion trains offered a welcome respite for hardworking Midwesterners. For a relatively small fee, they could get away from home for a short time and enjoy scenic and natural sites that they might not otherwise see. Some of the most popular destinations for the excursion trains were Mammoth Cave in Kentucky, Hot Springs, Arkansas, and Niagara Falls. It was to this New York wonder that the T.P. & W. train was heading. When the railroad had posted handbills about the excursion earlier that summer, hundreds of people eagerly responded. The railroad, struggling to fill the coffers that had been plundered by Jay Gould, offered a round-trip ticket to Niagara Falls for only $7.50.

The Toledo, Peoria & Western line stretched across Illinois from Warsaw on the Mississippi River to Peoria and then west to a town called State Line (now Effner) on the Indiana border. The line had long offered a valuable east-west service across the state. The "Niagara Special" started at LaHarpe in Hancock County and most of the large crowd of excited travelers came from Galesburg, nearby Iowa, and Peoria.

The train traveled eastward after departing Hancock County, picking up baggage-laden passengers in some of the towns along the way. The cheap fare had not only attracted hard-working vacationers, but a number of thieves and pickpockets, as well. The tourists would be carrying most (if not all) of the money that they had and

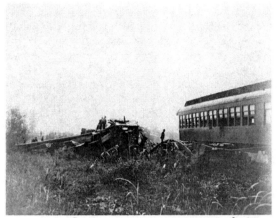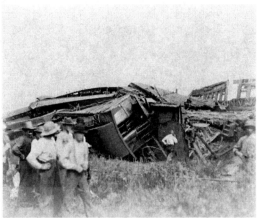

Contemporary newspaper photographs of the devastation at Chatsworth.

were easy targets for robbers. An hour after the train pulled out, Superintendent N.E. Armstrong began to receive reports of handbags and valises that had mysteriously disappeared. Armstrong became preoccupied by the reports of pilferage on the train and ordered some of his men to investigate. While this was going on, no one was paying attention to the condition of the tracks – or the dim glow of flames that could be seen flickering ahead of them on the dark prairie.

With all of the stops along the route, the train was running about two hours behind schedule. It was nearly midnight by the time it reached Chatsworth and it roared through town without stopping. They had no idea what lay ahead of them.

About two miles east of town, the lead locomotive crested a small hill and from this vantage point, the lead engineer spotted flames ahead on the rails. Horrified, he realized that a wooden trestle ahead of them was burning – and there was no time to stop the train.

The trestle was close to where Tim Coughlan and his work crew had been burning prairie grass that afternoon. It was a 15-foot wooden bridge that spanned a six-foot gully. Beneath it lay several bales of hay that had been stored by a local farmer. The patches of grass that had been burned that day had apparently not gone out after all. The smoldering fire had somehow spread, eventually igniting the hay bales. The old wooden trestle also began to burn.

The engineer applied the manual brakes – air brakes were available, but were much too expensive for the bankrupt line – just 300 yards from the burning trestle. It was simply too late. The lead engine raced over the bridge at 35 miles per hour but the second engine, operated by Edward McClintock, was too heavy for the weakened structure and it crashed downward through the flames. McClintock was killed instantly as nine cars behind his engine slammed into one another and pitched forward into the gully. The cars piled into the overturned locomotive and collided with one another, shattering as they came forward. Metal screamed with a horrific grinding noise and wood splintered and broke. Even in the darkness, many would recall seeing a rolling cloud of soot, cinders, ash and dust. The railroad cars slammed into one another with a telescoping effect, each coach slicing into the one in front of it. The flying metal whirred like the blades of a saw, producing a grisly death toll. Large numbers of passengers were cut into pieces, their bodies savagely sliced apart. Many more were crushed and died instantly.

As the wreck finally ground to a halt, 11 of the railroad cars now occupied the space that was once occupied by two. The sound of tearing metal faded and was replaced by a chorus of human screams and wails. The survivors of the disaster began to stumble about, looking for family members, friends and anyone else who might have lived through the terror. Mass confusion ruled the scene as in the distant skies, lightning began to flash.

The lead engine had somehow made it across the burning bridge and the engineer climbed down from his cab and stared in awe at the unbelievable wreckage that loomed behind him. Only the dim light of burning fires illuminated the scene, but the flames showed him more than he ever wanted to ever see. Two firemen from the lead engine took over the controls and rushed east to Piper City, their whistle blowing, to carry the awful news of what had happened. A brakeman took off in the opposite direction, running back to Chatsworth.

The horror began to grow worse. The wreckage caught fire, trapping many of the injured inside. As screams filled the night, other survivors who had managed to make it out of the ruined cars, desperately started throwing handfuls of dirt onto the flames. As rescuers began to arrive from Chatsworth, and from nearby small farms, they joined the battle and clawed at the dirt with their bare hands to keep the blaze from spreading. Meanwhile, telegrams were sent out from Piper City and Chatsworth and rescue trains began steaming toward the accident.

Then, around 3:00 a.m., the summer drought finally broke and torrents of rain began to fall from the sky. The storm, which had been only flickering lightning in the distance at the time of the wreck, reached the awful scene and unleashed its fury on the survivors, the rescuers and the dead. The rain managed to put out the remains of the fire but it also turned the nearby fields and dirt roads into a muddy swamp, making them nearly impassable.

By sunrise, Chatsworth was swarming with volunteers and curiosity-seekers. People came from all over to provide comfort and aid and also to see the carnage for themselves. Over the days that followed, the gruesome task of removing and identifying the dead was carried out. The twisted metal coaches made this job nearly impossible and newspapers repeatedly used the word "pulp" to describe the condition of the human remains.

Many of Chatsworth's buildings were turned into temporary morgues and so anxious were the crowds who came to view the remains that armed guards had to be posted at the doors. Fanned by sensational newspaper reports and wild rumors, terrible stories spread through the area. The rumors included reports that belongings had been stolen from the dead and that the bridge fire had been deliberately set. Responding to the public's anger, Tim Coughlan was arrested and blamed for the fire but was later released. No official cause for the fire was ever determined.

The robber baron had his millions and the cash-strapped railroad had -- thanks to its economic plight -- ultimately caused a disaster that left 81 people dead and another 140 injured. It was one of the worst railroad disasters in Illinois history but the authorities quickly closed the files and seemed to forget that it ever happened. The local people incorporated the tragedy into folklore and the story became a maudlin ballad by T.P. Westendorf called "The Bridge was Burned at Chatsworth." One melodramatic stanza went:

A mighty crash of timbers
A sound of hissing steam
The groans and cries of anguish
A woman's stifled scream.
The dead and dying mingled
With broken beams and bars
An awful human carnage
A dreadful wreck of cars.

1892: INDIAN TERRITORY MINE DISASTER

Coal mining has proven to be one of the nation's most dangerous forms of employment. The list of coal mine disasters that have taken place in our country is a long one and during the twentieth century alone, more than 100,000 coal miners were killed in accidents. Hazards included suffocation, gas poisoning, roof collapses, fires and gas explosions. It was not a safe occupation – and often still isn't – but when you consider that many miners in the early 1900s started working as young as 12 or 13 years old, the litany of bloody disasters becomes even more tragic.

"Firedamp" is a word used for flammable gas that is found in coal mines. It's a name that is given to a number of flammable gases, especially methane. The gas accumulates in pockets in the coal and adjacent strata, and when they are penetrated, the release can trigger explosions. These explosions became the common source for accidents that occurred in mines in the late 1800s and early 1900s, including one that occurred in the Indian Territory – present day Oklahoma – in 1892.

Mine #11 at Krebs was owned by the Osage Coal and Mining Company and it had long been known as a mine that constantly seeped gas. It was also plagued with problems that had arisen from the coal dust, the fine, powdered by-product of crushing, grinding and pulverizing coal. Coat dust that is suspended in the air can be explosive, due to the fact that the dust has more surface area per unit weight than chunks of coal, and is more susceptible to spontaneous combustion. As a result, a nearly empty coal store is a greater explosion risk than a full one. The worst mining accidents in history had been caused by coal dust explosions, a fact that was known to the owners of the Osage Coal and Mining Company. Rather than lose revenue, supervisors at the mine believed that they could alleviate some of the danger by having "shot firers" carry out their blasting work only after the shafts had been cleared of the miners at the end of the shift. Usually, this meant that a crew of shot firers would descend into the empty mine around 5:30 p.m. This was considered safe since the mine was always empty by then – or at least it was supposed to be.

What became the worst industrial accident in Oklahoma history occurred in the small town of Krebs in 1892. The town was named in honor of Judge Edmond Folsom Krebs around 1873. Judge Krebs was of mixed German and Choctaw Indian ancestry and served as a judge for the Choctaw nation in the 1880s.

The Missouri, Kansas and Texas Railroad built a rail line through the area that is now McAlester in 1872 and with the line came scores of new settlers and the need to tap into the area's most valuable resource – coal. Not only would it heat the homes of the local residents, it would run the locomotives and could be shipped out to other regions as a money-making commodity. The Missouri, Kansas and Texas Railroad formed the Osage Coal and Mining Company and then harvested the coal it needed to operate and sold the excess on the open market.

The richest coal deposits in the Indian Territory lay beneath Krebs. The deposits stretched from McAlester eastward to the Arkansas border and most of the small towns along that line owed their existence to coal. Much of the land belonged to and was leased from the Choctaw, which made the mines exempt from federal government laws and regulations. By the early 1890s, there were 15 coal mines operating in Krebs alone.

The initial workforce was made up of immigrants from England and Ireland. Later, Russians and Italians flooded the region and added to the legion of workers that were needed keep the mines operating around the clock. The mining company had an indifferent attitude toward safety and there were more than enough men looking for work that few upgrades were ever carried out.

The Osage Coal and Mining Company's #11 mine was notorious for being the worst of the local mines. The poor conditions were well known and for this reason, it seemed to attract only men who were desperately in need of work. This led to a high turnover of workers, so the company routinely hired unskilled labor, providing little in the way of training to get them up to speed. This was true for even the most dangerous jobs, like handling explosives and munitions, among them the shot firers who were sent into the mine at the end of the work day to set off charges so that coal could be loaded the following morning.

On January 7, 1892, the blasting crew arrived early, which would prove to be disastrous to the men who were still in the mine. The mining crews were lined up at the bottom of the main shaft and were just being lifted to the surface in cages as the shot firers were laying their explosives. Five cages had been raised and about 30 of the nearly 500 men working below had left the mine. At 5:04 p.m., either in haste or because of carelessness, one of the munitions crew set off a tremendous explosion that echoed through the mine and was heard for miles around. The mine, already polluted with gas and coal dust, erupted into flame. The elevator cage, which was sitting at the top of the shaft, having just released six men onto the platform, was blasted 50 feet into the air and through the roof of the mine tower. A pillar of fire and smoke belched from the mine shaft with a monstrous roar.

Hundreds of men still at the bottom of the shaft were badly injured. They began climbing out, some of them so badly burned that the flesh of their hands peeled off as they held onto the ladders. One man made the 450-foot climb with a broken leg. A father sent his son up the ladder while he searched for another son in the hellish tunnels below. They were later discovered dead in each other's arms.

Almost 400 of the men miraculously made it out of the mine, which was by then filled with lethal gas, as well as smoke and flames. Hundreds of miners from other operations in the area stopped work and rushed to the scene. As rescuers descended into the hot and stinking shaft, they reeled back in horror, having found piles of corpses, mutilated by the explosion and burned by the fire, littering the base of the shaft. As one reporter described the scene, "Heads, arms, legs, hands and feet were in many instances torn from the trunks. Their clothes were either partially or entirely burned away... and in several instances the flames had literally roasted all of the flesh on the body."

The corpses – or portions of corpses – were hauled up out of the mine in baskets and taken to a nearby blacksmith shop, where weeping relatives attempted to identify what was left of their husbands, sons, fathers, uncles and cousins. There was not a single household in Krebs that was not affected in some way by the disaster.

Meanwhile, rescue and recovery crews continued their grim work inside the mine. The horrific discoveries continued, as one newspaper rported: "Heads and hands or legs were found protruding from the mass of fallen rock... A number of burned lamps, caps and dinner buckets completed the desolation of the scene. The bodies were removed with all possible care, but this did not prevent an arm or leg, almost severed from the body, from being completely torn off when taken from under the wreckage."

Amidst the carnage and chaos, a race riot nearly erupted over the presence of a number of African-Americans who responded to the alarm at the mine. Blacks had sought work in the mines of the Indian Territory, but the white men had refused to work with them. When the black men arrived and then refused to assist in moving bodies out of the mine, some of the white miners grew angry. Allegedly, some of the black men stated that "it served the miners right to have been killed." Hearing the remark, the white miners turned on the blacks and the recovery project turned into a brawl. It was finally broken up by a U.S. Deputy Marshal who arrived with some of his men to "drive the colored men from the place with Winchesters."

The men and boys who died in Mine #11 were buried in a mass grave in McAlester. It would not be until 2002 when a memorial was finally placed in remembrance of those who lost their lives that day. The final death count remains unknown because many of the bodies could not be identified but it is said to be somewhere between 65 and 100.

The Osage Coal and Mining Company continued to do business in Mine #11 and in the other local mines, although things grew tougher after the disaster. Unions began to organize, rallying behind safer working conditions. Striking miners hampered company operations, most notably in 1894, when work stoppages shut down most of the mines in the Indian Territory. But even with the miners organized, deaths continued. At least 44 more men died in Osage operations before the company closed down.

It was the Great Depression that finally brought an end to Mine #11. Broken and bankrupt, the company shut down the mines at Krebs and auctioned off all of its equipment.

The story of the 1892 disaster lived on for years and is still remembered today as the worst accident of its kind in Oklahoma history. Almost every family in Krebs lost a friend or a relative in the explosion, which may explain the superstitious fear in which many of the miners held #11 after they returned to work there. The men had to feed their families, so they had no choice but to return to the place where so many had lost their lives.

According to the legends, the mine was haunted by those who died in the explosion. Italian miners especially complained of hearing voices and cries in the darkness at the bottom of the shaft. Eerie screams, moaning wails and terrifying calls echoed in the shadows, frequently on days when blasting was scheduled. Some believed that the ghostly voices served as a warning to the miners working in the shaft, pleading with them to get out of the mine on time so that they would not fall victim to a similar fate. Others believed that the spirits were simply reliving their own deaths on days when the shot firers returned to Mine #11.

1896: "DEATH TRAP" DISASTER
The Atlantic City Railway Disaster

Railroad disasters have been documented to have many causes over the years, from faulty switches to collapsing bridges, but perhaps the most common – and most preventable – cause is that of human error. Engineers, switchmen, brakeman and signal operators often misjudged distances, failed in their duties and sometimes even made mysterious errors that had no explanation, leading to the deaths of scores of people on the rail lines. The Atlantic City disaster of 1896 was one of the times when human error lent a hand to the Grim Reaper on an American railroad.

The "Death Trap" was what railroad men called a crossing in Atlantic City where many tracks intersected. Engineers on both the Reading line from Pennsylvania and the West Jersey Railroad gave the ominous name to this worrisome crossing because of what were described as the "heavily loaded trains dodging each other at that point for years." In the end, it was never really determined who was entirely to blame for the horrible wreck that occurred on the evening of July 30, 1896, but Edward Farr, engineer of the Philadelphia Express, was officially responsible.

At that time, leaving Atlantic City, the tracks of the West Jersey Railroad were parallel to those of the Camden and Atlantic Railway until they crossed a drawbridge where they switched off to the south, crossing the Reading line at an odd angle.

As Farr approached the crossing that night at about 7:00 p.m., his throttle wide open, it was claimed that he ignored the red signal shining from the control tower that overlooked the crossing, manned by signal operator George Hauser. At the same time, a seven-car excursion train from Atlantic City driven by John Greiner, carrying members of the Improved Order of Red Men and their friends, also made it to the crossing. Greiner proceeded through the crossing, since Hauser had given him the white (go-ahead) light. His engine had barely rolled into the crossing when the excursion train was hit by Farr's locomotive, slamming into the cars with a grinding scream of twisted metal.

When Greiner saw the other train approaching, he assumed that it was going to stop. When it didn't, he panicked. "My God, Morris!" he shouted to his fireman, Morris Newell, "he's not going to stop!" Greiner scrambled out of his seat and started to jump from the train, but had second thoughts. He jumped back into the cab, saving his life. If he had jumped, he would have been buried under the wreck. Newell was uninjured in the wreck. When the Reading engine struck his train, the first car was snapped off and the locomotive, which shuddered and pitched, remained on the track and continued on the line. After he managed to bring the train to a stop, Greiner ran back to the scene of the accident. What he saw there unnerved him completely. "I shall never forget the sight of that Reading engine as she rushed toward us..." he later said.

The last thing that Edward Farr saw that day was the side of the West Jersey train as he went speeding toward it. His engine rammed into the side of the first car at 50 miles per hour, knocking it off the tracks with such force that it went down the embankment and sank into a marsh. The second car was also torn off the tracks and it too collapsed down the embankment. The third and fourth cars telescoped into each other, tearing apart their occupants.

Farr's engine skidded to the opposite side of the tracks, dragging its first car along into the ditch. Almost immediately, surviving passengers began clambering out of the twisted doors and shattered windows, only to meet death as the boiler of the Reading locomotive exploded, scalding many to death and casting a boiling spray over many of the already injured passengers. Most of the wooden cars, both on and off the tracks, were burning. Survivors who watched from inside the cars of both trains never forgot the gruesome death scenes that played out in front of them.

Charles Blue, a passenger on the excursion train, later wrote:

After the crash, there was an indescribable scene... I do not know how I escaped being killed. Two children sat in front of me. They were crushed into a shapeless mass, while I was merely turned around in my seat. I noticed one family in particular who were sitting at the center of the car. The family consisted of a father, a mother, and two children. The father evidently saw there was going to be a collision, and just before the shock came, he seized the youngest child and threw it out an open window. Then followed the collision and the rest of the family was killed. The child was found apparently uninjured... A number of people escaped by jumping from windows before the cars came together."

As soon as the news of the crash reached Atlantic City, hundreds of people rushed to the scene. The road leading to the collision was choked with hackney carriages, omnibuses, bicycles, and all kinds of vehicles, while thousands of pedestrians hurried along the path to render what assistance they could. Men swarmed over the wreck, pulling the living and the dead from the flames. John Meyer, owner of the Union Market, was one of those who rushed to the accident site to lend assistance. He plunged into the tangle of cars and then recoiled in horror when he looked down to see a small girl sobbing, "I won't leave you, Mama." The blood-covered little girl had her arms wrapped around a headless corpse.

Rescuers found a mother and father who had covered their daughter with their own bodies so that she would survive. She, too, had to be torn away from her dead parents. As darkness began to fall, the work of rescuing the injured and recovering the bodies of the dead was carried out by the light from huge bonfires that were built by onlookers.

The flickering light made the scene even more horrific. One party of searchers, stumbling through the ruins of a destroyed Reading Railroad car found a human heart impaled on a splintered section of wall. They also found a man's severed leg, which was later identified as belonging to engineer Edward Farr. The impact had occurred with such force that his leg, blown off by the exploding boiler, was hurled the entire length of the first car behind the engine.

Fire raged through the fourth car of the excursion train as passenger Charles W. Seeds smashed his way through a window. He stumbled out and then pulled his wife out after him. She begged him to go back inside and pull out the others who had been traveling with them. With blood pouring from his cut legs, Seeds worked his way back into the car. He found a small girl pinned between two seats and pulled her out. Seeds made several trips through the car but aside from the girl, no one was left alive. Refusing to leave the bodies to be consumed by flames, he pulled 11 corpses from the wreck before the car was finally devoured by fire.

Julius B. Price, on his way to Atlantic City for a leisurely stay on the boardwalk, was in the smoker of the Reading train's second car. Moments after the crash, Price, uninjured, made his way forward on the wrecked train. Other men joined him and when entering the next car, Price saw "half a dozen people lying about amid the wreckage of the seats. It was here that we fully realized the horror of the accident. The first woman we took out had her leg cut off between the knee and the ankle. A man we took out afterward had evidently had his back broken... We got out as many as we could, but the doors were so smashed that it was impossible to remove all by the doors."

Price and the other men climbed onto the roof of the second car and broke through. Men inside lifted as many of the injured through the hole as possible. Price then walked down the embankment where dozens of bodies were laid out along the tracks. He heard the screams of those still trapped in the wreckage and tried to help them before realizing that only heavy equipment (which arrived later) could save them. Price later remembered, "I helped carry a man who had been internally injured to a spot where a number of others lay who had been hurt. On the way, he told us in broken words that he feared that his entire family was destroyed – his wife, his child, his wife's mother and father. As we lowered him to the ground, a woman all bandaged up came up panting and sank beside the sufferer. It was his wife. She was alive."

Crowds continued to gather throughout the night and rescuers roamed here and there through the wreckage, helping those who could be helped and dragging out the bodies of those who could not. The mangled and burned dead were carried from the wreck and laid out in a long like on the gravel bank near the tracks. There was nothing to cover them with except for a few newspapers, which were collected from the passengers.

Hundreds of injured and groggy passengers, propped up by Atlantic City locals carrying torches and lanterns, searched the debris for their families and then were escorted to the city. Some were taken by train and others by wagon to the Atlantic City Hospital. One man, delirious, babbled how he had been in the demolished second car from Philadelphia and how, on impact, bodies had been thrown the length of the car. A reporter leaned down and asked the man who he was. "When he was asked his name," the reporter stated, "he stared in a silly manner as if his tongue had suddenly forgotten to speak. On this point, his memory faded entirely."

Six of the injured died soon after they arrived at the hospital and two others died within a day, joining the 42 that had been killed at the collision scene. The old Excursion House at the foot of Mississippi Avenue was converted into a morgue, and the dead were taken there. The streets around the Excursion House, and the hospital, were soon packed with people anxious to learn the latest news.

By morning, the famous Atlantic City boardwalk was cluttered with bandaged survivors, many of them still searching for missing friends and relatives. A young man named Henry Muta had searched all night for his father and sister. He finally went to the temporary morgue at the Excursion House, where the dead were being placed in crude, wooden boxes. The first two boxes that were opened contained the bodies of his father and sister. Muta immediately fainted.

At dawn, the recovery crews were still at work. The last corpse removed from the wreckage was that of Edward Farr. It required two men to pry Farr's hands from the throttle and air brake.

The last fatality of the Atlantic City Railway Wreck was recorded miles from the scene of the accident. Authorities stood on the porch of Mrs. Edward Farr and told her that her husband had just been killed. Unable to withstand the shock, she fell to the floor dead.

The inquest into the accident became a confusing affair.

Atlantic County Coroner William McLaughlin, upon hearing of the accident, immediately went to the scene. He went directly into the tower and questioned signal operator George F. Hauser. Hauser told him that he thought the excursion train had time to cross the tracks of the Reading before the express got there and he set the "clear" signal for the West Jersey train. Before Hauser could make a further explanation to the coroner, he received an order from the railroad officials not to say anything else. He stopped talking and, pending an investigation, he was arrested. He was later released on a $500 bond.

A jury was impaneled the following day and on August 4, testimony was given that implicated the dead Reading Railroad engineer, Edward Farr. His action in running at a speed of more than 45 miles per hour past a danger signal seemed inexplicable to those present at the inquest. His reputation was that of an experienced engineer and a man of exceptionally good moral character. Only two weeks previous to the accident his train was signaled to stop at that very crossing, and he obeyed promptly.

The coroner's jury returned verdicts on August 7. Six jurors merely stated the manner of the passengers' deaths. Three found that "Engineer Edward D. Farr of the Atlantic City Railroad failed to have his engine under proper control on approaching [the] crossing, and that Tower Man George F. Hauser, in giving the excursion train of the West Jersey Railroad the right of way over a fast express used bad judgment... [and] that Engineer John Greiner of said excursion train erred in not exercising greater care on crossing ahead of said fast express." Three others found that "the cause of the collision was the failure of Edward Farr, engineer of Train No. 23, to give heed in time to the semaphore signals and crossing under the rules...the tower man, George F. Hauser, may have used poor judgment in his estimate of the distance away of the Atlantic City Railroad train when he gave the white boards to the West Jersey and Seashore Excursion Train No. 700."

In the end, it seemed that everyone was blamed but Edward Farr was held the most responsible. There was little that could be done to him, aside from tarnishing his reputation, since he had lost his life in the crash. For the survivors, it was a last bit of irony connected to an event that forever changed their lives.

1900: DEATH AT THE WINTER QUARTERS MINE

The early morning stillness of Utah's Pleasant Valley was broken by the voices of miners, raised in song as they left for work on May 1, 1900. Spring has finally come to the valley, and the thriving town of Scofield, and the bitter cold weather that had helped to give Winter Quarters its name had finally passed. On the minds of many of the men that morning was the coming evening's celebration to open the new Odd Fellows Hall. In addition, it was Dewey Day, a commemoration of Admiral George Dewey's naval victory over the Spanish in Manila Bay two years previously.

But instead of a celebration that evening, local residents would be stunned by the deaths and injuries of 200 miners. Parties and dinners would be canceled and the people of Scofield would be in mourning instead.

Pleasant Valley was a welcoming place in the 1870s. There were a number of settlers who lived in the area, most of whom grazed cattle on the lush valley grass. Coal was discovered in the dark canyon beyond the valley in 1875 and two years later, a small mine was opened on the western slopes of the canyon and the coal was transported out along narrow roads. The winter of 1877 came early and was very severe, stranding the miners in the coal pit and keeping them snowbound until the following February. The ordeal led the miners to name their forced camp "Winter Quarters" and this became one of the first commercial coal mines in the state.

Winter Quarters in 1900

Two towns, Winter Quarters and Scofield, sprang up around the mine and began to thrive. Many called them the most impressive cities in Utah. Only the ruins of a ghost town remain at Scofield today and it's hard to tell just how important the town once was. The business district was more than a mile long and boasted dozens of substantial stone buildings, many of them as fine as any in Salt Lake City. As the mine and the community grew, new and more efficient methods were sought to move the coal from the mines and so the Utah & Pleasant Valley Railroad was constructed, running from Springville to Winter Quarters and Scofield. It connected with the Denver & Rio Grande line in Colton, about 20 miles away. Businesses in

Colton included Covington's Hotel, Higney's General Store and five saloons. Colton was so bustling that it actually burned and was rebuilt three times! But the future of this town was tied directly to the future of the Winter Quarters mine. Unknown to both, the future was not to be a bright one.

In 1882, the Utah Fuel Company took over the mine and it became a subsidiary of the Denver & Rio Grande Railroad. The region continued to thrive until 1900, when there were several hundred men working in the mines and the local population numbered as high as 1,800. The Winter Quarters mine was considered the safest in the area. According to reports, it was free of the gasses that plagued so many other coal operations. But this would not be enough to save it from disaster...

The miners at Winter Quarters reported to work as usual on the morning of May 1. The men arrived at the mine carrying their tools. They were paid by tonnage rates, instead of

The Winter Quarters Mine

hourly, and supplied their own tools and blasting powder. Some of them started work in the No. 1 section of the mine, others in No. 4, which was located on an incline that opened high above the valley where the settlement was built.

An errant spark caused the disaster. It touched off the fine haze of coal dust deep underground and the No. 4 mine exploded with fury. One hundred men were killed instantly and another 99 died from the poisonous afterdamp, making this one of the worst coal mine disasters in history. That one moment of time left 113 widows and 306 fatherless children behind.

The explosion occurred a half mile inside of the mine and the force of it was so powerful that it completely leveled a shack that stood outside and tore out the motors and drums for the mine cars. John Wilson, a driver who was working at the mouth of the mine, was knocked 820 feet down the ravine and landed with a crushed skull and a splinter of board impaled in his abdomen.

A hastily assembled rescue party of 20 miners, led my mine superintendent Thomas J. Parmley, tried to get into the No. 4 mine through No. 1 but were driven back by the "black damp," the gaseous air that is left in the mine when all of the oxygen has been displaced by fire or explosion. The rescue party then charged up the hill to the mouth of the damaged mine. Smoke was pouring out of the entrance and it was partially blocked by fallen timbers. It took the men nearly 20 minutes to gain access to the mine's interior.

Townspeople, startled by the thunderous explosion and by the fire and smoke belching from the mine, rushed to the scene. While the crew was clearing the entrance, other volunteers searched the area and found driver John Wilson on the hillside. An engineer, who would have been in the demolished shack at the time of the explosion if he had not been a short distance away replacing a derailed car, was also found. The engineer only suffered minor injuries. Another man, also working outside, was found with his foot crushed, his shoulder dislocated and other, more severe injuries. An assistant helper with a broken jaw and crushed head and a miner with a broken arm, broken leg and internal injuries, were found outside of the mine entrance. The men were taken to a home in the valley where their injuries could be treated.

Once the crew could enter the mine, they found the first – and only – survivors. The first man found was Harry Belterson, who was badly burned and died later that night. Nearby was William Boweter, who managed to escape with only minor injuries.

Mass funerals and burials followed the disaster. The victims of the Winter Quarters Mine were buried in the cemetery in Scofield, which can still be visited today.

The rescuers worked to clear each section of the mine, carrying the bodies of their dead comrades to the entrance, where they were placed in rows. There weren't enough men left in Scofield or Winter Quarters to carry the dead into town.

Miners from Clear Creek and other settlements in the area descended on Winter Quarters to help bring the bodies down the steep hill that led up to No. 4. The town's school, boarding houses, churches, hotels, and barns were cleared out to receive the victims. As each corpse was carried down, wives, children and relatives rushed forward, calling out names. The air echoed with the screams of women as they saw the remains of their burned and mangled husbands.

The rescue party moved from No. 4 to No. 1, where they found men both burned and suffocated. The bodies were stacked on carts, sometimes 12 high, and moved out of the mine. Most of the dead in No. 1 succumbed to the "black damp," or were buried under dirt and debris. The rescue workers believed that most of them had been taken by surprise and may have thought the explosion was set off to celebrate Dewey Day. Some of the men were found were their tools still in their hands. One man, who sat down to smoke his pipe, was found with the pipe still in his hands.

Trying to cope with the disaster stretched the resources of the two towns to the limit. Daisey Harrom, a professional nurse from Salt Lake City, ran an infirmary for the injured until a train filled with doctors could arrive. The few survivors were taken back by train to Salt Lake City on May 2, where they could be better cared for. It was there that John Wilson had a steel plate inserted into his head.

There was chaos among the dead. Mistakes were made when the bodies were identified and many of the men were buried under the wrong names. Grave markers were made up in such a hurry that many of the men's names were misspelled. When word spread of the tragedy, every available casket in Utah was sent to Winter Quarters. This did not prove to be enough and the shortage had to be made up from a shipment of coffins from Denver. Graves were dug by volunteers in Scofield, while other coffins were shipped out to graveyards across Utah and in other states.

The mine company's manager, William G. Sharp, canceled all of the debts owed by the victim's families at the company store, a total of $8,000, and paid a $500 death benefit to each family. On May 5, Utah's governor, Heber M. Wells, called for the people of the state to contribute to a relief fund and over $110,000 was collected but the amount actually given to the families never reached that amount. Many of the widows left the area with the onset of winter and never received their share of the relief funds.

The terrible tragedy cast a pall of sorrow over the valley and the deaths of the miners seemed to signal the slow death of Winter Quarters. The gloom never lifted, although the mine remained in operation until 1928. Changing standards lowered the worth of the coal in the valley and eventually, it could only be used for inexpensive locomotive fuel. The cost of running the mine, and transporting the coal, finally doomed the mine. By 1930, most of Winter Quarters had been abandoned and residents had fled to Scofield and beyond. Only caved-in cellars, a few foundations and a single crumbling structure remain of Winter Quarters today.

In the early 1990s, I had the chance to live for an extended time in Utah. It was not long before I discovered that the state, which is one of the most beautiful in the country, is also one of the most haunted. I found tales of Indian spirits, slain pioneers and the weird history of the Mormons, but I had to look hard for them. Hauntings are easy to find in Utah, but are not often talked about. During my time in Utah, I spent many weekends hiking, exploring, seeking out ghost towns and half-heartedly looking for lost treasure. Nearly every one of my explorations introduced me to a ghost story or two and one of my adventures led me to the ruins of Winter Quarters.

To reach the site of the former town, I had to pass through Scofield, which is only a shadow of the boomtown that it was decades ago. It wasn't a ghost town, but it was getting there. I was told that I might also want to see another former coal camp at Hale, which is just north of Scofield. Its site was marked by the remains of a few shacks at the edge of a hillside. Some of the mines at Hale were located downstream from the Scofield Reservoir, a small nearby lake. Since I planned to camp overnight, I was told to consider camping at the Hale site rather than the shadowy canyon at Winter Quarters. I asked what was wrong with the canyon? "The ghosts of the dead miners," I was told, "are not likely to make for good company."

Apparently, there had been stories about ghosts at Winter Quarters for years, dating back almost to the time of the disaster. An article from the January 17, 1901 edition of the *Utah Advocate* newspaper read:

The superstitious miners, who are foreigners, have come to the conclusion that the property is haunted, inhabited by a ghost. Several of them have heard strange and unusual noises, and those favored with a keener vision than their fellow workmen have actually seen a headless man walking about the mine and according to their statements have accosted the ghost and addressed it -- or he.

At other times the headless man would get aboard the coal cars to which mules and horses are worked and ride with the driver to the mouth of the tunnel when he would mysteriously vanish and again reappear in the mine. Many supposedly intelligent men have claimed this and some twenty-five or forty have thrown up their jobs in consequence.

These same people and others have seen mysterious lights in the graveyard on the side of the hill where many victims of the explosion of May are buried... Efforts to ferret out the cause have been fruitless though close observations have been made by reputable citizens of the camp. These lights are always followed by a death, so it is alleged by others than the miners who might be disciples of the supernatural.

Tombstones where the light appeared have been blanketed but the light remains clear to the vision of those who watch from town.

I found Scofield easily enough and then had to ask for directions to the dirt road that would take me out of town. About a half mile along, I had to leave the car and cross an old barbed wire fence and walk another half mile or so along the railroad bed to reach to reach the town site. There wasn't much left to see there, except for sections of the walls that made up the former Wasatch store, in what was once the center of town. Antique photos show stacks of coffins piled outside the store in the days following the 1900 disaster. I walked through what was left of the town and started up toward the mine site.

However, I soon found that I was not alone. The ghost town remains very popular with treasure hunters due to the fact that so many of the men who were killed at Winter Quarters were bachelors. It is thought that many of them had what were called "post hole banks" in which they stashed their savings dug into the ground near their cabins. Any money that had been secreted away was never recovered. When the town was abandoned, many believed that some of these caches were left behind, hidden and forgotten.

This is what I was told by two young men who had hiked into the site with metal detectors. They told me that they had been coming out to Winter Quarters for a couple of years and just a month before had found a

The Wasatch Store at Winter Quarters in 1900, when the town was still thriving. And (below) how it looked the last time I visited the valley.

metal box that contained old silver coins. In the past, they had also turned up odd coins, a few tools, a pocketknife, a hand mirror and a rusted straight razor. I explained to them what I was doing around the town site and asked them if they had ever heard or seen anything strange in the area.

One of the young men, who identified himself as Mike, glanced at his friend. I could tell they were both a little uneasy about the question. "Actually, yes," Mike finally spoke up. "We were camping out here one night last spring and heard some pretty weird sounds coming from the direction of the mine."

"Weird sounds -- like what?" I asked them.

Mike's companion, Josh, spoke up. "I woke up in the middle of the night and went outside the tent to go to the bathroom and I heard voices coming from the canyon. At first, I just thought that maybe someone else was camping out here but..."

"We never saw anybody and we were out here all day," Mike said.

Josh added. "And we didn't see any fires, either. I woke up Mike and well, you just never know who might be out here. Then it started to get a little stranger. The only way that I can describe the sounds is that it was like people moaning and crying."

"It sounded like a big group of people, moving around, talking -- real weird," said Mike. "I know there was some sort of accident out here or something, I don't know -- maybe that had something to do with it."

His friend agreed. "I have to say that I never really gave much thought to ghosts and stuff, but I don't know what else this could be. I guess if you decide to camp out here, I don't suggest that you do it up the canyon anywhere."

I talked to Josh and Mike for a few minutes and then wandered off on my own, contemplating the fact that this had been my second warning about camping in the canyon beyond the town site. I had heard that the cemetery where the miners were buried in Scofield might be haunted, but apparently the mine site was too. I became determined to spend the night in what turned out to be a rather frigid canyon. To say that it was cold out there that night would be an understatement. The tent that I had brought with me offered little shelter from the wind that came blowing through the canyon and my sleeping bag provided little comfort from the cold. I stayed up most of the night and I do believe that I heard the weird sounds that had been described to me by the treasure hunters.

When I heard the weird noises, it was well after midnight. I heard them coming from the darkness near the old mine site. The best way for me to describe it is to say that it was an odd crying sound, almost like an animal in pain. I wondered for a moment if it might actually be a wounded coyote or something that was out of sight beyond the light from my fire, but then I dismissed this. The sound was farther away than that and then it seemed to be joined by another voice, then another, until there was a chorus of them. Perhaps my imagination as at work, but it sounded to me like a group of women, crying and moaning. In my mind, I could picture the dozens of women who must have come to the mine on the day of the explosion, weeping for the dead and searching desperately for their husbands as the victims were pulled from the depths. The sound faded and dipped and then came back strong again.

Was it the wind? I don't think it was -- but whatever it was, I have never forgotten that sound and for more than a year afterward, I would awaken at night having dreamed about it. It was one of the most unnerving experiences that I have ever had. To this day, I cannot give you a rational explanation that would explain the eerie sounds that I heard that night.

And yes, I did search for an explanation. I gathered my courage and armed with only a flashlight, I set off in search of a source for the sound. As I started up the hill toward the mine site, the sound abruptly ceased. It did not return that night, leaving me to ponder the mystery of what lingers at Winter Quarters.

1903 - 1908: "TWO TRAGEDIES IN FIVE YEARS"
The Hanna Mine Disasters

Hanna, Wyoming, was a company town, owned by the Union Pacific Railroad. Its dirt streets were straight and orderly and its small houses were nearly all alike, with four rooms and a privy out back. The streets ran up the low hills away from the railroad and into the sagebrush. Front Street, a row of small stores and a boarding house, ran along the tracks' north side.

The town had been built by the railroad for one purpose only – the mining of coal.

All of the mines in Hanna were underground. The Hanna No. 1 mine was a death trap, as all the men knew, but the wages were good and so they worked there anyway. The mine was much like other coal mines, with main tunnels, called slopes, that traveled down to side tunnels, called entries, leading off to either side. The entries led to pitch dark rooms underground. To light his work, each mine wore a small lamp with an open flame inside it on the front of his helmet.

The rooms had walls of solid coal as much as 30 feet high. Holding a hand-cranked steel drill at shoulder height, one miner drilled a hole into the coal. At the same time his mate, on the ground with a pick, worked to undercut the face of the wall of coal. Then they filled the hole with blasting powder. A fuse was lit and they hurried out of the room before the blast brought the face down. The men then loaded the loose coal into small cars, which ran on tracks through the entries. Some of the cars were pulled by mules, others were hauled up with cables that were connected to steam engines outside.

It would be two explosions – seconds apart – that caused the first disaster at the Hanna mine. The second would come five years later after a mine fire had been left burning for weeks. The two tragedies would lead to the deaths of 228 men and leave behind a haunting that echoed through the mine for years.

The Union Pacific Railroad needed a constant, steady supply of coal. The coal deposits at Carbon, near Medicine Bow, at Rock Springs, and at Almy, near Evanston, had determined the railroad's route across Wyoming. In 1868, mines were opened at Carbon and Rock Springs and a year later, in Almy. In the early years of the mines, most of the workers were English and Irish. Later, after these miners went on strike, the company brought in Chinese workers to Rock Springs and Almy, which led to the Rock Springs Massacre in 1885, where 28 Chinese miners were killed. Strikes and walkouts continued as the company tried to keep wages low.

The work was back-breaking and dangerous. There were few safety features in the mines and the Union Pacific operations were notorious for lacking extra airshafts for ventilation, extra exits in case of cave-ins and a lack of strong enough timbers to safely hold up the roofs in the tunnels and rooms. It would take large numbers of deaths to make the company realize the real dangers – and even then, it wasn't enough. Most of the first deaths that came were in scattered accidents, claiming one or two lives, but in 1881, an explosion and fire killed 38 men in a mine at Almy. Five years later, 13 more men died in the same mine from another fire.

The state of Wyoming passed new safety laws, which required a state safety inspector to inspect evey mine at least once every three months. Boys under the age of 14 were prohibited from working underground. In the belief that fatigue was the main cause of accidents, it was decided that workdays in the mines should be limited to eight hours. The Union Pacific ignored this requirement until 1907, when the newly organized Mine Workers of America won the right to an eight-hour workday for Union Pacific miners after a labor dispute.

Even with a few new safety regulations, accidents continued to happen in Wyoming mines. In 1895, 62 miners were killed in an explosion near Evanston and in February 1901, another 26 men were killed in a cave-in at Diamondville in Lincoln County. Eight months later, 22 more were killed in the same mine. The state legislature passed more laws and the state mine inspector was given the power to hire deputies to help with his overwhelming task. Inspections began to be required even after non-fatal accidents but accidents still occurred.

Meanwhile, the Union Pacific Railroad continued to grow and become more efficient. The tracks were rebuilt across Wyoming with curves being straightened and steep grades lowered. By the end of the 1890s, the mines at Carbon were nearly played out. In 1902, they were closed for good. The new railroad route ran through Hanna, 12 miles to the north, where new mines had been opened a few years before. Most of the miners simply moved over to Hanna and went right back to work. In the new town, though, they found themselves in a much different place. Where the town of Carbon had been scattered and disorganized, with more shacks than houses, Hanna had been planned by the railroad. The Union Pacific Coal Company owned everything in town – the houses, the store, the boarding houses and the community hall – the miners were forced to rent from the company and the rent was deducted from their pay.

While safety conditions were often questionable, the pay at the Union Pacific mines was good. Rent and purchases at the company store were deducted from their weekly paychecks but for most of the men, there was plenty left over to save or to mail home to relatives. Most of the workers in Hanna were Polish, Chinese or Finnish, with black miners making up the rest of the workforce.

The Finns were the largest group of immigrants working the mine. They were hard workers and saved their money to make seasonal trips back home every few years, but they invariably returned to Hanna. Town authorities were happy to cater to them and the towering wooden hall of the Finnish Temperance Society dominated the landscape of Hanna. The men were sober and thrifty, took good care of their families and labored long hours in the local mine.

Most of the Finns were working on the day shift on June 30, 1903, when the first disaster occurred. Around 10:30 a.m., blasting set off a tremendous explosion about one-and-one-half miles into the shaft. Another explosion followed two seconds later, when gas in the mine ignited. Great bursts of flame roared through the mine, knocking men down, scorching and burning others in the path of the flames. At the first explosion, the timbers at the mouth of the mine blew outward like kindling. Fire raged from dozens of entry points into the mine, leaving only one entrance where rescue workers could descend. One miner, a black man named William Christian, worked in this narrow entryway for hours, pulling out more than 20 men before he collapsed in exhaustion.

During the next 24 hours, 46 men were rescued from the burning mine, but 169 perished in the flames. Tragically, it was an accident that was completely unavoidable. Using a system called "gouging," the company had mined the coal as it dug the hole. That is, the entries off the main slope were opened and mined as the slope was dug farther downwards. This meant miners were always working below and beyond big areas empty of coal but very likely to fill with gases that might explode at any time. The correct way to do it, mine inspectors later stated, would have been to dig the main slope all the way down first, and then mine back upwards. Then the abandoned rooms could be allowed to fill with water, and the miners would never be working below empty spaces filled with dangerous gas. Only greed led the company to begin gouging coal as soon as it opened the mine.

And company greed forced the miners back to work a short time later. The mine was almost immediately re-opened, although the most damaged portions stayed closed for five months. No additional safety precautions were put into place after the mine started operating again.

Only one level of the mine – the fourteenth – was never re-opened. It had been too badly damaged in the blast and recovery efforts had failed, leaving the body of one miner to be sealed forever in the empty level. But did he remain there in peace? Workers at the mine – *superstitious* workers, mine managers stressed – claimed that they sometimes heard the sound of hammering from the abandoned section of the mine. In addition to the sounds of tools pounding the wall, they heard clanking sounds as if machinery was in operation and according to some, the mournful cry of a man. The miners claimed that the sound sent chills up the spines of even the most hardened men.

The reports of the ghost continued for the next five years, as conditions at the mine deteriorated further. Newspaper editorials railed against the lack of safety equipment and the company's failure to improve the mine. Editors at the *Independent* wrote, "We should... demand for these miners the same protection of life which we would ask for if we were working underground at Hanna."

On March 28, 1908, death came to Hanna once again. Unbelievably, gas fires had been burning in the lower depths of the mine for six days before more explosions killed another batch of miners. Half shifts had continued to work the upper levels while the fires – believed to be non-threatening – burned below. The company kept the miners working until a second disaster occurred.

The ground beneath the town of Hanna trembled and shook as another thunderous explosion rocked the mine. Huge rocks and splintered timbers erupted from the entrances, spewing thick, black dust. The main entrance was sealed off by the blast but rescue workers managed to get into the east entrance. The men quickly organized into two groups. One group went into the mine and the other worked to clear rocks and debris from the main entrance. The first group descended into the blackness, looking for survivors and corpses.

Unknown to the rescue party, volatile gases were building in the mine, swirling toward the flames that had been burning for days. Suddenly, a second explosion shook the mine. Eighteen men had been trapped underground by the first blast. There were 41 more underground when the second explosion came. The two blasts left 31 new widows, and 103 children without fathers.

Recovery workers were only able to pull 32 of the dead from the mine after the 1908 explosions. The rest were left inside when the mine finally closed down for good.

The Hanna mine was gone but coal mining in Wyoming remained dangerous. Between 1912 and 1938, 160 more miners were killed in Wyoming in accidents involving five or more men. Others continued to be killed in ones and twos. The worst disaster in those years came in August 1923, when 99 men were killed in an explosion in a mine near Kemmerer. The legislature continued to pass more laws strengthening safety rules and giving the inspectors more authority, but it was too late to save the lives of those who had been lost.

As the years have passed, many of the mines have been forgotten. Wyoming's coal-mining towns, some abandoned, some struggling to get by, one or two still thriving, have big, empty spaces beneath them. These spaces – the slopes, the entries and the many rooms – were once filled with men struggling to survive as they eked out a living from the unforgiving earth.

But are those spaces really empty? Do the spirits of the slain men still walk – as the miners from the past once claimed – through those dark spots, still reliving their last days over and over again?

1918: THE MALBONE STREET DISASTER
Death on the Brooklyn Rapid Transit Train

The early 1900s were marred by scores of labor strikes across the country. There was no question that workers of the day often labored under deplorable conditions. They worked long hours in often unsafe factories and, in many cases, labor unions were the only relief they had from the greed of big companies who would work their employees until they literally broke under the pressure. But in some cases, labor strikes had fatal consequences – as they did in Brooklyn, New York, in 1918.

The Malbone Street Wreck occurred after a strikebreaker lost control of a Brighton Beach train during the evening rush hour on a steep grade down Crown Heights, between Park Place and a tunnel under Flatbush

Avenue at Malbone Street (renamed Empire Boulevard after the disaster.) Ninety-three people died and many more were injured. To this day, it remains the worst wreck in the history of New York City's subway system.

Previously known as the Brooklyn, Flatbush and Coney Island Railroad, the Brighton Beach line dated back to the 1870s. It was one of several steam railroads that linked Brooklyn to the seaside resorts. By the early 1900s, the Brooklyn Rapid Transit system controlled the line, along with streetcar and elevated lines throughout the area.

During 1918, the last year of World War I, tensions escalated between Brooklyn Rapid Transit (BRT) and the Brotherhood of Locomotive Engineers. At least 20 men had been fired because of their membership in the union. The union responded by filing a grievance with the National War Labor Board, a federal review panel that had been created to strengthen the war effort on the home front by improving labor-management relations. In late October, the board recommended that the BRT re-hire the workers with back pay, but the board had no power of enforcement and the BRT ignored the recommendation. In fact, they even refused to meet with the union's delegation. Finally, a strike was called started at 5:00 a.m. on Friday, November 1, 1918.

The strike crippled the rail line. Supervisors and clerks with little or no hands-on training were thrown into empty locomotives to work as motormen. Among the strike-breakers was Edward Luciano, 23, who worked under the name of Billy Lewis to avoid the anti-Italian prejudice that was prevalent at the time. He had been a dispatcher for the BRT for two years. Earlier in 1918, he had received two hours of classroom instruction to become a motorman. Just before he was assigned to a locomotive, he had spent two days riding as an observer to gain practical experience in train operations. Needless to say, this scant training fell far short of the BRT's usual 60 hours of on-the-job training, in addition to a 90-question exam, 60 hours of apprenticeship on board trains, a physical exam and further testing and certification. After all of that, neophytes would be permitted to take empty trains on practice runs in and around the yards and terminals before finally being allowed to operate a train that was carrying passengers.

At 5:00 a.m. on November 1, Luciano began a long, eleven-and-one-half hour shift. When it ended at 4:30 p.m., he was offered a $20 bonus and the promise of a post-strike raise to pilot a rush-hour train from Kings Highway to Manhattan and then back to Brooklyn over the Brighton Beach line to Coney Island. Luciano had never ridden on the Brighton line, let alone driven a train there, but he gladly accepted. "A man has to earn a living," he later told the *New York Times*.

In the aftermath of the disaster, William Brody, a BRT trainmaster, stated that Thomas Blewitt, the BRT superintendent responsible for certifying motormen, had represented Luciano as being "properly qualified." Ironically, according to the standards set by the company in the midst of the strike, he probably was. Men with similar "qualifications" had been running trains on the line all day. Supervisors decided to take a chance with Luciano. At the yard, he was given a train with five cars attached. Each car had a steel underframe and a wooden body and roof. Four of the cars were at least 30 years old.

At 6:08 p.m., Luciano's train arrived at the Park Row terminal, the vaulted train shed that stood at the Manhattan end of the Brooklyn Bridge. Six minutes later, Luciano began his return trip to Brighton Beach. Charles Darling, a lawyer riding in the first car, later said that the train moved with sudden starts and stops and sped around a curve at Sands Street, the first station in Brooklyn. The train then rumbled onto the Fulton Street elevated line. Walter H. Simonson, a civil engineer who was on board, recalled that the car was jammed to near standing room only.

At 6:29 p.m., Luciano departed Grand Avenue for the junction at Franklin Avenue. The switch there was incorrectly set, keeping the train on the Fulton Avenue line toward East New York, rather than turning it southward toward Brighton Beach. After some delay, Luciano managed to back the train up and route it onto the Brighton Beach line at 6:38 p.m. Two minutes later, the train left Park Place Station.

As its name indicates, Crown Heights is located atop a crest of land. Between Park Place, at the top of the Heights, and Prospect Park, the station at the foot of the hill, the track dropped 70 feet over a distance of less than a mile. After the drop came an S-shaped curve that was known as "Deadman's Curve" even before the accident. It was a hazardous place where experienced motormen had to stay alert. By this time, Luciano was probably exhausted. He had been fortunate enough to have recently recovered from the deadly strain of influenza that targeted mainly young adults in the wake of World War I, claiming an estimated three percent of the world's population. In addition to having been ill, he was finishing up a double shift at an extremely demanding job for which he had been inadequately trained. His conductor signaled a stop at the next station -- Consumer's Park (now Botanic Garden) -- but Luciano rushed through without stopping. Passenger Walter Simonson felt the train accelerate, as if to make up for lost time. The next stop was Prospect Park, on the other side of Flatbush Avenue.

Luciano found it simple to accelerate the train but not so easy to stop it. Braking a subway train safely and smoothly – and aligning it with the station platform so passengers can safely board and depart – was a difficult task that could only be achieved with experience. The brakes operated with compressed air. By maximizing air pressure in the train's main brake line, a motorman had to release the brakes. In other words, he permitted the air to push the brake shoes from the wheels so the train could move. When he wanted to slow the train, he applied the brakes by reducing air pressure, permitting the brake shoes to make contact with the wheels. Air brakes took time to apply and to take effect, which meant that trains often traveled hundreds of feet before stopping. A motorman who knew from training and experience how his train would respond to a particular uphill or downhill grade could gauge when to begin braking. Luciano had no such experience. He had never run a train on the Brighton Beach line --- or any other line -- before that morning.

At the bottom of the hill, the tracks curved sharply, entering a short tunnel beneath the intersection of Flatbush Avenue and Malbone Street. The posted speed limit for the curve was six miles per hour. Luciano later stated that he had been traveling at 30 miles per hour. After the crash, the *New York Times* quoted a naval officer who estimated the train's speed at 70 miles per hour when it left the track. Many of the surviving passengers later admitted to feeling frightened as Luciano picked up the pace to try and make up for lost time.

As Luciano approached the curve, he claimed that the air brakes failed, after which he applied the emergency brakes and threw the train into reverse. Investigators from the New York Public Service Commission and the BRT found after examining the wreckage that the brakes had not failed, the emergency brakes had never been applied and the motors were never reversed. No one could explain what Luciano had been doing in those final seconds but it was obvious that he was totally unprepared for the challenges that faced him that day.

It was 6:42 p.m. when the train reached Malbone Street and roared into the curve, the first car derailed, ripping up the third rail in a burst of blue sparks. The car left the rails a few feet in front of the opening to the tunnel and rammed one end of a concrete partition that separated the north and southbound tracks. It was thrown at right angles across the roadbed, its front and rear corners crashing into the tunnel wall. The windows of the car shattered, spraying glass at the screaming passengers. Packed together in the flimsy wooden box, the passengers were crushed and cut to pieces.

The two following cars had swung wider. One of them struck the edge of the tunnel's mouth and ripped along its inner wall, where steel girders that supported the tunnel roof and Flatbush Avenue above protruded from the concrete surface. The girders tore into the car's roof and left side and it splintered and shattered into bits and pieces of wood, steel and flesh. Great gashes were cut into the side of the car, which was still traveling at high speed, mowing down the passengers who were standing, and decapitating some of them.

The left sides of both the second and third cars were stripped away. Scores of men, women and children were flung against the girders and the concrete wall, where they were either killed instantly or crushed under the wheels after falling onto the tracks. Some of those remaining inside the car were killed inside when they fell onto the twisted iron of the seats, broken timbers, and iron beams that projected through the shattered bottom of the car. People standing on the platforms were nearly all killed instantly. One dead man was found impaled on a broken metal rod that had run underneath the car and had snapped, shoting upward in the crash.

In the third car, Walter Simonson felt the car rise beneath him. It tilted to the left, striking the concrete pier at the mouth of the tunnel. In the moment before the lights went out, Simonson saw the left side of the car break apart and the wooden seats shatter, their riders stuck and savaged by splintering car timbers. He saw passengers beheaded by the tunnel girders and watched in horror as the car's roof crumpled. By all accounts, the carnage happened in seconds. Simonson was flung against a remaining piece of the car's left side, which kept him from flying into the tunnel.

With an agonizing shriek of metal, the train finally came to a stop. Only 10 seconds had passed – it was still

A crowd gathered outside of the tunnel where the wreck occurred and (right) the scene inside of the tunnel, where Brooklyn commuters lost their lives because of negligence.

6:42 p.m.

The last two cars had not derailed and most of the passengers riding in them escaped without serious injury. However, nearly all of them had been cut by flying glass or were bruised from being thrown from their seats. They were packed so tightly in the two rear cars that the force of the wreck was not really felt. Many women on board became hysterical when they learned what had happened in the front cars. The passengers were in complete darkness since the derailing cars had torn out the power lines in the tunnel. They could see nothing, but could hear the screams of the dying and injured in the blackness ahead. Would-be rescuers who tried to reach the forward cars found their way cut off by masses of broken wood and twisted steel. There was no way to get to the survivors who were pinned to their seats or crushed in the ruined cars.

Firemen who took part in the rescue work said that the second and third cars had fallen over on their sides and the passengers lay heaped together, some dead and some dying, some slightly injured and some unhurt, but all tightly gripped by the wreckage. Bodies were smothered to death found with only slight marks of injuries.

The last cars had survived the disaster and the locomotive was also largely intact. Attorney Charles Darling watched as Edward Luciano emerged unscathed from the cab. The lawyer asked him what had happened. "I don't know," Luciano reportedly replied. "I lost control of the damn thing, that's all." Then he stepped from the car and walked up the track to Prospect Park station. A newsboy waiting for a train who had heard the crash saw a man – presumably Luciano -- walk out of the tunnel and wander away. Luciano arrived home later that evening, having taken a trolley.

Because of the position of the wreck and the nature of the accident, there was a delay in spreading the alarm. Police and firefighters were not notified for nearly 20 minutes. The first rescuers to arrive on the scene found the tunnel jammed with debris "so tightly...that no crevice or opening was left," reported the *New York Times*. With lanterns in hand, they began removing wreckage one piece at a time. Police officers and firefighters set about removing the wounded from the tangle of steel, glass and shattered wood, "which stuck out like bayonets in all directions, some of them having already pierced those in the cars," the *Times* reported. Those who could walk staggered from the tunnel. Others had to be carried out. Cradles of burlap were made for the recovered bodies, which were hoisted by the rescuers to the street and laid out in rows before being taken to the morgue.

As word about the accident spread throughout Brooklyn, there was little detail about when or where it had happened. Those waiting for loved ones traveling home during rush hour began to panic. When it was finally realized where the tragedy had taken place, a crowd began to gather. Most were there to try and learn the fate of friends and loved ones, but ghoulish curiosity-seekers also swelled the ranks of onlookers. As the bodies of the dead were lifted out of the tunnel, reserves from six police precincts were sent to keep order. Ambulances arrived from every hospital in Brooklyn and scores of doctors and nurses were sent to the scene.

As darkness fell on the city, conditions in the tunnel grew even blacker. Automobiles were commandeered and their headlights were pointed at the wreckage. The Brooklyn Gas Company and the Brooklyn Edison Company sent gangs of men with searchlights to illuminate the site. Down in the tunnel, surgeons were working by lantern light, side by side with priests administering last rites.

Tens of thousands of people flocked to the police stations and to the morgue where the bodies were taken. The large numbers of those searching for missing relatives made identifying the dead a slow process. Telephone service in Brooklyn became overburdened as frantic calls were made to try and track down loved ones who usually traveled on the BRT line and had not yet arrived home. The wreckage stopped all Brighton Beach traffic, holding up thousands of passengers on the trains that followed. Many of those delayed had to walk long distances to overcrowded streetcars. Commuters arrived home more than two hours late, usually to empty homes. In many cases, their families had become alarmed and had gone to the site of the wreck in search of news, delaying their reunions until late in the evening.

In the early morning hours of November 2, Edward Luciano was arrested at his home on 33rd Street in Brooklyn. He was taken to the Snyder Street police station, where he was questioned by the district attorney, the police commissioner and the mayor. The young man quickly broke down when faced with such intimidating interrogators and blurted out a nervous story that turned out to be largely untrue. New York City Mayor John Hylan, himself a former railroad man, indicated to reporters that he believed Luciano had been criminally negligent. He told the press, "This man confessed that he had never run a train on the Brighton Beach line before.

He also admitted that when running around that curve, he was making a speed of thirty miles an hour."

Ironically, the mayor had been fired from his position as a locomotive engineer for taking a curve too fast and nearly hitting a supervisor who was crossing the tracks. He protested his dismissal, but to no avail. The experience left him with a bitter hatred of private rail systems and their owners.

When it was pointed out that a sign on the curve warned motormen to go no faster than six miles per hour, Luciano shrugged and had no reply. When he was asked why he had taken a job for which he was unfitted, he answered, "A man has to earn a living." He told the men that he had no intention of running away from the crash. He said he remembered nothing until he found himself at home after the accident. He did not know how he got out of the wreck, or how he got home. He said that he had a vague

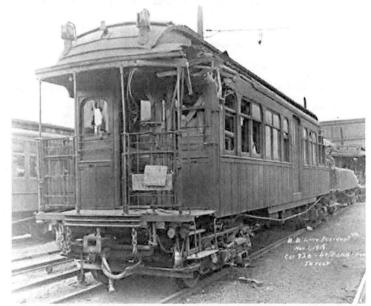

One of the only intact cars is returned to the Brooklyn Rail Yard after the disaster. Despite a lengthy investigation and several indictments, no one was ever held responsible for the disaster.

recollection of having boarded a trolley car, but could not remember what car it was. Detectives stated that Luciano was "as pale as death" when they reached his home and he appeared to be on the verge of collapse. His replies to questions about the details of the accident turned out to be lies: The brakes had not failed, the emergency brakes had never been applied and the motors were never reversed.

His wife pled his case to the newspapers. "Three weeks ago, my husband had an attack of influenza. The next Friday, our baby died… now this terrible accident," she wept. But the general public had little sympathy for Luciano, or for his bosses who operated the rail line.

Luciano and five officials from the BRT were indicted for manslaughter after the accident. Before the trial began, the BRT's lawyers obtained a change of venue from Brooklyn to Nassau County. Mysteriously, although the prosecution knew that Luciano had perjured himself by lying when he said that he had applied the brakes, that part of his statement was never used as evidence. All cases ended in hung juries, acquittals and dismissals. No one, including Luciano or the men who put him into his deadly position at the train controls, was ever held responsible for the deadly disaster.

The controversy over the disaster raged for months, culminating in a charge by Public Service Commissioner Travis Whitney that Mayor Hylan was responsible for the deaths in the tunnel. He said that it was the mayor's fault that the decrepit wooden cars – which were pulverized in the wreck while the steel cars came through unscathed – were still being used. Hylan, Whitney insisted, had done nothing for 10 months with an agreement awaiting his signature that would compel the line to use only steel cars. His charges were dismissed as nothing more than political posturing and eventually, the finger-pointing faded from the headlines.

In December, just a month after the accident, the Brooklyn Rapid Transit line went into receivership. This delayed payment of any claims against the line for over three years. Eventually, the company paid out damages totaling $1.6 million. The largest payout was $40,000, which went to the widow of George W. Holmes, the only railroad worker to die in the disaster. In 1923, the BRT was reorganized as the Brooklyn-Manhattan Transit Corporation. It, too, went into receivership and was dissolved on November 1, 1941, the twenty-third anniversary of the accident.

After Luciano was acquitted in 1919, he moved and went into the real estate business. He faded from history and what happened to him after that is unknown.

1919: "THERE WAS NO ESCAPE FROM THE WAVE"
The Boston Molasses Flood

The story of the "Great Molasses Spill" had its start in 1915, when the Purity Distilling Company constructed a huge storage tank in Boston's North End. It was designed to hold shipments of Caribbean molasses that could be distilled into rum and industrial alcohol. Located on Commercial Street, near Boston Harbor, the immense tank towered over the nearby neighborhood of homes and businesses.

In the years that followed the tank's construction, Purity and its parent company, U.S. Industrial Alcohol, had thrived thanks to the wartime demands for industrial alcohol, which was used in the production of weapons during World War I.

Those who lived and worked near the tank watched it with growing concern. The immense structure shuddered and groaned each time it was filled. Molasses seeped through the tank's seams, running to the ground in thin, sticky rivulets. Purity Distilling responded by painting the exterior of the tank brown, making it harder to see the leaking molasses.

There was grumbling that something terrible was bound to happen one of these days….

Like most of the rest of the country, Boston had a good feeling about it in January 1919. The Great War in Europe had finally come to an end and the peacetime economy was starting to thrive. Sailors and soldiers were returning to civilian life and it seemed as though the world was finally getting back to normal.

In Boston's busy harbor, the Navy training ship *Nantucket* was docked at Battery Wharf, within walking distance of the Charlestown Navy Yard. Along Commercial Street in the North End, freight terminals were humming with activity. Another 600,000 gallons of molasses had just arrived on a ship from Cuba and was added to the huge storage tank at the Purity Distilling Company. Located on the waterfront side of the street, close to the playground in North End Park, the 100-by-40-foot container held 2.3 million gallons of molasses that would eventually find its way to the company's plant in Cambridge.

January 15 was an unseasonably warm winter's day for Boston – close to 40 degrees -- and many people were out and about. Robert Burnett was at home on Commercial Street eating dinner with his family. Ralph Martin and Dave Spellman were relaxing in North End Park, sitting on an automobile. Bridgett Cloughtery, her daughter Theresa and her son Stephen, were eating in their dining room at 6 Copps Hill Terrace. Bridgett's son Martin, who worked nights, was asleep in the next room. Earlier, Mrs. Cougherty had been hanging laundry outside and had stopped to wave at a neighborhood child, little Maria DiStasio, who was gathering firewood.

Things were quiet in the nearby business establishments. William White, the custodian of the giant molasses tank, locked up and headed uptown to meet his wife for lunch and shopping. At freight house No. 4 of the Boston & Worcester Street Railway Company, freight agent Dorley worked with a crew of three clerks in a small office above the warehouse.

In the recreation room of a nearby firehouse, the men from fireboat No. 31 were passing the afternoon. Hoseman William H. Connor, who had just returned from the war where he had served aboard the *U.S.S. Kearsarge*, was playing cards with fellow firefighters Nat Bowering, Patrick Driscoll, Frank McDermott and George Lahey. Lahey later recalled that one of the fireman remarked on how quiet the day had been with no alarm all morning.

Daily life in the neighborhood continued just as it was supposed to. Horses pulled freight wagons down the street. Children from the nearby homes finished their lunches and told their mothers goodbye, walking back to school after the mid-day break. Workmen finished their lunches and returned to their labors. A railway train rattled past on the elevated tracks just west of the giant molasses tank.

Then, suddenly, the lives of those who lived and worked near the tank changed forever.

Most of the witnesses later agreed that the first sign of disaster came not with an explosion but with an ominous rumbling sound. The cause of the accident remains a mystery to this day, but whether it was a tank failure or an explosion makes little difference – the deadly results were the same. The giant tank suddenly ruptured with such force that its three-quarter-inch steel sides blasted into the elevated railway tracks. According to the *Boston Post*, the tank "smote the huge steel girders of the 'L' structure and bent and twisted and snapped them as if by the smash of a giant fist." More than 100 feet of the elevated tracks were utterly destroyed in a matter of seconds.

Every gallon of the thick molasses weighed almost 12 pounds. In a few moments, more than 27 million pounds of molasses was freed from the tank. A sticky wave more than 30 feet high gushed out of the tank and bore down on the homes of Copps Hill Terrace. After the wave smashed against the brick structures at the base of the hill, it swirled with deadly force back toward the harbor.

Robert Burnett, who had been at home with his family eating dinner in their second-floor dining room, told the *Boston Post*:

I thought it was an elevated train, until I heard a swish as if the wind was rushing. Then it became dark. I looked out from the windows and saw this black wave coming. It didn't rush. It just rolled, slowly as it seemed, like the side of a mountain falling into space. Of course, it came quickly... We snatched open the door of the hall and molasses was already at the top of the 14-step flight of stairs. I slammed the door and we ran for the roof.

At 6 Copps Hill Terrace, Martin Cloughtery woke up when he heard a slight rumble outside. He later told the newspapers that he "could see nothing but blackness all around with a few flashes of light. I seemed to be smothering when I got a breath of fresh air. I did not know where I was. I thought I was in the water... I found

The aftermath of the Boston Molasses Spill, which left more than 150 people dead.

what turned out to be part of my house resting on my chest."

Martin's mother, Bridgett Cloughtery, was killed when the wave of molasses struck their home. Reports stated that she had been "blown through the walls of her home and buried under the debris of her dwelling."

Martin McDonough lived in another apartment in the same building. The last thing he remembered hearing was a crash as he was taking a bite of mashed potatoes. He was later found unconscious in the street. The entire building had been flattened when the molasses spill swept it more than 100 feet off its foundation.

The body of little Maria DiStasio was found buried beneath wreckage near the elevated train tracks where she had been gathering firewood.

At the freight office, agent Dorley knew exactly what the sound was when he first heard it. "The molasses tank is gone," he cried to the other clerks in the office. He told the *Post:*

The words were barely out when the avalanche came. We heard the crash of the steel tank as it hurtled to the ground. The broken parts of the tank missed our shed by only a matter of inches... Parts of the tank struck other houses and they crumpled like eggs... We were trapped in the office. Beneath us surged the flood, sweeping everything before it. Men and horses about in the yard were caught up and tossed here and there like so many logs in a torrent.

Twenty-one people died in the disaster and another 150 were injured. Many others escaped death by sheer luck. A police officer who was walking his beat felt some liquid hit the back of his uniform and was able to duck around the corner of a brick building before the force of the wave hit. A sailor who had been standing on a corner chatting with a girl was swept away, but only slightly injured. The girl was listed among the missing. In North End Park, Dave Spellman watched as the wave of molasses washed his friend Ralph Martin into the harbor. He tried to save him but was unable to fight his way through the thick and sticky goo. A workman unloading a load of lard was severely injured and his horse killed when the wave of molasses struck his delivery wagon. Another workman, who was loading a wagon at the street railway terminal was thrown to the pavement and his horse and wagon crushed. An oil tanker was completely demolished. Two girls, ages nine and eleven, didn't return to school after the noon break and it was realized they were lost in the wave.

Most of the deaths that resulted from the disaster were caused by suffocation. There was simply no escape from it. As the molasses swept over its victims, they were unable to run, swim or even move. Once it washed over a person's head, there was no way to breathe or get free from the sticky mass. To die in such a way was undoubtedly terrifying.

Lieutenant Commander William Copeland was on the upper deck of the training ship *Nantucket* when he saw the tank burst open. Within five minutes, his crew had rushed to the scene with stretchers, first-aid kits and sailors to aid in the rescue of survivors. From the Charlestown Navy Yard, Commander William Rush sent crews from the minesweepers *Starling, Breaker* and *Billow*, which were anchored off the North End pier. Two Navy tugboats and a submarine chaser hurried to the scene and an Army hospital in Roxbury sent a medical detachment of 80 men. The Boston Red Cross also rushed to the accident site to offer support services.

What the rescue crews found was a huge sticky mess. Reeking, waist-deep molasses sloshed through the ruins of houses, freight terminals and warehouses. Wagons and railroad cars had been shattered and overturned by the heavy tide. Stunned survivors staggered in the morass, shaking and bogged down by the thick liquid. The sludge was so sticky and impenetrable that medical personnel on the scene and at the local hospitals were unable to immediately determine the gender of the survivors that were brought to them. As it slopped onto the floors, the molasses fouled the wheels of the hospital gurneys and dirtied the hallways and exam rooms.

Rescuers waded through tangles of debris, the hazards of which were hidden under the mess. They risked their own safety as they slogged through the wreckage. Their rubber boots became a hindrance as they filled with the oozing slime and men could be seen in their stocking feet as they chopped at debris with fire axes or cut through metal with acetylene torches.

During a day filled with valiant efforts, the most harrowing rescue occurred at the fireboat No. 31 firehouse. George Lahey had just left the card game and was going upstairs to check on the crew's boat when the wave of molasses hit. The tide actually lifted the three-and-a-half-story firehouse and then slammed it on the ground again. The force of the blow threw Lahey back down the stairs to the recreation room and sent him sprawling. Molasses and pieces of metal tank crashed through the firehouse and overturned a huge slate pool table, pinning Lahey to the floor.

Meanwhile, before the impact, fireman William Connor saw a wall of molasses that he guessed to be 150 feet high approaching the station like a cyclone. He yelled at the other men to jump and Patrick Driscoll hurled himself headfirst through the closest window. But Connor and Nat Bowering, along with Lahey, were not so lucky. They were knocked down on the floor and trapped in the building when the second story collapsed. The only thing that kept the men from being crushed to death by the second floor was a few chairs and a piano. There was barely 18 inches between the trapped men and the floor that loomed above them. Connor knew that if anyone attempted to rescue them – and entered the second floor – they would be killed instantly.

The prospect of being crushed to death was only one of the men's worries. The building had barely escaped being washed out into the harbor. Stuck at the edge of the wrecked dock, the fire station was directly in the path of thousands of gallons of molasses as it flowed downward toward the water.

Trapped on their backs, the three men would see out of a narrow opening and quickly realized the danger they were in. The flood of molasses, deadly in its own right, carried crushed pieces of wreckage with it as it flowed toward the place where they were trapped. If they were not crushed by the building collapsing, they could be drowned in the molasses or cut to pieces by the debris that came along with the wave.

Connor was able to grab hold of Lahey's foot, which was sticking through a partition that separated them. Lahey pleaded for help. The molasses was flowing in around him and was nearly up to his neck. Connor was also stuck but knowing that the men would be drowned if the molasses was not allowed to flow through the building, he crawled to an opening and kicked out a tangle of boards that were stuck over an open hold in the side of the firehouse. The level of the molasses dropped as it seeped through the ruins. "It seemed like weeks that we lay there," Connor later recalled. "The flood of molasses at times flowed up to our ears. We bumped out heads on the floor above, always trying to keep our nose and mouth above the fluid."

Finally, after about 30 minutes, a sailor from the *Nantucket* saw Connor's foot moving in the ruins. He signaled his fellow rescuers and they began a two-hour effort to work the firefighters loose. Not worrying about their own safety, a team of sailors smashed into the building and worked their way inside. With saws and their bare hands, they tore away the beams that imprisoned Bowering and Connor. Sailors pulled the two men to safety and then went back for Lahey. They desperately cut away a portion of the wood floor beneath him and rescuers were able to make contact with the trapped man. With Lahey's fading voice directing their work, a team of 50 men used torches and cutting saws to remove the iron and steel that held him in place.

Sadly, the rescue came too late. Just minutes before the sailors reached Lahey, he had lost consciousness. His head dropped into the molasses and he drowned.

Lahey did not die alone in the disaster. Another 20 people joined him in an early grave. Crews spent months spraying the area with fire hoses to clean molasses off the bricks and cobblestone streets of Boston's North End.

The question of who was responsible for the tragedy languished in the courts for years. The distilling company argued that some outside force caused the tank to explode. Prosecutors called it a "ghostly defense," laughing that the company seemed to think that "ghosts and hobgoblins" were responsible for the rupture. In the end, most came to believe that the tank was simply not strong enough to contain the massive load of syrup. The company paid out nearly $1 million in claims, an insufficient amount to make up for the lost and shattered lives caused by something as simple as molasses.

1924: CASTLE GATE MINE DISASTER

For well over a century, steam kept this country moving. In a way it still does: It keeps the lights on and the television playing in most of the country, anyway. But until the 1920s and 1930s, steam really did run just about everything -- tractors, trains, ships, industrial machines, and even some cars. Steam provided the power and boiling water provided the steam but it was coal the kept all that water boiling. Coal also kept people warm in their homes and fired the giant steel mills that helped make our country the industrial powerhouse that it was.

Coal was king, and the digging of the stuff made some men rich as kings. Coal provided meager livings for hundreds of thousands of men and boys, and fabulous wealth for a few. With all the money there was to be made in the coal industry, it is not difficult to believe that many business men wanted to become involved with that lucrative prospect. Coal was the original "black gold."

During the nineteenth century and into the early part of the twentieth, coal mines were opened all over the country. Although ten states provide ninety percent of the coal in the U.S., at least 27 states had (and still have) active coal mines. Early on, it seemed that coal couldn't be pulled from the ground fast enough, but as we moved through the early decades of the twentieth century, the coal boom was starting to decline. The coal industry had moved into a period of over-expansion and over-production. Too many mines had been opened and mining technology allowed for more coal to be pulled from those mines. It wasn't just men with picks and horse drawn coal carts anymore. Other forms of energy, such as gasoline and diesel fuels, were being introduced and used. The automobile was firmly established as the newest and most popular mode of transportation.

The result was decreased orders for coal from mines all over the country. Coal certainly wasn't hearing its death toll, as many billions of tons were still being produced, but some mines were hit harder than others. Some mines shut down temporarily and others reduced their work force. Such was the situation in March of 1924 in east central Utah.

A reduction in orders for coal meant layoffs and closings. Utah Fuel Company's Castle Gate Mines were no exception. Although Castle Gate had not declined which mines it needed to close, it furloughed many of its miners. To keep as many families in the area fed as possible, they laid off young, single miners and those without dependents and even hired some married family men who had been laid off when area mines had temporarily shut down. The miners knew the Castle Gate Mines were known for being dangerous, but they were happy to have jobs. Two weeks later, disaster struck.

Castle Gate Mine No. 1 opened in 1886 in Willow Creek Canyon, 90 miles southeast of Salt Lake City. It was named for a unique rock formation at the entrance to Price Canyon. Initially, boxcars were used to bring

The distinctive stone formation at the mouth of Price Canyon known as the Castle Gate, for which the Castle Gate mines were named.

in the first miners, who used them as their homes until the boxcars were needed elsewhere. Then, the company put the men up in tents until suitable housing could be built. After the first few houses were completed, the makeup of the Castle Gate began shifting from single immigrant and American-born men to more families. The town of Castle Gate was incorporated in 1912, the same year the second mine was opened. Castle Gate No. 2 was located on the opposite side of the canyon, one mile apart from the No. 1 mine.

Castle Gate Mine No. 1 had reasonably good coal quality, which was baked into coke for smelting plants to use in the production of steel. But when No. 2 was opened, the coal was of supreme quality, some of the best in the state, or even the region. This coal was destined for use in steam locomotives and steamboats. In 1922, Castle Gate Mine No. 3 opened and coal production went into full swing.

All three Castle Gate mines had been running smoothly with rotating shifts. For two weeks, some new men had been working together after many had been laid off and others hired. It was very unusual for such a high percentage of the miners to be married with children, but the company was trying to do right by the family men. And so, when 171 men walked into Castle Gate Mine No. 2 bright and early on Saturday morning, March 8, 1924, they were happy to be there and grateful to have jobs. It would not be long before their happiness would turn to terror.

A check board was positioned next to the entrance of each mine. On the board were a series of tiny hooks with small brass number plates hanging from them. As every miner walked into the mine to work, he would take in with him the brass plate bearing the number he had been assigned. This system was used to keep track of who was in the mine and who was not. If a man's number plate was gone from its hook, he was in the mine. It was a simple, commonly used system that had been adopted by many mine companies. As each man passed into the mine on that Saturday, he carried with him his brass number plate.

Inside the mine, the men walked down deep below the surface into rooms where different groups would be removing the coal that the shift before them had knocked loose. The coal mined in Castle Gate No. 2 was very brittle. The new "short wall" mechanical equipment that they had been using to dig out the coal created a large amount of coal dust when it was used with brittle coal. This mine had a sprinkler system to dampen down the dust, but it had not been sufficient to keep the dust down that day. Consequently, when the men went to work that day, the air and floors were heavy with light, fluffy black powder. In some mines, the men had to work hunched over because the room and tunnel ceilings were so low. In No. 2, however, the coal seams were very deep and wide, allowing for the ceilings in some rooms to be as high as 12 to 16 feet.

Two of the men were loading coal in Room 2, about 7,000 feet from the entrance. This room was known to have some of the poorest safety conditions in the mine, and it had with a particularly high ceiling. A few minutes before 8:00 that morning, the fire boss working Room 2 climbed up to investigate a pocket of gas at the ceiling. As he did so, his open carbide head lamp went out. He stopped to relight the lamp with a match, and in doing so, he ignited a deadly combination of explosive gas and coal dust. The force of the explosion that followed was monstrous.

The blast roared up the drift and burst out the entrance of the mine with such tremendous force that it tossed railcars about as if they were toys. One mining car, several telephone poles and some heavy equipment near the entrance were thrown across the valley to the other side of the canyon, nearly a mile away. The steel gates inside the drift near the entrance were twisted and ripped free, tearing the heavy hinges from their concrete foundations. These gates were also blasted across the valley and were found embedded in the rock of the opposite canyon wall. The damage inside the mine was as bad, if not worse. Heavy support timbers were ripped out and the steel rails were twisted like so much string.

A few minutes later, a second explosion burst through the mine. This time, the force of the blast was directed in a different direction, nearly destroying the fan house and leaving the fan itself extensively damaged. It was supposed that the force of the first explosion likely extinguished the carbide headlamps of the miners working in the other rooms. Plunged into utter darkness, it would not have been long before someone tried to re-light his own headlamp with a match, which set off the second explosion. This explosion was the one that likely killed any of the miners who had survived the initial blast. It is quite likely there were survivors, as the energy from the first explosion was directed outward. Even if there had been no second explosion, it does not necessarily follow that these men would have come out of the mine alive. The first explosion would have rapidly burned off most of the oxygen in the mine and "afterdamp" would have been left behind. Afterdamp is made up of hot toxic gasses left behind after the explosive gasses and the coal dust had burned, mixed in with a large amount of carbon dioxide - a lethal combination.

The catastrophe was not yet complete. About 20 minutes after the second explosion, the earth shook one last time as a third, spontaneous explosion detonated. This final explosion did extensive internal damage to the mine. The first and second explosions had blown out many of the timber roof support beams, allowing the third explosion to cause extensive collapses and cave-ins throughout the mine.

Family members and off-duty miners knew exactly what must have happened as the earth below them shook. They ran directly to No. 2, trying to get as close to the entrance as they could. The bosses set their emergency plan into action by calling the area mines to let them know what had happened. Trained rescuers would be arriving within the half hour.

Every mine had its own trained rescue teams and rescue equipment on hand. If ever there was a fire, explosion, or cave-in within any of the area mines, these rescue teams would be immediately alerted and sent to the mine in distress. The men on these teams were all miners themselves and very often when the call for help went out, they would be called out of their own mines. No matter what mine was in trouble or what company owned the mine, help would always be on the way when needed. No matter how bad the situation appeared when the rescuers arrived on the scene, they always went to work believing that there would be living men trapped inside. Unfortunately, when they arrived at the No. 2 Mine, they had no way of knowing how many men were inside at the time of the explosion. The check board containing that information was blasted into splinters and brass tags were blown all over the valley with the first blast.

The first men to enter the mine after the third explosion were 22-year-old Thomas Hilton of Helper, Utah, and two other men. Hilton, who later spent over 55 years working coal mines, had just been certified in mine rescue and first aid and had been laid off from No. 2 two weeks earlier. The men needed to get to the water shut-off valve for the eight-foot water line leading into the mine. There were worries that if the line had burned through, men could possibly drown if they were holed up in a low-lying room. Wearing breathing helmets, the men entered the mine while holding a rope so they could be pulled out in case they were overcome with gas. They were able to get as far as 100 yards but were only about halfway to the water valve. Hilton began feeling dizzy. He jerked his lifeline to signal that he was in trouble and turned toward the exit. After walking a short distance, his legs began to feel unstable and he began to run. In sight of the exit, he collapsed into unconsciousness. Two company managers who were holding the lifelines, covered their mouths with wet handkerchiefs and ran in and dragged Hilton out. The next thing he knew, he was lying in the Castle Gate cemetery, propped up against a tombstone, breathing clean fresh air.

Hilton took some time to recover and then headed back to continue with the rescue effort. The rescue team leaders were careful to keep him away from the area where his father had been working until after his father's body was removed. Hilton lost his father, an uncle, a cousin and other relatives in the blast.

The afterdamp in the mine was tremendously thick and there was no way to get it cleared; the force of the explosions had collapsed the airshafts and the ventilation fan was all but destroyed. The rescue teams were in possession of the latest emergency equipment in the forms of breathing helmets. These would allow the rescuers to work for fifteen minutes or more in areas saturated with afterdamp. But in this case, the afterdamp was so extreme that even with rescue helmets, the men were being overcome and frequently had to be dragged from the mine.

Of the 171 men who walked into the mine that Saturday morning, there were no survivors. Then the mine took one more life. George Wilson of Standardville, the head of the rescue crew, was in the first group to enter the mine. These men went in on Saturday afternoon, knowing full well that there had been no opportunity to ventilate the mine. They were focused on finding any trapped miners that could still be saved. It was believed that Wilson's breathing apparatus had somehow malfunctioned or that the device shielding his nose had slipped. Within the first 100 yards, he fell to the mine floor, asphyxiated from the toxic afterdamp. The other five men on his team also collapsed and had to be pulled from the mine. They were all unconscious but all but Wilson were later revived. The afterdamp was too strong even for the rescue breathing helmets.

Repair work had begun on the giant fan but it could not be put back into service before Sunday afternoon. Helmeted teams repeatedly tried to enter the mine but were turned back by the heavy afterdamp. Eventually, efforts to enter the mine were stopped until the fan could be repaired the following day. In the meantime, miners worked at and around the entrance, laboring to remove as much debris as they could, but their efforts were hampered by the massive crowd that had developed on the road leading to the mine. Police and mine officials were tasked with trying to push the crowd back so the others could work more efficiently. On Sunday, Utah National Guardsmen were called in for crowd control, and they were eventually able to move the crowd back down the road. After that, no one was allowed up to the mine unless they were known rescuers, had proper credentials, or were from the press.

A special train arrived at 3:00 p.m. at Castle Gate from Salt Lake City with five doctors and many nurses. With rescue and medical personnel in place, the Red Cross quickly arrived to help care for the families of the miners. They were provided with much-needed supplies and food, and with volunteers to help with such mundane household chores as child care, cooking and cleaning because many of the miners' wives were too distraught to function normally. Mothers and wives of the entombed miners did little more than stand silently and sadly, looking toward the mine.

Saturday night, a helmeted crew was able to penetrate the mine as far as 500 feet, but no bodies were found. Later that night, another helmeted crew made it as far as 1,000 feet, but found no one, and no evidence of anyone left alive.

Sunday, March 9, started with great expectations. The fan was to be repaired and would begin ventilating the mine, making it easier and safer for the rescue crews to do their work. Those high expectations were dashed that afternoon as a fire broke out in an emergency exit and rescuers were once again evicted from the mine for several hours until the fire could be extinguished. While the fire burned, there were more cave-ins in the main entrance, dropping tons of debris that would have to be cleared out before the operation could get underway once again. A further hindrance was a bitterly cold wind that blew steadily throughout Saturday, Sunday and Monday. Bonfires were built to help keep the teams warm.

Several more rescuers were overcome by the gas and had to be hauled out, but there were no more deaths. As an added precaution against gasses, where the afterdamp was not visibly present, the rescuers took caged canaries in with them. That was an old miner's trick for detecting many types of hazardous gasses, primarily carbon dioxide. The gasses would affect the birds long before the humans, so when a miner would see that his canary had fallen dead, he knew that it was time to leave quickly.

After the fire was out, the first ten bodies were found and gently carried from the mine. Horribly charred and mutilated, it was instantly evident that these men had been killed instantly. Soon after, two more bodies were found, headless and badly charred, it was impossible to identify them immediately. About 6:00 p.m., twenty more bodies had been located but the recovery team was unable to reach them before much debris was moved. All but the faintest of hopes of finding anyone alive were lost. The afterdamp had penetrated even the farthest reaches of the mine and it continued to hamper the men recovering the bodies. As more of the mine was being ventilated, and they ventured deeper into the mine, the helmeted workers would locate and carry the bodies to an area that had been cleared of the afterdamp, and pass them on to miners without need of breathing helmets. Then, with the aid of horses, the bodies would be carried to the surface.

When the rescuers accepted the fact that none of the miners were coming out alive, rescue shifted to recovery. They needed to find a place to store the remains and to make identifications. The Knights of Pythias Hall was used as a morgue and all the remains were then taken there and placed gently on the floor, with any clothing or belongings that were found near the bodies. Undertakers from area towns flooded in to assist in preparing the bodies for burial. The company had already sent out a mass order for coffins, to be delivered within a few days.

It took nine days to recover all 172 bodies. Mass funerals were conducted and burials took place in three cemeteries: Price, Helper and the largest number in the Castle Gate cemetery. One man, who was found headless, had to be dug up so his head could be put in the coffin after it was found several days later. On March 24, the sorrowful sound of "Taps" was heard echoing through the canyon as long funeral processions carried dozens of coffins to their final resting places.

A group of children who lost their fathers in the explosion

The Castle Gate miners had been an ethnically diverse group. Among the dead were 49 Greeks, 22 Italians, eight Japanese, seven English and Welsh, six Hungarians, two Scots, one Belgian and 77 Americans (including several African-Americans). These men left behind 110 widows and 258 dependent children. The oldest to die that day was 73 and the youngest was just 15.

Death benefits were paid by the newly established Utah State Workmen's Compensation Fund. Each dependent received $5,000 over time, with payments of $16 per week for five years. Several of the very young continued receiving payments well past the five-year cutoff. The company cancelled all of these families' debts to the company store and gave them ample time to find other lodgings. Governor Charles Mabey used the national press to plead for donations to be sent to help the families. He raised an additional $132,445.13. He then hired a social worker to work with the families to determine how the money would be delegated.

The widows dealt with their losses in different ways; some remarried, some returned to the "old country" and still others held fast to their sorrow and remained in mourning for the rest of their lives. Steve Sargetakis, who was only 18 months old in 1824, was too young to remember the disaster, but he remember well how it affected his mother and his life growing up: "My mother wore black for the rest of her life, we had black curtains at our windows and we had no parties or celebrations." He explained that he and his brothers worked hard delivering newspapers and doing odd jobs to make extra money to help support the family.

The Castle Gate No. 2 mine was cleaned, rebuilt and reopened. Coal was pulled from No. 2 until it was closed down for good on February 4, 1960, the same day that Castle Gate No. 4 was opened.

The mine and the land around it have changed hands several times, with different parcels sold separately. The land under the town of Castle Gate remained company land until it was sold in 1974. The town was dismantled and some of the houses were moved to nearby Helper. The remaining 200 Castle Gate residents were relocated to 60 newly built homes in the new Castle Gate subdivision, later absorbed into Helper. The remainder was bulldozed, leaving not the least hint that there ever was a town there.

Castle Gate is officially listed as a Utah "ghost town" but the truth is that there is nothing much left to see there; just level, graded ground. There are still several of the old mining buildings left from No. 2, but they have fallen into disrepair. At some point over the years, the old mine wheelhouse had a sinister local nickname of The Devil's Playhouse attached to it, but no one around seems to remember how or why it came to be called that. But they do stay away -- just in case.

Other than that of the Americans, the largest ethnic group killed in the disaster were Greeks. They were a very close-knit community and held a single large funeral for their dead in the Greek Fraternal Hall. Of the 49 Greeks who were buried that day, 29 had families who were too poor to afford headstones. These men lay in unmarked graves until many decades later, when Andrew Hillas raised $1,500 to purchase a new headstone inscribed with the names of all 29 men.

Of all the miners scheduled to work in No. 2 on that fateful Saturday in March, there was one man who was not there. Frank Mangone, who worked as a plumber in the mine and the buildings outside the mine, inexplicably decided to stay at home the day of the explosion. His daughter, Lea Haslam, who was nine years old then, clearly recalls her mother asking him if he was sick. He reportedly replied, "I'm not sick; I'm just not going." Lea said that she and her brothers and sisters were delighted that they would have their father home with them on a Saturday, something that almost never happened. Their joy was not to last for long, for when the mine exploded, her father joined the other miners in trying to rescue to save their friends. They never knew why he stayed home that day, only that he had never done anything like that before, and never did it again.

Hopefully most of the miners who died so suddenly and violently that day have gone on to their rest, but at least a handful of the miners who went back to work in No. 2 after the disaster believed that some of the spirits of the dead remained in the mine. The cleanup and rebuilding was all done by experienced miners who knew how to put a mine back together. As they went about their work, they found little mementos and reminders of their lost colleagues mixed in with the rubble. On a few occasions, they were reminded by their friends themselves! Most of the men believed that their old friends were trying to protect them as they did their work, more than once whispering a warning or giving a slight shove that kept them from being harmed by falling rocks or timbers. Although frightening when it happened, none of the miners regretted the protection.

1940: THE "DOODLEBUG DISASTER"
Death on the Rails in Ohio

Head-on collisions were common from almost the start of American railroading. At a time when almost all railroads consisted of a single track, it was tragically inevitable that trains would occasionally collide. A company's only method of controlling rail traffic on these single lines when trains traveled in both directions was the timetable. To avoid collisions, each railroad devised its own timetable to establish exactly where each of its trains was to be on the line at a particular time – but it didn't always work.

Later on, telegraph lines were added, along with signal lights and telephones. Eventually, even more sophisticated methods began to be used. Unfortunately, though, accidents still sometimes continued to happen. No matter how careful the employees of the railroads were, and how advanced the techniques to prevent accidents became, there were times when everything was supposed to work, but didn't. Why? The answer is simple: In almost every case, human error prevailed over warnings, signals and technology. In those instances, the common sense that usually prevents our complex world from dissolving into bloody chaos failed.

This is the terrible story of how it failed at Cuyahoga Falls, Ohio on the last day of July in 1940.

July 31 was a pleasant summer evening in northern Ohio as the Doodlebug made its way along the tracks toward Akron. No one knows how, or why, the Doodlebug earned its name. "Doodlebug" was a slang term given to several species of insects and perhaps the shape of the gas-electric motor coach, with its bulging gas tanks and the smooth, roundness of a trolley car, was why it was dubbed with such a comical name. Whatever the reason, by 1940, the word was an accepted term in railroad jargon for the one-car commuter service that ran the 12 miles between Hudson and Akron. The business commuters who used the car referred to the Doodlebug with affection and rode it back and forth daily between home and work. It provided an invaluable service to them, but it was no match for the Pennsylvania Railroad freight train that it slammed into on that fateful summer night.

The Doodlebug was carrying 46 passengers and crew, plus several hundred gallons of fuel, when it collided with the Pennsylvania train. The train, with 73 loaded freight cars, outweighed the Doodlebug by several million pounds. They collided at the Front Street crossing at Cuyahoga Falls and the metal skin of the Doodlebug peeled back "like a melon," as one witness described it. The lead locomotive of the freight train telescoped its way into the crowded Doodlebug, smashing through seats, windows and passengers, plowing relentlessly forward with the sound of screaming steel. Forcing the Doodlebug backward along the screeching rails, the train, with its own brakes wailing, didn't come to a stop until it had pushed the twisted

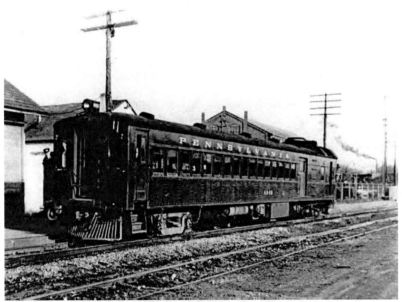

The "Doodlebug" before the disaster

commuter car almost 500 feet back from the point of impact. Even as the train and the car shuddered to a stop, still locked together, the gasoline tanks of the Doodlebug exploded, showering the car and train with a hot torrent of burning gasoline. In front of the horrified eyewitnesses, the crushed Doodlebug and its human cargo began to burn in a pillar of flame that spread out for 25 feet on both sides of the wreck and leaped 25 feet into the air.

How did such a terrible disaster happen? Everyone later agreed that it shouldn't have...

When the Doodlebug left Hudson at 5:49 p.m. on its regular run to Akron, its route and orders were clear. Engineer Thomas L. Murtaugh had a copy, as did conductor Harry B. Shaffer. According to the orders, the Doodlebug had a "meet" order with Engine 4454 (the Pennsylvania Railroad train) at the No. 1 switch at Silver Lake, several miles north of Cuyahoga Falls. The section of the Pennsylvania Railroad used by both trains was a one-track line, so it was part of the ordinary course of events for the southbound Doodlebug to lay over on a rail siding at Silver Lake while any northbound train passed by. The Doodlebug could then continue south, but only after it called Hudson for permission to continue on to the next section of tracks, which were south of Silver Lake. Operator O.L. Rickey had personally given the "meet" orders to Murtaugh and Shaffer at Hudson and the crew of the Pennsylvania Railroad train was given identical orders at Arlington at some point after 5:00 p.m.

To this day, no one knows what happened. Engineer Murtaugh brought the Doodlebug to the No. 1 switch at Silver Lake right on schedule. But instead of switching to the siding and calling Operator Rickey to get block permission, he just kept right on going on the main track. Murtaugh himself would not remember the accident, so why he kept going south toward the oncoming train remains a mystery. Oddly, neither conductor Harry B. Shaffer, brakeman A.L. Bailiff, nor baggage man Charles Bilderback, all of whom were familiar with the route, said anything about the failure to stop. Shaffer later recalled that he was too busy taking tickets from the passengers and checking them off his list to notice anything unusual. But just before 6:00 p.m., he happened to glance at his watch and see the outskirts of Cuyahoga Falls instead of the siding at Silver Lake, where the Doodlebug was supposed to be. After the wreck, he gave an interview from his hospital bed. "I jumped up to go up front and find out from Murtaugh why we had passed the siding. Just as I got to my feet, I looked out and saw the locomotive of the freight train rounding the curve ahead, coming towards us. I knew we were going to hit. We were going 50 to 55 miles per hour. I ran back into the baggage compartment and yelled, 'We're going to hit! Jump!' Then I jumped."

Shaffer wasn't the only one who saw disaster looming ahead. As the lead locomotive of the freight train pulled out of the curve just south of the Front Street crossing, engineer O.M. Lodge and fireman E.N. Reynolds suddenly spotted the Doodlebug coming right at them. Reynolds hit the brakes, but it was too late. He watched in shock as his locomotive sliced open the front of the Doodlebug and began driving it backward up the track. At the same time, Lodge and Reynolds heard the crump of the explosion as the Doodlebug's fuel tanks exploded. Burning gasoline showered over the locomotive and the first two dozen cars of the train. Stumbling out of the cab and frantically smothering the burning fuel on their clothing and skin, they ran toward the ravaged Doodlebug.

Eyewitness Weley Payne probably had the best view of the wreck. He was sitting in his 1935 Buick at the Front Street crossing gate, watching the Doodlebug pass by. He didn't see the freight train coming until it plowed into the commuter car, but had a clear view as they collided with a terrifying crash, burst into flames and started moving northward on the tracks in a blazing, squealing mass of metal. Jumping out of his car, he began running for the nearby Cuyahoga River along with other bystanders, some of whom had been splashed with gasoline and were on fire. As he tripped and fell down a ravine, Payne injured his leg and was later stitched up at St. Thomas Hospital. Shaken by what he had seen, he told reporters, "I served in the World War and fought in active battles in France, but the confusion and turmoil that followed the explosion was more horrible and ghastly than anything I saw in the war."

The initial impact of the locomotive had smashed virtually everything inside of the Doodlebug, scrambling seats and shattering windows and other debris into a chaotic tangle of metal. At the same time, almost all of the passengers were thrown forward toward what was left of the front of the car. They were probably all dead long before the first rescuers arrived. Those who rushed to help remembered that the most unsettling and eerie aspect of the horrific scene was the unearthly quiet that had settled over it; there was not a cry, moan or a scream to be heard, only the sound of flames in the wreckage. The rescuers could see the passengers inside, crammed up

(Left) The "Doodlebug" in flames (Right) Smoldering corpses can be seen through the burned and broken windows of the wrecked car.

against windows, slashed, cut and covered with blood, but none of them were moving. Perhaps it was best that they had died right away because it took hours to remove all 43 bodies from the wreckage. The force of the collision had bent and crumpled the sides of the Doodlebug so badly that it took crews with acetylene torches many hours to cut through to reach the dead. When they found them, they had been cut and burned beyond recognition. Jewelry, dental work and pieces of clothing had to be used to identify them.

Amazingly, there were three survivors of the crash. One of them was engineer Murtaugh, who apparently saw the freight engine coming and jumped out of the driver's cab before the wreck. He fractured his skull and sustained minor injuries but survived. His memory was filled with holes, though, and he was unable to remember why he had driven the Doodlebug to its doom. He was delirious when he was taken to the hospital and repeatedly moaned, "Get me out of here; I've got to get back to work."

Another who survived was conductor Harry Shaffer, who had cried out a warning and then jumped from the baggage section. Tod E. Wonn, a Pennsylvania Railroad section hand who was riding free of charge as a "deadhead" passenger in the baggage car later reported that he was startled by Shaffer's entry into the baggage car and heard him yell out, "Jump, boys, it's a crash!" before he flung himself out of the car. Wonn didn't have time to wake his friend, Bruce Kelly, who had dozed off in the seat next to him. The trains had already collided when he jumped and his clothes were on fire when he hit the ground. Rolling around in the brush, he managed to extinguish the flames. Then, covered with blood and in shock, he stumbled into a nearby filling station run by Fred Eckman. "My buddy! Oh, my buddy!" he murmured over and over again. Wonn refused to let Eckman's wife, Molly, treat his wounds. Instead, he ran out of the station and went back to the railroad tracks, searching for his dead friend. Wonn survived the wreck and was in better condition than Harry Shaffer, who lost his right hand and foot, probably when the Doodlebug was pushed by the freight train.

Within minutes, local policeman and sheriff's deputies arrived at the scene. The sound of the crash drew scores of civilians, most of whom pitched in to help. However, there was little for them to do. L.P. Seller, the Cuyahoga Falls fire chief reported, "I was there two minutes after the wreck and the Doodlebug was already a furnace. I heard no screams and realized everyone inside was dead. Some victims were hanging partly out of the windows and they were on fire. Some were pushed out by the force of the freight and they littered the tracks on either side. They were all shattered, bleeding and burnt. The interior looked as though a tornado hit it."

Many of the people who lived nearby did what they could to help as recovery crews slowly removed the bodies from the twisted metal of the crash. Molly Eckman, wife of the filling station owner who had tried to help

Tod Wonn, had been washing dishes when she heard the familiar sound of the Doodlebug going by. She was stunned moments later by the crash. When she looked out and saw the car burst into flames, she ran to her linen closet and gathered all of the towels she could carry and ran towards the wreck. "I knew they would need bandages," she later explained. Another who reacted without thought to his own safety was Reverend Joseph Butler, an assistant priest at St. John's Cathedral in Cleveland. He had been visiting friends in Cuyahoga Falls when he heard the sirens and went to the scene of the crash. Standing by the ruined car, he offered prayers for any Catholics who might have been on board and offered absolution to each of the bodies that were brought out of the wreckage.

But not all of the bystanders were there to help. The recovery team's efforts were constantly hampered by the ghouls and curiosity-seekers who gathered to gawk at the wreckage. Before the day was over, as many as 20,000 people converged on the scene, bothering the rescue workers to the point that police officers repeatedly had to drive back the crowds by force.

The aftermath of the tragedy was supervised by Summit County Coroner R.E. Amos, who remained there for the long hours needed to bring out the dead. Amos had workers stack pocketbooks, glasses, briefcases, and burned clothing in careful piles, knowing that the items would be needed to identify the victims. An inquest was started the following morning, even though Murtaugh and Shaffer were too badly injured to testify. Amos used the information that he had to file a report the following day blaming Murtaugh and Shaffer for the crash since they had disobeyed their written orders. This finding was largely based on the statement of F.W. Krick, the Pennsylvania Railroad division superintendent, who testified, "Apparently, both the engine man and the conductor had proper orders to wait at the Silver Lake siding and let the freight train pass. But apparently both of them had a mental lapse at the same time."

Unfortunately for the families of the victims, Summit County Prosecutor Alva R. Russell ruled that Murtaugh and Shaffer could not be prosecuted for any crime because the wreck involved "no specific violation of any statute." The entire matter was said to be a case of mass "accidental death." Additional investigations by Pennsylvania Railroad officials, the Ohio Public Utilities Commission, and the Interstate Commerce Commission added nothing significant to the mystery of the Doodlebug disaster.

Harry Shaffer blamed the disaster on Murtaugh and Murtaugh himself couldn't remember anything. But the engineer's wife defended him in the newspapers. "I'm sure that if he took the Doodlebug on the main line that he was doing it under orders," she said. "I know him well enough to be sure that if he had orders to stop at a siding he would have stopped. I am certain that if he was able to defend himself from these charges he would say that he had no such orders."

There was bad news for Murtaugh when Shaffer's duplicate copy of his orders was found in the wreck, confirming Shaffer's opinion that Murtaugh had, for whatever reason, ignored his orders. But both Murtaugh and Shaffer had defenders during the flurry of blame that surrounded the crash. Speaking for the Brotherhood of Railway Trainmen on August 15, legislative representative George A. Fox blamed the accident on the Pennsylvania Railroad's recent cost-cutting practices. He stated that there had been three signalmen stationed on the Hudson-Akron line but that their positions had been eliminated during job cuts. He believed that if the men had still been on duty, the tragedy would never have happened.

But who can say? The cause of the disaster remains a mystery.

The wreckage was removed from the tracks and while many of the wooden ties were burned, the steel rails remained intact. The dead were eulogized and buried, the wreck was largely forgotten and a Doodlebug was soon returned to the Akron-Hudson route. It ran for 11 more years until it was discontinued on July 31, 1951 – the anniversary of the deadly crash.

1946: GHOSTS OF THE GREAT NAPERVILLE TRAIN WRECK

Railroads provided the first means of mechanical transportation in American and ushered in an era of swift and relatively comfortable travel. For nearly two decades, the railroads were mostly free from serious mishaps, but by the 1850s, the primitive signals, unpredictable locomotives and hastily laid lines conspired to bring about accidents, disasters and deaths. As time passed, faster moving trains, faulty warnings and unreliable human nature claimed the lives of thousands of passengers and crew members on American trains.

Few times in American railroad history have such near-criminal negligence been demonstrated as in the horrendous crash that took the lives of 47 people, most of them passengers, in Naperville, Illinois, in April 1946. Not only does the true cause of the crash remain a mystery to this day, but it is also a disaster that has left lingering spirits behind.

Throughout the history of American railroading, collisions have been the leading cause of death for crewmen and passengers alike. In the early days, front-end collisions were common, mostly thanks to poor signal markers and confusing schedules, but after the Civil War, things began to change. In 1882, an editorial in *Scientific American* magazine noted quite dramatically: "Collisions, in fact, like the assassin's stab, are now to be more dreaded from the rear than from the front."

After 1865, America's railroads changed from the early period of small, light trains into an era of long, heavy trains that were crowded with passengers. As traffic increased, it became necessary on heavily traveled roads to run many trains close together and with that, the threat of rear-end collisions greatly increased. If the number of passengers on a scheduled run exceeded the capacity of a train, the company would just put another train on the tracks behind the first one. This meant there would be two trains for the one that was actually scheduled. The second train would follow the first at a distance of about 100 yards and the trains were always in sight of one another, except when the first disappeared for a time around a curve.

The danger of rear-end collisions was slight as long as the speed of the two trains was slow – usually about 15 to 20 miles per hour. Later on, when train speeds began to increase, the very real danger of rear-end wrecks began to grow. Clearly, the practice of operating two trains together in such a manner was dangerous, as it was difficult to coordinate speeds and distances with the trains running one behind the other. Often, collisions resulted when the first train stopped, slowed or broke down. Old-fashioned hand brakes were still in use on most lines until the 1890s and in those days, trains were hard to stop in an emergency. Because of frequent accidents, companies began running trains at intervals of five minutes between them, but this also had inherent problems. How was an engineer to know that he was precisely five minutes behind the train ahead of him when communications were questionable at best? Disastrous accidents occurred when the time intervals between the two trains failed, and for five decades between 1870 and 1920, rear-end collisions were the single worst type of railroad accidents, according to *Scientific American.*

In the event of a breakdown or the unscheduled stop of a train, a flagman was sent out to warn any other train on the line that there was danger ahead. In the days before automatic signals, which came into use around 1880, "flagging" was essentially any kind of signal, including flags, lanterns or any kind of bright light. Any delay in protecting a stopped or disabled train could lead to a disaster.

But sometimes, even in the modern era of railroading, flagging wasn't warning enough.

April 25, 1946 was a pleasant spring day in Naperville, Illinois. At 1:03 p.m., Northern Pacific train No. 11, called the Advance Flyer, was on its way from Chicago to Omaha. It pulled thirteen cars, all filled with passengers, many of whom were servicemen returning home after the end of their enlistments after World War II. The train was speeding westward when it was signaled to stop at Naperville by a brakeman who thought he saw a large object shoot from beneath the train as it traveled along the tracks. What this object might have been remains a mystery as nothing out of the ordinary was ever found.

The train made an unscheduled stop at Loomis Street to check for damage. While it was being inspected, the rear brakeman, James Tagney, jumped down from the train with a red flag in his hands and ran back along the tracks for a distance of about 800 feet. Although the track was level and straight and the afternoon was clear and sunny, Tagney waved the flag back and forth as a warning about the halted train on the tracks ahead. His efforts, though mandatory according to railroad regulations, were really supplementary since the entire route was marked

by signal lights – all of which were red while the Advance Flyer was in the Naperville station.

Three minutes behind the Advance Flyer, and on the same track, was the Chicago, Burlington & Quincy train No. 39, the Exposition Flyer, which was racing toward San Francisco. Tagney could see the train coming in the distance but he assumed that it would stop in time. At the throttle of the train was M.A. Blaine, a 68- year-old engineer with many years of experience.

When he realized that the Exposition Flyer was not slowing down, Tagney began to panic. He jumped up and down and shouted, even though he knew his voice would be lost over the sound of the oncoming locomotive's engine. The Exposition Flyer kept coming and its speed was later estimated at between 80 and 86 miles per hour. All along its route, the approach signals were blinking red but Blaine either did not see them or chose to ignore them. Crew members on No. 39 later testified that they felt a slight decrease in speed, as if the service brakes had been applied, but it was not enough to slow down the speeding train.

With one last wave of the flag and a loud cry, Tagney jumped out of the path of the oncoming train. He saw its fireman jump down the stairs from the cab, swing outward for a moment while holding onto a safety bar and then, moments before No. 39 smashed into the stopped Advance Flyer, fall to the ground. His body was hurtled outward from the speeding engine and he was killed when he hit the ground.

Train No. 30 tore into the rear of the Advance Flyer at full speed. Its weighty diesel engine ripped into the last car, slicing through the middle of it with the sound of screaming metal. The locomotive refused to stop, ramming halfway into the next car and sending it hurtling with such force that it buckled the next car, a lighter weight dining car, into the shape of a U, killing almost everyone inside. The next car was thrown onto its side and the remaining cars all derailed.

A total of 47 people were killed in the disaster, most of them mangled so horribly that they were barely recognizable as human. Passengers had been crushed to death, ripped into pieces and heads and body parts were severed. Rescue workers were stunned by the horrific condition of the bodies as they began pulling them from the wreckage of the two trains. In addition to those killed, 125 people were severely injured.

Peter Kroehler, owner of the Kroehler Manufacturing Company across from the railroad tracks on Fifth Avenue, closed down the factory for the day and allowed his workers to aid in the rescue efforts. The factory floor was used as an emergency triage hospital for the wounded. Students from North Central College brought over the mattresses from their dorm rooms for the injured to be placed on. Throughout the day and into the night, ambulances ferried the victims to hospitals in Aurora and Wheaton.

The dead were laid out in long rows on the lawns of homes along Fourth Avenue, parallel to the railroad tracks. The grim line of bodies stretched for almost a full block, from Loomis Street to the Naperville train station. Additions to the line were stopped at 3:00 p.m. when children were let out of nearby Ellsworth Elementary School and came running over to see the scene of horror. Rescue workers scrambled to move the corpses across the tracks to the Kroehler factory where they were laid out in a room on the west side of the large brick building.

To this day, the 1946 Naperville train wreck ranks as one of the worst railroad disasters in American history – one for which no one was ever really held to be responsible.

M.A. Blaine, the engineer of No. 39, had stayed in his cab at the moment of impact and had somehow survived. He was called before a board of inquiry but he could give no satisfactory answer as to why he had not stopped the Exposition Flyer in time. He was later charged with manslaughter, but a county grand jury did not indict him, due to insufficient evidence. With no real answers as to why the disaster took place, the cause of the Naperville crash remains unsolved to this day.

The cause of the crash is just one of the mysteries that lingers in regards to the disaster. Perhaps the most compelling question is whether or not the victims of the wreck are still wandering the streets of Naperville where the accident took place. Two blocks of Fourth Street, directly across from the old railroad line, are said to haunted by strange happenings that include eerie voices, ethereal figures, cold spots and touches by phantom hands. It was along this stretch of street where the bodies of the accident victims were laid out in long rows before being taken to the Kroehler factory on the other side of the tracks. Did the spirits of the victims stay behind near their bodies, only to be left in limbo when the corpses were hurried away to another site? Many believe this to be the case, especially those who claim to have seen dark figures approach them in the twilight, only to vanish without a trace.

The old Kroehler factory building is also believed to be haunted. The building was first constructed in 1897 and was home to the Naperville Lounge Company, which made handcrafted furniture. The owner, James Nichols, hired one of his former college students, Peter Kroehler, to handle the business end of the company and by 1895, Kroehler had bought out the other shareholders to become sole owner. After a devastating

The old Kroehler Manufacturing Company as it looks today

fire in 1913, Kroehler repaired the structure and painted its new name, Kroehler Manufacturing Company, across the factory's south wall. The business thrived, making leather sofas, divans, and daybeds for many years but cheap mass-production later replaced handmade furniture and the company was closed down in 1982. It stood empty for many years until developers turned the place into a combination shopping mall, restaurant complex and loft-style apartments. It re-opened as Fifth Street Station – home to upscale shopping and living and, according to some, a number of ghosts.

Business owners and tenants began telling eerie tales of resident spirits believed to be linked to the Naperville train crash due to the old factory being used as a temporary hospital and morgue. It was not hard to imagine that the weird goings-on could be linked to the macabre history of the building. Stories told of phantom footsteps, cold spots, whispers and voices, strange knocking sounds, unexplained locking of doors, slamming sounds and first-hand accounts of being touched and pushed by unseen hands. The former factory building was – and is – a very active place when it comes to the spirits of Naperville's haunted past.

1950: "TROLLEY OF DEATH"
Chicago's Green Hornet Trolley Disaster

The fates of 33 people were tragically changed in 1950 because of a rainstorm. On the night of May 24, a sudden torrential downpour flooded the 63rd Street underpass at State Street on Chicago's South Side, making the road impassable for the electric CTA trolley cars. No one knew what horrific events would follow the rainstorm or how simply missing a signal would send the occupants of a trolley along a path of no return.

During the first half of the twentieth century, electric streetcars were a familiar sight on Chicago streets. Trolleys had first appeared in the Windy City, pulled by horses, back in 1859. By the 1890s, electricity had replaced the horses and the cars began to travel along steel rails that had been fitted into the city streets. Trolleys were so popular that during World War I, Chicago operated the largest streetcar system in the country.

And while many riders relied on trolleys to get them to and from work each day and to allow them to travel throughout the city, the vehicles had drawbacks. The most obvious problem was that they lacked the ability to maneuver around accidents and flooded areas, causing the cars to have to be diverted to alternate routes. For this reason, among others, they were eventually replaced by buses. The fact that trolleys were unable to change routes with ease would later lead to the worst loss of life involving a motor vehicle in America.

On the morning of Thursday, May 25, the low-lying underpass at State Street remained flooded with rainwater from the storm. A flagman stationed there throughout the day detoured southbound cars to a turnaround track on the east side of State Street, making 63rd Street the temporary end of the line. At rush hour, the area remained closed, but this fact was apparently missed by Paul Manning, driver of the one of the trolleys called "Green Hornets" due to their speed and distinctive green paint job. The trolley that Manning was driving was known for being one of the newest and sleekest vehicles on the CTA line, and it was in perfect working order. Only a terrible mistake could be blamed for what happened that night.

Manning was driving the Green Hornet at an estimated 35 miles per hour, which some believe was too fast for the wet conditions. The CTA flagman was still in place at 62nd Street, one block north of the turnaround. When he saw Manning's trolley come into view, he frantically began signaling the driver to slow down. Instead of slowing, the vehicle continued along the street. The flagman continued to wave frantically, attempting to warn Manning that a switch in the track was open for a turn that would put the Green Hornet directly into the path of oncoming northbound traffic.

In the opposite lane, heading north, a semi-trailer truck driven by Mel Wilson was quickly approaching the viaduct. The truck was hauling 8,000 gallons of gasoline destined for South Side filling stations.

Why Manning failed to see the flagman's signal is unknown, but we do know that he was unaware of the closed underpass and also of the open switch that was being used to bypass the trolleys. It's likely that he simply

The smoldering ruins of the Green Hornet Trolley

thought that the car would clip right along on the route he normally took. However, when the trolley hit the open switch track, it violently swung to the left, throwing its passengers to the floor. Manning was last seen throwing up his hands and screaming in terror as the streetcar hurled through the intersection and rammed into the tanker truck. The impact ripped open the tanker's steel skin, creating a shower of sparks that immediately ignited the gasoline that was flooding onto the street. The two vehicles erupted into a single fireball that incinerated the trolley.

At the time of the accident, every seat on the Green Hornet had been filled. The passengers lay dazed on the floor, trying to figure out what had happened, when they suddenly felt a wave of tremendous heat as fire swept through the car. In the terror and confusion that followed, the trapped and burning victims pushed against the side doors, but they refused to open. The windows were covered with steel bars, making them useless as an escape route. Somehow, 30 people managed to crawl away from the scene, leaving 33 others behind to die. The fortunate few who survived were treated for severe burns at Provident Hospital.

Meanwhile, the explosion shook the entire neighborhood as flames soared two and three stories into the sky. The burning gasoline engulfed seven buildings on State Street. The fire was so hot that it twisted metal, fused windows and melted sections of asphalt on the street. The walls of several buildings collapsed, although the occupants managed to escape. Drivers who had been lined up in traffic somehow also managed to escape serious injury.

More than 30 fire companies were called to the scene, and it took more than two hours to get the worst of the fire under control. It would be a long time before a sense of calm could be restored to the area, though, and the smell of scorched flesh hung in the air long after the debris was cleared away. According to newspaper reports, as many as 20,000 people lined the streets hoping to catch a glimpse of the fire, the destroyed vehicles, and the blackened bodies that were taken away to the morgue.

It's likely that some of the emergency workers who had to deal with the carnage would have gladly traded places with the curiosity-seekers. When they forced open the rear doors of the trolley, they were met with a ghastly scene. "In some cases we found only the skulls and parts of limbs," Fire Marshall Albert Peterson later recalled. "We had to remove all of them and make a temporary morgue on the sidewalk."

A number of the passengers escaped the trolley thanks to a 14-year-old girl who had thought quickly enough to pull a red safety knob that opened the center doors. However, the rear doors had no such device and were in fact designed to be entry doors only, unable to be opened from the inside. When the recovery crew opened the doors, they found a mass of bodies that had been literally fused together by the heat.

In the investigation that followed, it was found that the Green Hornet had been in perfect working order, as had the gasoline truck. Mel Wilson, the driver of the truck, had been burned to death in the accident. Most pointed fingers of blame at Paul Manning, who had been involved in 10 minor accidents during his career, but the real problems lay in the design flaws in the trolley itself. These included the lack of safety pulls (now standard equipment on buses and elevated lines), the steel bars that blocked an emergency escape through the windows, and doors that would not open from either side. It took the deaths of 33 innocent victims to correct simple mistakes that should have been immediately apparent from the start.

In the years that followed the Green Hornet crash, trolleys slowly began to disappear from Chicago streets to be replaced by buses. The final run of a Green Hornet trolley took place on June 21, 1958, closing a chapter on mass transit – and death – in Chicago.

1951: "DEATH CAME FOR CHRISTMAS"
The Orient No. 2 Mine Disaster

The history of Illinois began not in the cities and industries of Chicago and the northern part of the state but among the fields, rivers and rolling hills of southern region. It was in southern Illinois where the first French settlers made their homes and where the first real wealth was discovered as "black diamonds" of coal.

The existence of coal in Illinois had been known since 1673, when explorers Marquette and Joliet first came to the region. Many later travelers noted its presence in outcroppings of rock and in creek banks, but it was not until the middle 1800s that explorations for this natural resource began in earnest. In 1840, the state was only producing about 17,000 tons of coal each year, with only 152 men engaged in coal mining. By 1860, annual production had jumped to more than 728,000 tons. The reason for the increase was due to the expansion of the railroads. During the 1850s, the railroads greatly expanded across the state, and not only did they haul coal cheaply to surrounding regions, the locomotives also burned it.

Railroad building, which was interrupted by the Civil War, resumed in 1865 Illinois began to transform itself from an agricultural state to an industrial one. The standard of living rose and coal fed both the boilers of the great factories and the furnaces that heated homes. Coal production shot upwards to 2.6 million tons in 1870; 6.1 million tons in 1880; 15.2 million tons in 1890, and in 1918, Illinois coal's peak year, 90 million tons were taken from the ground.

There were 48 coal mining counties in Illinois, most of them in southern Illinois, where companies like the St. Louis and Big Muddy Coal Companies flourished. It became a violent place of accidents and strikes, where clashes between the coal companies and the United Mine Workers of America (formed in 1890) frequently occurred.

Lying between West Frankfort and Benton was the New Orient No. 2 mine. It was opened in 1922 and was said to be the largest shaft mine in the world. It was a fitting place for such a mine since West Frankfort was a town that was literally built by coal. The place had been nothing more

Frankfort's Orient #2 Mine

than crossroads store when the railroad went in a bit to the west of the nearby town of Frankfort. Early settlers had once built a fort there called Francis Jordan's Fort, later changed to Frank's Fort, then Frankfort, then Frankfort Heights. When the railroad bypassed Frankfort Heights, business left. The town of West Frankfort started in 1897, about the same time that speculators sank test holes in search of the rich No. 6 seam being mined to the south between Johnston City and Carterville. The seam was nine feet thick at a depth of about 500 feet. When local investors began looking for coal, about 100 people lived in West Frankfort.

The first coal shaft was sunk in 1904 and mine after mine opened in the vicinity in the years that followed. West Frankfort grew quickly, its population eventually topping 20,000. But through it all, it remained an average southern Illinois coal town. There was nothing special about West Frankfort to make it stand out from all of the other towns like it in the region.

There was nothing out of the ordinary about it until December 21, 1951, when death came calling at the Orient No. 2 mine.

Downtown West Frankfort was aglow with holiday lights on December 21. The residential streets, lined with modest, working class homes, had decorated trees glowing in their windows. It was the Friday night before Christmas and there was feeling of happiness and good cheer in the air. That night would be the last working shift at the Orient No. 2 mine before the miners' Christmas vacation was to begin. When the late shift gathered at the shaft entrance that night, they saw a jovial message chalked on the board: "Merry Christmas to the Night Crew."

As the men filed forward, each of them retrieved his metal tag punched with his specific and his headlamp from a board in the lamp house. After that, the men went down into the mine, load after load, in the clanging, creaking steel elevator cage that took them deep beneath the earth. As the men waited their turn in line, the mood must have been light and festive. There were likely excited conversations about the holidays and family gatherings and a general happiness about the mine being closed until after Christmas. As the elevator landed, each man departed to his assigned work location in the mine.

The miners were only hours away from the start of their vacations when, at 8:30 p.m., an explosion ripped through the tunnels. It was an accident that should never have occurred. The mine, owned by a Chicago firm called the Wilmington & Franklin Coal Company, had been thoroughly checked out by two federal mine inspectors in July 1951. They strongly urged that abandoned workings in the No. 2 mine be either sealed off or ventilated separately from the areas of the mine that were still being worked.

Mine superintendent John R. Foster declared that the federal recommendations were "controversial," adding that he was under no legal obligation to follow such advice. The Illinois Mining Code did not ban the reuse of air, fouled or not by methane gas. It would be this air that exploded that night while 281 men were at work in the shaft.

The explosion shattered support timbers for three miles in the sprawling mine. One of the survivors described the blast as "so terrific that it knocked cars weighing several tons off the tracks." Paul Donahue, a night dispatcher at the mine, tried to spread the alarm when the explosion occurred. He told reporters the next day, "There was a terrific sound, like a thud. It numbed my ears; I yelled, 'Boys, there's an explosion, we better get out!'" He said that he attempted to warn the men working in the mine but was unable to do so because the switchboard power had been cut off. Four or five minutes later, he said there was a terrific roaring wind, which filled the tunnel with dust. Plunged into darkness and searching for a way out, Donahue followed a railroad track to the elevator in the main shaft before he lost consciousness. He was later rescued.

A warning did go out to those outside of the mine. A whistle at the shaft alerted everyone in the surrounding area that an accident had occurred and rescue workers from all over southern Illinois converged on the scene. As word spread throughout Franklin County, family members desperate for news about their loved ones rushed to the mine. Many of them kept round-the-clock vigils until they received definite information about their men, waiting, praying and hoping for good news. A high school basketball game in West Frankfort's gym had been interrupted by news of the accident and later, the gym was converted into a temporary morgue for the bodies of the dead. Many of the dead men were fathers of the boys who, hours before, had been playing ball on that same court.

The explosion had a devastating effect on the mine. Mine cars were derailed, sturdy support timbers were snapped like twigs and entire sections collapsed. The force of the blast extended the full length of two passageways, more than a mile, and was followed by clouds of dense smoke that permeated the mine and hampered the efforts of the rescuers. The recovery workers included brothers, sons and fathers of trapped miners, who worked feverishly to reach the men. They first concentrated on searching for anyone who might still be alive but as they advanced through the gas-filled tunnels along which the bodies of many miners were lying, they realized how futile this task was. They recovered the bodies of 28 men during the first 24 hours after the explosion. That grim work, carried out under extremely difficult conditions, went on for three days. Wearing gas mask and with their miner's cap lamps providing the only light in the black, smoke-filled tunnels, the rescue teams worked their way through miles of underground passageways, carrying out bodies one by one. They sometimes had to crawl on their hands and knees and drag bodies more than two miles before they could be loaded onto underground motorcars. They groped through pitch dark, rock-choked tunnels and quickly erected temporary barricades to act as air stops to protect them from the carbon monoxide that filled the air. Many of the recovery workers were overcome by gas and others narrowly avoided being killed by additional cave-ins. But the men bravely returned to their work again and again, always hoping that one of the miners might still be found alive.

The bodies recovered from the mine were taken to the junior high school gym, which had been converted into a temporary morgue. Terrified, grief-stricken family members walked between the rows of bodies covered by tarps. The tarps were pulled back, one by one, until each body was recognized and identified. Identification was seldom easy. The bodies bore marks that indicated that they had been hurled against walls or machinery. Many were charred and their clothing burned from the initial blast. Investigators later stated that there had not been enough oxygen left in the mine to support a fire after the explosion. Those not killed by the explosion died from carbon monoxide poisoning in the minutes that followed.

The explosion killed most of the men in the immediate area instantly, but a few survived for a short time afterwards. One man, Cecil Sanders, miraculously made it 60 hours before he was rescued. He later described his ordeal:

We knew the only thing to do was find a fresh air course. There were eight or nine men in my bunch and we began to put up brattices. We tried to put up canvas curtains so the gas would go around us. But the gas current was so strong it caught us between two air courses. We knew the only thing to do was find a hole and hope the gas would go over us. We ran back into the rocks just as far as we could go. But it wasn't far enough. The gas seemed to cover us. Then a little while later - I don't know just when - I lost consciousness. When I came to, I was on a big pile of rocks. I tried to stand up but all I could do was sit up. How long I had been in that shape, I don't know but after a long time I saw a beam of light and there were men coming through the smoke." "'Help me, boys, help me,' I called. Somebody said, 'My God, there is a man alive.'

The prayers of Cecil Sanders' family were answered that day but for 119 other families, hope turned to despair. Prayers for the lives of their loved ones turned to prayers for their souls as the bodies of the dead men were finally all recovered from the mine. The heart-wrenching task of burying the dead began Christmas Eve when 18 funerals were held. There were 24 more held on Christmas Day and the rest on December 26, the day the men were originally supposed to return to work after their vacation.

John L. Lewis, the President of the United Mine Workers of America, John Forbes, Director of the U.S. Bureau of Mines, and Oscar Chapman, Secretary of the Interior, flew in from Washington, D.C. on December 23 and went below the surface with rescue workers for a personal inspection of the damaged sections of the mine. Chapman ordered one dozen federal mine inspectors to open an investigation into the tragedy. Walter Edie, Illinois Director of Mines, and Illinois Governor Adlai Stevenson also visited the mine in the days following the disaster. Stevenson was angry when he spoke to reporters after returning from the mine. He said that he had pushed to no avail to have a modern mine-safety code adopted in Illinois. "I presented such a code, the work of many months, at the last session of the legislature, but neither the union, the operators, nor the senators from southern Illinois would support it."

The federal inspectors blamed the abandoned portions of the mine for the disaster, which they had warned the company about months before the tragedy. A team of six inspectors concluded that the caving in of the roof in the abandoned areas of the mine, plus the partial short-circuiting of the air current due to the opening of a ventilating door, caused a "large body of gas" to push out of the abandoned area into the active working section. The single ventilating door, which was open to allow cars and locomotives to move through, also allowed the gas through, as well. Investigators said that it was evident that a moving cloud of gas, rather than a standing of body of gas, was ignited because of the blast pattern from the explosion. The gas had apparently reached two shuttle cars and two electric drills in succession, which cause the gas to ignite. The explosion spread along the line of the gas cloud but was halted when it reached more active areas of the mine where there was enough rock dust to retard the flame. These conditions made it possible for the men in unaffected regions to make their way to the surface uninjured. Four other men were rescued, one of whom later died at the hospital.

If the mine company had followed the recommendations made by the inspectors in July, it's possible that the disaster would never have happened. However, the company had not broken any laws by ignoring the inspectors. Illinois Representative Melvin Price said shortly after the explosion, "Federal inspectors could only recommend that these safety violations be corrected. Had the federal law the teeth it required and a bill which I have pending in this Congress, H.R. 268, will give to it, the mine operators would have been compelled to comply with the inspector's recommendation or be subject to strong penalty, and if the inspector found imminent danger the legislation provides authority to close the mine."

Newspaper editorials railed against the lack of safety conditions in the mines. The editor of the *Nation* wrote: "Once again tragedy has struck against the mining community because profits were placed above safety... We hope that the West Frankfort tragedy will move Congress to action before more blood is smeared on our coal."

The disaster did force a change. In 1952, Congress amended and strengthened the 1941 Coal Mine Health and Safety Act. The amendment gave federal mine inspectors the power to close a mine if they deemed it unsafe. It's impossible to know how many deaths were prevented by the amendment, but the numbers were likely in the thousands.

1951: THE WOODBRIDGE TRAIN WRECK
The Crash of "The Broker"

It had been an ordinary Tuesday, nothing special. The day was cold and damp, with light rain falling off and on most of the day. People remarked that it could have been worse; it could have been snow. It was February 6, 1951. The workday was ending and people were heading home. Thousands of people were making their way to the closest commuter train station.

Many of them would never make it home alive.

On a Pennsylvania Railroad (PRR) track in Jersey City, New Jersey, a nine-car commuter train known as "The Broker" waited to begin its express run to Bay Head. The Broker would soon be carrying homebound commuters, mostly from New York City offices, to their homes in Red Bank, Long Branch, Asbury Park, and other communities along the New Jersey's wealthy shoreline. The Broker was so named because most of the regular riders were bankers, lawyers, stockbrokers and other businessmen, as well as office workers.

Engineer Joseph Fitzsimmons was already on the train, going through the necessary preparations and building up steam prior to getting underway. Fitzsimmons was 52 years old and had been working on trains his entire adult life. He had spent 33 years on the rails without a single accident.

The Broker's nine passenger coaches carried an average of 900 people on a typical weekday evening. This Tuesday however, was not going to be a typical evening. There was another railroad line that ran the same basic route, the Jersey Central. However, switchmen working for the Jersey Central Railroad had called a "sick call strike" and most of their commuter trains were not running. The Broker's usual passengers load had swollen by several hundred. The train was seriously overcrowded and the aisles were packed. The Broker pulled out of the Exchange Place station in Jersey City at 5:10 in the evening.

Earlier in the day, the rail line the train would normally follow had been slightly altered. In Woodbridge, a small New Jersey city 30 miles south of New York, the train would be taking a short detour. Work had begun on the construction of the New Jersey Turnpike, and where the train passed through Woodbridge, paralleling Fulton Street, a new temporary wooden trestle had been built to accommodate workers building the turnpike below. The new trestle shifted the track roughly fifty feet from the original line to pass over Fulton Street, on an embankment 20 feet above the street. The trestle had been put into service that afternoon, about five hours before The Broker was scheduled to cross it. It appeared to be solid and safe, as six PRR trains had already passed over it without incident. Because of the shift in the line, a "go slow" order had been posted in the PRR alert

PRR Engineer Joseph Fitzsimmons before the Woodbridge wreck.

board, requiring a reduction in speed for the approach and crossing of the trestle. Under normal conditions, trains would speed through that section between 50 and 60 miles per hour. The "go slow" order reduced the speed limit to 25 miles per hour until the trestle was cleared.

The trip had gone smoothly as Engineer Fitzsimmons pulled his train away from the Newark platform and began picking up speed as he drove through the darkening winter evening. Fitzsimmons later said that as the train neared the new trestle, he had tried to slow down but was having great difficulty. The rails were wet and slick, and the train was terribly overloaded, making it much heavier than usual. The additional weight and slick rails created a situation where the train took much longer to slow down sufficiently. The train was heading into the curve approaching the new trestle at over 50 miles per hour. At 5:43 in the evening, just 33 minutes after the train had left the station, Woodbridge experienced the worst train wreck to take place in the United States in 32 years. The speed and weight of the overloaded train as it rounded the curve onto the trestle had shifted the tracks, causing the train to derail. By the time the sun rose to chase away the darkness, 82 people would lie dead on a garage floor, and over 500 people would be injured, many of them seriously.

From his hospital bed, Fitzsimmons described what happened next: "The moment the engine passed over the trestle and lurched sharply, I felt the rest of the coaches would never make it. I hit the trestle at about 25 miles an hour and the speed of the train certainly couldn't be blamed for the crash. When I started to sway, I applied the brakes, but it apparently was too late."

Passengers interviewed after the wreck insisted that the train had been going much faster than Fitzsimmons had reported. Several days after the accident, the devastated engineer tearfully admitted that his train was traveling over 50 miles per hour, but that there had been no yellow signals warning of a "slow down" before reaching the altered track, and he had been caught off guard.

Attorney Irving Teeple, a passenger or the ill-fated train, reported: "I heard him throw on the air brakes three times as she came down a grade and onto the temporary tracks. He was doing his level best to hold her back."

Momentum carried the engine and the first three coaches over the chasm before falling down the end of the embankment and onto the street below. Norman Mertz related: "It just went bounce, bounce, bounce -- and then there was a terrible noise."

The engine flew from the tracks in an arc and fell more than 20 feet to the pavement below. The first five

(Right) Aerial view of a section "The Broker"
(Left) The force of the speeding, overloaded train ripped the rails from the temporary trestle, but the trestle remained standing.

coaches after the engine whipped back and forth, ending in a horrible tangle of ripped steel. Eight of the coaches had been derailed. The first two lay on their sides in the mud of the wet embankment. The third and fourth cars had telescoped into each other and were the most badly twisted and smashed. The largest number of deaths and serious injuries occurred in these cars. Still others remained upright but were horribly twisted and smashed, with one car was bent into a U-shape. Inside the coaches, passengers were tossed around like rag dolls as the cars jerked and rolled. Metal stressed and tore, mutilating and crushing the passengers inside. Newspaper accounts reported that some were "...mangled to bits under the grinding weight of the sharp, broken metal. Others survived or died in tomb-like crevasses of steel, as some of the coaches were bent by the terrible force of the crash."

At first, the air was rent with the sounds of the train as it smashed and crashed and the scream of the metal as it was torn and twisted in a thousand places. Then came a terrible quiet -- everything was still. The quiet lasted only a moment, for very soon moans and screams shattered the silence. There were chilling cries of: "Help me, help me please..." Moans and sobs of men and women writhing in pain, if they could move at all, were heard from every part of the twisted hulk.

The coaches in the center, specifically the fifth, sixth and seventh cars, were left fully or partially suspended over the street below. In these cars, many of the passengers who were able to move on their own, crawled toward the windows looking for a means to escape. The train's route crossed over rivers at several points and many of these people believed they had crashed over a river. The view out the windows at the street below, with streetlights reflecting on the dark, wet asphalt, confirmed that belief to many disoriented and injured people. William M. Hall was one of these. He later said: "All I wanted to do was get out. But I thought I was over water and wanted to dive out." Fortunately, Hall chose not to dive out, as several of his fellow passengers did just that. They leaped or dove from the wrecked coaches, expecting river water to soften their landing; instead they hit hard, unforgiving pavement. These people had survived the train crash, but died in an attempt to save themselves.

The wreck occurred in a heavily populated area so help was very quick to arrive. The Woodbridge fire and police departments were the first official rescue agencies to appear. They found it extremely difficult to climb up the slick, muddy embankment to get to the wrecked coaches, and nearly impossible to pull the injured from the train and back down through the mud. Ladders were laid down on the embankment and the rescuers used the rungs as a sort of stairs. The Woodbridge Fire Department used their ladder truck for nearly the same purpose, except they were able to extend the ladder over the embankment and directly onto the coaches.

Ambulances, first aid squads, and medical personnel came from at least twenty neighboring communities and cities. The Perth Amboy General Hospital, the nearest urban hospital, was alerted that there would be a large influx of injured passengers. Perth Amboy went into full disaster mode and received nearly all the people whose injuries were serious enough to need immediate and intensive medical care. First aid squads assisted those injured who were able to walk with treatment at the site. The number of injured and dead passengers was so great that a local grocery supplier had its trucks pressed into service as additional ambulances, and later as hearses.

Within thirty minutes, an enormous crowd had arrived and surrounded the crash site. Some volunteered to help, but the majority had come out of morbid curiosity to watch the bloody drama unfold. The vast numbers of onlookers, pushing in on each other, rapidly became a calamity within itself. Ambulances experienced great difficulty getting in or out. Rescue workers had to struggle to get through the crowds. Vital rescue equipment was smashed under the mass of feet. Seeing how the behavior of the crowd was delaying the rescue operation, and possibly costing the lives of victims in dire need of immediate attention, Governor Alfred Driscoll called in the New Jersey National Guard for crowd control. The Guardsmen stood side by side, arms linked, forming a human chain, after which the rescue and recovery efforts moved forward at a rapid pace.

The whole area was lit with acetylene torches and countless flashlights could be seen bouncing about as the rescuers searched for anyone still clinging to life. When a survivor was found, a call went out for assistance. The rescuers would work in a group to chop, cut, or pry away any obstructions that might be pinning the victim, then they would be loaded onto a stretcher and carried down the ladders to the street.

Some victims were able to leave the wreck by themselves, whether they had received medical treatment and been released or had been uninjured. Many people living near the crash site opened their homes to these stunned and shocked individuals. They were offered food, warm blankets, and most importantly for some - the use of telephones. They needed to call home to assure their families that they were alive and to find transportation home.

Pearl Sullinger, a survivor of the wreck, briefly described her ordeal when she wrote in on the comment page of an online article: "When I woke up, dead people were lying on top of me. Blood was all over me. My collarbone was broken; my left arm was broken. There was so much smoke in the air I thought the train was going to catch on fire. I climbed through a window and sat down in the mud. A man from the neighborhood brought me into his home and took me to Perth Amboy hospital."

As it became apparent that the number of dead would be high, a place had to be found to store the bodies until identifications could be made. There was no place large enough that could accommodate the huge number of bodies being pulled from the wreckage. It was decided that the garage at the Woodbridge Fire Department would serve as a temporary morgue, but the idea of laying bodies on the dirty floor of a garage was repugnant. The problem was solved when a local butcher donated large rolls of waxed brown paper. As each body was brought into the garage, a sheet of the brown paper was unrolled and the blood-spattered workers gently placed the body on the paper. Then another sheet of paper was cut and laid over the body. Witnesses described how "the feet of the dead sprawled limp, uncovered by the paper shrouds."

Some of the bodies brought into the morgue were so severely mutilated that it took hours to identify them, and then only by an article of clothing or a personal belonging. As word of the morgue's location spread, terrified family and friends of anyone who was supposed to be on the train that evening lined up outside, hoping against hope that their loved one would not be lying on the floor.

One of the last living victims to be freed, his body partially crushed, found trapped under one of the heavy steel wheels that had been ripped from one of the coaches. The rescue and recovery continued nonstop until the last body had been removed from the wreckage. It took over seven hours. The National Guardsmen stayed to watch over the site throughout the night to prevent looting and keep souvenir hunters from climbing on the wreck and getting hurt.

The day after the crash, the FBI opened an investigation looking for evidence of sabotage. Finding none, the case was closed.

The Pennsylvania Railroad (PPR) conducted its own investigation and laid the entire blame at the feet of Engineer Joseph Fitzsimmons. The PRR was accepting no culpability, even though they had failed to install any yellow warning lights to signal a change in speed ahead, or to signal an unexpected change in the track conditions, such as a shift of 50 feet and a new temporary trestle.

The Interstate Commerce Commission was ordered to make an investigation into the cause of the wreck. A public hearing was convened the day after the crash. A string of witnesses including PRR employees, passengers, expert engineers and community members who witnessed the crash. Fault was found with the operational practices of the PRR. New rules and guidelines were put in place in order to reduce the possibility of a repeat accident of this kind.

The Middlesex County prosecutors office found the fault lay with the PRR for the accident. It was discovered that the PRR had a company safety rule that yellow signals were to be installed at all go-slow areas, regardless of paper notices posted in the offices. It was further discovered that the PRR branch that operated along the north Jersey Shore had a practice of ignoring the rule.

The assistant prosecutor voiced outrage that the PRR was using Fitzsimmons as a scapegoat. He brought 85 counts of manslaughter against the PRR. However, the charges were later dropped when it was determined that the cost of the court proceedings would bankrupt the county. In the end, they agreed to an out-of-court settlement.

A year after the accident, the bridge had been rebuilt and all debris, wreckage, and evidence of the crash had been removed and the trains were "back on track." In preparation for the anniversary of the crash, a group of survivors requested that the rush hour train would stop at the site of the crash just before 6:00 p.m. for a brief ceremony to commemorate the loss of life. Administrators at the PRR denied the request. Instead, the group stood at the rear of the train and threw out a spray of 85 flowers onto the track as they neared the crash site -- one flower for each life that was lost.

Sixty years after the crash, the granddaughter of a man who was killed when The Broker jumped the tracks, was asked by an interviewer how her family had felt about the train's engineer, Joseph Fitzsimmons. She replied: "This poor man and his family had to live with this ordeal every single day, people pointing the finger at him. How terrible a feeling of guilt that he lived with, even though he did everything to ensure the safety of the situation. I really wanted to find his family and give them some sort of comfort in the fact that my family held no ill will towards him. It was an accident -- the whole thing was in God's hands, as every act is. I just wanted to tell him that he is not to blame; he was made the fall guy and what a damn shame the PRR could not fess up to the fact that they made the dreadful mistake."

Decades after the accident, a Pennsylvania resident recalled an experience from childhood. It happened on a summer evening in the mid-1960s, just at dusk in the Francis Street Park, located next to the train tracks in the Little Budapest neighborhood in the northeast corner of Pennsylvania.

A group of children had been playing in the park for most of the day, but their playtime was rapidly coming to an end as daylight faded toward night. It was then that they noticed "...a young boy of about 12 standing at the far side of the park near the railroad tracks. None of us had ever seen him before. One thing that stuck out about him was the way he was dressed in old fashioned clothes but in a somehow realistic manner." He just stood there looking at the children. They debated going to him and asking who he was and where he came from, but just when they decided to approach him, an ice cream truck pulled up, and getting ice cream suddenly became their priority. When they came back to the park with their ice cream, the boy had gone and they thought no more about him.

A few weeks later, some of the same children were visiting an older woman who lived alone on Thomas Street, near the Francis Street Park. In the past, she had offered the children a quarter to pick up her grocery order. One day, she asked them to bring the groceries inside her house. They did as she requested, and as they walked through her living room, they noticed a photograph of a young boy hanging on her wall. They told her that they had seen him in the park a few weeks earlier and asked if he was her grandson, or some other relative. She didn't answer for a while, just stared at them, seeming to have gone into a daze. After a long pause, she explained that there was no way that they had seen the boy; he was her son and the photo had been taken over 15 years earlier. He and her husband had been killed in a terrible train wreck in Woodbridge, New Jersey, in 1951.

Her husband had taken their son into the city for a special outing for his birthday, and they were returning home when the train had crashed. She told the children that she had had a strange feeling that morning that something bad was going to happen. She made her son promise that he would be careful and come home safely. He promised, kissed her, and ran off to catch up with his father. That was the last time she saw her son, except in dreams where he had somehow escaped the wreck and walked home uninjured.

The children left the house in silence and they began wondering if they had seen the same boy or not. None of them had ever heard of the train wreck that had killed the woman's husband and son, but they did know that the tracks running next to their park were the same ones that ran through Woodbridge.

Was the boy in the park the woman's long-dead son, and had it taken him all that time to keep his promise? Or had he been there all along, still trying to find his way back home? No one will ever know but hopefully the sighting gave a heartbroken mother some peace.

AIR

1847: DESPERATE PASSAGE
The History & Hauntings of the Donner Party

All of us have dark stirrings of doubt and fear whenever the Donner Party is mentioned. In such extremis what would we do? Snow-trapped and starving in the Sierras with no hope of relief, would we fall to devouring each other? Our fathers? Our children? Our lovers? How close to the animal are we? How far from the desperate beast? In the purely physical realm of survival, what justifies what?
James Dickey

"In prosecuting this journey," warned an 1849 guidebook to the West, "the emigrant should never forget that it is one in which time is everything." No truer words would ever be written in regard to the wagon trains that made their way to the mountains, meadows and open ranges of the American West. Time spelled success for most of them and doom for many others during the middle decades of the 1800s. Nothing had prepared most of these travelers for the ordeals of the trail. They had pictured building new homes in the bright, shining lands of the West but the strain of getting there proved to be far worse than any guidebook had hinted at.

Life on the trail was a story of an increasingly difficult adventure, of failing food and water supplies, of bone-wrenching weariness and accumulating miseries of every sort. The pioneers pushed overland, perhaps as slowly as 15 miles each day, and many of them lost sight of the vision that had set them on the road in the first place. That shining vision was replaced with the tragic signs of the families that had preceded them -- the wolf-pawed graves of the dead, the rotting carcasses of mules and oxen, splintered wrecks of abandoned wagons and once-precious household items that had been cast away like refuse once travel became too tough. The weight of their own privations was enough, on occasion, to bring tears to the eyes of the women and to buckle the knees of the men and yet they kept going.

The long trail to the West, from the Missouri River to the West Coast, ran more than 2,000 miles, with constant detours for pasture and water. The distance in miles however, mattered less than the distance in time. It usually took about four and a half months to reach the Far West, and the trip became a race against the seasons, in which timing made the difference between success and failure.

Late April or early May was the best time to depart, although the date had to be calculated with care. If a wagon train started too early in the spring, there would not be enough grass on the prairie to graze the cattle. On the other hand, a train that left after other trains had already departed would find campsites marked by trampled grass and fouled water holes. And if there was one thing that all of the guidebooks to western travel agreed upon -- it was not to get caught in the mountain passes when winter came to the high elevations. Such a dilemma would be sure to bring tragedy and disaster to even the most hardened group of travelers.

Time, the pioneers were assured, waits for no man and death comes on swift wings for those who do not heed its warnings.

The golden age of westward immigration began in the 1840s. After the opening of the Oregon Territory in 1846, settlers began to look to the West as a place of new hope and bright futures. One such man was George Donner, a well-to-do farmer from Riverton, Illinois. Donner was no ordinary emigrant, hoping for free land and open range in the West. He had been married three times, sired 13 children, and now, at the age of 62, was headed for California on one last great adventure. Donner traveled with his third wife, Tamsen, his five youngest children and three wagons. He also brought 12 yoke of oxen, five saddle horses, numerous milk and beef cattle, several hired hands, a dog and $10,000 in bank notes that had been sewn into a quilt. His older brother, Jacob, aged 65, had a similarly affluent train. The Donner brothers shared leadership in the expedition with James Reed, a Riverton neighbor who farmed and was known as a furniture maker. Reed, age 46, traveled with his wife, mother-in-law and four children. He also believed in traveling first class. He had stocked two support wagons with an assortment of fine foods and liquors. His main wagon was equipped with built-in beds and a stove. The Reeds, Donners and a number of other Illinois residents left Springfield, Illinois, by wagon train on April 14, 1846.

The expedition was a disaster from the beginning. The Donners and Reeds made every mistake that travelers could make. Not only did they overload their wagons but they left Springfield too late in the season. On the date that they departed, their schedule should have had them heading out from western Missouri. Then, at Fort Bridger in Wyoming, they decided to take an untested route to California.

The party made this decision based on a guidebook that had been published the year before by Lansford Hastings, a zealot for California settlement. He hoped to overthrow California's weak Mexican government by bringing in enough American settlers to start a revolution that would end with himself as president of the new independent republic. His guidebook, written to boost emigration, was the first step in that plan but the Donners and Reeds were completely unaware of this.

The shortcut that Hastings recommended directed parties to leave the main Oregon Trail at Fort Bridger, well before the usual turn to California at Fort Hall. It went directly west across the Wasatch Mountains, down into the Salt Lake Valley and across the Great Basin to join the standard California Trail along the

James Reed and his wife, Margaret

Humboldt River, thus saving a distance of nearly 400 miles. Unbelievably, Hastings had never taken his own shortcut before publishing the book. He had gone west on the Oregon Trail in 1842. He never doubted his judgment, though, and tried the route backwards in 1846, carrying his gear and provisions on pack mules. He had no trouble and arrived at Fort Bridger a few weeks before the Donners. After arriving, he stayed a short time and persuaded a company of 200 emigrants and 66 wagons, guided by an old Indian fighter named Captain George Harlan, to follow him back to California. He was sure that wagons traveling westward would have no more trouble on the route than his mules had experienced coming east.

Cutting across the Wasatch Mountains, Hastings led the emigrants through the narrow gorge of the Weber River, a passage so close and treacherous that the wagons had to be pushed and dragged along the riverbed. The men in the party moved boulders and hacked away brush, and when the riverbed became too narrow they were forced to hoist the wagons onto the bluffs using block and tackle. On the average, the luckless wagon train moved at a rate of a mile or less each day.

As the wagon train managed to get beyond the mountains and into the Great Basin, travel became even rougher. The wagons traveled for two days in the desert without a sign of any water or grass. Many of the oxen simply fell down and refused to get up. Others ran about crazed with thirst and then died. A number of the wagons were abandoned but they finally made it across the trackless wastes to the Humboldt River. Unfortunately, it took them three weeks longer than the emigrants who had taken the usual route by way of Fort Hall. Rallying what resources they had, the group continued on across another dry stretch to the foot of the Sierra Nevada, hauled the wagons up and down sheer cliffs and arrived in California's Sacramento Valley as the first snow was starting to fall. Miraculously, only one pioneer died in the bungled effort.

The Donners would not be so fortunate.

When they arrived at Fort Bridger and heard that Hastings himself had started down his shortcut with another wagon train, they saw no reason not to follow. By now, a large number of other pioneers had joined their expedition and on July 31, 1846, they set out with a contingent of 74 men, women and children and 20 overloaded wagons.

The party followed the wagon tracks of the earlier company into the Wasatch, where they were joined by 13 other pioneers and three wagons, bringing the total number of the party to 87. Almost immediately, though, the expedition got into trouble. They lost four days trying to get through the Weber River gorge, which had been so bothersome for the Harlan party. The Donners decided that it was impassable and turned back to try and find an alternate path over the mountains. It took them 28 days to reach the Great Salt Lake -- a distance of only about 50 miles -- but they relentlessly pushed on.

The desert exacted a terrible toll on the Donner party. It took them six days to travel across this wasteland, during which time 100 oxen died and many of the emigrants, including James Reed, were forced to abandon their wagons and supplies. Legend has it that George Donner buried his money somewhere in the desert with plans to return for it, but never did. It is said to still be out there somewhere, long forgotten. By the time the group reached the Humboldt River on September 30, the Harlan party was more than 300 miles ahead of them.

Time was now running out for the expedition. Short of food, growing desperate and near the limits of their endurance, the emigrants added to their problems with constant fighting and bickering. On October 5, near the end of a hot day along the Humboldt River, aggravations boiled over. The wagons were stretched out in two columns and in the rear unit was John Snyder, a young, well-liked teamster. As he pushed the wagons along, he lashed furiously at some tangled oxen. James Reed, also in the rear, ordered him to stop. Snyder's anger at the oxen shifted to Reed, and he threatened the older man with his whip. Reed drew his hunting knife, a move that prompted Snyder to reverse his whip and begin flailing at Reed with the heavy handle. As the two men grappled, Reed plunged his knife into Snyder's chest. The teamster sank to the ground and bled to death.

Those who witnessed the incident were stunned. Snyder had been popular and Reed, although acknowledged as one of the leaders of the expedition, was arrogant and aloof. Many of the party members wanted to hang him on the spot. After further deliberation, though, the company decided to expel Reed from the wagon train, forcing him to leave his wife and four children with the expedition. Reed rode ahead to the lead unit, picked up a friend and struck out for California. After enduring days of hunger, the two men eventually caught up to the earlier party led by Hastings. They soon reached Sutter's Fort and began organizing an expedition to fetch Reed's family and to bring food and supplies back to the Donners. Reed was surprisingly forgiving about his ouster from the party and was more concerned with helping his friends than with his own injured feelings.

Far back on the trail, the emigrants were suffering and near starvation. Two days after Reed had been expelled, an elderly man named Hardkoop had fallen far behind. By then, many of the wagons had been abandoned and Hardkoop, along with many other men, had been forced to walk across the desert. Too weak to keep up and unable to find anyone who would let him ride in a wagon, he had simply given up. No one had the strength to go back and look for him and after some discussion, the emigrants decided that he was expendable and left him to die. A few days later, Patrick Breen, the father of seven children, refused a cup of water to William Eddy, who wanted it for his three year-old son and infant daughter. Threatening to kill Breen, Eddy took the water by force. Two days later, Eddy came to Mrs. Breen and a Mrs. Graves for food for his famished children, and they turned him down. It had become a case of survival of the fittest and everyone was looking out for themselves with little disregard for anyone outside of their own families.

Eleven weeks after leaving Fort Bridger on the Hastings shortcut, the battered remnants of the Donner party reached the meadows along the upper Truckee River, in the eastern shadows of the Sierra Nevada. It was now October 20 and far too late to attempt to cross the mountains. Early winter snows could be seen on the ridges ahead and a cold bite could be felt in the night air. For whatever reason, the expedition felt that they had no choice but to continue on. The emigrants voted and decided to push on. After grazing their emaciated cattle on the lush meadows for five days, they prepared for the final journey across the mountain range.

The trail led about 50 miles into the hills, just beyond Truckee Lake, and then climbed to its highest and most difficult point at Truckee Pass, the last major barrier between the emigrants and the Sacramento Valley. It was vital for the party to cross this pass before more snow made travel impossible.

The first three families to arrive at Truckee Lake were the Patrick Breens, the William Eddys and the Lewis Keseburgs. On October 31, they camped near the lake and in an inch of snow, made the first attempt to cross the pass. By afternoon, they were floundering in five-foot snowdrifts and could make it no farther. The three families turned back to the lake and set up camp as a cold rain began to fall. The Breens moved into an abandoned cabin that had been left by earlier pioneers and waited for the other groups to arrive.

On the second day, during a pounding rain, a second group of wagons arrived at the lake. With this party came Charles T. Stanton, a diminutive bachelor who, weeks earlier, had ridden ahead to Sutter's Fort and returned with food, mules and two Indians to serve as guides. On the morning of November 3, Stanton led another assault on the pass. The storm that had drenched the lake had brought even more snow to the higher elevations and the wagons quickly bogged down. The party struggled to continue on foot, with adults carrying the children, but only Stanton and one of the Indians reached the summit of the pass. They returned when they saw that

The Donner Party reached Truckee Pass, the last major barrier before the Sacramento Valley, but could make it no further.

the others could not make it. That evening, another storm came up, and pelted with sleet and snow, the small party spent the night around a tree that they had cut down and set on fire. When morning came, they retrieved their wagons and descended to Truckee Lake.

By this time, it was plain that they were going to have to settle in at the lake and so shelters began to be constructed. A large lean-to was erected against the old cabin, which the Breens continued to claim it as their own and would allow no one to share. Two double cabins were built nearby.

Meanwhile, the far end of the wagon train had troubles of its own. They were stuck in a crude camp about five miles from the lake at Alder Creek. In this group were George Donner, his brother Jacob, their families and hired help and a widow, Mrs. Wolfinger -- 21 people in all. George Donner's wagon had broken an axle and they had fallen behind trying to fix it. Even more unluckily, Donner had gashed his hand while trying to carve a new axle, and while a small injury, it refused to heal. The storm that had swamped the other members of the expedition at the lake had also hit the Donner party at Alder Creek. For shelter, they had erected tents and a lean-to covered with brush, blankets and clothing. Huddled in these fragile shelters, they decided to stay put.

The snow continued to fall, on and off, for the next two weeks. When it ended, the emigrants at Truckee Lake made several more attempts to get through the pass but to no avail. It had become painfully obvious to everyone that they were imprisoned on the backside of the California mountains and would have to remain there all winter. There were 81 people desperately trapped in the two camps and 41 of them were children.

On the western side of the mountains, James Reed and his rescue party fared no better. They were trying to make their way eastward with food and supplies from Sutter's Fort but were also being bogged down by the snow. The Indian guides had deserted with three of the pack horses and soon the remaining animals dropped from exhaustion and died in the snow. The saddle horses also gave out and for a short time, the men pushed ahead on foot, with a single mule carrying the supplies. Within a day, they knew that it was useless to go on and they returned to the fort. Captain John Sutter, who had no other men to send, consoled them with the assurance that the Donner party could survive the winter on ox flesh and beef.

By December, though, the conditions in both camps were grim. Ignorance and carelessness had doomed the food supply when the oxen and cattle left to range on their own had wandered off and vanished in the deep snow. Their carcasses could not be found and it was realized that the remaining meat would not last until Christmas. A few cups of flour were hoarded to make a thin gruel for the infants and a little sugar, tea and coffee remained, but no salt. The trout in the lake had burrowed in for the winter and refused to bite. The deer had disappeared for the lower elevations but William Eddy shot a coyote one day and an owl the next. He wounded a bear on another day and when it fought him, he valiantly clubbed it to death. The small amount of meat did not last long among all of the settlers and the emigrants took to boiling hides and eating the glue that resulted. In one cabin, children cut up a fur rug, toasted it and ate it. At the camp on Alder Creek, water dripped continuously into the shelters and put out the fires that were supposed to keep the occupants warm.

The deepening winter brought more storms, less to eat -- and death. The first to die was Baylis Williams, a hired hand of the Reeds, on December 15. The shock of the young man's death sent a wave of panic through the stranded travelers at Truckee Lake. The following day, a small contingent of the strongest emigrants made another frantic effort to conquer the pass.

Ten men, five young women and two boys -- an escape party that called itself "the Forlorn Hope" -- set out on snowshoes fashioned from rawhide and hickory oxbows from the wagons. They each carried a blanket and had among them one rifle, a couple of pistols, a hatchet and finger-sized strips of meat that were meant to last for six days if each person only ate two strips three times a day. Stanton and the two Indians led the way, accompanied by William Eddy, "Uncle Billy" Graves, Sarah and Jay Fosdick, Uncle Billy's daughter, Mary, William and Sarah Foster, Lemuel and Billy Murphy, ages 12 and 11, and the recently widowed Harriet Pike. Amanda McCutchen joined them, as she was anxious to see her husband in California. She left her baby behind, likely in the care of Aunt Betsy Graves. Sarah Foster had left her own child and Harriet Pike had left two. It was a heartbreaking decision to have to abandon them, but it would have been impossible to carry young children through the snow. They were, of course, assured that the children would be safe. The remainder of the party included "Dutch

Charley" Burger, Antoine the herder, and Patrick Dolan.

The Forlorn Hope started off in single file, the leaders breaking a trail for the others. Even with the snowshoes, they sank halfway to their knees with each step. There were not even enough snowshoes to go around, so Burger and the two Murphy boys brought up the rear, carefully stepping in the tracks left by the others. The snow rarely held them up and they found themselves stumbling and floundering in the drifts. They only made it four miles on the first day and young Billy Murphy gave up and decided to head back. Dutch Charley gave up, too, but no one noticed his absence for some time. They assumed that he had headed back with Billy but he actually got lost. He did make it back to the lake a day after the boy did.

The party valiantly made it to the top of the pass and after traveling six miles, was too exhausted to go any further. The snow at their campsite was 12 feet deep but the Forlorn Hope knew how to make a fire in such conditions. The trick was to cut down two green saplings and lay them parallel on the snow a few feet apart. More green wood was placed across them to make a platform and then the fire was built on top of this. As long as someone kept the fire going all night, the travelers could stay warm in their tents, even with only one paltry blanket each.

As they climbed over the pass on December 18, they reached the open, downward slope. They traveled only short distances at a time, blinded by the glare of the sun on the snow. Stanton, the worst affected by the glare, began to fall behind. He would often wander into the camp each night after sunset. Since he was the only one among them who actually knew the trail, his misfortune affected all of them.

By now, the travelers were not only starving but close to mental unbalance as well. They began to hallucinate as they dragged themselves through the snow, hearing strange sounds, eerie cries in the woods and seeing drifting shapes that appeared and then disappeared before their eyes. They began to believe that the ghosts of those who had died on the expedition were calling to them.

On the morning of the sixth day, the last for which the party had food, Stanton sat by the campfire as the group prepared to move on. He was asked if he was coming and he answered that he was coming soon and would catch up later. The Forlorn Hope started off, guided rather uncertainly by the Indians, who had only been on the trail once and then there was no snow on the ground. As it turned out, the Indians took them in the wrong direction, which would cost them many painful days and miles. They didn't realize just how lost they were for more than a week. That night, they used up the last of the beef strips and waited for Stanton to come in to the warmth of the campfire -- but he never arrived.

The next day, they had traveled only about a mile before a heavy snow began to fall. They stopped and made camp and spent the day with no food, again waiting for Stanton. They watched for him but the little man still did not come staggering in through the snow. By nightfall, they gave him up for dead. A gentleman and a hero to the very end, Stanton had sacrificed his own life rather than endanger the lives of his friends by holding them back.

The following day, December 23, they climbed the barren, rocky surface of Cisco Butte, the highest point in the area, and tried to get their bearings. Without Stanton to guide them, they had to plot their own route. The easiest way appeared to be toward the south, where the mountains looked less fierce than in other directions. Unfortunately, this led them badly off the trail, but they had no way of knowing this at the time. The party continued on and survived by subsisting on a half-pound of bear meat that Eddy's wife had secretly placed in his pack. She had deprived herself and her children to provide extra food for the expedition.

Back at the lake, where the last of the livestock had been slaughtered and eaten, the miserable families gnawed on boiled hides and bones seasoned with pepper. Margaret Reed, accustomed to the comforts of her family wealth, killed the family dog, Cash, to feed her four children. They ate everything they could from his carcass and lived on the animal for an entire week.

Meanwhile, the Forlorn Hope struggled down the west face of the mountain through a series of horrific snowstorms. For several days, they were totally without food and shortly after, a series of gruesome events began -- events that would earn the Donner party a unique place in the annals of the West.

The painful journey continued on Christmas Eve, when another foot of snow fell. They limped along for two or three miles before finally sitting down to hold a meeting. All of the men except for Eddy wanted to give up and return to the camp at Truckee Lake but he argued that this was a foolish and suicidal plan. They had not eaten for

William Eddy, who became the leader of the "Forlorn Hope" rescue party

two days and in their weakened state, they would die before they made it back. Eddy, along with the women, stood firm on this point and vowed to go through with the mission or die.

Finally, Patrick Dolan, a formerly carefree bachelor, voiced a thought that had crossed all of their minds -- that one of them might die to save the rest. Dolan proposed that they draw lots to determine who might be killed so that the others could eat but William Foster opposed this plan, not wanting to take the risk that he might draw the bad lot. Eddy offered a compromise, suggesting that two of the men take revolvers and shoot it out until one of them died. This sporting proposition was also voted down. Eddy then spoke up again and suggested that perhaps they should let nature take its course and continue on until someone died. After some argument, the others agreed and they staggered on into the storm for another few miles.

The night that followed this miserable day was one of disaster. First, the snow and wind made it almost impossible to get a fire started. When the flame at last caught, the travelers piled on enough wood to make a blazing bonfire. Even though they had nothing to cook at least they could be warm. But one of them did not enjoy the fire for long. Antoine, the cattle herder, lay in an exhausted slumber near the fire and in his sleep, he flung out an arm and his hand landed in the hot coals. Eddy saw it happen but was too tired to move and help the sleeping man. He thought sure that the heat from the burns would wake Antoine but they did not. Antoine was so bone-weary that he continued to sleep and his hand doubled up and began to roast. This was more than Eddy could bear, and he dragged himself forward to pull the unconscious herder from danger. Antoine soon flung out his arm again and Eddy realized that it was no use to try and help him, Antoine died without ever awakening from what, under normal circumstances, would have been excruciating pain.

Shortly after this, a terrible storm of wind, snow and hail swept down upon the camp. At the same time, the fire began to eat its way down into the snow, devouring the blazing logs, platform and all. When the supply of firewood ran out, one of the men took the party's lone hatchet and went to cut more wood. But as he chopped at a log, the head of the hatchet flew off and was lost to the depths of the snow. It was impossible to find in the darkness of the storm, even if he had managed to summon the strength to dig for it.

One small piece of luck occurred, however, when the fire managed to keep burning. It was shielded from the snow by the shelter that it had melted itself into, about eight feet below the surface of the snow. The emigrants were forced to crouch around it with their feet in ice-cold melted snow. They knew that the fire would soon sputter out in the water so a few of them stood the half-burned foundation logs on end and rebuilt the fire on top of it. At this point, one of the Indians stood up to get closer to the warmth, and clumsy with cold and weariness, lurched against the new platform. The rickety structure fell over and the fire hissed out in the icy pool of water in which the party was standing. It looked as though they were finally doomed to perish in the cold. Despair set in and everyone began to pray to God for a merciful death -- except for Eddy and one or two of the women.

Eddy, always resourceful, finally persuaded his companions to try a trick that he had heard about from someone on the trail. He prodded them all out of the pit made by the fire and made them spread their blankets on the surface of the snow. They then sat on their blankets in a tight circle with their feet in the center while Eddy dragged himself across the circle and spread other blankets over them. He then slipped into the circle himself, and the blankets, with the snow that fell on top of them, formed a snug, insulating tent that held in their body heat and kept them warm. It was simple enough to do but some of the emigrants were so apathetic that it took Eddy nearly an hour to bully them into position. Uncle Billy Graves had been growing weaker throughout the evening and he now told Eddy that he was dying. With his last words, he urged his daughters to eat his body when he was gone. He knew that it was the only way that they could survive.

The next day, on Christmas, Patrick Dolan also died. As a storm raged outside their tent of blankets, Dolan became delirious and began to babble incoherently. He then pulled off his boots and most of his clothing and shouted to Eddy to follow him down to the settlements --- they would be there in just a few hours, he promised. With great difficulty, the others managed to overpower him and subdue him under the blankets. He thrashed about as they held him down until eventually, his energy exhausted, he became quiet. He drifted into death, his companions later said, looking as he was enjoying a calm and pleasant sleep.

On December 26, Eddy tried to start a fire under the blanket tent with gunpowder but his cold hands were clumsy and a spark caused his powder horn to explode, burning his face and hands. Amanda McCutchen and Sarah Foster were also burned, but not seriously. The burns did not stop Eddy from creeping out from under the tent later that afternoon. The storm had passed by now and as he looked around, he discovered a huge, dead pine tree standing nearby. Using some scraps from the cotton lining of Harriet Pike's coat as tinder, he started a small fire with sparks from flint and steel and soon was able to set fire to the pine tree. The emigrants lay down around the burning tree to enjoy the warmth and were too weak and uncaring to dodge the big, burning limbs that began falling in their midst. Luckily, no one was injured.

As the day wore on, the survivors huddled under their blankets close to the fire, half-crazed with hunger but unable to take that final step toward cannibalism. Finally, late that afternoon, they gave in. Unable to look one another in the eye, they began to roast and eat strips of flesh from Dolan's body. Only Eddy and the two Indians, overcome by guilt and grief, refused to take part in the feast. The others dried what they did not eat and saved it for later. Within days, Eddy and the Indians, now almost mad from a lack of food, surrendered and ate some of the meat.

The depleted survivors stayed at this site for the next four days and more death followed. Sarah Murphy Foster and Harriet Murphy Pike tried to feed a little of Dolan's flesh to their little brother, Lemuel, but he was beyond hope by this time. He grew steadily weaker and then died in the early morning hours with his head in Sarah's lap. The living members of the Forlorn Hope were not far from death themselves and looked like walking skeletons. They had resigned themselves to dying. When Eddy, hiding his own fears, tried to cheer them up, they responded with sighs, tears and moans. But the meal of human flesh, as loathsome as it was, had given them new strength. The women regained a bit of spirit but most of the men continued to sulk.

On December 30, the Forlorn Hope left the "Camp of Death," as they called the spot, and moved on. They carried with them the dried pieces of meat that had been carved from their dead friends and relatives. Although the first taboo against eating human flesh had been broken, no one touched the meat that had been carved from his or her own kin. The group struggled down the trail, barely able to walk. Their feet had become so swollen that the skin had burst. They wrapped their feet in rags to try and cushion them but the pain was so bad that the expedition could only travel short distances at a time.

On December 31, they traveled along a high-crested ridge and somehow, accidentally blundered back onto the trail that Charley Stanton had started them on. The Indians had confessed to Eddy a few days earlier that they were lost but he chose not to tell the others, believing they had no choice but to continue. But while the party was back on the right track, it was the most terrifying portion of the journey so far. They walked along the edges of icy, rock-strewn cliffs and crossed ravines on fragile bridges of snow. They teetered precariously on their clumsy snowshoes but their luck held out. After what seemed like an eternity of picking their way along, they reached a high point on the ridge and paused to take in the view. In the distance, to the west, they could see the vast, green plain of the Sacramento Valley. The sight gave them hope but their joy was dampened by the mountains and canyons that still lay in their path. Subdued, but not broken, they continued on.

Late that afternoon, they made it to the end of the ridge. Before them was a slope that plunged 2,000 or more feet to the bottom of a canyon. They could see that the canyon on the left made a bend below them and joined the canyon on their right. Unable to continue on that day, they made camp.

New Year's Day 1847 brought the emigrants no more cheer than Christmas had, save for the fact that there were no storms and no one died. The entire day was spent negotiating the canyon. They worked their way down the slope by squatting on their snowshoes and sliding down to the bottom, usually ending up in a snowdrift. The fierce cold had frozen the water below, the Bear River, and they were able to cross without difficulty. Climbing up the other side of the canyon was a nightmarish task. For the first 50 feet or so, the hunger-weakened men and women had to cling to cracks in the rock to keep from tumbling back down the steep slope. As it became less vertical, they dug their snowshoes into the snow and stair-stepped upwards, moving slowly and leaving blood from their damaged feet behind them on the trail. That night, after making camp, they ate the last of the human flesh they had brought with them.

They spent the next two days crossing a broad plateau over mostly level ground. The snow was firm enough that they could walk on it without their snowshoes but their feet could not heal while walking in the snow. To make matters worse, Jay Fosdick had become sick and his weakness forced the whole group to move slowly. One of the Indians was in even worse condition and the ends of his frostbitten toes began to drop off.

Things began to look more encouraging on January 3. The snow remained firm and it looked like they were coming down from the upper elevations as oaks could now be seen among the conifer trees. When they camped that night, the snow was only three feet deep, which was a cause for celebration. Believing that they would no longer need their snowshoes, they toasted the rawhide strings that held them together and ate them for dinner. Eddy also cooked a pair of worn-out moccasins and shared them with the group.

They set out again the next day with no food. Fosdick was now so weak that they were only able to travel about two miles. The only good news was that they camped that night for the first time on bare ground and in a grove of oak trees. After several days without food, William Foster proposed killing the two Indians so that the rest of the party could eat. To most white Westerners, an Indian was not quite human and so no one was shocked by the suggestion except for William Eddy, who was adamantly against it. To him, the two young men were not only fellow human beings, but faithful companions. To kill them would be an unjust reward for them having brought food over the Sierra Nevada with Charley Stanton a short time before. He argued with the others and finally realizing that he could not change their minds, he secretly warned the two young men. Horrified, they vanished into the forest.

The Forlorn Hope still had its lone rifle and a meager supply of ammunition, so Eddy became determined to take the gun and go hunting. If he had some luck, he knew he could save the lives of his remaining companions but if not, they would be no worse off. When he mentioned his plan to the women, they wept and begged him to stay with them, realizing that without him they would be lost. But Eddy's mind was made up and he started off the next morning. Harriet Pike threw her arms around his neck and implored him not to go. The others joined in, convinced that he was abandoning them and not coming back. The once-beautiful and now-emaciated Mary Graves decided to accompany Eddy; she was the only one left who was strong enough to keep up with him.

They trudged through the forest for more than two miles, keeping an eye out for signs of deer. Eddy was an experienced hunter and when he eventually found a place where an animal had laid for the night, he burst into tears. When he explained what he had found to Mary, she also began to weep. They continued on and, not much farther into the woods, they saw a large buck. Eddy raised the gun but found to his dismay that he was too weak to aim it. As much as he tried to hold it still, the gun wavered back and forth and dipped too low to fire. He changed his grip and tried again but failed once more. He heard Mary sobbing behind him. Eddy whispered for her to be quiet and she explained, "Oh, I am afraid that you will not kill it." Then, she fell silent.

Once more, Eddy lifted the rifle to his shoulder and raised the muzzle above the deer. As his weak arms started to let it fall, he pulled the trigger with the deer in his sights. The rifle thundered and the deer leaped three feet into the air and stood still. Although Mary feared that he had missed it, Eddy knew that his aim had been true. The deer dropped its tail between its legs, a sign that it was wounded, and began to run. Eddy and Mary limped after it until it crashed to the ground about 200 yards away. The animal was still alive when Eddy reached it and he cut its throat. Mary fell to Eddy's side and the two famished survivors drank as the animal's warm blood gushed out.

They rested a bit and then rolled the carcass to a spot where they could butcher it. They built a fire, and with their faces still covered with blood, ate part of the deer's liver and some of its other organs for supper. They gorged themselves on the heavy meat and that night, for the first time in many days, they enjoyed sleep without dreaming of food. During the night, Eddy fired his gun several times to alert their companions. At the camp, Fosdick heard the first crack and knew what it meant. "Eddy has killed a deer!" he weakly cried. "Now, if only I can get to him, I shall live."

But Fosdick's hopes were not meant to be. He died during the night and Sarah, his wife for less than a year, wept as she wrapped his body in their one remaining blanket and lay down on the bare ground to die next to her husband. But death did not claim her. She survived the frigid night and in the morning, she felt better. To her horror, though, she saw two of her traveling companions -- likely William and Sarah Foster, although no records ever stated for sure -- approach her campsite to make sure that she and her husband had both died during the night. They planned to help themselves to not only their flesh, but to their jewelry, money and watches too. Embarrassed at finding Sarah still alive, they turned back to their own campsite and there they met Mary and Eddy, who had emerged from the forest with venison for everyone.

As Eddy dried the remaining meat on the fire, Sarah and the two Fosters returned to Jay Fosdick's body. Sarah gave him one last kiss and then, in spite of her entreaties, the Fosters, now numb to the atrocities they were committing, cut out Jay's heart and liver before her eyes and also took his arms and legs, the meatiest parts of the body. The young widow, only 22 years old, made a little bundle of her valuables and returned to the campfire with the two people who had just callously butchered her husband. Uncaring, they skewered Jay's heart on a stick and began to roast it in the fire as Sarah looked on. When she could stand it no more, she fled to Eddy's campsite a short distance away.

Over the next couple of days, the survivors made it to the north branch of the American River and crossed. They had to climb another steep canyon wall on the other side but when they made camp that night, they were cheered by the fact that the weather was good and sat down peacefully to eat the last of the venison. Eddy made a speech mourning their lost companions -- tactfully avoiding any mention of cannibalism.

After supper, William Foster took Eddy aside. From the time of the first hardships experienced by the group, Foster had been strangely unhelpful and weak, unable to make a decision on his own and totally dependent on Eddy. Suddenly seized by initiative, he asked for Eddy's approval to kill Amanda McCutchen. His excuse was that she was a nuisance and could not keep up but in truth, he had acquired a taste for human flesh and deep down, his guilt over it had driven him mad.

Needless to say, Eddy was shocked and revolted. He told Foster that Amanda had a husband and children and besides, she was one of their companions and depended on them for protection. Foster continued to argue until Eddy told him sternly that he was not going to kill her. Foster than turned to the sisters, Sarah Fosdick and Mary Graves. He pointed out that neither of them had children and Sarah no longer had a husband. At that, Eddy walked away in disgust and returned to the fire. He loudly warned Sarah and Mary of Foster's plans for them in front of the entire company.

At that, Foster became angry and said that he did not care what Eddy said for he could do whatever he wanted. Eddy, losing patience, challenged Foster to settle their differences on the spot. He grabbed a large stick, banged it on a log to see that it was solid and then tossed it to Foster, ordering him to defend himself. Sarah Fosdick gave Eddy her late husband's knife and he went for Foster as quickly as his weakened condition would permit. Eddy was ready to kill him when all of the women except for Sarah, two of whom Foster had just proposed to kill and eat, seized Eddy and dragged him to the ground. They took his knife away but luckily, Foster just stood there in a daze.

When Eddy recovered, he warned Foster once more that he would kill him if he ever again showed the slightest inclination to take the life of any member of the expedition. If anyone were to die, it would either be Foster or himself, he said. And they would settle the question in a fight to the death, since Foster had never been willing to draw lots, which Eddy believed was the only fair way of selecting a victim.

On January 8, they left the campsite and continued on. They had walked about two miles before coming on the bloody tracks of the Indian guides who had wisely deserted them some time back. Foster, now obviously deranged, vowed that he would track down the Indians and kill them. Another mile or two farther they found the two men on the trail, near death. Eddy wanted to let them die in peace, for they could not last more than an hour or two, but Foster, now in an almost manic state, refused to wait. He shot the two Indians in the head and then butchered their bodies. Then he cut the flesh from their bones and dried it over the fire.

That night, Eddy ate only dried grass, refusing to eat the flesh of the Indians. And from that night on, only Foster's wife and Harriet Pike camped with Foster. The others kept a safe distance away with one of them remaining on watch at all times, afraid of what their former friend might do next.

As they continued on and passed through the forests, they saw numerous deer but Eddy was so weak that he could no longer aim and the rifle. He was still living on nothing but handfuls of grass, as he refused to touch the meat taken from his Indian companions. They all staggered as they walked and were so weakened and weary that they could only travel for a quarter mile or so before they had to stop and rest. The slightest obstacles would cause them to stumble and fall. A cold rain began to fall on the wretched wraith-like figures and did not stop.

At last, on January 12, they reached an Indian village in the foothills. The occupants burst into tears of pity when they saw the skeletal figures. They hurried to bring the survivors their own staple food of acorn bread but the emigrants' stomachs were unable to handle it and many of them got sick. Eddy was forced to go back to eating grass. The next day, the village chief sent runners ahead to a nearby encampment and told them to take care of the travelers and to have food ready for them. An escort accompanied them with two Indians walked with each of the party to support them and help them along. In this way, they passed from village to village toward the white settlements.

On January 17, they reached a village and one of the men had collected a large handful of pine nuts. For some reason, after eating them, Eddy felt miraculously restored and with this new energy, he pushed his comrades on. But the others gave out after a mile and collapsed on the ground, ready to die. The Indians were greatly distressed but were unable to get them to continue.

All Eddy could think about was his wife and children starving in the mountains and he resolved to make it through or die trying. One of the local Indians agreed to accompany him to the closest white settlement but after five miles, Eddy's strength gave out. Luckily, another Indian passed by and with the promise of tobacco, agreed to help Eddy continue on. They managed to make it another five miles before Eddy collapsed again, this time for good. His strength had completely failed but the Indians half-carried him along, dragging his bleeding feet on the ground.

At about a half hour before sunset, Eddy, starved beyond the point of recognition, came upon the home of a settler named M.D. Ritchie, who had arrived late in the fall of 1846 and had built a cabin to spend the winter in. Several other emigrants, who planned to claim their own spreads in the spring, lived in other winter quarters nearby. Ritchie's daughter, Harriet, heard a noise outside of the house and went to the door. There, she saw two Indians supporting a hideous-looking bundle between them. The shape lifted its head and, speaking in English, asked her for some bread. Harriet burst into tears and let the Indians bring Eddy into the house. Her family put him to bed, fed him and heard his story. He remained in bed for four days, too beaten to even turn over. He had traveled 18 miles on foot that day and he had been on the trail for 31 days.

Harriet Ritchie ran immediately to the neighbors with the news of starving travelers on the trail behind Eddy. The women collected all of the bread they could spare and added sugar, tea and coffee to go with the beef that had been butchered from California's immense herds. The men rode back and forth between the cabins bearing messages and collecting food. Four men took backpacks loaded with as much food as they could carry and set off on foot, for they did not want to risk their horses by riding at night. They were guided by the Indians and found the remaining members of the Forlorn Hope around midnight. One man stayed up all night cooking for them. Eddy had warned the rescue party not to give them too much to eat but the survivors wept and begged for food so pathetically that they could not deny them. As a result, gorging caused all of them to vomit.

In the morning, more men came with food, this time on horseback. They had no trouble following the trail for the last six miles were marked by Eddy's bloody footprints. The rescuers could not believe that he had covered such a distance, amazed at what had to have been a superhuman effort.

That night, the rest of the party was brought down into the California settlements. Of the 17 people who had left the lake camp a month earlier, only Eddy, Foster and five of the women had come down from the mountains alive.

A massive rescue operation was organized to try and reach the emigrants still on the other side of the mountains at Alder Creek and Truckee Lake. On February 4, the first expedition started out and began a journey into the mountains. Eddy, whose wife and children were still at the lake, started out with the rescuers but his ordeal had left him so weak and emaciated that he was forced to turn back. Two weeks later, the relief team reached the encampment with packs filled with food. A woman staggered out from one of the cabins and cried "Are you from California or Heaven?"

The situation at the two camps was hideous. Thirteen people had died, including Eddy's wife and daughter. At the Alder Creek camp, Jake Donner and three of his hired men were dead. George Donner lay dying as the wound on his hand had become infected with gangrene. Many of those still living were on the verge of insanity. Cannibalism had become commonplace in the mountains as well. The emigrants had no other food at their disposal and after some brief objections, began eating the dead. It was almost too much for most of them to bear.

The rescuers headed back to California with 21 people, as many as they could safely take. Tamsen Donner refused to leave her dying husband and Mrs. Reed was forced to leave her son, Tommy, behind, as he was still too weak to travel. Young Patty Reed stayed behind to take care of him. "If I do not see you again, Mother," she said, "do the best you can."

Halfway down the west side of the Sierra Nevada, the first relief party met a second band of rescuers, this one led by James Reed. After spending only a few minutes with his wife and the two children she had managed to bring with her, he continued on to the east. Reed's party gathered up 17 more survivors from the Alder Creek and lake encampments, most of them children, but almost as soon as they crossed the pass, a storm struck and snowed them in for two days and three nights. The fire they had built sank into the snow and was snuffed out and soon, the food supply was gone. Five-year-old Isaac Donner died during one dark night.

When the storm finally passed, Reed tried to get the party moving again but the Breens and the Graves family refused to go on. He had to leave them behind in a crude, snowy encampment, where they remained for six days until they were found by a third relief party from California. By that time, Elizabeth Graves and her son Franklin were also dead. Parts of their bodies were found boiling in pots when the rescuers arrived and Elizabeth's infant daughter was discovered wailing next to her mother's half-eaten corpse.

In this new rescue party was William Eddy and, surprisingly, William Foster. They had both recovered from their journey and Foster had also recovered from the madness that had gripped him on the trail. He had repaired his friendship with Eddy. Both men had come back because they had left children behind at the lake camp and hoped to save them. Unfortunately, they were too late. When they arrived, they were informed by Lewis Keseberg, a German immigrant and member of the party, that he had eaten Eddy's and Foster's sons. Grief stricken, the two men collected George Donner's children and quickly departed. Donner, unable to walk, stayed behind to die and Tamsen remained with him. Lavina Murphy, nearly blind, stayed with Keseberg, whose wife had left with the first rescue team.

George Donner died on the night of March 29 and it was said that Tamsen went mad with grief. She ran all of the way from Alder Creek to the lake cabins to see if anyone there was left alive. On the way there, she fell into a stream and her clothing froze. Shivering and weak, she managed to make it to the cabins, where she found Keseberg. When she arrived, she was coughing and sick and burning up with fever. She told Keseberg that she had to see her children in California and she was willing to cross the mountains on foot, at that very moment, if necessary. The German realized how sick she was and put her to bed in the cabin.

When a fourth relief expedition arrived at Truckee Lake in April, the only survivor was the emaciated and spectral Keseberg. He was found lying unconscious next to a large pot that contained the liver and lungs of a young boy. He had been living on nothing but human flesh -- despite the fact that some supplies remained from the earlier rescue parties. There were also the carcasses of cattle that had been lost in the winter storms that were now thawing in the melting snow. Their meat was untouched because, as Keseberg explained to his rescuers, the oxen meat was "too dry eating." The German's mind was obviously completely gone. He was

Donner Lake is said to be haunted by the restless spirits of the doomed emigrant party

eventually charged with six murders but was reunited with his wife and settled in Sacramento.

The Reeds later settled in the area outside what would become San Francisco. Margaret Reed lived in relative peace and happiness until she died in poor health, several years later.

William Eddy, the hero of the Forlorn Hope, remarried and had children in Petaluma, California.

The Donner children were left as orphans. Some of the younger Donner children were adopted by various families, while the older girls, some as young as 14, married young Californians. The remaining Graves suffered a similar fate as the Donners. The more fortunate were adopted, while some had to survive without any home or family of their own. Sarah Fosdick later remarried, and she and her sister, Mary Graves, tried to support and care for their younger siblings when they could.

The various families of the Donner Party almost never saw each other after they were rescued and it's easy to understand why. They had endured a horrific experience and during the ordeal had engaged in what is still considered as one of the greatest human atrocities -- cannibalism. Some of the survivors lived as unhappy recluses, while some like William and Mary Graves, Virginia Reed, and Eliza Donner published accounts describing their ordeal. Virginia Reed was even featured in a 1891 magazine article.

Eventually, the cabins, shelters and bodies left behind at Alder Creek and Truckee Lake were erased by time. The chilling reminders of the Donner Party encouraged settlers to hurry along the trail for years to come, avoiding untested shortcuts, until the railroads put an end to the Oregon and California Trail. Time -- that great enemy of the Western emigrants -- defeated the physical remnants of the Donner Party's suffering but it could not erase the memories.

Of the 81 travelers who had made camp east of the pass on the night of October 31, only 48 survived. The area around Truckee Lake, later renamed Donner Lake, became known as a shunned and cursed place, and is it any wonder? Who could find a better place for a haunting?

As the years have passed, the legends of the lake state that the restless ghosts of the doomed expedition still wail and cry in fear and starvation here. There have been many tales told of travelers who, not knowing what had occurred in the ruined cabins along the lakeshore, stayed the night before crossing the pass and experienced the phantoms of those who died, or were murdered, years before. These same stories tell of mournful wails and ghostly figures whose confused spirits still roam the area.

Many years after the horrible events, the ruins at the site were turned into a monument of sorts to the tragedy that occurred. The crumbling stone walls of the Murphy cabin were marked with a monument, as were the sites of the Breen and Keseberg shelters. It is near the Keseberg cabin that an inordinate amount of strange activity has been reported over the years. Many believe that it may be the ghost of Tamsen Donner who lingers here, perhaps because of the mystery surrounding her cause of death. According to Lewis Keseberg, she had come to the shelter already sick from a fever, likely caught after falling into the creek and then running through the cold woods at night. Keseberg would later admit to cannibalizing Tamsen but some believe that he may have murdered her, rather than wait for her to die. He was charged with her murder but the case never went to trial. Eliza Donner always believed Keseberg's story that her mother had died from the fever, but the truth will never be known for sure.

These unanswered questions are what allegedly cause Tamsen's spirit to continue to walk. In recent years, there have been reports of an apparition sighted nearby that looks like a woman dressed in white. In addition, ghost researchers have also recorded voices and sounds with recording devices that sound like a woman weeping. Could these sounds be the voice of Tamsen Donner, still crying out from the other side?

Another active site is the former location of the Murphy cabin. The cabin is long gone now but a large stone remains that was used as a fireplace wall. This has long been thought to be the most eerie location in what is now a state park, dedicated to the Donner Party.

A number of years ago, while living in Utah, I took a trip to Donner Lake to see where the ill-fated expedition came to an end. I had been interested in the story of the emigrants lost in the wild for quite some time, and the promise of ghostly activity made the trip all the more inviting. As it turned out, though, my night at the lakeside camp was without incident -- and perhaps that was for the best.

I would be hard-pressed to think of a group of people who more deserved to rest in peace. The horrible days that they endured at the lake, and along the trail to the Sacramento Valley, were terrible enough that they should not be subjected to an endless purgatory here on earth. I would hate to think that the spirits of heroic figures like William Eddy or Charles Stanton are still lost out there, somewhere in the wilderness, forced to repeat their most hellish days over and over again.

Perhaps some ghost stories, and the ghosts who create them, just deserve to fade away.

1888: THE CHILDREN'S BLIZZARD

On January 12, 1888, a blizzard broke out over the Great Plains that changed history. Out of nowhere, a dark cloud appeared on the horizon. The air grew still for a long, eerie moment and then the sky began to roar and a wall of ice dust blasted the prairie. Every house, barn, fence row, wagon and living thing was instantly covered with shattered crystals, blinding, suffocating, smothering and burying anything exposed to the wind. The cold front raced across the open landscape, freezing everything in its path.

It swept across Montana first, and then buried North Dakota around the time that farmers were doing their early morning chores. South Dakota was frozen as children were finishing their morning recess at school and in Nebraska, school clocks were nearing the time for dismissal. In three minutes, temperatures in every region dropped more than 18 degrees. As night fell, the temperature kept dropping steadily, hour after hour, deluged by the cold from the northwest.

The cold front brought snow, ice and subzero temperatures – and it also brought death.

By the morning of Friday, January 13, hundreds of people lay dead on the Dakota and Nebraska prairie, many of them children who had fled – or been sent home from – country schools at the same time the wind shifted and the sky was exploding.

It was a disaster created by bad luck and bad timing. The January 12 blizzard – which has become known as the "Children's Blizzard" or the "Schoolhouse Blizzard" – affected an entire region and its population. There was not a family among the farmers, settlers and town-dwellers on the prairie who was not personally affected by death caused by the storm, or who at least knew another family that was. It was a terrifying event and after it passed, the region was never the same again.

The series of events that created the Children's Blizzard began in the frigidly cold sections of western Canada, where the month of January is typically brutal. In the winter days of late 1887 and early 1888, the chilling fields of

the Canadian northwest were particularly intense and a great mass of arctic air slowly expanded southward and continued to cool over the snow-covered plains. By the start of the second week of January, the cold air mass sat over the western Canadian prairies with temperature readings at places like Medicine Hat in Alberta resting at 18 degrees below zero.

Unfortunately, there was little warning for residents of the American prairie about the cold temperatures that were coming. In the late 1880s, weather observations were few across most of the continent and even sparser in the western lands away from the coast. In those days, the U.S. Army Signal Corps provided weather services for the nation, including a daily weather map series that was started in 1871. Using telegraph messages, weather stations across the country reported in to a central hub that compiled the readings for the map. While they did not provide the kind of accuracy that we have today, the maps did show the broad features of the march of weather across the continent. Tragically, that was not enough. Those in charge of preparing and disseminating the "indications" (as forecasts were called in those days) did not see the danger of the cold front and the storm until it was too late. But the men of the Signal Corps were not trained meteorologists by today's level of accreditation -- few in America were. The state of the science of weather forecasting was in the early days of development in 1888.

There was no one to blame for the storm – it was merely deadly bad luck that claimed so many lives.

In early January, a small storm system developed over western Colorado and it dragged some of the frigid Canadian air into Montana and Wyoming. Meanwhile, on January 11, a mass of unseasonably mild tropical air moved out of the Gulf of Mexico and streamed northward over Texas and Oklahoma. The morning temperatures on the Plains began to rise. Those who lived in the region were thrilled with what they believed was a "January thaw." The temperature continued to rise throughout the night, and on the morning of January 12, it was downright balmy. Children went to school wearing light coats and farmers went about their chores without the gloves and mufflers they had needed for the last few weeks.

The warm air surged north from the Gulf as the pool of cold air to the north remained intact. The proximity of these two very different air masses could be compared to holding a burning match next to a powder keg. High above the earth, a strong jet stream blew over the boundary between the two fronts, pushing the match ever closer to the gunpowder until finally it was lit. The result was an explosive storm that made history.

As the storm finally came together, it moved at a breakneck pace throughout the day, from Montana in the early hours of January 12, crossing the Dakota Territory in the late morning and racing into Nebraska by the middle of the afternoon. The rise in temperature overnight was followed by an even more rapid plummeting of the mercury in the wake of the storm. The winds began to rise in the fury of the storm. A Signal Corps observer named Frank L. Harrod wrote: "Sudden and fierce change of wind from south to north." Then, "heavy blinding snow." The litany of "fierce winds," "blinding snow," "heavy drifting," and "bone-chilling drops in temperature" was repeated over and over again in the Signal Corps reports as the storm system rushed to the south and east.

The forecasters of the Signal Corps had their barometers to warn them that something terrible was about to happen but out on the prairie and in the one-room schoolhouses and on the streets of the hastily built railroad towns, the blizzard took people utterly by surprise.

To those who happened to be standing outside, it looked as though the northwest sky was suddenly bulging and ripping open. In nearly every account of the storm, there runs the same thread, often in the same words – there had never been anything like it before. Settlers who had been on the plains for years had seen plenty of bad storms in the past, including one they called the "Snow Winter" in 1880-1881 that literally buried the region under dozens of feet of snow, but they had never seen a storm come up so quickly or hit so violently.

Allie Green, a 15-year-old boy who lived in Clark County in the eastern Dakota Territory later wrote: "My brother and I were out snowballing on a bank. We could see the blizzard coming across Spirit Lake. It was just as still as could be. We saw it cut off the trees like it was a white roll coming. It hit with a 60 mile an hour wind." H.G. Purcell, who lived in neighboring Codington County recalled that the blizzard was "like a gray wall."

A newspaper story carried an account by an unnamed Dakota schoolboy who said, "We were out playing in our shirtsleeves, without hats or mittens. Suddenly we looked up and saw something rolling toward us with great fury from the northwest, making a loud noise. It looked like a long string of big bales of cotton, each one bound tightly with heavy cords of silver, and then all tied together with great silvery ropes. The broad front of these cotton bales looked to be about twenty-five feet high; above them it was perfectly clear. The phenomenon was so unusual that it scared us children, and several of us ran into the schoolhouse and screamed to the teacher to come out quickly and see what was happening." When the storm reached the schoolhouse a few minutes later, it hit "with such force that it nearly moved it off its cobblestone foundation. And the roar of the wind was indescribable."

A schoolteacher named Norris E. Williams from Jerauld County, west of Sioux Falls, was standing in front of his schoolhouse with a group of students during a late morning recess when the storm arrived. He later wrote, "I was just saying that I ought to dismiss school and go to Woonsocket for coal when a sudden whiff of cold air caused us all to turn and look toward the north, where we saw what appeared to be a huge cloud rolling over and over the ground, blotting out the view of the nearby hills and covering everything in that direction as with a blanket. There was scarcely time to exclaim at the unusual appearance when the cloud struck us with awful violence and in an instance, the warm and quiet day was changed into a howling pandemonium of ice and snow."

Darkness fell…. "darkness that might be felt," as one farmer wrote. "You could hardly see your hand before you or draw your breath and that with the intense cold roaring wind and darkness it would appall the stoutest heart."

Many wrote that the arrival of the storm was preceded by a loud roar, like that of a train approaching on the empty landscape. It was a roar that they not only heard but felt inside their guts. The sound was the wind at the knife edge of the cold front, smashing the snow into powder. The turbulence behind the front was so incredible that the air was rolling over at the same time that it was coming down. The effect was like putting snow and ice into a grinder.

By 1:00 p.m. on January 12, the cold front had spread over almost all of the Dakota Territory, the western two-thirds of Nebraska and the northwestern edge of Minnesota. Over the next two hours, it picked up speed as it spread over the most populated section of the prairie. There was no way of warning anyone of the danger that was coming. The weather stations hoisted cold wave flags, to warn of impending temperature drops, but they were useless except for those who lived near the Signal Corps outposts. Even then, visibility was so bad during the storm that the flags were largely invisible unless someone was only a few feet away. The cold wave warnings were meant as a public service, but the people of the region were on their own when the blizzard hit.

This was especially true with the schoolteachers, many of whom were barely older than the children they taught. As the blizzard broke against the northwest walls of the schoolhouses, every teacher was faced with the choice of keeping their children at the school or sending them home. Many of the teachers were familiar with the danger of winter storms but didn't have the necessary fuel for the school stoves that would keep the children warm. They believed they would be safer at home. At some point, it became a choice of freezing where they were or attempting to go out into the storm and seek other shelter.

Others had enough fuel to make it through the night. Teacher Seymour H. Dopp of Pawnee City, Nebraska, kept his 17 students at the schoolhouse overnight. The building stayed warm and the following morning, worried parents managed the snow-drifted roads to find the safe but hungry students had been sheltered from the storm. That afternoon, Dopp returned to his home in Table Rock to find the teacher at the school in that community had made a different decision. His 11-year-old daughter Avis and her classmates had been released from school. She suffered frostbite on her one-block trek home.

But not all of the teachers on the prairie could keep their children warm during the bitter night of January 12. Minnie Mae Freeman, who was still in her teens, was one of the many teachers who faced the problem of freezing or fleeing in the storm. She had 16 students, some of them almost as old as she was, at her country schoolhouse near Ord, just east of the Nebraska Sand Hills. The schoolhouse was made from sod, which was unusual for a school on the prairie, and had a crude door attached by leather hinges and a roof of tarpaper with sod laid over it. Around noon, the first blast of the storm tore the door off its hinges and blew it back into the schoolroom. A couple of the boys helped Minnie get the door back up, but it quickly blew off again. This time, she had them nail it shut. Minnie knew she had enough coal to heat the schoolhouse all night and she was determined to stay there and to keep the children inside.

But that plan quickly fell apart. A gust of wind ripped off a section of the tarpaper where the sod had fallen away and Minnie realized that they would all die if they tried to stay in the school. The family with whom she boarded lived a half mile north of the school and she decided that the best plan was to take them there for the night. Legend has it that she found a length of rope and tied the children to one another before they set out, but others claim this tale was cooked up by the newspapers in the aftermath of the storm. Regardless, all of Minnie's students stayed together and made it safely to the home where she boarded. Later, Minnie Freeman always insisted that she had done what anyone would have done that day, but in fact, many older and more experienced teachers failed to act as quickly and as sensibly.

The storm descended on the town of Wessington Springs soon after it hit Ord. From noon until 4:00 p.m., teacher May Hunt did her best to carry on in the eerie, blowing twilight with the seven students who had come to school that day. When the fuel ran out that afternoon, May and the children were suddenly faced with the choice of freezing or fleeing. May Hunt chose to go...

Just 140 yards west of the school, on the other side of a large ravine, was a farmhouse that belonged to the Hinner family. The children in school that day – Fred and Charles Weeks, the three oldest children of Reverend S.F. Huntley and his wife, Abi, and Frank and Addie Knieriem – all lived at least three-quarters of a mile away. The Hinner house looked as though it was the best and safest option.

The ravine was what worried May the most. It was five feet deep and the sides were steep. There was a makeshift bridge that had been placed across it, but it would be hard to find in the blinding storm. If they missed the bridge, the children could fall into the ravine and with the drifting snow, the little ones would have a hard time getting out. May counted herself lucky that Fred Weeks had come to school that day. At 18, he was her oldest pupil, a big, shy, dark-haired farm boy, and when May told him her plan, Fred volunteered to go scouting. If he could find the bridge, he'd clear a path and then come back for the others.

Fred was gone for a half an hour while the rest of the group waiting around the embers of the dying fire.

When he finally came back, the younger children cheered. He had found the bridge and had walked back and forth two times between it and the school in order to clear a path. They would do fine as long as they followed close behind him. Once he got them across the ravine, they would be able to make it to the Hinner house.

It was 4:30 before the students were ready to leave. Addie Knieriem, one of the youngest girls, was wearing thin, dainty little shoes (it had been warm when students came to school that morning), so May wound scarves around her feet to keep them from freezing. Fred ventured back outside first and everyone joined hands behind him in a human chain. In just the few minutes after Fred's return, the storm had grown worse. The tracks that he had made in the snow were completely drifted over. There was no sign of the bridge that he had managed to find two times.

The school and the Hinner house were only separated by 140 yards – the length of a football field and a half – and on a clear day, even the youngest child could have walked it in less than 10 minutes. But in the storm, blinded, deafened and barely able to breathe in the cold wind, the best-laid plans went awry. It was the ravine that brought on the initial panic. Stepping out where he believed the bridge to be, Fred fell through the snow that had drifted into the ditch and dragged the others down with him. They crashed into the cold snow in a tangle that would have been funny if not for the horror of the storm and the terror being felt by the children. As they wrapped themselves back in their coats and scarves and struggled out of the snow, precious minutes and body heat were wasted during their efforts.

Somehow, they managed to make it up out of the ravine, determined to march to the rest of the way to the Hinner house. Fred led the way, praying that he was going in the right direction. With every step, he expected to catch a glimpse of the house ahead of them through the gray snow. By now, the sun had set and what little light remained was rapidly fading from the sky.

Their dogged determination drained the energy from their bodies until they became exhausted to the point of near collapse. It was only 100 yards to the house but they fought the elements in thin cotton clothing with their eyelashes caked with ice and frozen shut and masks of ice hanging from their faces. They plunged ahead in a storm during which cattle died standing up, perishing from suffocation before they froze solid. When they had climbed out of the ravine, the students were soaking wet and nearly blind. Most had lost the use of their fingers. Addie Knieriem had no sensation in her toes. Panic had stolen what little heat remained inside of their bodies and within minutes, all of the children except for Fred and his brother were ready to give up.

Fred pushed them on and when suddenly he stumbled on the flax straw pile that belonged to the Hinners, he believed they were saved. The party could shelter inside the straw for a few minutes while he went to look for the farmhouse. Then he could come back and lead them to safety. By pure luck, Fred found a pitchfork in the snow and enlisted the help of his brother, Charles, to help him dig out a cave in the sheltered side. It took them some time to hollow out a space for Miss Hunt and the children and when it was done, he pushed them all inside. Huddled together, shivering from their time outside, the claustrophobic interior of the hay pile was much better than being out in the wind.

May insisted that Fred should not go out looking for the farmhouse alone. Charles would go with him and Ernest Huntley volunteered as well. Before they set out, someone had the idea of making a guide rope for them to use. Several of the girls had worn aprons to school that morning and May collected them and tore them into strips. When all of the pieces were tied together, they had a good length of rope. Fred would take one end and May would hold tight to the other. When they found the farmhouse – which based on the proximity of the hay pile should have been only a few yards away – they would follow the rope back and find the others. Or, if they failed to find the house, at least they wouldn't be lost in the storm.

Fred and the two other boys went back out into the storm and began to walk around the straw pile in ever-larger circles. One time around, then a few steps farther, and they'd circle it again. They shouted as loud as they could and held out their arms in front of them, hoping to brush against the side of a building, a piece of equipment, anything at all. They looked as hard as they could but could see nothing. They heard nothing but the howling wind. At least they had the rope from the aprons to guide them back to the hay pile because without it, they would have surely wandered into the storm and froze to death.

May Hunt refused to give up. All eight of them shouted for help, praying the Hinners would hear them, until their voices gave out. No one came to their rescue. When the smaller children began to shiver, May directed Fred to dig deeper into the hay pile, making a larger cave where all of them could pile together and ride out the storm. He did the best that he could with the pitchfork and they all settled in. Without being asked, Fred took the place at the mouth of the hay cave, which was the coldest and most exposed spot. He did the best that he could to shelter the others. They had not eaten since noon. They had no adequate clothing, no blankets or gloves, and few had even worn hats. For a while they told stories and sang songs, but eventually the children began to fade. May did all that she could to keep them awake, even when they wept from fear, hunger and cold.

Fred Weeks, whose extraordinary bravery would be lauded following the storm, kept guard at the mouth of the hay cave and climbed out every few hours to check on the progress of the blizzard. At 4:00 a.m., he went out to see that the air had cleared, there were stars overhead and there, less than 100 yards away, was the Hinner farmhouse for which he had searched so desperately. He staggered to the house on frozen feet and shouted and pounded on the door until Mr. Hinner answered.

Fred and Mr. Hinner returned to the haystack as quickly as possible, bringing lanterns and piles of blankets. They called to May to bring the children to safety. At first, the smaller children were groggy and slow to react. They shivered uncontrollably as soon as they got outside. Fred, despite the condition of his hands and feet, wrapped the children in blankets and shawls and sent them staggering into the farmhouse.

Soon, they were all toddling inside, except for Addie. In the excitement of the rescue, no one noticed at first that something was wrong with Addie Knieriem. She was unable to stand up and had to be pulled out of the hay pile. They quickly realized that it was her feet. They had gotten wet when she fell into the ravine and after taking shelter in the haystack, her shoes and stockings had frozen solid. As she huddled in the cave, the warmth drained out of her feet and they remained encased in ice, wool and leather all night. At some point, her feet turned into ice.

Fred carried her into the house and they removed her shoes and stockings. May Hunt was appalled – she had never seen human flesh that looked like that before. Frostbite had set in and Addie's feet looked like grayish purple marble. In those days, the standard home remedy for frostbite was to rub the frozen flesh with snow and then let it thaw gradually in warm water. Things would be done differently today, using warm water, rehydration with warm fluids and antibiotics, but even modern medicine likely could not have saved Addie's feet. Eventually, gangrene set in and one foot was amputated. The other was saved, but she lost all of her toes.

We will never know how many spent the night out on the prairie, but it was likely in the thousands. They were stranded in the southern and eastern parts of the Dakota Territory, in the eastern part of Nebraska and in southwestern Minnesota. The northern section of Dakota was largely spared because the storm came through so early that people stayed home and kept their children inside. Iowa, although it received the heaviest snow, suffered few casualties; the storm didn't arrive there until late in the day, when night was falling and the farmers and their children were safely at home. But in southern Dakota and Nebraska, the timing of the storm could not have been worse and many of those overtaken by the storm perished – and more than 20 percent of them were children.

Their suffering was terrible. They froze alone or with their parents or died in a mad, frantic search for loved ones. They died with the frozen skin torn from their faces, where they had clawed at the mask of ice that covered their flesh with numb fingers. Some had died within hours of becoming lost while others lived through the night and then died at first light. They were found standing waist deep in snow drifts with their hands frozen to barbed wire fences, clutching at their clothing, buried under wagons, on their backs and facedown in the snow with their arms outstretched as if trying to crawl to safety. Women died sitting upright in their homes with their children gathered around them. Their fires had gone out when the last bits of wood, hay and broken furniture had been exhausted and the hearth had gone cold.

A young couple in Minnesota died kneeling side by side with their hands held high above their heads.

A Nebraska boy named Roman Hytrek, age nine, was walking the prairie with his dog when the storm overtook them. The dog showed up that evening, scratching at the door of a neighbor's house. Roman's coat was found in March but his body was not discovered until days later. He died alone leaning against the side of a hill.

The search party speculated that he had unbuttoned his coat to try and keep his dog warm but the wind had torn it from his back.

William Klemp, a young Dakota newlywed, left his pregnant wife at home and went out into the storm to care for their livestock. He never returned. A few weeks later, Klemp's wife gave birth to a son. It was spring before Klemp's body was found in a sod shanty a mile from the house.

A young Nebraska schoolteacher named Lois Royce huddled all night on the prairie with three of her students, two nine-year-old boys and a six-year-old girl. The children cried themselves to sleep. Lois stretched out on the ground, lying on her side with her back to the wind and the children sheltered in the hollow of her body. She covered them with her cloak. The boys died first. Lois felt one of their bodies stop moving as the breath left him and he went cold. The second boy died a few hours later. The little girl, Hattie Rosberg, had begged her teacher through the night for more blankets and died at daybreak crying, "I'm so cold, Mama, please cover me up!" When the air had cleared enough for her to see, Lois left the three dead children lying together and crawled a quarter of a mile on her hands and knees to reach the nearest farmhouse.

In Dakota's Beadle County, a farmer in his thirties named Robert Chambers was outside watering his cattle with his two sons and their Newfoundland dog when the storm hit. The older boy, who was 11, suffered from rheumatism, so Chambers sent him home before the weather got too bad. He thought that he and his nine-year-old boy, Johnny, could get the cattle into the barn by themselves. The dog would know the way. But in the horror of the storm, the father and son became confused and lost and soon realized that they had no hope of making it to the house. Chambers burrowed down into a snowdrift and wrapped Johnny in his jacket and vest. Neither of them had worn a coat outside on that balmy morning. Robert placed the boy in the snow shelter and then stood in the storm and shouted for help for as long as his voice held out. The dog barked frantically in unison, but neither of them could be heard over the wind. By evening, Chambers was too cold to do anything but lie down in the snow next to his son. The dog lay next to them, providing a little extra warmth. Johnny later recalled how cold his father's body was and he urged him to get up and look for the line of trees that they had planted by the house. But Chambers would not leave his son.

As the night wore on, father and son spoke of death and Chambers assured Johnny that they would survive and repeated over and over again that the boy needed to lie still. Johnny knew that his father was freezing. At some point, the boy dozed off and when he woke, his father was still alive, but only barely. Chambers told his son to pray and he would pray with him.

At daylight, a rescue party heard the Newfoundland barking and found them. The snow had drifted so deeply that Johnny was completely buried. Robert Chambers was dead. The dog was standing guard over them both.

Before dawn on Friday, January 13, 1888, the blizzard blew itself out over the Dakotas, Nebraska and southwestern Minnesota. The last gusts of wind pushed at the drifts and hollows of snow and then a high pressure system moved in and the air grew pure, dry and bitterly cold. The temperature plunged even further and when morning came, a bright sun made the landscape shimmer with white light. A southern Dakota farmer named Thomas Pirnie wrote, "It was a beautiful but awe-inspiring scene. The frost sparkled like myriads of diamonds and the sun dogs were beautiful as a rainbow. Overall, there was a death-like stillness, not the sounds of a dog barking, a cow bellowing or a horse neighing. The hills which had been sharply outlined were now but rounded knolls. Ravines had almost disappeared. Everywhere there was perfect whiteness. The smoke from the house chimneys went straight up in round columns high into the sky. This was the only sign of life about us."

Towns and cities across the region were paralyzed. The streets were drifted over, the stores and schools closed, the railroad yards deserted. Residents later wrote that no team or vehicles of any kind moved about. There were reports of drifts that were 20 feet high. Trains were abandoned on impassable tracks. Locomotives equipped with plows set out from Aberdeen, Sioux Falls, Omaha and Lincoln along the major routes but were unable to break through the wind-packed drifts. Heavy snows pulled down the telegraph wires and not a word came or went from most of western Iowa.

Across the prairie, nothing moved. Every object that was large enough to raise a profile above the landscape had been turned into a drift of snow. The exposed northern and western faces of these objects, though, had been scoured clean by the wind. The first rays of the sun brought color to the open fields, but no warmth. At odd intervals in the vast, smooth white surface, dark and irregular specks could be seen – these were the cattle that had not been brought to shelter the previous day. They had frozen in the pastures, still standing upright. As the sun gleamed, smaller objects began to appear in the whiteness – the gray sleeve of a coat, a boot, a tangle of hair, a child's small hand.

It seems incredible that a person could survive that night without shelter or food, yet many did. Although some of them survived the night only to die in the new light of day.

Two children, Amelia Shirk and Omar Gibson, had lived through the night because of a horse blanket. They buried themselves beneath it and managed to make it through the storm, even though the horse it had belonged to had vanished into the blizzard. Amelia was 12, Omar, 16, the younger brother of the girl's stepfather. They weren't blood relatives but Omar tenderly cared for the girl. He wrapped her in the blanket and when she could not stop shivering, he gave her his jacket as well. The snow covered them, providing some barrier between the wind and bitter cold. They were both alive at sunrise. In fact, Omar was strong enough to get to his feet without help. He told Amelia that he was going to search for their horse, took a few slow steps, and then died on his feet. He fell to the ground, facedown in the snow.

The same thing happened to a boy named Jesse Beadle in Dakota's Jerauld County. Jesse and his grandmother had ridden to his school the day before in a horse-drawn sleigh. His grandmother was filling in as a substitute teacher for a few days at the school. The blizzard struck late in the morning and at first, his grandmother decided they should wait out the storm in the schoolhouse, but as the blizzard raged on, she and Jesse began to worry about the safety of their horse, which was still hitched at the south end of the building. The grandmother's house was only three miles from the school, to the southeast, which meant they would have the wind at their backs. They got most of the way there before the horse floundered in the deep snow. Jesse unhitched the animal and freed it from the drift, but the sleigh was stuck. Disoriented by the whiteout conditions and unable to walk through the deepening snow, Jesse turned the sleigh on its side so that it could break the wind. He gave his grandmother the blankets from the sleigh and huddled down beside her.

They endured the night and at dawn, Jesse saw a house about a half-mile away. He told his grandmother to wait for him in the shelter of the sleigh while he went for help. He pulled himself to his feet and saw the horse standing and looking at him across the snow just a few yards away. Jesse managed to stagger a short distance toward the house before he collapsed. He, too, died moments later.

Jesse and Omar died of cardiac arrest caused by shock. All night long as they lay in the snow, their bodies fought to keep warm by drawing the blood away from their skin and exposed extremities and pushing it deep into the core. In the morning, when the boys stood up and tried to walk for the first time in hours, the sudden change of position and unaccustomed movement triggered a massive drop in blood pressure. Blood from the cores of their bodies cooled as it moved into the cold extremities. Their pumping hearts caused this cold blood to circulate and when it reached their hearts, the organs instantly seized. Instead of contracting and releasing in steady beats, the lower chambers of their hearts began to quiver without coordination or effect. They stopped pumping and the blood stopped circulating through their bodies. Jesse and Omar blacked out and a few seconds later, their erratic hearts ceased to beat altogether.

A cold heart can be a dangerous thing. If a body is roughly handled, sometimes even by something as slight as feet touching the ground, it can immediately seize. Coming in out of the cold can also stop the heart. This happened numerous times after the blizzard. Doctors would later call this rewarming shock.

It was what killed Frederick Milbier, age 18. Frederick had been caught out in the storm in an open bobsled with his sister, Christina, her husband, Jacob Kurtz, and their baby. They were on their way home from dinner at the home of Jacob's parents near Yankton in southeastern Dakota Territory. When the horses refused to walk in the wind, Jacob left his wife, child and brother-in-law in the bobsled and went for help. He only made it a few yards before he was knocked down by the wind. Unable to get up, Jacob lay on the snow and slowly lapsed into unconsciousness.

Trapped in the bobsled, Christina unbuttoned her dress and her blouse and placed her baby next to her naked skin. This probably saved both of their lives. In the morning light, Christina and Frederick saw a farmer in the distance, gathering hay from the pile near his house. Frederick climbed out of the bobsled, and unable to walk, he began to crawl towards the farmer. Alerted to their predicament, the famer and his family quickly got Frederick, Christina and the baby into their house. Wrapped in blankets and given warm drinks, Frederick died soon after in the comfort of the farmer's home.

Rescuers went out to look for Jacob Kurtz and found him buried in the snow. They reported that he was entirely frozen "except for a sphere of warmth surrounding his heart." Jacob might have been revived in a modern hospital but in those days, he was beyond hope. The search party brought him to the farmhouse and like his brother-in-law, he died from heart failure as he slowly thawed out.

For most, the suspense of the night ended on that bright sunny morning – one way or another. In the clear light of day, husbands tracked down wives who had wandered out into the storm. Wives found husbands who had gone out to bring in the cattle and had not come back. Dogs returned home, with or without their masters. Parents rushed to country schools where their children had spent the night huddled around fires made from burning desks and chairs. Or the schools were empty, the children missing, the teachers frantic with grief and remorse. News of the missing, the living and the dead was carried into towns on foot or on horseback and spread from the hotels, the Western Union offices and the railroad station agents. One terrible story after another circulated back east to the newspapers offices in the cities and small towns:

Mr. Sterns, a Dakota schoolteacher, had taken his three children to the school where he taught in De Smet and never returned home.

A Nebraska farmer named Closs Blake found a bobsled turned upside down and buried in a snowdrift. When he righted it, he found the body of a little boy frozen underneath.

In the country, south of Sioux Falls, Peter Wierenga gathered his neighbors to help him search for his four children. The men walked the route the children took home from school and spotted Wierenga's 17-year-old daughter first. She was in a grove of saplings with her back to a tree. She had frozen to death standing up. Her brother and two younger sisters were huddled at her feet. All of them were dead.

Peter Heins, a farmer who lived nearby, lost three boys. Crazed with grief, Heins was on his way to the schoolhouse to kill the teacher who had let them leave in the storm. But a neighbor whose children had survived stopped him and told him what had happened. When the storm came, the teacher begged the children to stay in the school and she even locked the door. But the children refused to obey her. One of them, a strong boy of 17, overpowered the teacher and managed to open the door. They fled for home into the storm. Heins' sons were among them. The boys made it two miles before they collapsed in a pasture and died.

There was a cruel aftermath to the blizzard. In addition to the hundreds of funerals, there were the surgical amputations of those who lost fingers, ears, toes, feet and noses to frostbite. There were also those who survived the night, only to die soon after from illnesses caused by exposure to the elements.

The precise number of the dead was never determined. Estimates published in state histories and local newspapers have ranged from 300 to 500 souls. The southern and eastern parts of the Dakota Territory suffered the majority of the casualties. Undoubtedly, many of the deaths that occurred in the lonely places that were far off the beaten path were never reported at all. Many died in the weeks after the storm from pneumonia and from infections contracted after amputations. For many years afterward, gatherings of any size in Dakota or Nebraska always included people who walked on wooden legs, held fingerless hands behind their backs or hid missing ears under hats. They were all victims of the Children's Blizzard – but were those who had escaped with their lives.

In 1909, South Dakota historian Caleb Holt Ellis wrote, "The dark, blinding, roaring storm once experienced remains an actual living presence that has marked its pathway with ruin, desolation and death. The 12th of January, 1888, is, long will be, remembered, not only by Dakotans, but by many in the northwest, not for the things we enjoy, love, and would see repeated; but for its darkness, desolation, ruin and death, spread broadcast; for the sorrow, sadness and heartache that followed in its train."

There is no question that the prairie was devastated by the January 1888 blizzard and to those who survived it, it truly did remain an "actual living presence." Every pioneer who wrote a memoir and every family that recorded its history included a story of someone who died in the blizzard. Every story was heartbreaking – but some were stranger than others.

There were tales of the dead who lingered after the storm. It was not uncommon to hear weird and eerie tales of specters that were seen during the storms that came after the January 12 blizzard. Often, they were faces and figures that seemed strangely familiar but should not have been there – for they had died weeks before.

One family told a story about a stormy night later that winter when a lost loved one came calling. A Dakota farmer named Peter Klein was gathered around the fire with his wife and their two surviving children one cold night in February. A storm had come up after dinner, blowing and buffeting against the house and conjuring up bad memories of the night when their 12-year-old son lost had been lost in the blizzard. The three Klein children had tried to walk a mile home from school after their teacher released them and the oldest boy had died. The other children had somehow survived, buried under a wagon, nestled against their brother's body. The other children had both lost toes from frostbite and were slowly recovering at the time this second, much quieter storm, swept across the prairie.

Late that night, after the children had fallen into a fitful sleep, Klein and his wife heard an odd noise outside. Klein was convinced that it was someone calling out in the storm --- and it sounded as though the voice was calling out "papa." Mrs. Klein was startled by the sound and tried to convince her husband that the voice belonged to their dead son. Klein adamantly did not believe in spirits – their son had been taken to be with God – but was shaken himself when he heard a knock on the door.

"It must be a neighbor," he assured his wife. Klein went to the door and opened it, only to find a ribbon of snow, swirling in the wind. There was no one there, he thought, until he lifted his lantern and caught the white oval of a face in the darkness. Stifling a cry, he rushed out into the storm. It was his son! His boy had somehow returned!

But as he stumbled out into the snow, the face vanished – if it had ever been there at all.

The Kleins were not the only ones who claimed to be visited by those who died in the blizzard. A widow from near Sioux Falls claimed that she saw her husband walking out of their barn one day. He had vanished in the storm and his body had not been found. Elated that he had somehow survived and had come home, she ran out to greet him, but there was no one there. She had seen a man walking, she stated, but he left no footprints behind. She was convinced that the man had been her husband, although his body was found in March at the bottom of a ravine where he had apparently fallen during the storm.

The Children's Blizzard left an indelible mark on the history of the American prairie and its effects lingered in both sorrow and hauntings for many years after the last physical effects of the storm had long since passed. It can perhaps be best summed up by the words of Sadie Shaw in a letter to her relatives back east. From her Douglas County homestead, she lamented: "I have seen the Dread of Dakota. Oh, it was terrible. I have often read about Blizzards but they have to be seen to be fully realized."

1906: "TYPHOID MARY"
The Sad Tale of Mary Mallon

The year 1906 marked a turning point in American medicine. It was the year when the new science of bacteriology gained public attention when it was used in the investigation of a typhoid outbreak in New York City. It was a disaster of another sort, a strange one that led the authorities to a healthy woman who was unknowingly spreading the disease. As these same authorities struggled to convince her that she was infecting the people she worked for, they eventually quarantined her for 26 years, despite the fact that she was later identified as one of several healthy carriers.

The story of "Typhoid Mary" has had a lingering effect on American history. Her name alone has become a metaphor for fear of contamination from contagious disease and her plight now symbolizes the need to balance the civil liberties of disease-carrying individuals when the population at large is at risk.

Her story has had other lingering effects as well, namely on the place of her confinement, a now-abandoned hospital on New York's North Brother Island. Is one of the ghosts that still walks the hallways of the hospital that of Typhoid Mary? Perhaps, for hers was a strange history...

The tale of Typhoid Mary began in the summer of 1906, when New York banker Charles Henry Warren rented a summer home for his family in Oyster Bay, Long Island. The house was rented from George Thompson and a large staff was hired, including an Irish immigrant named Mary Mallon, who was employed as a cook.

On August 27, one of the Warren's daughters became ill with typhoid fever. Soon after, Mrs. Warren and two maids also became stricken with the same symptoms of high fever, diarrhea, vomiting, chills and a rash. Days later, another daughter became sick, as did the Warrens' gardener. In all, six of the 11 people in the household came down with typhoid.

Since the most common way that typhoid

Mary Mallon, who became known as "Typhoid Mary"

was spread was through food and water sources, the owners of the house feared that they would not be able to rent the property again without first discovering the source of the outbreak. The Thompsons first hired investigators to look into the situation, but they were unsuccessful in finding the cause. Then, they hired George Soper, a civil engineer who had experience with typhoid fever outbreaks. It was Soper who believed that the recently hired cook, Mary Mallon, was the cause of the sickness. Mallon left the Warrens about three weeks after the outbreak and went to work for another wealthy family. Soper began researching her employment history, looking for clues.

Mary Mallon had been born on September 23, 1869 in Cookstown, County Tyrone, Ireland. According to what she told friends, Mary came to America at the age of 15. Like many Irish immigrant women, she found work as a domestic servant. She became a cook, which paid better than most domestic service positions.

Soper traced Mary's employment history back to 1900 and found that typhoid outbreaks had followed her from job to job. From 1900 to 1907, Soper found that Mary had worked at seven jobs in which 22 people had become ill, including one young girl who died from typhoid shortly after Mary came to work for her family.

Soper was convinced that this was not a coincidence, and yet he needed stool and blood samples from Mary to prove that she was a carrier. The idea that someone could be healthy and still carry a disease – and spread it to others – was a concept that had been announced by Robert Koch but had not yet been proven in any individual. Mary, Soper knew, might be the first such person discovered by science.

In March 1907, Soper found Mary working as a cook in the home of Walter Bowen and his family. Soper needed samples from Mary and he confronted her at her place of work. She was shocked, as anyone would have been. As far as she knew, she was quite healthy and now she was being approached by a stranger who not only told her that she was spreading some sort of disease that was killing people, but wanted her to give him samples of her blood and her feces. Mary not only refused, she became quite angry.

Soper later wrote:

I had my first talk with Mary in the kitchen of this house. . . . I was as diplomatic as possible, but I had to say I suspected her of making people sick and that I wanted specimens of her urine, feces and blood. It did not take Mary long to react to this suggestion. She seized a carving fork and advanced in my direction. I passed rapidly down the long narrow hall, through the tall iron gate . . . and so to the sidewalk. I felt rather lucky to escape.

But Soper was relentless in his pursuit. He followed Mary to her home and tried to approach her again. This time, he brought an assistant, Dr. Bert Raymond Hoobler, for support. Again, Mary was enraged and made it clear that they were unwelcome. She cursed at them as they made a quick retreat. Soper, now realizing that it was going to take more persuasiveness than he was able to offer, handed his research and theories over to Hermann Biggs at the New York City Health Department. Biggs agreed with Soper's theories and sent Dr. S. Josephine Baker to talk to Mary.

After Soper's clumsy attempts to obtain blood and stool samples from her, Mary was now extremely suspicious of doctors and health officials. She refused to listen to Baker and sent her away. Baker returned a short time later, this time with five police officers and an ambulance. When they arrived at the house, Mary met them at the door with a long kitchen fork in her hand (likely the same one she had chased away Soper with) and lunged at Dr. Baker with it. As Baker stepped back, colliding with police officers behind her and knocking them down the steps, Mary slammed the door shut and made a run for it. By the time they got the door open and followed in pursuit, Mary had disappeared. Baker and the policemen searched the house but found nothing. Eventually, footprints were discovered leading from the house to a chair placed next to a fence. Mary had apparently escaped into a neighbor's yard – or so they thought at first.

They searched both properties for the next five hours until, finally, they found what Dr. Baker later described as "a tiny scrap of blue calico caught in the door of the areaway closet under the high outside stairway leading to the front door."

Mary was dragged from the closet "fighting and swearing" and even though Dr. Baker spoke to her calmly about the specimens that she needed, Mary refused to listen. Dr. Baker wrote, "By that time she was convinced that the law was wantonly persecuting her, when she had done nothing wrong. She knew she had never had typhoid fever; she was maniacal in her integrity. There was nothing I could do but take her with us. The policemen lifted her into the ambulance and I literally sat on her all the way to the hospital; it was like being in a cage with an angry lion."

Mary was taken to Willard Parker Hospital and there, the specimens were finally taken. Laboratory results showed that Mary indeed had typhoid bacilli in her stool – she was a carrier of typhoid fever. As the first healthy typhoid carrier in New York City, Mary was made an example of by public health officials and was punished for her resistance to their tests. She was promptly detained and was quarantined on North Brother Island, located in the East River near the Bronx, which housed hundreds of individuals infected with highly contagious tuberculosis and other conditions. The otherwise healthy Mary Mallon was confined in a cottage on the island, making newspaper headlines and creating her infamous nickname of "Typhoid Mary."

Mary had been taken by force and was being held against her will without a trial. She had not broken any laws but, because of the fact that she was a lowly Irish immigrant with no money or political clout and also because she was infected with an illness that people dreaded at the time, she found few to rally to her cause. Mary believed that she was being unfairly persecuted. She could not understand how she could have spread disease and caused a death when she, herself, seemed healthy. She wrote, "I never had typhoid in my life, and have always been healthy. Why should I be banished like a leper and compelled to live in solitary confinement with only a dog for a companion?"

Public officials felt they had every right to lock up Mary indefinitely, basing their power on sections 1169 and 1170 of the Greater New York Charter, which read:

The board of health shall use all reasonable means for ascertaining the existence and cause of disease or peril to life or health, and for averting the same, throughout the city. [Section 1169]

Said board may remove or cause to be removed to [a] proper place to be by it designated, any person sick with any contagious, pestilential or infectious disease; shall have exclusive charge and control of the hospitals for the treatment of such cases. [Section 1170]

The charter was written before anyone knew that "healthy carriers" – people who seemed healthy but carried a contagious form of disease that could infect others – could even exist. But the health officials of the early 1900s believed that healthy carriers were even more dangerous than those that were sick with a disease because there was no way to visibly identify a healthy carrier so that they could be avoided or quarantined. For this reason, they had no issues with locking Mary away for as long as they deemed necessary.

Mary was initially confined for two years on North Brother Island, during which time she wrote letters and filed a legal suit pleading for her freedom and release from the island.

A scathing story about Mary Mallon in the *New York American* in 1909 subjected her to public scrutiny.

During the time of her confinement, health officials had taken and analyzed her stool samples about once a week. The samples mostly came back positive with typhoid, but not always. For nearly a year, Mary also sent samples to a private lab, which tested all of her samples negative for typhoid. Feeling healthy and with her own lab results in hand, Mary believed that she was being unfairly held.

But in truth, Mary did not understand much about typhoid fever and, unfortunately, no one tried to explain it to her. Not all people have a strong bout of typhoid fever; some people have such a weak case that they only experience flu-like symptoms. Because of this, Mary could have had typhoid fever without knowing it. Though it was commonly known at the time that typhoid could be spread by water or food products, people who are infected by the typhoid bacillus could also pass on the disease by not washing their hands after using the bathroom. For this reason, infected cooks (like Mary) or food handlers had the most likelihood of spreading the disease.

In 1909, Mary argued to the Supreme Court that she was never sick and was never given due process before her confinement. The court ruled against Mary, setting the precedent for the courts to rule in favor of public health officials when individual liberties were at stake. Mary was remanded to the custody of the Board of Health of the City of New York and went back to her isolated cottage on North Brother Island with little hope of ever being released.

In 1910, however, the new health commissioner of New York decided to release Mary as long as she agreed to regularly report to the health department and to promise that she would never work as a cook again. Anxious to regain her freedom, Mary accepted the conditions. On February 19, she was let free.

Mary vanished into obscurity after her release – but not for long.

In January 1915, the Sloane Maternity Hospital in Manhattan suffered a typhoid fever outbreak in which two people died and 23 others became sick. During the investigation, evidence pointed to a recently hired cook, Mrs. Brown – who was actually Mary Mallon using a false name.

Some believe that Mary never had any intention of following the conditions of her release, but most likely she found that not working as a cook forced her into domestic positions that did not pay as well. Feeling healthy, Mary still did not believe that she could spread typhoid. Mary first worked as a laundress and at a few other jobs, but for some reason that has never been documented, Mary eventually went back to working as a cook.

If the public had shown Mary any sympathy during her first period of quarantine because she was an unknowing typhoid carrier, it disappeared after she was locked up again. This time, Typhoid Mary knew of her carrier status – even if she didn't believe it – and so she willingly and knowingly caused suffering and death to her victims. The fact that she had been using a false name made her look even more guilty.

Mary was sent back to her cottage on North Brother Island and she remained there, imprisoned on the island, for the next 23 years. The exact life that she led on the island is unclear but it is known that she helped around the island's Riverside Hospital, earning the title of nurse in 1922. In 1925, she began helping in the hospital's lab.

In December 1932, she suffered a stroke that left her paralyzed. She was then transferred from her cottage to a bed in the hospital's children's ward, where she stayed until her death six years later on November 11, 1938.

In the years that followed her death, the term "Typhoid Mary" stopped referring to Mary Mallon and became a term for anyone who has a contagious illness. People who change jobs frequently are also sometimes joking referred to as a "Typhoid Mary." Mary Mallon changed jobs frequently. Some believed that it was because she knew she was guilty, but it was likely because domestic jobs at the time usually didn't last long.

But how did Mary become such a legend? Yes, she was the first healthy carrier to be found, but she was not the only once discovered at the time. An estimated 3,000 to 4,500 cases of typhoid fever were reported in New York City alone and it was estimated that about three percent of those who had typhoid fever became carriers, creating more than 90 new carriers a year.

Mary was also not the most deadly. There were 47 cases of typhoid connected to Mary, while Tony Labella (another healthy carrier) caused 122 people to become sick and five deaths. Labella was only isolated for two weeks and then was released.

Mary was also not the only healthy carrier who broke the health officials' rules after being told of her contagious status. Alphonse Cotlis, a restaurant and bakery owner, was told not to prepare food for other people. When health officials found him back at work, they agreed to let him go free when he promised to conduct his business over the phone.

Mary Mallon's cottage on North Brother Island

So, why was Mary singled out? Why was she the only carrier isolated for life? These questions are impossible to answer. Some historians believe that it was prejudice that contributed to her extreme treatment by health officials. She was Irish; she was a woman, uneducated, a domestic servant, had no family and was basically a "nobody." She didn't have the money or the position to fight back and when she did, she was dismissed by the courts for all of the same reasons. Despite Mary's temperament and her violation of the conditions of her release, one has to wonder if the "crime" really deserved the punishment she was given.

The question remains unanswered today, which is perhaps the reason why her spirit is still said to linger at the abandoned hospital where she spent her final days.

The ruins of Riverside Hospital on North Brother Island

North Brother Island is a place of ghosts.

It lies on 13 acres just southwest of Hunts Point in the East River. It is a remnant of a long-forgotten era in New York history. The island has been abandoned since 1963, when the city closed down Riverside Hospital, which had opened in 1886 to treat and isolate victims of contagious diseases. It gained its notoriety during the tenure of Mary Mallon and remains a mysterious place today, off limits to the public because it is the nesting place of a species of rare black-crowned herons.

It is, without question, a spooky place – and some say a haunted one. Time seems to have bypassed North Brother Island's gaslight-lined streets, brownstone hospital buildings, crumbling doctor's houses and sandy beaches littered with cookware and heavy glass tonic bottles.

Tragedy first bloodied the island's history in June 1905 when the *General Slocum* disaster took the lives of 1,141 people, most of them German immigrants from the Lower East Side. They were on their way to a Sunday picnic on Long Island when the overcrowded steamer was accidentally set ablaze. The ship ran aground on North Brother Island and doctors and patients from the hospital ran to try and save the hundreds of passengers who had jumped from the burning ship. For hours after the tragedy, bodies continued to wash up on the island's shore and the beaches were strewn with victims.

For decades after, island residents spoke of seeing the ghosts of these victims as they wandered the grounds, weeping for their lives and those of loved ones lost in the disaster.

Perhaps these spirits do not walk alone…

Riverside Hospital was closed as a quarantine hospital in 1942. It was abandoned for a short time before briefly being used as housing for World War II veterans who were studying at New York colleges. It was serviced by two ferries that regularly stopped at the western slip, but this proved inefficient and expensive, and when cheaper housing was found for these men, the island was abandoned again.

In 1952, it opened again, this time as an experimental juvenile drug treatment facility that was offered as an alternative to going to jail. The tuberculosis pavilion of the hospital (which was built in 1942 and never actually used to house tuberculosis patients) became a dormitory and then a main residence and treatment building for the program. The doors to many of the rooms were retrofitted into seclusion rooms with sheet metal reinforcement and heavy deadbolts that could be used for withdrawal management.

The experimental plan would take a patient, newly arrived and addicted to heroin, and place him in one of these rooms with no conveniences except for a bare mattress and a mess bucket. They would be forced to undergo withdrawal in the seclusion room without any kind of medicine. After several days, when withdrawal was complete, the patient would be introduced into the general population. It was believed that this harsh return to reality, followed up by a stay of no less than 90 days on the island, and bolstered by athletics and education, would provide the best chance against relapse.

All of the buildings on the island were renovated. The services building became the school, the nurses' residence became the girls' dormitory, and the tuberculosis pavilion became the admissions hospital and boys' residence. The building next to the tuberculosis pavilion – originally the hospital's children's ward, where Mary Mallon spent her final days – was turned into a library and annex to the school.

The grand experiment was a failure. Recidivism rates were extremely high, and even at the isolated island hospital, patients still found means of obtaining and using drugs. There are accounts of boyfriends making the trip to the island in order to visit in the middle of the night; accounts of orderlies getting paid in cigarettes to smuggle heroin on the ferries; and accounts of physical and sexual abuse on and by patients. The hospital was shuttered and the island was abandoned in 1963 for the final time.

The lost souls of this era certainly left an indelible mark on the island but the most famous troubled spirit that may linger is that of Typhoid Mary herself. Mary was first quarantined on the island in 1907 after causing a number of outbreaks of typhoid fever. She was set free in 1910 but returned to the island five years later after an investigation into an outbreak of typhoid at a Manhattan hospital revealed that she was once again working as a cook, under an assumed name. She was send back to her cottage on the island, this time for good.

Mary never understood that she was a carrier of a possible deadly disease. Instead, she felt she was a victim of persecution at the hands of officials who could neither prove that she was the source of these outbreaks nor explain to her why she felt so healthy and why she seemed free of any of the typical symptoms of typhoid. In 1938, she died on the island due to complications from a stroke she had suffered six years earlier.

Mary's cottage was demolished after her death – officials felt that it was unsafe for habitation – but she spent much of her time working, and later dying, at Riverside Hospital, where her ghost is still believed to walk.

Over the years, visitors to the island – those who brave the river and the warnings against trespassers – have reported the spirit of a woman who wanders the corridors of the crumbling old hospital. She has been seen a number of times by a wide variety of people, including staff members at the hospital during the era when the drug treatment program was in place. One account details an orderly who followed the woman down a corridor, only to see her walk into one of the rooms. Thinking that one of the inmates had gotten out of her room, the orderly hurried down the hall and entered the exam room – only to find there was no one there!

Was this woman one of the many tragic spirits of North Brother Island, or could it have been the ghost of Mary Mallon, unable to rest after nearly three decades of punishment that she never felt she deserved?

No one will likely ever know for sure.

1925: "DAUGHTER OF THE STARS"
The Crash of the Airship Shenandoah

The name *Shenandoah* was painted on the gleaming hull of the first great United States dirigible, a name that literally meant "Daughter of the Stars" in the language of the Algonquians. But this helium-filled creation of early

American aeronautics would from the grace after her deadly plunge to the earth on September 3, 1925, an air disaster that was later shrouded in volatile criticism, anger and bitterness.

The *Shenandoah* was constructed in 1922 and patterned after the *L-49*, one of the German zeppelins that were already all the rage in Europe. The $2 million airship was 680 feet long and made of Duralumin, an aluminum alloy. Her tanks were filled with helium, making her the first dirigible to use gas. Unfortunately, the airship's short life was filled with harrowing near disasters.

Weather alone made the *Shenandoah,* and her sister airships, questionable vessels. Many aviators of the day saw little use for the slow-moving, unwieldy vessels. One of them, a wealthy New York lawyer and author named Laurence La Tourette Driggs, wrote, "When the heavy winds blew, she could neither leave nor enter her hangar. When ordinary storms broke about her, she was in peril. When no mooring mast was handy, she required 500 men to catch her and hold her to the earth. When raindrops clung to her envelope, she feared to attempt landing under their weight until they evaporated. When every condition was favorable, she sailed through the skies majestically --- but to what purpose?"

The purpose, it seemed, was to convince the public that the shaky experiments of the Zeppelin engineers had merit, and that the giants of the sky could provide a safe method of transportation while also gathering important scientific information on weather conditions. Concern for safety caused engineers to fill the *Shenandoah* with helium, a less flammable gas than the conventional hydrogen, but this slowed the airship's maneuverability in flight and especially hindered her ability to climb out of deadly storms.

Shenandoah made her first one-hour flight on September 2, 1923 but the first real scare in her history came just a few months later on January 16, 1924. Berthed at a newly designed mooring mast at Lakehurst, New Jersey, the ship was suddenly assaulted by a massive weather front with winter winds of more than 65 miles per hour. The *Shenandoah* suddenly broke loose and the rigid airship began drifting toward a row of pine trees, which would have sliced into the hull and tore the ship apart. The skeleton crew was trapped on board. Led by Lieutenant Commander M.R. Pierce and Captain Anton Heinen, a German builder and pilot of dirigibles, the crew managed to save the ship. Even though the two forward gas bags had been ripped open as the ship tore loose from her mooring, Heinen and Pierce wrestled with the controls and managed to steady the airship. Fuel and ballast loads were quickly redistributed and the dirigible's engines were started just moments before she would have reached the trees. She pulled upward and the crew kept her aloft until dawn, when they were able to steer the *Shenandoah* back to the mooring mast.

This was hardly the way to make good headlines, so the Navy scheduled a long-distance flight for later that same year. This 9,137-mile voyage would take the *Shenandoah* back and forth across the United States to show off the military's prized airship. Lieutenant Commander Zachary Lansdowne, 36, considered the most experienced dirigible pilot in America, was placed in charge of the flight. Lansdowne was graduated from the United States Naval Academy in 1909. He began a stellar aviation career at

The officers lost on board the airship *Shenandoah*

Pensacola Air Station in 1916 and learned how to pilot dirigibles in England during World War I. He was aboard the British airship *R-34* when she made her historic Atlantic crossing on July 2, 1919. It was Lansdowne who had piloted all of the memorable flights that the *Shenandoah* had made, so he was the logical person to be placed in command on her transcontinental voyage from Lakehurst to Los Angeles and back in a record 19 days and 19 hours. A number of minor mishaps occurred on the trip, but the weather remained favorable throughout the journey. Keeping to a southerly route, *Shenandoah* serenely sliced through the skies over the southwestern desert.

The scheduled flight that was to take the ship across the Midwest the following year was another matter entirely. The weather would likely be poor in September and Lansdowne more than once complained to his wife that he was being forced to make the trip by the naval authorities for "political purposes." Shortly before the ship went to her doom, one of Lansdowne's fellow officers bitterly remarked, "There's a string of county fairs throughout the Middle West right now, and all of the politicians are pulling wires to have *Shenandoah* fly over their hometowns as part of the circus."

Despite his misgivings about the flight, Lansdowne was at the controls as the ship moved away from her moorings on September 2, 1925. The dirigible proceeded steadily west toward her destruction.

At 4:00 a.m. on September 3, strong headwinds began to buffet the *Shenandoah,* and she could make little headway, even though all five engines were running. Lansdowne ordered the engines opened up to full capacity, and directed the ship's bow to be nosed downward at 18 degrees. Even with her rudder hard over and the elevators hard down, the ship still climbed from 2,000 to almost 7,000 feet. During the rapid ascent, *Shenandoah* began to shred to pieces. When the officers and crew finally managed to stop the upward surge, the ship, then too heavy for the altitude, abruptly plunged downward.

As the dirigible began to fall from the sky, Commander Lansdowne shouted out his final words, which were recalled later by surviving crew members: "Let every man stick to his post, regardless!" The commander ordered the jettisoning of tons of water ballast, but the giant aircraft, moving at an estimated 1,400 feet per minute, was dropping too fast. Two engines stopped. The crew worked frantically, dumping overboard any heavy equipment, fuel tanks or other objects that could be stripped from the dirigible.

Lieutenant Commander Charles E. Rosendahl was in charge of trying to lighten the ship. Oddly, he apparently had some sort of premonition of disaster (or perhaps a death wish) before the flight began. According to reports, he muttered, "I hope I get killed" as he stepped into the cockpit on the day that the flight departed. It was later learned that Rosendahl's fiancée had recently been killed in an auto accident, and her death had left him deeply despondent. "I don't care what becomes of me," he reportedly told one of her friends as her funeral.

However, in the midst of the disaster, Rosendahl rose to the occasion. He calmly scrambled into the keel of the ship where, using a hand valve, he released a great quantity of helium. Six other men worked frantically alongside him. Rosendahl survived the crash, but whether he was disappointed or relieved is unknown. He later reported, "At the moment there was a crash. I heard the struts breaking and saw the nose of the ship parting from the control department. A second later, I heard another crash, which must have been the control compartment hitting the ground. It was in this compartment that Commander Lansdowne and the [ten] others were killed."

The ship broke into two pieces. The nose, with Rosendahl and his six companions hanging precariously from the struts, sailed off at a speed of about 25 miles per hour. It shot upward to almost 10,000 feet, but Rosendahl and the men managed to release more helium and the bow section gradually drifted to the ground. "We handled the nose as if it were a free balloon," Rosendahl related, "and landed safely in Sharon [Ohio]..."

Chief Machinist's Mate Shine S. Halliburton was among those who rode the nose portion down with Rosendahl. He recalled that he "was just reaching for pliers to cut the stay-wires on the [fuel] tanks and let them drop out of the ship when she parted. Then she began to drop."

Meanwhile, a farmer named Ernest Nichols watched in amazement as the nose portion of the *Shenandoah* drifted down onto his land. A neighbor telephoned to tell him that an airship had broken up, and that it appeared to be heading toward Nichols' house. The farmer ran outside and later recalled, "...and here it came right through our orchard, headed straight for the house. I looked up, and there was my oldest boy – I have six boys and one

The remnants of the *Shenandoah*, spread over the Ohio landscape.

girl – sticking his head out the upstairs window. I knew I had to stop the thing or the house would be smashed and my kids would be killed."

From the tumbling section of the ship, Nichols could hear Rosendahl and the others yelling, "Grab hold! Grab hold! Turn her south!" Nichols jumped up and grabbed a cable that was dangling from the hulk and quickly wrapped it around a fence post – which promptly snapped. Nichols clung to the cable and this time, looped it around a large maple tree stump. To his chagrin, the cable slipped off the stump and the ship continued scooting violently along the ground. It tore off the top of a grape arbor, ripped away the roof on a shed and splintered the wheel on a well. But Nichols clung doggedly onto the cable and finally, he managed to wrap it around a sturdy tree. As he pulled hard, he soon had helping hands. His children had fled the house and ran to help their father tie off the massive hulk.

Nichols added, "Even then it didn't stay where it was, for we had to tie it again several times during the day." Halliburton later borrowed a shotgun from the farmer and shot holes in the remaining helium bags so that the wreckage wouldn't drift off in the wind.

Sharon, where the front section of the *Shenandoah* landed, was about 12 miles from where Lansdowne and the others plunged to their death. Ironically, it was only a short distance from Greenville, Ohio, where Lansdowne had been born and where his mother still lived.

The aft section of the ship had also floated free like a balloon with 25 men still clinging to it. Among them was Ralph Joneson, on duty in Engine Car 3. He later reported that when the airship broke in half, he sat down near the engine, shut his eyes, and clung as tightly as he could to a strut. "First thing you know, I was walking around on the ground. Then she blew away again and there I was alone in a field," he said.

His incredible escape was repeated over and over again by other members of the crew. Frederick J. Tobin had just awakened and rolled out of his wildly swinging hammock as the storm raged against the dirigible. He started for the control car and was only a few feet away from it when it disappeared downward into the night sky. He later spoke excitedly to reporters, "The first thing I knew was that where I started to step for the control car was space, 7,000 feet of it. I crawled back to the catwalk, aft of the break. Soon the silver cover was ripped off, and I stood there, thousands of feet in the air, holding on a slim brace. I thought I might as well look down. I did, and I've never seen trees rush so in my life. They seemed to be rushing straight for me. When I could see the green of them, I got ready to jump, but the section I was in bumped once and rose again to drift another half a mile. When I did get out, I saw nothing but twisted steel.

The last man to leave the control car was Lieutenant J.B. Anderson. His survival was the most incredible of all. At one point, the car had literally dropped beneath his feet. He said later, "Commander Lansdowne told me to release 800 gallons of gas to lighten her, and that was when I started for the ladder. After I reached the catwalk, she dropped dizzily to 2,500 feet, groaned in every girder and fell apart."

Anderson felt himself falling. He dove for a strut and held on, dangling over empty space. Lieutenant R.C. Mayer, who was in the bow section with Rosendahl, saw Anderson about to fall, grabbed a rope, and threw it "with the accuracy of a plainsman" and lassoed Anderson just as he was about to plummet to the ground. Anderson shot downward and was then jerked upward by the rope. Several men ran over to help Mayer pull him to safety.

Another officer, Lieutenant W.L. Richardson, who had been on board to make a photographic record of the flight, rode the aft section all of the way to the ground. He had gotten out of bed at 4:00 a.m. to get a drink of water and decided to go to the front section of the ship to see if the weather conditions were good for taking photographs. Then he looked at his watch and, seeing it was too early, decided to go back to bed. It was a decision that undoubtedly saved his life. "The control car dropped clear of the ship," he later said, "and dropped through space like a comet, killing all who were in her."

After Richardson returned to his berth, the pitching of the ship turned more violent and the nose started to drop. The *Shenandoah* shot high into the air, dropped, and then rose straight up again before breaking in two. "One section, the forward part, carrying the control car, shot straight up," he reported. "The other section, on which we were, dropped rapidly downward. It seemed to flutter down like a falling leaf. First the point end, then the rear end, would be on top. A part of our section was torn away before we landed. I managed to save myself from sliding into space by grabbing wires and girders near my berth. Then as soon as possible I started to the after part of the section.

Richardson grabbed onto a gasoline tank, but it broke free from its moorings. Then he grabbed onto some girders. Through an open hatch, he could see treetops speeding beneath him only a few feet away, and then he saw the ground. He jumped, even though the remains of the ship were still moving quickly. On his way down, a wire snagged around his leg and dragged him down a hill behind the ship. "I finally got loose," he said, "and ran up the hill out of the way of the rolling bag."

The men who survived the crash felt that a miracle had taken place. Those in the engine car, the control car, and those who were unable to hang on were not so lucky. Fourteen of them were dead when the *Shenandoah* finally came to a rest on the ground.

One of the survivors, cook John J. Hahn, sent a telegram to the naval authorities to alert them to the disaster. News of the *Shenandoah's* end was soon flashed around the country, provoking a firestorm of angry statements. Zeppelin Captain Anton Heinen, who knew first-hand the shortcomings of the airship, pointed out that certain automatic valves had been removed from the ship before the trip. He went so far as to label the disaster "murder." Colonel Billy Mitchell charged that the *Shenandoah's* final flight should have never been made since it was nothing more than a propaganda trip. Mrs. Lansdowne was quoted as saying that her husband was compelled to make the flight. "He had to go," she said, "because the Secretary of the Navy wanted to play politics by sending the ship over Middle-Western cities... My husband was very much opposed to making the flight this time because of weather conditions he knew so well. He asked officials in Washington to delay the flight until a better season."

A court of inquiry ignored the criticism that was pouring in and concluded that the *Shenandoah* had broken apart and crashed because of "large, unbalanced, external, aerodynamic forces arising from high velocity air currents." An investigation of the accident was hampered by souvenir hounds, who swarmed over the remains of the dirigible, picked clean the dead men's effects, and carried away parts of the wrecked structure. The material was never returned for examination. The Ohio members of the American Legion finally sent out armed guards to drive away curiosity-seekers and vandals. At one point, they had to fire their guns in the air to drive them off. One newspaper grimly commented, "The sole complaint that we lodge against the legionnaires is that they did not shoot straight."

In the end, the story of the *Shenandoah* became a forgotten part of American history. Never truly explained, other than just to say that dirigibles were unstable in the first place, the deaths of heroic Commander Lansdowne and 13 other men have gone unanswered for more than eighty years.

1925: THE TRI-STATE TORNADO
The Deadliest Tornado in American History

There's never been another tornado like it: not in America, not anywhere else in world.

On March 18, 1925, the Tri-State Tornado rode a straight path for three-and-one-half hours across 219 miles of Missouri, southern Illinois and Indiana, making it the longest single tornado track anywhere in the world. It loomed a mile wide, and when it was approaching, it appeared to be even wider than it was tall. When it arrived it obliterated entire towns, sent thousands to the hospital and claimed more than twice as many victims as the next-deadliest tornado in American history, which happened in Natchez in 1840.

The Tri-State Tornado has never been forgotten; even though weather forecasters weren't allowed to use the word "tornado" in those days, it changed the history of the weather service -- and the entire region -- forever.

In the spring of 1925, the U.S. Weather Bureau didn't even have the word "tornado" in its vocabulary. The word had been banned since 1887, when the U.S. Army Signal Corps managed the country's weather predictions. Tornadoes were utterly unpredictable, according to the current logic, and forecasting what they might do or where they might go was utterly pointless and would simply spread panic. Forecasters weren't allowed to study tornadoes, or even publicly acknowledge that they existed.

The forecast for the central Midwest on March 18, 1925 was for rain showers and cooling temperatures: nothing out of the ordinary. While tornado forecasting didn't exist at the time, the weather bureau had been tracking a cold, low-pressure system that dropped down from Western Canada into Wyoming and made it all of the way to the Oklahoma-Texas border before curving back towards southeastern Missouri. The jet stream wasn't discovered until World War II when Japanese scientists were experimenting with transoceanic balloon bombs, but most likely its path on that day mirrored that of the storm front. The winds of the jet stream were likely very strong, given how fast the tornado traveled.

A warm front from the Gulf of Mexico raised temperatures by 10 degrees across the region, causing warm air to rush skyward and providing what forecasters today call the tornado's "lifting mechanism." The storm systems merged and then transformed into a tornado-producing spiral as the gray skies over southeastern Missouri turned an ominous shade of black.

At 1:00 p.m., a funnel cloud near the town of Ellington, Missouri, formed into a twisting column and killed a local farmer. Traveling at a speed of 72 miles per hour, it took 14 minutes to hit the town of Annapolis, where it killed four more people and destroyed almost every building in town. An hour later, the monstrous tornado spun off two adjacent funnels before it moved through Biehle. It reformed into a single system a few miles later, as it tore its way across rolling farmland toward the Mississippi River. The tornado left Missouri having traveled 80

miles through mostly rural farmland and killed as many as 13 people in just 83 minutes. Illinois would fare much worse.

At 2:26 p.m., the tornado approached the tiny town of Gorham, Illinois, a railroad town that was nestled next to a huge bluff that rises mysteriously from the flat land that surrounds it. The storm began throwing golf ball-sized hail as it advanced on the town. "There was a great roar," local resident Judith Cos told the *St. Louis Post-Dispatch* two days later. "Like a train, but many, many times louder. 'My God,' I cried. 'It's a cyclone and it's here.' The air was full of everything: boards, branches of trees, garments, pans, stoves, all churning together. I saw whole sides of houses rolling along near the ground." Cox had been having lunch at a local diner when the storm approached. When she tried to leave the restaurant, she was blown back inside as the building collapsed. The restaurant's cook was crushed to death, but Cox was pulled out of the ruins alive, along with a cow that had been picked up and deposited on the roof. The storm killed 37 of the town's 500 residents and destroyed every single building, many of which have never been rebuilt.

The next town in line was Murphysboro, an emerging industrial town with a population of about 12,000 on the banks of the Big Muddy River. Because it bore the brunt of the twister's wrath, it's more closely associated with the history of the Tri-State Tornado than any other town. Murphysboro would eventually count 234 of its inhabitants among the dead. There were 8,000 people left homeless and with the destruction of many of the local factories and businesses, more than 2,000 jobs disappeared. Entire residential blocks were either leveled or obliterated. Churches, schools, hotels and other buildings were completely destroyed.

Author Wallace E. Akin, who went on to become a tornado scientist, was two years old when the tornado struck his family's home in Murphysboro. Akin's mother shielded him with her body in the family room when the tornado struck. He later recalled, "The house began to levitate and, at the same time, the piano shot across the room, gouging the floor and carpet where I had played only moments before. The walls began to crack as the roof ripped free and disappeared, joining the swirling mass of debris. But the walls and the floor held as we and the house took flight." Akin, his mother, and their entire home landed on top of their garage, which landed on top of another house.

At the Longfellow Grade School, children rushed out of the building as it collapsed, trapping roughly half of the 450 students. A block away, at the railroad repair yard, 35 men were killed as the tornado laid waste to the shops. Some of the survivors from the railroad shops rushed to the school and began removing rubble to try and free the trapped students. Many of the seriously injured were put aboard an emergency train that left for St. Louis about three hours after the storm tore through town. Hundreds of others were injured, some of them requiring surgery. Years later, some would recall amputations being carried out, even after the supply of anesthetic had run out.

Furnaces with fires burning inside were tossed into the storm, and after the winds calmed down, the ruins of Murphysboro were in flames. As night fell, there was a hellish glow in the sky and the horror grew worse. Many people who were trapped in the wreckage burned to death in the fires that followed. In a desperate attempt to put out the fires, officials used dynamite.

The town's near-complete destruction, the fires, the awful haze of smoke, the cries of the dead and dying, the rumbling of the explosions, the wandering people who called out for help as they searched for missing friends, families and loved ones, all combined to create a scene of absolute devastation.

Devastation in Murphysboro, Illinois during the 1925 Tri-State Tornado.

The tornado depressed the economy of Murphysboro for nearly 20 years. The railroad repair center moved to Alabama, and then the Great Depression hit. It wasn't until World War II that most of the abandoned lots were rebuilt and the town began to prosper again.

Murphysboro may have seen the greatest destruction, but the twister had another two hours and 130 miles to go before it was finished.

Minutes after leaving Murphysboro, the tornado ripped into the small town of DeSoto, destroying a school building filled with children. It killed 69 of the city's residents, left only three structures intact, and sparked a series of fires that swept through the rubble. The tornado then ravaged the village of Bush, which had been leveled by another tornado 13 years before. Then it crossed over the Big Muddy River and struck the tiny town of Plumfield.

The twister then swept on to West Frankfort, where miners working under the town were forced to climb out of a 500-foot underground shaft after the tornado cut power in the area. When they reached the surface, they found their community had been blown to splinters. Of the 127 people dead, most were women and children. Most of the miner's homes had been destroyed and their families killed.

The principal of the public school at Parrish, located to the east, saw the approaching storm, locked the doors, and kept all of the children inside. Almost 90 percent of the town was destroyed and a third of the populace was killed, but the Parrish school was one of the few buildings that were spared.

The tornado missed all of the other urban areas in Illinois, passing over open countryside into Indiana. It crossed the Wabash River and left the town of Griffin in ruins, killing 25 and injuring 202. As the storm continued across the landscape, witnesses reported that three separate funnels swirled away from the larger maelstrom. It continued on a collision course toward Princeton, Indiana, where it destroyed a large section of the town and killed 45 people. The Tri-State Tornado continued on for another 12 minutes after leaving Princeton before it blew itself out. By then, it had claimed 695 lives, injured thousands, and demolished more than 15,000 homes.

The single biggest thing that happened as a result of the Tri-State Tornado was the increase in public awareness about tornadoes. Even though the National Severe Storms Laboratory had a ban on using the word "tornado," the tornado-spotter network began in the aftermath of the terrible storm. There were no official programs, but newspapers began to mention the spotters after 1925. These programs contributed to the steady decline in the number of tornado deaths in subsequent years.

It was to be another 23 years before modern tornado forecasting was born, however. On March 20, 1948, a tornado struck Tinker Air Force Base near Oklahoma City and General Fred Borum asked two of his meteorologists, Captain Robert Miller and Major Ernest Fawbush, to look into predicting future tornadoes for the base. Their first major test came five days later, when they informed General Borum that the weather looked much like it did on March 20. Borum gave them the chance to issue the first ever "tornado watch" and the two men sent out the alert. And they were right; another tornado tore into Tinker but this time, the planes had been tucked away in hangars and air traffic diverted, sparing most of the damage to the base.

Soon after, the U.S. Weather Bureau dropped its ban on the use of the word "tornado."

But these were not the only legacies left by the Tri-State Tornado.

A look at the storm's progress across southern Illinois shows an eerie path that was marked with schools. It would be difficult to draw another straight line through the sparsely settled region that included as many school buildings. Most were totally destroyed, resulting in an unusually high percentage of fatalities among children. The first school destroyed was in Gorham, and then three more in Murphysboro (Logan, Longfellow and the high school), the DeSoto school, and a school in Griffin, Indiana. The twister barely missed the schools in Caldwell and Parrish.

Another chilling fact is that, because this was a coal-mining area and many of the men were working underground in the mines when the twister struck, more women than men were killed or injured. In an ironic reversal of fate, this time it was the miners who were spared while their women, who were at home cooking and taking care of the house, became easy targets for the killer storm. Few men were injured in the mines, although the tremendous drop in air pressure caused a number of concussions that were similar to injuries sustained during mine explosions. Doors were ripped from their hinges and some of the ceilings collapsed.

In the days that followed, the rest of the nation slowly became aware of the horror that had struck this rural section of the Midwest. Newspapers across the country carried the terrible details and aid began flowing into the area. Supplies arrived by the trainload; the Red Cross set up emergency headquarters in several of the devastated towns; the National Guard offered tents to use as temporary shelters and large amounts of cash were donated to help those who had lost everything. A caravan of 2,000 farmers formed and traveled throughout the region rebuilding homes and farms. Unfortunately, scores of looters were also attracted by the disaster and the curiosity-seekers and sightseers hampered the efforts of those trying lend assistance and to recover from the devastation.

As time passed, the storm entered the folklore of Missouri, Illinois and Indiana. Stories were told of children being torn from their mother's arms; of people carried off into the sky, some to die and others to somehow survive; of pieces of straw driven into fence posts and tree trunks; of railroad cars blown off their tracks... and more. For months afterward, objects that had come from homes and towns far to the west were still being retrieved and in some cases, returned to where they had come from before the storm.

And for years, the people of the ravaged area would mark the passage of time by referring to events as having taken place before or after the Great Tornado of 1925.

1926: LIVING & DEAD IN SUNNY FLORIDA
The Horror of the Great Miami Hurricane

The 1920s have long been considered one of the golden eras of American history. The Jazz Age, the Age of Wonderful Nonsense, the Roaring Twenties, it was a time that embodied the beginning of modern America. Many Americans were buoyed by the end of World War I, by surviving a worldwide influenza epidemic and the economy was "roaring" thanks to an insane law that prohibited alcohol from being bought, sold or manufactured. For the first time in many Americans' lives, they openly broke the law by having a drink or buying alcohol from the local bootlegger. It was a time of exuberance, expansion and a great time of change.

One of the areas of the country most affected by the changes of the 1920s was South Florida. The swamps, farmland and orange groves of the region were in the midst of a development boom as people began escaping the cold weather in the north and snatching up parcels of land in the sunshine. Towns began springing up, filled both with cheaply constructed houses and stone mansions.

By September 1926, though, it was all gone – swept away by a storm like nothing that South Florida had ever seen before.

It seemed like everyone came to Florida in 1925. It was the beginning of one of the greatest frenzies of real estate speculation in American history, and making a fortune was easily accomplished. It often took little more than a few dollars spent on brochures and a billboard or two in some northern city advertising an escape to sunshine and warm weather. Millionaires were made overnight.

Tiny, remote villages in sparsely populated parts of Florida were converted by real estate speculators into booming, exotic cities, promising tropical warmth and year-round sunshine. Coral Gables, started by real estate magnate George Merrick, was turned into an "American Venice," replete with man-made canals. Hollywood-by-the-Sea, St. Petersburg, Orlando, Fort Lauderdale, Winter Park and, of course, Miami and Miami Beach became some of the most fashionable places in the country to be.

Brothers Addison and Wilson Mizener used their wealthy connections to become enormously successful real estate developers. Their subdivisions ran to Spanish-style homes in pleasing stucco hues of pink, light blue and cream. The houses had little touches like ornate

A booming Miami in the 1920s

grillwork and imported tile roofs, making them attractive to a public enamored with the fantasy of an exotic tropical lifestyle. The brothers advertised widely and raked in millions of dollars. Unfortunately for the homebuyers, the quality of construction in the subdivisions can best be imagined by Wilson Mizener's oft-quoted remark: "Never give a sucker an even break." The Mizeners' homes looked good but were about as sturdy as cardboard. Most of them, along with 5,000 other houses, fell down in the hurricane that came just one year after they were built.

To the delight of the Mizener brothers and others like them, the "suckers" came to Florida in droves – 4,000 by train each day, 3,000 by automobile and 200 by ship; and during the 1925 boom, nearly 2.5 million people began calling the state home. Those who flocked to Florida were frenetic in their lust for land. And it is any surprise? One advertising brochure from 1925 that was widely distributed in the chilly northern states rhapsodized:

Florida is bathed in the passionate caresses of the southern sun. It is laved by the limpid waves of the embracing seas, wooed by the glorious Gulf Stream, whose waters warmed by the tropical sun, speed northeast to temper Europe. Florida is an emerald kingdom by southern seas, fanned by zephyrs laden with ozone from stately pines, watered by Lethe's copious libation, decked with palm and pine, flower and fern, clothed in perpetual verdure and lapt in the gorgeous folds of the semitropical zone.

But paradise began to grow stale by the turn of the year. Swindles and frauds were rampant, and the National Better Business Bureau began to create uproars – and quick departures – with its investigations. Stock in Florida real estate plunged on the New York Stock Exchange. A mass exodus began, the roads leading north filled with the disgruntled, the angry and the financially ruined. All through 1926, the promoters intensified their pleas for money and there was a little renewed investor interest by September when it all came to an end with the arrival of a monster storm.

The hurricane's life began in the southern Atlantic near the Cape Verde Islands. It stalked past Puerto Rico

Miami was devastated by the storm, stripping palm trees and wiping homes and hotels off the beach

on September 15, and three days later, it came ashore at Miami. Its winds reached 138 miles per hour and the cheap subdivision houses of the so-called "emerald kingdom" were swept away, carrying with them the victims that had lured by the palm trees and sunshine.

At Fort Lauderdale, the storm unraveled the beach and established a new shoreline about 100 yards farther inland. The intensity of the storm was described in the account of a Fort Lauderdale man who tied his wife to a tree and struggled for four hours against the roaring ten-foot waves and horrific wind to travel a few blocks in search of help. The rescue party took just as long to return to the woman, who was miraculously saved. In Coral Gables, heaps of the dead floated through the ruined "Venetian" canals.

But the real nightmare was in

**(Left) Ships were pulled off the water and dumped on the beach
(Right) A terrified Miami resident sought shelter in a bathtub, only to have the walls ripped from their home, luckily leaving the tub behind.**

Miami.

A story told of a hysterical woman who ran from house to house, four in all, as each successively collapsed behind her. The hurricane's first fury struck the city at 3:00 a.m. on September 18. At one of the lavish beachfront hotels, several hundred guests in tuxedos and evening gowns nervously clustered around a piano as they eyed the windows and doors. The pianist tinkled out a steady litany of popular tunes, as one woman shouted, "Play louder, louder!" as if to drown out the sound of the shrieking hurricane. Eventually, though, the storm proved too much for even the hardiest guests. All at once, a huge wave crashed onto the breakers, which were only about 300 feet from the hotel, and the angry ocean battered down the building's huge front doors and rushed into the lobby, swamping it under three feet of water. Screaming, the guests fled the hotel.

The storm hammered the city for the next five hours, but by 8:00 a.m., all was quiet. Believing the storm to be over, many of the tourists donned bathing suits and waded happily out into the sea. Hundreds, even thousands, from the luxury hotels wandered out into the water, splashing, laughing and commenting on the storm, which upon inspection had not been so terrible; some roofs were missing from the hotels and a few houses were down, but that was all.

But that wasn't the end of the storm. The tourists and would-be land investors had no idea what to expect from a hurricane and were ignorant about how these fearsome storms behaved. They were relaxing in the calm eye of the hurricane and within the hour, as they paddled about in the increasingly rough surf, they became puzzled as they watched the sky turn black. Soon, the other side of the hurricane was upon them. Once again, the wind and waters pounded Miami, and many of those who were playing in the water were trapped, unable to swim back to the beach. Many perished in the waves and on the streets of the city. Flying pieces of wood, broken glass and pieces of demolished homes swept into the air, killing and injuring those foolish enough to be out in the elements. Hundreds were dragged into the sea, never to be seen again.

The pounding waves and terrifying winds ripped through Miami, drenching anyone caught outside and making battered hulks of scores of automobiles. Elegant yachts were torn from their berths and were sent careening for blocks inland onto city streets. The Fleetwood Hotel's manicured rooftop gardens were shredded and torn away. The dome of the Flamingo Hotel was completely torn off. A ship, *Magic City*, named in honor of Miami was split in two, one half sinking into the bay, the other sent out to sea with six men on board who were never seen again. Apartment buildings, flimsily built in the first place, began to collapse. One of them went down with more than 100 people inside it.

A tourist named Ruth Anderson, from Lexington, Kentucky, and another young woman raced into a house just ahead of a wall of water. Dozens of snakes and rats, also seeking shelter from the storm, filled the house, as terrified as the two girls. Part of a wall collapsed and the other girl's spine was broken. Ruth built a raft from debris that she found inside the house and placed the girl on it, where she floated for two hours before being rescued.

R.T. Freng, a pilot, put his weight against the wind and tried to make his way down a Miami street. But the winds, estimated at more than 140 miles per hour, blew him into a gutter and there, hanging onto a sewer grate, he stayed for more than three and a half hours. Freng had earlier tried to save the life of a woman who had just given premature birth. He and two friends carried her from a collapsing home as her husband was crushed to death by a falling telephone pole right in front of them.

While hiding in the gutter, Freng saw all manner of debris fly past him in the air: lumber, metal pipes, trees, and even small automobiles. Children separated from their parents screamed helplessly as they were blown past him down the street. He attempted to reach them and pull them to safety but his efforts were wasted against the horrendous winds.

A man named Kirby Jones was inside a large building with about 150 other people when the roof caved in and showered them with broken boards, beams and timbers. He later reported, "All of us ran to a schoolhouse a block away. It was a pitiful sight to see that crowd running through the driving rain, barely able to make headway against the terrific force of the wind... Women were crying hysterically, and old men whimpering that they did not want to die, their voices almost inaudible over the roar of the wind. And all the while flying timbers and glass were falling all about us."

Miami wept in the wake of the storm. The city was in ruins. Fires burned and voices cried out in the rubble. A schooner was found in the center of the street, blocks away from the harbor. Houses were torn off at their foundations. Rows of palm trees had been reduced to splinters.

At the door of the Miami Morgue, George Fielding kept count until 56 bodies had been brought in. At that point he could not continue his grim addition and hurried past a long line of volunteers holding more corpses. "I cried," Fielding later wrote, "at the sight of children having broken limbs set and deep wounds sewed without narcotics to deaden the pain."

For many of the real estate speculators who had flocked to the city to make their fortunes, it was all over. One man, with more than a $1 million invested in ruined homes, committed suicide by walking into the sea. More than 300 people were killed in the storm and 2,000 more were injured, many crippled for life. At least 5,000 homes, many of them brand new, were blown down by the hurricane, bringing Miami's golden era of the 1920s to an end.

1938: THE VOICES OF CHILDREN
Ghosts of the Great New England Hurricane

The monster hurricane that struck New England in September 1938 was born somewhere in the West Indies. It grazed the Bahamas and the Florida Keys before traveling along the Atlantic coast, striking inland at North Carolina, New Jersey, New York and then devastating New England. It was for many people one of the greatest storms they had ever experienced, and nearly 400 souls were lost in the horror of the hurricane – although some believe many of them have never left this earth.

The great New England Hurricane remains one of America's most devastating storms. Measured in terms of its destructive power, it remains one of the top 10 hurricanes to make landfall in the United States. It moved northward quickly, aided by a low-pressure system that accelerated the storm at speeds never seen, before or since. It hit the Northeast without warning, causing billions of dollars in damage and considerable loss of life. Memory of the storm became a part of folk legend in New York and New England for generations.

The word *hurricane* is Spanish, derived from a place of legend. Early explorers of the Caribbean, Mexico and the West Indies experienced first hand the tropical storms of the region and heard about them in the creation legends of the Mayan civilization of Mexico. According to their mythology, the god whose physical manifestation was the hurricane created the earth and the celestial bodies. According to the Mayans, the god visited often, just to remind the people of his power.

The New England hurricane began as most hurricanes begin – as winds blowing off the west coast of Africa and across the Atlantic toward the Caribbean. When the disturbance reached the tropical waters northeast of Puerto Rico on September 16, 1938, the U.S. Weather Bureau classified it as a hurricane and warned that its path could put it on a collision course with southeast Florida. Four days later, however, the storm slowed and veered northeast, not an uncommon occurrence. At this point, most hurricanes left the warm waters of the tropics, lost their energy source and began to dissipate. The Great Hurricane of 1938, though, behaved differently, thanks to a boost from an unlikely source.

High velocity winds carry cold air from the Arctic southward in search of the warmth and humidity of the Gulf region, a meteorological phenomenon known as the Great North American Trumpet. The high winds that sweep across Canada and the Great Lakes region of the United States are evidence of such polar winds pulled southward by tropical conditions. Although this common weather pattern is well documented, the upward movement of air creates strong upper-level troughs. Warm air turns into clouds and rain, and cold air creates dry conditions and clear skies. These troughs get their energy from the interplay of warm and cold air moving eastward in the direction of the Gulf of Mexico. By midnight on September 20, 1938, a stronger than normal weather trough with increasing wind speed over the Caribbean began to propel what became the Great Hurricane in a northward direction. Despite leaving the warm waters of the Atlantic Gulf Stream for colder northern ocean waters, the jet stream ahead of the trough created what hurricane analysts called the "Long Island Express."

With a forward speed of at least 70 miles per hour, it remains the fastest traveling hurricane in recorded history. The storm slammed without warning into Long Island on September 21 at about 3:30 p.m.

In an age of weather satellites, radar and instant communication, it is difficult to imagine a time when a

Devastation from the Great New England Hurricane of 1938

hurricane could strike without any real warning, but that's exactly what happened to the New England region in 1938. In those days, storm warnings were pieced together using barometric readings from many locations. Charting such information told forecasters that a center of low pressure was heading north along the coast, but their charts told them little about the intensity of the storm. The common belief was that hurricanes went out to sea and never passed through New England. The U.S. Weather Bureau had been keeping records since 1871, and it hadn't happened yet.

Throughout that week in September, radio stations continued their regularly scheduled programs and received no weather news worthy of reporting. Coastal weather observation centers and ships at sea provided tracking information about the storm and fishermen along the New England coast knew they were in for a good blow, but no one was prepared for the monster storm that was coming.

As if these circumstances were not bad enough, the low-pressure frontal system had begun to drop several inches of rain on coastal Long Island and New England for a week before the hurricane arrived. With the land saturated with water and with the rivers swollen, any additional volume of water would place the region in flood stage. In addition, the autumnal equinox in September caused higher than normal tides as the gravity of the new moon tugged at sea levels. These tides reached their height on September 21.

While the hurricane bolted from the Carolinas up the east coast, a center of high pressure moved over Nova Scotia. The usual path of northeast storms was blocked. The hurricane only had one place to go: It turned left out of the Atlantic Ocean, crossed over western Long Island and curled north over the Long Island Sound. The hurricane's eye was taking a track parallel to the Connecticut River Valley, but a few miles to the west.

It had struck Long Island just a few hours before flood tide. The storm was 50 miles wide and packed wind gusts of 180 miles per hour. After making landfall, wind velocity dropped, reducing the storm from a Category 5 to a Category 3, which was still very dangerous. The forward motion of the storm propelled by the upper-level jet stream caused it to move so rapidly that many areas in New York, Connecticut, Rhode Island and Massachusetts were struck at the same time. The combination of wind, rain and tides caused a near-total destruction that shattered the record books.

The storm surge, with waves 30 to 50 feet high, dumped millions of tons of seawater on shocked and unprepared residents along the coast. Tides that were 14 to 18 feet above normal extended along most of the Long Island and Connecticut shoreline, and 18 to 25 feet above normal from New London, Connecticut, to Cape Cod. The downtown section of Providence, Rhode Island, was submerged under a surge of water 20 feet deep, while sections of New Bedford and Falmouth, Massachusetts, were under eight feet of water.

Boston was hit hard by the storm. Tens of thousands of trees were uprooted throughout the city and in the surrounding area. According to the *Boston Post*: "By the time the anger of the wind and water had somewhat abated [the Public Garden] presented the appearance of a jungle." The Arnold Arboretum suffered "inestimable damage." Falling trees and bricks killed several people in greater Boston. Shattered windows littered the streets with glass, and more than 200,000 homes lost electrical power.

On the coastline of Buzzards Bay, the terrible winds took their toll on the town, but it was the lack of advance warning and a "tidal wave" that did the most damage. The *Falmouth Enterprise* reported that, "the first intimation to people along Main Street, Falmouth, that the storm was becoming dangerous was at 4:00 p.m. when a large limb parted from a tree… and crashed to the ground." At the same time, Robert Neal, a station agent at the steamship wharf, realized that the storm was more threatening than anyone had been led to believe. The tide was as high as he had ever seen it, and yet high tide was not expected for another three hours. He started clearing people out of the station, fearing the worst.

For many residents on the shore of Buzzards Bay, though, it was already too late.

A woman named Eleanor Brooks went down to Falmouth Beach with a few other sightseers to watch the crashing surf. The sea had begun to flood the road, sweeping through the bathing pavilion and washing toward higher ground. The group panicked when they suddenly found they were in water up to their knees. Someone noted that there were two cars stalled near the Bath House. "We hoped the people had left them in time," Brooks later recalled, "and suddenly realized there *was* a figure, moving slowly, pulling itself along the strong fence with its cement posts and steel cables that bordered the beach road."

One her companions ran for a telephone. Brooks sent another car to the nearby fire station. "We could see the figure by the fence, not moving one way or the other. The surf was drawing nearer. We watched helpless," she wrote.

While the bathing pavilion was torn apart by the sea, two boys drove up in a car. One stripped off his shoes, rolled up his pants, and was promptly knocked down by the surf. The boy exhausted himself trying to rescue the distant figure until firemen arrived. They roped themselves together and waded through breakers into the water up their shoulders, but there was nothing they could do.

The figure trapped in the surf had been a woman named Alice Maurer, who had been spending the weekend at her parents' home in Falmouth. Maurer and her nephew, Henry Maurer III, had been running errands, and their car had run out of gas along the shore. Henry had hitched a ride into town to get more gas and his aunt planned to wait in the car until he returned. She was trapped by the pounding waves, and eventually tried to make it to safety but was lost in the storm.

She was not the only one who perished that day. Mr. and Mrs. Andrew Jones owned a home on Silver Beach. When the ocean crashed into their yard around 6:00 p.m., they tried to escape in their car, but it wouldn't start. The couple ran back into the house. When the water flooded into the first floor, they retreated upstairs. When the tide continued to rise, they climbed out onto the roof. The *Falmouth Enterprise* continued their story: "When Mr. and Mrs. Fritz Lindskog saw the Jones roof sweeping past their building, they tried to tie blankets together to throw a life line to the elderly occupants. But the wind swept away their frail attempt." The Joneses rode on top of the roof until it crashed and broke into pieces in the surging water.

Bernice Fitzgerald was lucky enough to survive the night. While she and her sister prepared dinner by oil lamp, since the electricity had gone out, one of them happened to look outside. The surf was pounding over the seawall and the only road off their seaside island was covered by the ocean. By the time they got their things together to make an escape, the road to the mainland was completely washed out and they were stranded.

The Fitzgeralds were not alone; there were 22 other residents of the beachfront community that were trapped on the small island. They watched helplessly as their cars were washed out to sea. Every house and building on the island was inundated with water or had collapsed, except for one. On a small rise in the center of the island was an empty, two-story cottage. The entire group rushed for the small building, broke a window and pushed their way inside. The tide was still rising, but with the rest of the island washed out and in shambles, the cottage was their last hope. Bernice Fitzgerald later told the *Boston Post*, "We had only been in the place a short time when the water began to lap at the stairs, then came up level with the porch. We decided then to go upstairs. We had to go upstairs, all 22 of us... There were no lights of any kind. We found crackers and tonic. There was no other food."

During the flood, Bernice ventured partway down the stairs and saw furniture floating in the living room. The water reached the top of the fireplace. But the tide turned about 7:00 p.m. and the water slowly began to recede, saving those who sheltered in the cottage. By 11:00 p.m., rescue crews from the mainland were able to make their way to the island.

News reports blamed a "tidal wave" (today referred to as a "storm surge") for the destruction in Buzzards Bay. Observers saw boats tossed high onto the shore and estimated that a rogue tide had run as high as 15 feet. In Somerset, a giant oil tanker was pushed upriver from its mooring and landed on a garage owned by one of the town's officials.

Reports from nearby towns were just as shocking. Of the 100 cottages at Horseneck Beach, none remained. At Crescent Beach in Fairhaven, five summer homes survived out of 178. In Wareham, 316 homes and cottages were washed away or destroyed by the force of the water. On Cape Cod, 33 people were killed, and 15 more died in Falmouth and Woods Hole. There were 57 killed around Fall River.

Many more would have died if not for the courage of dozens of unsung heroes. Up and down the New England coast, volunteers climbed into rowboats and skiffs to try and rescue their friends, neighbors and complete strangers. Three of the dead in Woods Hole were coastguardsmen who were washed into the harbor by a rogue wave while they were trying to save other boaters.

The storm also descended on Providence, sending wind and flooding into the city during the evening rush hour. The seas swamped everyone aboard buses and trains, those in automobiles, and anyone unlucky enough to be on foot. People trapped in buildings dropped sheets and ropes to those being swept past them in the raging waters. More than 90 people died in the city. Faced with massive destruction, officials imposed martial law on Providence to prevent looting. Cleanup operations, using unemployed laborers who worked for $2 a day, took place in the days that followed. Hundreds of telephone and electrical employees labored to restore services to the northeastern part of the city, the hardest hit. Later, the city constructed a series of locks and dams to protect it from future storm flooding.

With the loss of hundreds of millions of trees over a six-state area, the environmental impact of the Great Hurricane was devastating. In addition, with the storm coming on the first day of autumn, apple orchards across New England lost their entire crop. The coastlines were changed and in some places, new inlets replaced old ones that had been filled with shifting sands and debris during the storm. The hurricane destroyed almost 9,000 homes, summer cottages and commercial and public buildings. More than 15,000 more needed major repairs. It sank more than 2,600 boats and damaged another 3,300. The New England fishing fleet suffered substantially. While the industry recovered in the long run, the hurricane cost fishermen 2,605 vessels, with damage to another 3,300. In today's dollars, the damages exceeded $20.8 billion. It is still considered one of the most devastating hurricanes in our nation's history.

As with so many disasters, doubts exist about the true number of storm-related deaths. Some bodies were never recovered, because individuals were swept out to sea, buried beneath the shifting sand, or dismembered by flying debris. Estimated fatalities range from 564 to more than 690 but the real losses – like the horror of those who suffered through the storm – will never truly be known.

The rapid movement of the hurricane carried it north across New Hampshire and Vermont. By 9:00 p.m. on September 21, about five hours after first striking Long Island, the Great Hurricane passed into Canada and ended its day of destruction in the Arctic.

The *Boston Globe* summed up the days that followed:

In the work of reconstruction, clearing the debris of thousands of trees, wrecked homes, fallen wires, washed-out roadbeds and tracks, thousands were engaged today. The WPA in Massachusetts suspended all projects to throw 80,000 workers into the breach and speed the cleanup. Transportation and communication facilities were at a standstill. Bridges are gone, rivers have climbed their banks to create inland flood conditions as menacing as the great flood of 1936. And along the seas, where a tidal wave of typhoon proportions smashed its way 1,000 feet inland, the shores are strewn with dead bodies.

And what of the ghosts left behind by such massive loss of life? Stories emerged of shadowy figures seen walking on the beaches at night, only to vanish when approached. Tales circulated of haunted summer cottages, where the corpses of hurricane victims had been found after the storm had passed. It is said that many of those who died did not rest in peace.

One such place where tales of ghosts are still told is the Lighthouse Inn, overlooking Long Island Sound in New London, Connecticut. Originally built as Meadow Court in 1902 for Charles Strong Guthrie, a steel tycoon from Pittsburgh, and his wife, Frances Amelia, the mansion has endured into the present in the thriving seaside town. Designed by renowned architect William Ralph Emerson (with landscaping by Frederick Law Olmsted, who also designed New York's Central Park), the house was supposed to "capture sunlight and the exterior world of nature." The lush grounds reached all of the way to the shoreline and were so acclaimed that they were featured in the 1912 issue of *American Homes & Gardens.*

Guthrie died at age 46 in 1906. His wife continued to live at the house during the summer until 1925, when the property was subdivided and sold.

In 1927, Meadow Court re-opened as the Lighthouse Inn. The inn became a popular spot for well-to-do locals and the cream of New London society. Many appeared in the *New London Day,* the regional newspaper that chronicled the daily lives of the inn's most noted guests. The inn's proximity to local theaters attracted guests like Joan Crawford and Bette Davis, adding to its appeal.

A year after the inn opened – and continuing for the next decade – a private school called the Pequot Day School operated in the building. It was said to be a happy to learn and play until September 21, 1938, the day of the Great New England Hurricane. The storm would cause the deaths of two of the students at the school -- two children who are said to have never left the premises.

The hurricane struck without warning and changed the face of the region forever. Waves rose to incredible heights, rushing, crashing and bringing death to the Connecticut coast and the entire New England shoreline. Winds roared at speeds of over 120 miles per hour and the storm devastated New London. Not only was the city slammed by the storm, but the next day, it was ravaged by a terrible fire, believed to have started in one of the warehouses that were wrecked in the hurricane. It took more than 10 hours to battle the blaze, and when it was over, the entire waterfront was a smoking

The Lighthouse Inn, formerly Meadow Court and the Pequot Day School

ruin. Any beach houses not lost in the storm were burned in the fire. The hurricane's force actually moved a 240-ton ship from its berth in the harbor, dragging it into the city. More than 75,000 structures were damaged or destroyed. At least 98 people died in Connecticut, 100 went missing and over 2,500 were injured. Makeshift morgues sprang up, many of them containing only parts of bodies. Survivors would later recall that the wind was so fierce and high-pitched that it literally sounded as though it was screaming.

Laughter and running footsteps are the sounds connected to the two children who are said to haunt the Lighthouse Inn. The children were among the storm casualties. The school never re-opened after the hurricane, but it is said that the spirits of the young victims are still there.

Current staff members at the Inn still claim to encounter the ghostly children today. A food and beverage manager reported, "Everyone hears them running up and down the stairs and around on the third floor, bouncing a ball off the wall and laughing." They seem to stay there, trapped in time, perhaps re-living the happy days before the Great Hurricane.

1956: GHOSTS OF "CRASH CANYON"
The Grand Canyon Airline Disaster

At around 10:30 a.m. on Saturday, June 30, 1956, two passenger planes, Trans World Airlines Flight 2 and United Airlines Flight 718, collided over the rugged eastern end of the Grand Canyon. All 128 passengers and crew on both planes were killed. The two aircraft involved – TWA's Super Constellation and United's DC-7 – were the largest commercial planes in service at the time. The death toll in this horrific collision outnumbered previous aviation accidents, prompted the government to create the Federal Aviation Administration, and gave birth to a haunting that still lingers today in one of the most mysterious places in the American West.

TWA Flight 2 and United Flight 718 both left Los Angeles International Airport just after 9:00 a.m. on June 30. The TWA flight was bound for Kansas City and followed a route just south of that of United Flight 718, which was headed for Chicago. The planes were actually supposed to come near one another at one point over the Painted Desert in Arizona, directly above the Grand Canyon. The pilots of both planes stayed in communication with air traffic control as their aircraft gained altitude. In 1956, most civilian flights followed Instrumental Flight Rules (IFR) during and after takeoff, but pilots could switch to Visual Flight Rules (VFR) once they were "on top," or above cloud level. Aircraft and crew employed the rudimentary system of "see and be seen" once they switched to VFR, in which case, the pilots flew mostly by sight. Air traffic control rarely denied the request to fly by VFR. The Civil Aeronautics Agency, the predecessor to the FAA, lacked the funding and facilities to expand the scope of IFR. Consequently, vast area of uncontrolled airspace, not covered by any type of radar, prevailed in 1956. Above the clouds, pilots relied strictly on their eyes to fly.

TWA Flight 2 radioed the Los Angeles Air Traffic Control Center at 9:21 a.m. and requested permission to climb from 19,000 to 21,000 feet. An air traffic controller in Salt Lake City recognized that this would intersect the path of the United plane and told the controllers in Los Angeles to deny the request. The TWA pilot then asked for 1,000 feet "on top" and a switch to VFR, which Los Angeles approved. The TWA flight entered uncontrolled airspace at about 21,000 feet. In short, while air traffic control would not approve the elevation climb, the switch to VFR in effect permitted it to occur. The pilot of United Flight 718 radioed the Los Angeles tower shortly after takeoff, reporting that he was "on top." The air traffic controller granted United 718's request to continue under VFR.

The pilot of each plane contacted air traffic control again just before 10:00 a.m. At 9:58, United Flight 718 reported an altitude of 21,000 feet over the Needles, a rock formation in Utah's Canyonlands National Park. The pilot estimated that he would pass over the Painted Desert at roughly 10:31. The TWA's crew reported its position in Las Vegas at 9:59. The plane had just passed Lake Mohave, Arizona, at 1,000 feet "on top," or 21,000 feet. TWA Flight 2 was also due over the Painted Desert at 10:31.

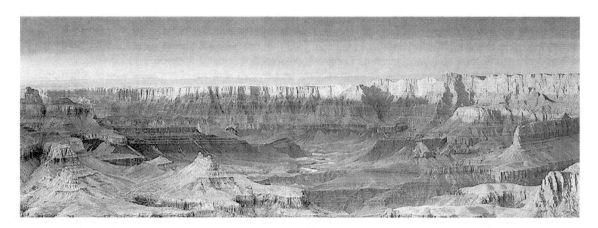

Flight 2 was never heard from again.

The United plane issued a final radio message at 10:31 a.m. Radio operators in San Francisco and Salt Lake City were unable to translate the message, but after the crash, the broadcast was discovered to be: "Salt Lake, United 718... ah... we're going in!"

The Civil Aeronautics Agency issued a missing aircraft alert at 11:51 a.m. There had been no eyewitnesses to a crash, or at least none that could be found, so officials had little idea of where to begin the search. Late that evening, though, a local pilot who took tourists on scenic flights spotted wreckage of the TWA plane. Air Force helicopters arrived at the site on July 1 and the CAA began its investigation of the crash.

TWA Flight 2 had crashed upside down on the northeast slope of Temple Butte. The stone formation was located in a wild and remote section of the Grand Canyon. United 718 had struck Chuar Butte, opposite the Little Colorado River. The investigation determined that a collision had taken place in midair. The evidence showed that paint from the United plane was visible on the wreckage of TWA Flight 2, and the propeller incisions on the TWA plane exactly matched the size of the United plane's propellers. The planes had been traveling at speeds greater than 300 miles per hour, and had plunged about four miles into the canyon. It was discovered that the left wing of the United plane had hit the rear fuselage of the United plane, rendering the aircraft inoperable. With the fuselage blown open and the rear cabin opened to the sky, passengers and luggage were sucked out of the plane. A mere 30 seconds after the collision, TWA Flight 2 crashed. The United plane stayed airborne approximately 90 seconds after the initial impact, but was unable to clear Chuar Butte. The force of the collision with the rock wall obliterated the aircraft, the passengers, and everything on board. Investigators were left with only the carnage and debris of TWA Flight 2, which was strewn across Temple Butte. The remote location and the vertical cliff face made the investigation – and the recovery of the corpses – nearly impossible.

The disaster exposed many of the flaws that existed in air traffic control in 1956. Air traffic had increased dramatically during the 1950s, straining the capacity of the Civil Aeronautics Agency to keep pace. Both the CAA and the Civil Aeronautics Board had jurisdiction over phases of air transportation, a situation that hampered regulation. The CAB formulated rules of aviation, while the CAA oversaw their implementation. Safety matters fell to the CAB, even though the CAA was better suited to determine safety guidelines. The military answered to neither agency, further complicating air traffic coordination.

The results of the investigation into the crash were released on April 17, 1957, highlighting this regulatory confusion. The most critical part of the report concerned the heavy reliance on VFR, a technique that had become outdated. The "see and be seen" practice had been adequate in an earlier era when the skies were relatively open. But air travel rose sharply after World War II, greatly congesting the skies. The CAA noted that the technical capability to reduce aircraft collisions existed, but that a lack of funds and personnel kept it from being put into place.

President Dwight D. Eisenhower appointed Edward P. Curtis, a veteran of aviation planning, to recommend improvements in air traffic control. Curtis proposed a single agency that would "regulate not only the system of airways, including the nationwide system of electronic aids to navigation," but all safety matters, including the certification of pilots, operators and aircraft. Congress created the Federal Aviation Agency (FAA) in December 1958, instructing that it create equitable zones of military and civilian airspace. Even so, it would not be until 1967 that the FAA managed to help institute the VHF Omi-Directional Range system across the United States, which allowed pilots the electronic capacity to determine the location of other aircraft.

It was another case of an unthinkable tragedy exposing a flaw in the system that has since saved an unknown number of lives.

Without question, the Grand Canyon is the most mysterious place in the American West. For centuries, it has been the focus of stories of lost cities, missing treasure, unexplained disappearances and, of course, ghosts. The first white explorers to witness the magnificence of the canyon were stunned by the size, beauty and terror of what has been considered one of the seven wonders of the natural world. The canyon had a way of creeping up on these intrepid explorers. A mountain could be seen for miles, but the Grand Canyon remained hidden until the very moment that one stepped to the edge and the world dropped away into a crevice 300 miles long, one mile deep and 10 miles wide.

In 1857, the U.S. Army sent Lieutenant Joseph Ives and his men to explore the area. When Ives returned two years later, he submitted a report to Congress. In his report, Ives compared his descent into the canyon with entering the gates of Hell... "the corresponding depth and gloom of the gaping chasms into which we were plunged imparted an unearthly character... Harsh screams issuing from aerial recesses in the canyon sides and apparitions of goblin-like figures perched in the rifts and hollows of the impending cliffs, gave an odd reality to this impression."

In the 1860s, John Wesley Powell conquered the canyon – in the only way that man can truly conquer nature – and it has been the scene of both tragedy and mystery ever since. In 1909, reports surfaced that an explorer for the Smithsonian Institution named G.E. Kinkaid had discovered a cache of Egyptian treasure hidden in a cave inside of the canyon. The discovery was carefully described and publicized and then vanished from the papers without a trace. It was allegedly found in a section of the canyon that is closed to hikers and outdoor enthusiasts today.

While many have vanished in the canyon over the years, perhaps the most famous disappearance was that of Glen and Bessie Hyde. The young couple were attempting to navigate the canyon in a boat on the treacherous Colorado River and were never seen again. No trace of their boat, their bodies or any of their belongings ever turned up.

What is it about the Grand Canyon that makes it such a strange place? Is it merely the deaths and tragedies that mark its history? Is it the rugged majesty of the terrain? Or is there something far deeper in its makeup that makes weirdness seem to surround the region? The Hopi Indians believe the canyon is a gateway to the underworld. Their mythology tells the story of a god who appears, on his good days, as a handsome young man with long hair who wears and indigo-hued breechcloth. On bad days, though, he appears as a monstrous, burned corpse with an enormous head and a mouth filled with jagged teeth. The god is called Maasaw and he has hollow eyes that burn with fire. The Hopi believe that if you see a light moving in the darkness, it might be the Maasaw coming for you. Or you might hear the tap-tapping sound of the claws on his toes and he walks in the shadows. Maasaw is a complex god, both feared and loved, and is the keeper of death. The sight of him can paralyze one with fear and his breath is said to drain one of one's energy. Maasaw is so feared that many Hopi are terrified of encountering him in the dark and refuse to speak his name. According to legend, he dwells in the canyon and guards the passage from this world to the next.

There are a number of ghost stories connected to the Grand Canyon. One of them involves the foreman of a trail crew, one of the unsung heroes of the national park. His name was Rees Griffiths and on February 6, 1922, he and his crew set off a dynamite charge to cut a new route for the North Kaibab Trail. The blast loosened a huge boulder, which fell on Griffiths and crushed him. A nurse and chief ranger hiked down the dangerous trail in the dark to try and help him, but Griffiths died before they arrived. Before he slipped away, he asked his crew to bury him in the canyon he loved so well. The National Park Service honored his request and today the trail foreman rests under a pile of reddish-black rocks at the base of the cliffs where he was killed. But does he rest in peace? Not according to trail crews, who claim that an eerie light is often seen above his grave. They believe that the light is the ghost of Griffiths still watching over his beloved canyon.

The ghost of a wandering woman has been seen near the Grand Canyon Lodge. She is a spirit spawned by a tragedy that occurred on September 1, 1932. On that day, an early morning fire destroyed the interior of the lodge and legend has it that a woman perished in the flames. She has since been seen wearing a white dress printed with blue flowers, roaming the canyon's North Rim near the rebuilt lodge. Employees claim that she won't allow a particular door in one of the hotel's corridors to remain open. Whenever a staff member closes it, the woman slams it shut. Numerous visitors and employees say that they have heard her mournful wails outside of the cabins at night, and at least three park rangers have reported encountering her after dark along Transept Trail.

Along the canyon's South Rim is the Hopi House, an adobe gift shop that is said to be haunted by the spirits of two Native American boys. Employees claim that if you stay late in the evening, you can hear them running around upstairs. They are said to knock over merchandise, turn off computers and toss rugs on the floor.

Adjacent to the Hopi House is the Grand Canyon's most luxurious hotel, the El Tovar. Perched high on the edge of the canyon, the El Tovar has been the scene of violence over the years, including two gun deaths. A sheriff's deputy shot an armed robbery suspect outside of the hotel in 1951, and in 1984, a well-intentioned stranger was accidentally shot when he tried to break up a fight between a local man and his girlfriend. There have been a number of eerie occurrences that have taken place at the hotel. Several tourists have hurriedly checked out of a certain room after seeing what they described as "death head" faces looking back at them from a mirror. Two staff members who were vacuuming the dining room saw an eerie ball of light push open the kitchen doors, float across the room, and then vanish out a window toward the canyon. An apparition of an old

man said to be that of Fred Harvey, the hotel's former operator, roams the halls in a black hat and a long coat. The ghost of a woman in a 1930s-style dress once startled a night watchman so badly that he fled the hotel.

But the most haunted location within the confines of the canyon is the area that came to be known as "Crash Canyon" after the air disaster that occurred in 1956. The planes went down on either side of the narrow side canyon, slamming into Temple and Chuar buttes. The cliffs were so inaccessible that Swiss mountain guides were hired to recover the remains of the passengers on Temple Butte. Some of the bodies had been forced into narrow rock crevices, and the entire site

Eerie "Crash Canyon", where the two planes went down in 1956 -- and where ghosts of the victims are still said to linger.

was subjected to 100-plus degree heat for many days after the disaster. There was some controversy over whether or not the bodies should even be recovered, but workers from the park service made sure the recovery was accomplished. A mass grave on the canyon's South Rim, west of the Yavapai Overlook, contains bodies of the victims.

There is no easy way to reach Crash Canyon. In order to reach the short path that leads to the crash site (where debris is still occasionally found), you must travel there on the river. It is near this site where strange things are reported to happen...

A few years ago, a park ranger named K.J. Glover told author Andrea Lankford about her own experiences in Crash Canyon. Glover was on the third night of her patrol on the Colorado River and decided to make camp at the mouth of the little side canyon between Temple and Chuar buttes. She knew nothing of the history of the area at the time. She pitched her tent above the beach and after dinner, went to bed.

She was awakened later that night by the sound of voices. Through the mesh window of the tent, she saw 12 or 15 men and women walking toward her from a narrow trail that led away from the camp. The men and women walking past her tent wore "city clothes" inappropriate for the rugged surroundings: the men in button-up shirts and the women in knee-length skirts. They were having quiet, muttered conversations as they passed by, and eventually disappeared into the darkness. She might have been dreaming, but Glover adamantly said, "I really thought I was awake."

As she would later find out, she was not the only one to experience eerie visions while camping between Temple and Chuar buttes. Another ranger was camping on the beach across the river from Crash Canyon when he was awakened by the sound of someone calling for help. He climbed out of his tent and looked across the river, where he saw moving lights, as if a large group of people with flashlights was walking along the river. The ranger found this odd since there was no trail along the edge of the river and the only way to reach the canyon was by boat. He yelled out across the water, but got no response. Eventually, the lights moved upstream and disappeared around a bend in the river. The ranger, assuming that the group was part of a river trip making their way back to camp, got into his tent and went back to sleep. The next morning, he asked all of the river rafters that he saw if they had been hiking with their clients across the river the night before.

None of them had.

FIRE

1868: 'SEVEN INMATES PERISH IN THE FLAMES'
The Haunting Fire at Ohio's Central Lunatic Asylum

The ghost that got into our house on the night of November 17, 1915, raised such a hullabaloo of misunderstanding that I am sorry that I didn't just let it keep on walking, and go to bed. Its advent caused my mother to throw a shoe through a window of the house next door and ended up with my grandfather shooting a patrolman. I am sorry, therefore, as I have said, that I ever paid any attention to the footsteps.
James Thurber

Stories of fiery disasters and lingering ghosts seem to go hand in hand. It is quite common to hear tales of burned-out public buildings, homes and theaters that contain spirits that remain behind after a blaze has taken place. In the case of a former mental hospital in Ohio, the dead not only remained behind at the site of the destruction, but became an inspiration for a short story by one of America's favorite authors.

The Ohio Central Lunatic Asylum was first organized on March 5, 1835 with Samuel Parsons, William Awl and Samuel McCracken appointed as directors. They selected a tract of land in downtown Columbus, about a mile northeast of the state capitol building. The 30-acre piece of land fronted south on what is now Broad Street, and

The original Ohio Central Lunatic Asylum, which burned in 1868

its western boundary ran along what would later become Washington Avenue. The next three years were spent building an institution that would accommodate about 120 patients. It was the first institution for the treatment of the insane west of the Alleghenies, and William Awl was named as medical superintendent. The first patients arrived on November 30, 1838.

The massive place contained 153 single rooms and offered what little the state could do for the mentally ill. Prior to 1900, mental health care barely existed. In those days, anyone suffering from a mental disorder was simply locked away from society, either at home or in an asylum. Many of these institutions were filthy places of confinement where patients were often left in straitjackets, locked in restraint chairs, chained to walls or even placed in crates or cages if they were especially disturbed. Many of them spent every day in shackles and chains. Even the so-called "treatments" were barbaric. Patients were given cold-water baths to shock their systems, were wrapped tightly in wet sheets to relieve tension, or worse.

Not surprisingly, such techniques brought little success and patients rarely improved. In those days before psychiatry and medication, most mental patients spent much of their lives locked up in an asylum. Things began to change around 1905, when new laws were passed and psychiatry began to promote the fact that the mentally ill could actually be helped, not just locked away and forgotten. Unfortunately, the Ohio Central Lunatic Asylum was opened long before that…

Doctors came and went and the hospital was severely overcrowded most of the time. When a fire broke out in November 1868, there were 314 patients in rooms that had been intended for nearly one-third of that number.

The asylum was almost completely destroyed by the fire that broke out in the evening of November 17, 1868. The fire originated in the north dormitory of the east wing. Most of the patients were assembled in the recreation room at the time. An alarm was telegraphed to the engine house and the entire fire department was almost immediately dispatched to the grounds. The flames spread rapidly and most of the efforts of the firemen were directed toward rescuing the inmates – seven of whom never made it out alive.

The water used to fight the fire was pumped from cisterns on the grounds, but by 10:00 p.m., the wells were exhausted. There was little to do but watch the asylum burn. The scene on the grounds was like a hellscape from the paintbrush of Hieronymus Bosch. Frantic inmates ran from the burning building, the entire east wing of which was now in flames, coming from their beds in various states of undress. They flung themselves from windows and ran through doors. They screamed, cried, howled and shouted gibberish. The light of the fire danced across the open lawn, illuminating the firemen at work as they searched for more water, shouted, and rushed from one side of the lawn to the other.

By midnight, walls and ceilings had begun to fall, and yet relatively few curiosity-seekers flocked to the scene. Every omnibus and carriage in the city was ordered to the asylum and the inmates were transferred to the Deaf and Dumb Asylum, where they were locked away and taken care of to the best of the staff's ability. No serious accidents occurred and no escapes took place. The mental patients were later removed to other facilities.

When the water in the cisterns surrounding the asylum had also been exhausted, water was forced from other tanks in the city, but it did little good. By then, the fire was burning to the point that it was nearly out of control. The flames extended along the roof of the east wing, then along the front part of the main building at the extreme west end. For a time, the wings extending north were free from fire, but when the cisterns dried up, these sections also began to burn. The firefighters soon realized that the building was lost. After the surviving patients were rescued, efforts then turned to salvaging as much of the furniture as possible.

The *Ohio State Journal* wrote of the fire: "The disaster is one of the most terrible kind. The announcement will strike the people at large, as it did the citizens of Columbus last night, with a terror that cannot be spoken."

The origin of the fire was – and still remains – a mystery. It was first discovered at the north end of the east wing, which was occupied by female inmates. The smoke first appeared issuing from the wards and cells that housed the "incurable" patients.

About 200 of the inmates were out of their cells and were taking part in an entertainment provided by musicians and benefactors from Columbus who volunteered to help ease the plight of the mentally ill. The recreation hall was filled that night with music and laughter as both the sane and insane mingled together for a pleasant event.

When it was first discovered, the fire caused no serious alarm. It was thought that the flames could be easily put out, but when the firemen arrived, they realized it was a serious blaze. They were able to do little to check the progress of the flames, especially after the cisterns ran dry. Water was thrown onto the building's tin roof, where it ran down like rain. Unfortunately, the bars over the windows kept the water from penetrating the rooms except in the form of a light spray. The firefighters quickly realized that the asylum was lost and the great building was abandoned to its destruction.

A reporter on the scene from the *Ohio Journal* wrote, "One of those indescribable scenes followed, which are beheld but once in a lifetime, a faithful impression of which cannot be conveyed to those absent from the appalling spectacle."

The flames cut off communication between the extreme end of the east wing and the main building, so that the only hope of rescuing the incurable female inmates was by breaking through the heavily barred windows, or by cutting a passage through the tin roof. Ladders were thrown up against the asylum's walls and the strong iron bars were torn away. In moments, screaming and shrieking women were scooped up in the arms of the fireman and carried down the ladders to the ground. Others were led carefully along the steep roof of the conservatory building and then handed down to the men below. Firefighters cut holes in the ceilings of the cells and passed the occupants out to other men on the high roof of the building.

"They moved through the storm like specters walking in the air or on the sea," the reporter described the scene. "Many of these unfortunate women were almost entirely nude. Some had nothing on but their night clothing, some had sheets or blankets wrapped about their heads; others with their hair streaming in the wind, looked like furies let loose. The feet of almost all were without covering, and not a few were without covering upon the upper portion of their persons."

If possible, the hellish scene became even stranger. The women who had been rescued were secured in the recreation hall so that they could not escape. Almost all of the guards and attendants were busy saving other patients and carrying property from the building, so the insane were left to their own devices. Some crouched on the floor and silently prayed, some cried out loudly for God to save them, while others, believing that the flames around them to be the fires of hell, begged for forgiveness and an end to their torment. Others laughed, screamed and swore. They lifted their eyes in supplication and danced in an ecstasy of delight. One large woman jumped onto the piano at the head of the room and danced and stomped on it until the instrument was completely destroyed.

When the raving women were finally taken away in carriages and omnibuses, they were mostly quiet and cooperative, except for a few who manifested an unaccountable desire to rush back into the flames from which they had been rescued.

The seven inmates who perished in the fire were suffocated by the thick, black smoke that choked the rooms. Their lifeless bodies were snatched from the flames and, wrote the *Ohio Journal* report, "lay stretched amid the falling snow, upon the grass, rendering more ghastly and ghostly the harrowing scene."

As the fire gained momentum, the flames shot into the sky and attracted the attention of people all over the city. The alarm bells had failed to rouse them earlier but now, as the spectacle grew greater, more than 10,000 people reportedly rushed to the scene. Almost 1,000 of them began to try and save the furniture and other movable property inside the asylum. Beds, chairs, tables, pianos, desks, mirrors, blankets, quilts, dishes, books, musical instruments and paintings were carried out at the doors or hurled from the windows.

By the following day, the massive walls stood hollow and blackened, teetering on the edge of total collapse. The institution, the newspaper wrote, "which for thirty years has been the pride and glory of our noble state, has passed away. But it will reappear again, grander in its proportions, broader in the charities and more boundless in its blessings to the brotherhood of man."

Whether the asylum actually provided any "blessings" to its wretched inmates is doubtful, but the newspaper was right on one account: On April 23, 1869, an act was passed by the legislature for the re-building of the asylum on the old grounds. Work began on the foundation in October but winter brought the construction to a halt. The site remained abandoned until spring, when a new act was passed that authorized the sale of the old land and required a new hospital to be built elsewhere. No explanation was ever given for this decision. The land was eventually purchased by a real estate developer who began building homes on the site of the old hospital.

The original asylum was all but forgotten after the new hospital opened, but it would not stay forgotten for long. Residents who moved into the houses that were built where the former asylum once stood soon found that some memories of the old place refused to go away.

One of those residents would go on to earn a place in history as one of the great humor writers of his era. His name was James Thurber, and he wrote a famous story about the comedy of errors that happened when a ghost "got in" his home one night. It was based on a real event that happened at the house where he and his family lived from 1912 to 1917. The house is located at 77 Jefferson Avenue, on the site of the old Ohio Central Insane Asylum. Stranger still, the incident occurred on the 47th anniversary of the fire that destroyed the hospital and claimed the lives of seven patients.

The Thurber House, located on the site of the burned asylum

The house today is known as the Thurber House, in honor of its famous former occupant. Built of brick in the Italianate style, it made for a charming rental property in its day, attracting a number of tenants, including the Thurber family. James Thurber lived there with his parents and his eccentric grandfather, all of whom he later featured in his stories. He was the middle son of the three Thurber boys. The three of them were undoubtedly a handful. In fact, James lost the sight in his left eye after one of his brothers accidentally shot him with an arrow. He went totally blind later in life.

The house was one of three in which the Thurbers lived in Columbus, but it has become the most famous. During the time the family lived on Jefferson Avenue, James was attending Ohio State University, making the 45-minute streetcar ride to school each day. Because his eyesight was too poor for him to complete the required ROTC course at Ohio State, he wasn't able to graduate. His natural talent and gift for drawing and storytelling opened doors of opportunity for him, even without a college degree. Although best known for his cartoons and witty short stories, Thurber wrote 32 books, including collections of essays and modern commentaries, fables and children's stories. His literary contributions saved the house from the wrecking ball at a time when other homes on the street were being torn down to make room for new structures. The Thurber House is used today as a museum and literary center, and to many of those on staff, there is no question that it is haunted by spirits of the past.

James Thurber, who turned his time in a haunted house into one of his entertaining short stories.

Are all of the ghosts who linger at the Thurber House connected to the hospital that once stood on the site? Perhaps not... After the Thurbers moved out, the house stopped being rented for a time and in the 1920s was the Wallace Collegiate School and Conservatory of Music. In 1946, it became a boarding house for many years until, in the 1970s it was donated to the Jefferson Center for Learning and the Arts, which offers the house to the public today.

Thurber wrote that he did some asking around in his old neighborhood about the possible source of the ghostly footsteps that inspired "The Night the Ghost Got In." Someone told him that prior to the Thurbers' residency, the house had been the scene of a suicide. It seems a man received an anonymous call at work one day informing him that his wife was having an affair. The caller went on to say that if the man went home early, he would catch his wife in the act. He supposedly did so, and overheard his wife making love to another man. The revelation left the man completely shattered. He allegedly paced around the dining room for awhile before running up the back stairs to a room on the second floor where he shot and killed himself, but not before outlining his actions in a note. The note was allegedly destroyed by the man's family, and the suicide was hushed up.

Whether there is any truth to the tale of the betrayed husband is unknown, but Thurber evidently believed it enough to record it as a possible explanation for the ghostly footsteps that inspired his famous story.

Strange activity has been reported nearly everywhere in the building, from the living room and dining room on the first floor, all the way to the third-floor apartment occupied by the writer-in-residence. Books fly from shelves, doors refuse to stay closed, windows slam, voices are heard and – just as when James Thurber lived there – pacing footsteps are sometimes heard, ringing heavily on the wooden floors.

1872: "SIXTY ACRES OF RUIN"
The Great Boston Fire

In October 1871, a fire nearly destroyed the entire city of Chicago. Thirteen months later, another fire swept through Boston, which was no more prepared to handle the inferno that gutted the city's business district than Chicago had been the previous year. Instead of eating through the ramshackle homes of the poor, as the fire in Chicago did, the Boston fire struck down department stores, office buildings, and the mansions of the wealthy. In no other city were conditions more ripe to produce a deadly blaze than in Boston.

During Boston's gaslight era, public transportation was supplied by horse-drawn streetcars. With ringing bells

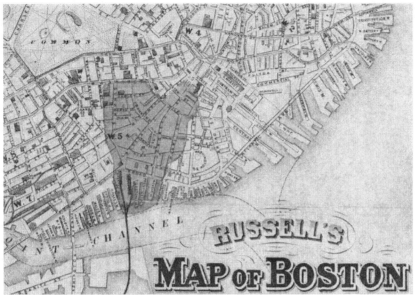

A vintage map of Boston with a darkened area showing the section that was destroyed by the 1872 fire.

and clip-clopping hooves, the horse-drawn vehicles carried Bostonians throughout the city. But in the fall of 1872, most of the horses in the city became sick with distemper. Without the teams to pull them, the horse-drawn streetcars were useless. Boston's fire department lacked horses, too. With no teams to pull them, the city's new steam-engine pumpers had to make it to fires the old-fashioned way. It became a common sight to see groups of gasping firefighters hauling their equipment through the streets on foot. None who saw these men could begin to imagine the heroic tasks the entire Boston Fire Department, 28 engine companies from neighboring towns, and nine units from three other states would soon undertake.

The evening of November 9, 1872 was a pleasant one. Saturday shoppers walked from store to store, theatergoers hurried downtown, afraid of missing the opening curtain, and strollers filled the city streets as people enjoyed the unseasonably mild temperatures. Soon, though, a crowd began to gather on Washington Street, trying to see what was happening down Sumner Street. This was where the business district began. It was an area tightly packed with office buildings, their mansard roofs crowding one another on a narrow thoroughfare that dated back more than a century. Down the street, spectators pointed out glowing billows of smoke pouring from the top of one of the roofs. Within minutes, flames began shooting from the windows of the building.

Across the river in Charlestown, two policemen were the first officials to note the glow of fire coming from Boston. It was 7:08 p.m.

None of the onlookers on the street turned in a fire alarm, each believing that someone else had already done it. It was not until a Boston policeman who was walking on Lincoln Street heard the shouts of the onlookers, saw the fire, and ran a block to the nearest alarm box that city hall was given the news of the blaze. An alarm operator notified firehouses throughout the city and then recorded the time — it was 7:24 p.m. The fire had been raging in the heart of the business district for at least 15 minutes before firefighters were informed. The delay would turn out to be disastrous.

By the time the first contingents of firemen arrived, almost all of the buildings along Sumner and Kingston streets had been devoured by the fire. The flames had jumped the narrow streets until buildings on Otis Street and others were also burning. A strong wind was fanning the flames, making the situation even more dangerous.

The fire started in a new, five-story granite building on the corner of Kingston and Sumner streets. The lower floor and basement were occupied by a wholesale dry goods dealer. A company that dealt in hosiery, gloves, lace and similar small wares had the second and third stories, and the fourth and fifth floors were used by a corset and hoop skirt maker. The fire had started in the elevator engine room, which was located in the basement. It spread upwards, devouring the woodwork that lined the elevator shaft, before moving to the rest of the building. The flames roared as they climbed to the mansard roof, and within 10 minutes, fire was pouring from every window in the building.

Chief John Damrell heard the alarms and hurried from his home on Temple Street to reach the fire on foot. When he arrived, he immediately sounded a general alarm that summoned every firefighter in the city. At that point, only one piece of equipment – steamer 7 – had arrived and the men were battling the blaze alone. Steamers 4 and 10 arrived a few minutes later, pulled by men who already looked exhausted. The men from steamer 4 connected their pumper to a nearby hydrant and tried to hold the line in the face of searing heat, flying glass and exploding chips of stone. They risked their lives to try and extinguish a five-story building fire with hoses that only spit water as high as the fourth floor.

They fought valiantly until a massive block of granite smashed onto the sidewalk and severed the company's hose. As steamer 4 retreated, flames burst from the upper floors of the brick buildings across the alley. The heat was so intense that it passed through the brick walls of adjoining buildings and the fronts of warehouse on the opposite sides of the streets.

By 8:00 p.m., the fire had jumped across Sumner Street and was now being attacked by almost the entire Boston Fire Department. They knew that defeating the fire at the corner of Sumner and Otis streets was the only way they could keep it from raging out of control and destroying the city. Firemen on Otis dragged hoses up ladders while their comrades struggled up stairways to reach smoke-filled upper stories of buildings on Sumner. But as they turned on the nozzles from their hazardous locations, the men found almost no water pressure at all. Chief Damrell worked fast, ordering pumpers in other locations to be shut down in the vain hope that enough water pressure could be channeled to Sumner and Otis. Unfortunately, men who found themselves facing the searing flames at the shut-down locations had no protection from the heat and the flames. They cried for more water, but the water never came. Within minutes, the heroic battle at the corner of Sumner and Otis became futile. Chief Damrell sent telegrams asking for aid from any city or town within 50 miles of Boston. He feared the fire would engulf all of Boston if it continued burning out of control.

As the inferno burned through Devonshire, Federal, Congress and Pearl streets, firefighters from outlying towns rushed into Boston. The fire was sweeping east from where it started. To the south, the fire would eventually burn itself out on the city docks. To the north and east were the historic landmarks that stood in the heart of the city. Whatever it took, the fire had to be stopped before this section was destroyed. The broad avenues of Washington and State streets became the areas were the fire crews established their defense. Many of the men drenched the perimeter while others fought on Milk, Otis and other streets to try and slow the advancing flames.

Shortly after midnight, throngs of men descended on the mercantile blocks that were in the path of the fire. They were intent on removing the valuable goods from the warehouses and saving them from destruction. Piles of salvaged goods were dumped on the Boston Common, where hastily erected signs announced new locations where businesses would be resumed if the fire continued to spread. Many assembled to watch the chaos, some weeping, others apparently celebrating. As a precaution against the spectators getting out of hand, the rum shops were closed down.

Trinity Church caught fire and burned in minutes. The offices of the *Boston Transcript* were gutted. The editor, his writers and printers desperately attempted to save their type and important papers by rushing armloads to the basement, which housed the press, in the belief that the fireproof first story would offer some protection. It did, but only for a few hours. The blaze tore through the newspaper offices with such ferocity that all the entire building collapsed onto the first floor, caving it in and instantly reducing the printing presses to wreckage.

The fire threatened the granite sides of Boston's new post office building, alarming Postmaster General William L. Burt. While most other officials were so dumbfounded by the disaster that they failed to act, Burt took charge. He ordered all of the mail removed and placed it in the custom house, far away from the path of the fire. Hundreds of postal employees struggled with sacks of mail, dragging them down the streets and carting them on wagons and in carriages. Not one letter was lost to the blaze, and on Monday morning carriers were already in the streets and making deliveries – although most of the addresses they sought had been lost in the fire.

By 2:00 a.m. on Sunday, General Burt was convinced that drastic measures were needed to combat the fire.

A panoramic view of downtown Boston after the devastating fire.

After summoning the mayor and Chief Damrell to city hall, Burt held a meeting behind closed doors. He convinced the other men that explosives were needed to stop the spread of the flames to the north. They would create a firebreak and destroy anything along the line that could burn and add fuel to the fire. He left city hall with nine volunteers and the promise of enough gunpowder to meet his needs.

With assistance from engineers from the nearby Navy yard, General Burt secured three wagons filled with explosives and went to work. Reports were that as many as 15 buildings on Washington, Devonshire and Water streets were blown up to try and stop the spread of the fire. The explosions were not universally well received. While many considered Burt a hero, firefighters were less enthused. Most of them believed the explosions had done nothing to slow the fire. By noon on Sunday, Chief Damrell had revoked the authority to blow up any more buildings, including several on the south side of State Street that had already been mined with powder.

The fight against the encroaching flames continued on Washington Street during the early morning hours. As the sun was rising, buildings were still continuing to fall. The firefighters had managed to slow the inferno, but they hadn't stopped it. Many of the men gave their lives for the fight. A dozen firemen were killed during the battle and many more were injured.

By daybreak, the tide was starting to turn. With an army of engines battling on the north and torrents of water flowing through the charred streets, the firefighters saw a reason to hope when they managed to save the Old South Meeting House. As water was being sprayed over the lower roof, a burning fragment blew across the street and landed in the belfry. The roof was just beginning to burn when a steamer from Portsmouth, New Hampshire, came charging up Washington Street to lend assistance. The steamer had just arrived in the city on board a special train and the crew had rushed to the scene. Almost singlehandedly, they managed to save the historic structure.

Chief Damrell's original strategy was working. The eastward advance of the fire on Washington Street was stopped at the Old South Meeting House and the destruction was starting to slow. The new post office was next in line but it was saved. The building was made from granite, and suffered only minor damage.

The fire was now focused directly on State Street. After a 12-hour battle, the fire crews managed to beat back the flames two blocks to Devonshire and State streets. The fire had been burning all morning from the back of the Merchants Exchange building that fronted State Street. With pumpers from dozens of cities and towns throwing heaving streams of water on the roofs and walls, managed to knock the fire down. By Sunday evening, the crisis had passed.

The National Guard's ninth regiment and four companies of cavalry were called out to control the trainloads of spectators and bring about some order to the scene. They joined the Boston police in attempting to keep order – and it was good that they did for post-fire Boston was plunged into chaos.

Criminals descended on the city by the trainload. As soon as news of the fire was telegraphed to other cities, they began to arrive. While firemen were still attempting to contain the blaze, thieves intent on burglary skirmished with the police as they tried to enter the burning business district.

The reaction to the fire by the crowds was bizarre. While firemen, heroically trying to stem the blaze, were dying from smoke inhalation or were being crushed to death by falling walls, spectators enjoyed themselves. *Harper's Weekly* later reported:

> *Pressing against this line of police all the way around the sixty acres of ruin was a crowd of sight-seers peering curiously into the smoke and dust, pleading for passage through, or begging for some relic of the great fire; and beyond, in the streets nearby, on the piers on one side and the paths of the Common the other, strangers thronged unceasingly from morning till night, looking contented, interested and happy, watching the cavalry as they cantered by, examining the wares of itinerant peddlers on the Tremont Mall, studying the smoky sky through the big telescope, or trying the lung-testers – carrying themselves for all the world to see, rather than the destruction of a great section of a great city by fire.*

On Monday, the business district was a "broad plain of ruin." Spectators continued to arrive, filling the hotels and buying all sorts of odd souvenirs from street urchins. Pieces of twisted iron culled from the burned-out business district brought a nickel each. Broken pieces of crockery were sold, along with scraps of leather from the gutted shoe manufacturing district and even blackened hard-boiled eggs.

By the time the fire had been put out, flames had consumed more than 900 buildings. Estimates of the loss varied from $100 million to $150 million, but Bostonians took an optimistic view from the start. Unlike the Chicago fire, few homes were lost in Boston. The people of the city had lost warehouses and employment but dry goods and jobs were replaceable. The smoke was still clearing as decisions were being made about Boston's future. The post office would expand; new business would be developed; the narrow, crooked streets would be replaced by wide avenues and the city would become more modern.

And, like Chicago, a new city emerged from the ashes.

1877: THE MAKING OF HEROES
The Southern Hotel Fire

The morning of April 11, 1877 dawned clear and bright as the luxurious Southern Hotel in downtown St. Louis lay in ruins. The massive hotel had catered to the rich and famous for only eleven years before meeting its tragic end. At about 1:20 a.m., a hotel watchman found a burning pile of mattresses in the corner of a basement storeroom. Unable to extinguish the fire, it swept through the hotel with startling speed. Within 45 minutes, the fire had spread to every floor, and soon the entire building was engulfed. Fire will seek any means of moving quickly and unimpeded. This particular fire found an open elevator shaft next door to the storeroom. The elevator shaft acted as a chimney, carrying thick, toxic smoke into the upper hallways and corridors, and most critical of all, it provided the fire with easy access to all six floors of the hotel. As the fire took a firm hold throughout the building, few who held out hope of saving the hotel. All attention was soon directed toward saving those trapped inside "the hotel that almost wasn't."

Twenty years earlier, a group of affluent St. Louis citizens got together to discuss the need for a new hotel, a very special hotel. As St. Louis continued to grow, already populated with nearly 350,000 people, city fathers had their eyes on the future. In order for their city to grow in the direction most beneficial to them, they would need to draw in a higher class of visitors -- people with stature and money. They wanted St. Louis to become a prime

The Southern Hotel in St. Louis, one of the city's grandest lodging palaces.

destination for wealthy visitors and investors. To entice these visitors to remain, they would need an elegant place for their families and associates to stay while in the city.

A company was formed, money invested, land purchased, excavations completed, cellars constructed --- and then nothing. The project's momentum slowed, then it came to a halt. Some investors and interested parties suggested that the land be subdivided and sold to help recoup their expenditures. Before this could happen, however, a group from the development company persuaded the state legislature to grant a tax abatement for the first 10 years (yes, businessmen were wrangling for tax breaks even a hundred and fifty years ago) and the project was on again.

But the year was 1860 and more pressing concerns were about to take over as the country was ripped apart by the Civil War. Whether Missouri's future was to be with the Union or the Confederacy, St. Louis was determined to be a driving force and projects like the Southern Hotel would prove that to the rest of the country. Despite the many hardships caused by the war, including difficulties getting materials, transportation problems, lack of skilled laborers, funding limitations, and long delays in construction, the Southern Hotel was finally completed.

The grand opening of the Southern Hotel was held on December 8, 1865. Dignitaries and socialites from around the country and the world were in attendance at the elegant ball held for the occasion. What they saw was simply magnificent. The hotel was one of the largest in the country. It was six stories high (very tall for that time) and took up nearly a full block, fronting on four streets. Its exterior was in the Italianate style and on the inside the level of opulence was stunning. The public spaces had lofty ceilings of carved woodwork and gilt ornamentation. The furnishings were upholstered in velvet with gold tassels. The foot of the grand staircase opened in a wide arc under a fabulous rotunda, which would later become a popular meeting place for guests and visitors. The 361 guest rooms were equally beautiful, with every possible amenity for the convenience and comfort of the guests. On the sixth floor, along with some of the largest guest rooms, there were several smaller rooms that provided living quarters for many of the employees.

The hotel was a huge success; many people came to stay for no other reason than to see it. The hotel rapidly became so successful that its initial investors sold it to Colonel Robert Campbell less than a year after it opened. Campbell continued to operate the hotel until that fateful night in 1877 when all was lost to the fire.

Before the advent of the smoke detector, large public venues used watchmen to patrol less-traveled areas inside buildings. Their job was to watch for fires, alert others, and to work to put the fire out. The watchmen were not the only employees that were to be on the lookout for a fire; each employee was to watch for fires as they went about their regular duties. On the night of April 11, the Southern Hotel reportedly had fifteen employees on duty including seven watchmen in the cellars, a night clerk, two bellboys, two bootblacks and three watchmen on the second floor. If a fire was found, the plan was for the employee to immediately sound the alarm to his fellow employees. Together, they would put out the fire. If that was not possible, the desk clerk would use a special telegraph box that was connected directly to the fire department to call for help. In the meantime, the others on duty would spread out and alert everyone in the hotel of the fire and facilitate a rapid and safe evacuation.

Unfortunately, on this night, nothing worked as planned. By the time a watchman first found the fire, it was well beyond his power to extinguish, and the smoke had already spread into the upper corridors. Rather than notifying the staff of the danger, he instead tried to put the fire out himself. He was soon aided by other employees on duty, who had been alerted to the fire by the spreading smoke. Together, they worked for 20 or 30 minutes trying to contain the fire, while the hotel guests and off-duty employees slept, unaware of the impending disaster. When they finally acknowledged defeat, flames had reached all the way to the top of the building by means of the elevator shaft. To add to the deteriorating situation, the desk clerk was unable to notify the fire department because the special telegraph box put in place for just such an event was either missing or broken. Either way, it wasn't used, causing another 10-minute delay in sounding the alarm. As the fire had already spread to the upper floors, no one made it past the second floor to alert the sleeping guests and employees.

When the fire call finally went out, the first firemen arrived in only five minutes. They were accompanied by six engines and two hook and ladder companies, and were soon followed by the entire fire department. Fire Chief Sutton, one of the first to arrive, described seeing heavy smoke pouring from every level of the hotel, and flames coming from sixth-floor windows and shooting up through the roof. He notified his men that the building could not be saved; they were to work solely on rescuing the several hundred people believed to still be inside the hotel.

Inside the hotel, many guests were aroused from sleep not by the staff, but by the growing commotion in the hallways and the smell of smoke. One man however, Charles Kieffnict, the head waiter, was seen on the fifth floor running from room to

A *Leslie's Illustrated* sketch of firefighters battling the blaze at the Southern Hotel

room, waking people and spreading the alarm. Sadly he was never heard from again and his body was never recovered.

The Southern Hotel was the tallest building in that part of St. Louis and the flames were visible for miles. This brought out numerous spectators who had an unfortunate tendency to get in the way and hinder the efforts of the firemen. At one point, there was such a crowd blocking the street that a vital piece of rescue apparatus was completely covered under their feet, and it took several minutes to move the crowd back enough to put it into action. But not everyone was just there to watch. Several private citizens joined in the rescue efforts, some even bringing along their own ladders. Many instances of heroism were reported among these citizens and lives were saved due to their efforts. One such hero was Charles Tiernan, a popular member of the St. Louis sporting community. He lost his life trying to force his way into the building while rescuing a trapped group of people.

Firemen and police found their rescue efforts very difficult and dangerous because of the height of the building, making the upper two floors of the hotel inaccessible to their equipment. This problem was apparent to many of the people trapped on the upper floors. As panic set in and was escape seemingly cut off by the fire, people began to fall or jump from upper floor windows.

George Gouley, Grand Masonic Secretary of Missouri, was killed when he fell from his fourth-story window. His body fell into a burning area of the hotel, and his remains were found in the ruins days later. Similar stories played themselves out on all four sides of the hotel. Henry Hazen of New Castle, Pennsylvania, was killed after falling from his third-floor window onto Walnut Street. Three of the hotel's live-in housekeepers made their way from their tiny rooms on the sixth floor down to the fifth floor in the south wing. Once there, they found themselves trapped. They climbed out a window and leapt to their deaths together. At the same time, on the Fourth Street side of the building, Rev. A. Adams, a vicar from Berkshire, England, said a short prayer before plummeting from his fourth-story window.

Two women survived their dramatic falls. A lady whose last name was Scott was found unconscious and broken on the sidewalk, and was rushed to the nearest hospital. After two days at death's door, she rallied and eventually recovered. An actress named Frankie McClellen jumped from her fourth-story window, landing on the roof of a tavern abutting the hotel. She was reported as having sustained "a severe concussion of the brain and spinal cords. She also has cuts on her face and head, two penetrating wounds in the groin, a fractured rib, and several minor injuries." Though her injuries were severe, she survived her ordeal and returned to the stage a year later.

As bodies fell from the burning hotel, firefighters and police worked frantically to rescue those still trapped inside. They risked their lives by moving through any part of the building not yet burning, searching for survivors,

Ruins of the Southern Hotel

pulling them from their rooms, and escorting them to safety. One policeman heard two gunshots as he moved down a hallway checking rooms for people too afraid to leave. He ran to the room from which he heard the shots, where he found the bodies of a man and a woman lying dead on the floor. Police and firefighters stayed in the building until the floors began to collapse.

On the outside, rescues were problematic. The fire department's tallest ladder could reach only as high as the fourth floor windows, yet many people were still visible, leaning out of windows on the fifth and sixth floors. Some brave individuals took charge of saving their own lives and those of their families by fashioning ropes from bed sheets and lowering their wives and children to the floors below, or into waiting firemen's arms before climbing down themselves. J. H. Reese used a rope to lower his wife and two maids from their fifth-floor room to the fourth-floor level, where they were carried down ladders by waiting firemen. After the women were safe, Reese lowered himself to the ladder and to safety.

Many people were saved or saved themselves this way but at least two of these attempts ended in tragedy. W. S. Steward was in the process of lowering his wife, Jennie, with a rope made from their bed sheets, when the sheet ripped and she plummeted to the pavement below. On the Elm Street side of the building, Andrew Einstinan found himself alone in a room on the fifth floor. Fashioning his own rope of bed sheets, he climbed out over the edge of his windowsill, intending to lower himself to safety; instead, he too fell to his death.

As the fire raged on and terrified people still leaned from windows high above, two firemen found the courage to do to the extraordinary and thus distinguished themselves as heroes. Fireman Phelim O'Toole climbed to the topmost rung of the fire department's highest ladder on the Skinner Escape Truck (an early horse drawn hook and ladder truck). He called to guests on the floor above, and had them tie sheets to bed posts and lower the ends down to him. O'Toole was able to climb the sheets to the fifth floor. He then used more sheets to swing from window to window, pulling people from their rooms and lowering them to waiting firemen below on the ladder. In this way, he rescued 12 people from certain death. His last rescue came just minutes before the walls supporting that part of the hotel collapsed.

Miss Joanna Halpin, when testifying at the coroner's inquest, described her daring rescue by O'Toole after having to hold her head out the window in order to breathe: "That fireman Phelim O'Toole jumped into the room and I will never forget him. He was like an angel sent down from the very heavens to us. There didn't seem to be any escape for me. Still we hoped against hope, and the roof over our heads was all on fire."

Fireman Michael Hester, using the same technique as O'Toole, was able to get all the way up to the sixth floor, where he found eight women who worked for the hotel as domestic servants, huddled in one corner of a room. He lowered them, one by one, down two stories. They were each caught by waiting firemen and carried down the ladders to safety. Hester lowered himself to the ladder just as part of the roof and wall collapsed inward.

After the fire, most of the firemen agreed that if only those people who jumped to their deaths, rather than stay and die in the fire, had waited a while longer, they might all have been saved.

As the last of those to be rescued reached safety, the building began to crumble. No one knew how many had perished in the fire. The fire burned for so long and with such intensity that authorities believed the true number would never be known. The heat from the fire was so great that some of the bodies would be completely burned to ashes.

As the firemen and police were forced to retreat, unable to continue their rescue efforts, the only thing left to do was to work to contain the fire and keep it from spreading to surrounding buildings. One by one, the floors caved in and the walls collapsed, leaving a massive heap of smoldering debris.

The last person to die as a result of the fire was a man who had originally escaped relatively unharmed. William Felix Munster, a 28-year-old visitor from the Cork County, Ireland, fought his way through the flames to safety, only to find that his wife was still inside the hotel. After searching through the crowd for her for hours, he wandered to the home of a friend on the corner of Fourth and Olive streets, and locked himself in a bedroom. Munster became mentally deranged at the idea of losing his wife and sobbed uncontrollably for a time before shooting himself to death. His wife's body was never found.

As the sun rose on what was left of the hotel, huge crowds were forming at newspaper offices and police stations, waiting for more information. At the site of the fire, vast numbers of spectators paraded past the rubble, some worried about missing friends and family and others just wanting to bear witness to such a notable event in their city. Still others waited for hours in morbid curiosity, hoping to catch a glimpse of a burned body being pulled from the ruins.

The fire continued to burn through the following day. At 1:00 p.m., St. Louis Mayor Henry Overstotz ordered 100 men to begin the search for bodies after the unstable walls were pulled down to help protect the searchers. As the men moved slowly through the ruins of the grand hotel, the heat was at times unbearable. They were repeatedly forced to withdraw in order to douse hot spots and flare ups with water.

The first area ordered searched was at the base of the grand staircase, under the rotunda. As this was frequent used as a meeting spot, it was thought that it might also have served as a rallying place as families fled the flames, and many bodies were likely to be found there. Yet five hours into the search, only one tiny body was discovered. The head and feet had been burned away, but since it had been wrapped in the remains of a quilt, it was believed that the body was that of a child who had been asleep when the fire started and had most likely suffocated from the smoke. The child's remains must have fallen from one of the floors above when the floors collapsed.

The searchers had no idea how many bodies they would recover. The hotel's register had been lost in the fire so there was no way to determine who had not made it out alive. There was also no definite list of employees who had been staying in the hotel that night, as many may have gone home to sleep. It was also found that as some people made it to safety, they simply left the area and never returned. The police made repeated requests in the press pleading for anyone who had been in the hotel to please give their names as survivors. They also requested that anyone who was thought to be in the hotel during the fire but was not for some reason, including hotel employees, to do the same. Despite these requests, several guests and employees were never heard from, though they were not definitely determined to have died in the fire.

As the search progressed through the following days, more bodies were discovered. A set of remains were discovered on the third day under the fourth-floor balcony. The body was badly charred, with the face and two-thirds of the upper part of the head burned away completely. Nothing remained of either arm below the elbows and the legs were burned to a crisp, falling to cinders as the men tried to move the body. Enough of one breast was left intact to indicate the body was that of a woman. Most of her clothing was burned away but a bit of her dress remained. She was later identified as Abbie Clark, wife of H. J. Clark, who was also among the missing. A few hours after the discovery of Mrs. Clark's body, the body of a man was found five feet from hers. It was believed that this was her husband. Horribly burned, and without even the smallest remnants of clothing, the only means of identification were a pocket watch found next to his body. The child found early in the search was believed to be that of the Clarks' child but the child's nurse was never found.

Another "fragment of a male body" was believed to belong to H. S. Adams of Massachusetts. He was never positively identified but Adams' watch chain and keys were found nearby.

Over 300 people survived the fire, and each of them most assuredly had his or her own harrowing story, but quite possibly the strangest story of survival was that of J. C. Keeler of Cincinnati. Though he was originally thought to have perished, Keeler was later found to be among the survivors. He had made it safely out of the burning building and was watching from the street when a man on the sixth floor fired a gun out his window to draw the attention of rescuers. The ball struck Keeler in the head and he crumpled to the street. Fortunately, the ball had spent most of its energy by the time it struck him and he was not severely injured.

The Southern Hotel was a popular lodging place for actors appearing in local theatre productions. On the night of the fire, there were at least five actors in residence. Among them was Frankie McClellan, who was seriously injured after jumping from her fourth-floor window. Three other actors, Rose Osborne, M. P. Clinton, and Milton Nobles, all escaped unharmed but lost everything they owned in the fire. The most notable of these thespians, also a survivor of the fire, was Kate Claxton, whose most famous role was that of Louise in "Two Orphans." Just four months earlier, Miss Claxton was performing that role to a sold-out crowd in the Brooklyn Theater when it too caught fire, killing over 300 people. After surviving both fires, she was harassed by the press in articles and cartoons as being bad luck. Years later, she was to survive a third theater fire in Erie, Pennsylvania.

But these actors were troupers in every sense of the word. The night following the fire, all four were back at work, appearing in a play at the Olympic Theater. Three days later, they performed in a benefit dedicated to the five actors who survived the fire. Everyone from the actors to the orchestra donated their services. Mr. Spalding, owner of the Olympic and fellow survivor of the Southern Hotel fire, donated the use of the theater.

As the recovery efforts turned to cleanup efforts, the official number of those killed was 21. This number was determined based on the number of human remains recovered from the ruins and of those who jumped or fell to their deaths. The hotel reported that 20 of its employees failed to report back to work, and 38 guests remained unaccounted for in the days following the fire. It will never be known how many of those missing died in the fire, or simply left the scene to recover at home.

After all bodies had been removed, additional teams of searchers were hired to dig through the rubble, looking for any valuables that may have survived the fire. J. H. Morril of New York had left a jewelry sample case in his room with contents valued at over $17,000. He hired men to dig in the area below his room and they were able to recover about $600 worth of jewels. He then had three barrels packed with the ashes from the same area were the jewelry was found and shipped them back to his firm in New York to be melted down. A few other personal items were recovered but for others, it was a total loss.

A coroner's inquest was convened in which 92 people gave testimony. There were general complaints about the way the hotel handled the emergency including the time it took employees to alert the building's occupants. They also complained about the firemen seeming disorganized when they arrived. The official verdict was released to the public on April 27. Part of it read: "As to the cause of the fire, we have no testimony sufficient to base an opinion on, but from the dryness of the woodwork and the inflammable material in the storeroom, wine-room, and carpenter-shop, all situated in the basement of the hotel, it would have required only the slightest spark in a very few minutes, if not discovered, to have caused a fire of such magnitude as to be beyond ordinary control."

Fireman Phelim O'Toole, one of the heroes of the Southern Hotel fire, received a citation for bravery and a reward of $500 from the city of St. Louis. This was quite a significant sum as his monthly fireman's salary was $75. O'Toole donated the money to help the orphans of St. Louis. His career as a firefighter lasted only two more years. Answering an alarm for a small fire in the basement of an empty house, a fire extinguisher exploded in his hands and blasted into his chest, killing him instantly. Of O'Toole, Fire Chief Clay Sexton said: "He was one of the bravest men who ever lived. The bravest of the brave." St. Louis honored the bravery of O'Toole by naming its fire marine rescue unit's fireboat the "Phelim O'Toole" (the fireboat sunk following an accident).

Fireman Michael Hester, another hero of the Southern Hotel fire, had a long and distinguished career in the St. Louis Fire Department. Hester lived to age 89. He and O'Toole had saved 20 people from certain death in the early morning hours of April 11, 1877.

In honor of their bravery, Harry Banks wrote and published the song: "Phelim O'Toole Southern Hotel Fire Hero." He dedicated it to Phelim O'Toole and Michael Hester.

A book about St. Louis history that was published in 1883 contained the following description of the fire's aftermath: "The

Heroic firefighter Phelim O'Toole

Phelim O'Toole Southern Hotel Fire Hero
Respectfully Dedicated to Phelim O'Toole and Michael Hester of the St. Louis Fire Department
By Harry Banks

There's brav'ry in battle, when cannons resound,
And men who in shipwreck are steady and cool;
But never has an equal been found
To the courage and brav'ry of Phelim O'Tool.

He's brave and he's gallant without knowing why;
He cares not for science; he cares not for rule;
His philosphy's [sic] this: To save, he will die;
There is but one Phelim, and he's an O'Toole!

To save helpless women, at the word of command,
He bravely came forward, for duty he strived;
Ascending the ladder, his life in his hand,
Defying the fire fiend, while hope now survives.

Brave Phelim O'Toole mounts higher and higher,
And reaches the high elevation at last;
He bears fainting women from torturing fire
Down the perilous ladder the danger is past.

Full many an ev'ning these girls have all sought,
The angels of mercy in heavenly glow;
They never imagined, the never once thought,
An angel of safety would come from below.

The example of brav'ry, where can it be learned?
Who is the teacher? Where is the school?
Where can the highest position be earn'd?
Go take your first lesson from Phelim O'Toole!

He'll tell you in heaven he always relies,
And then calmly waits for duty to call;
When time comes for action, grim death he defies,
No dangers deter him, no terrors appall.

When others are losing their reasoning powers,
Be watchful and careful, be stead, keep cool;
Care not tho' ev'ry one falters and cow'rs,
But March boldly forward like Phelim O'Toole.

The sheet music for Phelim O'Toole, Southern Hotel Fire Hero (The lyrics to the song are to the left)

blackened ruins and the crumbling walls remained a ghastly memento of this awful disaster for two years..." A group of businessmen and concerned citizens gathered to develop a plan to rebuild the Southern Hotel. Using lessons learned from the destruction of the first hotel, the design for its replacement would be built of as many non-flammable materials as possible, with the most up-to-date means for detecting a fire, warning the guests and employees, and providing for the most rapid means of escape. After the building was completed, the builders pronounced the second Southern Hotel to be "the most thoroughly fire-proof hotel structure in the world."

The new Southern Hotel held its Grand Opening with a ball on May 11, 1881. The hotel remained one of the grandest in the Midwest for many decades until it was demolished to make way the most prosaic of structures -- a parking garage.

On one corner of the parking garage is a small bronze plaque that describes the brave actions of Phelim O'Toole in the early morning hours of April 11, 1877. This is the only thing left to mark the disaster that took place there unless, of course, you happened to be parking your car in the parking garage on one of the days when the smell of smoke is particularly strong. Is it a warning, or a memory? It's difficult to say for sure, but anyone who has taken the time to read that plaque as they walked away from the garage just might understand a little bit more than most.

There was one more possible remnant of the fire a few blocks away from where the hotel stood. For years after the fire, in a house on the corner of Fourth and Olive streets, sometimes late at night in the spring a man could be heard, sobbing uncontrollably. Then would come a bang, followed by silence. The house is long gone now, and we can only hope that William Munster is no longer lamenting the loss of his wife, and has found peace.

1883: "A SCENE OF WILDEST CONFUSION"
The Newhall House Hotel Fire

The six-story, 300-room Newhall House Hotel in Milwaukee, Wisconsin, was a veritable death trap. Built from brick in 1857 with an interior of wood, it had a myriad of partitions and a maze of hallways to confuse guests who were unfamiliar with the building's layout. If that weren't enough, there were only two fire escapes. These design flaws assured the deaths of 71 people when a started on the morning of January 10, 1883. The flames raced up an elevator shaft, and destroyed most of the hotel. The building had been so poorly constructed that none of the local insurance agents would issue it a policy.

The tragedy came as no surprise to William E. Cramer, editor of the *Wisconsin* newspaper. Cramer had the bad luck to be inside the hotel when it caught fire, and was badly burned. Ironically, he had once written that the hotel was "doomed if it ever got on fire in the night."

What may come as no surprise to some is the lingering haunting that surrounds the site of the former hotel, and the fact that many of the victims refuse to rest in peace.

If we ignore history's warnings, we tend to make the same mistakes over and over. This was the case of the fire that destroyed the Newhall House Hotel in 1883. The owners of the hotel should have taken warning from the fires that had already occurred on the property. One of the structures that stood on the site before the elegant Newhall House was the lavish, rambling, United States Hotel, which was gutted by a blaze in 1854. The hotel was a death trap, constructed totally from wood. It offered almost no escape for those trapped in the building on the night of the fire. It burned to the ground, leaving charred remains behind.

Three years after the fatal blaze, Milwaukee's leading financier, Daniel Newhall, ordered the construction of what he believed was the most impressive hotel in the Midwest. The result was the previously mentioned Newhall House, a six-story building of

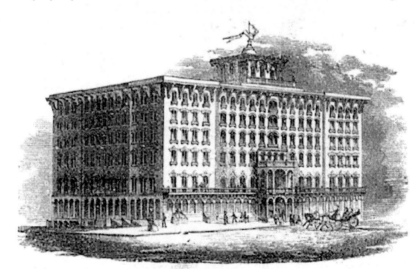

Milwaukee's Newhall House

cream-colored brick. The interior was handsomely carpeted and decorated with thick oak paneling with gold-painted trim. Despite its elegant appearance, the hotel was, according to one account, "a regular tinderbox." The partitions that created a maze of hallways in the building were not filled in with bricks to create a firewall, the woodwork was "exceedingly dry," and there were only two fire escapes – which were nearly inaccessible. When a fire started in the kitchen and raced to the hotel's roof on January 10, 1880, almost $7,000 damage was done to the top north section of the structure. After that, local insurance agents refused to insure the building.

Three years to the day after the first Newhall House fire, a blaze began at about 3:30 a.m. at the bottom of the one of the elevator shafts. The flames shot upward and swept across the roof. In the initial minutes after the fire's discovery, no alarm was issued. The owner had given strict instructions not to arouse the guests in the event of another fire because the one in 1880 – which turned out to be minor – had caused considerable panic. This "no alarm" policy eventually led to the loss of many lives.

An alarm was not sent out to the fire department until after 4:00 a.m. By that time, the entire six stories were burning. When firemen, accompanied by a huge, unruly crowd, arrived at the hotel, there was little they could do to help the guests who cried out from the windows, where flames and smoke billowed out behind them. Telegraph wires that had been thickly strung around the hotel impeded the rescue work and served as deadly snares for those who were either brave enough – or terrified enough – to jump.

Leslie's Illustrated described the horrifying scene:

A scene of the wildest confusion ensued. The unfortunately inmates were in many cases only aroused from their slumbers by the noise of the flames, and found their escape already cut off. Men, women, and children rushed up and down the halls in the dense suffocating smoke, missing in their frantic efforts the stairways and windows leading to the fire escapes. In despair many leaped from the windows of their rooms to the pavement several stories below, although such a leap meant death or shattered limbs. A few leaped upon an outstretched canvas held by citizens, but only to receive fatal injuries. The maze of telegraph wires encircling the building on the south and east sides played sad havoc with those who made the frightful leap for life. Several of the bodies were cut deep into by wires and then the torn and bleeding forms dropped to the ground. Others struck the wires crosswise, rebounded, and were hurled to the ground with a dreadful crash.

A newspaper sketch of the Newhall House during the blaze.

The helpless firemen were stunned and shocked by the grotesque heaps of mangled bodies that were beginning to form on the street. As they tried to prevent more guests from leaping to their deaths, one of the firefighters pointed to a group of figures that had appeared on the roof. Several dozen hotel employees, mostly cleaning women who occupied rooms on the top floor, lined the roof, pleading for rescue.

But there was no way to reach them.

The hotel roof was burning out of control.

Before the flames engulfed the women, many of them jumped from the edge, plunging downward toward the alley. Rescuers rushed to the scene, only to find a mound of writhing, broken-limbed women, all of whom died within minutes.

More than a dozen waitresses and other female employees were trapped in a wing on the sixth floor. Their plight seemed helpless until two heroic firemen, Edward Ryemer and Herman Strauss, appeared on the roof of the bank building located across an alley the hotel. Both firemen had tried to reach the upper floors of the burning building with an extension ladder that had been brought to the scene by their company, but the ladder could not be extended to that height. Abandoning the idea, the two men broke into the bank and ran up the stairs carrying a ladder. Strauss later stated that he almost went mad hearing the "shrieking and calling for help." He and Ryemer used the ladder to make a bridge between the two buildings. It slid sharply from the roof of the bank and smashed into a window of the hotel.

Strauss scrambled across the precarious bridge. Below him, thousands watched and loudly cheered. While Ryemer held the ladder steady, Strauss pulled a woman onto his back and crawled slowly across the ladder to the roof of the bank. He made twelve trips across the ladder, each time bringing back a woman dressed in badly singed nightclothes.

It wasn't long before the end of the ladder began to burn and Strauss knew that he could not make many more trips before the whole thing went up in flames. During the final trip, as he was crawling across the ladder, the woman on his back fainted, slipped off his back, and began to fall. Amazingly, Strauss reached out and snagged her by the ankle. She dangled there in mid-air as the spectators below gasped in disbelief. With what must have been a herculean effort, he managed to pull her back up onto the shaking bridge and dragged her to the safety of the bank's roof. Strauss' feats that night earned him the respect of the entire fire department, and the people of Milwaukee. He received honors and awards for years to come.

Fire Company No. 1 had many heroes that day. A fireman named Van Haag dashed into the hotel and ran to the top floors, knowing that the guests lodged there were in the most danger. As groups of terrified people groped their way along the dark, smoke-filled and maze-like hallways, Van Haag appeared, shouting to them and directing them to safety. When confused guests questioned his ability to get them out, he yelled back at them, "If you value your lives, you'll follow me!" Most of them did, and he led them to the almost-hidden fire escapes.

It was Van Haag who was credited with saving the lives of P.T. Barnum sideshow star General Tom Thumb (Charles Sherwood Stratton) and his wife, Lavinia. The celebrated little person was staying at the Newhall House that night, preparing for a show with his troupe the following day. Van Haag burst into the Strattons' suite and swept up Charles and Lavinia. He carried them under his arms down a burning hallway to a fire escape. The celebrities were safe, although one of the members of their troupe died of smoke inhalation.

For almost two hours, as the hotel was being devoured by flames, Van Haag continued his rescue work until he was killed by the fire. His end was spectacular. In full view of those who lined the streets below, a wall collapsed, and the fireman rode it downward, holding a screaming child in his arms. As chunks of brick, plaster, and wood toppled onto the telegraph wires, Van Haag still had the presence of mind to toss the child into an outstretched section of canvas that was held by his fellow firefighters. The child was saved. Van Haag crashed to the ground, having seemingly escaped injury until two telegraph poles, their wires tangled into the debris, fell on top of him, crushing and killed the courageous father of nine children.

Seventy other people lost their lives in the inferno, including Milwaukee business leader Allen Johnson and his wife, who jumped to their deaths from the third floor window of their room; New York businessman Thomas E. Van Leon; James Vose, respected government engineer; and – most tragically – 43 people who were never identified. Their bodies were later buried at Milwaukee's Forest Home Cemetery.

The Newhall House Hotel was lost on that day, but it lived on for many years as one of the deadliest hotel fires in American history. But is that the only way the story of the hotel lived on? Some don't believe so; they believe that some of the victims of the fire have remained behind at the place where they met their untimely ends.

The Ardor Pub & Grill opened on North Broadway in Milwaukee long after the doomed hotel had become a footnote in the city's history. Soon, staff members and customers began to realize that strange things were going on in the bar. According to Allison Jornlin, who conducts research into Milwaukee's haunted history, as well as ghost tours of the area, waitresses at the Ardor Pub claimed to report strange noises – voices, knocks and footsteps – that could not be explained. They also told her of seeing weird streaks of light in their peripheral vision. When they turned to see what was there, the place was always empty.

Did the tremendous loss of life that occurred at the site of the fire in 1883 leave an indelible mark on the history of Milwaukee? It seems that it did. History is not the only thing that reminds of mistakes that were made in the past – sometimes the spirits are just as eager to make sure that we never forget.

1900: GHOSTS OF THE BURNING SHIP
The Hoboken Docks Fire

On a Saturday afternoon in June 1900, a smoldering fire in a stack of cotton bales ignited 100 barrels of whiskey on a Hoboken, New Jersey, pier. The inferno that followed set fire to four ocean liners that were tied up at the docks. The unbelievable fire burned the ships, along with the piers and dozens of other boats and barges. More than 300 people were killed and scores of others were badly injured.

One of the most badly damaged ships – which also saw the greatest loss of life – was the *S.S. Saale*, a steamer that somehow managed to survive the blaze and return to sea as an American cargo ship. During the next two decades of her existence, though, strange tales haunted her decks and sailors came to believe that the dead of the Hoboken fire had never found peace.

The Saturday when death came to Hoboken was a beautiful, sunny day. It was June 30, 1900, and the area was filled with tourists who flocked to the waters that lapped against the Jersey shoreline. In 2001, 111 years and a few months later, people would come to the same shoreline to see the destruction of the World Trade Center, just a short distance across the water in Manhattan. But on this day, they would bear witness to destruction of another kind.

Groups of smiling vacationers climbed aboard four large ships tied to the docks belonging to the German Lloyd Line. Most of the ships' crew members were ashore on leave, but hundreds of carpenters, longshoremen, stewards and stewardesses were busy preparing the vessels for departure. Mingling among the passengers and

The *Kaiser Wilhelm der Grosse*, one of the ships that burned at the Hoboken docks

crew were New Yorkers who had come over from Manhattan with their families for an afternoon "open house" on the luxury liners.

At Pier 2 was the liner *Main*, which had completed her maiden voyage just a few months before. Next to her was the pride of the German commercial fleet, the *Kaiser Wilhelm der Grosse*. The 648-foot-long ship had set the Atlantic crossing record at five days, 17 hours and eight minutes. Tending to these two ships, along with the other two vessels, were 18 canal boats and barges laden with oil, cotton, coal and gasoline.

On Pier 3, where the two other Lloyd Line ships, *Saale* and *Bremen*, were docked, workers had stacked a tremendous number of cotton bales. They towered above the wooden piers, looming next to 100 barrels of whiskey that were waiting to be loaded aboard one of the ships. Somewhere in the huge pile of cotton bales, a fire began to smolder. What started it – perhaps a careless cigarette or match – was never discovered. At 3:55 p.m., a small fire had taken hold, and soon a huge column of yellow and red flames began shooting upward from the cotton bales. As the fire spread, it swept into the stacks of whiskey barrels, and they also began to burn. The whiskey ignited with an explosive whoosh and the docks began to burn. The flaming whiskey rolled like a fireball, devouring the wooden docks and rushing toward a group of panicked longshoremen who had been hard at work just moments before. The workers cried out as they rushed toward the end of the pier. As they ran, the flames swept along with them, behind, beside and finally, in front of them, cutting off their escape. In seconds, they were overtaken by fire and smoke.

The shooting flames and billowing smoke began to rise, causing the more than half-million bathers and sightseers that normally lined the Manhattan and Jersey shores on such days to hurry to view the spectacle. For most, it was an exciting interlude during an otherwise uneventful afternoon. But beneath the clouds of dark smoke and colorful flames, people were roasting to death.

All of the German ships had caught fire. Flames that reached more than 100 feet high jumped from Pier 3 to Pier 2, then on to Pier 1, belonging to the Thingvalla shipping line. Great storehouses, which had been built at a cost of $1.5 million, were gutted in less than nine minutes. Flames raced up the wooden gangplanks and swept onto the decks of the *Saale, Bremen, Main* and *Kaiser Wilhelm*.

It was soon clear that only *Kaiser Wilhelm*, her decks loaded with hundreds of sightseers, had a chance to escape the inferno. Her bow was in flames as hundreds of tugs from both shores hurried to her rescue. A dozen lines were tossed up to the ship's crew. The tugboats began to pull the ship away from the flames. Fire still swept across the ship, setting the stern ablaze. Despite the screams of the terrified tourists, the crew bravely stood their posts. Some of the officers beat down the flames with their uniform jackets as the sailors doused the fire with buckets of water. None of them ran for safety. To further illustrate the kind of discipline seen on board *Kaiser Wilhelm*, reports circulated that her captain stood stoically on the bridge, a pistol in each hand, uttering not a word or command. He didn't need to: his men knew what to do. No lives were lost that day aboard the *Kaiser Wilhelm* ship.

It was a different story on the other three liners. None of them had been able to push away from the dock in time, and all of them were soon burning from stem to stern. Tugboats, manned by stubborn, valiant seamen, hovered about them, attempting to draw them away from the pier. Tragically, many of the tugs caught fire, too. One of the supply ships, loaded with gasoline, drifted off and sailed into a Manhattan pier, which caught fire. Luckily, the flames were quickly extinguished.

The tugboat *Nettie Tice* was almost swamped as she pulled 104 people from the burning *Bremen*, at the same time trying to drag the ship into deeper waters. The tug *Westchester* rescued 40 men from the *Saale* as that ship, too, was hauled away from the doomed pier. Nothing could be done for the *Main*, which was consumed by fire. Several tugs tried in vain to pull her away from the docks, but she was stuck fast. The ship was thoroughly gutted, and by nightfall, her hull was glowing with an eerie red color.

Then the horror truly began.

Hands and faces began to appear at the portholes of the *Saale, Bremen* and *Main* – portholes that were much too small for anyone to climb out. Passengers were trapped below decks by the fires above them and searched desperately for a way off the blazing ships. The men on the tugboats on the ocean below looked at them helplessly, unable to climb aboard and bring them to safety. As a woman appeared at a porthole on the *Main* one

A newspaper photo of the Hoboken docks during the blaze.

of the men tried to save her by tossing a rope onto the ship's deck. He clung to the steaming side of the ship and inched toward the porthole as his companions sprayed water over him. The flames burned through the rope, and he fell, just moments before the woman in the porthole was swallowed by fire and smoke.

She did not die alone on the ship. Scores of passengers perished and below the decks, stokers, engineers and stewards died miserably, waiting for death as flames roared over the heads and then ate through the decks to devour them.

It was the same on the *Saale*. Dozens of pathetic figures appeared at the portholes, unable to escape. Women and children waved frantically for help, but there was nothing that could be done for them. Twenty tugs fought desperately to put out the fires on the ship. More than 100 men climbed on board with hoses and axes. Some of them doused the decks with water, while others chopped at the wooden decks, hoping to cut their way to those who had tried to find a safe place below. The tugboat men ripped away rails and pulled helplessly at those reaching through the portholes, trying to yank them through holes through which no one could fit.

It took three hours for those trapped on board the *Saale* to die. Men on the decks and in the tugboats went mad with their inability to save anyone. One tug captain broke down and wept, bitterly shouting as each face disappeared into the flames behind the portholes: "My God, my God, will it never stop?"

By this time, hundreds of thousands of people on board ferries and lining the shore were watching the disaster in shock. People screamed, cried, fainted and took photographs of the deadly scene. Others behaved more curiously, like an excursion boat loaded with students who had returned from Poughkeepsie, N.Y., that afternoon. They insisted that their ship's band provide musical accompaniment to the nightmare before them.

The fire on *Kaiser Wilhelm* was extinguished with only minimal damage. Her captain could not bear to watch his sister ships go down in flames, so he jammed his guns in his pockets, went into his cabin and locked the door. He wept there in private.

His close friend, Captain Mirow of the *Saale*, was already dead, burned on his bridge as he vainly tried to save his ship, which eventually came free from the docks, drifted and ended up grounded in the mud off Ellis Island. It was still smoking and smoldering hours later.

The *Bremen*, on which dozens of people burned to death below decks, went aground on the Jersey side, just below Weehawken. The ship continued to burn into the night, aided by the same southwest winds that had helped to spread the flames on the piers.

The piers and the docks burned into the night, casting a flickering light that could be seen from miles away above the city of Hoboken. Then, at 11:00 p.m., a small miracle occurred that, for a moment, lessened the impact of the tragedy. Even though the *Main* was sunk at her dock and all hope had been lost, the captain of a tugboat that happened to be passing by her saw a small oil torch signaling from the dead ship. Coming alongside, the tugboat crew heard knocking on the hull and immediately began cutting into the metal. Fifteen men had somehow survived inside of what must have been an oven. For eight hours, they had hidden in an empty coal bunker in the deepest bowels of the ship. The heat was so intense that all but one of the men lost consciousness. The sole crewmen who was still conscious managed to get his scorched arm through a porthole and signal for help with the oil lamp. They were cut out of their oven within the hour and only one of them, an elderly seaman, was seriously injured – he had gone blind from the incredible heat.

The bodies of the dead began to be collected the following day. There were 65 dead on the *Saale*, dozens more on the *Bremen*, scores on the *Main* and myriad corpses were found floating in the sea. Searchers found 34 bodies bunched together at a single bend in the river. One account stated, "There were those who had died on the decks when another step would have meant safety; there were those of whom but a bone remained. Some have been sadly charred; some were not even blemished... A little heap of white ashes told the whole pitiful story better than words."

A rough, conservative count of the dead reached as high as 326, with more than 250 injured, but most authorities believed the numbers were much higher. To this day, it remains one of the most disastrous nautical fires in history.

As the newspapers spread the story of the Hoboken disaster, officials of the Lloyd Line were stunned. But with taciturn deliberation, their public statement announced, "We will rebuild our piers. This time, we use steel."

And they were true to their word. The Hoboken piers were replaced with larger, stronger and more fireproof structures – each constructed from steel. The new piers were known as Hoboken Pier Numbers 1, 2 and 3. Unbelievably, all the damaged ocean liners were returned to maritime service. The *Saale*, which saw the greatest number of deaths, sailed under a different name, the *S.S. J.L. Luckenbach*.

The ship was rebuilt, fitted with new engines and turned into a cargo ship of American registry in 1902. She became known as an unlucky ship – and a haunted one. Over the course of the next two decades, strange stories were told by the men who worked aboard the vessel. Eerie voices and screams were heard from empty corridors and passageways, and disembodied footsteps were also reported. According to reports, apparitions of sailors and men and women wearing civilian clothing were sometimes seen lurking in various corners of the ship. But perhaps the most disturbing incident – which sailors believed was directly connected to the ghosts of the Hoboken pier fires – occurred on October 19, 1917, during World War I. The *J.L. Luckenbach* was carrying a load of cotton in the North Atlantic when it came under fire from a German submarine for three hours. The attack set the cargo on fire. An American destroyer, *U.S.S. Nicholson*, arrived on the scene and drove off the U-boat, then helped to extinguish the fire and make repairs to the ship. When the convoy that the *Nicholson* was escorting caught up to the two ships, the *Luckenbach* followed and made it safely to France two days later.

During the fire on the ship, sailors on board the *Luckenbach* claimed that they heard screaming coming from what turned out to be an empty hold. As smoke and flames swept across the deck, images of what appeared to be women in long, burning dresses ran past the crew and vanished. A few on board who knew the story of the terrible fire believed the figures were the ghosts of those who had perished on board more than 20 years before.

Perhaps most eerie of all, though, were the reports from those on the *Nicholson* who had come to the aid of the burning ship. Sailors who came aboard to help fight the fire hurried below decks and were puzzled because they found no passengers there. When they were asked who they were searching for, they told the men on the

Luckenbach that they had seen women waving for help from the portholes on the sides of the ship!

The ship never really recovered from its "unlucky" reputation. Despite continued efforts to re-name her – she became the *S.S. Princess* in 1922 and the *S.S. Madison* in 1923 – the ship was finally broken up at Genoa in June 1924.

1908: CLEVELAND'S GREATEST SHAME
The S.S. Kresge Fireworks Explosion

One of the greatest tragedies in the history of Cleveland, Ohio, occurred on July 3, 1908. It is a date that is largely forgotten today but for those who suffered through the S.S. Kresge fireworks explosion and fire, it was a horrific nightmare that they lived over and over again for the rest of their lives. They would forever recall the fiery holocaust that brought death to seven, injuries to dozens of others, and a day of horror, tragedy, heroism and shame to the city of Cleveland.

In the aftermath of the explosion and fire, the newspapers of the era created a cast of characters – some tragic, some heroic – to tell the human side of the horrible disaster. The stage was set for the fateful day during the early morning hours, when sisters Anna and Freda Trefall rose at 6:00 a.m. in order to be at work on time. They were scheduled to arrive at the S.S. Kresge store at 2025 Ontario Street where they were employed as sales clerks before the store opened at 9:00 a.m. sharp. Anna, 24, and Freda, 17, were very close – a fact that would be proven during the terrifying day to come.

Ed Bolton also rose early that day. Bolton was a shipping clerk at the W.P. Southworth grocery store, located next door to S.S. Kresge. He had a huge stack of orders that needed to be processed before the July 4 holiday, and expected to be at his desk most of the day.

Mary Hughes' job as an assistant to a downtown dressmaker would also take her to Ontario Street that morning. She had run out of some fabric, and S.S. Kresge was the best place to buy it.

Luther Roberts was the janitor at the Ontario Street Kresge store. From all accounts, Roberts was a quiet, self-effacing man who worked hard and mostly kept to himself. Few of the other employees at the store knew him well, but they would soon have cause to think of him with great admiration. His incredible courage that day would win him fame throughout the city.

Winifred Duncan also worked at Kresge's. She was excited when she arrived for work that morning. Only 18, she was one of many teenaged clerks at the five and dime store. She usually sold postcards on the first floor but today, she had a special assignment, oe that would cause her to leave a permanent mark on the history of Cleveland.

Jimmy Parker, the four-year-old son of George and Minnie Parker of Hampden Avenue, was also excited that morning. George had promised Jimmy that he could join in the noisy fireworks celebration at the Parker home the next day. But first, Jimmy had to go shopping downtown with his mother. Their destination was the S.S. Kresge store.

The store occupied the first two floors of a four-story building on Ontario Street. There was a restaurant in the basement and offices on the third and fourth floors. In the center of the store, towards the back, there was a stairway that led to the second floor. It divided halfway into right and left landings. The left side had stairs that led to the store's upper floor. On the right side, a balcony stretched out over the right rear of the store, forming a mezzanine where the manager's office was located. The second floor had wide windows at the front and back. The front windows overlooked Ontario Street, and the rear ones led to a fire escape over an alley. The store seemed to be a safe enough place – except for one small thing. There was a rear exit that was accessible from the left side of the stairs, but even though it looked identical, there was no rear exit on the right. The mezzanine ended at a set of three windows, which were partially blocked with temporary shelving and secured with steel bars, iron netting and sheet-iron doors to prevent break-ins from the alley. Under normal circumstances, this would not have been a problem, but if someone was in a hurry to get out of the back of the store and turned down the right hallway instead of going up the stairs to the left, it might mean the difference between life and death.

Because of the confusion of the fire, no one really knows the exact sequence of events as they occurred that day. It is known, however, that at about 10:50 a.m., Minnie Parker and her son, Jimmy, entered the store. Jimmy was drawn by the sight of Winifred Duncan, who was demonstrating a sparkler near the store's front window. D.E. Greene, the store manager, had asked her to do so, assuring her that sparklers were "harmless." Winifred stood in a three-foot-wide aisle that separated the postcard department where she usually worked from the holiday display of firecrackers, Roman candles, rockets and sparklers. This incendiary bounty was typical of the array of fireworks stocked by discount stores during the early twentieth century, an era of virtually unregulated Independence Day mayhem.

While Jimmy and Minnie Parker were watching Winfred cheerfully waving her sparkler, Greene was in his office with cashier Celia Zak, looking through the day's mail. Fannie Frank, from Collinwood, was shopping on the second floor with her four-year-old granddaughter, Grace. Mary Hughes, the dressmaker's assistant, was perusing the goods in the sewing section on the second floor. Ed Bolton was next door at the Southworth Company, working on his orders. Carrie Bubel, 18, was working at her sales counter on the second floor. Erma Schumacher was pacing the floor, keeping an eye on the 50 or so clerks who worked there. Although only 18, Erma had recently been promoted to floorwalker, and it was widely known that she aspired to rise even higher in the company's ranks. Muriel Mayes, one of the second floor clerks was also at her counter. Freda Trefall was there too, while her sister, Anna, worked downstairs. A cleaning woman named Mary Podowski was waiting for change from the $20 bill that she had just handed a clerk. Andrew Lempke was on a ladder trimming lamps on the first floor. The key players in the drama had unwittingly taken their places. Staff pianist Hazel Thompson, one of several pianists employed by Kresge to demonstrate sheet music for the customers, launched into a popular tune by songwriter Harry Williams: "Turn Up the Lights; I Don't Want to Go Home in the Dark."

To the tinkling sounds of the piano, hell arrived at the five and dime store.

The tragedy began near the front door, where Winfred had the bright, sputtering firework in her hand. Jimmy was transfixed by the sight but Minnie was not too sure about it. Winifred soothed her fears, repeating what she had been told by her manager: The sparkler was "perfectly harmless." A moment later, as she turned sideways to let Minnie and Jimmy pass her in the aisle, Winifred accidentally brushed against an American flag hanging above one of the fireworks displays. Sparks from the firework in her hand ignited the fabric of the flag, which in turn set fire to Mrs. Parker's dress. As the two terrified young women attempted to put out the flames, sparks fell onto the adjacent boxes of fireworks, and explosions erupted from the display. A burst of flame shot upwards to the ceiling and colorful streamers of fire flew in every direction. The store contained almost $30,000 worth of fireworks and, within seconds, the entire stock ignited in an inferno of blazing colors, thick smoke and terrifying explosions. In less than a minute, the entire first floor was a fiery deathtrap, with more than 200 employees and customers frantically searching for a way out of the store.

Max Zucker, a customer on the first floor, was near one of the fireworks displays when the explosion occurred. He later told a newspaper reporter that he had been looking at a box of sparklers when "I heard a sputtering noise – a skyrocket whizzed past my face and darted over the heads of the crowd and set fire to combustible materials on the counters. People around me stood aghast for a few seconds. A giant cracker exploded with a roar that set all into a mad dash for the front and rear exits."

The fire spread with shocking speed, setting merchandise ablaze as it leapt from counter to counter, aisle to aisle, throughout the entire store. The *Cleveland Plain Dealer* wrote, "Big piles of fireworks exploded and added to the noise and confusion. Giant crackers pounded and boomed, skyrockets whizzed through the crowded room, roman candles sputtered and flashed. It was a mimic battle, magnificent if it had not been so full of terror and death."

On the blazing first floor, customers fled in three directions. Those near the front headed for the Ontario Street exit. Those toward the rear rushed to the staircase to escape the flames, and then turned toward the right and left landings, which they believed would lead them to safety. This was true of the exit to the left, which led to an unlocked door to the alley but the corridor on the right led only to the rear of the store and to the barred windows that were blocked by shelving.

Things were better for those already on the second floor. When it became apparent that the first floor was on fire, the customers rushed to the front and rear windows, the elevator and the staircase. The elevator was not working, and it was immediately abandoned after one attempt to use it. Most of the shoppers and clerks fled to the front and back windows and most survived, although they were certainly injured and traumatized. Those who tried to escape down the stairs did not fare as well. The crush and hysterical panic of people trying to come up and go down the stairs at the same time caused a collision of screaming, suffocating women, girls and children on the stairs, the landing and on the ground floor. All of them were pulled out or managed to get free, only to stagger into the inferno on the first floor.

The fire department was immediately called to the scene and arrived soon after the fire began. Even so, by the time the fire companies arrived, Kresge's was already a blazing pyre, with smoke pouring out of every door and window. Employees and customers were running out of the exits, and frightened women were leaping out of the second floor windows. Firemen quickly deployed ladders and nets. The nets saved lives, but could not prevent some terrible injuries. Because of the heavy smoke, many of those who jumped could not clearly see the nets below and misjudged, plummeting past them and landing on the pavement instead. A number of people jumped at the same time, injuring each other and bringing the nets crashing to the sidewalk.

Little Jimmy Parker had disappeared into the interior of the store during the first few panicky moments after the explosion. Minnie, although badly burned, frantically searched for him until a rescue crew pulled her from the store. She was told that her son had been pulled alive from the store, and so she was persuaded to leave and go home. By the time she got there, her husband had already identified Jimmy's corpse at the county morgue.

D.E. Greene, the store manager, did his best in the disaster. As he was in the middle of sorting mail, an exploding firecracker alerted him to the danger. He immediately seized Celia Zak and rushed her to safety outside on Ontario Street. He then returned and tried to save others from the fire until the flames and smoke forced him out to the street for good.

The hero of the fire, though, was Luther Roberts, the store's janitor. Realizing that the elevator was useless, he began to smash open the windows on the second floor. He then went to the fatal staircase, which was clogged with screaming, panicked people and began to drag them out, bodily carrying women to the back windows on the second floor and shoving them out onto the fire escape. He returned to the staircase over and over again until finally, the heat and the smoke drove him back. He was "blinded and dizzy," he told the newspapers, but somehow, he had cleared everyone from the staircase.

Roberts' courage, if not his fate, was matched by that of Anna Trefall. When the fire started, Anna was working with several clerks on the first floor. Her companions immediately seized her and tried to drag her out with them onto Ontario Street. But Anna resisted, screaming that she had to find her sister. She broke away from them and ran back into the store, determined to get up the staircase to find Freda on the second floor. Her first attempt to make it up the stairs failed. The hysterical sea of bodies pushed her back toward the Ontario Street exit. But she again freed herself from the crowd and resumed the search for her little sister. Meanwhile, Freda was trying to get out of the smoke and fire on her own. She was the last person to make it down the stairs from the second floor but was overwhelmed by the mass of bodies at the bottom of the stairs. An eyewitness saw Anna try to pull Freda out toward the Ontario Street exit, but then saw both sisters go down the right-hand corridor where the manager's office was located.

There was no way out.

Anna and Freda died with the rest of those who had been trapped by the barred windows at the end of the mezzanine, their arms around each other's necks. Freda's face was so distorted by fear that her fellow employees were at first unable to identify her corpse.

Mary Hughes died along with them. The dressmaker's assistant was in the wrong place at the wrong time that day. She survived the crushing pile-up on the stairs, only to die with the others by the three barred windows.

Ed Bolton also proved to be a hero that day. After hearing the alarm raised, he ran into the burning building to help. He dragged several people out of the store and then crawled back inside on his hands and knees to search for others, until the smoke and flames finally drove him out again. He then helped hold nets for those who jumped from the second floor. His bravery nearly got him killed. As a girl prepared to leap from an upper window, she opened her umbrella like a parachute to aid in breaking her fall. By the time Ed shouted at her to not worry about the umbrella, it was already too late. As the young woman landed in the net, her umbrella struck Ed's arm, breaking it and forcing him to seek a doctor. But it was impossible to keep Ed Bolton down. After having his arm set, he returned home to change out of his wet clothing and then resumed work shipping out orders for the Southworth Company.

Fifty-year-old Fannie Frank was another heroine of the fire. On the second floor with her granddaughter, Grace, Mrs. Frank quickly led the child to a window and out onto a ledge. From there she jumped, holding onto Grace so as to shield her from the impact of the fall. Fannie was injured when she hit the ground, but Grace came through the ordeal unscathed.

Erma Schumacher, the newly promoted floorwalker, also died in the blaze. When the fire started, she tried to calm the panicking employees, but to no avail. Her body was discovered near the barred windows, where the Trefall sisters and Mary Hughes was also found.

Muriel Mayes, a second-floor clerk, was one of the first to escape from the upper floor. At first, she thought the explosions downstairs were the work of mischievous boys setting off fireworks in the street outside, but she eventually made her way to the front windows, and was the first person to jump into the firemen's nets below. She survived the jump, but was badly injured by the falling bodies of people who refused to wait for her to get out before jumping into the net after her.

Emma Schaef, another store clerk, also fled to the second-floor windows. There was a woman and her child there, blocking the window, afraid to jump through the smoke toward the waiting nets. So Emma gave them a shove and pushed them out the window. The woman missed the net and hit the sidewalk. Then Emma jumped – and missed the net too. The child, luckily, was unhurt.

Store clerk Carrie Bubel was paralyzed with fear for several minutes after the fire broke out. By the time she got to the window, everyone else had jumped. She followed after them, missing the net and breaking her left leg and spraining her right ankle.

Mary Podowski, the cleaning woman who had been paying for a purchase when the explosion occurred, was at first disoriented by the blast. As she recovered her nerve, she began searching through the smoke-filled, burning store for the clerk who had taken her $20 and not returned her change. After fighting her way through the terrified crowd, she seized hold of the young woman who had taken her money and demanded that it be returned to her. The clerk, who must have been amazed at Mary's request, simply replied that she did not have it. The two were carried out of the store with the surge of customers who were rushing for the exit. After the fire was finally extinguished, Mary could be seen in front of the smoldering store, weeping over her lost $20 bill.

The fire was over in a little over an hour. It had gutted both floors of the dime store and turned the building into a smoldering ruin. Outside on the street, firemen, policemen and scores of curiosity-seekers milled about, looking at the bodies of the dead and hovering around those that had been injured. The initial belief was that everyone had been rescued from the burning building but around 12:30 p.m., Fire Chief George A. Wallace and a crew of rescue workers entered the smoking hulk and found seven bodies in the right rear corridor by the three barred windows. Captain James Granger of the Cleveland Fire Company No. 1 later described the hideous scene to a reporter from the *Cleveland Plain Dealer*.

"I heard what sounded like the mewing of a cat. I had heard that sound before, however and I shuddered... [There] was a mass of humanity, it seemed, intertwined. There were [six] women. It seemed they had all huddled together in the belief that they would get air at that particular point, and when the fumes of the powder and paper became too strong all had given up at the same time. The arms of [most] of them were free, but their legs were intertwined so that it would have been impossible for anyone to have dragged herself out. At the farther end of the bunch was a little lad. He was living..."

The boy was Jimmy Parker, who died soon after being taken from the store. The fact that he was still alive when he was found may have led to the false report that convinced his mother that he had survived the blaze.

In the early afternoon hours, it began to rain. The bodies were removed and laid out in the muddy alley behind the store. To the horror of the bystanders, it became apparent that two of the badly burned women were still breathing! Two nurses forced themselves through the police line and tried to revive the two young women. Their efforts proved to be in vain and the girls, Erma Schumacher and store clerk Elizabeth Reis, both died.

The terrible day was not yet over. While police and firemen searched the ruins of the store and questioned the survivors, a scene of heartbreak was unfolding at the morgue. The remains of the seven victims had been taken there, and through the rest of the day and into the night, a mournful procession of family members, survivors and the morbidly curious streamed past the bodies. When he caught sight of his dead son, George Parker collapsed, sobbing "My son! My son! My poor Jimmy!" Two sisters of Mary Hughes identified her corpse by her teeth, and then became hysterical and had to be led away. Throughout that grim July afternoon, a sad line of men and women stumbled through the morgue, searching for their loved ones among the dead.

An inquest followed the fire. It began on July 9 and featured a parade of witnesses, rigorous cross-examination and a lot of contradictory testimony. Winifred Duncan testified about her "safe" sparkler demonstration, but denied that it was the cause of the fire. All of the witnesses corroborated her belief and that of the store manager that sparklers were "harmless." Testimony revealed that no one knew the right rear windows were barred – or even that there were windows at the end of the corridor. Testimony also showed that there had never been a fire drill carried out at the store, not that they legally required. As to the displays of fireworks, officials and witnesses agreed that it was in full compliance with Cleveland's fire and safety laws. Thanks to this, Coroner Thomas Burke, who headed the inquest, had to state, "I am satisfied that the law was violated in spirit, while it seemed no one was legally culpable. It was morally wrong for that condition to be permitted to exist." The inquest concluded with the finding that, while the fire occurred due to "careless handling of fireworks," no one was legally at fault because everyone involved acted under the belief that the sparkler was harmless.

But the public was not ready to let matters lie. Cleveland newspapers stoked the public's outrage over the fire for several weeks afterward. The enduring legacy of the Kresge fire was an end to the kind of deadly mayhem that had previously existed when it came to July 4 and fireworks. On July 6, 1908, a new ordinance was passed that banned the sale and possession of fireworks in the city. The legislation gained national attention and led to similar ordinances being passed in other cities and states – saving the lives of countless others who always believed that simple fireworks were "harmless."

1931: "48 PERISH IN OLD FOLKS HOME FIRE IN PITTSBURGH"
The Little Sisters of the Poor Home Disaster

Perhaps the most devastating fire in the history of Pittsburgh, Pennsylvania, occurred in 1931 when the Little Sisters of the Poor Home for the Aged burned to the ground. The crumbling building, which had been constructed in the 1870s, was home to 213 men and women, all over 60 years of age. Combustible materials in the basement ignited, sparking a six-alarm fire that brought 22 companies of firefighters and scores of ordinary citizens to the scene. In the end, 48 residents of the home died, and none of the survivors escaped without injury.

Death was a common visitor to the Little Sisters of the Poor Home. The "old folks home," as it was often referred to, had been serving as the final residence for many Pennsylvanians since 1871. Since all of them were elderly and many of them were infirm, it was a regular occurrence for the nuns who cared for the residents to find that not all of their aged charges survived the night. But on the dark night of July 24, 1931, death claimed many more than its usual number of victims when a ghastly fire swept through the building and carried 48 people to their doom.

The fire first came to the attention of Sister Agatha, mother superior of the Little Sisters of the Poor, around

10:00 p.m. She was awakened from a deep sleep by the sound of thumping canes pounding on the floor above her. Although she was 80 years old herself, she was still spry and alert. It took her very little time to dress and hurry out of her room – only to find the hallways choked with heavy smoke. The smoke filled the four floors of the building, spreading upwards from the fire that was burning in the basement. Sister Agatha immediately rang the alarm bell, but precious minutes would pass before the fire department was alerted since there was no telephone in the building.

The cause of the fire remains a mystery, although it undoubtedly started in the basement. Initially, the newspapers reported that the fire had started in the men's infirmary but fire officials later stated that the basement floors had just been oiled and polished, and an oil-soaked mop had caught fire.

After Sister Agatha rang the alarm, the other 16 nuns in the building were roused and began working to rescue the home's inmates, many of whom were crippled with rheumatism and other ailments. The formed the bewildered and screaming residents into lines and led them to doors and windows as quickly as the darkness – broken only by the glare of the flames – would permit. Once the fire department arrived, ladders were extended up to the third- and fourth-floor windows to help the residents escape from the inferno.

Twenty-two fire companies answered the call to the fire at the home, located at Penn and Aiken Avenues. Before their arrival, scores of passersby had spotted the blaze from the street and rushed to the gates of the home. Finding the tall iron gates locked, many climbed the eight-foot-high brick walls surrounding the grounds and ran up the hill to the building where dozens of elderly patients were crying out for help. Several gangs of young men, who had been hanging around on the street corner, as well as a mob of men from a nearby poolroom, were among the first to see the fire. They came on the run, joining in the rescue operations. The young men joined in with the firemen, risking their lives in the flames as they carried out dead, dying and helpless old men and women.

The fire department broke open the gates when they arrived and rushed their trucks to the building. They were shocked to find young men and nuns already hard at work carrying the patients to safety.

Sister Agatha recounted the rescue to the newspapers on July 25:

They were so helpless. There were no lights – only the horrid reflection of the flames. As we went into the dormitories, some of them were panicky. We did everything possible to get them moving. They did pretty well, but every once in a while, one broke from the lines, wanting to go back for her shawl or her slippers. But that awful crackling of the flames brought them back. As soon as we got the women moving, we went to the men's dormitory...

As people flocked to the scene, drawn by the glow of the flames and the screams and cries of the injured, automobiles began to be commandeered to transport victims to the area hospitals. They rapidly began to fill with the injured – volunteers and firemen among them – and a temporary field hospital was set up on the grounds of the home. Emergency and resuscitation equipment was obtained from the fire department and the bureau of mines, but the strain was too much for many of the patients, and they died. The nuns, although many of them were also injured, stood by their posts, refusing all offers of aid until their charges were cared for.

In addition to automobiles and ambulances, a fleet of about 40 taxi cabs responded to the fire. The cab drivers had a hard time getting through picket lines that were striking against the city's cab firms. One cabbie who was stopped by two strikers wielding clubs was quoted as saying, "Don't stop me now, buddy. I'm going out to haul some of the old people hurt in the fire at the home." The strikers tossed aside their clubs and hopped in the cab. All three men helped to carry the injured from the building.

A number of patients were trapped in the men's dormitory wing, and some of them began jumping from the second and third floor windows. Policemen rushed to those who were preparing to leap and urged them to wait until nets could be brought by the firemen. None of the men who waited for the nets, mostly held by the young pool hall toughs, were injured after jumping.

After the fire, the newspapers carried many stories of heroism and bravery.

Edward McMenenin and Harold Lauer were among the first rescuers to reach the building. Each was able to carry out three women before smoke drove them out of the building for the last time and firefighters with smoke masks took over the task. Lauer recounted the events he witnessed:

We saw people hanging out of the windows, crying for help. Some were coming down the fire escapes. We ran up a fire escape and reached the second floor. I grabbed one old woman. She was dressed only in her nightgown, and I carried her to the ground and made two other trips. When I got out with the second woman, a nun was there helping. I don't know how she got there but she cried for us to go back and we did.

By that time, more rescuers were coming and things were going along pretty good. Then the smoke got so thick that we couldn't see. It spread down the walls of the building. Everything got confused and mixed up. My buddy rescued three and then firemen wearing smoke masks took up the work.

W.H. Schulte was passing by the home that night when he realized the place was on fire. He was one of the men who climbed the walls and hurried to the building. According to witnesses, he managed to carry 20 people to safety before someone noticed that he was injured and forced him to go to the hospital. He was interviewed on his hospital bed (where he insisted that he was just tired and wanted to return to the scene and help) about what had occurred the night before:

I heard men and women screaming. I couldn't stand it so I ran in. It was a terrible sight. The poor old men and women were frantic. I helped one old woman out into the street. Then I went back in. I don't know how many I helped. But I'll never forget the sight nor the screams. I saved several women. I don't want credit for that. I was just helping.

Mary Maloney, a 73-year-old resident of the home gave thanks to her rescuer. She was interviewed from her bed at St. Francis Hospital:

God bless the man that saved me. I was lying on the floor, being trampled. I was almost unconscious. All of the sudden I felt someone's arms around me. It was a man I never saw before. He carried me from the building. Please get me his name so I can pray for him.

Mary Lang, another survivor, told her story:

In all of my 80 years, I have never seen a sight so awful. Old women crying and praying all at once. When I first went into the hall the smoke made me want to go back but I couldn't. The women were being herded out like sheep. I remember Sister Louisa urging us toward a fire escape. Finally we crawled out the window and we carried down the fire escape. I thank the Good Almighty for getting me out safely.

Miss Mary Shannon said that after being awakened by the warning cries and pounding on the door of her room, she was shaking so badly that she was unable to put on her clothes. She told a reporter:

So I pulled a blanket over me, took my cane and groped my way through the hall to a fire escape. Smoke rolled all around us in the dark. Only sometimes there was light from the awful fire. A woman who was moving along the hall with me became hysterical. She grabbed at my blanket and nightgown and almost tore the nightgown from me. We did reach the fire escape and some man carried us down. I don't know who knocked on that door but I would have died if I hadn't heard it. I'm crippled with rheumatism and it takes me twice as long to move about.

Sister Agatha refused to speak about her part in the rescue to the newspapers but others were quick to recount her heroism in the face of the disaster. She refused to leave the building or be rescued, said Eugene Cummins, one of the passersby who hurried to the scene to try and help. He ran into the building to help and encountered Sister Agatha on the second floor, helping old men and women from their rooms. Cummins took it upon himself to grab her and start down the stairs with her. He told a reporter, "As soon as I got outside, she grabbed me by the shirt, tore it off my back and then ran back into the building." Cummins hadn't realized it, but his shirt was on fire. He was badly burned on the back and hands, and it's possible that Sister Agatha had saved his life.

Anne Daly lived in an apartment directly across the street from the home. She and her daughter allowed rescuers to bring some of the fire victims into their home. "My daughter directed four women victims into our place," Mrs. Daley recounted. "As I bent over one woman who was badly burned, I heard her say 'I wonder if my husband is all right.' Then she died."

John Ryan and John Reynolds were driving past the home when they realized that it was on fire. They abandoned their car and ran to the building to try and help. The pair climbed to the second floor and began carrying and helping people from the burning home. "People were lying all around, gasping for breath," Reynolds said. "Others were at the windows calling for help. I'll never forget the scene. I guess I carried out 12 people." Ryan added that he "supposed he carried out about 14 people," but neither of the men wanted to be recognized for their bravery.

Harry Seigert reached the fire in the early minutes after the alarm went out. Flames were shooting out of the basement windows on each side of the front door. "Several of us broke down the door," he said, "and about 25 of the old men and women were coming downstairs. The nuns led them out and we ran upstairs and helped some others."

Ray Harry made several trips up the fire escape to aid in the rescue work. He described the bravery of the nuns to the newspapers, "One nun I saw almost collapsed and I grabbed her by the shoulder and started to lead her down the stairs of the fire escape. She jerked away from me and insisted staying at the window with several other nuns until all of the inmates gathered there had escaped."

Sister Mary Louise even insisted on accompanying deputy coroners through smoke and flames to save the institution's records so all of the names of the residents would be known.

Some of the stories were especially tragic. Sarah Carlson was taken out of the third floor trapdoor as flames engulfed the women's wing. Suddenly, she broke away from the firemen and, to their astonishment, ran back into the fire, calling out her husband's name. Her husband was also a resident of the home. Both of them perished in the inferno. Their bodies were later found together, hand in hand.

It took more than six hours to put out the fire, leaving the aging building a smoldering, blackened ruin with 48 dead and another 175 injured. The city was shocked by the horror of the night and many wondered what would happen to those who survived the blaze. It was the early years of the Great Depression. People in Pittsburgh were out of work, children were going hungry and the elderly had been all but forgotten at a time when people didn't have jobs, food, a decent place to live or much hope for the future.

The bodies of those who had died were taken away for burial by their relatives. All of them, that is, except for eight victims who lay in the morgue, unknown and unclaimed. The Sisters of the Poor Home had been a place for the elderly poor, and many were without anyone to bury them. They were homeless when they came to the hospital, with nowhere else to go. Bishop Hugh Boyle of Pittsburgh, stepped in and brought the remains to St. Paul Cathedral, where he planned to preside over a funeral Mass for the unclaimed victims.

At the Mass on August 3, the eight victims were remembered by one of the largest crowds ever to gather at the cathedral. The people of Pittsburgh filled every pew, spilling out onto the sidewalks and into the street. Catholics, Protestants, and non-believers sat and stood side by side. They came together to pay their respects to the unknown dead in their donated coffins.

A week after the funeral, Bishop Boyle went on the radio to ask for help. The Little Sisters of the Poor, and the elderly patients they served, were homeless. While it seemed fruitless at a time when so many had nothing of their own, the Bishop asked for donations to build a new home for the nuns and the people that cared for. He said they would need $300,000 to rebuild. Unbelievably, in the midst of the Depression, within three months the people of Pittsburgh gave that much – and more.

A new home was constructed for the Little Sisters of the Poor and the old site was forgotten for many years, which leads us to the even more tragic part of the story.

The former home of the Little Sisters of the Poor is unrecognizable today from the way it looked 80 years ago. There are a number of old buildings that remain from the time of the fire but residences and a recently constructed children's home have come along to replace what used to be standing at the corners of Penn and Aiken avenues. For a number of years, the site where the hospital stood was empty, neglected and forgotten – or at least it would have been forgotten if not for the memories of the tragedy and the eerie tales that were told in the neighborhood. According to the stories, some remnants of the terrible fire remained behind, making their presence known with screams, cries and the unearthly voices of people who sounded as if they were being burned to death.

Great tragedies sometimes leave an impression behind on the atmosphere of the place where they occurred. Some believe that all of the energy expended during those times soaks into the earth, and any buildings on the site, occasionally releasing and replaying itself in the form of noises and visions. In many cases, these hauntings eventually wear themselves out over time, which was apparently happened with the Little Sisters of the Poor fire. For years, locals spoke of the voices and weird sounds that were heard at the former site of the hospital, and then the stories just seemed to stop.

Did the haunting finally come to an end, or did the rest of the city just finally move on and leave the story of the disaster behind? Old stories, like that of the great fire, are like old ghosts – if we stop thinking about them, perhaps after a time, they simply disappear into the mysterious fog of yesterday.

1940: AMERICA'S FORGOTTEN NIGHTCLUB FIRE
The Rhythm Club Fire of Natchez, Mississippi

Much has been written over the years about the deadly fire at the Coconut Grove Club and other famous nightclubs (see countless books and our own book, *And Hell Followed With it*) but there has been little written about another devastating nightspot blaze, the Rhythm Nightclub Fire, which occurred in Natchez, Mississippi, in April 1940. It was a bit of mystery to us as to why no one has taken a closer look at this fire before now (a documentary about the fire was produced in 2010) but when we started researching the story, the answers became clear: All of the victims were African Americans.

We have never been believers in the idea that racism is behind everything in America, but when looking over the newspaper articles that pertained to the fire, the writing style in them made the situation pretty plain. The Rhythm had been a Negro club, staffed and owned by Negroes, patronized by Negroes ("imitating their white counterparts by dressing in evening clothes," as one contemporary news report sneered) and the tragedy was not taken as seriously in 1940 as it would have been today. Mississippi was still a segregated state, plagued by the Jim Crow laws, and many white residents had little use for the blacks that lived among them, alive or dead, unless they cleaned their homes, mowed their lawns or proved themselves useful in some other way.

It was a devastating event when 216 African American music lovers lost their lives on the night of April 23, 1940 – but far too few people seemed to care.

The Rhythm Nightclub Fire occurred on St. Catherine Street in Natchez. It was an area referred to as the "Negro section" of town, on the edge of the downtown business district. The wooden, oblong structure was built in 1925 to serve as a church, which later closed. It was used as a garage for a time before being converted into a nightclub in 1938. The building was ramshackle and run down and had only one entrance, located at the back. A stage had been erected at the front, where the altar of the church had been. In an attempt to decorate the place, the club's proprietor, Ed Frazier, had draped the walls and rafters with Spanish moss. It hung down above the customers, giving the place a moody, bayou-like atmosphere that must have appealed to the late night revelers.

Tragically, it would prove to be the club's undoing.

The Rhythm Club had numerous windows on both sides of the building, dating back to its construction as a church, but thanks to a problem with what the owners referred to as "gatecrashers," shutters had been nailed over all of the windows to keep non-paying customers out. The shutters would also serve a more sinister purpose – they would keep everyone inside.

The evening of April 23 was an exciting night for the black community in Natchez. One of the biggest names in Negro entertainment, Walter Barnes, was playing at the Rhythm Club with his 15-piece orchestra. It was bound to be one of the big shows of the year and the club attracted the cream of the local

Walter Barnes and the Royal Creolians

African American society. Present that night were black attorneys, physicians, teachers, social workers and scores of other community leaders. They were packed into the place, elbow-to-elbow, with more than 300 other customers, some having come from as far away as Louisiana to hear the Chicago orchestra.

Walter Barnes was a native of Vicksburg, Mississippi. He was born in 1905, and had moved to Chicago in 1923, where he began studying reed instruments with classical teacher Franz Schoepp. He took further studies at the Chicago Musical College and the American Conservatory of Music. He took over as the bandleader from the Detroit Shannon outfit in 1924 and re-named the band the Royal Creolians. He traveled across the country and recorded music with the band in 1928-1929 for the Brunswick label. Barnes made a name for himself by taking dance music to small Southern towns, where most other big name entertainers rarely performed. Barnes recruited musicians from several different states for his tours and was always popular in Mississippi.

When he arrived in Natchez in April 1940, he was on the last leg of his current tour. He brought with him a 15-piece band, including a female singer. After Natchez, they only had two more stops on the tour, Vicksburg and New Albany, Mississippi, before returning to Chicago.

The fire broke out around 11:35 p.m. According to Ernest Wright, an elevator operator who came to meet his wife at the club after getting off work, the fire was started by a careless cigarette. He told the police that he saw two girls come out of the women's room near the front of the hall and heard one of them say: "Now you did it. You set the place on fire."

Wright said that he didn't see anything for a minute and then he saw blinding sheets of flame. "In a moment," he said. "The whole place was on fire."

Fire officials believed that a cigarette had inadvertently touched one of the streamers of Spanish moss, which were hanging from the rafters. The dry moss had been hanging there for nearly two years, and instantly burst into flames. A cry of "fire!" went up from the crowd. Someone managed to slip outside and contact the fire department, which arrived less than five minutes later. Even then, however, it was too late for scores of people trapped inside.

Once the people jammed into the club realized that the place was on fire, they immediately went into a panic. There were shouts, screams, cries and curses, and in moments, the crowd became a clawing, fighting mass as they tried to get out of the single door. Almost 150 people escaped before the thrashing, terrified victims became jammed into the doorway, unable to break loose and blocking all means of escape for everyone still trapped inside.

The fire department arrived at 11:40 p.m. Frightful screams came from the towering flames that now engulfed the building from wall to wall. A few moments later, the tin roof fell in and the crash sent a shower of sparks and flames soaring into the dark sky. The firemen immediately went to work, dousing the fire with water, and working frantically to try and pull the trapped people from the building.

Meanwhile, inside, it was a hellish scene. People fought, punched, kicked and scratched, struggling to get out of the door. There was simply no place for them to go. Many of those who were pushed away cowered near the stage at the front of the club, hoping that they could somehow avoid being burned to death. Unfortunately, an exhaust fan near the front of the club pulled the smoke and fire in the direction of the bandstand. It was there that Walter Barnes, and some of the members of the orchestra, was trapped. Two members of the band, plus Alton Barnes, the bandleader's brother and the band's manager, had escaped from the club. Walter was not so lucky, but in the aftermath of the fire, he was hailed as a hero. When the fire first broke out, he tried to calm the crowd while he and the band continued to play the song "Marie." His body was later found, among dozens of others, at the front of the building.

The inferno was out within 10 minutes. It had reduced the club to a pile of smoldering ashes. Smoke rolled out from beneath the hot tin roof, which had collapsed onto the grisly scene. White men came running to the scene from the nearby business district and aided the blacks and the police in taking the injured to one of the nearby Negro hospitals. Men and women were found wandering in the street, practically naked and in a daze. Their clothing had been either burned off or torn off in the fight at the door. Officials believed that about 150 people escaped from the club and that between 50 and 100 of them were injured. The hospitals were soon filled to overflowing.

The bodies of the dead that could be easily reached were taken to the three Negro undertakers in the district, where police officers began counting them and laying them out for identification. The coroner suggested a plan of embalming the bodies and putting them on display so that friends and relatives could identify them later. The grim task continued for weeks after the fire.

The initial estimates of more than 150 dead were quickly upgraded. By the following day, many of the burned victims had died in the hospital, raising the death toll to 212. More would be added before it was all over. Coroner R.E. Smith visited the scene the next morning and blamed most of the deaths on the fact that the building only had one door, as well as the fact that the windows had been boarded over to keep people from sneaking into the shows. He described the horribly gruesome scene to the newspapers:

The bodies were piled up like cordwood. The skin was peeling from faces, blood oozed from mouths and flesh was broken. From my examination, it appeared that most of the people died from suffocation. A majority of the victims were 15 to 16 years old. There were about as many youths as girl victims.

The bodies were piled up in funeral parlors and no identifications have been made yet. The undertakers told me that they would embalm the bodies and line them up and let relatives file by to identify kinsmen.

Coroner Smith, who was also the managing editor of the *Natchez Democrat*, said that the paper's janitor, Julius Hawkins, had been at the show that night, and had been standing near the rear. Hawkins had escaped but didn't know what had started the blaze. Smith quoted him as saying, "All I thought about was getting away from there."

V.H. Jeffries, a photographer who reached the scene a short time after the disaster, pointed out that the club had been completely gutted. He also spoke to reporters about what he saw:

Great quantities of dry moss had been hung on the walls for decoration. This caught fire in some way and the intense heat and fumes probably suffocated the victims. Men and women were sprawled grotesquely about on the floor like dead chickens, their clothing burned away and their flesh seared. The fire started near the entrance and it seemed that the crowd fled to the rear, where they could not escape.

By the following afternoon, the rest of the city was feeling the shock of what had occurred. It was estimated that very few of the African-American families in Natchez were unaffected by the fire. At that time, the population of the city was nearly 18,000 people – 60 percent of them were black.

Angry white voices began to be heard in city government, incensed that the club had been allowed to operate with only one exit door. They demanded a city ordinance requiring dance venues to have at least two exits, which would effectively put most Negro clubs in the city out of business. This didn't seem to bother anyone, especially after news spread that the police had arrested several black men who had been recruited to pull bodies out of the ruins of the club. They were allegedly stealing from the dead, or so sheriff's deputies claimed.

Instead of bringing the city's residents together, the fire had served to drive whites and

The Rhythm Club turned out to be a fiery deathtrap for scores of people who gathered there. (Below) The burned out interior of the club.

blacks even farther apart. It would be decades before Mississippi ended segregation, and it was just as long before safety measures began to be required in what were referred to as "Negro dance halls." Not surprisingly, with attention fading quickly about the tragedy, the Rhythm Nightclub Fire was soon forgotten by the press, Natchez officials, and by history.

But the families of the victims didn't forget, nor did the generations of blues singers who told the story of the fire in their songs, or the group of aging women who make up the Watkins Street Cemetery's preservation society. They care for the mass grave where the fire victims were buried. When the number of bodies overwhelmed city authorities, they buried them in trenches in the Watkins Street Cemetery. There was no way to identify many of them. A few markers have been placed over the years, but mostly, it's just a large grave where the bodies have been placed side-by-side. Their names have been forgotten, as have their lives.

But the dead still remember.

In 2010, a small museum was erected in honor of the Rhythm Club Fire, and according to the stories, strange occurrences have been happening there "almost daily" ever since. Voices have been heard, as well as music, and the sounds of doors opening and closing. Photographs that are displayed on the walls sometimes fly off and can be found in odd positions across the room. The museum was set up on the concrete slab that once marked the foundation of the Rhythm Club. The rest of the slab serves as the museum's parking lot.

Intrigued by the reports, Adams County Deputy Sheriff Michael Chapman, who also runs the Natchez Area Paranormal Society, and a few of his team members decided to check out the site of the fire in September 2011. They set up recording equipment, as Mike wrote, "to see if we could get responses to any questions, knowing we were literally standing on top of the remains of a building where over 200 people died in a very short time with what had to be a lot of fear, panic and intense physical and emotional agony as they could not find a way out of the burning structure."

After a short time, they recorded a number of eerie responses, such as "Couldn't get out," "I'm from Alabama," "Get out, cracker!" and "open up the Rhythm nightclub." They were surprised by the intense responses, but as Mike added, "On the other hand, considering just how powerful the tragedy was, it isn't so surprising."

The story of the Rhythm Nightclub Fire may be only a footnote in American history, but to the people of Natchez and those directly affected by this horrendous event, its legacy lives on. It is a story worth telling – and remembering – and maybe someday the victims of the fire will finally rest in peace.

1946: GHOSTS OF AMERICA'S GREATEST HOTEL FIRE
Horror & Hauntings of the Winecoff Hotel

As has been proven time and time again throughout the years, words like "unsinkable" and "fireproof" seem to mean very little when it comes to the power of the forces of nature. Ships sink and theaters and hotels burn – but few of them burn with the kind of horror seen at the Winecoff Hotel on December 7, 1946. The hotel, with 285 guests crowded into 194 rooms, was gutted by a six-hour fire that claimed the lives of 119 guests and injured another 90, making it the worst hotel fire in American history.

There were 285 guests that checked into the hotel that night and it's possible that even after death, many of them have never checked out.

The Winecoff Hotel in Atlanta, Georgia, was built at Peachtree and Ellis streets by W. Frank Winecoff in 1913. After he retired, Winecoff continued to reside at the hotel that he loved. He was convinced that it was a safe place, as were city officials, who deemed the hotel "fireproof," a term that has since been discontinued by the National Board of Fire Underwriters.

Like most hotels in Atlanta in those days, it had no sprinkler systems and no outside fire escapes. It had been built with a central staircase winding around an enclosed bank of elevators and, aside from the elevators, the staircase was the only method of escape from the building. In spite of this, the hotel was pronounced safe when it was inspected only a short time before the disastrous blaze by the city's fire marshal. The building was supposedly of fireproof construction, which merely meant that the framework of the building would remain sounds after a fire – it said nothing of the contents and unfortunately, people are not fireproof.

The hotel was 15 stories tall with the floors numbered consecutively except for number 13, which was eliminated from the numbered system for the usual superstitious reason. The structure was protected by a shielded steel frame, and the roof and floors were made from concrete. The exterior was composed of 12-inch-thick brick panels, and inside partitions were constructed of tile plastered on both sides, ensuring that the structure would remain stable. Unfortunately, the walls and hallways were covered with painted burlap from the wooden baseboards to the chair rails, above which they were papered. Corridor floors had wall-to-wall carpeting over felt padding. Doors to rooms were of light panel wood, with wood frames and transoms. The rooms were wallpapered, some with as many as five layers of paper, and ceilings were painted. A few of the guest room windows were fitted with wooden venetian blinds, but most were fitted with ordinary cloth drapes. While the building itself was indestructible, apparently little thought was given to its contents, which were, of course, highly flammable. A kitchen stove, for example, is a "fireproof" device that contains flame for controlled use and function, but it can still burn flesh if anyone were unwise enough to try and climb inside.

The hotel's design also included many openings, mostly vertical, such as ventilating shafts. These openings also had a hidden use: In the event of a fire, they would serve as chimneys and fans to draw oxygen-seeking flames onto all 15 floors. The hotel was also equipped with transoms above the guest room doors, which, when opened, would also help to spread flames in the case of a fire.

The two elevators shafts, as mentioned, were centrally located with a single staircase wrapping around it up and down the length of the building. The stairs began on each floor as a single staircase, and then branched off into opposite directions halfway up, each stairway leading to two long corridors that ran parallel to each other. Since the elevator shafts were enclosed with fire resistive materials, a blaze, should it occur, would probably proceed up the staircase, feeding on the burlap wallcovering, wallpaper and woodwork.

Atlanta's Winecoff Hotel was the scene of a deadly fire in 1946. Many believe that some of the victims still linger behind.

On the morning of December 7, 1946, the Winecoff Hotel was filled nearly to capacity with almost 300 guests on the hotel register. It was 3:30 a.m. when the hotel's night clerk, Comer Rowan, who was sitting in for his wife, noticed the switchboard light for Room 510 was blinking. The guest asked for some ginger ale and ice. Rowan rang for Billy Mobley, the only night bellhop on duty. Mobley took the items up in the elevator and was joined on the trip by the night engineer, who was making his routine nightly check. When they arrived at Room 510, they had to wait for three minutes because the guest was in the bathtub.

Meanwhile, the elevator operator, a young woman, slowly took the car back downstairs. Around the third floor, she thought she smelled smoke and took the elevator down to the basement. From there, she ran up to the main floor and told Rowan. He told her to go to the fifth floor and find Mobley and the engineer. Leaping over the desk, Rowan raced up the stairs to the mezzanine and saw flames reflected there in a mirror. He dashed for the telephone and called the fire department. It was 3:42 a.m. and within a few minutes, three ladder and four pumper companies pulled away from their station, two blocks away.

On the fifth floor, Mobley and the engineer emerged from Room 510, where they had spent a few minutes talking to the night-owl guest. As they opened the door, flames and dense clouds of black smoke swept toward them. They slammed the door closed.

Rowan plugged in every guest telephone as fast as he could, shouting "Fire! Fire! Fire!" Then, the switchboard went dead. The guests that had been sleeping peacefully in their rooms were now on their own. There was no fire alarm in the "fireproof" hotel. By the time the firemen arrived, the building was in chaos, filled with rushing, frenzied people – many of them ready to jump from the windows high above the street.

The firemen urged them not to jump, even though the hotel, from the third to the fifteenth floor was a blazing inferno. The firemen were faced with the dilemma of fighting the fire or saving the frantic guests who were shrieking from the window ledges above them. They chose rescue, hurried to their ladders and sent them up. More fire brigades began to arrive, until the city's complete 60-piece fire department was surrounding the burning hotel. Their ladders, though they reached to the tenth floor, could not be elevated quickly enough.

Everything inside of the hotel was burning – drapes, wooden trim, furniture, bedding – and with no sprinkler system to douse the blaze, the hungry flames swept through hallways and blasted up staircases and elevator shafts. Most of the transoms above the guest room doors were open, as were the windows, which created even more drafts to feed the flames.

With no way to escape, the heat of the flames drove the guests to the windows. One woman appeared on a seventh-floor ledge holding her two children. A ladder shot up to meet her, but before it came within reach, she threw her small son into the air, followed by her daughter. Then fell into the darkness, hurting toward the street below. A newspaper reporter on the scene wrote about what happened next:

Her nightgown shone white against the flames behind her as she stood on the window ledge, high above the street. Then it, too, caught fire. She jumped. But she missed the net stretched by the firemen. She landed astride overhead wires. There she hung in flames. Finally, her body broke loose and toppled to the ground.

A fireman reached one woman on the fifth floor just as she was losing her grip on the window ledge. He swung her around the ladder and onto his back. As he backed downward with her, another woman jumped from a ledge several floors above. She struck the fireman and the woman on his back and all three of them fell to their deaths.

Even though firemen and spectators on the street urged those on the ledges not to move, scores of bed sheets tied together to form ropes began to be tossed from the windows and half-crazed guests began to lower themselves down toward the street. One girl crawled two floors downward on one of the makeshift ropes. A fire ladder swung over to get her and holding the sheets with one hand, she lunged for the ladder. But a split second before she could grab it, the sheets came apart and she crashed to the pavement.

The firefighters and the spectators held out safety nets, hoping to catch anyone who fell or jumped from a window. One man missed a net by inches after jumping from the tenth floor.

On the eighth floor, a woman stood on a window ledge, begging for someone to save her four-year-old son. As flames roared from the window behind her, she flung the little boy into the air. One of the spectators saw that there were no firemen near the place where the boy would land and he raced to the spot. Miraculously, he caught the boy in the air and the child was saved without injury. The mother fell a few seconds later, but was killed in the fall.

After seeing others leap to their death, a suicidal frenzy spread among the endangered hotel guests. Perhaps they believed that a certain death on the concrete below was better than burning to death or worse, surviving with permanent injuries. Others began to jump, sometimes regretting the decision – after it was too late. A girl scrambled for a ladder two floors below as searchlights swept over her, highlighting a face that was filled with terror. She groped for the ladder, blinded by the light, and missed. Her body fell crazily, spinning out of control, and smashed through the hotel's marquee.

Another woman climbed out onto one of the makeshift bed sheet ropes and began to lower herself. It

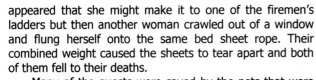

After seeing others leap to their death, a suicidal frenzy spread among the endangered hotel guests. A Georgia Tech student snapped this photo of a woman leaping from the building.

(Left) Bed sheets were hung from the windows to be used as ropes but were far from the ground.

appeared that she might make it to one of the firemen's ladders but then another woman crawled out of a window and flung herself onto the same bed sheet rope. Their combined weight caused the sheets to tear apart and both of them fell to their deaths.

Many of the guests were saved by the nets that were spread out by the firemen below. However, a few of them hit the nets with such force that the handles were ripped from the would-be rescuers' hands, and hurtling bodies struck the earth. There was nothing that could be done for those who hit the pavement under those circumstances.

A girl on the seventh floor had been patiently waiting for rescue as the flames began creeping out of the window behind her. A net was finally arranged below. Spectators heard her shout, "I hope I live! I hope I live!" and then she jumped. She lived – although she broke a hip, one arm and one leg.

The suicidal mania that had gripped the guests stopped after 20 or so of them fatally plunged to their deaths. More and more of them crept out onto the window ledges to escape the deadly heat, flames and gas and waited their turn for rescue. Heroic firemen worked swiftly to get them down from the building safely. A number of the rescuers were injured during the effort and 25 of them were later hospitalized for smoke inhalation.

While many of the firemen had set to work trying to rescue the hotel guests who were clinging to the window ledges on the sides of the building, others had rushed inside to try and get control of the blaze. Inside of the lobby, a section of firemen began battling their way up the main staircase from the second floor, their hoses blasting the flames with water. They could hear the screams of trapped guests burning to death in the rooms above them. One man tried to seal off his room, taking his family into the bathroom. He turned on all of the water faucets but the heat from the flames almost instantly turned the water into steam. The toilet exploded, as did many others, and the man was found later asphyxiated with his head in the shower. His wife, holding onto their children, lay next to him. All were dead.

One couple that was trapped on the fourteenth floor was determined to live. As flames shot through the transom over the door and ignited the room, they crawled out onto the window ledge and slipped into the room next door, where the transom was closed. The couple there was trying to barricade the door. The man and woman on the ledge climbed into the room and tried to help. Both couples jammed a mattress against the door, constantly soaking it with water from the bathroom. For two hours, they soaked the mattress as the room filled with steam – but they lived.

A military officer, Major Jake Cahill, was in another room with his wife. He had sealed the transom and then had waited anxiously until a ladder reached the seventh floor window ledge of their room. Cahill's elderly mother was in the room next door, but he was unable to reach her because of the fire. After he climbed down the ladder to safety behind his wife, Cahill immediately rushed into the Mortgage Guarantee Building next door and ran up the stairs to the seventh floor. He went from window to window until he saw his mother's room directly across an alley. He obtained a long plank from somewhere, extended it between the two buildings and then crawled across it. He then led his mother back across the shaking board to safety.

Cahill alerted other guests about the plank and one of those saved by this method was Major General Paul W. Baade, who had commanded the 35th Army Division in Europe during World War II. He managed to bring his wife with him into the building across the alley.

For six hours, the firemen fought their way, floor by floor, through the fire, extinguishing blazes on each floor before continuing upward. None of them had ever experienced a fire with such intensity, and as they broke into one room after another, they discovered scenes that were beyond their comprehension. Brass doorknobs and telephones had melted. Light bulbs were fused. Heavy metal elevator doors were twisted. In some rooms, only the bedsprings remained, the rest of the furnishings having been completely consumed by fire.

The dead were everywhere. Bodies sprawled in hallways, smothered by the smoke and lack or air. A dead woman was found at an open window. She was untouched by the fire, seemingly asleep, with only a trickle of blood at the corner of her mouth. Room after room contained corpses of those who had died in bed, never realizing the hotel was ablaze around them.

Yet, in the midst of all of this, the hotel stood, its structure still sound and "fireproof."

When the pale winter sun rose that day in Atlanta, crowds assembled to see the firemen carry away the corpses of 119 people. Another 90 people were taken away on stretchers to area hospitals. The worst hotel fire in American history was finally over.

Among the dead was W. Frank Winecoff, suffocated in his tenth floor suite. Although he had sold his beloved hotel in 1937, he continued to live there in his retirement, insisting until the day that he died that Atlanta's finest hotel was completely "fireproof."

The building that was once the Winecoff Hotel survived the fire. Although nearly gutted, it reopened in the 1950s as the Peachtree on Peachtree hotel and then saw another incarnation in the 1960s as a retirement home. After changing hands several times, it sat vacant for years, dwarfed by the modern hotels and office buildings around it. More renovations were done in the 1990s and it is now open once again as the Ellis Hotel – a place that has its share of ghostly tales.

Stories have circulated for years that lingering remnants of the fire remain behind at the new hotel. Some of these stories even date back a few years to when the Ellis was being renovated. At the time, workmen on the job claimed that they were hearing footsteps and voices in empty rooms and that their tools often disappeared from where they had been left, mysteriously turning up on odd places. More recently, guests and staff members have also reported footsteps, along with loud cries and noises in the corridors, as if a group of people were frantically running down the hall. When they look out from their rooms, or turn a corner in pursuit of the noisy guests, they find that no one is there. The hallway is empty and deserted. Some also claim that they have been awakened at night to the smell of smoke, only to find that nothing is burning.

Perhaps most disconcerting, though, are the faces – eerie apparitions of people's faces that have been reported peering out from the hotel's windows. The tales regarding these ghostly visages began many years ago, when the building was abandoned. The faces were first believed to be those of homeless people or squatters, sleeping in the place after it had closed down. Security officers who searched the building, however, found no one inside.

As the years passed, the faces remained and are still sometimes reported today. These chilling images are distorted and unreal, human but inhuman, and some claim that appear to be screaming in terror. Are they real, or the result of fevered imaginations? Some believe the faces are nothing more than simulacra – the result of people's ability to perceive familiar images in random patterns (such as the play of light and shadow upon a window). There are others, though, who believe the images are real and that they are the horror-filled faces of the people who died screaming at the Winecoff Hotel in 1946.

Those who spend the night at the Ellis these days can judge for themselves.

1990: ONE GALLON OF GASOLINE AND TWO MATCHES
The Happy Land Social Club Fire

The date was March 25, 1990. It was the eve of Punta Carnival, the Honduran equivalent of Mardi Gras. A group of mostly Honduran immigrants were celebrating the holiday at the Happy Land Social Club on Southern Boulevard in the Bronx, New York. The club was located on the cramped second floor of the building, and on that night, was filled well beyond capacity as the revelers drank and danced. As the party wore on toward the early morning hours, a madman with a gallon of gasoline and two matches saw to it that 87 of the partiers at the club that night would never see the sunrise. He left only five survivors to tell the tale, a tale that had started ten years earlier in Cuba.

The "Freedom Flotilla"
Freedom Flotilla was the name given to the hundreds of boats and ships involved in the boatlift that transported Cuban refugees to the United States between May and September of 1980.

For decades, Cuban expatriates living in the U.S. had been lobbying anyone who would listen for the release of their families and the hundreds, if not thousands of political prisoners filling Cuban prisons, prisoners whose only crime was opposing the politics and the cruel, iron-handed rule of dictator Fidel Castro. Hundreds had likewise been fighting for their freedom from within Cuba. Finally, on April 20, 1980, after months of violence all around Cuba involving other countries like Peru, Costa Rica and the U.S. -- Castro announced that all Cubans wishing to emigrate to the United States were free to leave the country by boat from the port of Mariel Bay. Within 24 hours, dozens of boats were leaving from Florida, carrying Cuban Americans headed to Mariel Bay to pick up relatives and friends before Castro could change his mind. Thus began the Freedom Flotilla.

But Castro had ideas beyond simply allowing dissidents, troublemakers and possible revolutionaries to be removed from his borders, and not all the Cubans headed for the U.S. were traveling on American boats. Fidel included a few boats of his own, though none were particularly seaworthy. Hidden among the over 200,000 Cuban emigrants, now dubbed Los Marielitos, departing from Mariel Bay between May and September, Castro presented the U.S. with inmates of his prisons and mental hospitals. Beginning on May 15, 1980, he instructed his soldiers to begin the emptying of Cuba's prisons and insane asylums, sending them on a forced march through the oppressive tropical heat to Mariel Bay, where a number of rusting, leaking excuses for boats awaited them.

This group of convicts, including many political prisoners, was also composed of thieves, rapists, murderers, the mentally ill, the criminally insane, drug dealers, drug addicts and general thugs. Among them was Julio González, a 25-year-old petty criminal, incarcerated for a minor crime this time, though he was no stranger to jail cells. Julio had been imprisoned years before for desertion. He was uneducated, penniless and starving. His sole possessions were the rags he wore. Word had spread through the prisons that there was to be a mass evacuation of the worst of the prisoners, bound for a boatlift that was headed to some unknown location. Julio, eager to get out and go somewhere -- anywhere -- lied to the guards, telling them he was a drug dealer so he would be included.

No one knew where they were going, though there were rumors that it was to be the United States. But how could that be? It couldn't be possible that President Jimmy Carter would be willing to take in the worst of the worst criminals from another country, could it? The answer to that was simple: No one knew, until it was too late, just who made up the human cargo on those mundane boats arriving from Cuba, alongside the thousands of other boats arriving from the same port.

By early June, U.S. immigration officials had figured out what Castro had done. The federal government made an official request that he accept the return of his criminals. As might be expected, this request was met with a hearty laugh and a strong refusal.

Most of these criminals were quickly imprisoned in American detention centers, where some languished for years with no real expectation for release. Others, however, were deemed non-violent, and after only a few months in the overcrowded centers, were released to live as free people on American soil. Julio González had lied about his crimes to get shipped out of Cuba, and then barely survived the two-week trip in a leaking boat with almost no food. He now found himself a free man.

After a brief time spent bouncing around Miami, González followed the example of many of his fellow Marielitos and made his way to New York City. Despite having little education, no money or possessions and no friends or family, he managed to assimilate into his new surroundings without too many problems. He stayed out of serious trouble as he worked his way through a series of low-paying jobs over the next decade. Julio was a free man in America, but he continued to live in poverty.

He did manage to make a few friends, and in 1984 he found himself in a relationship with Lydia Feliciano, a woman ten years his senior. Their relationship could best be described as tumultuous. Julio and Lydia lived together off and on for a few years, with Lydia earning most of their money, and Julio drinking and unable to keep a job for long. They were barely able to scrape by and often had trouble paying the rent.

After years of fights and beatings, Lydia finally had enough. She threw Julio out for what she proclaimed to be the last time, and tried to move on with her life. She had begun working on weekends as a coat-check girl at the Happy Land Social Club, one of the many unlicensed social clubs operating throughout New York's five boroughs. This particular club was in a largely Honduran neighborhood in the Bronx.

The Happy Land Social Club
In 1980, it was estimated that there were over 1,000 social clubs being illegally operated in New York. Some sprang up overnight and vanished just as quickly, while others thrived for months or even years. Many of these clubs were vital to immigrant communities, providing a place for people from the same country or ethnicity to meet, mingle and reminisce about home. This was often the only meaningful interaction that many of these immigrants had with people with whom they could relate and converse with in their own language. They were opened in spaces in otherwise-empty buildings, and most of the time these spaces were not designed to hold large numbers of people. The cover charges were high but the booze flowed freely and there was always music and dancing.

Happy Land was unlicensed but the New York City Fire Department had inspected the building in which it was housed. The club was deemed a fire hazard and received a shutdown order. There were no fire exits, no fire alarms, no sprinklers in the club area, and sadly no follow-up by the fire department. There were only two functioning exits on the ground floor. The fire exit on the second floor, where the actual club functioned, had a metal cage door that had been welded shut to prevent gatecrashers.

The building itself was quite small, only 20 feet wide and 60 feet long. The main entrance door opened into a small vestibule with a flight of steps directly ahead leading to the club on the second floor. To the side of the vestibule was the coat check room and an area for a bouncer to collect the cover charge. The only other door was behind the tiny coat-check room and opened into a service area.

After breaking up with Lydia, Julio wasn't faring too well. He lost his job as a warehouseman at a lamp factory, and had drunk up his last paycheck. Now he was facing eviction, unable to pay the rent at his rooming house. He found himself wandering the streets of the Bronx in the early morning hours of March 25. At about 2:30 in the morning, he entered the street-level entrance of the Happy Land Social Club, where Lydia was working. Her little coat-check room was right next to the entrance so he didn't have to look far to find her.

Julio was in a surly mood. He was drunk and broke and looking for a fight. He demanded that Lydia give him money. When she refused, he began arguing with her -- shouting and calling her names. She still wouldn't give him any money and tried to get him to leave. Growing more and more angry, he then insisted that she quit her job and leave with him. When she refused this as well, he grabbed her by the arm and tried to pull her from the building. It was at this point that the club's bouncer stepped in, throwing him out into the street. It was now approaching 3 o'clock in the morning.

Furious, Julio yelled at the bouncer from a safe distance on the sidewalk: "She's my woman, not yours!" He then screamed up at the building: "*Regresare, ha cerrar esto!* I will be back! I'll shut this place down!" The bouncer waved him off and went back into the building, returning to the second floor where the party rolled on.

But Julio wasn't through with Lydia just yet. He would show her and her friends at the club. No one was going to treat Julio González that way! He walked a couple of blocks to an Amoco filling station on the corner of 174th Street and Southern Boulevard. Outside the building, he found a discarded hydraulic fluid jug which he filled with a gallon of gasoline. Edward Porras, a 23-year-old college freshman, was the attendant working the station that night -- his first night on the job. After watching Julio's drunkenly stumble as he carried the jug inside, Edward refused to sell him the gasoline. However, after a customer in the station vouched for Julio, Edward finally relented and sold him his dollars' worth of gas. It was a decision that would haunt young Edward for decades to come.

Having walked the few blocks back down Southern Boulevard to the Happy Land Social Club, Julio stopped and stared up at the building. The street was empty. Only the music and shouting and laughter coming from the second floor gave notice that the party was still in full swing. It was now 3:30 a.m. Only an hour had passed since Julio had entered the club and argued with Lydia. He was about to enter the club once again, but this time with a different purpose in mind.

Julio poured the gasoline on the vestibule floor just inside the entrance, and on the stairs leading to the club on the floor above. The door at the top of the stairs was closed and no one saw what he was doing or guessed what was about to happen. Julio retreated to the vestibule at the bottom of the stairs and struck a match. It sputtered and went out. He struck another match and threw it. The gasoline on the floor ignited with a whoosh, and the fire raced up the stairs. Julio backed out onto the sidewalk and crossed the street to watch.

At first, the fire was trapped between the closed door at the street level and the door at the top of the stairs. Julio was disappointed at the seemingly minimal effect of the fire, but then it quickly gained in ferocity and he was soon satisfied with how his well his plan had worked out.

Ironically, Lydia Feliciano was the first to see the flames outside her little room. Terrified, she tried to warn others by shouting "*Fuego! Fuego!*" (Fire! Fire!) No one in the club above heard the warning. The music was loud and the door was closed.

Lydia found she was not alone at the bottom of the stairs. A group of patrons had just come down to collect their coats and leave. Roberto Argueta, Orbin Huez Galea and their lady friend (or two lady friends -- police were unable to determine) saw the vestibule and stairs fill with flames, cutting off their only exit, or so they thought. Lydia called them to the back of her coat-check room and showed them the door to the service entrance. The door leading outside was in the form of a metal cage, with a steel roll-up door behind it. The group was able to reach through the cage door and force the steel door up and out of the way. They raced out into the street and turned to see one more person stumble out of the building. Meanwhile, the fire ate its way up the stairs toward the party, where the celebrants continued to dance, oblivious to the danger heading their way.

A Pale Horse was Death — Page 169

Ruben Valladarez, the club's DJ, was the only other survivor. His station was uniquely placed in the front and he was able to look down at the entrance and see the fire in the stairway, which by that time was burning so fiercely that the door began to glow a dull red. Ruben turned off the music, turned on the lights and shouted a warning that the club was on fire. A few of the patrons near his area also saw the fire and tried to escape down the stairs, but the fire was too hot and the smoke too thick. Ruben decided to do whatever it took to save himself. He passed those gathered at the door, ran down the stairs through the fire, and rolled out the outside door and onto the sidewalk. Most of his clothes had been burned off and he was severely injured, but he was alive.

Strangely, the first people to escape, including Lydia, were so confused and in shock that they left the area and simply went home. They were believed by many to have perished in the fire until late in the afternoon.

True crime writer Mark Gado described what was to follow: "Now that the door was opened, oxygen poured into the fire and a powerful draft was created. The effect was very similar to a chimney. The fire exploded to life and charged up the wooden steps and into the room. The people on the top of the steps screamed and fled in terror. "*Fuego! Fuego!*" they screamed. Within seconds, a huge cloud of toxic, black smoke filled the staircase. As the blaze began to feed upon itself, the heat increased dramatically. The realization of a fire then became immediate to everyone. Soon the crowd on the dance floor was in a full panic as the black smoke poured unobstructed into the room. There were no windows in the 60' by 20' club. People instinctively fell to the floor face down where at least they could breathe, if only for seconds. For some, it was already too late. Those sitting at the tables had already inhaled the poison gasses and a few breaths of such a mixture is all it takes."

With the upstairs door now open and providing oxygen to feed the flames, the revitalized fire screamed through the club, carrying with it extreme heat and dense, toxic smoke. No windows meant no ventilation, so within three minutes the room was completely filled with smoke. As the fire continued to burn, the smoke became highly concentrated with lethal gasses from the burning plastic that covered the chairs, booths and walls. For a few seconds, people nearest the stairs screamed and tried to escape down the stairs, but the fire was too intense. These were the first to die.

As the smoke thickened, dozens of people on the dance floor became disoriented as they staggered and dropped, knocking over tables and chairs as they fell. Most were dead before they hit the floor. The super-heated gasses raced through the room, suffocating everyone along the way in rapid succession. Death came so quickly that some were found dead where they were sitting when the fire started. Three minutes after the fire burst through the door to the sound of panicked screams, there was only a terrible silence.

The first fire alarm sounded ten minutes after Julio struck his second match. It took only four minutes for Ladder Company 58 to arrive on the scene. The firefighters saw that the flames were already burning themselves out but everything was strangely quiet. No screams. No shouts for help. No signs of anyone on the sidewalk outside and no sounds from within. The only person they saw was the DJ Ruben Vallardares lying in the street barley conscious with the

The burned-out vestibule of the Happy Land Social Club, where the fire was started.

remains of his clothes still smoking. Could it be that they were there for a simple structure fire with no other lives at stake? It was the middle of the night, after all. They had no way of knowing of the carnage that lay just inside the building's brick walls. Not until they broke down the street-level door did they get a hint of what awaited them. In the vestibule and on what remained of the stairs lay a pile of charred bodies, 19 in all. The tangled pile was so dense that the bodies had to be removed before the firefighters could move to the second floor. They were somewhat relieved that the worst appeared to be over; they just needed to make sure the second floor was clear and all remaining residual fires were extinguished.

When the stairs were cleared and the path upwards was open, the first few firefighters cautiously walked into the club. The room was extremely dark. Taking tentative steps, not knowing how badly the floor had been burned, they noticed that the floor felt strangely lumpy and soft under their feet. They began to stumble and trip over what seemed to be bundles of clothes and charred piles of debris. As flashlights snapped on one by one, the firefighters realized to their horror that they had been treading on human bodies.

Bodies were everywhere. Those nearest the top of the stairs were lying in burned, smoldering heaps. As the searchers moved through the room they saw bodies draped over chairs, slumped across tables, propped up against walls or just heaped on the floor where they fell. It was a horrific sight, but worst of all were the dead still sitting at the tables, their hands still grasping their drinks. Some were holding hands, some leaning against each other, and some just facing forward as if waiting for the next song to begin and the dance floor to fill with friends. The flames had hardly touched these people; they had simply taken one or two breaths of the toxic gasses and died.

After the last of the fires were out and the toxic gasses and smoke was ventilated from the building, the firefighters had time to really take in what lay before them. Assistant Chief Frank Nastro described Happy Land: "The scene was paralyzing. We stood there numbed. No one spoke. There were 69 bodies spread about this 24 by 50-foot area. They all could have been sleeping." The "Happy Land" sign still hung overhead, seemed to mock the men below as they bore witness to the dead. Lt. Richard Bittles, one of the first to arrive with Ladder Co. 58, described what he saw on the faces of his fellow firefighters as they struggled to go on with their work: "In their eyes was the hollow and distant look of men who could not believe what had occurred."

One by one, the bodies were carefully removed from the scorched building. The magnitude of the disaster had come upon them so unexpectedly that it took time to organize transportation and find morgue space for such a large number of human remains. Each body was placed gently on the sidewalk or street and covered with a sheet. Terrible grief and confusion arose as many in the gathering crowd noticed that many of the dead were

The sidewalks outside the burned-out building as they filled with bodies. The Happy Land sign, singed but readable, hangs over the scene in grim irony.

unburned, lying there with no sign of how they had died. Somehow, this made everything seem much more grotesque.

After starting the fire, Julio had moved across the street, slowly drinking a beer as he stood watching. He watched as a small group of people ran from the service entrance, unaware that his ex-girlfriend was among them. He watched as Ruben Vallardarez tumbled from the doorway, his clothes still burning as he lay in the street. He watched as the first of the fire trucks arrived. He watched as the first few bodies were pulled from the building. Then he grew tired and decided it was time to go home.

As Julio made his way home, remorse began to set it. When he got to his building, he woke Carmen Melendez, one of his neighbors. He told her he had killed his girlfriend and burned down Happy Land. Carmen, angry at being awakened by this sloppy drunk, told him to go sleep it off and slammed her door in his face. Julio retreated into his tiny, one-room apartment and dropped onto his single bed, pausing only long enough to strip off his gas-soaked clothing. He slept soundly until he was awakened by loud knocking at his door later that afternoon.

Beginning almost before the fire was out, Detectives Kevin Moroney and Andy Lugo were bombarded with questions from witnesses, victims' family members, the press and politicians. It wasn't until later in the afternoon that the two detectives finally got a chance to interview Lydia Feliciano. Until then, they had no idea that she had any involvement in the case other than being one of the few survivors. As they questioned her, she told them about Julio, her former boyfriend. She explained how he had come to the club early that morning, and had become abusive. She described how he had been kicked out by the bouncer and the threats he had shouted back at them before he left. Moroney and Lugo now had a viable suspect.

The two detectives were finally able to get away from their office in the 48th Precinct about four o'clock that afternoon. They drove directly to a rundown tenement building at 31 Buchanan Place. As they climbed the steps to the third floor, they started smelling the strong odor of gasoline. The smell grew stronger as they approached the door belonging to Julio González. On the other side of the door, Julio was still asleep, just as he had been for the past twelve hours. They knocked, and after a time, González answered. The odor of gasoline in the room was almost overwhelming. They waited while Julio got dressed and put on his gasoline-soaked shoes -- the only shoes he owned. The detectives escorted Julio back to their station house for questioning. Apparently, he didn't need much prodding. Within minutes of being read his Miranda Rights, in English and in Spanish, he broke down sobbing and confessed to everything he had done. He was quoted as saying: "I don't know; it looks like something bad got into me. It looks like the devil got into me!"

In the wee hours of the following morning and long after darkness had fallen, González was arraigned in Bronx Criminal Court. Following his arraignment, he was immediately transferred to a nearby psychiatric hospital and placed on suicide watch. Charged with 87 counts of murder, he was officially accused of being the worst mass murderer in American in history at that time.

And it didn't escape notice that the date of the Happy Land fire was shared with another historic New York fire. Exactly 79 years earlier the Triangle Shirtwaist Company factory burned, killing over one hundred people. Most of them were immigrants, just like the Happy Land victims.

The *New York Post* dubbed González "The Monster," a sentiment that was repeated thousands of times throughout the Bronx, the state and the nation. The grief that engulfed the surrounding neighborhoods was a pall upon the Honduran community and the city as a whole. Nearly seventy percent of the dead were Honduran. Ninety children lost one or both parents. Forty parents lost one or more of their children. Roosevelt High School lost five students. The list could go on and on, tabulating the impact of that unimaginable event. Regardless of how the magnitude of the terrible tragedy is measured, the undeniable fact remains that eighty-seven innocent lives were cut short by a drunk seeking revenge.

On March 28, the funerals began. The largest of the funerals centered around 17 caskets lined up inside St. Joseph's Church. Over a dozen funeral homes played host to thousands of mourners over the next few days, closely controlled by police barricades. A memorial of flowers, mementos, candles and signs began forming outside the Happy Land building. The names of those who died that night may some day be forgotten but the tragic loss will be felt for generations.

Psychologists who examined González found him to be mentally ill and not responsible for his actions on that fateful night, but a jury found him sane and criminally responsible. Julio would stand trial for his crimes.

The trial of Julio González took place in August of the following year. Judge Burton Roberts worked hard to guarantee him a fair trial, but the outcome was inevitable. There was just too much evidence, including multiple long and detailed confessions by Julio himself. In the end, he was found guilty of 87 counts of murder and 87 counts of arson. The jury foreman responded with the word "guilty" 174 times as the verdict was read on August 9, 1991.

Julio González during his trial.

A month later, González learned his fate as he received a sentence of 25 years to life for each of the 174 guilty verdicts. His combined sentence of 4,350 years was the longest in New York history. González was sent to the Clinton Correctional Facility in Dannemora, N.Y., where he remains today. According to New York state law, multiple sentences received for multiple crimes committed during the same event or action are required to be served concurrently. Because of this, he will be eligible for parole in March of 2015, but few believe that he will ever again be a free man. Julio González will likely die in prison.

Lydia Feliciano, a 45-year-old mother of two at the time of the fire, is rapidly approaching her 70s and is in ill health. She has had open-heart surgery and is on dialysis. Her family says she looks much older than her years and sorrow shadows her face.

Judge Burton Roberts presided over the class action civil suit filed against the owners and operators of the Happy Land Social Club building. The suit was finally settled in 1995 with an award of 15 million dollars, to be divided equally between the victims' families -- roughly $172,000 for each death.

The victims of the Happy Land Social Club fire are memorialized at the site of the fire with a traffic circle containing an eight-foot-high granite obelisk surrounded by an ornate iron fence. The names of the dead are inscribed on the memorial. The site has been named "The Plaza of the Eighty-Seven." The fire was also immortalized in song including Duran Duran's "Sin of the City," Joe Jackson's "Happy Land" and Tom Russell's "A Dollar's Worth of Gasoline."

The once-strong and vibrant Honduran community disintegrated shortly after the fire. Some went back to Honduras but most simply moved away, unable to withstand the daily reminder of all they had lost.

The building that housed the Happy Land Social Club still stands. For the most part, it remained empty and padlocked for the better part of 17 years. The debris from the fire had been hauled away and the damage repaired, but for all those years no one felt it appropriate to start a new business on the ashes of so many who died in such a horrible fashion. Others avoided the building, fearing that the boarded-up storefronts hid from view the *espíritu de los muertos*: the spirits of the dead.

Only recently were the storefronts were filled. Today an accountant and tax business is on the left and a unisex barbershop on the right. The second floor remains empty, at least of living inhabitants.

The proprietors of the two businesses on the first floor, along with several of their customers began hearing footsteps overhead, almost as soon as they moved into the building. On some occasions, the footsteps are accompanied by the sounds of murmuring voices and faint strains of calypso music. Upon investigation, no one has ever been found on the second floor who could be responsible for the strange noises.

There is more evidence that not all the patrons of Happy Land left the club when their bodies were removed after the fire. On separate occasions, employees working on the first floor have looked up to see a young man and a young woman walk past them, holding hands and huddled close together. It is not until they fade to nothing that the witnesses remember the burned edges on the young couple's clothing, and recognize the smell of singed hair. How sad to consider the many years this couple have walked the floors of the lonely and deserted building before life returned to the little store fronts bringing living people to finally bear witness to their presence. One can't help but wonder how many others may still linger unseen, bound to the site by their violent deaths.

Espíritu de los muertos.

WATER

1838: DEATH ON THE OHIO RIVER
The Explosion of the Moselle

In the early 1800s, steamboats were rapidly becoming the most popular mode of transportation on American rivers. Inventor Robert Fulton first conceived of a commercial line of steamboats, and made that idea a reality in 1811. Shipping and travel began growing at a fantastic rate. Fulton's first regular shipping route was on the mighty Mississippi River between New Orleans and Natchez, Mississippi, with his first steamboat, the Pittsburgh built New Orleans. In 1814, New Orleans saw 20 steamboat arrivals in a single year, and by 1834, she was welcoming over 1,200 landings annually.

As steamboat travel on inland waters became more common, scores of new routes were developed to take advantage of America's abundance of rivers. These routes expanded to include travel up and down the coastlines as well, but were never as popular. Somehow, traveling on rivers felt safer, without the possibility of being washed overboard by giant waves should an oceanic storm arise without warning.

These steamboats, also known as paddle boats or river boats, were equipped with large boilers below decks to create the steam to drive the paddle wheels. As these boilers were early in their development, they weren't always as reliable as the operators would have wished. Although river travel was much more relaxing that traveling on land, it carried with it its own dangers. If the boilers were not well designed, poorly constructed or improperly maintained, they often failed. When a steamboat boiler failed, everyone knew it because a failing boiler was an exploding boiler. The boats themselves virtually never survived a boiler explosion, the result of which was

The *Moselle*, as she set off on her maiden voyage

like a bomb going off in the belly of the wooden-hulled boats.

Wherever the route took these boats, they rarely traveled in any other condition than fully loaded. They were equipped to carry all sorts of cargo including livestock, bales of cotton, manufactured goods, raw materials and people -- lots of people. A hundred years later when traveling on large ocean liners, the poorest passengers were berthed in steerage deep down inside the hull. It was quite different with the early steamboats. Steerage passengers traveled on the open decks; eating, sleeping and visiting was all done on deck if you couldn't afford a ticket for a cabin. So when a boiler exploded, the poorest passengers were the first to die, either from being ripped apart by the explosion or scalded to death by the spray of steam and boiling water. The reality was that it didn't really matter where you were on the boat if the boiler exploded, because your chances of surviving were low. Men wore heavy suits and women were encumbered with long, heavy skirts, neither of which were conducive to swimming in the fast-flowing and often frigid rivers. Even if they had time to strip off some of their clothing, it rarely made a difference. Very few men, and almost no women at that time knew how to swim. If a person was not killed by the explosion or the steam, and if they were unable to catch hold of a piece of floating debris, more often than not they drowned before reaching the shore.

The hazards of steamboat travel notwithstanding, it became more popular than ever. As these boats began carrying more passengers, and a more affluent class of passengers, new designs and technological improvements were introduced. There was also a growing demand for greater cargo space, making each trip more profitable.

When the steamboats could get no larger for river travel, the focus shifted to speed. The lumbering steamboats became faster. In 1816, it took twenty-five days to steam from New Orleans to Louisville, Kentucky. By 1850, the same trip took only four and a half days. Speed was increased by installing bigger boilers and MORE boilers. These additional boilers took up extra cargo space below deck, but that wasn't a big concern since the faster they ran, the more trips the boats could make. The number of boilers installed increased to two, three and even four on a single boat.

The boats were designed and built with a specific capacity calculated, but as there were no laws and no one to oversee that the capacities were followed, they were largely ignored. The common practice was for the captains to load the boats first with cargo, then with passengers, until there was not much more than standing room only on the decks. The captains personally profited from the excesses: The overflow of passengers meant more coins in their pockets. Since steamboat captains were usually a confident, if not an arrogant bunch, believing they could handle whatever came up, extra passengers were certainly nothing to worry about.

Captain Isaac Perrin was one such captain. He had learned his trade as an officer on the steamboat Missouri Fulton. Now at age 28, it was time to for him to master his own steamboat. On March 31, 1838, he took possession of the *Moselle*, straight from the boat builder. He was to be owner and master. Construction of the

Moselle had begun on December 1, 1837 in the Cincinnati boatyards. Four months later she was steaming the Ohio River with Perrin in command.

The *Moselle* had been built for speed, and she had four large boilers under her foredecks. In just her first month on the river she was already setting speed records. She was described in a local newspaper as being "The swiftest steamboat in America." A contemporary report describes her as "Regarded as the very paragon of western steam boats; she was perfect in form and construction, elegant and superb in all her equipments, and enjoyed a reputation for speed which admitted of no rivalship." She completed her first voyage by steaming the one hundred and ten miles from Portsmouth to Cincinnati in a record-breaking seven hours and fifty-five minutes. Her last voyage had been a much longer steam: that of seven hundred and fifty miles from St. Louis to Cincinnati in two days and sixteen hours. This trip had broken the previously held record by several hours.

The *Moselle* had a mighty reputation for having been in the water less than a month. Crowds gathered wherever she landed and on the shorelines, just to watch her fly past. Captain Perrin was keenly aware of the name he had made for himself and his beautiful steamboat. He was becoming well known as a racing captain, one who was unwilling to allow any other boat to pass him or beat his times, unaware that his love of speed would prove to be his doom.

And so it was that on April 25, 1838, Perrin and his beautiful *Moselle* were docked at the Cincinnati landing, preparing for a speed run to Louisville and St. Louis. Her cargo had been loaded and she was taking on passengers. His love of speed was one thing, but Perrin also loved money. The weather that afternoon was pleasant, and the crowd at the landing was unusually large; they all wanted to board the illustrious *Moselle*.

Perrin allowed passengers to continue boarding until the very last minute. When he pushed off from the landing between four and five o'clock, he was carrying at least 280 passengers, and some witnesses estimated as many as 300. Her hold was nearly full with livestock and other cargo. Almost all the passengers were out on deck, taking in the last of the afternoon sun and likely anticipating an exciting trip aboard the famous steamboat.

Before heading to St. Louis, Captain Perrin had to make a short trip up-river to Fulton to take aboard a family of German immigrants and their belongings. This was only a little more than a mile out of his way, but as he was leaving the Cincinnati landing, a rival steamboat was also leaving for St. Louis. This little trip in the wrong direction would slow him down. Even though he would be well behind the other steamboat by the time he cast off from Fulton, Perrin fully intended to keep his position as the swiftest boat on the river; in fact, he had a plan...

Fulton was small and had only a simple log wharf. Perrin edged the *Moselle* up to the wharf, allowing the passengers and their cargo to be boarded. As he did so, a newspaper later reported he "madly held on to all the steam that he could create, with the intention, not only of showing off to the best advantage the great speed of his boat as it passed down the river the full length of the city (Cincinnati), but that he might overtake and pass another boat."

As the boat sat at the small wharf, steam continued to build. People in the crowd who had come out to view the *Moselle* began to comment to each other about the strange noise coming off the steam. At the same time, passengers became uneasy with what they thought was "injudicious management of the steam apparatus" and several openly begged the captain to back it off. The heat in the boilers was rising to the point that passengers noticed that the deck boards beneath their feet were getting hot. One man became so distressed that he chose to leave the boat.

When the new passengers and their meager cargo were aboard, the bow of the *Moselle* was pushed off from the shore and Captain Perrin engaged the paddle wheel at maximum steam. Before the wheel had time to make one full revolution, all four of the boilers violently exploded in unison.

The blast was so powerful that the forward portion of the boat just beyond the wheel was completely demolished. Pieces of the boat and boiler, along with cargo and passengers were blown high in the air. As body parts and large pieces of boilerplate flew overhead, a collective scream rose from the crowd on shore. With the front half of the boat blown to splinters, the remaining passengers began jumping into the freezing river. They had no time to think about their plight as the remaining half of the boat immediately began to founder. The sinking hulk was caught by the current and carried a hundred yards downstream, where in only a few moments, she met the river bottom. The sole part of the *Moselle* remaining above water was the uppermost peak of her

The *Moselle* explodes with a such tremendous force that pieces of boilerplate weighing hundreds of pounds flew over 800 feet.

cabin. She had been cast into her watery grave at the tender age of twenty-five days.

Upriver, where the explosion had taken place, the water's surface was awash with struggling survivors and their baggage. There was no chance of a rescue by other boats as there were none. This location was only used for brief on or off loadings and was not a place where other boats collected. The spectators on the shore were helpless to assist those in the water, able only to render aid to the individuals who were carried to the shore by the force of the blast or to those fortunate enough to have been able to paddle to safety.

Witnesses recounted seeing between sixty and seventy persons in the water after the wreck had sunk. Some held fast to debris, trying to stay afloat, while others splashed about in panic. Of the large number in the water, less than a dozen made it to shore alive.

One young boy was found battered but alive, frantically pacing the shoreline. He was sobbing and begging for anyone around him to help his family. His mother, father and three sisters were in the water, struggling helplessly to get to shore. Sadly, they were out too far for assistance, and all five disappeared beneath the surface, one by one, as he watched. Later that evening, that same young boy experienced what many observers deemed a true miracle. After watching nearly his entire family drown in the river, his infant brother was found unharmed, floating on a piece of hurricane decking.

The sight on shore was heart-rending. Bruised, scalded and broken, between twenty and thirty corpses were strewn along the riverbank. Many of them had been blown into the air by the explosion and lay where they had landed. Among them were scattered various arms, legs, heads, fingers, toes and even internal organs such as hearts, kidneys and lungs -- all having been viciously ripped from the unfortunates who had been standing on the deck directly over the boilers. One victim was blown off the boat with such force that his body flew over a hundred yards and landed on top of a house. The impact was so violent that his head and upper torso pierced the roof and dangled, blood dripping, inside the house.

Captain Perrin was also one of those who had been standing on that particular part of the deck, though his body was found somewhat intact. He had been blown nearly eighty feet from the spot where he stood. Perrin had been talking to a member of the crew at the time of the explosion, but his companion was simply knocked onto a surviving part of the deck, and survived the ordeal unharmed. There were rumors that the captain's body had landed on the Kentucky bank, nearly a quarter of a mile across the river. Another story told of his body being found near the top of a large tree at the edge of the water. Both rumors were dispelled by witnesses testifying at the Cincinnati investigation into the event.

The explosion was so sudden that for quite some time no one knew who had been killed and who had survived. Women searched for husbands and husbands searched for wives. Parents called for their children. Children cried for their parents, brothers and sisters. A majority of those traveling on the *Moselle* that afternoon were families, and no family was left intact.

When word of the tragedy reached Cincinnati, hundreds of people rushed to the site to help however they could. Some set to work giving aid to the injured, others dragged the dead and dying from the water, and some stood in stunned silence, unable to do anything but watch. The devastation was tremendous but nothing prepared them for the sight of the human wreckage around them, and the broken spirits of those who had lost loved ones.

A father had been able to save himself and one of his sons, but later found that his wife and his other five children were lost. A young woman could not be calmed as she cried for her family, repeatedly crying out "Oh, my Father! Oh, my Mother! Oh, my sisters!" Two boys of about five or six were holding tightly to each other and sobbing. One cried for his lost father and the other for his entire family.

One man lost his wife, eight children and everything they owned to the river. Another man seemed to have become completely deranged. He was found lying on the ground, holding a severely injured child on one side and the corpse of his dead daughter on the other. At his feet lay his dying wife. No one could coax him from his macabre position. A physically uninjured young man lay crying in a heap and could not be consoled as he cried for the loss of his wife and five children. Similar stories repeated themselves up and down the shoreline.

Not every story was a sad one. A woman pulled from the water dropped to her knees and gave thanks that her life was spared, then dropped the rest of the way to the ground, crying out for her child. The baby had been found floating on a pile of debris and was taken to her mother, alive and well. Occasionally, a cry of joy was heard as one family member found another alive, but sobs quickly followed as they took stock of whom they had lost.

Eva Weiss, her husband Jacob Weber and their children had sailed from Bavaria to America to start a new life. They were making the final leg of their trip to a farm in the Midwest. From the family history of the Weber Sauer family, this remarkable story of survival from the *Moselle* was published: "*Fortunately, Eva was wearing a hoop skirt, and as she was blown into the Ohio River, it caught air. Some of her children used it as a life preserver to cling to while awaiting rescue from the chill, swift-moving water. Every belonging the Weber family had owned -- everything they brought with them from the old country -- their money, clothing, personal items -- everything was gone. But that didn't matter as most of their family had survived.*"

The force of the explosion was enough to destroy half the ship and send people flying through the air. But bodies weren't the only thing flying that day, and it was truly remarkable that none in the crowd on shore were injured. The massive pieces of boilerplate were the most damaging, smashing through house walls and roofs as they went. A piece of plate weighing 450 pounds was thrown 170 feet. Another weighing 336 pounds flew 480 feet. Still another piece of plate, weighing 236 pounds, was found to have flown over 800 feet and landed on a brick sidewalk, pulverizing the bricks.

Many of the steerage passengers were German and Irish immigrants taken aboard in Cincinnati and never registered, so their names were never known, and their bodies never identified. Whole families may have lost their lives. There was no exact count of passengers, but the best estimate was between 280 and 300. The number of known dead was 160. Some bodies weren't recovered for over a month. The body of Lt. Col. John Fowle, an Army officer headed for his new post in Florida, was found three weeks later and 100 miles downriver. It is assumed that there were many poor, unnamed passengers whose lives were lost that day, and whose bodies were lost forever.

The day following the disaster, a public meeting was held in Cincinnati with Mayor Samuel W. Davies presiding. Survivors and witnesses gave testimony of the day's events. The purpose of the meeting was to discuss the facts of the event, determine a cause and find solutions. At the end of the day, several resolutions had been passed. The most important made note of "The great and increasing carelessness in the navigation of steam vessels." They urged that Congress to look into this problem. They further felt the tragedy was caused by "reckless and criminal inattention to their duty on the part of those who had the management of the Moselle, nor was there any attempt to palliate their conduct."

Following a complete investigation initiated by a citizens' committee in Cincinnati, Judge James Hall wrote: "The recent explosion of the steamboat *Moselle* at Cincinnati affords a most awful illustration of the danger of steam navigation, when conducted by the ignorant and careless."

The good people of Cincinnati worked hard to care for the survivors and recover the victims of the terrible explosion of the *Moselle*. They then worked equally hard to bring the hazards of steamboat travel without government regulations, or anyone to oversee how these boats were operated, to the attention of the public and to the government. Sadly, their hard work was to no avail. Over the next several decades, steamboat boilers continued to explode and travelers continued to die.

Steamboat explosions didn't really stop until river travel fell out of favor as roads and railroads became more popular. Unfortunately, this trend did not change before the worst steamboat explosion of all time occurred twenty-eight years after the *Moselle* disaster, almost to the day. On April 27, 1865, the *SS Sultana*, steaming on the Mississippi River near Memphis, suffered a fatal boiler explosion that sent her to the bottom of the river. This proved to be the most deadly maritime disaster in history - even today. There has never been a more deadly accident on the water as the nearly 1,800 souls that departed this life with the wreck of the *SS Sultana*.

1860: THE *TITANIC* OF THE GREAT LAKES
The Wreck of the Lady Elgin

One of the greatest horrors to ever occur on the Great Lakes was the sinking of the steamboat *Lady Elgin* on Lake Michigan in September 1860. She was struck by the lumber schooner *Augusta* not far off the coast of Chicago's North Shore and sank in just 20 minutes. Although records are unclear, she may have been carrying as many as 700 passengers when she went down. Of these, only 98 were saved.

The double-decked wooden side-wheel steamer was built in Buffalo, New York, in 1851 and was named for the wife of Lord Elgin, the governor-general of Canada. *Lady Elgin* was one of the largest and most opulent passenger steamships on the Great Lakes, but she quickly broke apart when struck by the other vessel, casting passengers into storm-tossed waters. Although many of them made it to shallow water on makeshift rafts, hundreds died in the breakers just offshore. The *Lady Elgin* was considered the *Titanic* of her day, and the wreck forever changed the social fabric of Milwaukee, Wisconsin.

The disaster occurred at a time of unprecedented tension in America, with a divisive presidential campaign going on and a war quickly approaching. Wisconsin was known as a fervently abolitionist state, and had threatened to secede from the Union if the federal government did not abolish slavery. When it began to look like Wisconsin's secession might really happen, the state Adjutant General surveyed all the state's militia companies to determine which would support the state and which would support the federal government if it did. Milwaukee hosted four main militias; the German Green Jagers, the German Black Jagers, the Milwaukee Light Guard and the Irish Union Guard of Milwaukee's Third Ward. When the question of the militia's loyalty was posed to Captain Garrett Barry, the commander of Milwaukee's Irish Guard and a Democrat, he replied that even though he was opposed to slavery, he considered any stand against the federal government to be treason. When the reply reached state officials, Governor Alexander Randall promptly revoked the militia's commission and disarmed them. But Barry and his men refused to disband, and were determined to raise money to buy new weapons. With the help of the local Democratic Party, they decided to commission an excursion to raise money and lift political spirits. They booked passage for the militia and their guests on *Lady Elgin* for a cruise to a Democratic rally in Chicago, where they would go on parade and hear a speech by Illinois Congressman and presidential candidate Stephen A. Douglas.

Tragically, many of the Irish Guard would never return home.

The excursion left Milwaukee during the early morning hours of September 7, 1860, and docked in Chicago at dawn. That morning, the men went on parade and then toured the city. The attended a debate and later in the evening, went to a dinner dance where they listened to a speech by Stephen Douglas. By 11:00 p.m., the Guard had returned to the ship, and were ready to return to Milwaukee, but Captain Jack Wilson of the *Lady Elgin* was worried about the weather. Wilson was a veteran sailor on the Great Lakes and knew that weather in September could be treacherous. However, his passengers were eager to get home and pressure to maintain a mail delivery schedule finally convinced him to get underway.

Several new passengers were taken on board, and by 11:30 p.m. *Lady Elgin* had cleared the Chicago Harbor and was steaming out into the open lake. The records and reports vary, but contemporary accounts suggest that between 600 and 700 people were on board when the steamship departed. She was not overcrowded, though. The steamer had been designed to handle a large passenger load, even if some of them were not supposed to be on board. There had been several parties taking place while the *Lady Elgin* was docked, and since she departed with little warning, a numbered of guests didn't have a chance to disembark.

As the ship sailed off into the dark waters of Lake

The *Lady Elgin* tied up at the dock, waiting for her passengers

Michigan, many of the excursionists, exhausted from their long day, turned in for the night. Meanwhile, the parties continued and people danced and reveled in the ship's spacious salons, completely unaware that danger and death awaited them. A few hours after the *Lady Elgin* left Chicago, the wind began to pick up, eventually reaching gale strength, and turning the slightly choppy waters of Lake Michigan into great rolling waves. *Lady Elgin* weathered the storm well and continued on toward Milwaukee.

At 2:30 a.m., the steamship was about seven miles off Winnetka, Illinois, when a tremendous crash was felt throughout the ship and she suddenly lurched onto her port side. Passengers who looked out of the portholes reported seeing the lights of a vessel rapidly bearing down on *Lady Elgin,* and they braced for a collision. When the other ship rammed into the side of the excursion ship, all of *Lady Elgin's* oil lamps went out, plunging the passengers and crew into darkness and adding to the confusion on board. Captain Wilson and First Mate George Davis had been asleep in their staterooms and dressed quickly. Wilson went below and found water gushing into the engine room, while Davis rushed to the pilothouse and ordered the ship turned toward the Illinois shore. When Captain Wilson returned to the pilothouse, he pulled Davis aside and privately told him that *Lady Elgin* would never make it to land.

The ship that had come out of the darkness and collided with the *Lady Elgin* was *Augusta*, a two-masted schooner bound for Chicago with a deck load of lumber. Despite the strong winds, *Augusta* was still flying most of her canvas and was sailing out of control. As she raced through the water, the heavy load of lumber had shifted and she was nearly sailing on her side. Fearing that she might capsize, her crew worked frantically to gain control of her --- failing to spot *Lady Elgin* until it was too late. Her second mate, John Vorce, was the first to spot the other vessel. He spotted *Lady Elgin's* lights from a considerable distance and reported it to Captain Darius Malott. Unfortunately, though, in the confusion and chaos of the storm, Malott gave no orders until *Lady Elgin* was almost directly in front of them. At the last minute, his orders finally came, and he yelled to the helmsman, "Hard up! For God's sake, man! Hard up!" But time had run out and the schooner shattered the side of *Lady Elgin*, slamming into her just aft of the port paddle wheel.

Lady Elgin was still plowing along through the rough water, and as *Augusta's* bow was buried deep into her side, she careened along dragging the schooner along with her. The wood on *Lady Elgin's* side splintered and broke, and as *Augusta* was carried along, she tore loose the steamer's paddle wheel and ripped apart the wooden hull. A few moments later, the schooner dislodged and *Lady Elgin* pulled away.

Captain Malott and his crew were immediately concerned for their own vessel, fearing that she might have extensive damage below the waterline. When they looked about for *Lady Elgin*, they could no longer see her, causing Malott to remark, "That steamer sure got away from here in a hurry." Believing that they had struck only a glancing blow to *Lady Elgin*, and fearing that they might founder, *Augusta* immediately continued on for Chicago.

But *Lady Elgin* had not escaped. Her lights had gone out, making her invisible in the darkness of the storm. It was pandemonium on board as the crew worked feverishly to save her. There had been 50 head of cattle in pens below deck, and the crew drove them overboard in an attempt to lighten the load. Other cargo, including heavy crates of iron stoves, was moved to the starboard side in order to raise the gaping hole in *Lady Elgin's* side above the waterline. An attempt was made to launch one of the lifeboats, but it was lowered into the water without being secured and had no oars. Those on board watched helplessly as it drifted away from the steamer with only the First Mate and a few crewmen on board. Another lifeboat leaked so badly that it couldn't be used at all. Some of the workers in the engine room used a mattress to try and stem the flow of water by lodging it in the hole, but they were unable to hold back the rush of the water. As *Lady Elgin* sank, she began to break apart, cutting off most of the passengers from reaching the life preservers. Passengers began taking hold of anything that would float and Irish Guard men, who also served as firefighters in Milwaukee, began chopping the hurricane deck with axes in order to make a raft. Captain Wilson, crew members and passengers chopped down doors in order to rescue sleeping passengers. *Lady Elgin* sank stern first and the air rushing forward caused her upper works to explode as she came apart and sank below the waves. Within minutes, the broken vessel had sunk to the bottom of Lake Michigan. Only her bow and two large sections of the decking remained afloat. As *Lady Elgin* vanished, the skies opened up and poured rain on the survivors with flashes of lightning illuminating the horror of the scene.

The unlucky passengers of the *Lady Elgin* were left in the wet blackness of the night, and scores of them would not survive.

As dawn broke the sky, there were still hundreds of survivors clinging to various pieces of debris and decking. The lake was still very rough, and the large deck sections slowly came apart in the surging waves. Captain Wilson had taken charge of an infant and was sheltering it from the wind and waves. He reached out to hand the child to a woman who was nearby so he could try and rig a sail. Just then, a wave washed over their crude raft and swept the child from the woman's arms to its death.

Two large hull sections, with over 100 people clinging to each of them, remained afloat for nearly five hours before they neared land. First Mate George Davis' lifeboat reached shore first, just below the bluffs at Hubbard Woods. He scaled the cliff and woke the Gage family, who sent word of the disaster to Chicago via the Chicago & Milwaukee railroad station. By 8:00 a.m., student volunteers from Northwestern University were on the scene as the wreckage and the rafts approached the shore. The survivors began to be filled with cheer, incorrectly believing that they would soon be safe.

Unknown to them, the storm had generated a massive surf with a powerful undertow just offshore. When the flimsy rafts reached the breakers, they immediately disintegrated, pulling their human cargo deep under the water. Perhaps as many as 400 survivors reached the shallow water, but fewer than a hundred were saved, with the rest drowning in the churning wreckage and surf.

There were numerous acts of heroism among both the rescuers and survivors. Captain Wilson was lost while trying to save two women caught in the undertow. He was dashed against the rocks by the waves and killed. His body was not found for three days, when it washed ashore at Michigan City, Indiana, 60 miles away.

Captain Garrett Barry of the Irish Guard was also lost while trying to save survivors. He drowned less than

The sinking of the *Lady Elgin*

100 feet from shore, valiantly trying to fight his way through the waves. Exhausted, he passed out and sank beneath the water.

One of several distinguished people lost in the disaster was Herbert Ingraham, a member of the British Parliament, and the owner of the *London Illustrated News*. Among the best-known heroes was Edward Spencer, a student from Northwestern University. He was said to have repeatedly charged into the surging water to rescue people, despite receiving numerous injuries from floating wreckage. He was credited with saving 18 people, after which he collapsed in delirium, repeatedly asking bystanders, "Did I do my best?" He was allegedly confined to a wheelchair for the rest of his life and was the inspiration for the establishment of the Evanston, Illinois, U.S. Lifesaving Station, which was constantly manned by Northwestern students. A plaque in his honor remains on display at the university today, commemorating his heroic efforts.

Many other survivors made it shore on their own. One of them washed ashore on the carcass of a dead cow, while another climbed into one of the Irish Guard band's bass drums and rode the waves to shore. Another man climbed into a steamer trunk and paddled it to shore like a canoe.

But the small numbers of those who survived paled when compared to the hundreds who perished. It was a tragedy like nothing anyone in the region had ever seen before.

While passengers and crew members of *Lady Elgin* were fighting for their lives in the churning waters of the lake, *Augusta* was sailing into port. She was leaking badly and her bow was crushed. When Captain Malott learned that *Lady Elgin* had gone down after the wreck, he was horrified. He promptly gathered his crew and stated his case to shipping officials. He claimed that the configuration of lights on *Lady Elgin* was incorrect, which caused him to misjudge the distance. He also explained that he believed that he had only damaged the steamer's trim and feared for the safety of his own struggling vessel, which is why he left without offering assistance.

Despite his pleas and excuses, public outcry against Captain Malott was harsh. The newspapers attacked him, suggesting that he was an agent of the burgeoning Confederacy, or perhaps working for pro-Confederacy Britain, where Malott had lived for some time. Rampant speculation accused him of ramming *Lady Elgin* as part of a plot to kill the Irish Guard. Angry mobs began to gather and the crew of *Augusta* went into hiding. Captain Malott was arrested and held for formal hearings, during which no evidence was found that the wreck had been anything other than an accident.

The bodies of the *Lady Elgin* passengers continued to wash up all around Lake Michigan – some as far away as 80 miles from the scene of the wreck -- well into December. Of all of those lost, nearly half of them were never found. Some of the victims could not be identified and ended up in a mass grave in Winnetka. Others were returned to Milwaukee, where scores of gravestones were inscribed with the words "Lost on the Lady Elgin." Because no official passenger list survived the tragedy, and it was known that many unticketed passengers were on board, the exact number of passengers and victims will never be known.

The disaster was said to have orphaned more than 1,000 Milwaukee children, and the entire city mourned the tragedy. Most of the Irish Guard members belonged to the parish served by the St. John Cathedral in Milwaukee, and the church continues to hold a memorial service for the *Lady Elgin* victims on September 8 each year. Milwaukee's Irish Third Ward was decimated by the tragedy, and it permanently changed the city's social and ethnic make-up. The Irish population in Milwaukee never truly recovered.

The disaster prompted popular songwriter Henry C. Work to pen the song 'Lost on the *Lady Elgin*," which became an enduring piece of pre-Civil War American music.

The disaster served to increase tensions in America at the time, mostly due to the newspapers fanning the flames of conspiracy and suggesting the Irish Guard were victims of a pro-slavery plot. Wisconsin's Governor Randall was portrayed as a villain by many for disarming the Irish Guard in the first place, which forced them to journey to Chicago to raise funds for replacement weapons. While suggesting that the governor was part of a larger conspiracy was almost comical, the continued newspaper stories fanned the flames of conflict over slavery and issues of states' rights.

Officially, there was no one to blame for the disaster. An inquest exonerated both captains involved and blamed the rules of lakes navigation instead.

Lady Elgin herself remained a problem for many years to come. Her bow remained afloat for a time after the wreck, and drifted until her anchors dragged several miles off Winnetka. The upside-down hull section remained a hazard to navigation for some time before finally sinking into the waters of the lake.

After that, the ship was largely forgotten by all but historical societies until the middle 1970s when Chicago salvager Harry Zych began hunting for her remains. He eventually found them on the bottom of the lake in 1989, beneath 60 feet of water. The wreck became the subject of an extended legal battle with the state of Illinois, which Zych eventually won. *Lady Elgin* is now the only privately owned historic wreck on the Great Lakes, and research and salvage work continues today. More than 200 artifacts have been brought up from the site – from swords to a chandelier – but as of this writing, no museum has been found to host or fund an exhibit.

What will become of *Lady Elgin's* remains is still unknown.

There are many stories of ghost ships and related hauntings in Lake Michigan. And while *Lady Elgin* has never mysteriously appeared as an ethereal vessel, steaming across the lake for eternity, there have been a few ghost reports connected to the wreck. According to a number of legends at Northwestern University, students of the past frequently encountered people on the beach, stumbling up out of the water and asking for help. These soaking and bedraggled figures appear in early September and seemed to come from nowhere. When witnesses turned away for a moment, the apparitions disappeared.

But the weirdest – and some say supernatural – events connected to the crash don't involve *Lady Elgin*, but the ship that struck her, *Augusta*.

Maritime superstition claims that any ship's name ending with the letter "A" brings bad luck, and the history of *Augusta* certainly seems to bear that out. Her entire sailing career was so filled with misfortune that she was eventually renamed, although sailors also regard changing the name of a ship as bad luck, as well. If you combine the history of *Augusta* with the ill-fated *Lady Elgin*, it seems almost tragically fitting that the two doomed ships were fated to meet in the storm-tossed waters of Lake Michigan.

Some believed that *Lady Elgin* was doomed from the start. Because her boilers and engine once powered a slave trading ship called *Cleopatra*, some said she was cursed from the moment of her launching in 1851. In 1854, *Lady Elgin* hit an uncharted reef off Manitowoc, Wisconsin, while carrying hundreds of passengers. The following year, problems with the ship's machinery led to her being towed to Chicago. Two years later, a fire caused severe damage to many of the ship's staterooms and hurricane deck. In 1858, she once again hit a reef, this time near Copper Harbor, Michigan. She had to be towed again in 1859 due to broken engine parts. And then, of course, in 1860, she went to her watery grave after her collision with *Augusta*. Few ships could boast such an impressive run of bad luck – although *Augusta* would come close.

After the crash, *Augusta* delivered her load of lumber to Chicago, unaware of the disaster that has since been called one of the greatest maritime horrors in history. Captain Malott, who had turned 27 years old on the day of the accident, was subsequently arrested, but a trial cleared him of charges of negligence. He had only recently taken command of *Augusta* and had not yet learned that she was difficult to steer when carrying cargo. The wreck had been an accident, and if there was any blame to be laid, according to the hearing, it was on the fact that the two ships were not well lighted. If any good resulted from the tragedy, it was the ruling four years later that all sailing vessels had to carry running lights.

Already rumored to be a bad luck vessel, *Augusta* was now seen as cursed. After spending the winter in dry dock in Detroit, *Augusta* set sail the following spring under the name *Colonel Cook*. But perhaps more attention should have been paid to the superstition about not giving a ship the name of a vessel that has been lost to the lake. Three years earlier, a schooner called *Colonel Cook* had departed from Detroit bound for England. It never arrived, wrecking en route in the St. Lawrence River.

The owners had also ordered the ship to be painted black, but a name change and a new paint job weren't enough to conceal her past. When she arrived in Milwaukee with a cargo of lumber, word quickly spread that the ship that had killed so many Milwaukee Irishmen nine months earlier was now in the harbor. The former *Augusta* had to rapidly set sail before an outraged mob burned the ship while she waited in port.

Colonel Cook sailed out of the lakes and began working along the Atlantic Coast, eventually returning to the Great Lakes a few years later. But due to her reputation as a cursed ship, it was always difficult to hire a crew. It seemed that every sailor knew how many people had died when *Augusta* ripped open *Lady Elgin*. Those men who did sign on as crew members told tales of hauntings on board the unlucky vessel. Strange lights were reported on the night deck, mysterious footsteps were heard, as well as scratching sounds on the wood planking as though people were trying to claw their way to safety. Finally, on September 23, 1894, *Colonel Cook* became stranded on in Lake Erie, breaking apart near Euclid, Ohio.

The unlucky *Augusta* was no more.

This marked the end of the curse, which had already claimed its most famous victim nearly 30 years before: Captain Darius Malott.

It had taken some time, but Captain Malott and his crew had eventually found work on another ship, a bark called *Mojave*. Strangely, *Mojave* disappeared without a trace on September 8, 1864, exactly four years after the *Lady Elgin* disaster. All but one of the crew lost on *Mojave* had also been on *Augusta* when she rammed *Lady Elgin*. Whatever happened to *Mojave* is one of the unsolved mysteries of the Great Lakes – although some have suggested that the vanishing was perhaps a case of justice finally being served. The ship may have simply foundered in northern Lake Michigan, but legend has it that history finally caught up with the captain and crew, and they were murdered by those avenging the deaths of the Irish Guard. No one will ever know which version of the story is true, but it does lead us wondering if perhaps they merely cheated fate the first time around.

Or perhaps, *Augusta* really was a cursed ship after all.

1874: THE MILL RIVER DISASTER

Before the horror in Johnstown, Pennsylvania, in 1889, the most devastating dam collapse in American history occurred in the Mill River Valley of western Massachusetts. It happened early one morning in May 1874, when a reservoir dam suddenly burst, sending an avalanche of water roaring down a narrow valley lined with small towns, factories and farms. Within an hour, 139 people were dead and four towns had been washed away. The death toll would have been even higher if not for the bravery of three men who relayed the warning down the valley, racing ahead of the surging waters in wagons and on horseback.

The Mill River Flood instantly became one of America's biggest newspaper stories, and people soon learned of destruction, daring escapes and the horror of searching for the dead among acres of debris. Not surprisingly, investigations into the disaster showed that the dam had collapsed due to poor construction and negligence by the companies that built it to power their factories. But as with so many other disasters in the nineteenth century, no one was ever held accountable.

The factory owners and wealthy industrialists who developed the Mill River Valley in western Massachusetts knew that water was their greatest asset. The steeper the river, the faster the flow, and the more energy it could produce. They knew that the narrow, fast-moving Mill River that dropped 700 feet from its headwaters in Williamsburg to the Connecticut River in Northampton would provide more than enough energy to power their factories and mills. Along the seven miles of the rocky riverbank, they built canals, mill ponds, water wheels and turbines, each harnessing the flow of water. Controlled and channeled, the small but mighty Mill River supplied the power for button factories, brass works, and mills that produced silk, cotton and woolens.

In the early 1800s, four villages lined the banks of the Mill River: Williamsburg, Skinnerville, Haydenville and Leeds. By that time, there were more than 5,000 people living in the valley.

Many of the villagers worked in one of the 64 mills that drew power from the river. They were not on the same scale as larger mills in more populated places like Lawrence and Lowell, but the people of Mill Valley lived comfortably. The local mill owners resided in large homes and were active in banking and politics, effectively controlling the local economy. They built company housing, schools and churches, knowing that a moral and educated workforce was good for the community and good for business. They had harnessed the power of the water, and by doing so had made themselves powerful. Their mistake was in believing that nature could be controlled.

Summer droughts sometimes caused problems for water-powered mills. As a solution, mill owners often

The Leeds Silk Mill #3, one of the many thriving operations along the Mill River in the 1870s

A Pale Horse was Death – Page 186

joined together to build their own reservoir dams. After getting permission from the state legislature, mill owners constructed large earthen dams, allowing them to control the flow of water as they saw fit.

The Goshen Dam had controlled the headwaters of the West Branch of the Mill River since its construction in 1852. Holding spring rains for release during the dry summer months, the Goshen Dam and reservoir ensured that the mills in the valley would continue running throughout the year.

By 1864, businesses in the Mill Valley were expanding and the mill owners decided that they needed more power. The Civil War had created huge demands for the products made in the local factories, and more water power was needed to keep the mills running around the clock. The east branch of the river was surveyed for three miles above Williamsburg, and a site was chosen for the new Williamsburg Dam by a man named Joel Hayden. Hayden also happened to be lieutenant governor of Massachusetts, as well as the owner of a cotton mill and a combination gasworks and brass factory, both of which were powered by the river. Hayden, along with other mill owners including William Skinner, Onslow Spelman, Lucius Dimock and William Clark, had no trouble securing a state charter and financing for the dam.

Work began on the site. Initially, the mill owners rejected three different plans drawn up by engineers as being too expensive. They got together and devised their own plan for an embankment dam that cost 80 percent less than the first proposals.

Embankment dams need a solid core to keep water from filtering through the structure. Instead of a solid masonry wall or one built of heavy timbers, the newly formed Williamsburg Reservoir Company settled on a common New England stone wall set on hard soil and rock. This type of dam requires a gradual slope of compacted earth piled over the core wall to keep the pressure of the water in the reservoir pushing down rather than out against the walls of the dam. Instead, the mill owners decided to save money by using less fill and creating a steeper slope.

The new dam was 600 feet long and 43 feet wide. It flooded more than 100 acres, creating a reservoir capable of holding 600 million gallons of water. It seemed to be the answer to all of the mill owners' problems, but instead, it was trouble from the start. Water seeped from the downstream base, making the ground around it swampy and wet. Large chunks of muddy soil slid off the face of the dam after each spring rain, so during the first three years of its existence, the owners piled up brush and drove timbers into the core to try and stabilize it. They added 1,000 pounds of extra fill to increase the slope of the face and hauled in crushed stone to try and prevent the soil from eroding. They spent nearly half as much on improvements to the faulty dam as they spent on its original construction.

Meanwhile, Joel Hayden was quietly troubled. He knew that the condition of the dam jeopardized the safety of the valley's residents and endangered the mills and factories where most of them worked. On rainy nights in the spring, Hayden often rode out alone on the muddy roads to check on the dam. Unable to sleep, he checked the reservoir levels, inspected any leaks at the base of the dam and reassured himself that everything was secure. As a precaution during stretches of bad weather, his friend and partner William Skinner moved his valuable supply of raw silk from his mill to higher ground.

Hayden hired a caretaker named George Cheney, who lived with his family in a cottage beside the dam. Following Hayden's instructions, he kept the water in the reservoir at a moderate level so that it would not put too much pressure on the wall of the dam. It held for years and, except for Joel Hayden, most people in the valley forgot about the danger.

Then, in November 1873, Joel Hayden died. His son, Joel Hayden, Jr., did not share his father's concerns about the safety of the dam. After his father's death, the spring rains of 1874 were allowed to fill the reservoir to capacity. It seemed to hold and only George Cheney continued to have doubts about the dam and its many leaks.

The cool, damp Saturday morning of May 6, 1874 was just another day of work for the people of the Mill River Valley. George Cheney was up and out of his house around 6:00 a.m. to look over the dam. The reservoir was full – water lapping at the edges – but everything looked secure and in order. Cheney walked back to his house to have breakfast with his wife, their children and his elderly father. They were just finishing their meal when, around 7:15 a.m., they heard a loud noise that signaled the beginning of the horror. Cheney's father cried out in terror when he saw a 40-foot section at the base of the dam break apart and washing downstream.

Running along the base of the collapsing dam without concern for his own safety, the caretaker threw open the gate in the vain hope of draining the reservoir fast enough to prevent the catastrophe that Joel Hayden had feared for years. Cheney turned to run back toward his house and got his first good look at the face of the dam. The *Springfield Republican* recounted what he saw: "...it could hardly fail in a few minutes to give way entirely; streams of water as large as a man's arm were forcing their way, new ones appearing every moment, the wall was constantly crumbling away, and its utter downfall was evidently only a matter of minutes."

Shouting at his father to warn the neighbors, Cheney ran to his barn, bridled his horse and, riding bareback, bolted along the stream toward Williamsburg. During this three-mile ride, Cheney passed homes that would certainly be destroyed by the flood but he knew that he did not have time to stop and warn each of these friends and neighbors individually – he had to make it to the village.

Onslow Spelman saw the caretaker ride up to his house and he met Cheney outside. Spelman, the mill owner who supervised the dam, thought that Cheney was exaggerating the danger. When Cheney assured him that the dam was giving away, Spelman argued that it was impossible. It took several precious minutes for Cheney to convince the man why he believed the dam was failing. Finally, Spelman sent Cheney to the livery stable for a fresh horse and went to tell the employees at his button factory to head for high ground. At the livery, Cheney met the man that the newspapers of the day would portray as the greatest hero of the disaster.

One of the heroes of the flood was Collins Graves, who operated a milk delivery business. He used his milk wagon to warn hundreds of people in the path of the flood.

Collins Graves was a lifelong resident of the Mill River Valley and cared deeply for the community. The son of a dairy farmer, he operated a milk delivery business and kept his supplies in an icehouse in the basement of Spelman's mill. Cheney told him what was happening and he required no further explanation – Cheney's word was good enough for him. If the dam was breaking, people needed to know. Graves climbed onto his milk wagon and sped away to warn the hundreds of workers in the largest mills downstream in Skinnerville, Haydenville and Leeds.

The destruction of the dam was truly a catastrophic event. Unlike many other dam failures, where a reservoir overflowed and water washed over the top of the dam, the Williamsburg dam literally exploded when the immense pressure of the water in the reservoir blew apart the structure's base. The contents of the entire reservoir were released in an instant. Complete destruction was assured by the steep, narrow channel of the Mill River, which funneled the immense power of the water through the populated parts of the valley.

Church bells began ringing a warning in Williamsburg village. Then, at 7:45 a.m., the flood tide hit. Onslow Spelman had just reached high ground when he heard a terrifying roar that finally convinced him that Cheney had been right. Witnesses told of a giant wall of water that rose to between 20 and 40 feet high, followed by a wave that took nearly 20 minutes to pass. Like an ocean surge that strikes the shoreline and creates a wave, the wall of reservoir water was slightly slowed by trees, rocks and buildings, causing it to grow in mass and height. Most terrifying of all, the witnesses told of seeing a dark, murky form that was not water – it was debris. The water propelled a massive table of trees, roof beams, livestock, mud, rocks, mill equipment, and household furniture ahead of it, scouring the landscape down to bare rock.

Harper's Weekly told of the effects of the flood tide:

Trees and drift-wood obscured the waters. Spelman's button factory did not stand a moment. It rose up on the crest of the wave, and collapsed as though made of card-board. [In Williamsburg] a dozen houses lined the valley, and the inmates were forgotten in the general alarm. The waters lapped them up. Entire families were destroyed in a moment... Fifty-three persons lost their lives in three minutes after Cheney's alarms were given.

As he bolted away from Spelman's mill, Collins Graves didn't look back to see the destruction behind him. He slapped the reins on his horses, driving the wagon at breakneck speed. He shouted as he dashed down the narrow road: "The reservoir is right here! Run! 'Tis all you can do!" Graves continued downstream to warn the factory workers. He knew that the people in the houses and on the streets would hear the cry, but the roar of the factories would drown out the warning for anyone inside.

Graves' first stop was the silk factory in Skinnerville, about a mile downstream. He clattered into the dooryard, his milk cans rattling, and shouted to the company's bookkeeper. He was on his way again in seconds, racing toward Haydenville, which was another mile downstream. He stopped first at the brass works and crashed into the office of superintendent Charles Wentworth. When he told him that the reservoir was coming, Wentworth scoffed and told him that even if the dam really had broken, the water would not be there for days.

Graves walked back outside, doubt filling his mind. After all, he hadn't actually seen any of the floodwaters. Perhaps the situation wasn't as bad as Cheney thought it was. Exhausted, he turned his horses back upstream and suddenly saw a horrible sight – the wall of water was coming! Truly believing that he was about to die, he whipped his horses uphill and made it to high ground with only seconds to spare.

Graves had arrived in Skinnerville only five minutes before the flood. By the time he reached Haydenville, the water was just two minutes behind him. The few minutes Graves lost while arguing with Wentworth tragically cost lives. Newspapers reported that only four died in Skinnerville, thanks to the fact that workers in the silk factory were evacuated before the brick building was utterly destroyed. But in Haydenville, where the floodwaters used smaller houses like battering rams to destroy a foundry and the massive brass works, the death toll was 80 lives.

With only seconds to escape, many people who saw the flood coming were simply frozen with fright. Those who tried to run were snatched up by the water or crushed by the debris. Many died in their homes when the structures collapsed. One family was lucky to survive when apple trees in their front yard caught so much debris

The aftermath of the deadly Mill River Disaster

that they diverted the flood and kept the water from carrying away their house.

The most heroic effort of the day, at the greatest risk of his own life, was performed by a man who received little attention in the press. His name was Myron Day and he drove an express, or delivery, wagon in the valley. When he arrived in Haydenville that morning, he heard the warnings being given in the village. Day urgently wanted to warn his friends in Leeds, but the flood was nearly on top of him. To deliver a warning to the next village, he would need to race a mile downstream on a road through a narrow ravine that channeled the river and offered no escape. He knew that if he attempted this, there was little chance that he would escape with his life. It was ride hard, or die, for there would be no way out.

In his heart, Day knew he had no choice but to try. He lashed his horse and roared off toward Leeds. Rocking and creaking, the wagon sped through the ravine and Day made it to Leeds in the nick of time. Passing the Nonotuck Silk Company, Day broadcast the alarm and did the same at George Warner's button factory, while the flood was sweeping away the silk company at the other end of town.

Myron Day's bravery saved many lives, but in spite of this, 51 people were killed in Leeds. Where the button factory once stood, only a chimney remained on the scoured rock of the valley floor.

Below Leeds, the slope of the valley eased as the Mill River prepared to meet the Connecticut River near the village of Florence. Although the village was spared from total destruction, Florence became the dumping ground for most of the corpses and wreckage that had been carried away by the flood.

The final toll was 139 dead, countless injured and 146 families left homeless. As town halls and churches became makeshift shelters and morgues, help arrived from all over New England. The search for bodies lasted for an entire week as volunteers and survivors attacked the debris with axes, ropes and teams of horses. Newspapers from across the region were quick to cast blame, calling the dam a "trap of destruction" and stating that the "builders of the dam were murderers."

The people of the Mill River Valley reached different conclusions, though. There was plenty of blame to go around – the builders, the mill owners, the state legislature. They knew who had built the dam and knew that it had been constructing shoddily and cheaply. But more important to them than casting blame was the resumption of their lives. The mills were rebuilt, as were the homes of the workers. Mill owners hired back their employees as quickly as possible, and a relief committee paid compensation of $300 per family and $50 for every working man. Most people gladly accepted the money, eager for a fresh start. After all of the loss of life and devastation, there were no indictments, no fines and no subsequent lawsuits. A year after the flood, in 1875, Massachusetts passed its first legislation regarding reservoir dam design, construction and liability. Considered weak by today's standards, the law was at least the first step toward safer dams.

Cheney, Graves and Day received medals for their heroism on the day of the disaster and lived the rest of their lives in the Mill River Valley.

Americans of the era saw the Mill River Flood as a terrible calamity but it was just one of hundreds of disasters – including steamboat explosions, railroad bridge collapses, and mill fires – caused by the carelessness and dishonesty of business owners and industrialists. It took disasters like the Mill River Flood to expose such negligent practices but in 1874, there were decades more of such tragedies still to come.

1893: THE SEA ISLANDS HURRICANE
Death and Destruction Along the Southern Atlantic Coast

Eighteen ninety-three would long be remembered as the year of storms. Gales blew through the islands as they rose and fell, rose and fell. Tornadoes battered the Atlantic coast, killing and destroying as they moved across the land. Cyclones formed in the tropics and blasted the Atlantic coast as they moved northward. And then there were the hurricanes, 10 of them in all, five of which were considered major.

For the first time in recorded history (and it has happened only one time since), there were four major hurricanes active on the same day: August 22. There was almost a fifth, but it had dissipated on the 21st. The

San Roque Hurricane was the first to form, followed by the New York Hurricane, then the Sea Islands Hurricane. The fourth was simply denoted as Hurricane No. 7 (before the first hurricanes were named in 1950, they were numbered). The New York Hurricane had strengthened to a Category 3 on the Saffir-Simpson Hurricane Scale, but had dissipated to a Category 2 by the time it made a direct hit on New York. Hurricane No. 8 moved across the Gulf of Mexico before it devastated the coast of Louisiana on September 7, killing 2,000 and destroying hundreds of homes and businesses before blowing itself out over land.

Mixed in with all these horrific storms was the Sea Islands Hurricane, officially Hurricane No. 6. Some references have labeled this storm the Savannah Hurricane of 1893, but the greatest loss of life and destruction and continued suffering was tied to the Sea Islands. This was the second-most deadly hurricane in American history, after the Galveston Hurricane of 1900, in which 12,000 people lost their lives.

Just how many people were killed during the Sea Islands Hurricane is difficult to say. Some sources list the number as low as 1,000, but times were different then. In 1893, the Jim Crow laws were in full force, especially in the Southern states. When there was a disaster in which many lives were lost, it was common practice to only count the white casualties in the lists of those killed and injured. It was very rare for black victims to be included. It was as if they didn't count enough to be counted. In the case of the black Sea Islanders, they had the added complications of isolation and almost no forms of communication with other communities on nearby islands or with the mainland. After careful research taking into account the lives lost on the "black islands," the death toll has been adjusted to nearly 3,000, but it could have been as high as 3,500. Most of these were black Sea Islanders who were drowned by the tidal wave or what we now refer to as a storm surge. Another complication with trying to determine an accurate count of lives lost is the unknown number of islanders who succumbed to exposure, starvation, dehydration or malaria after the storm had passed.

The Sea Islands are a group of small, isolated barrier islands off the Atlantic coast of Georgia and South Carolina. During the eighteenth century, wealthy planters on the Sea Islands imported large numbers of kidnapped Africans as slaves. Thanks to slave labor, the islands became home to some of the largest plantations in South Carolina. These plantations grew rice, indigo, and a strain of high-grade cotton called Sea Island cotton, with unusually long, silky fibers. When President Lincoln signed the Emancipation Proclamation in 1863, the 5,000 slaves living and working on the Sea Islands suddenly found themselves free men and women. At the end of the Civil War, these freed slaves hoped they would receive land somewhere where they could farm and become self-sufficient, but this was not to happen. Instead, almost all of them stayed on the islands, the only home they had ever known, and continued to work for their former owners as laborers, tenant farmers, or sharecroppers.

The former slaves and their families who stayed on the Sea Islands lived in shacks as they eked out a meager subsistence on land they would never own. They were free, but they were still tied to the islands. They were incredibly isolated and impoverished. They had only their own community to rely on as the world that had left them behind went on around them.

There were a few white neighborhoods on the islands, and these were very different from the black communities. They were made up of pleasant houses and even mansions in some cases. They had railroad lines and telephones to connect them with the outside world. They had fire departments and police forces, libraries, schools, post offices, and specialty shops – all things that the black communities did not have.

Having lived their entire lives, for many generations, on these isolated islands, the black Sea Islanders grew very close. They developed their own Gullah culture and language (also called Geechee), which still survives on the islands. Today, the Sea Islands provide the setting for some of America's most popular coastal resorts. There are high-end residential areas where millionaires live. The Sea Islands have become playgrounds for the rich and famous, and vacation destinations for a multitude of tourists, but this was not the case in 1893.

Hurricane No. 6 started out as a tropical storm that had formed on August 15 east of Cape Verde, off the coast of Western Africa. The storm built up strength as it crossed the Atlantic Ocean and on August 19, between Cape Verde and the Lesser Antilles, it moved into hurricane status. The hurricane continued to move west, where it reached Category 3 status on the August 25. It appeared to be heading for the Bahamas when it changed course to a west-northwest route. By August 26, the southernmost Sea Islands started feeling the effects of the approaching storm in the form of rain and increasing winds. Conditions on the islands grew treacherous as the hurricane passed over as it turned north, following along the Atlantic coast of Georgia.

Hurricane No. 6 made landfall on August 27 at Savannah, Georgia. When it finally hit the mainland, wind speeds were reported as a sustained 120 miles per hour. The hurricane continued up the coast of South Carolina on August 28, moving northward until it dissipated into a extra-tropical storm over Canada.

As severe as the hurricane itself was, bringing death and damage with its winds, the real horrors rode in on the storm surge that reached as high as 16 feet above sea level. Many of the Sea Islands were just a few feet above sea level and were completely overrun by the tidal wave. On most of the islands, there was not a single building that was not completely swept away or damaged beyond repair. This was especially true for the islands populated by the Gullah (black) communities, where the homes were often little more than shacks. The tidal wave did great damage along the coastline, but the Sea Islands took the brunt of the surge.

Tybee Island was one of the islands with a sizable white population. The Savannah public library has on file a letter written by a woman, known only as M.S. Workman, who lived on Tybee during the hurricane. In this letter to her uncle, she describes her ordeal as she and her family fled their home to save their lives:

"Death and disaster seem to have overtaken this summer. Sunday night about 10 o'clock it began to blow and rain, increasing steadily, so that the [railroad] track was completely covered with sand, and the trains could not pass our cottage...Mr. Graham called to us to come and look at the big wave coming. Just then, Mrs. Ulmer came running in, telling us that we must leave the house...we took the children and servants and started out. When we locked the dining room door, the water was rushing up to it then and the bath house was floating way up to the house.

We waded over to the plank walk and as we got up to the Ryans' house, a man rushed in saying the police barracks had fallen, and the horse smashed to death. I don't know how I did it, there is always an opportunity for us to come out strong.

The Ryans tried to hold me, for the ocean was then surrounding their house. I saw if we remained longer we would be cut off entirely...so we started out again. The water had risen so that the track was covered knee deep and over. This time it was plunge in or get cut off altogether, so in we went up to our knees. The wind, sand and rain were blinding us. People were fleeing to the woods to get into trees for safety as we passed along. Glancing back, we saw a house on fire, but we trudged on, little caring if it was ours or not.

We reached the Blun house...it was the strongest house on the island. Each man in the party had planned to take one woman or child when the house fell, and swim out if possible as we were surrounded by eight feet of water then. Every gust seemed more terrific -- the intensity and force with which they struck the house seemed as thought it must fall.

The next morning...we all went down to the cottages to see what damage had been done, the water having almost receded. What desolation met us on every side -- articles of every description, remnants of chairs, mattresses, baskets, trunks, pieces of furniture...and not a sand dune to be seen...

The track was so completely demolished we knew it would be weeks before we could get up to town again...A man came out and told us that the mayor had sent a tug, which was then...four miles and one quarter away and would take all the women and children and as many men as they cold up to Savannah if we could walk that far.

Such a walk I will never forget. There is hardly a house left, and under some of the wreckage were the remains of four people who were drowned. The track is torn up and twisted, even the road bed is gone. Ships turned bottom up on one side of us, and on the land side a house [was] all splintered. You can imagine the forlorn feeling that you have literally nothing."

Mrs. Workman and her intrepid band of survivors made it to the tugboat and on to Savannah that same day. Nothing more is known of her, nor where her house was located, but we can assume that she was fairly well off, as her letter mentioned taking her servants with her when her family fled their home.

The approaching storm had been closely monitored by the weather service and warnings had been sent out three days before the hurricane arrived. Some families took heed of the warning and left the islands to seek safety on the mainland. Unfortunately, the warnings only went out to the islands where the residents had radios and telephones. There was no effort made to warn the thousands of black Sea Islanders who were among those at greatest risk. They were left to ride out the storm, cut off from the mainland and unprepared for the devastation that was bearing down on them.

The storm first struck the Sea Islands in Beaufort, North Carolina. There was considerable damage in Beaufort, it was far enough from the beach that it did not get the full brunt of the storm surge. Photography had come into its own by this time, and cameras designed for the general public were readily available but strangely, very few photographs seem to have been taken of the damage incurred by the hurricane. The reason could be that the greatest damage was to the islands where the residents were too poor to own cameras. It may also have been due to the fact that the hurricane season had been so devastating, and the storms so continuous, that no one was interested in recording this particular storm for posterity. For whatever reason, very few photographs exist today to visually describe the destruction that the storm wrought on the Sea Islands.

The Sea Islands are very low in elevation and lie open to the sea. They are barrier islands that provide great protection to the mainland, but there is nothing to protect the islands themselves. The islands that suffered the most were those between Port Royal and Charleston. When the tidal wave hit, some were swept clean while others were left with nothing more than remnants of what was once there. The storm hit just as the islanders were about to harvest their most valuable crop: Sea Island cotton. The cotton balls were saturated with seawater and then blown from their stems. Seawater flooded the fields, ruining the potato and sweet potato fields that were the islanders' second most important cash crop.

The black islanders fought hard for their lives and the lives of their families. Despite their struggles, over a thousand of them were killed outright or drowned. One young man spent 36 hours clinging to the bottom of a dredge that had been capsized in the storm. Utterly exhausted, he gave up and slid down the side and into the water. He rode the tide to Beaufort, where he was thrown onto the shore and deposited on a pile of debris just outside his mother's door. After many hours wrapped in warm blankets and with something hot to drink, he survived to tell the tale. Not many others were so lucky.

Entire families were washed away and never seen nor heard from again. Hardly a family was left unscathed or without loss of life. A mother of five lost three of her children to the sea. After the storm passed, she spent many long hours walking the seashore and the marshes, hoping to find their bodies and give them a decent burial. In the chaos and confusion of the violent winds and rising waters, this poor woman had been able to get herself and all five of her children up into a tree. But as the worst of the storm was ripping and lashing through the woods, the tree toppled, hurling the family into the tumultuous floodwaters below. Three of the children were ripped from their mother's grasp and carried on the giant waves past the marshes and out into the raging sea. Despite everything, she was thankful; many of her neighbors had lost all their children.

After the storm, the grieving mother stood before the spot where her little house had once stood. The only thing that remained was the blackened hearthstone; everything else had been swept away. Except for that stone, no one could have guessed that her house, or any of the other houses near hers, had ever existed. The family that had lived next to her had 13 children. When she ran to the trees, she had called to them to run too, but the raging storm had muffled her cries. The family had remained in their house and had all been drowned as their house was smashed to kindling and washed away.

Throughout the Sea Islands, the monster had arrived carrying terror before it and leaving death and destruction in its wake. As far as the eye could see lay the evidence of the storm's destruction. Houses that had remained somewhat intact were tossed on their sides like children's toys. Giant dredges weighing hundreds of tons had been plucked from the water and flipped onto the land. Groves of live oaks had been flattened, and ships were carried hundreds of yards from the shoreline. Smaller boats were simply gone.

Nearly 2,000 Sea Island residents had drowned. When the tides were kind, their bodies were returned to shore or captured by the sedge the grew in the marshes. Cruel tides carried the bodies away forever. Overnight,

30,000 black islanders had seen their homes and belongings obliterated, their food stores washed away, their crops ruined, their wells filled with salt water, their boats blown away and tons of marsh sedge deposited on the only land that was suitable for cultivation. They had essentially been left with no shelter, no water, no food, and no means of livelihood.

On the island of St. Helena, the storm had brought a gift that helped the islanders survive. Just off shore, the steamer *City of Savannah* had been wrecked. Her passengers and crew were rescued, but the ships that carried them away had ignored the black islanders in need of assistance. The islanders made their way to the wrecked ship and took the provisions that had been left behind.

The day after the storm had passed, word of the death and destruction laid upon the inner coastal cities of Georgia and North Carolina spread across the country on telephone and telegraph wires. The heart-wrenching stories of survival and loss experienced by the white population were known by the nation in a matter of hours, but the Sea Islands remained mute. With no means of communication or transportation, their plight remained completely unknown to the outside world.

Conditions among the white population of Beaufort and Port Royal were not known until two days after the storm, when an Atlanta newspaper reporter made his way onto the islands and wrote about their struggles. As the townspeople were immersed in the task of pulling their own dead from the waters, they began noticing that some of the black corpses looked vaguely familiar. Two men were thought to be from the far side of Ladies Island, and a black woman looked like a woman someone knew from Coosaw. These were only guesses, as the bodies had been in the water for a few days by then, but the idea was starting to form that the black islanders might be in trouble.

The isolation of the islanders was so complete that no one had thought to go and check on them. The islanders would come to market in their little boats and then leave again. They didn't have close ties to anyone on the mainland and their trips there were infrequent.

On September 2, six days after the storm, information about the horrific conditions on the Sea Islands finally reached Charleston. Word arrived in Beaufort and Port Royal about the same time. Two men who lived on one of the islands had found a damaged canoe and had used it to go to the mainland for help. One man rowed while the other man bailed water.

Immediate calls for assistance went out but only a few volunteers responded. Medical doctors were sent to make their way from island to island to treat the sick, but so few doctors were available (or willing) to help that many islanders waited for weeks to receive medical attention. The Red Cross finally came to the islands with much-needed aid on October 1. The reason for the delay is not known, but it is supposed that their resources were stretched thin from rendering aid to victims of a hurricane that had struck the Florida panhandle in June.

Among those who provided aid to the black islanders were former slave owners. They had been responsible for these people's welfare when they were slaves, and as one published account pointed out, they "still felt the pressure of that old habit of responsibility."

The former slave owners had known the black islanders their entire lives and undoubtedly felt a bond with them. To white outsiders, however, the dark-skinned islanders, with their incomprehensible dialect and reticence toward strangers, seemed both mysterious and unsettling.

A writer for *Scribner's Magazine* interviewed some of the islanders after the hurricane and commented approvingly that they seemed subdued, not shouting or singing boisterously as he expected black people to behave. He wrote in the February 1894 issue:

"Gentle, patient, smiling and good-humored, the Negros have no complaints to make. They discuss the storm among themselves, but not in a way to impart much information to a white listener. They speak in monosyllables and get to the core of words. Their shyness is pathetic, and their smiling patience is in the nature of a perpetual appeal to those who come in contact with them."

Within a few weeks of the storm, malaria outbreaks blanketed the islands. A doctor who visited eight of the largest islands to inspect their sanitation reported that 3,709 individuals had been sick and were treated. Of those, 2,542 had malaria. One can only imagine the extent of the disease on the dozens of islands not included in the report.

Early on, there had been rumors that the black islanders had left their dead to lie in the sun and rot rather than bury them, but this turned out to be a wild exaggeration. The widespread malaria epidemic had left thousands of people terribly weakened, with very little food and water. With so many bodies to bury, some were simply wrapped in quilts or whatever could be found and quickly buried in shallow graves where the tides would come in and uncover the bodies. The reality was that the islanders were quick to bury their dead, but due to an island tradition, the graves were dug in the wrong place. The islanders had long held to a saying that went, "Die by water, lie by water." As most of the victims had drowned, they were buried as close to the shoreline as possible. Without realizing their mistake in time, the islanders had buried many bodies where the tides could expose them, which added to the malaria epidemic.

When the Red Cross finally arrived to set up their distribution centers, administrators and supervisors met to determine how to disperse the supplies. Donations from around the country had been heavy during the first week after the storm, when the public was full of pity for the people of Charleston, Savannah, and the surrounding towns. But donations had dropped off dramatically when word of the horrific conditions and great need of so many black people were publicized, despite a personal plea by Red Cross founder Clara Barton.

So when the Red Cross arrived, supplies were lower than normal and food was tightly rationed to the black families. It was determined that although the Red Cross had been caring for individuals and families in need following disasters for many years, this was a special case. The administrators were fearful that if these families were given enough to eat, they might become lazy and would not take steps to better their plight themselves. They felt that if the families were not technically starving, but were still very hungry, the head of the household would work hard to supplement their food supplies. Thus, a week's ration for an average family of six was a peck of grits and one pound of meat -- usually pork. The extreme rigidity and economy also stemmed from the fact that since donations were dramatically down, they simply didn't have as much food as usual to give out. We must also remember that without the Red Cross, many thousands more would have died before much more time had passed.

Eventually, the fields were cleared of seawater and sedge. New crops were planted and harvested and life returned to the way it had been before the storm, but not for long. Soon, wealthy people would begin to notice the beauty of the islands and want a piece of it for themselves. What were once isolated and forgotten islands became prime real estate. The black Sea Islanders were shunted aside to make room for progress. The Sea Islands will never return to the old quiet, simple ways and time marched on, as it always does.

There are hundreds of tales and legends of haunted sites and ghost-riddled shores throughout this entire region. Certainly Charleston and Savannah have as many ghost stories as anywhere, but there is one legend that stands out as a cautionary tale for islanders facing an oncoming hurricane. This is the story of the Grey Man of Pawleys Island.

Pawleys Island is a small island off the coast of South Carolina, only four miles long and a quarter of a mile wide. Because of its size and low elevation, it is particularly vulnerable to hurricanes. For over a hundred years, a mysterious man dressed in grey has been said to wander the beaches during hurricane season, warning residents, or anyone he may meet on the beach of impending storms. He is supposed to be so reliable that he has frequently warned of hurricanes before the weather service does.

Although the Grey Man has frightened and startled many of the people who have chanced upon him, his warnings are sincere. In actual fact, meeting the Grey Man is very good luck because, according to the legend, if you heed his warning and leave the island, you and your home will be spared.

The first recorded encounter with the Grey Man was in 1822, when he approached a young woman and told her to leave because a storm was coming. Her father took the family off the island and they missed a terrible storm that raged for two days. He was next seen in 1893 as the Sea Islands Hurricane was approaching. He warned a local family of the impending disaster. They left the island and their home was still standing when they returned.

Reports of the Grey Man can be traced throughout the twentieth century as well. Supposedly, he appeared twice in 1954; once before a tornado and the second time before Hurricane Hazel struck the area. He was seen again in 1989 just before Hurricane Hugo.

No one knows where the Grey Man comes from, why he warns people about hurricanes and bad storms, or ever why he protects Pawleys Island. There are many theories, however. Some say he is the ghost of Percival Pawley, the first white man to live on the island. Another tale describes a pair of star-crossed lovers, a poor man from Charleston and a wealthy young woman from the island. After interference from her parents, he joined the Navy and sailed off, not to be seen again until he washed onto the beach of Pawleys Island, barely clinging to life after his ship had capsized in a storm. Upon learning that his love had found another, he walked to the beach and out into the ocean, where he drowned.

Another version of the story tells of a young man from Charleston who was in love with a woman from the island. In this tale, the young man is concerned about the safety of his lover as a terrific storm approaches. He set out on foot, trying to make his way to the island, but is washed away and drowned by a freak wave. His lady survived the storm unscathed and now, the young man must walk the shores of Pawley's Island, forever, watching for storms, and saving those fortunate enough to receive his warning.

Regardless of how the Grey Man came to be there or why he watches for storms, he has proven to be a better alarm system than the National Weather System and is a welcomed and well-loved member of the Pawleys Island community.

1896: DEATH ON THE CUYAHOGA
Cleveland's Whiskey Island Disaster

One of the most obscure disasters in Ohio history occurred one July day in 1896 when a crew from the Cleveland & Pittsburgh ore docks left Whiskey Island and met their fate in the surging Cuyahoga River – leaving tales of ghosts and hauntings behind.

The men labored long and dangerous hours, toiling their lives away at the manufacturing and shipping industries of the day. And there were few tougher places to work than Whiskey Island. It was there that much of the iron ore was unloaded by sweating, under-paid men to feed the smoldering steel mills located farther down the Cuyahoga River.

Is it any wonder that they were in such a hurry to escape their workplace on the hot summer evening of July 16, 1896? Tragically, though, many of the men would never escape at all. They still linger at the site of their deaths, never free to cross over to the other side.

On the night of July 16, the day shift workers had been laboring throughout for days, emptying tons of heavy ferrous metal from the hold of the ship *Sir Henry Bessemer*. Most of the men were German immigrants who lived in the Clark Avenue-Selden Avenue neighborhood and by the end of the day, were anxious to get home to their families. It was brutally hot that afternoon and the men wanted nothing more than a bath and a cold glass of beer before supper.

Until recently, the men had left Whiskey Island each day by crossing the Willow Street Bridge, which spanned the river just south of Whiskey Island and took them to the West Side. But the city had torn down the old bridge and the men now preferred to be ferried across the river, rather than walking farther to the Valley Railway Bridge, which the Cleveland & Pittsburgh company had leased for their convenience. The ore workers had chipped in a few pennies each and had purchased an old, broken-down boat from the nearby Murphy & Miller shipyard. The young boys who were hired to bring water to the thirsty men during the day were also expected to row them across the river after their shift ended.

Given their work patterns and this makeshift form of commuting, the tragedy that occurred was likely inevitable. For one thing, the boat they had purchased was old, unstable and extremely unsafe. It was not built to hold as many men as it usually carried and it leaked badly. It wouldn't take much to upset such a boat, and the river in that area was in constant motion with tugboats, bulk carriers and larger ships. They all jockeyed for space on the water at all hours, crowding the 250-foot-wide river. All the ingredients were in place for disaster when the doomed men laid down their tools at 7:00 p.m. and ran for the boat that would carry them toward home.

One of the first to reach the scow at the Whiskey Island dock was a man named Ed Patten. He usually helped water boy Martin Corrigan with the heavy oar. But Patten began to have second thoughts about the wisdom of crossing in the first boatload as at least 40 men jumped into the boat after him. As Corrigan prepared to cast off, Patten noticed that the sides of the scow were only a few inches above the river. For whatever reason – perhaps common sense or perhaps an eerie premonition – he hurled himself out of the scow and just managed to scramble back on the dock. A moment later, a body hit him from behind. A young man named Ed Savage had shared his hesitation and he also jumped out of the boat.

The scow shoved away from the dock and ran into its first problem – a steamer called *Lagonda*. The ship was being towed eastward toward the main Cuyahoga channel by the tugboats *W.D. Cushing* and *Chamberlain*. The men in the scow couldn't see the steamer or the two tugboats; they were blocked from view by *Sir Henry Bessemer*, which was on the right side of the ferry boat as it pushed off from Whiskey Island. The men on the lead tug, *W.D. Cushing*, were unable to see the scow, then about 100 feet away from the northeast shore of the island. The first mutual sighting occurred at the same moment that the first surging wave, created by the tug's powerful propeller, turned the scow sideways and dumped water into the overloaded boat.

After that, things happened very quickly. Because of the filthy condition of the ferry, most of the men were already standing up, many of them on top of the three long seats that ran the length of the narrow craft. As the wave filled the boat with water, the men began to scream and shout in fear as the boat rocked from side to side. Seconds later, some of them rushed to the side of the scow, making the craft even more unstable. Then, one of the men tore off his coat and jumped into the river.

It was as if the other frightened men were just waiting to see who would go first. They suddenly began leaping into the water, their hats and lunch pails gripped in their hands. Some of them immediately sank like stones to the bottom, which was about 18 or 19 feet deep in that part of the river. Most of the others, screaming and thrashing about, grabbed onto their fellow workers who were also struggling in the water. This only added to the general peril and sent the men into hysterics. A moment later, the scow flipped over and the few men still left in it were also thrown into the river.

A few of the survivors told their stories to the *Cleveland Press*. Bernard Patton, age 16, was able to swim but he had not gotten more than a few feet from the overturned boat when four desperate men grabbed hold of him. He kicked and struggled against them, but it was only when they all sank together that he was able to struggle free underwater and make his way to the south shore. Another workman, John Perew, did even better. He was an excellent swimmer and quickly and easily made it to shore, only to go back into the water and save two men who would have died without rescue. Perhaps even more heroic was Pat McGinty, who also swam to shore and then returned to help his struggling companions. He saved two men by bringing them life preservers before he was exhausted and pulled himself up on the riverbank.

Those on board *Sir Henry Bessemer*, *Lagonda*, *Chamberlain* and *W.D. Cushing* were quickly aware of what was happening. They began throwing life preservers, ropes, wood and anything else that would float into the cluster of struggling men. A man named Dwyer even jumped into the water from *W.D. Cushing* and saved two men. Richard Masten, though, was one of the workers who didn't need help. Along with a few others, he had the presence of mind to remember that the overturned boat would still float. So, while most of the other men were pulling each other down to a watery death, Masten and the others clung to the bottom of the upside-down scow until they were rescued.

It was all over in less than five minutes. Eyewitnesses later agreed that a number of the men sank as soon as they hit the water and never came to the surface again. Others struggled for two of three minutes, clinging to their equally terrified – and doomed – friends. The river had been turned into a frantic, thrashing scene of chaos for only a few minutes, and then it was over. By 7:15 p.m., the only obvious evidence of the tragedy was the overturned scow and the silent evidence of a dozen or so hats floating on the surface of the water. All of the bodies of the workmen were later found on the bottom of the river, within 20 feet of where the boat had overturned. Evidence of the horror that possessed the victims was offered by the first body pulled from the river.

As it was pulled to the surface of the water, horrified spectators could clearly see the hands of a second corpse still clasped around the neck of the first.

The men who were thrown into the river could be excused for their behavior -- clinging to their companions in terror and accidentally drowning them in their panic – but the aftermath of the tragedy brought out the worst in the people of Cleveland. Ambulance men from competing private morgues in the city fought for possession of the bodies, even fighting with the bereaved relatives. Within minutes of the accident, hundreds of people lined the riverbanks, gawking at the corpses that had been retrieved from the water and interfering with the police and rescue workers. Most ironic was the fate of William Buelow, a curiosity-seeker who rushed to the scene with friends as soon as he got word of the tragedy. While running along the dock area at the foot of Detroit Street, he fell into the river and drowned.

Although the authorities could never be sure since many of the German immigrants' identities were only vaguely known or documented, at least 16 men drowned in the accident. There were 27 who survived and most of them, albeit bruised and shaken, were back at work unloading ore at the docks the next day. Crews with grappling hooks worked late into the night bringing the dead men up from the river bottom. They worked from small rowboats, each fitted with lanterns. The dead were all taken to nearby morgues and given proper burials. They left behind widows, many children, and very little in the way of savings. No payments were made to the families by the Cleveland & Pittsburgh company since the men had technically not been working when they went to their deaths.

The coroner's inquest into the accident was perfunctory at best and simply repeated conclusions that had already been formed. These included the fact that the boat had been overloaded, that most of the men could not swim and that they had panicked when they fell into the water. It also noted, however, that the skin, hair and clothes of the workers were so impregnated with iron that they might as well have been carrying metal weights when they went into the river.

In the months following the tragedy, strange stories were told about the section of the river where the accident occurred. Some attributed the stories to the superstitions of the ore workers – who avoided the area at all costs, choosing to go out of their way to the Valley Railway Bridge to go home – but it became hard to explain away the stories told by ship workers who knew nothing of the tragic history of the place.

The stories were all remarkably similar and told of hearing cries for help coming from the river. Others claimed to see men splashing about, desperately thrashing their arms before finally sinking under the surface. There were numerous times when passersby and ship workers actually jumped into the river, fearing that someone was drowning, only to find no one was there. The shouts, cries and apparitions were usually noticed around dusk, just about the time the accident occurred.

After dark, more eerie sights were reported. People claimed to see glowing lights traveling on the surface of the water when no boats were present. Some attributed these lights to a ghostly recreation of the search for bodies that took place on that hot July night. Others simply dismissed the images as reflections of streetlights on the river, turned into a "ghost story" by those with overactive imaginations.

But was this the case? No one can say. The haunting near Whiskey Island has not been reported for many years now. It's as if the events of that day left an impression behind that has slowly faded away over the years until it has been forgotten altogether.

1898: THE PORTLAND GALE
Wreck of the Steamer Portland

It was a perfect storm in the making, a monstrous nor'easter that happens only once in a century. Two high-energy, low-pressure weather systems were headed on a collision course for New England. The year was 1898 and no one could have predicted the power and intensity of the storms as they met, one from the west and one

The *Steamer Portland*

from the south. It was to be the most violent and damaging storm the region had ever seen and it remains today the most deadly maritime storm in New England history.

On November 25, 1898, a low-pressure weather system was forming over the western Great Lakes. As it gained energy, it began moving east. At the same time, a larger low-pressure system was moving through the Gulf of Mexico, gaining strength as it went. The Great Lakes system picked up a cold front from Canada and the Gulf of Mexico system brought along high humidity.

The following day, November 26, Boston greeted the day in sunshine with a slight breeze. It was cold and the sky was clear and blue, but by early evening snow began to fall and the wind intensified. The two weather systems were about to collide with a warmer high-pressure system stalled over New England. Together, the three systems created a perfect storm...

The storm battered New England and the coastal waters for over thirty hours. When the sky finally cleared and the sun returned, the area was buried in two feet of snow, but the worst damage was from the high winds, at times reaching 100 miles per hour. Entire neighborhoods were destroyed and several coastal buildings were washed away. At least 450 people had lost their lives in New York, Connecticut and Massachusetts, many of whom were drowned in the Atlantic. Over 400 boats and ships sank or were washed aground, decimating the local steamship and fishing industry. The storm was officially named "The Gale of 1898," but because of the devastating loss of one particular ship, it will forever be known as "The Portland Gale."

Before the Storm

The steamer *Portland*, launched in 1889, was one of the largest sidewheel steamships in New England. She was built in direct competition with the region's railroads, providing the most luxurious way to travel between Boston and Portland, Maine. She was 281 feet long and 42 feet wide and was equipped to carry cargo, but her main purpose was providing elegant and comfortable accommodations for up to 800 passengers. According to the *Boston Herald*, her main saloon was the height of style for the era. It was lighted by a beautiful domed skylight and decorated with thick carpeting and carved mahogany furniture upholstered in plush wine-colored fabric. Her hull was white oak and she drew only ten feet of water, allowing her access to shallow harbors and rivers, but her shallow draft also made the *Portland* vulnerable to rough waters in the open ocean.

The *Portland* served a regular route between Boston and Portland. Departing at 7:00 o'clock every evening, she made a one-way trip every day, back and forth between Boston's India Wharf and the Franklin Wharf in Portland. The voyage was roughly one hundred miles and took between nine and ten hours in reasonable weather. Passengers could board in the evening, sleep comfortably through the night and arrive at their destination in the morning. The cost of a one-way ticket was $1 per person.

In 1898, the *Portland* was captained by Hollis Blanchard, a seasoned officer in his mid-fifties who had recently been promoted to the position. Both Captain Blanchard and The Portland Steamship Company were respected for their reputation for safety and caution.

The Doomed Voyage

It was Saturday, November 26. The Thanksgiving holiday had provided a chance for people to visit friends and family, but now it was time to go home. Anyone who needed to get back to Portland for the beginning of the week would need to board the *Portland* on Saturday, or they would not be able to get home until Tuesday morning. They gathered at the India Wharf where the *Portland* was moored, waiting to board and get warm.

Much earlier, there had been word that a storm was headed toward Boston, blowing northward from the deep South. Captain Blanchard was aware of the approaching storm and had been checking the weather conditions throughout the day. He knew the storm was to be fairly strong, but that was really all he knew. As 7:00 p.m. approached and the passengers were all boarded, he discussed the situation with his superiors. Should they depart or should they stay in the relative safety of the harbor? Blanchard decided that if he left on time and pushed a little harder, he would be able to outrun the storm and arrive safely in Maine. He could deliver his passengers and cargo, and weather the storm in Portland before returning to Boston as scheduled the following night.

A light snow had begun to fall on Boston Harbor as the *Portland* got under way. She carried just under two hundred passengers and crew. It must have seemed ominous to those watching on shore that as the *Portland* steamed out of the harbor, dozens of smaller vessels and ships were racing back in, seeking the shelter of the harbor as the storm moved in. As the *Portland* reached the open ocean, the swells were already so high and the wind so strong that it would have been impossible for Blanchard to turn the boat around without being capsized. He now had no choice but to put on the steam and do what he could to stay afloat until the storm passed or they reached Portland, whichever came first.

Throughout Saturday evening, lighthouse keepers and crews on board other ships struggling to maintain their own vessels in the storm, spotted the *Portland* in varying positions between Cape Cod and Cape Ann. The storm system had developed over Massachusetts Bay much faster than any of the mariners had expected. Meteorologists at Boston's Blue Hill Observatory measured an average wind speed of 45 miles per hour through the night, with gusts of up to 100 miles per hour, and snow was falling at a rate of over 1.5 inches per hour. The conditions on land and at sea were deteriorating rapidly.

At approximately 10:00 p.m., the *Portland* was spotted again, steaming north just off of Thatcher's Island, thirty miles north of Boston. By 11:00 she had been blown well off course and farther from shore, where she narrowly missed colliding with the fishing schooner *Grayling*. Between the time of her near miss with the *Grayling* and 11:45 p.m., the *Portland* was spotted three more times, now southeast of Thatcher's Island, being driven even farther off course by the storm. She had already sustained visible storm damage with the most serious damage to her superstructure (the portion of the ship above the deck).

Cape Cod's Outer Cape coastline was once lined with lighthouses and life saving stations. These were occupied with crews watching for ships in distress, ready to put rescue boats and rescue swimmers into immediate action if needed. Samuel O. Fisher was a lighthouse keeper and member of the Race Point Life Saving Station crew at the northern tip of Cape Cod. Fisher happened to be on duty early Sunday morning, November 27, 1898. As he scanned the waves from the lookout tower during a lull in the storm, he heard four short blasts of a steamer's whistle. At that time, four short blasts meant a mariner's distress signal. Fisher immediately readied the rescue boat but before he could launch it, the whistle stopped. He would have no way to find the distressed ship in the heavy surf. The early morning was too dark and stormy to see the ship, but it was believed to have been the *Portland*, and for very good reason, but that was not to be determined for another dozen hours.

The *Portland* was reportedly spotted a few more times, roughly between 9:00 and 10:30 that morning. She appeared to be wallowing out of control between five and eight miles off shore, again near the northern tip of Cape Cod. That was the last time anyone ever laid eyes on the *Portland* while she was

Old Point Race Life Saving Station. One of nine stations set up along the beaches of the Outer Cape. Each station included living quarters, an observation tower and storage for the surf boats as seen in the foreground.

still afloat. She wasn't seen again for a hundred years, and when she was, she was lying on the sea floor under four hundred feet of water.

As Sunday dawned, the people of New England looked out on a devastated landscape. There were two feet of snow, disabled railroads and downed telegraph and telephone lines. The shores were littered with ships and boats either smashed against the rocks or washed ashore, many lying on their sides on the beach. No one could go anywhere and no information was getting in or out. It was later determined that over 140 ships were lost in the storm and 260 grounded or washed ashore; but on the morning after, there was no way of knowing which ships had survived and which were lost.

On the northern shoreline of Cape Cod's Outer Cape, between the Race Point Life Saving Station and the Peaked Hill Bars station, a lifesaver named John Johnson was watching the surf on his regular shore patrol when he found debris that was washing ashore. First there were several empty 40-quart dairy cans from the Turner Center Creamery in Maine, then a life vest with "*Str. Portland*" printed on it. It was 7:30 p.m., just a little more than 24 hours since the *Portland* had steamed out of Boston Harbor.

Over the next two hours, the waves deposited additional pieces of wreckage such as doors and carved woodwork onto the shore. At 11:00 p.m., the rising tide brought with it more and heaver pieces of wreckage, along with several bodies. There were pieces of timbers, a large amount of furniture, planking and other mangled and splintered pieces of a ship. It was impossible to tell how the *Portland* had met her end. Had she capsized, been broken apart by a wave, collided with another ship or even suffered a boiler explosion in the churning seas? No one knew and no one could guess from looking at the debris washing onto the northern Cape Cod beaches.

The only thing that could be learned was determined from the bodies recovered from the water. Many of them were wearing wristwatches and all of the watches had stopped at or about 9:15 o'clock. The only thing anyone knew for sure was that the passengers had gone into the water around that time, making it the estimated time of death for the *Portland*.

In Portland, Maine, anxious friends and family members of passengers and crew on board the *Portland* were gathering at the wharf. The ship was over 12 hours overdue. With telegraph and telephone lines down all over Massachusetts, there was no way to contact Boston to determine if the *Portland* had left Boston Harbor the night before. Even as bodies and wreckage were washing up on Cape Cod, the gathering crowd in Portland was being told not to worry; everything would be fine and to just be patient.

Charles Ward, a reporter for the *Boston Herald,* was on Cape Cod during the storm. When he heard about the bodies and items that identified the wreckage as being from the *Portland,* he realized that she had been lost, and that no one in Boston could possibly know. He was determined to carry the horrible news back home. It was to be quite an undertaking. First, he took a train as far as he could, and then hiked through the snow until he was able to hire a horse which he rode nine more miles to another train station. Once there, he rode the train several miles until finally arriving in Boston on Tuesday morning with the news. The headline on the special edition published by the *Herald* read: STEAMER PORTLAND SURELY LOST. The *Boston Globe's* special edition screamed 100 LOST: Steamer Portland Wrecked off Highland Light. This number turned out to be an understatement by half.

The people of Portland were hardest hit by the loss of the steamer. The ship's home port was there and almost all of her crew lived there. A majority of the passengers were also from Portland, as they were nearly all returning home after the Thanksgiving holiday. There was hardly a person in Portland who hadn't lost a relative or who didn't know someone who had gone down with the ship. Captain Blanchard lived in Portland with his wife and two children.

Family and friends waited a week for confirmation of the tragedy, hoping against hope that the news had been wrong and that at least someone had survived. But the sea had taken them all -- every last one.

It seemed like everyone in Portland had a sad story to tell of those they were missing. Emily Cobb was scheduled to perform her singing debut in a Portland Church. Greg Kenniston had spent Thanksgiving with his sister and was on his way to see his brother in Yarmouth before returning to his studies at Bowdoin College. Jes and Jessine Schmidt, along with five-year-old Jorgen and four-year-old Anton, had almost made it home; they were returning from a trip to Europe to visit family. Maine Senator E. Dudley Freeman had been en route home to spend time with his wife and children. Charles Thompson, owner and operator of the Thompson Grocery Store, perished with his wife and their three-year-old daughter. Oren Hooper ran a Portland furniture store and was headed home with his thirteen-year-old son. The Portland schools lost several teachers. A majority of the steamer's 65 crew members were African Americans living in Portland. They also left families behind.

Only 35 bodies were ever recovered. Most families were left with nothing to bury. The lives and property losses from the wreck of the *Portland* were tremendous. Long after the dead were laid to rest and the debris cleared, the human toll continued to mount.

Many, if not all, of the crew members were the sole providers for their families. Watchman John C. Whitten left behind his wife, Lettie, three sons and one daughter. After his death, his wife applied for and received $35, his last month's wages. She was soon so impoverished that she was unable to care for her family and was forced to put her daughter up for adoption. At age 32, Lettie Whitten moved into an "invalids home" in Portland. According to the Maine Historical Society, this institution was where "self-supporting (unmarried or widowed) women could be cared for at a nominal price when by reason of overwork or illness they required the rest and nursing which could not be secured elsewhere." In other words, it was an asylum. Two of John and Lettie's sons were sent to Good Hill Farm in Fairfield, Maine: the county poor farm. What became of the third son is unknown. What is known is that John Whitten's family became destitute after his death and was ripped apart.

Arthur Johnson left his wife, Ellen, to care for their three children alone. Ellen suffered a double loss as her sister was also working on board the *Portland* that fateful night. Ellen filed for the back wages of both her husband and her sister. This helped her to hold her family together for a few years before they too became impoverished and were forced to separate,

Similar stories of families broken apart after the breadwinner went down with the *Portland* came from all corners of the city. The crew members who died had nothing to leave their families except one month's wages, certainly not enough to keep a family safe and fed for long. Making the loss even greater, it was a time when few women could find employment that paid enough to support a family on their own.

Many civil lawsuits were filed against the Portland Steamship Company on behalf of the estates of passengers killed on the *Portland.* The company filed a petition for limitation of liability in the U.S. District Court in Portland. The petition languished for a time until the court ruled the sinking was an act of God. This relieved the company of all responsibility and the lawsuits were dropped, as the plaintiffs now had virtually no possibility of winning.

The actual number of people aboard the *Portland* as it steamed out of Boston Harbor on her final voyage will never be known. All passenger records were kept aboard the ships, and the records aboard the *Portland* went down with her. No paperwork was ever recovered. Many names of those lost were known only because they were supposed to be traveling to Portland and never arrived. The names of the crew, or at least most of them, were discovered when family members applied to the shipping commissioner for the back wages of loved ones who were working on the *Portland* when she sank. The average monthly wage for men who worked on the steamship was $35; for women it was $20 to $25.

There has never been any conclusive evidence as to exactly when the *Portland* lost her battle with the storm, other than 9:15, as indicated by the stopped wristwatches found on many of the recovered bodies. What remained unclear was whether they stopped at 9:15 a.m. or 9:15 p.m. Historians and maritime experts have tried to resolve this mystery but their conclusions are contradictory. There are good arguments for both possibilities.

Records indicate that there were several sightings of the *Portland* wallowing five to eight miles off the northern tip of Cape Cod sometime between 9:00 and 10:30 a.m. that Sunday morning. However, it remains unknown what the exact times were, as records list only approximations.

If the ship was definitely still afloat after 9:15 that morning, then she must have survived throughout day and not sunk until 9:15 Sunday evening. If the *Portland* had lasted that long, then she would have been at sea, battling the storm for over 26 hours. That seems unlikely since she would have run out of coal to fire the boilers long before that. Keeping the boilers fired and the sidewheels turning would have been critical in maintaining control of the steamer and staying afloat. Without power, the pounding waves would have easily pushed her around, forcing her to come abreast of the waves. She would then have capsized with a single large wave.

One theory suggests that when their supply of coal had been exhausted, the crew could have burned other flammable materials such as furniture, and then stripped off the wooden trim, the doors, and even burned the cargo to keep the boilers fired. The ship needed power to keep the bow pointed into the waves to avoid capsizing. However, it is strongly believed that this was not done because of the massive amount of furniture and other pieces of flammable wreckage that washed ashore. Also, many experts do not believe that the Portland could possibly have held together for that long a time, considering the terrible weather conditions and the relentless pounding of the waves.

Others argue that if she had gone down as early as 9:15 in the morning, it would not have taken a full twelve hours for major debris to begin washing ashore that night. The long delay in the debris field's making landfall seems to suggest that the *Portland* hadn't succumbed to the sea until Sunday night. A wreck in the morning would have meant that debris would have been washing ashore all day. It's likely that no one will ever know whether the Portland was lost in the morning or that night, but we can be sure that she began her journey to the ocean floor, taking with her nearly 200 passengers and crew, on Sunday, November 27, 1898.

Following the wreck of the *Portland*, steamship lines took a hard look at some of their practices. The age of large side paddle wheel steamships running on coastal waters was rapidly drawing to a close. The *Portland* was one of the last of her kind to be used on the "outside" or "Down East" routes. They continued to be used for many decades but were limited to inland waterways. Shipping companies realized that for travel on coastal waters, they needed a different kind of vessel to regain the public's confidence, ones that could hold their own in rough, stormy seas. They quickly shifted to more stable steel-hulled ships driven by propellers instead of paddle wheels.

Another change was generally embraced, though it had nothing to do with safety but everything to do with the possibility of sinking. Most captains instituted a practice of sending a list of passengers and crew to their office on shore before leaving port. In case of disaster - no one might die unknown or unremembered.

The Search for the Portland
Several attempts were made to locate the wreck of the *Portland*. The first was in 1899, a year after the sinking, when an expedition was funded by the *Boston Globe*. This search centered on an area off Cape Cod known as Peaked Hill Bar. The system used was a simple one: Two boats dragged a cable between them along the bar. They found nothing.

Almost fifty years later, in 1945, a second search got underway when Edward Rowe Snow, a New England maritime historian, launched his own expedition. He and a partner hired a diver to search a wreck that had been found previously off the northern tip of Cape Cod. They hoped the diver would be able to identify it as the *Portland*. The diver was able to descend the 140 feet to the wreck and looked around. When he returned to the surface, he claimed that the wreck was indeed that of the *Portland*. The identification was based solely on the diver's word, as he was unable to bring up any artifact or evidence to confirm the identification. This caused much doubt from rival historians. Regardless, Snow stood by the diver's claim and published his views on the subject for many years after.

John Fish mounted the next expedition. He is a noted maritime historian and specialist in underwater search and recovery. He was also vice president of American Underwater Search and Survey based out of Cape Cod. In 1981, Fish and his partner, Arnold Carr, put together a team and began their search for the missing steamship, this time looking farther north. After thousands of hours spent scanning the ocean floor, and nine years of study and calculations, they discovered what they believed to be the remains of the *Portland* in 1989. The location where they found her is designated as part of the Stellwagen Bank National Marine Sanctuary at the mouth of Massachusetts Bay. She is sitting upright in 400 feet of water, but they were unable to absolutely confirm the identification.

Using coordinates and data provided by John Fish's expedition, the National Oceanic and Atmospheric Administration (NOAA) returned to the wreck site in a joint venture with the National Undersea Research Center and the University of Connecticut. Using towed side-scan sonar towed by a surface vessel, they were able to photograph the wreck and definitively identify it as the *Portland*.

While scanning the area for the *Portland*, they found the wreck of a smaller fishing schooner believed to be the *Addie. E. Snow* lying less than a quarter of a mile from the *Portland*. The *Addie. E. Snow* was also lost during The Portland Gale. After analyzing the bow of the schooner and the distinctive damage to the *Portland*, they concluded that the two vessels had collided and sank together in the storm.

Cape Cod has long been one of the most haunted locations in New England. Many houses and inns date back to the 1600s and 1700s, and have a rich history of reported visits from ghosts of former residents. But some of the most haunted places to visit aren't inside these beautiful old structures. Stories of encounters with spectral mariners and phantom ships have been passed on for centuries. This should be of no surprise to anyone with an understanding of the history of the place. The shores of the Outer Cape have born witness to the wrecks of countless ships. The waters near the shallow rips a few hundred yards off shore have created a graveyard containing the remains of over three thousand shipwrecks. This underwater graveyard holds more than rotting old ships, as over ten thousand people went into the water here when their ships went down. Some washed ashore, but many are still down there, locked away in cabins or tangled in decayed rigging.

A solitary walk along the beaches of the Cape Cod National Seashore may not be solitary for long. If someone joins you, or if you see someone wandering the dunes, regard them carefully. Especially if they seem a little lost or out of place. There's a good chance that your companion may not be just another person out for a stroll, at least not another *living person*. And if you find yourself walking on one of the beaches far to the north, between where the old Race Point Life Saving Station and the Peaked Hill Bar Life Saving Station used to be, pay very close attention. The lost souls who haunt these sands may not be the remnants of old sailors. You may see mothers, fathers, brothers, sisters and children -- many children. They just might be the long-lost passengers of the steamer *Portland*, looking for their lost loved ones or just trying to get home.

1913: THE GREAT OHIO FLOOD
Ohio had always been a state that flooded, and flooded often. Spring floods were just a way of life and the people of Ohio had become accustomed to the flooding as routine. Rivers and creeks rose, spilled out of their banks, covered the flood plains, then receded back to where they belonged. Year after year, decade after decade, the waters went through their cycle. But then came the big one: the flood to top every other flood. In March of 1913, Ohio experienced its greatest weather disaster in history in the form of a statewide series of devastating

floods.

During a very long three days, between March 6 and March 9, 11 inches of rain fell across the state. Temperatures fluctuated wildly between 60 degrees and 20 degrees Fahrenheit. Flood waters rose to as much as 27 feet above flood level in some areas and rushed through cities at a depth of up to 20 feet. Over 40,000 homes were flooded and 20,000 more were destroyed outright. Explosions and fires brought on by natural gas leaks consumed entire city blocks. The losses from damage to homes, businesses, industries and farmlands surpassed two billion in today's dollars, but the highest cost was measured in the loss of human lives. The exact number of lives claimed by the flood will never be known but at the very least, 600 men, women and children were swept away and drowned by the icy cold waters of the Great Ohio Flood of 1913.

Early spring was mild and wet throughout March of that year, but on the whole, the weather had been fairly pleasant. As the Easter weekend approached, people were busy with plans for holiday dinners and visits to family. Children eagerly anticipated a visit from the Easter rabbit and the brightly colored eggs and candy that awaited them. Unfortunately, most of Ohio would not be celebrating Easter that year. Instead, it would be a weekend of terror, loss and mourning.

Ohio was about to be pummeled by three storms in three days, the aftermath of which would be the stuff of which legends are made. What transpired that week in March of 1913 was thought to be the defining event of a lifetime for an entire generation of Ohioans. For the rest of their lives, they would ask each other: "Where were you during the Great Ohio Flood?"

Bad Weather's a-Comin'

The first of three consecutive storms slammed across the region on March 21, carrying with it rain and high winds. The winds blew in unseasonably warm temperatures reaching over 60 degrees. The ground soaked up the rain till it became soggy, and then it rained some more, but not so much as to worry anyone. It would just be a wet, muddy Easter.

The following day, Saturday, March 22, dawned warm and sunny. But as the day wore on, dark storm clouds moved in, and with them more rain. Temperatures across the state plummeted to 20 degrees or below. The rain-saturated ground quickly froze. The second storm had done its part in preparing the region for the catastrophes to come.

March 23 was Easter Sunday and the third and most devastating storm was already gathering over the plains of Ohio. A torrential rain began to fall, and continued nonstop all day and throughout the night. The frozen ground couldn't absorb the rain as it fell. As a result, over 90 percent of the rainwater falling across the Ohio River Valley ran directly into adjoining tributaries and rivers. The water flowing across the frozen watersheds for the Sandusky, Muskingum and Great Miami rivers were filling those rivers at an alarming rate. In some cases, river levels rose a foot or more per hour.

Over the next two days, cities and towns all over the Ohio River Valley were inundated with floodwaters. As the ground froze, watersheds continued to drain and the rivers and tributaries continued to swell and overflow their banks. Death and destruction followed in every flooded community.

Severe Weather Turns to Tragedy

In each flooded city, the stories were the same. Thousands of residents became trapped in their homes, unable to evacuate because of the swift currents of the floodwaters. They had to move higher and higher to escape the rising waters. People in single-story houses were forced onto their roofs, some having to chop holes in the roofs to gain access. Others who were caught off guard outside were forced to climb into trees or cling to telephone poles and wait, hoping and praying for rescue. Making matters much worse, while huddled together on rooftops or in trees in the frigid temperatures, they were pelted first with rain, then sleet, and finally snow.

In Cleveland, the Cuyahoga River flowed into industrial regions of the city, washing away docks, lumberyards, trains, rail yards and factories, disrupting shipping by rail and on Lake Erie for months. The Tuscarawas River flooded most of Massillon, south of Cleveland. The Muskingum River rose to 27 feet above flood stage and overran Zanesville, where the water was 20 feet deep in some downtown areas. In Defiance, the Maumee River

(Above Left): Massillon, south of Cleveland, is flooded by the Tuscarawas River.

(Above, Right): After the flood waters had receded in Marietta.

(Left): Downtown Zanesville, guarded by Ohio National Guardsmen.

topped out 10 feet above flood stage and covered 268 homes with water.

The Sandusky River flooded 550 homes in Freemont, but here the police had been closely watching the conditions on the river. They were able to warn residents to evacuate the area before the flood hit. Some left but far too many stayed in their homes. A major problem in Freemont was the Ballville Dam, a hydroelectric dam that had been completed the year before. The churning water washed out the foundation and the dam collapsed, releasing a wall of water that washed away entire buildings. Dozens of people were rescued from rooftops and plucked from trees. Of the three lives that were lost one was a man who was said to have rescued hundreds of people before he was drowned.

Upriver from Freemont, the Sandusky River overflowed into Tiffin. Here too, people trapped in their homes moved onto their roofs and into large trees. The Sandusky was not as merciful in Tiffin as it had been in Freemont. Over 500 Tiffin homes were damaged or destroyed completely, sending many people scrambling to their roofs or clinging to trees. While families waited on rooftops for rescue, 19 people were killed when several houses and trees collapsed into the river, sweeping entire families away with the remains of their homes.

The flooded Ohio River made its way south, passing through Portsmouth and Cincinnati. Portsmouth had been protected by a series of levees. The raging river first topped, and then washed away the levees, leaving 4,500 homes flooded. In Cincinnati, the Ohio rose 21 feet in 24 hours, flooding business and residential districts in a matter of hours.

In central Ohio, Columbus and Chillicothe fell victim to the Scioto River. Chillicothe's downtown district was completely flooded. It was much worse in Columbus, where early on March 25, the water reached between nine and 17 feet when the levees failed. The residents had no warning that the river was approaching the top of the

(Left): Fire rages out of control through a Columbus industrial building. The Scioto River blocked the fire department and the building was left burn itself out.

(Right): A fire department wagon races to a Columbus fire, where the floodwaters of the Scioto River were shallow enough for them to pass.

levees and a result, over 100 people died. Several died of cold and thirst while waiting on their rooftops for rescuers who never came.

Martha Louise Riser was 11 years old when the 1913 flood swept through Columbus. She described how her father ran into their home as the waters started to rise, rushing the family out with the intent of getting them to higher ground. Unfortunately, the water was rising faster than they could flee, and they had to take refuge in a business building with a dry goods store on the first floor. They quickly climbed to the second floor of the two-story building as the water washed into the store. To make matters worse, the store below them caught fire.

Martha's father pulled a door from its hinges and carried it to the roof. He used the door as a bridge between the roof of the burning building and the roof of the building next door. The terrified family crawled, one by one, across the makeshift bridge to safety. The building where they took shelter housed a grocery store and they helped themselves to food. There was no fresh water, however, and they only later realized that they could have collected rainwater for drinking. For the remainder of that day and all of the next, Martha's family watched from second-story windows as rescuers in small boats tried to collect people and take them to safety, or else deliver food and supplies where rescue was impossible. For those two days, a majority of the boats they watched pass by got caught up in the rushing currents and were capsized. Still, the rescue and aid attempts continued. When Martha's family was finally able to return home, they found that their home, was destroyed, but they

The bridge between Main Street and High Street in Hamilton. The bridge was quickly topped and as debris washed down from Dayton. It smashed against the steel trusswork then broke apart and was washed away shortly after this photo was taken.

A Pale Horse was Death — Page 207

had survived and they had each other.

Hamilton, just south of Dayton, had the misfortune of being built on the banks of the Great Miami River, which had been picking up water for hundreds of miles. The river had also been picking up hundreds of tons of debris, carrying it along as the flooding river moved into Hamilton. The flood had struck Dayton ahead of Hamilton, so many of the residents there had some warning of what was headed their way. Dr. O.H. Thomas left his house and ran to his horse that was tied to a post in his front yard. Just as he untied the reins, a wall of water came surging down the street. The horse was washed away but Dr. Thomas was able to cling to the hitching post as the water rushed past him. The current was so fierce that it lifted his body till he was parallel to the ground. Thomas held fast to the post for over an hour, until the current slowed enough that he was able to wade to safety in a nearby building.

The warning alarm may have helped Hamilton; although there was massive destruction, far fewer lives were lost there than in Dayton. One particularly sad death was that of Captain Isaac Floro, from Port Clinton. He had heard of the disaster and had ridden to Hamilton to assist in the rescue operations. After repeatedly taking a small boat into the floodwaters, and retrieving many people trapped inside their homes or on rooftops, he drowned when his boat became caught in a strong current and was capsized.

The Worst of the Worst - Dayton

Dayton was the hardest hit by the flooding, so hard in fact, that while all the other floods throughout the state were given the collective name of The Great Ohio Floods of 1913, the flood here was distinguished from all the others with the name The Great Dayton Flood. Dayton residents came to call it simply The Flood.

Israel Ludlow had been a government surveyor in the late eighteenth century. When he was sent to the southern part of the Ohio Country (Ohio was not yet a state), he was to survey the lands, laying out specific land grant tracks and proposed sites for future cities. This was done in aid of the young country's westward expansion. Ludlow was therefore responsible, by default, for founding Cincinnati, Dayton and Hamilton by choosing the sites where these cities were to be built.

At that time, travel and shipping on major rivers was a growing prospect and Ludlow wished to be proactive by choosing locations along Ohio's southern rivers. In doing this, he increased the possibility that these cities would become major shipping and travel destinations. Unfortunately, he unwittingly increased the probability that these cities would experience frequent flooding. As he surveyed the proposed site for Dayton, he was repeatedly warned by local Native Americans that the area he had chosen was prone to frequent flooding. Ludlow ignored their warnings and his proposal was approved. Dayton was built exactly where he planned, as was Cincinnati along the banks of the Ohio River, and Hamilton on the Great Miami River.

In the center of downtown Dayton, the Stillwater River, the Mad River and Wolf Creek converge with the Great Miami River. The idea that the 4,000-square-mile Great Miami watershed drains into the Great Miami River and passes through downtown Dayton is even more stunning when we consider that a majority of the downtown area lies in the Great Miami's natural flood plain. The result was that severe flooding occurred in Dayton nearly every decade, with five major floods striking during the nineteenth century. Even after all those floods, none would ever compare to what was about to happen to the unsuspecting city on that Easter weekend in 1913.

The Dayton area had experienced the same three storms that had moved across most of Ohio, dumping an enormous amount of rain on the Great Miami River's watershed. Having experienced so many floods in the previous century, a series of dry levees had been built in strategic locations around the city to hold back floodwaters and protect downtown Dayton. The levees did add a certain level of protection but they also had an adverse psychological effect on the residents, as they developed a false sense of security. They were aware that the rivers were rising, but they believed that the excess water would be channeled away and they would be safe and dry. And the levees did do their job...for a while. They held back the water for one day, Monday, March 24, until the deluge proved to be just too much.

Dayton police had been closely monitoring the rising height of the waters and the condition of the levees. Just after midnight on Tuesday, March 25, the Herman Street levee was visibly weakening and the police started spreading the alarm. The air about Dayton was suddenly filled with sirens, bells, whistles and shouts that a flood was imminent. Unfortunately, far too many people ignored the warnings, choosing to rely on the protection of the levees.

Gaylord Cummin, Dayton's city engineer, was also watching the rising waters. At 5:30 a.m., the water had reached the top of the levees and Cummin determines that the flow rate was 100,000 cubic feet per second. He knew that the levees would be topped in minutes, and when that happened there would be nothing anyone would be able to do.

Half an hour later, water flowed over the levees and began to appear in the streets of Dayton, small streams of yellowish water at first, followed by a sheet of dirty water began to fill the streets. Less than two hours later, the south side levees experienced catastrophic failure and water rushed into the city's downtown area.

This photo, taken soon after water began filling downtown Dayton as indicated by the lack of floating debris and live horses. The water is already raging through the streets, but will rise another 12 to 15 feet before cresting.

The water levels rose quickly, and continued to rise all day. This was not the peaceful sort of flood where the water rises, soaks everything down, then calmly recedes in its own time: This was a raging flood, violently tearing at everything in its path. The heavy masonry buildings downtown compounded the problem. Most of them survived the currents, but they created canyons that restricted the flow and increased the velocity of the water pouring into the streets at a speed of over 25 miles per hour.

The conditions in Dayton were unprecedented. Fourteen square miles of the city were under water. In some of the lower elevations downtown, the water was over 20 feet deep. The total amount of water that passed through Dayton in that three-day period was greater than the amount of water that flows over Niagara Falls in a month!

As the water level rose, storefront windows burst from the water pressure or from being struck by floating debris. Once the windows were gone, the floodwaters washed much of the contents of the first floors, and sometimes even the second floors, into the streets. As the floodwaters began filling with debris, the danger increased dramatically. Observers watching from upper windows saw as all manner of flotsam pass in front of them. They saw crates, barrels, lumber, and pieces of houses slam into each other and against the buildings. When the floodwaters flushed out the contents of a music store, a parade of pianos floated down one city street. A group of small houses, still whole, were seen bobbing about in the water and down the river channels.

At one point, a trolley loaded with passengers was swept down the street. Most of those on board believed that there was no hope for them and the trolley would soon sink, taking them with it. But before that could happen, the trolley slammed up against a pole and became wedged. A young man who witnessed the calamity from an upper story window, tied a rope around his waist and flung himself into the raging torrent in an effort to get to the trolley. He quickly became exhausted and was pulled back to safety. Three other men tried to do the same but were also thwarted by the strong current of the icy water. A fourth man made one last attempt to reach the trolley and was successful. Using the rope, he helped the passengers to safety.

For reasons unknown, whether no one thought about it or whether it was just left too late, the city's natural gas was left flowing long after the downtown flooded. As debris smashed into buildings and some were dislodged from their foundations, gas pipes were cracked, spewing natural gas freely. The resulting fire caused severe

More of an entire city block in downtown Dayton was destroyed by natural gas explosions and fire.

damage throughout the city, but the worst was in the business district where fire destroyed more than a full city block. In one case, a large group of people had taken refuge on an upper floor of an office building when one side of the building was suddenly blown away. Survivors in a building across the street watched helplessly as they scrambled to the roof, making their escape onto the roof of the next building. Too frightened to climb lower, they remained on the rooftops, exposed to the extreme cold with little or no food and water.

Solitary explosions and fires rocked entire neighborhoods, as fires raged throughout Dayton. The Whitmore family watched from a hill behind their home. Mr. Whitmore later recalled: "You could see those fires burning and there was nothing they could do; all the fire equipment was under water. It just had to burn down to the water line."

A cluster of witnesses in a residential area watched as a number of people on top of a mass of wreckage floated past, caught in the swift current. Several people risked their lives trying to rescue them, only to find they were mannequins that had been washed from a clothing store nearby. Another group told of seeing a dining room table float by set for breakfast with dishes, silverware and even the tablecloth still in place. Shortly after, the matching set of chairs sailed by.

In residential areas, the velocity of the water flow was not quite as great as it was in the downtown districts, but it still devastated many neighborhoods. Mrs. Myers Morgan, who was 15 in 1913, later summed up the feelings of most of Dayton's residents: "That awful flood came with a savage rush, and stole so much from so many."

As water began filling the streets, fathers and mothers left work, shopping, or whatever they were doing and rushed home to their families. In some places, the water rose so quickly that when these worried parents began their trek home, they splashed through ankle-deep water, but soon found they were struggling through water up to their waists. Many were overcome by the currents and were swept away, having never reached their homes. -

Charles and Viola Adams lived in a low-lying neighborhood. Aware that their house would be among the first to flood, they fled their home, taking with them their 11-month-old twins, Charles Jr. and Lois. As they tried to make it to a relative's house on higher ground, they were overtaken by the rising water. Charles Adams hailed a rescue boat and the little family was pulled in. Almost immediately, the boat was caught in a strong undercurrent and it slammed into a pole, knocking everyone into the water. Baby Lois was swept away but somehow, Charles managed to hold onto his son. A second rescue boat almost immediately picked up Charles and the baby but it, too, capsized. This time, baby Charles wasn't so lucky. Like his twin, he was swept away.

Up and down countless streets, groups of people were experiencing the same struggle to survive. Within two blocks of where the two rescue boats carrying the Adams family capsized, the babies were seen by a group of strangers and both were plucked from the water, still alive. The Adams family survived their ordeal, but the babies were far from well. They had been nearly drowned and when pulled to dry ground, Dr. D.E. Miller, who happened to be among the witnesses, was able to resuscitate the twins. They hovered near death's door for weeks, both nearly succumbing to pneumonia. In the end, the twins pulled through and each lived long, happy lives; Lois dying in her eighties and Charles living well past ninety. They were known for the rest of their lives as the Flood Twins.

Other families found themselves trapped in their homes when the water rose too quickly for them to escape safely. As the water climbed higher, they retreated to the safety of their homes' second floors and others retreated into their attics. The time they spent hoping for rescue was terrifying. Many survivors did their best to put their harrowing experience into words, trying to describe not only what had happened, but also to capture the emotions they were feeling as they waited, not knowing if they were waiting for rescue or for death.

William Mathews wrote of climbing to an upper floor of a neighbor's house, where he sheltered when he was unable to get to his own home: "By that time water was coming in, bubbling up through the floors, like a fountain." Mathews carefully logged the water levels as they rose and fell, peaking at 17 feet. He believed that the explosions and subsequent fires were the biggest threat. During the night on his third day trapped, fatigue, hunger and terror were taking their toll on his emotions. He

This small house was ripped from its foundation and deposited precariously between two other homes.

described his feelings: "It appears very much like the end will come soon as the city is surely doomed with fire."

Some families tried to save at least some of their possessions by carrying their best pieces of furniture, china, and treasured photographs upstairs. All too often, there just wasn't enough time and they ended up scrambling up the stairs for their lives. As the main floor below them filled with water, they could hear their waterlogged furniture banging against the ceiling below their feet.

Reaching the 'higher ground' of upper stories or roofs did not necessarily mean safety. They were safe, but only for the time being. Fires burned all over the city, and at any time, the wind could shift, carrying with it burning cinders that could set their own homes alight. Residents held hostage in their own houses by the raging floodwaters watched helplessly as houses around them collapsed, or were torn from their foundations and sent tumbling through the current. They never knew when or if their house might suffer the same fate, carrying them and their families with it. Not much sleep was to be had during those days and nights of horror.

An anonymous person wrote what is perhaps the most poignant and terrifying description of those stranded days and nights:

Rescue boats plucked those who were most exposed and took them to safety. Some people were left hanging onto a pole for days before anyone could reach them and help. A sense of isolation settled over each building, as if they were each marooned in the middle of a vast ocean, left to fend for themselves. Most folks had little food, and ate what they could scrounge out of crates floating in the floodwater. The city's water supply was undrinkable, so basins and pans were set out to collect rainwater.

In the afternoon of the second day, temperatures plunged well below freezing and snow began to fall. Later that night, a violent storm brought lightning and thunder. Great bullets of rain pelted those who were still exposed and the storm stirred the floodwater. For those holed up indoors, the sounds that night were nearly unbearable. They heard people screaming for help and the bang of debris hitting the side of the house. The bumps in the night were especially ominous because no candles or matches could be lit, for fear of an explosion from a gas leak. People groped through the darkness, the only light coming from distant fires and the occasional flash of lightning.

In another part of the city, young Harry Jeffrey, his sister and brother, his parents, grandmother, aunt and uncle had all gathered in the front bedroom of their home's second floor. The dirty brownish-green floodwater had risen to within two inches of the second-story floor. Their solid brick house was at the bottom of a steep hill, and they were surrounded by wood frame houses that they feared would catch fire. A rescue boat had come to their home but the current was so strong that the firemen at the oars were unable to keep the boat in position. There was nothing the Jeffrey family could do but stay put and pray.

At age 92, Harry Jeffrey, by then a retired Dayton attorney, was interviewed about the night his family spent trapped by the flood by the *Dayton Daily News*. He called it the most frightening night of his long life.

Our plight was steadily getting worse. The rain fell incessantly, and it was bitter cold. No one dared to even strike a match for fear of starting a fire, for by now the pungent odor of escaping gas filled the air. Less substantial frame houses began to give way under the strain and were torn from their foundations. Barns, horses, furniture and autos and articles of every imaginable description floated past the house in an endless stream.

The crash of an explosion shook the air. We rushed to the windows in time to make out a great mass of wreckage hurled into the air. Bricks were thrown hundreds of yards. The apartment house half a square away had been blown up. Screams of men, women and children pierced the air. The building above the water had become a mass of flames. The fire soon spread to neighboring houses. The occupants of those houses fled from one house to another over roofs and masses of floating wreckage.

A group of people had gathered on top of the hill above the Jeffrey house. They shone searchlights down to help light the area. A man with his baby tied to his back with a sheet led his wife through the water till they reached a telephone pole. Using the telephone wires, they were able to pull themselves the two blocks to the hill and safety.

Another man tossed a rope onto the Jeffreys' second-story balcony. Harry Jeffrey's father and uncle then used the rope to pull 28 stranded people into their house, one at a time. They were relatively safe there but the biggest worry was still the fire spreading in front of them. The Jeffreys were saved from having to flee their home when the wind changed direction just as the last frame house burst into flames.

Jeffrey continued:

"By 3 a.m., the water level began to recede. At last thin streaks of gray began to appear in the east, but that dawn did not seem cold and cheerless to the silent watchers in the house. Anything would have been a relief after the experiences of that night, a night which had assumed an eternity."

The Jeffrey family and the people they had saved were eventually rescued after the water had receded and the current had lost some of its velocity. A line of boxcars were sent down the hill on the streetcar tracks to the house. A pontoon bridge of sorts was used to connect the boxcars to the house. One by one, the 36 occupants of the house crawled across the bridge and into the boxcars, which were then pulled back up the hill to dry land. Their longest night had finally ended.

Two of Dayton's most famous citizens, Wilbur and Orville Wright, were staying with their father when the flood hit. Their home was completely flooded when a rescue boat approached the house. Wilbur and Orville insisted that their father climb aboard but they stayed behind. The brothers eventually made their way to their factory, which was on high enough ground to avoid the flood. They were worried about the safety of their records, photographs, calculations and designs for the Wright Flyer that were in the office of the factory building. The factory turned out to be safe and the records were untouched, but the building next door, which housed the actual Wright Flyer, caught fire.

Amos Crow lived and worked in downtown Dayton where he operated a restaurant and wholesale store. Two weeks after the flood began, he wrote the following personal account:

This is the most awful sight I ever saw and do not care to see another soon. We have been living very slim since the flood but are glad to get anything. We look around and see people in worse shape that we are. We saved everything at home but lost the wholesale place and the restaurant. The walls washed away from the building we were in. Our horses were drowned. We had them in a livery barn close to the wholesale house. There were about 100 horses in that barn and all drowned; 27 of them never got out of the barn...I saw one horse hanging up by the heels on a guy wire with just his head touching the ground. People climbed up in trees and stayed there for 48 hours in all that rain and sleet without shelter or drink. The water was 13 feet deep on my restaurant floor... I saw houses go down the river and people on top of them.

At the time of the flood, the largest single industry and employer was the National Cash Register company, with nearly 7,000 employees. When the level of death and destruction caused by the flood became apparent, John H. Patterson, the company's owner, sprang into action. He wired the *New York Times* with the message: "Situation here desperate. All people except on outskirts imprisoned by water. They have no food, no drinking water, no light, no heat for two days." He knew this would be the fastest way to spread the news of the plight of the people of Dayton.

Next, Patterson converted part of his factory for building small rescue boats. His employees were able to assemble nearly 300 flat-bottomed boats. He organized teams to set out in the boats to rescue people who were stranded in exposed areas such as trees, poles and roofs first, then on to people who were only a little better off, trapped in upper floors of their homes. Patterson himself, though 70 years old, went out on a boat for several of these rescues. They were able to bring in thousands of stranded citizens, though some had to wait until Thursday, March 27. Quickly realizing that the victims would have no place to go, he converted his Steward Street factory into an emergency shelter. There, flood victims were provided with food, water, blankets and a place to stay. Patterson also organized medical professionals from Dayton, and those arriving from around the country to assist in the care of the sick and injured.

John Patterson paid for everything personally and never asked for a dime in return. He is credited for the survival of hundreds of people who would surely have died if not for his quick action and the bravery of so many of his employees.

As word of the floods spread across the state and the nation, people were desperate for news -- but the news sources in the hardest-hit cities had ground to a halt. Newspapers across Ohio were left to speculate and build on rumor. As a result, many of the reports were vastly inaccurate. One such example appeared in the *Zenia Daily Gazette* on March 26. The headline screamed:

THOUSANDS DEAD IN DAYTON FLOOD
Citizens Warned by Blowing Whistles, Bells.
River Running 3 Miles Wide Through Heart of City
Levee Breaks While Children are on Way to School, Drowning Hundreds

The next day, March 27, The *Mansfield News* led with its version of the situation in Dayton: "The crowded north side of the river where it is feared there may be thousands of foreigners dead and dying is still far beyond reach. No one speaks of it, the immediate needs of the known survivors calling for every attention. If the downtown section is relieved by night it may permit the city authorities to get together with the militia and the relief committees and make some organized attempt to give aid to the north side.

The industrial area on the north side of the city was very heavily damaged but the death toll was no worse than in other parts of the flooded city. There were odd stories of pockets of stranded groups and their survival stories. At the Dayton's Union Station, a trainload of 300 passengers found themselves marooned for several days in the cars. One person happened to have with him a case of chocolate cremes. All 300 survived for two days by

(Left): Simple houses ripped apart and deposited in massive piles.
(Right): The receding waters left behind the bodies of 1,400 horses, all victims of the flood.

sharing the chocolate cremes and drinking rainwater."

Food was in short supply throughout the city. John Patterson sent out an order for: "...every available motor car and truck to scour the farmhouses south of the city and confiscate all available food supplies. While farmers in the vicinity have contributed so heavily their bins are believed to be nearly empty. It is hoped to obtain enough potatoes and vegetables to prevent immediate starvation here."

This wonderful photo depicts two aspects of the flood. On the right, we see a huge debris pile. On the left, a symbol of the indomitable spirit of the people of Dayton as a store owner proclaims that they will reopen in a few days with the message: Don't Worry. Dayton is Alright. Get Busy

As the floodwaters began to disappear from the streets of Dayton, the real work began. Ohio Governor James Cox ordered that the city be placed under martial law and brought in the Ohio National Guard to protect the belongings of the citizenry as they worked to recover. Food, drinking water and aid supplies were being trucked in from all over the country. Relief stations were set up throughout the city, caring for 85,000 people. Drinking water was carried from house to house in water carts.

As the flood victims were being cared for, the able-bodied citizens of Dayton went to work, starting the job of cleaning up their city and getting their lives back in order. The people rose to the challenge and dug in. The one complaint echoed from one cleaning crew to the next: Absolutely everything was covered with a thick layer of gooey, oily, smelly black mud.

Tens of thousands of homes and businesses were destroyed and twice that number were seriously damaged. The streets were clogged with wreckage of every conceivable sort.

Automobiles were smashed into the piles of debris left behind, but horses were still the prime means of transportation. Many had been were trapped in barns and stables and had drowned where they stood. Others were caught up in the raging waters and were swept away to their deaths. The flood left 1,400 horses dead, their carcasses strewn throughout the flood plain, in the streets, in family yards and even deposited inside ruined stores.

Afterward

Dayton was eventually cleaned up, the burned-out shells of buildings were demolished, and the debris was carted away. The city recovered from Great Ohio Floods of 1913, as did the rest of Ohio. Time marches on and lives return to their routines. Plans to prevent such a massive disaster from ever happening again moved forward with the adoption of the Miami Conservancy District. Dams and levees were constructed in some places and some existing ones were removed. Floodgates were installed and river channels dredged. In one case, the entire town of Osborne was relocated, one building at a time, to a position on higher ground next to the town of Fairfield. The process took three years to complete. Eventually, the two towns merged and changed the name to Fairborn.

Major floods continue to ravage parts of Ohio. The state has always been prone to flood but there has never been a repeat, either in damages or loss of life, to the Great Ohio Floods of 1913.

Today in Dayton, the water is gone and the mud is cleared away. Many residents believe that only memories and photographs remain to mark this tragic event, but others believe differently. As when any event occurs that brings with it a great and violent loss of life, spirits remain behind. As the flood progressed, emotions ran very high, leaving behind residual impressions on the space. A variety of unexplainable events are still said to occur around the city that many believe are directly linked to the flood.

None of the buildings that comprise Sinclair Community College in downtown Dayton were around in 1913. The entire campus was constructed over the figurative graves of buildings that were destroyed by the floods. Lives were lost there, and people huddled in terror for three terrible days in March. Blair Hall is Sinclair's theatre building and is considered to be the gem of the campus. Many unexplained events have been reported in Blair Hall, starting almost as soon as it opened.

The sound of babies crying occasionally echos down the quiet corridors on otherwise lonely nights. Locked doors suddenly swing open and a cold wind often blows through the theater itself. But the phenomenon that may possibly be the most closely linked to the era of the flood is the mysterious appearance, and disappearance, of men and women in old-fashioned clothing of the style commonly worn in 1913.

A house in east Dayton near Xenia Avenue may be caught in a residual loop. On random nights throughout the year, someone or something pounds on the front door just after midnight. A hundred years ago, on that cold, rainy night of March 25, the police monitoring the levees protecting downtown Dayton agreed that it was time to alert the residents of the impending disaster by blowing sirens, ringing bells, and pounding on doors -- just after midnight.

John H. Patterson, former owner of the National Cash Register company and hero of the Great Dayton Flood is apparently still spending time in his former home on Brown Street. The Patterson Homestead was donated to the city in 1953 and is now operated as an archival center and museum. According to employees and volunteers working there, Patterson never left the old home place -- even after he died. A black shadow in the shape of a man has been seen in his old bedroom, and a man in military garb has been seen on the third floor. Patterson was known as a demanding taskmaster in his factory, but he tended to be a mischievous trickster at home. He is apparently continuing with the tricks as rocking chairs rock by themselves and cold breezes blow through closed rooms, but the most humorous trick played by old Mr. Patterson is when he moves around his own carved bust!

No doubt, other spirits still linger around Dayton who remember the great flood. It would be comforting to believe that they are watching the waters of the Great Miami River, ready to warn the residents should the waters once again start to rise...

1934: "A MADMAN ON THE DECK"
The Morro Castle Disaster at Sea

"Such a disaster could never happen at sea," a newspaper writer stated while describing the dock fires that occurred on Hoboken, New Jersey, in 1900. And yet, 34 years later, one of the most horrendous disasters to ever occur on an ocean-going vessel took place on a luxurious ocean liner known as the *Morro Castle*. Just six miles off the New Jersey coastline, the ship burned to a gutted shell and out of the 455 passengers and crew members on board, 133 people were either drowned or burned to death.

In the wake of the tragedy, acting Captain W.F. Warms was tried, convinced and sentenced to prison, but this ruling was later overturned. The disaster, fraught with mystery, intrigue and possible arson, remains an enigma to this day.

The *S.S. Morro Castle* was an 11,520-ton passenger liner that was operated by the New York & Cuba Mail Company, a subsidiary of the Ward Line. She was a swank, top of the line, luxury vessel, launched in 1930, soon after the start of the Great Depression. She sailed between New York and Havana for the benefit of the fortune few who could afford to take a seagoing vacation at a time when the rest of the country was in severe financial straits. But *Morro Castle* was not unaffected by the climate of the country in the early 1930s. In fact, for those who served on the ship, there was an air of fear – if not outright terror – from the start of the voyage. The entire voyage turned out to be one of mystery, mutiny, danger and unknown evil.

The fact that such a pleasure ship was operating at all during the Depression incited the crew to near-mutiny over having to work for starvation wages. Labor problems had reached a violent point with the anti-union Ward Line in the early 1930s. The crew demanded not only better pay but, almost more importantly, decent food. Crew members were fed little more than table scraps while customers and officers enjoyed lavish meals in the dining parlor. The crew was unhappy with the working conditions on board and thanks to this, some took matters into their own hands to correct the situation. Smuggling on the ship was rampant. Captain Robert R. Wilmott had become a one-man police force, searching out illegal caches in hiding places throughout the ship. Narcotics were

The *S.S. Morro Castle*

hidden everywhere, and Wilmott conducted daily searches of the holds and crew quarters, sometimes finding bags of heroin and cocaine that had been bought in Cuba, which was then a way station for drugs coming in from Europe, the Middle East and Latin America. No matter how hard he tried, though, Wilmott was unable to stop the smuggling. It was simply too profitable for seamen, many of whom, according to authorities, bought their jobs on *Morro Castle* for high prices so that they could bring in drugs.

And narcotics were not the only things smuggled aboard the ship. Prior to the end of Prohibition, Cuban rum was also frequently stashed on board. On one occasion, Wilmott found several cases hidden at the bottom of an elevator shaft. He had them thrown overboard in front of the crew.

Morro Castle was also a haven for political refugees and illegal aliens attempting to sneak into the United States. Times were desperate in America, but things were even worse in Cuba. Fleeing a purge by Cuban dictator Gerardo Machado, General Julio Herrera escaped the island in 1932 by paying a sailor $5,000 to hide him in the *Morro Castle's* wine cellar. He was eventually offered asylum in the United States. To supplement their monthly salaries, both crew members and officers smuggled scores of people about the ship and helped them escape when the ship reached New York. Captain Wilmott did everything he could to prevent this illegal activity, too. On several occasions, he found clusters of terrified aliens and had them put off the ship at a port before leaving Cuban waters.

Nothing on board *Morro Castle* seemed to run smoothly for the captain. Gambling was everywhere and when an engineer complained to Wilmott that he had lost all of his wages in a fixed game, the captain stormed into the crew's quarters to discover a small casino, complete with card tables and a roulette wheel. He gathered up all of the gambling equipment, carried it up on deck, and angrily hurled it into the sea.

With all of this activity going on, Wilmott faced an angry, resentful crew on the ship's last voyage. He also had to contend with officers whom he distrusted and feared and who, in return, considered him to be ill-tempered, sickly and mentally unbalanced. The captain was inexplicably terrified of chief radioman George Rogers, the tall, obese wireless operator. On one occasion, watching the radioman lumber across the deck, Wilmott remarked to another officer: "There goes a very bad man." Rogers, in the decades to come, would prove that Wilmott's opinion was correct, but there was no way he could have known that at the time. Wilmott was also convinced that junior radio operator George Alagna was a "communist." Evidence of this was provided by the fact that he had attempted to start a union on board *Morro Castle* and throughout the Ward Line. Wilmott had repeatedly asked Ward Line authorities to remove Alagna from the ship.

Wilmott also had concerns about the fitness of his chief mate, William F. Warms. Though he had his master's papers, Warms had shown in the past that he often fell apart when called upon to make hard decisions. He was unsure of himself and often seemed to be confused by his duties. The fact that Captain Wilmott, who bossed the ship from stem to stern, was a hard taskmaster did not alleviate Warms' feelings of insecurity. On one occasion, Warms was suspended for 18 months for failing to hold fire drills on a freighter operated by the Ward Line. After that, Warms had a penchant for safety exercises. He would roust the crew from their quarters, sometimes battering down bolted doors to get them moving. Most of them drilled slowly, largely because they were drunkards who consumed huge amounts of liquor each day and slept in a stupor at night.

On the last night of the cruise from Havana to New York on September 7, 1934, it wasn't only the crew that was drunk; many of the passengers were too. There were 138 passengers on board from the German-American Concordia Singing Society, a group of wealthy businessmen from Brooklyn. They had been treated to an exotic tour of Havana's most popular nightclubs, guarded by Machado's soldiers armed with machine-guns. They drank for hours before being chauffeured back to the ship, where most of them retired to their quarters in an alcohol-induced haze.

The first unusual thing to occur that night took place when the normally gracious Captain Wilmott declined to dine with the guests at the captain's table. This was a nightly ritual that Wilmott rarely missed. When he failed to appear, some of his officers became concerned. Wilmott ordered steak and vegetables sent to his cabin, where he dined alone. At 7:00 p.m., he called the ship's doctor, DeWitt Van Zile, and asked him to bring up medicine for indigestion. When the doctor arrived at the captain's cabin, he found Wilmott had collapsed halfway into the bathtub. He was dead from what Van Zile, and several other physicians on board, believed was a heart attack.

Chief Officer Warms was summoned and told of the situation. He then went to the bridge and wired the home office to inform them of Wilmott's death. Warms told one of the officers on the bridge, "Tell everyone that I'm in command of the ship." But, as events would prove, he was not in command of much of anything at all.

Morro Castle's luck grew worse as she made her way up the Atlantic coastline and ran into a howling gale that sent huge waves washing over her bow. Chief Mate Warms, now acting captain, was terrified by the rough seas. Passengers in the dining room moved into the grand ballroom to ease their own nervousness, consuming gallons of mixed drinks. Others retired to their staterooms for brandy and cigars and crew members broke out their own hidden stores of liquor.

As the storm increased throughout the night, passengers became ill and staggered to their cabins. At least six women, all dead drunk, passed out and were carried bodily to their cabins. A group of men, also drunk, sat in the writing room and flipped lighted cigarettes into a basket to amuse themselves. After starting a small fire on a rug, the group was chastised by watchman Art Bagley. He quickly put out the tiny blaze and inspected the writing room for any other damage. He didn't find any, but it was impossible to ignore the fact that almost everything on *Morro Castle* was flammable, even her steel plates, which were slathered with 14 coats of paint. In the cabins, dining room, ballrooms, saloon and writing room were overstuffed chairs, carpets and thick wooden paneling.

The party began winding down during the early morning hours. Around 2:15 a.m., on September 8, a passenger named Paul Arneth, dressed only in a bathrobe and pajamas, went looking for his roommate. He wandered into the writing room and noticed that smoke was seeping out from beneath the double doors of a large locker where 150 extra blankets were stored. The blankets, made highly combustible by the fluids used to clean them, rested against a wall that was backed by one of the ship's smokestacks, which, it was later deduced, was hot enough to become a possible source of the horrific fire that swept through the ocean liner.

Before a fire alarm was raised, Arneth summoned a steward, who threw open the locker doors. A rush of flames shot out into the room, instantly igniting the wood paneling, the carpets and the furniture. A number of officers and crew came running with a hose a few minutes later but there was no pressure and very little water trickling out. This was because Captain Warms, when hearing about the fire, had ordered all of the hydrants on board to be opened up, thus lessening the individual pressure for each one. Warms was so preoccupied by the storm battering the ship that he didn't notice smoke drifting out of a small ventilator on the bridge until another officer pointed it out to him. After that, Warms simply shut down. According to another officer, he began to "act like a man who had lost his senses."

As the fire spread through the ship, orders were given and then reversed. Passengers were alerted to danger and told to stand by, but Warms was a man without direction. George Alagna, the second radio operator, waited at his post for orders from the captain to send out a SOS. None came, so Alagna went to the bridge to ask for his orders. He reportedly found Warms in a befuddled daze. The radio operator was unable to get any orders from him so he returned to the radio room and told Rogers what had happened. A report that he filed later stated that the officers on the bridge acted like "madmen." He claimed that he made no less than five trips to the bridge before he managed to get an order for the sending of an SOS. This caused a crucial delay of 20 to 30 minutes before the ship's fate and position were made known to other ships in the area and the authorities on shore.

Captain Warms failed to send out a timely emergency call but he did order the ship to continue at top speed against a screaming wind. This was a bad decision because it forced the fire through the ship to the stern. The smoke became so thick on the deck that no one could see farther than a few feet. People burned to death

The *Morro Castle* as she burned at sea

in their cabins and their screams, for the most part, were ignored by crew members hurrying topside to save their own lives.

Acting Third Officer Howard Hansen reached the bridge and insisted that Warms make for shore. In his book *The Morro Castle*, author Hal Burton reported that Warms told Hansen that the ship could make it to the New York harbor but Hansen knew that the ship's only chance for survival was to be beached on the New Jersey shore. He exploded at Warms: "You damned fool! That's forty miles away! We've got to stop this ship. We won't last that long."

As he shouted, he struck Warms in the face and knocked him down. A sailor rushed onto the bridge and asked, "Where's Warms?"

Hansen replied, "The bastard's on the deck."

After Warms got to his feet, several men asked him what he was going to do. He ordered them to drop anchor, at which point the ship was stopped six miles off Asbury Park. Warms gave the order to abandon ship with blasts from the foghorn and *Morro Castle* was lost.

No serious attempt was ever made to try and fight the fire. Even though *Morro Castle* was equipped with the most modern fire-detecting devices available, the crew on board exhibited a profound lack of knowledge about their use. As soon as Warms gave the order to abandon ship, a general policy of "every man for himself" was adopted. Discipline among the crew was non-existent. There was no efficiency and seemed to be no authority. Courage was a quality that had never been expected of them and it certainly did not reveal itself during the fire. Officers and hands alike thought only of their own safety, running, hollering and shoving their way to the lifeboats, and completely disregarding the passengers on board.

The chief engineer, Eban S. Abbott, never once joined his below-decks crew after the fire started. Instead, he

Thousands lined the beaches of the Jersey Shore to see the burned-out hulk of the ship

ordered them by telephone to stay at their posts – and then ran for a lifeboat. His behavior was typical for most of the crew on board. In one lifeboat that reached shore, there were 31 crew members and one passenger. In another, 19 crew members and one passenger rowed to the beaches of Asbury Park. The remaining passengers fought among themselves to get into the lifeboats, but as the flames overtook the ship, many jumped into the water and drowned. A majority of them were simply too drunk to swim. Those sober enough to stay afloat were forced to swim several miles in order to save themselves after being abandoned by the ship's crew.

The tragedy was complete when *Morro Castle* drifted to shore later that morning. Thousands of people lined the beaches along the New Jersey shore, gaping at the gutted hulk with smoke still streaming from her burning holds. There were 133 people dead, either still on board, burned beyond recognition, or floating face-down in the sea.

Inquiries were launched as a shocked public demanded to know how so many people had died about the luxury vessel. A special board for the Bureau of Navigation and Steamboat Inspection investigated the tragedy. The ship, it was determined, had all of the required safety apparatus on board, which meant the disaster could have only be caused by the fact the undependable crew failed to act properly in the time of need. Testimony indicated that early efforts were made to try and extinguish the fire but with no officers on hand to direct the operation, the efforts were quickly abandoned.

The Ward Line, in an attempt to escape from blame and possible lawsuits, attempted to blame the fire on arson. They claimed that union agitators on board (namely radio operator Alagna) had set the fire to get back at the non-union company. The claims were dismissed, although they would become troubling later on when more information about one of the crew members came to light.

The biggest question in the investigation concerned the delay in sending out the SOS. No call for help was sent until many of the passengers had already jumped to their deaths in the sea. Despite the storm, the fire could be plainly seen from the Jersey shore, just six miles away. Boats from much greater distances sent radio calls inquiring about the fire long before the SOS call was ever sent.

As a result of the investigation, Captain William Warms, along with four others, including chief engineer Abbott, was charged with negligence. Warms was blamed for delaying the SOS call, failing to stop the ship even after it was obviously on fire and failing to direct effective measures to put out the fire. Charges against Abbott and three other officers had to do with the fact that they have saved their own lives without regard to saving the passengers.

George Rogers

Warms was found guilty at trial and sentenced to two years in prison. Abbott received a four-year sentence. However, all of the sentences were later reversed by higher courts and none of the men responsible for the disaster ever went to prison.

A sort of footnote to the disaster emerged many years later, thanks to research done by author Thomas Gallagher, who wrote a book about the tragedy called *Fire at Sea*. He learned that one the men connected to the disaster eventually did go to jail. George Rogers, the radio operator who was so feared by Captain Wilmott, turned out to have a long criminal history. Rogers, first hailed as one of the rare heroic figures in the *Morro Castle* disaster, was responsible – according to a theory created by Gallagher – for not only setting the ship on fire but for poisoning Captain Wilmott as well. There was no evidence other than Rogers' sordid history to back this up, however, but Gallagher's findings were certainly enough to create a reasonable doubt. After the fire in 1934, Rogers was involved in several murders and went to prison. Could he have had something to do with the deadly disaster? No one knows, but it certainly added another mysterious element to this already troubling case.

BLOOD

1704: THE DEERFIELD MASSACRE

Today, romantic images of colonial New England villages are almost storybook in nature. We visualize peaceful, tidy thatched-roofed cottages lining a peaceful, tidy road, and cows peacefully munching on grass in nearby fields while children sit quietly and respectfully at a table, working on their studies. We imagine the villagers' primary concerns revolved around keeping within the boundaries of their strict Puritan faith, putting food on the table, and staying warm in the winter. We also like to think that, being human, the Puritans engaged the always-interesting activity of keeping track of what the neighbors were up to.

The harsh reality faced by these villagers was quite different from the romantic image. Although they did have to face concerns about faith and food, these were only two in a long list of problems. True, these people were stalwart and productive, but their lives were rarely peaceful. Threats of attack from all sides were constant.

Colonial New England was frequently a place of deadly violence and often, of war. Repeatedly, villagers found themselves caught up in conflicts that originated in Europe. Since New England and New France (Canada) were considered extensions of their governing counterparts across the Atlantic Ocean, they were expected to carry on with the European wars in the Americas.

The New England colonists did their fair share of stirring up trouble as well, becoming embroiled in inter-colonial wars. Between battling the French to the north and various Native American tribes all around, they were, by necessity, always on their guard.

In the hundred years before the American Revolution, six wars were conducted on North American soil: King Phillip's War (1675-76), King William's War (1689-97), Queen Anne's War (1701-13), Father Rasle's War (1724-26), King George's War (1744-48) and the French and Indian War (1754-63). In between were smaller, shorter battles or skirmishes so obscure they weren't even named.

More often than not, these conflicts took the form of a series of small-scale raids carried out by small groups of men. Warring factions were often based hundreds of miles apart and so it was common for a group of armed men to traverse the distance, make a surprise attack, strike, withdraw, and return home. Episodes of fighting might be months apart. The number of deaths and amounts of property damage were usually small, but over time, they accumulated and took their toll.

Only rarely were entire villages or towns targeted, but it did happen. The goal was to kill, burn and capture. Though they occurred in different wars, targeted attacks were perpetrated against the towns of Salmon Falls and Oyster River in New Hampshire, York and Wells in Maine, and Lancaster, Haverhill, and Deerfield in Massachusetts. The most famed of these by far is the attack on Deerfield during Queen Anne's War, later labeled a massacre.

It has been said that history is made memorable by those who write it down. These targeted attacks on individual villages were all deadly, but the one most remembered was that of Deerfield. The reason is that someone wrote it down -- and that someone was a victim of the attack. Rev. John Williams chronicled the raid on Deerfield and the ordeal that followed as the captives were driven on a forced march back to Canada, and later ransomed and returned home. His memoir, "A Redeemed Captive Returning to Zion: A Narrative of the Captivity, Sufferings, and Return of the Rev. John Williams, Minister of Deerfield, Massachusetts, who was taken Prisoner by the Indians on the Destruction of the Town, A.D. 1704," was published in 1707, just three years after the massacre. Williams became famous and his book was an immediate bestseller that went on to be reprinted multiple times over the next 200 years. Thanks to Reverend Williams, the attack on Deerfield, unlike other village attacks of its kind, is remembered and has become a part of America's frontier story.

Alongside the Connecticut River, where it flowed through western Massachusetts Bay Colony, sat a village of Algonquian-speaking Pocomtuc Indians. In the early 1660s, following a vicious attack by the Mohawk nation, the Pocomtucs were virtually obliterated, leaving only a few survivors. In 1665 a group of colonists living in eastern Massachusetts were given a land grant by surviving members of the Pocomtuc nation. The colonists moved west and established Deerfield on the site of the former Pocomtuc village, in what was then the western frontier of the English settlements.

Within ten years of its founding, the population of Deerfield had risen to over 200 and the little village appeared to be thriving. It was 1675, and King Philip's War pitted the New England colonies against the area populations of Native Americans. Deerfield, being dangerously isolated, was evacuated. The evacuated residents became part of a series of attacks that ended in the Battle of Bloody Brook in which more than half of the men from the village of Deerfield were killed.

The abandoned village was seized and reoccupied by the warring Indians. The following year, the original colonial residents were joined with additional colonists in re-capturing the village and slaughtering many of the Indians camped there. The remaining Indians were forced to retreat north to French-controlled Canada, or into the western wilderness. Whether driven north or west, these fleeing Indians would remain the avowed enemies of the English who would ally themselves with any groups opposed to the New England colonists.

Queen Anne's War, initiated in 1703, essentially pitted New France against New England. For the first two years, New York and the other colonies were not involved in this particular dispute. The war started with a series of French-led Indian attacks along eastern coastal settlements in Maine and New Hampshire. The English countered with attacks on several Abenaki Indian villages. In the interim, the English had captured the French "pirate" Jean-Baptiste Guyon and were holding him in Boston. The French, however, claimed Guyon was not a pirate at all but one of their naval officers, and they wanted him back. Guyon, whether pirate or naval officer, was a driving force behind the attack on the tiny village of Deerfield.

With new uprisings between the French and the English, the residents of Deerfield were on the alert. In the late spring of 1703, New York Governor Lord Cornbury received a warning passed on to him by friendly Iroquois Indians. The information was that: "a party of French and Indians from Canada who were expected every hour to make some attaque [sic] on ye towns upon Connecticut River." There was no direct reference as to a specific target. Lord Cornbury forwarded the warning into Massachusetts.

Deerfield already had a small stockade fortified with a palisade (a high fence made up of pointed boards.) The residents went to work repairing, reinforcing and expanding the stockade. When complete, there were a dozen houses inside the stockade and roughly 30 outside. They also hired 20 militiamen for additional armed protection. With the new war and warnings of imminent attack, all 240 villagers plus the militiamen spent each night inside the stockade, leaving the unprotected houses outside the walls empty. Feeling that they were as prepared as they could be, the residents of Deerfield went on with their lives while remaining vigilant.

The Deerfield villagers spent a stressful summer and early fall, but nothing out of the ordinary happened. They continued to worry about their near-isolation, as they were relatively alone on the western frontier. The nearest English settlement of any appreciable size was 40 miles to the east. They had some neighbors to the south, but those villages were in the same predicament as Deerfield.

Things changed a little in October when a small band of Indians crept in and captured two Deerfield men who were working in a field. There was no actual fighting involved; it was more of a kidnapping, and the men were taken back to Canada and held as captives. This increased tensions in the area and the Massachusetts Militia responded by sending a garrison of soldiers to each of the three villages on the Connecticut River: Hadley, Hatfield and Deerfield.

The rest of that fall passed uneventfully and things stayed quiet well into December. The general in charge of the militia released the garrisons he had sent to protect the villages, sending them home in the mistaken belief that no one would be crazy enough to launch an attack during the harsh New England winter. Deerfield relaxed, but just a little. They kept on their hired militia, slept inside the stockade, and had a militiaman walk the perimeter at night, keeping watch.

The French Canadians had been eyeing the villages along the Connecticut River Valley as prime targets for an attack for years, but they didn't begin assembling an actual attack force until May of 1703. The raids were to be led by a French officer named Jean-Baptiste Hartel de Rouville but the force would be made up largely of Indians from various tribes. Indian spies for the English had gotten word of this to New York's governor, who passed the warning on to the Massachusetts frontier.

The original plan was never carried out, however. Queen Anne's War was being conducted on several fronts, and just as a raiding party was preparing to head south, the troops were divided into smaller groups and sent away. A large number were sent to help defend Quebec when rumors arrived of English war ships on the Saint Lawrence River. Hartel de Rouville took another group with him to attack English settlements in Maine. With most of the force and their leader gone, the plan was put on hold.

Some time after Hartel de Rouville returned to Montreal in the fall, the French again began to amass troops for a raid on western Massachusetts. The newly formed raiding force set out from Chambly, just south of Montreal, in late January 1704. The group was a highly diverse bunch. There were 48 Frenchmen, including four of Hartel de Rouville's brothers, and roughly 200 Indians including Abenakis, Iroquois, Wyandots, and Pocumtuc. As they marched south, they picked up another 40 Pocumtucs who were looking for revenge against the people of Deerfield, whom they saw as having taken their land. Their force was nearly 300 strong as they approached Deerfield in late February.

New France's Governor-General Philippe de Rigaud Vaudreuil had made the village the primary target of the raiding party. He knew it was the home of Reverend John Williams, a highly regarded Puritan minister. Vaudreuil believed that if Williams could be captured and held prisoner, the English might be induced to exchange Jean-Baptiste Guyon for him.

The French forces were nearly all experienced in wilderness travel and warfare. They were well equipped for the trip and wore snowshoes and had dogs and sleds which they used to carry supplies. They had come nearly 300 miles, crossing frozen lakes and rivers and traversing the Green Mountains. A surprise attack would be strongly in their favor, so they kept mainly to the woods, where the deep snow would muffle any noise they might make. When they reached a spot roughly 25 miles north of Deerfield, they left behind their dogs and most of their supplies, to be picked up on their return trip home. Traveling light, they moved out on their final trek. On February 28, they established a camp at a spot across the river from Deerfield, less than one mile west of their target. Here, the raiders prepared themselves for the battle ahead while waiting for darkness to set in.

The people of Deerfield had been on general alert for months, but they were completely unaware of the approaching raiders. As they had done every night since the warning of an impending attack, they went to sleep inside the stockade, leaving one guard on night patrol.

The Massacre

At midnight, the French sent out a scout to check on the village. When he returned, he told them of the watchman patrolling the stockade. A few hours later, the scout went back for another look. This time, no one was stirring. It appeared that the watchman had fallen asleep. The scout had even more good news: The villagers had allowed deep snow to accumulate around the wall surrounding the stockade and a large snowdrift reached nearly to the top.

The troops moved out under cover of darkness. They walked past the dark, empty houses outside the stockade, then headed directly for the fortifications. It was 4:00 in the morning on February 29, and all was quiet inside the stockade. The first troops that arrived easily walked up the snowdrift and dropped silently down inside the wall.

With the element of surprise on their side, the rest should have been easy, but the attack did not go quite as smoothly as planned. This was likely due to a communication problem between the different groups of attackers. They were to fan out across the enclosure with small groups splitting up to attack each house. The French were aware of the layout of the village, as they had sent in spies pretending to be trappers earlier in the fall. The home of Reverend Williams had been singled out ahead of time, as he was to be the prize captive. This house was where the assault was to begin.

With a piercing war cry by one of the Indians, the townspeople were ripped from their slumbers and cast into a night of terror. Many of them dashed about in panic but some had the presence of mind to elude the attackers by leaping from windows and running into the woods. Several boys, including young John Sheldon, were able to run to the neighboring villages of Hadley and Hatfield to summon help.

Reverend Williams and his family were roused from sleep by the violent pounding of axes and hatchets on the

An early artist's drawing of the Deerfield Massacre

doors and windows. Williams ran from his bed to awaken the two soldiers who were sleeping upstairs and then raced back downstairs to arm himself. In his memoir, he described what happened next: "The enemy immediately brake into the room, I judge by the number of twenty, with painted faces and hideous acclamations."

He managed to cock his pistol and aim it at one of the attackers, but the gun failed to discharge. At that, three Indians seized and bound him. With their prize captive in their possession, the Indians started "rifling the house, entering in great numbers into every room." None of Williams' family had yet been harmed, but this was not to hold true for long.

There would be killing as well as pillaging. Williams watched helplessly as "Some were so cruel and barbarous as to take and carry to the door two of my children and murder them [six-year old John, Jr., and six-week-old Jerusha], and a negro woman [a family slave named Parthena]." It was about 7 a.m. when Williams was finally allowed to dress, as were his wife and remaining children. Meanwhile, the raiders taunted him, "insulting over me a while, holding up hatchets over my head, threatening to burn all I had."

Throughout the village, similar events were repeated in nearly every household. Infants, the ill and the elderly, as well as children who were considered too weak to survive an extended marched through the wilderness were killed immediately. Anyone who appeared to be able-bodied or who would make desirable hostages were captured and held in the meeting house and another nearby home.

The descendants of Mary Catlin have passed the following story of the raid down through the generations: "The captives were taken to a house...and a Frenchman was brought in [wounded] and laid on the floor; he was in great distress and called for water. Mrs. Catlin fed him with water. Someone said to her, 'How can you do that for your enemy?' She replied, 'If thine enemy hunger, feed him; if he thirst, give him water to drink.' The Frenchman was taken and carried away, and the captives marched off. Some thought the kindness shown to the Frenchman was the reason of Mrs. Catlin's being the only one of her large family not killed or captured."

Later, it was told that the Frenchman she had taken pity on was a brother of Hartel de Rouville, the leader of the raiding party.

While a group of Indians were left to guard the prisoners, most of the others were charging around the village slaughtering livestock, destroying food stores, smashing the villagers' possessions and setting fire to their homes.

One house had thus far been able to ward off the attack. It was the house of the commander of the militia, Sergeant Benoni Stebbins. Inside the house, they were well armed and trained for battle. The Stebbins house was made of brick and the Indians were unable to set it on fire.

When a significant number of captives had been subdued, a group of them were taken from the stockade and marched to the attackers' camp across the river. The captives would be held there until the raiders were ready to return to where their dogs and supplies were waiting.

After two hours of hard fighting, the Stebbins household was nearing their breaking point. Houses were burning all around them and their house was surrounded by the attackers. The glow of the burning houses made a glow in the sky that could be seen for miles. As they contemplated surrender, thirty men from Hadley and Hatfield rushed into the stockade, fresh and well armed. This sudden and unexpected arrival of reinforcements startled the remaining raiders and they fled the village. Some ran in such panic that they threw down their weapons and stolen loot.

The villagers felt hope for the first time since the attack had begun. Twenty Deerfield men joined in with the Hadley and Hatfield men and they gave chase to the fleeing raiders. The English and the French troops skirmished in a field outside Deerfield. The French ran as they fought, still pursued by the English, but the chase was ill conceived and the English were unprepared as they were ambushed by the French troops who had left earlier with the first group of prisoners. Of the 50 English who had chased the French from the village, nine were killed and several were wounded.

The English collected their dead and wounded and retreated back to Deerfield to take stock of their losses. The French raiders rounded up their prisoners and headed north to collect the supplies they had left behind before starting the long march north to Canada.

The raid had taken a terrible toll on the people of Deerfield. Seventeen houses were destroyed and nearly all the rest had been ransacked and looted. The French and Indians had slaughtered 44 of the village's residents: 10 men, nine women and 25 children. Five garrison soldiers and seven Hadley men had also died during the battle. Of those killed, 15 were died as a result of the fires. Three children were burned to death while hiding in a cellar. A family of ten had suffocated in their cellar as their house burned over their heads. The other dead had been beaten with war clubs or hacked to death with hatchets or knives. Only 140 were left alive in Deerfield.

The attackers had taken 109 Deerfield residents captive, plus three Frenchmen who happened to be visiting the village. This represented nearly 40 percent of Deerfield's population. Almost half of the buildings had been burned.

When the men returned to the village after fighting with the French forces, the morning was still young. It was only 9:00 a.m. The raid had begun only five hours earlier. They had lost much in a very short time. As the fires were burning themselves out, the townspeople who had escaped at the start of the attack began wandering back into the village. One man who escaped after having been briefly taken captive had had his right index finger cut off, as some Indian tribes were accustomed to do to mark their captives.

After the wounded were cared for, the survivors faced the horrific task of burying their dead. A few of those who had been murdered had family members among the survivors who chose to bury their loved ones individually. With so many bodies left to bury, and the ground frozen solid, the rest were buried in a mass grave.

The English weren't the only ones who suffered losses. The men who had chased the French into the meadow and across the frozen river knew they had inflicted great harm by the amount of blood in the snow. There was evidence that many bodies had been dragged to a hole in the frozen river and pushed into the water. New France's Governor-General later reported that 11 raiders had been killed and 22 wounded.

The plight of the 109 captured villagers was a terrible one. Few of them were dressed for the extreme cold and they would not be warm for a very long time. They were just beginning a 300-mile trip to Montreal, on foot and in the dead of winter. Their captors, fearing the English would pursue them, pushed forward as hard and as fast as they could. The suffering and deprivation were felt on both sides. The French troops were low on food and the villagers were a further drain on the scant supplies. The French and Indians were also burdened with their wounded comrades.

The captors made it very clear that they would kill anyone who could not keep up with their pace. Reverend Williams' wife Eunice was the first to fall. She was still weak from giving birth six weeks before. The troops and captives had been traveling along the frozen Connecticut River. Not long into the journey, Mrs. Williams fell through a hole in the ice and was drenched. As she was weak, she was separated from the group, dragged a short distance away and killed with a single hatchet chop. Her body was left where it fell, exposed to the elements and to wild animals.

During the first few days, a few captives managed to escape. Hartel de Rouville pulled Reverend Williams aside and told him to inform the others that any escaped captives that were caught would be tortured to death. There were no more escapes. Over the seven weeks it took to reach Canada, 16 more captives were murdered and two starved to death, their bodies left by the wayside. In the end, only 89 of the original 109 captives survived to reach Canada.

As the travelers neared Montreal, Reverend Williams was taken by the French. The rest of the captives were taken by the Indians. Williams wrote that his five surviving children were divided up and tenderly cared for by the Indian families who took them in.

One of the main goals of the raid was to dishearten the English in the hope they would forfeit the war. Instead, the English launched into violent retaliatory attacks, destroying several Indian villages and inflicting major damage on several villages in Nova Scotia. The bounty for Indian scalps was raised from £40 to £100. The New England frontier towns were heavily fortified with garrisons.

Almost immediately, Deerfield and the neighboring communities started collecting funds to ransom the captives. Beginning in late 1704 and continuing into 1706, negotiations began for the release or exchange of the captives. In order to secure as many of the captives' releases as possible, Massachusetts Governor Joseph Dudley made a purely political move: He released French captives, including Jean-Baptiste Guyon, in exchange for prisoners from the Deerfield raid. All the captives who wished go home were back in Boston by August 1706.

While the captives were in the hands of the French and Indians, great effort was made to convert them to Catholicism, with some success. Several of the very young captives were adopted into Indian families and many chose to stay with their captors. Among these was Eunice Williams, daughter of Reverend Williams. She was eight years old when captured. In the two years she spent living with her adoptive family during hostage negotiations, she became completely assimilated into their culture and was given the name A'ongote. At 16, she married a Mohawk man and raised a large family. Fifteen other captives also chose to stay with their new Indian families. Still others chose to stay with the French Canadians for the rest of their lives. Over the years, many of them returned to New England to visit their families, but all returned to Canada of their own free will.

These "defections" were a source of great irritation for the English, as they wondered how these captives had been persuaded to stay. There was the suspicion that they may have been somehow forced. Most historians, however, do not believe this to be true. As most of the captives in question were young girls, the answer may have been simply that they were well treated, and even loved, within the Indian villages, in tribes where women could hold positions of respect. Deerfield, on the other hand, was a Puritan village. The Puritan way of life was especially harsh and restrictive for girls and women. The Deerfield girls who survived to reach Canada very likely lived much happier and personally fulfilling lives in their adopted communities.

It took several years before Deerfield recovered from the devastating attack. The threats of attack gradually lessened as time passed and the frontier pushed farther and farther west.

Deerfield has survived and remains a beautiful and tranquil New England village. Today, the site of the original village has been preserved as a living history museum. The main street is lined with lovely old houses. Some of these have been outfitted with historically accurate furniture and decor, and are open to the public. Though none of the structures remain from 1704, historical accuracy of the location is very closely followed. Visitors who choose to stay within the living history village can book rooms at the Deerfield Inn.

It should come as no surprise that with all the horrifically violent deaths that occurred in and around Deerfield, ghost stories have been passed among the locals for many generations. According to employees at the living history museum, there are frequent ghost sightings in many of the prominent buildings in the village.

A February 29 visit to the Old Burial Ground might present the visitor with an interesting, if unexplainable experience. Some witnesses over the years have described hearing a woman sobbing at the mass grave where most of the Deerfield Massacre victims were buried.

Eunice Williams, wife of Reverend John Williams and a victim of the Deerfield Massacre, was murdered with a hatchet along the Deerfield River by her French and Indian captors. Although her body was later recovered and buried in the Deerfield cemetery, she has been seen for many years haunting the site of her death.

A variety of ghostly occurrences have been recounted over the years by employees and guests of the Deerfield Inn. The most frequent story reported has been that of someone -- or something -- walking down the corridors of the inn, pounding on guests' doors and asking to be let in. There is also a little boy who wanders around the inn, creating mischief for the guests, who believe him to be a "real" boy until they turn and he has disappeared. The inn sits on land that would have been inside the Deerfield stockade.

1831: "BLOODY PROPHET"
The Slave Rebellion of Nat Turner

The Nat Turner rebellion of 1831 was the bloodiest, most devastating slave revolt in American history. In less than two days, 70 black insurgents killed 50 white Virginians – which in turn led to the retaliatory murders by whites of more than 100 blacks.

Even though Turner's rebellion ultimately failed, it changed the South forever. And few had any idea that the rebellion was inspired by the voice of a spirit.

Nothing struck deeper into the hearts of whites who lived in the pre-Civil War South, whether they held slaves or not, than the idea of a slave revolt. Contrary to the popular image of docile slaves working in peaceful servitude, there had been numerous small rebellions and slave uprisings, often in union with Indians or disaffected whites, dating back to the time of the Spanish rule in the New World. These were not limited to the South, as murderous uprisings also took place in colonial Connecticut, Massachusetts and New York. One of the bloodiest of these occurred in South Carolina in 1739, when slaves killed 25 whites under the leadership of a slave named Jeremy.

But the greatest horror for early America came from the Caribbean, where Toussaint L'Ouverture, a former carriage driver and a natural leader, led the slaves of St. Domingue (present-day Haiti and the Dominican Republic) in successful rebellion during the 1790s. Inspired by the revolutions in American and France, Touissant's rebellion led to more than 60,000 deaths and created an island republic of former slaves, which still managed to integrate the white minority into the island's new government. In 1800, Napoleon sent troops to retake the island, but they were no match for Touissant's army. He was not captured until he was lured to the French headquarters under a truce flag and taken away to die in a jail cell.

For many years, slave owners tried to keep the news of Toussaint and his rebellion from their slaves. In 1831, though, the name of Nat Turner began to be whispered. It was a name that would become the most dire threat imaginable to white control. Turner's rebellion followed two earlier unsuccessful uprisings by slaves. In 1800, a slave named Gabriel Prosser led an aborted assault on Richmond, Virginia, and in Charleston in 1822, a charismatic slave named Demark Vessey also attempted a mass rebellion, but was betrayed by some of his own people.

But it would be Turner's rebellion that would cause stringent new slave laws to be passed and strict censorship laws to be aimed at abolitionist material. To whites and slaves alike, Turner had mystical qualities that made him larger than life. Even after he was hanged, the slave owners were terrified of him.

Nat Turner was born on October 2, 1800, in Southampton County, Virginia. Under different circumstances – and in a different time and place – Turner could have gone far in the world. He was intelligent, had a quick and inquiring mind and had impressive leadership abilities. He was, however, a slave. Born into slavery, he was destined to be another man's property. The hardships of Turner's life steered him toward religion. He was a devout believer in God and learned to read at an early age. His parents strengthened him in his belief that he would grow up to be a prophet and a liberator of his people. Other slaves came to regard him with awe and wonder and when not working in the fields, he spent his time fasting and praying.

As he was plowing one day, Turner claimed that he heard a voice – a spirit voice – speak to him. He believed the voice was of divine origin, just like the voices that spoke to the prophets of old, and he vowed to listen to

Nat Turner

whatever it told him. The voice spoke to him on and off for the next two years, and Turner heard the same revelations over and over again, confirming in his mind that he truly was a prophet. He was to tell his fellow slaves of the truths that had been revealed to him and of the purpose for which he had been divinely ordained – a bloody liberation.

In 1825, a new overseer was hired by the plantation owner to whom Turner belonged. Turner fled, becoming a fugitive slave. Given his intelligence and courage, he could have stayed on the run and perhaps achieved freedom in the northern states. However, the spirit voice grew angry with him for running away and, to the surprise and consternation of the other slaves, Turner returned to bondage voluntarily. He realized that he was meant to lead his people from chains, not to simply encourage them to follow his example of running away.

Over the course of the next several years, Turner continued to have often disturbing revelations of fire, blood and violence. In 1828, the spirit informed him that "the serpent is loose" and Turner knew that the time was approaching when "the last shall be first." His work was to commence after a sign in the heavens. In February 1831, the sign was revealed during a full eclipse of the sun and Nat Turner knew that his time had arrived. If he obeyed the will of the spirit, he and his followers would be "led to Jerusalem."

On Monday, August 21, 1831, shortly after midnight, Turner and his followers killed slave owner Joseph Travis, his wife and children, and all of the other whites on the plantation. After they had traveled some distance from the blood-drenched house, they remembered that in the chaos, they had forgotten one of the children – an infant in a cradle who had slept through the slaughter. Turner sent two of his men back to the house and the baby was hacked to pieces.

The insurgents agreed that "until [they] had armed and equipped [them]selves and gathered sufficient force, neither age nor sex was to be spared." Turner and his small army made good on this promise. Believing that God was on their side, they moved from house to house across Southampton County, gathering weapons, freeing the slaves and killing every white man, woman and child they encountered. The victims that were shot were the lucky ones. Most of

One of the many drawings of the Turner Rebellion that was circulated in the wake of the attacks.

them were stabbed, cut or hacked to death with axes. They took horses, ammunition and guns and the force of insurgents began to grow. In a short time, Turner's band had grown to nearly 70 men, all mounted and armed with a variety of deadly weapons.

Turner and his men brought death and destruction to the countryside. As soon as word spread of the rebellion, local militia troops gathered to fight them. A running fight ensued but Turner managed to repulse the militia and continue with his rampage.

Escaped slaves rallied to Turner's army and white plantation owners, alerted to the menace, fled the countryside, leaving Turner and his rebels as the masters of the all they surveyed – for a short time. In other places, smaller slave revolts had broken out as news of Turner's rebellion spread. The greatest fears of the white southerners had been confirmed, it seemed, by Turner's revolt. But it would not last for long. As the rebels camped in the abandoned homes of the hated white masters, the militia was preparing for war. Turner would no longer be facing unarmed women and children, or families asleep in their beds, but well-armed men with the single goal of putting down the rebellion before it grew worse than it already was.

On Tuesday, August 22, Turner decided to head for the county seat of Jerusalem – where he believed the spirit had directed him. There was an arsenal in town and if the rebels could seize it, they would be more heavily armed than anyone who stood against them. After marching 20 miles, Turner's army was ambushed by the heavily reinforced militia three miles outside of town. Outnumbered and overpowered, the rebels scattered and the uprising collapsed only a short distance from the place that Turner had been promised his justification would come.

Retaliation came swiftly. On the same day, whites killed more than 100 members of the black community – some were members of Turner's band, but most were not. The heads of the slain were cut off and fixed on poles around the countryside as a deterrent to anyone who might have ideas of another rebellion. Turner's army had quickly scattered, but 19 of his men were captured and executed.

Turner managed to elude capture for nine weeks before being apprehended on October 30 by Virginia state militiamen. He was put on trial in November. During this time, a young attorney named Thomas Ruffin Gray interviewed him in his jail cell and transcribed a statement that became Turner's *Confessions*. Most historical knowledge about Turner – including his belief that he was motivated by God and a spirit voice – comes from this short account. Turner was sentenced to death and was hanged on November 11, 1831.

He met his end in the town of Jerusalem, Virginia. He had arrived there at last.

1835: THE TEXAS WAR FOR INDEPENDENCE

San Antonio de Bexar - The Battle of the Alamo
The Battle of Coleto and the Goliad Massacre
The Battle of San Jacinto

In the Texas War for Independence, there were certainly more than three battles but the Battle of the Alamo, The Goliad Massacre and the Battle of San Jacinto were the most important and without a doubt the most bloody. The "revolution" lasted a little less than five months, but in that short time, thousands died.

Mexico had become independent and had established a democratic constitution in 1824. After that time, settlers from America had been strongly encouraged to immigrate to Mexican Texas (then part of the Mexican State of Coahuila y Tejas) to establish settlements, colonies, businesses, farms and plantations. The Mexican government believed that this would accelerate the civilization of that part of Mexico. The American colonists were guaranteed protection and assistance by the Mexican government.

This practice continued without problem until the Texicans (or Texians, as they were called,) revolted when Antonio López de Santa Anna became President of Mexico in 1835. Upon coming into power, Santa Anna rescinded the democratic constitution of 1824, dismantled the state legislatures, and proclaimed himself as dictator, though he retained the title of president.

Large groups of Americans flooded into Texas to assist in the revolt, hoping to help the Texans achieve independence. Adding in to the growing army were Tejanos (Mexican Americans living in Texas) and Texians (American colonists). Though most of them were untrained for military operations, and could count their time in Texas by weeks rather than years, they were a dedicated group. Together, they moved to capture Mexican military outposts and garrisons in the area. After a major conflict on December 10, 1835, in which the new Texas army defeated the Mexican garrison at San Antonio de Béxar, they were able to drive out any remaining Mexican military from Texas.

After taking San Antonio, the spirited Texans declared their independence from Mexico, established a provisional government, and elected Davis Burnet as president. A capitol for the fledgling Republic of Texas was founded at Washington-on-the-Brazos. The Americans and Texian colonists who had volunteered to help drive out the Mexicans believed that the revolution was over and the Republic of Texas was in place. Most of them returned to their homes and families, leaving a skeleton army to maintain the new republic's independence.

Santa Anna, a man not to be crossed, did not agree. He saw the "revolution" as nothing more than an insurrection, and that needed to be put down immediately. With a strong show of force and a violent, unforgiving hand, he believed the Texians would suffer the consequences of their rebellious actions and not dare to rise up again.

Mexican President during the Texas War for Independence: General Antonio López de Santa Anna

The Battle of the Alamo
President Santa Anna gathered an army more than 6,000 strong. Within days of being informed of the loss of San Antonio de Béxar (simply

(Left to Right) -- Colonel James Bowie, 39 years old at the Alamo; Colonel William Travis, 26 years old at the Alamo; David (Davy) Crocket, 49 years old at the Alamo

referred to as Béxar by Texans and Mexicans), he assumed the title of general and personally led his vast army on a march into Texas. Once in Texas, he split his army, sending 900 men with General José de Urrea to San Patricio. Santa Anna continued the march to Béxar himself, as he wanted to be the one to personally put down the Texans and retake the fort, formerly a mission known as the Alamo.

After the Texans had overtaken San Antonio and evicted the Mexican military, protection from Mexican retaliatory attacks became the primary goal. Two forts blocked the entrances into Texas from the interior of Mexico: the Alamo in San Antonio de Béxar and Presidio La Bahía in Goliad. Both forts would remain frontiers outposts for the protection of the new republic. Colonel James W. Fannin was put in command of the fort in Goliad and Colonel James Neill was assigned to command the Alamo.

Colonel Neill worked hard to strengthen the former mission. The walls were thick and high but they were simple masonry. The buildings were not strategically designed for protection. Their principal efforts were directed toward placing the 24 artillery pieces inside the fort's walls for the greatest effect. There was also a severe shortage of supplies. The fort was seriously undermanned and low on both ammunition and horses. Neill complained to General Sam Houston that his men were underfed and exhausted. He sent a message to the provisional government stating: "Unless we are reinforced and victualed (provided with food and stores), we must become an easy prey to the enemy, in case of an attack."

Soon after, on January 19, Colonel James Bowie arrived with a small company of men. He was impressed with the work already done and he worked well with Colonel Neill. Complaints again went out stressing the lack of horses. There weren't even enough horses to send out scouts to watch for signs of the Mexican army. Again, a meager number of reinforcements were sent to the Alamo. Colonel William Travis arrived on February 3 with a small contingent of cavalry. Five days later, David Crockett arrived with a small group of American volunteers. Travis was unhappy to be given this post, but as a career army officer, he followed orders. Sadly, they were still significantly low on supplies and ammunition. The number of soldiers positioned at one of the two forts protecting the whole of the Republic of Texas had risen to a whopping 150 men.

At noon on February 23, 1836, Santa Anna and the forward part of his army reached the Alazon (crossroads), just outside of San Antonio. Pickets that had been positioned south of town came riding in hard with the news that what looked like the entire Mexican army was moving in. With Neill absent as the result of a family emergency, Travis and Bowie began giving orders. Some men were sent to collect what food stores they could find and others worked to drive their few head of cattle inside the fort. Most of the Mexicans living in Béxar were hostile to the Texans, but there were a few people living outside the walls of the Alamo who were invited inside for protection.

Two hours later, after a brief respite, Santa Anna marched his men into Béxar and sent word to Travis, demanding immediate unconditional surrender. Travis answered with a cannon shot. Santa Anna initiated a bombardment of the fort and gave orders that it continue around the clock. Travis sent off an express message to Colonel Fannin in Goliad, 90 miles to the southeast, where Fannin had a contingent of 300 soldiers. Travis described the situation at the Alamo and requested immediate assistance.

The 13-day siege of the Alamo had begun.

On February 24, Travis sent the following appeal to the provisional government for supplies and reinforcements. He and Bowie knew that without them, they had no chance of withstanding the attack:

COMMANDANCY OF THE ALAMO, Béxar, February 24, 1836
Fellow citizens and compatriots: I am besieged by a thousand or more of the Mexicans under Santa Anna. I have sustained a continued bombardment for twenty-four hours, and have not lost a man. The enemy have demanded a surrender at discretion; otherwise the garrison is to be put to the sword, if the place is taken. I have answered the summons with a cannon-shot, and our flag still waves proudly from the walls. I shall never surrender or retreat. Then I call on you in the name of liberty, or patriotism, and of everything dear to the American character, to come to our aid with all dispatch. The enemy are receiving reinforcements daily, and will no doubt increase to three or four thousand in four or five days. Though this call many be neglected, I am determined to sustain myself as long possible, and die like a soldier who never forgets what is due to his own honor and that of his country. Victory or death!
William Barret Travis, Lieutenant Colonel commanding.

P.S. - The Lord is on our side. When the enemy appeared in sight, we had not three bushels of corn. We have since found, in deserted houses, eighty or ninety bushels, and got into the walls twenty or thirty head of beeves. T.

The siege of the Alamo Mission

As Colonel Travis was composing his message, Colonel Bowie fell ill. He was believed to have fallen victim to what was then known as "hasty consumption" (rapidly active tuberculosis). Bowie would remain in his bed for the rest of the siege, except for the noon officers' meeting, when he would crawl from his bed to attend, and then crawl back to bed.

On February 26, a light skirmish between the fort's defenders and Mexican cavalry erupted but amounted to nothing. A storm had blown and the temperature dropped to 39 degrees. Santa Anna brought up more reinforcements and posted more guards around the Alamo. But the Texans were able to sneak out for wood and food and return safely. While they were out, they burned a few more houses. The bombardment of the Alamo continued.

Early in the day on February 28, Colonel Fannin and 200 men with four pieces of artillery left Goliad for the Alamo, leaving 100 men to guard the Presidio La Bahía. After marching only 200 yards, a wagon of supplies broke down. They decided to return to the Precidio La Bahia and Fort Defiance in Goliad. They would not be reinforcing the soldiers at the Alamo. The bombardment of the Alamo continued.

On March 1, Captain John Smith sneaked into the Alamo bringing 32 Texans with him. That brought the number of men inside the walls to 188; outside Santa Anna's troops numbered 5,000. The defenders were holding but the walls of the fort were weakening. The Mexican troops were rested and well fed while the Texans were starving and exhausted.

By the tenth day of the siege, March 3, Santa Anna's men had erected a forth battery to the north of the fort, within musket range. Travis sent off another desperate request for reinforcements and supplies. This was to be his last appeal to the president. By then, he had ceased expecting any help to come from Colonel Fanning. In a letter to a friend, carried by the same courier, Travis wrote of his concern for the future of his son.

"Take care of my little boy. If the country should be saved, I may make him a splendid fortune; but if the country should be lost, and I should perish, he will have nothing but the proud recollection that he is the son of a man who died for his country."

He continued with bitterness:

"I am still here, in fine spirits, and well to do. With one hundred and eighty-eight men, I have held this place ten days against a force variously estimated from fifteen hundred to six thousand; and I shall continue to hold it till I get relief from my countrymen, or I will perish in its defense of this place and my bones shall reproach my country for her neglect. We have a shower of bombs and cannon-balls continually flying among us the whole time, yet none of us have fallen. We have been miraculously preserved."

The final day came on March 6 when just after midnight, Santa Anna pulled his entire force into town and surrounded the fort. His troops had been supplied with scaling ladders and they waited quietly for the word to attack. At 5:00 a.m., they received the word. The troops moved forward and the ladders were placed against the wall, ready to scale. But the Texans were ready and brought down very heavy fire and the Mexicans were driven back. They made a second attempt with the same results, followed by a third and a fourth. Each time, they were repulsed by the Texans. For Santa Anna, the fifth try met with success.

The Mexican troops flooded up and over the wall and into the Alamo. Completely overwhelmed, the Texans had no chance, but they kept fighting. Travis was one of the first to be killed but still, the defenders kept fighting. They fought until nearly all lay dead in the dirt inside the Alamo. Santa Anna had given orders that the wounded were to be killed and many bayonets were bloodied that day. The Mexicans then moved through the fort, looking for anyone who might be hiding. During this search, the men came upon Colonel Bowie, still in his sickbed. Knowing he was one of the commanders of the fort, they butchered him.

After twelve days of bombardment, the Alamo was taken by the Mexican army in just 90 minutes. By 8:00 a.m., every fighting man who had defended the Alamo lay dead.

After the dead Texans had been collected and brought into the center of the courtyard, the bodies were looted for valuables. The bodies were then stripped of their clothing and stacked like cordwood and set on fire. Witnesses related that the piles smoldered for three days.

Despite the savagery of the attack, several people survived the day. Santa Anna distinguished between those who had fought against him and others who had not. The survivors were all released without harm. They included the wife of a slain officer and her infant daughter; Travis' black servant, and two Mexican women from Béxar, cousins of Travis' widow. Each of the survivors were given a blanket and two dollars and sent on their way.

The Alamo Today

The Mexican army stood victorious but at a tremendous cost. Records vary, but best estimates put the number of dead at nearly 500 and almost as many wounded.

The number of Texans and other defenders of the Alamo killed was historically thought to be 189. However, with ongoing research, historians suggest that the number was closer to 257. None of the wounded were left alive.

The battle that Santa Anna thought would frighten the rebels into submission became an inspiration to the Texans. Their battle cry for freedom became "Remember the Alamo!" But all too soon would come Goliad, another of Texas' greatest tragedies.

The Alamo and its mission chapel fell in and out of repair as several different uses for the structure were found -- from a military outpost to a police station and jail. In the early 1900s, the land was purchased by the state of Texas and the Daughters of the Republic of Texas were appointed as permanent caretakers. The site is visited by hundreds of thousands of people each year.

The Haunted Alamo

The Alamo was already 93 years old at the time of the famous battle. The first stones for the Spanish mission were laid in 1744. There were several hundred burials in what is now Alamo Plaza. In 1793, the Catholic Church moved the religious artifacts to a nearby mission and turned the property over to the town. It officially became the Alamo, the Spanish word for cottonwood, when it was used as a barracks for Spanish soldiers in 1803. The building was vacant and abandoned between 1825 till 1835, when General Cos of the Mexican Army made it into a military fort. It changed hands between the Mexicans and the Texans three more times, including the Battle of the Alamo in 1836. After that time, a variety of purposes was found for the structure until it was purchased by the state of Texas and opened to the public as a state shrine.

After so many different uses by so many different people, it is not unexpected that the old mission chapel and surrounding property is considered quite haunted. However, the primary reason that the Alamo is so haunted can be linked to the battle that occurred there in 1836, when between 800 and 1,100 people died violent deaths over a period of little more than two hours. Added to that, the bodies of the Texans were stripped, desecrated and burned, with no proper burial. Even the bodies of the Mexican soldiers were mishandled in ways that would have been considered improper in their religion and their culture. They were either burned, thrown into the San Antonio River, or left to rot as carrion for wild animals and vultures.

The land within and surrounding the old mission is essentially a cemetery. After the bodies were burned, their ashes and charred pieces of bone and teeth were raked out and mixed into with the soil. If there were a checklist for events that would most likely to lead to a haunting, the Alamo and Goliad (soon to follow), would certainly tick the top eight or ten.

There is no record of any hauntings or ghost sightings before the battle in 1836, but one of the most prominent paranormal legends stems from just a few weeks afterwards. General Santa Anna and the bulk of his forces stayed on at San Antonio de Béxar for a few weeks before leaving to chase down General Sam Houston and the Republic of Texas Army, leaving a garrison of men at the Alamo under General Andrade's command.

Shortly before leaving, Santa Anna ordered General Andrade to demolish the Alamo, leaving nothing standing. General Andrade then instructed Colonel Sanchez to get the job done. Colonel Sanchez took his men to the site of the Alamo. After 12 days of constant bombardment, the place was not much more than rubble. The only recognizable structure still standing was the mission chapel. Sanchez ordered the men to begin demolishing of the church and the men complied, although there was some grumbling among the ranks about it possibly being sacrilege to tear down a former Catholic church.

According to legend, as the men began to work, six ghostly forms emerged from the chapel walls. The soldiers immediately stopped what they were doing and backed away, crossing themselves and muttering "*diablos*" (devils) under their breath. The forms, often described as monks, slowly advanced on the soldiers, waving flaming swords and warning the men in inhuman voices, "Do not touch the walls of the Alamo!" Colonel Sanchez and his men ran screaming from the chapel, back to their encampment.

When Sanchez told General Andrade what they had witnessed, Andrade was furious and chastised Sanchez for his cowardice. Taking matters into his own hands, Andrade collected a detail of men and marched them to the Alamo to get the work done. As added protection, he took along a small canon and instructed the gunner to aim it directly at the front doors of the chapel. But before they could blast the doors, the six ghostly monk forms again took shape and issued their warning. Andrade's horse took fright and reared, throwing the general to the ground. Before following his men in retreat, he turned to look at the building again and saw giant flames blast up from the ground. The smoke curled and twisted into the shape of a huge man. The figure held balls of fire in each hand and threw them at Andrade.

General Andrade affected a hasty retreat and the phantom protectors of the Alamo won out, but this part of the legend is not borne out by fact. Apparently, Andrade was not frightened away for good, since he must have returned to complete his orders. According to official records and archeological investigations, much of what remained of the mission was demolished, including many of fort's walls.

In the 1890s, the Alamo chapel and some of the old barracks were used as a police station and local jail. Soon after moving into the old buildings, the prisoners and guards began complaining about a variety of unexplainable experiences. They reported that a ghostly sentry walked from east to west on the roof of the police station, formerly the old barracks. This and other events were described so frequently and fervently that the hauntings became news -- literally.

The *San Antonio Express News* published two articles, in 1894 and again in 1897, about the ghostly goings-on. These articles described several types of "manifestations" that were witnessed within the walls of the police station and jail. They saw mysterious man-shaped shadows moving about the rooms and corridors, and heard strange moaning sounds that could not be explained. According to the newspaper reports, these were frequent and frightening, so much so that many of the guards refused to patrol the area after dark.

As the stories of the hauntings became more well known, complaints were brought to the San Antonio City Council, where councilmen took the position that making the prisoners sleep in a building with ghosts roaming around and moaning amounted to "cruel and unusual punishment" and that it was unsafe for the public because of the guards refusal to walk their patrols after sunset. Shortly after the second article was published, the city moved the police station from the Alamo to a building that was not haunted.

Many of the same types of incidents that were reported in the 1890s are said to continue to happen today, except that now, the ghosts of the Alamo no longer seem to distinguish between night and day, but prefer to conduct their hauntings around the clock.

For decades, visitors, park rangers and passersby have described seeing a mysterious sentry walking his patrol. There have also been countless reports of unexplained noises: men screaming in pain, battle cries, and voices and whispers seeming to emanate from the walls of the chapel. People walking past the Alamo at night have seen distorted and disheveled human shapes forming right out of the exterior walls themselves.

A commonly seen apparition is that of a man dressed in clothing of the early 1800s, walking across the courtyard. Although visitors have described seeing this man many times over the years, the story was validated for Alamo officials by one of their own park rangers. The ranger noticed a man dressed in period costume walking toward the library. The ranger decided to follow him and see what he was up to. To his surprise, the stranger faded away to nothing as he approached the chapel.

Another commonly witnessed ghost is that of a blond boy who has been seen wandering the buildings and courtyard, but is most often seen in the gift shop. He apparently likes to interact with children and has been known to carry on conversations with them. He has told several children that he was present during the battle and believes he died there. He seems to selectively appear to specific people, with children waving goodbye to him while their parents see no one.

Another ghost often seen on the grounds is that of actor John Wayne. In 1959, Wayne directed and starred in a movie about the Alamo. The Duke portrayed Davy Crockett in the film. He was said to be obsessed with creating a movie set that was historically accurate, down to the last detail. Filming could not take place in the original Alamo, so an exact replica was built 125 miles away in Brackettsville, Texas. Wayne toured the real Alamo many times and he developed a passion for the place and the people who fought there. The reproduction that was built for the movie was so close to the real thing, it has become a tourist attraction in its own right called Alamo Village.

One last identifiable individual said to be haunting the site is none other than Davy Crockett himself. Crockett fought and died at the Alamo, either killed during the battle or slaughtered afterwards by some of Santa Anna's officers. His ghost is most often described as wearing a full set of buckskins and his famous coonskin cap. He has been seen all over the compound, but most frequently he is seen guarding the old mission chapel.

The Battle of Coleta and the Goliad Massacre

As General Santa Anna marched his army of 5,000 men toward San Antonio and the Alamo, his second in command, General José Urrea and his army of 900 Mexican Centralistas were marching up the gulf coast of Texas. While Santa Anna was carrying out his siege on the Alamo, Urrea was waging his own battle, albeit a much smaller one. He and his men had arrived at their first stop at the abandoned Irish settlement of San Patricio on February 27, 1836. There he surprised Private Frank Johnson, co-commander of the Texian forces protecting the area. Following a quick skirmish, Johnson and four of his men escaped and the remainder of the Texians were either killed or captured. Johnson and his four companions were able to make their way to Goliad, where they joined Colonel James Fannin's troops.

General Urrea continued on his assigned route through eastern Texas. He next came upon Private James Grant (the other co-commander) and his 28 men camped along the Agua Dulce Creek. On March 1, the general again initiated a surprise attack. Grant lost his life along with all but one of his men, who was taken prisoner.

With two easy battles down, Urrea headed for Refugio, the next town in line. This time was different, as the citizens of Refugio had been warned that they were in Urrea's path, but they were slow to evacuate and requested assistance. The nearest fort with a garrison of soldiers was the Presidio La Bahía in Goliad, commanded by 32-year-old Colonel James Fannin. Word of the enemy's approach reached Fannin and he immediately sent Captain Aaron King and 28 men to assist in the evacuation and protect the fleeing settlers. The following day, Fannin added to the Refugio reinforcements by sending Colonel William Ward and 150 more men. By March 12, Urrea's forces had increased to nearly 1,500 but the battle was not going to be an easy one. The Texas troops had arrived in Refugio before Urrea and had taken refuge in the old church. The building was in ruins but the walls were thick and strong and the men were able to barricade themselves inside. With loopholes to shoot through, the men were quite well protected.

Urrea attacked several times and suffered heavy losses, with over 200 killed or injured. Eventually, he pulled his troops back to camp, leaving a small contingent of men to guard the old mission church in case the Texians tried to sneak away in the night. That was exactly what the Texians planned to do, but three of their comrades had been wounded. They were loath to abandon them but had no choice. They killed the Mexicans guarding the well, filled some water bags for their wounded friends, and bid them farewell.

King and Ward separated their forces and headed for Goliad along separate paths. Urrea's men hunted them down and Ward and his men surrendered and were taken as captives. King was not so lucky. Instead of being held as prisoners of war, they were slaughtered on the road to Goliad. Their bodies were stripped and left in the dirt to rot in the sun.

After the fall of the Alamo, General Sam Houston realized that the likely next step would be for the Mexicans to take the Precidio La Bahia at Goliad, which Fannin had named Fort Defiance. Rather than risk losing the 350-odd soldiers posted in there, Houston sent orders to Fannin to evacuate the garrison and fall back to Victoria, on the Guadalupe, taking with him as much artillery as possible. Fannin was further ordered to blow up the fort rather than leaving it to be occupied by the Mexicans. Fannin received the orders on March 14 and again, just as he had been slow in coming to the aid of the besieged forces at the Alamo, he was slow to follow orders. After a delay of five days, he and his men were finally ready to leave Fort Defiance.

Fearing their low numbers would make them an easy target, Fannin sent a message to Colonel A.C. Horton at Matagorda, requesting that he join them with the 200 men under his command. Horton arrived on the 16th with just 27 mounted troops.

Colonel Fannin frequently complained that his men were mostly poorly trained volunteers. He blamed them for the lengthy delays both in reinforcing Travis at the Alamo and the slowness of the retreat to Victoria. After gathering wagons and carts, and burying some of the artillery pieces, they were finally ready to leave Goliad.

In the early morning hours of March 19, Colonel Horton and his mounted troops headed down the road to Victoria. Seeing the road was clear of the enemy, Horton sent word back to Fort defiance that it was safe to proceed. The last thing Fannin's men did was to dismantle the fort and burn the buildings.

There was one delay after another. A cart broke down and the load had to be redistributed into the other carts. Crossing the San Antonio River, the artillery pieces got stuck in the mud. Eventually, the men were on their way again. They marched for about eight miles before Fannin called for a short rest. His officers were outraged that he would stop to rest on the open prairie within sight of the woods along the Coleto Creek. Fannin was feeling secure and refused to believe that the enemy was near enough to catch them in the open.

Shortly after they resumed their march, a group of Mexican cavalry numbering at least 350 came riding out of the timber to the far right. It was evident that they were attempting to cut the Texans off before they could reach the Coleto crossing. Fannin ordered his men to retreat to a depression in the prairie and set their artillery in strategic positions. The depression was about seven feet deep and though they were hidden from plain view, they had little cover. The Mexicans dismounted and fired off several volleys, but as they were keeping their distance, their shots were harmless. The cavalry was soon supported with at least 1,500 infantry. Fannin warned his men not to fire back, saving their ammunition for the real fight. As Urrea's cavalry moved in closer, the Texans opened fire. The Mexicans fixed bayonets and charged, but were met with a barrage of artillery fire, cutting them down in large swaths. Colonel Fannin was wounded with a ball through his thigh. They were soon generally involved in battle, with the Texans holding their own, even though they were out in the open and outnumbered.

A witness to the battle during one of Urrea's charges offered this description:

"The scene was now dreadful to behold. Killed and maimed men and horses were strewn over the plain; the wounded were rending the air with their distressing moans; while a great number of horses without riders were rushing to and fro back upon the enemy's lines, increasing the confusion among them; they thus became so entangled, the one with the other, that their retreat resembled the headlong flight of a herd of buffaloes, rather than the retreat of a well drilled, regular army, as they were."

By early afternoon, the Texans had no more water to sponge down their cannon, which had gotten too hot to

Colonel James W. Fannin of the Republic of Texas Militia and commander of Fort Defiance (Precidio La Bahia).

Precidio La Bahia at Goliad

be fired safely, forcing them to revert to using small arms. As darkness drew in, Urrea pulled his troops back for the night. The Mexican Centralistas had started with roughly 800 cavalry and infantrymen against fewer than 300 Texans. Seven Texans were killed, several mortally wounded, and six seriously wounded. They estimated that the Mexicans had lost at least five times that many.

Horton and his cavalry had gone in advance of the infantry and were still in the timber when the fighting broke out. Unable to even get close enough to render assistance without engaging in a suicide action, they stayed out of sight and later retreated to Victoria.

As night fell and the fighting abated, Urrea's Centralistas took cover in the woods. The Texans used the darkness to fortify their position; building breastworks of the wagons, carts, debris and anything else they could muster. Why they didn't just pack up and head back to Goliad or simply find an easier position to defend was answered by Captain Shackleford, one of the physicians attached to the Goliad garrison. He wrote:

"It has been often asked as a matter of surprise, why we did not retreat in the night. A few reasons, I think, ought to satisfy every candid man on this point. During the engagement, our teams had all been killed, wounded, or had strayed off; so that we had no possible way of taking off our wounded companions. Those who could have deserted them under such circumstances possess feelings which I shall never envy. I will mention another reason, which may have more weight with some persons than the one already given. We had been contending for five hours, without intermission, with a force more than seven times larger than our own; had driven the enemy from the field with great slaughter; and calculated on a reinforcement from Victoria in the morning, when we expected to consummate our victory."

There is no historical record of why Shackleford thought reinforcements were on their way. They may have believed that either Colonel Horton and his cavalry would rejoin them, or that Horton had ridden to Victoria to summon assistance. Either way, help came. The same was not true for the Mexican Centralistas. During the night, General Urrea welcomed the arrival of Colonel Morales with 500 troops and three pieces of artillery from Béxar.

As the sun rose on the 20th, the sight that greeted the Texans must have been simultaneously shocking and horrifying. By 6:30 in the morning, Urrea had gathered his entire compliment, now numbering nearly 1,200 men, and surrounded the Texans. He had also strategically placed the newly arrived canon front and center.

Fannin and his men were in great jeopardy. They were out of food and supplies and their ammunition was critically low. Most disturbing was their lack of water. Without water, they would be unable to fire their canon more that a couple of times. The Centralistas had no shortage of water, which meant they could fire until their ammunition was spent at the flimsy breastworks the Texans had built through the night.

Fannin called his officers together to discuss their next move. They considered surrendering, since prisoners of war were usually moved to an enemy stronghold, held for a short time, then paroled and sent home. Even if there wasn't another shot fired, the Texans knew they could not hold out for long with no food and no water. They were particularly concerned for their wounded comrades. If they were to surrender, they believed they would survive and eventually get home. More importantly, their wounded would be cared for. After talking it over, they felt they were left with no alternative. They would surrender.

The Texans Surrender
The white flag was raised and was promptly answered. Major Wallace and Captain Chadwick marched out to meet with General Urrea, but Urrea would speak with no one other than their commander. Though Fannin had been wounded the day before, he rose and promised his men that he would negotiate only honorable terms of surrender. The terms he negotiated were indeed honorable and quite lenient:

1. *That the Texans should be received and treated as prisoners-of-war, according to the usages of the most civilized nations.*
2. *That private property should be respected and restored: but that the side-arms of the officers should be given up.*
3. *That the men should be sent to Copano, and thence, in eight days, to the United States, or so soon thereafter as vessels could procure them.*
4. *That the officers should be paroled, and returned to the United States in like manner.*

The Texans immediately relinquished their firearms. Those who could march were gathered together and marched back to Goliad. The wounded, including Colonel Fannin, were brought along at a slower pace and didn't arrive until two days later. The captured men were crowded into the old mission chapel where they were given water and a bit of beef. Fannin wrote to complain about the short rations to Urrea, reminding him of the terms of surrender they had both agreed to.

The following day, March 23, Urrea sent Colonel Heizinger, a German engineer in service with the Mexican army, to accompany Colonel Fannin to Copano to see if they could hire a boat large enough to take the Texans to the United State. Unfortunately, the only boat of sufficient size to do the job had departed port the day before the men had arrived in Copano.

The two men did not return to Goliad until the 26th, so Fannin had no idea of what had gone on in his absence. What had happened while he was away was of the utmost significance for the prisoners; the number of which had grown considerably. The day Fannin had left for Copano, two groups of prisoners of war had been brought to Goliad: Major Miller and 40 Texas volunteers who had just been captured in Copano, and Colonel Ward and his men, who had been captured in the defense of Refugio. The conditions for the prisoners had improved somewhat, but they were still getting almost nothing to eat and the old mission chapel was now crowded. The wounded prisoners had received some medical care and water, so they were faring a little better. Their spirits were improving, as they believed they would be going home soon. In fact, a few young men who could play the flute were entertaining their fellow prisoners in the evenings. A few of the Mexican guards had let it slip that there was a rumor going through camp that General Santa Anna himself would be arriving the next day, to personally free the prisoners.

The only prisoners missing from the chapel were the four physicians: Drs. Bernard, Field, Hall, and Shackleford and their four hospital assistants. They had been quartered in another building where they were ordered to care for the wounded Mexican soldiers.

Things were not going well for General Urrea at this point. He had sent a message to Santa Anna, proclaiming his victory over Fannin and his Texans and that they were now in possession of Goliad.

Furious that the prisoners had not been executed immediately after surrendering, Santa Anna fired back a message to Urrea ordering that they be killed immediately. Urrea wrote again to Santa Anna, requesting clemency for the Texans. He was having great difficulty contemplating this order, and wrote in his diary that he: "...wished to elude these orders as far as possible without compromising my personal responsibility." He then left Goliad, placing Colonel José Nicholas de la Portilla in command until he returned.

At about 7:00 in the evening of March 26, a special express message arrived from General Santa Anna for Colonel Portilla. In this message, Santa Anna bypassed Urrea and gave a direct order to Portilla to execute the

Texans immediately. Shortly after, he received a second message, this time from General Urrea, ordering him to: "Treat the prisoners with consideration, particularly their leader, Fannin, and to employ them in rebuilding Goliad."

Portilla was in a quandary. He did not wish to carry out the mass execution, feeling it excessive and brutal; but orders were orders, and this order was from his president. After much thought, he determined that Santa Anna's orders took precedence, and he set about planning the cold-blooded murder of over 300 men the next day.

March 27, Palm Sunday, dawned with fog blanketing the land as far as could be seen. At 6:00 a.m., Colonel Portilla had ordered all the able-bodied prisoners to pack their belongings and form a line in the quadrangle, so they could be counted. The Texans thought this was good news. It had to mean that they were being paroled sooner than they thought; that they would soon be taken to the port of Copano, and from there to the United States. There was laughter and singing. This was going to be a good day.

With all the prisoners gathered in one large group, Major Miller and the 40 or so Texas volunteers who had been captured with him in Copano were pulled out. These men, along with the four physicians and their four assistants, were marched back into their quarters. It was later determined that Portilla had exempted them from the executions because they had not engaged in any fighting, and therefore did not deserve to be executed -- yet.

The prisoners were then told to form three lines, with their officers at the head of the lines. Each line of prisoners had a line of guards on either side, with one to two guards per prisoner. Each group was told they were being taken out for a work detail.

The guards marched the prisoners out of the Precidio, then each group separated and headed in three different directions. Each group traveled between one-half and three-quarters of a mile from Goliad before being called to a halt. After they were all stopped, the guards opened fire on the unarmed men at almost point-blank range. The first group to be fired upon were caught unawares and cried out for mercy, but none was given.

When the shooting and screams started, the other two groups of prisoners realized that they were to be killed as well. A few of them feigned death while others ran for their lives. Most of those who ran were cut down or brought back and shot. Any of the men who were shot but had not been killed outright were either clubbed or bayoneted to death. The numbers vary, but on that early Palm Sunday morning, roughly 360 men were marched out of Goliad and none returned. Twenty-eight fled the firing squad and were lucky enough to escape with their lives. Twice as many Texas were killed in Goliad that at the Alamo and San Jacinto combined.

Years later, Captain Benjamin Holland, one of the men who escaped the execution squad, wrote of his experience that morning:

The Goliad Massacre

"The company of which the writer of this was one was ordered to go forward, and no more was seen of our unfortunate comrades: we marched out on the Béxar Road, near the burying-ground; and as we were ordered to halt, we heard our companions shrieking in the most agonizing tones "O God! O God! Spare us!" and nearly simultaneously, a report of musketry. It was when we knew what was to be our fate. The

writer of this then observed to Major Wallace, who was his file leader that it would be best to make a desperate rush. He said, "No---we were too strongly guarded." He then appealed to several others, but none would follow. He then sprung, and struck the soldier on his right a severe blow with his fist: they being at open files, the soldier at the other file attempted to shoot him; but being too close, was unable. The soldier then turned his gun, and struck the writer a severe blow upon the left hand. I then seized hold of the gun and wrenched it from his hand, and instantly started and ran towards the river. A platoon of men (I have been since informed, by two others who made their escape by falling when fired upon among the dead bodies of their comrades) wheeled and fired upon me, but all missed.

I then had a chain of sentinels to pass at about 300 yards' distance; they were about thirty yards apart, three of them closed to intercept my retreat, the central one raised his gun to fire---I still ran towards him in a serpentine manner in order to prevent his taking aim---I suddenly stopped---dropped my piece, fired, and shot the soldier through the head and he fell instantly dead. I ran over his dead body, the other two firing at me but missing, and immediately ran and leaped into the river, and while swimming across was shot at by three horsemen, but reached the opposite banks in safety; and after wandering six days without food in the wilderness, succeeded on the tenth of April in joining General Houston's army, after having been retaken by the enemy once, but succeeded in making my escape in company with a wounded man who had got off from La Bahia by falling among the dead."

After the execution squads had completed their duties, they returned to the church where Fannin and the other wounded prisoners had been left. They pulled the wounded prisoners out of the church, lined them up on the ground side by side, and shot them where they lay.

General Santa Anna had given special directions to Colonel Portilla for disposing of Colonel Fannin and Portilla followed them to the letter. Fannin had been saved for last so that he might know his men were being killed, and hear their death screams. After the wounded prisoners had been shot, Fannin was escorted from his room in the church and given a chair, as his wounded leg would make it difficult for him to stand. Facing his firing squad, Fannin made three final requests: that his personal belongings be sent to his family, that he be shot in the heart and not in the face or head, and that he be given a Christian burial. None of his requests were carried out. He was shot him in the face, the officer commanding the squad kept his possessions and his body was burned along with those of the other executed prisoners.

When all those who were to be killed were dead, soldiers were put to the task removing their valuables and stripping the bodies. Many of the naked bodies were stacked in piles, covered with dry brush and set on fire. The attempts to burn the corpses were done so poorly that most of the bodies were left only partially burned, some with hands and feet left untouched and others without any signs of charring. When the soldiers became weary of carrying the bodies to the fires, they left the rest lay where they had fallen, to rot in the sun and be gnawed on by wild animals.

Almost one month later, the Mexicans were routed at San Jacinto. Rumors flew from Mexican outpost to outpost that General Santa Anna had been captured. A few days later, the rumors were confirmed that he had been taken and further, that he had surrendered. Fearing retribution, the soldiers still stationed at Goliad went to where the mass murders of the prisoners had been committed. They frantically searched for body parts and bone fragments still laying about and tried to burn them in an attempt to eliminate as much of the damning evidence that they could. Then they abandoned the Precidio La Bahia and Goliad.

Almost immediately, a story began to circulate about a Mexican woman who had taken pity on the surviving Texans. According to the story, she pleaded with the officers to save the lives of the prisoners who had been spared from the mass executions. Many believed that these men had witnessed too much and they should be executed as well, to eliminate anyone who could spread word of the Mexicans' sadistic behavior. This woman was able to protect them long enough for them to survive the war.

No one knows for sure who this woman was, but most historians believe she was Francisca (or Francita) Alvaez, wife of Captain Telesford Alvaez, an officer in the Mexican Centralista army. She was described as a "high-bred beauty" -- the highest complement a woman of that age or nationality could receive. To Texans, she became

"The Angel of Goliad." Books and songs have been written about her and the state of Texas has honored her with a statue in the Goliad State Park.

The Haunting of the Presidio La Bahia in Goliad

There was no actual battle in Goliad, but a river of blood most definitely flowed through this tiny town on the eastern Texas plain. The killing fields of Goliad were spread wide. The river flowed from the old mission chapel in three directions. The Presidio and the lands that suffered the massacre are now within the Goliad State Park and Historic Site. The sacrifices of the men who were so brutally murdered on that memorable day in March have not been forgotten, nor has the role they played in Texas' bid for independence.

As the memory of what happened there has remained alive within the living, the memory seems to have remained alive with the dead as well.

Visitors who have wandered away from the Precidio La Bahia and out into the field area in the direction of one of the mass murder sites have encountered strange smells of burning flesh or rotting meat.

Most of the unexplained experiences seem to happen closer to the Presidio itself, centering around the old mission chapel and in the living quarters. Mysterious cold spots move through the living quarters, and visitors and employees have heard banging on the doors and walls. Lights are often seen burning deep into the night, long after the doors have been locked and everyone has gone home.

Strange sounds have been heard in and around the chapel. A baby's cry, a women's choir and a solo soprano have all been heard echoing down the chapel's nave. In the front, near the candle-offering rack, a woman dressed in black has been seen, apparently in great emotional distress.

Two different ghosts spend at least part of their time in front of the chapel doors. A short, fat monk dressed in brown stands watching and waiting for something apparently very important to him, but unknown to everyone else. When the monk is not making an appearance, a mysterious woman dressed in white sometimes paces back and forth in front of the chapel entrance. The woman in white has also been seen in the cemetery, particularly in the area where the unmarked graves are. She moves from grave to grave, as if looking for someone long lost.

With all this, perhaps the strangest, and most unexplainable ghost appears in the form of a hitchhiker. People driving past the park have looked in their rear view mirror to see a spectral form in their back seat as they are driving over the San Antonio River bridge. The ghost always disappears when they reach the far side. No one knows who this mysterious hitchhiker is, or even if it is a man or a woman, but it only appears to drivers as they pass the Presidio.

The Battle of San Jacinto:
Vengeance is Realized

The Battle of San Jacinto has been described as the decisive battle in the Texas War for Independence, and it turned out to be the culminating battle as well.

After the devastating news of the Battle of the Alamo and the Battle of Coleto, which ended with the Goliad Massacre, many rapid changes took place in the new Republic of Texas.

To General Santa Anna, these battles, along with several small skirmishes along the way, were symbolic of the Mexican military's superiority. He no longer wanted to simply put down the "rebellion;" he wanted to crush the Texans into submission in such as way as would keep them subdued for generations.

For the Texan army, the horrors that occurred at the Alamo and the massacre at Goliad only served to energize them. Losing fellow soldiers in battle has always been a fact of life in warfare, but this was different. Vengeance for their murdered comrades became the Texans' driving force as they planned for the annihilation of the Mexican Centralista army.

General Sam Houston had been placed in command of the Texas army and militia. In the short months that had elapsed since the first blood was drawn, his only duties had been involved in rebuilding his army, hammering out future military strategies and sending out orders in response to pleas for reinforcements. Unfortunately, David Burnet, the governor of Texas, was not one of Houston's supporters and they argued frequently.

After Goliad, the first action Houston took was to begin a slow removal of his army of 900 men to the east, away from Santa Anna's forces. Texans wondered if Houston was retreating without having seen battle. How could they defeat the Mexican army if they were running in the opposite direction? This angered President Burnet, who repeatedly ordered Houston to turn back toward Santa Anna and fight. Houston ignored every special message sent from Burnet. As the army moved farther east, the Texas capitol, Washington-on-the-Brazos, was left undefended. The government feared capture so they abandoned the capitol and moved their operations first to Harrisburg, and then to Galveston. They could flee no farther east without getting their feet wet in Galveston Bay.

General Sam Houston

The Texas settlers jeered and hissed as Houston and his army passed through on their slow march eastward. As the army continued on what appeared to be a retreat, the terrified settlers and colonists, Texians and Tejanos alike, fled in utter panic as they were no longer protected. Santa Anna and his troops would surely be following Houston's army, and they did not wish to suffer the same fate as Goliad. This mass exodus from Texas became known as the "Runaway Scrape." As they fled, the land they left behind was virtually uninhabited.

Some of Houston's officers turned on him, threatening to seize command if he didn't turn around and go after the Mexicans. Houston put out a general warning to all that anyone who moved to take command would be shot on the spot. The officers backed down but continued to try to persuade Houston to stop and fight.

Initially, Houston had headed his army toward the Sabine River, which bordered Texas and the United States. He knew that federal troops were stationed there in case Santa Anna tried to invade Louisiana. But instead, he turned southeast and headed toward Harrisburg, arriving at an area alongside the confluence of the San Jacinto River and the Buffalo Bayou. Houston moved his men into the woods and made camp. It was April 20, 1836, exactly one month after Colonel Fannin and his soldiers had surrendered to General Urrea on the grassy plains of Coleto.

Santa Anna had remained in Béxar after the Alamo had fallen. It was there that he began strategizing to wipe out what remained of the Texas army. He planned to pursue Houston and attack him in the center with one column of men, while flanking him on the right and the left with two other columns. After his army marched out of Béxar, he learned that the provisional government had fled the capitol. With that news, he changed his plans and determined to capture the fleeing government at Morgan's Point, half a day's march from Lynch's Ferry. Santa Anna personally led 900 of his men on the mission, but was unable to find any of the Texas leaders. He then turned his men toward Lynch's Ferry and made camp on another grassy plain, this one next to the San Jacinto River, just 1,000 yards below the camp of the Texas army. The date was April 20. The two armies were finally about to meet in battle.

Houston was by then well aware of the position of the Mexican army, but Santa Anna was not sure where the Texans were camped. He sent out scouts to probe the woods and the surrounding areas. They met with resistance from troops Houston had strategically placed around his camp. The scouting party that entered the woods was met by Colonel James Neill, who commanded the "Twin Sisters," two small brass cannon that had been donated by the citizens of Cincinnati, Ohio. The Mexican scouts were turned back without realizing that they were nearly upon the whole of the Texas army. For the first time, the odds would be even, with both armies having roughly the same number of men.

Santa Anna knew the Texans were near and believed he had them cornered. But he was overconfident. Instead of attacking, he decided his men needed a good long rest. They would stay in their camp for two days then attack the Texans on April 22. Early in the morning of April 21, General Martín Perfecto de Cos arrived with

The Battle of San Jacinto by Henry Arthur McArdle

500 reinforcements, bringing the total compliment of Mexicans up to 1,400 troops. Unbeknownst to Houston, he was about to face a force half again as large as his own.

The Mexican troops had spent the morning placing artillery and building a five-foot-high barricade of wagons, carts, baggage and other materials found around camp to protect them. After their work was finished, their encampment became a place of leisure. Most of the men retired for their afternoon siesta. Many of the men had gone into their tents with their camp followers. Others worked around camp in a leisurely manner. A few cavalrymen had ridden to the river to collect water for the evening.

At noon on that same day, Houston gathered his officers and held a war council. The question of the day was whether to attack immediately or wait until the Mexicans attacked them. Houston worried that Santa Anna would take his time to prepare, and gather his troops for a concentrated effort. He didn't want to provide him with the extra time.

In the end, Houston decided on a surprise attack that very afternoon. Most of his men would be advancing across open ground, moving toward the center of the Mexican camp. The cavalry would be heading off to flank them on the left. Every decision Houston made that afternoon was a risky one. He was going to attack a larger army, in broad daylight, over open ground, and he was further stretching his army by sending his cavalry off to work their way around the other side of the enemy. The Texas officers set about preparing for the attack and explaining the plan to their men.

Santa Anna, a man well known for his conceit and blood lust, once again displayed his overconfidence. As his camp began to settle down for the afternoon, he decided to take it easy too. But he had made a crucial miscalculation, most likely due to the reinforcements that had arrived that morning. He took his siesta without posting sentries or skirmishers. The entire Mexican army was spread across the grassy plain with its eyes closed.

Once the decision was made, the Texans wasted no time putting their plan into action. By 3:30 p.m., Houston had his men were steeling themselves for what was to come. Deaf Smith, a frontiersman turned Texas soldier, rode into camp with news that the first stage of the plan had been accomplished. They had burned Vince's Bridge, the only means of escape for either army.

Promptly at 4:30 that afternoon, what was left of the Army of the Republic of Texas stepped from the trees, marching toward victory or doom. They knew that the element of surprise was their only chance so they moved as quickly and silently as possible. As there were no enemy lookouts watching for them, they found themselves only a few dozen yards from the Mexican line and were still undetected. Manuel Flores took the lead and the men charged into the Mexican camp, screaming "Remember the Alamo!" and "Remember Goliad!"

The Texans, as they moved to within a few yards of the camp, fired their first volley then fell to the ground, expecting return fire. Manuel Flores shouted for the men to get up. Santa Anna's men were running! Thomas Rusk of the cavalry rode up at that moment and shouted to the men to get up and "give 'em hell!" The calls of "Remember the Alamo" and "Remember Goliad" echoed through the camp as the Texans ran from tent to tent, shooting the confused and unarmed Mexicans. General Manuel Fernández Castrillón gathered a few men and tried to resist, but he was shot and killed early on and his men scattered and fled.

A number of Mexican soldiers made a break for the nearby marshes and rivers. The Texas cavalrymen were the first to make it to the river and shot them as they floundered in the water. General Juan Almonte and the 400 men in his command surrendered, but the carnage continued all around them. A thick cloud of smoke hovered over the field as the gunshots continued.

General Houston had been at the head of the charge and was shot in the ankle, but he stayed in the heat of the battle. General Santa Anna's bravado turned to cowardice. Removing his ornate uniform, he donned the jacket of a private and crawled in the opposite direction from the fighting. He reached the high grass and crawled some more.

The great Santa Anna lay on the ground for the rest of the afternoon and through the night. He was still too terrified to move the next day and was eventually discovered by a group of Texans scouring the grasses for escaped Mexican troops. The Texans were unaware of his identity and believed that they had captured just another runaway private. They had no idea who they had until he was taken back to camp and the other prisoners stood at attention and saluted him as "El Presidente."

The surprise attack in broad daylight had been successful beyond anyone's wildest expectations. The Mexican army was thoroughly defeated in about 18 minutes, but the Texans were out for vengeance. Houston and a few of his officers tried to restrain their men but there was no stopping them. The chaotic slaughter went on for another hour or so, finally ending when the Texans became exhausted.

When the shooting ended, nearly 700 Mexican soldiers lay dead on the field, 208 lay wounded, and 703 were taken prisoner. Of the Texans, only nine lost their lives and 30 were wounded. Almost all of the Texas casualties occurred in the first few minutes of the attack.

Houston was determined to spare Santa Anna's life. Based on the Mexican general's behavior during the battle, Houston believed that the he would quickly surrender and try to make peace in order to save his own skin. He had proven time and time again that he was a ruthless man who cared little for the lives of others, even those of his own men. However, he did care greatly for his own life and he acted just as Houston believed he would.

Three weeks after the battle, on May 14, 1836, El Presidente Antonio López de Santa Anna signed the Treaties of Velasco. Officially, he agreed to have all Mexican troops out of Texas by June and that he would return to Mexico City and work to negotiate the recognition of Texas' independence. In return, he would be given safe passage back to Mexico.

General Urrea was furious. He was not present at San Jacinto as he was still maintaining several Mexican strongholds within Texas. Although he had argued fervently for the lives of the Texans at Goliad as a matter of honor, he still believed in the Mexican cause in Texas. He further believed that the war could continue with a good possibility of a Mexican victory, but Santa Anna had signed the treaty solely for self-serving reasons. Urrea had no option but to leave Texas as he had been ordered to do.

Santa Anna had expected safe passage home, but that was not to happen for awhile. He was held for six months as a prisoner of war and he eventually met with American President Andrew Jackson. He eventually returned to Mexico in early 1837, not as returning hero but with shame and dishonor. While he was held prisoner, the Mexican government had renounced him and nullified any agreement he had entered into. Regardless, the independence of Texas was set, even though Mexico did not agree officially until 1848 when, at the end of the Mexican American War, the Treaty of Guadalupe Hidalgo was signed.

The Haunting of the San Jacinto Battlefield

Visitors who have wandered away from the monument dedicated to the men who lost their lives there, and out into the field area in the direction of one of the mass murder sites, have encountered a smoky shape in the form of a man, sometimes several such shapes. The smoke may move toward the visitor before bursting and floating away. On rare occasions when multiple shapes have formed, they have been observed to come together to form a single shape seconds before dissipating in the wind.

1857: "NONE WILL BE SPARED"
The Massacre at Mountain Meadows

Legend had it that Mountain Meadows, located at the southern edge of the Wasatch Mountain foothills of Utah, were created by God as a resting spot for weary travelers who were trekking across the country to California in the middle nineteenth century. Located about 300 miles southwest of Salt Lake City, Mountain Meadows was a valley five miles long and only a few hundred yards wide. Fed by mountain streams that caused the grass to grow tall and green and the trees to stand thickly on the slopes of the rounded hills that overlooked it, it was a place of calm restfulness and a respite from the hot, dusty hardships of the trail. Before they reached Mountain Meadows, the settlers in their creaking wagons traveled across miles of rocky wasteland. After the meadow, they faced the rigors of the Mojave Desert. But for a few brief days at the meadows, while their livestock was watered and fed and their children played in the waving grass, it was as if they were given a taste of what awaited them in California.

One of the worst civilian massacres in American history took place in this peaceful valley on September 11, 1857. It was a crime of religious fanaticism that would not be equaled for almost a century and a half, when on September 11, 2001, other religious zealots would fly airplanes into the World Trade Center. A special report to Congress called the slaughter of 120 men, women and children from a wagon train that had stopped at Mountain Meadows "a hellish atrocity."

To make matters more shocking, the murderers were members of the Mormon Church, a once-persecuted religious movement that had always seemed somewhat mysterious to the majority of the American public. The actions of church members on that day caused an even deeper rift of mistrust between the rest of the country and the Church of Jesus Christ of Latter-day Saints, a chasm that still exists as the ever more powerful Mormon Church still attempts to absolve itself of responsibility for the bloody massacre.

The story that ended in the bloody grass at Mountain Meadows began with Joseph Smith, the founder of the Mormon religious movement. Smith was born in Vermont in 1805, but moved to western New York with his parents and eight siblings when he was 15. His father was a farmer and Smith grew up in an area that was rife with religious zealotry. Things were so bad that it had been given the derogatory nickname of "the Burned-Over

Mormonism founder Joseph Smith

District" because so many evangelists, revival meetings and religious renewals had hit the common folks that the religion had been "burnt out of them." But religion had not been burned out of Joseph Smith…

One day, while praying in his upstairs bedroom, the 17-year-old Smith claimed that he was visited by a figure that was bathed in light that was "as bright as the midday sun." The figure, an angel named Moroni, told Smith that God had work for him to do. The angel returned to visit Smith several more times in the years that followed and eventually led him to discover the golden tablets upon which were engraved the words that would become the basis of the Mormon Church. Smith was the only person to ever see these tablets (which could only be read with a pair of "magic spectacles") but by 1832, he had translated what became known as *The Book of Mormon*, which held that two tribes of Israelites had been guided by God to North America 600 years before the birth of Christ. These people had built a powerful civilization but then had turned away from God and had fallen from grace, regressing into the Native American tribes that the Europeans found living on the continent centuries later. The angel Moroni was the last of God's true prophets in North America and he had hidden the golden tablets until Smith could reveal the Mormon story to the world.

Perhaps unsurprisingly in an era of bizarre religious movements, these fantastical tales met a receptive audience and the ranks of the religion that Smith was calling the Church of Jesus Christ of the Latter-day Saints began to swell. Just as unsurprisingly, Smith and his followers began to meet resistance and persecution for their unorthodox beliefs.

Smith and his followers were driven out of western New York by mainstream Christians who felt they were blasphemous. They moved to Kirtland, Ohio, on the southern shores of Lake Erie where they made plans to start a new Mormon community. The Saints believed that it was essential that a new Zion be built in the American wilderness so that they could create a Mormon paradise on Earth that would be duplicated in Heaven.

At first, the 2,000 Mormons were met with open arms by the people of Kirtland, but it wasn't long before they wore out their welcome. Smith, a handsome, charismatic man, began to spread a philosophy of polygamy (he would eventually take on 49 wives of his own), although he called it "celestial marriage" and justified it by pointing to the great characters of the Bible who all had many wives. Polygamy became a source of conflict both in and out of the Mormon Church, especially in a frontier community where the men greatly outnumbered the women. The general public was horrified and fascinated with the practice and it would plague the church for many decades to come. Even today, fundamentalist Mormons who practice polygamy are seen as radical zealots, even by other Mormons.

But it would be money that would drive the Mormons from Ohio. As the bank panic of 1837 hit the United States, a bank that Smith had opened spread useless paper currency around the area. Facing criminal charges, he fled Kirtland in the middle of the night, first for Missouri and then for Illinois and the remote community of Nauvoo. The story was the same everywhere. As the ranks of the Mormons grew larger and larger, people began to resent them and violence broke out. The lieutenant governor of Missouri stated publicly that "Mormons are the common enemies of mankind and ought to be destroyed."

There were those who followed his suggestion. A band of vigilantes attacked a Mormon settlement at Haun's Mill, Missouri, in 1838 and gunned down an entire family, including a 10-year-old boy, in cold blood. "Nits grow lice," one of the men reportedly said before he put a bullet into the boy's head.

After real threats like these – as well as many imagined ones – Smith created an armed militia that he called the Army of God. The 2,000 troops were a quarter of the size of the standing U.S. Army at the time. Smith made himself a general and wore a uniform of his own design. He also selected a top-secret group of men to surround him called the Sons of Dan, or the Danites. These men were essentially Smith's personal assassins. Taking their name from the biblical prophet Daniel, they dealt out vengeance in the form of "blood atonement" to people inside and outside of the church who had crossed Smith in some way.

In 1843, Smith made his policies on plural marriage public and more and more people began to speak out against him and his church. In addition, people were complaining about being cheated by Smith's shady business dealings and word leaked out about the Danites. Eventually, Smith was arrested and killed by an angry mob while locked up in the Nauvoo jail. Once again, the Latter-day Saints were on the move, this time to Utah under the leadership of their new prophet, Brigham Young.

Brigham Young was a dynamic speaker and natural leader who had made numerous successful recruiting missions to England on behalf of the church. He began to rule the church with absolute authority and an iron hand. One of his first acts, according to Danite soldier John D. Lee, who would become a central figure in the Mountain Meadows Massacre, was to swear "by the eternal Heavens that I have unsheathed my sword, and I will never return it until the blood of the Prophet Joseph Smith is avenged.."

But even as fiery as Young was, he knew the Mormons could not remain in Illinois and prosper. He still needed to create the new Zion that Smith has espoused and he knew it needed to be far to the west in an unpopulated territory. With that decision made, Young led his people on a terrible journey in 1847 and settled them in the arid country around the Great Salt Lake in present-day Utah. It was not the biblical paradise that Smith had envisioned, but Young insisted that they begin irrigating the country on the day they arrived and gradually, Salt Lake City began to grow.

Brigham Young

Two years later, when gold was discovered at Sutter's Mill, Brigham Young controlled land that became a crucial link between California and the rest of the country. The Mormons were in control of every route into and out of Utah – every river, trail and mountain pass. By the early 1850s, he had created his own kingdom, apart from and beyond the control of the federal government. Finally, President Millard Fillmore was forced to surrender to the inevitable and make the Mormon leader Utah's territorial governor.

But even then, the Mormons acted as if the laws of the U.S. did not apply to them. In 1853, a federal surveying party was attacked and massacred because the Mormons did not want the government measuring their land. Federal judges were murdered. A settler who foolishly courted one of Young's daughters was butchered. But was it the Mormons who carried out these crimes? Not according to church members. In every case, the murders were carried out by Native Americans – or so it seemed. The victims were scalped and mutilated in what was presumed to be methods perpetrated by Indians and witnesses even stated that they had seen painted warriors fleeing the scenes of the crimes.

The Mormons may have thought they had thrown suspicion off the Danites, but not everyone was fooled. As the bloody incidents increased, outrage grew among the population back East, and the federal government, under President James Buchanan, decided to send soldiers to quell what Buchanan and others believed was a rebellion in the Utah Territory. As the soldiers departed for Utah, the fate of a peaceful wagon train that was headed for Salt Lake City was forever sealed.

The Fancher Train, named for its leader, Alexander Fancher, had originated in Harrison County, Arkansas. On March 29, 1857, the group of settlers had departed Arkansas, bound for California, where Fancher's brother John had already started a ranch. Fancher, age 43, was the epitome of the Western pioneer. Sober, industrious, a Mexican-American War veteran and a born leader, he had already led one wagon train to California and had returned to form another group made up of friends and neighbors to take with him to the rich lands of the West.

Many had begged to go with Fancher and he was able to choose whom to take with him. The final group was made up of people like himself, 20 to 30 close-knit families, who had an optimistic outlook and an excitement about starting new lives in California. They were a wealthy party, many of them having converted their life savings into gold, which they hid under the floorboards of their wagons and inside of featherbeds. Historians believe that the Fancher party may have been traveling with nearly $100,000 in gold coins.

The Fancher wagon train numbered roughly 200 men, women and children when it left Arkansas. A party of that size rarely ran into trouble with Native Americans. Even so, Fancher made sure that all of the men were well armed and schooled in how to use their weapons. They were not expecting problems, nor were they – as was later claimed by Mormon disinformation – wild and boisterous, "swearing and boasting... that Buchanan's whole army was coming right behind them and would kill every damn Mormon in Utah." They were, in truth, a group of ordinary families seeking a new start in a new place.

But there turned out to be nothing ordinary about their journey. As the Fancher party approached Salt Lake City, rumors were flying throughout the Mormon community that a force of U.S. soldiers was coming to forcibly remove Brigham Young from his position as territorial governor. In reality, Buchanan's army *was* preparing to march on Salt Lake City, but it would not arrive in Utah until November 1857, when a nearly bloodless war was fought between the Mormons and the U.S. government.

The Fancher party arrived in the Great Salt Lake basin in early August and found themselves greeted with hostility. No amount of money could purchase supplies and so a planned weeklong rest was shortened to only two days and then the wagon train moved out again.

At that time, there were two routes from Utah to California: a northern one, the California Trail through Salt Lake City and Nevada, and the old Spanish Trail, a southern route through the Mojave Desert. The Fancher Train had planned on taking the northern route but were convinced by a Danite named Charles Rich – who rode into their camp near Salt Lake City and gave them orders to leave the area the next day – that the southern trail was safer; there were fewer Native Americans, and there was more feed along the way, especially in a little valley called Mountain Meadows.

As the Fancher party headed south, their deaths had already been plotted. On September 1, Brigham Young met with Paiute Indian leaders in Salt Lake City. Using his son as a translator, he told the tribal leaders that all of the cattle on the Spanish Trail were theirs for the taking – a clear reference to the large and valuable herd that accompanied the Fancher wagon train. The next day, the Paiutes left Salt Lake City and headed for southern Utah.

While this meeting was taking place, the Fancher party was passing near Cedar City, Utah, about 35 miles from Mountain Meadows. On September 4, they were refused food and feed for their cattle, but were directed to the meadows as a place where they could rest and graze their livestock. Unknown to the members of the Fancher party, the Danite John D. Lee had already arrived at Mountain Meadows with a mixed force of Paiute and Mormons, the latter of whom had painted their faces to look like Native Americans. They observed the Fancher party enter the valley and make camp on September 6. When darkness fell, Lee and his men crept down from the hills and concealed themselves in the rocks and brush at the edge of the valley.

The morning of September 7, 1857 broke bright and clear. The travelers built up their cook fires and began making coffee and preparing their breakfast. They sat chatting near the fires and then, recalled one of the survivors, "While eating a breakfast of rabbit and quail, a shot rang out and one of the children toppled over." A second volley of shots struck between 10 and 15 of those gathered in the camp. Seven of them were immediately killed. Others, including Alexander Fancher, were mortally wounded.

Although taken by surprise, the well-trained men and women of the Fancher party took immediate action. They circled the wagons, dug ditches behind them, both as firing trenches and to offer protection for the children, and returned fire on the attackers. They assumed they were being attacked by Native Americans since they heard

The Mountain Meadows site, looking west.

(Right) Danite John D. Lee

horrible cries in the woods and saw dark-skinned men in war paint darting through the trees and brush, but were bewildered as to the cause of the attack. According to Fancher, who had traveled in the region before, the Paiutes were normally peaceful and owned relatively few firearms. The men who attacked the camp, though, were armed to the teeth and well stocked with ammunition.

But the settlers did not go down without a fight. The initial return fire killed three Paiutes and the Mormons and their allies realized that wiping out the Fancher party was not going to be easy. In fact, the Paiutes called off their attack. They told John Lee that this kind of bloodshed was more than they bargained for and abandoned the Mormons in the hills. Lee knew he needed more reinforcements and so he rode to nearby Cedar City to recruit more men. According to Lee, he received three wagonloads of "well-armed men" under the command of Major John Higbee. Higbee told Lee that their mission was no longer to simply frighten or harass the Fancher party, or to rob them of their belongings. Higbee told him, "it is the orders of the President [Brigham Young] that all emigrants must be put out of the way… none who are old enough to talk are to be spared."

During the time that Lee had been away gathering more men, the settlers had remained under siege. Despite their bravery, they were at a considerable disadvantage. They had not set up their camp near the stream that ran through the meadows because it was too swampy, so they had to travel more than 100 yards under fire to get water. As the days wore on, the little water they had ran out and they began to suffer from thirst. Desperate, two little girls dressed in "spotless white" ran to the stream with pails for water but this appeal to the humanity of the Mormons did no good – the two little girls were shot to death.

By Wednesday, Lee had returned with his reinforcements and now even more men were raining bullets down on the Fancher camp. More people were killed and the bodies of the slain lay stinking and swelling in the sun. In another desperate move, two men snuck out of the camp in the night, hoping to find another wagon train passing nearby that could help them. They slipped away from their attackers and rode until they saw a small campfire with three men sitting around it. Thinking they might be travelers, one of the men spilled their story of being attacked in Mountain Meadows. But the men around the campfire were Mormons – Danites, in fact – and one of the men from the Fancher party was gunned down in cold blood. The other man managed to get away and made it back to the wagon train. He told them what had happened. Any doubt that the Fancher party had about the identity of their attackers was now gone.

But when John D. Lee rode into their camp under a white flag on Friday, September 11, they had no choice but to trust him. They were nearly out of ammunition and their water was long gone. Lee told them that he was a major in the Mormon militia and that the Native Americans had gone wild and had attacked them. Lee promised to try to save the settlers by taking them to Cedar City under his protection. All they had to do, he explained, was give up their guns and ammunition so as to not incite the Paiute any further. Despite their suspicions of the Mormons, there was nothing else the settlers could do. They had perhaps 20 rounds of ammunition between them and a number of wounded who needed care. Alexander Fancher was dying and his nephew Matt was placed in charge of the party. He told his uncle what was taking place and Fancher gasped out weakly, "Good God, no, Matt!" They had no choice, though, and the remaining men in the Fancher party laid down their weapons.

Lee then organized the party into three groups. The wagons of the wounded were loaded first, followed by the women and children and then the men, walking in a single file about 10 feet apart, each accompanied by a Mormon guard. They were led by Major Higbee, astride his horse. After about a mile, he stopped his horse near an open area surrounded by scrub oak and ordered the column to halt. He then fired his pistol in the air and called out, "Do your duty!"

And each Mormon turned and shot the man he was guarding.

Chaos erupted in the meadow as the settlers attempted to flee, only to be gunned down by their captors. Among the Fancher party were several so-called "apostate Mormons," who had once been members of the church but had given up the faith. They were singled out for special treatment of "blood atonement." In 1856, Brigham Young had preached, "There are sins that men commit for which they cannot receive atonement in this world, or in that which is to come." The atonement of Jesus having shedd his blood for them would not apply. These were people, Young and other Mormons believed, who needed to be dealt with by the practice of blood atonement. They were not merely killed but were slaughtered by the practice of "having their blood literally spilled on the ground." In other words, their throats would be cut. During the massacre, Higbee sliced the throats of the former Mormons in the Fancher party.

When the shooting started, the women and children began to panic. Lee then gave the order to kill them all. Sallie Baker, a child who survived, later wrote, "From the survivors went up such a piercing, heart-rending scream – such a shriek of blank despair" that everyone who heard it remembered it always. Sallie also remembered how one Mormon gunman ran up to the wagon where the women and children had been placed and said, "Lord my God, receive their spirits. It is for Thy Kingdom that I do this!" He then began firing wildly into the wagon. Another man shot two badly wounded settlers who were huddled together on the ground. A 14-year-old boy was clubbed to death with a rifle butt to conserve ammunition.

Two teenaged girls, Rachel and Ruth Dunlap, ran into a cluster of trees where witnesses said they were raped by Mormons and shot by Lee himself as they begged for mercy and promised to "love him forever" if he spared their lives. Much of the killing was done by sword and knife, and the Mormons, crazed by bloodlust, were soon covered with gore. One young girl fell to her knees in front of a teenage Mormon boy, begging him to spare her. He said he would, but his father – which some reports claim was Lee – stabbed her to death in the boy's arms.

More than 50 years later, a woman who was a four-year-old child at the time remembered seeing her mother shot in the forehead and fall dead. Other witnesses saw "children clinging around the knees of their murderers, begging for mercy and offering themselves as slaves for life could they be spared. But their throats were cut from ear to ear in answer to their appeal." A survivor of the massacre who told her story many years later was asked how she could remember everything that happened in such detail since she was just a little girl at the time. She replied, "You don't forget the horror. And you wouldn't forget it either, if you saw your own mother topple over in the wagon beside you, with a big red blotch getting bigger and bigger on the front of her calico dress."

When the killing had ended, the Mormons were left with the problem of what to do with the children who were considered to be of "innocent blood," which was generally under the age of eight. Since the children had not attained the age of reason, the Mormons saw them as being innocent of whatever "crimes" their parents had committed. In the eyes of God, they believed, these children should be spared. However, it appears that the older children among the group (those nearer the age of eight) were the last to be killed that day because it was feared that they would carry the tale of the massacre with them.

The rest of the children, mostly age seven and under, were taken from the massacre site by wagon to a Mormon farming community called Hamblin a few miles away, just east of Mountain Meadows. The screaming and wailing of the children, most of whom were soaked in their parents' blood, was nearly unbearable to hear. The children were left in Hamblin until they could be parceled out to Mormon families – in some cases to the families of the men who had killed their parents and older siblings. By 1859, though, the federal government had managed to track down the children and sent them back to Arkansas to be reunited with relatives. Amazingly, the Mormons tried to demand money from the government for taking care of the children for two years.

The next day at Mountain Meadows, the Mormons returned to the stiff and twisted corpses of the Fancher party, tearing clothing and jewelry from the bodies and ransacking the wagons for gold and anything useful they could steal. Afterward, they made a half-hearted effort to bury the bodies by dumping them in a ditch and throwing some dirt over them. The remains of the Fancher Train were left to the wolves, the buzzards and the elements.

The killers swore a blood oath to keep silent about the massacre, but it wouldn't last. The enormity of what had befallen the Fancher party, once the bloodlust had left them, began to weigh on many of the men involved in their deaths. Higbee and his immediate superiors felt no shame, though. They blamed the massacre on the Paiutes, although since Mormons were in possession of the Fancher supplies, cattle, gold and surviving children, this seemed hard to believe. A few days after the massacre, Brigham Young wrote a letter, which he dated before the slaughter, ordering Mormons not to harass the settlers – an obvious attempt to whitewash his involvement in the affair.

Whispers and rumors of the massacre spread, and subsequent wagon trains stumbled on the remains of the Fancher party. Reports from travelers reached the California newspapers, and then spread to Washington. The American public demanded an investigation. Eventually, the Army sent Major James Carleton to investigate and to find the surviving children. Even as late as 1859, Carleton found the scene of the massacre "horrible to look upon." He collected baskets filled with women's hair, which were lying "in detached locks and masses" throughout the site. Bones and skulls were scattered about, as well as pieces of rotted clothing, leather and bits of metal. A pathologist who accompanied Carleton noted that, "many of the skulls bore marks of violence, being pierced with bullet holes, or shattered by heavy blows... or firearms disclosed close to the head."

This ended the lie spread by the Mormons that the victims had been killed by Indian arrows. Unfortunately, despite his best efforts, Carleton's report was not enough to bring about the prosecution of those involved in the massacre. The Mormon church was simply too powerful and Utah residents – Mormon or otherwise – were too scared to talk. It would be 20 years after the massacre before the federal authorities brought murder charges against John D. Lee and four others, including Major Higbee. Lee was the only one brought to trial. Most were convinced that he was a convenient scapegoat to protect Brigham Young. He was convicted and was taken to Mountain Meadows, where he was executed by a firing squad.

The Mormon church desperately wanted this to be the end of the matter. But the Mountain Meadows Massacre has never been truly forgotten and has always left a stain on the relationship between the Latter-day Saints and the rest of the country. Even now, long after the church has distanced itself from polygamy and other controversial practices of the past, the Mormons have still not convincingly answered charges that they were fully involved in the deaths of the innocent settlers passing through Utah. The church now admits that "local" Mormons took part in the massacre, not just Native Americans, but refuses to admit that Brigham Young ordered or had prior knowledge of the killings, as historians believe that he did. As far as the Mormons are concerned, that chapter in history is forever closed.

But the conviction of John D. Lee, and the church's official denial, did not close the book for everyone.

Almost from the time of the massacre, and the investigation that followed, stories circulated that Mountain Meadows was haunted. Even though the victims had been properly reburied by the military, they did not, it was widely reported, rest in peace. This blight on the history of Utah created a haunting that continues to this day – although it's often difficult to find people to talk about it. Stories of ghosts and hauntings are not widely accepted by those of the Mormon faith, and since the massacre was denied for years before being grudgingly accepted in recent times, this make is doubly hard to track down stories of strange events at the massacre site. Searching historical records, though, it's possible to find accounts of apparitions, eerie cries and screams that are connected to Mountain Meadows, which is now a part of Dixie National Forest.

The massacre became closely tied with the community of Hamblin, which was nothing but a quiet collection of homes and businesses in 1857 when the murders took place. Soon, though, it received national notoriety as the place where the children of the slaughtered settlers had been taken.

The town had been settled just one year earlier by a band of Mormons led by famous explorer Jacob Hamblin. It quickly grew into a thriving town with a fort for protection from Indians at one end of the main street. A church, schoolhouse and a co-op store were later added and it seemed that Hamblin was well on its way to a permanent place in Utah history. The town did leave a mark in history, but it was not the one that Hamblin and the other settlers had in mind.

After the massacre, the surviving children were brought to Hamblin and were given to local Mormon families to raise. Although the bloody events were meant to be kept secret, the story soon shocked the nation and people all over the country began to hear of Mountain Meadow and, of course, the small town of Hamblin. Jacob Hamblin had always been a peaceful man, a friend to the Indians and a generous supplier to the wagon trains that passed through the region. He had been unaware of the massacre and was appalled by the bloodshed.

Some said that Mountain Meadows was cursed after the massacre. The stream that once watered the meadow stopped flowing and the grass dried up, leaving large sections to be swallowed by the desert. Sagebrush grew where grass had once been, as though trying to hide the sight of the nameless graves. The town of Hamblin managed to survive the so-called curse – at least for a time. Eventually irrigation lines dried up, people moved away and before long, Hamblin was a ghost town. And even in those days, stories spread that the massacre site was haunted and ghosts walked the deserted streets of the town. Today, a rough dirt road leaves Route 18 in the southwest corner of Utah and winds its way to Hamblin Cemetery, which is all that remains of the unlucky town started by Jacob Hamblin — a town wiped out by a curse.

1859: "JOHN BROWN'S BODY"
The Bloody Raid on Harper's Ferry

John Brown's Body lies a-mouldering in the grave,
But his soul goes marching on...

On October 18, 1859, John Brown lay bleeding on the floor of an armory office in Harpers Ferry, Virginia, the "great work of his life" at an end. Just 36 hours earlier, he had launched a bold attack on the federal armory in an attempt to wage a campaign of slave liberation across the South.

Instead, Brown's crusade ended abruptly when U.S. Marines stormed his position in the armory's engine-house. Most of Brown's guerilla fighters were dead or dying, including his two sons. The few slaves freed in the brief uprising were returned to bondage after their liberator had been beaten to the floor of the engine-house by a Marine wielding a dress sword.

It was at the moment of his defeat that Brown became a legend. Under harsh interrogation, the wounded prisoner spoke with such eloquence that even his interrogators expressed stunned admiration. Virginia Governor Henry Wise told a reporter, "He is a fanatic, but firm, truthful and intelligent. He is a bundle of the best nerves I ever saw cut and thrust and bleeding an in bonds."

Brown's admirers knew how devoutly he held his cause for the abolition of slavery, but even they were afraid

John Brown in 1856

of him. Frederick Douglass once stated, "His zeal in the cause of freedom was infinitely superior to mine. I could live for the slave, but John Brown could die for him."

Brown had a similar effect on the Virginians who watched him hang six weeks after his terrorist attack on Harpers Ferry. He walked briskly up the scaffold steps, positioned himself beneath the noose, shook hands with the hangman and calmly requested, "Do not detain me any longer than is absolutely necessary." This last request was not granted, however, for the large contingent of soldiers guarding the gallows needed time to march into place. For an excruciating 15 minutes, Brown, with a hood over his head and a noose around his neck, stood absolutely still atop a trapdoor, awaiting the plunge to his death.

"He behaved with unflinching firmness," wrote Major Thomas Jackson, who would soon be nicknamed "Stonewall" for his own resolute bravery. Near him stood Edward Ruffin, a pro-slavery man who considered Brown a "robber and murderer and villain of unmitigated turpitude." But after witnessing the abolitionist's courage on the gallows, Ruffin wrote in his journal: "He seems to me to have had few equals." Brown never spoke on the gallows, but he did hand one of his captors a note. It read, "I, John Brown, am now quite certain that the crimes of this guilty land will never be purged away but with blood."

After his body was cut down, legend has it that those present were horrified by the expression in his eyes. They were said to shine brightly, as if he were still alive. The doctor that was present examined him three times to be certain that he was actually dead. Finally, candle wax was poured over his eyes to hide their eerie gleam.

John Brown was as frightening in death as he had been in life. He was a man who, even now, defies easy judgment. Many have tried to place him into ready-made molds: hero or villain, martyr or monster, prophet or madman. In 1859, the *New York Times* called him "a wild and absurd freak," but the man and his mission have never been forgotten.

And he left an indelible impression on Harpers Ferry that has left many believing that – more than 150 years after his death – his spirit refuses to rest in peace.

John Brown was born in Connecticut in 1800 and raised in modest circumstances on the Ohio frontier. He was a man of ferocious ambition and one who embraced the abolitionist cause with almost mystical fervor. A devout Calvinist who believed in a wrathful God, he saw himself as an Old Testament warrior battling the evils of slavery. In the early 1850s, he came to accept the idea that violence was necessary to end slavery in America.

In his personal life, Brown endured almost Job-like tribulations. He showed talent as a leather tanner and livestock farmer, but land speculation and poor money management drove him into bankruptcy. He recovered to become a leading wool merchant, only to overextend himself again and end up mired in lawsuits and debt.

He also suffered repeated family tragedies. His mother and his first wife both died in childbirth and he buried eight of his 20 children as infants or toddlers. His first wife and several of his children exhibited signs of mental illness, which many Americans would later suspect affected Brown as well.

In spite of his many trials – or more likely, because of them – Brown emerged in the mid-1850s as a renowned abolitionist who was not afraid to get blood on his hands. Unlike most slavery opponents, he was willing to take up arms and so he went to Kansas to join the free-state fight against the forces of slavery.

The events of "Bleeding Kansas" began with a compromise created by Democrat Senator Stephen Douglas that would allow Kansas and Nebraska to decide for themselves whether they wanted to be free or slave states. This single piece of legislation likely did more to push the nation toward Civil War than any other enacted at the time. It led to a rebellion in the Democrat party (leading to the death of the Whig party and the establishment of the Republican party) and a violent series of events out west.

More than 5,000 pro-slavery Missourians marched into Kansas and illegally seized the polling places, installing a legislature that made even speaking out against slavery a crime. The anti-slavery settlers quickly established their own government and were backed by abolitionists, who sent in reinforcement troops and plenty of rifles. Political bickering soon turned to bloodshed, with shootings, stabbings and murders occurring across the state. When a pro-slavery sheriff was killed in Lawrence, 800 of his supporters raided the town in search of his killer, leaving behind death and destruction in their wake.

The violence in Kansas even reached as far as the U.S. Senate, where South Carolina Senator Preston Brooks physically attacked abolitionist Senator Charles Sumner. Sumner had spent two days denouncing the actions of the pro-slavery mob in Lawrence before Brooks hammered him into unconsciousness with his gold-headed walking stick.

John Brown was enraged by the Lawrence raid and planned retaliation. On May 24, 1856, shortly after the violence in Lawrence, Brown and six of his followers (including three of his sons) executed five pro-slavery settlers at Pottawatomie Creek. These murders elevated the level of violence in the region and Kansas did not stop bleeding until more than 200 people were dead.

Brown continued the fight over the next three years. During this time, many more met with violence at his hands. He also liberated a number of Missouri slaves at gunpoint and escorted them to freedom in Canada. Mentally unstable or not, Brown clearly had a charismatic personality that attracted a loyal band of followers wherever he went. He was joined in Kansas, and later in Virginia, by a cross-section of society: farmers, artisans, lawyers, poets, shopkeepers and former slaves. Almost none of them hewed to Brown's fervent Calvinism and many of them bristled at his domineering leadership. What they shared, though, was a militant commitment to destroying an institution that felt violated the nation's founding promise of liberty and freedom for all. Based on letters written by some of the men involved in the Harpers Ferry raid, they were not suicidal zealots who blindly followed a cult leader to certain death; they were idealistic young men, willing to leave their farms and families behind for a cause they cherished – not unlike the men who took up arms in the war that soon followed.

Brown also had many supporters that did not fit the image of wild-eyed fanatics. His core financial backers were wealthy businessmen, ministers and reformers. Brown also drew covert support from Frederick Douglass, Harriet Tubman and other well-known black abolitionists. And while many in the North condemned Brown's use of violence, they were galvanized by his courage and his willingness to go to extremes in the fight against the institution of slavery.

But despite all of the support for Brown and his ideals, his plan to fulfill "the great work of his life" at Harpers Ferry was an ill-conceived one.

Over the course of three years, Brown developed the fervent belief that he could almost single-handedly free the slaves of the

Harper's Ferry in 1859

South by military force. He would lead his followers into Harpers Ferry, a strategic location on the Maryland border. At first glance, the town was an unlikely place for a slave revolt. It wasn't close to the vast plantations that held hundreds of slaves. In fact, most of the surrounding farms were owned by middle-class men who owned few, if any, slaves. The town was made up of mostly factory and government workers and ironically, nearly half of Harpers Ferry's residents were free blacks. But on the other hand, it was located at the junction of the Potomac and Shenandoah rivers and was a crossroads for major rail and road travel. Harpers Ferry also boasted a munitions factory and a federal arsenal. If Brown and his men could seize the arsenal, they could ship out arms for slave uprisings throughout the South.

All through the summer of 1859, Brown worked hard to gather militant abolitionists to his banner. He sent up a base of operations at a small farmhouse located south of Sharpsburg, Maryland. He gathered 400 rifles and 950 iron-tipped spikes with which he would arm his men. But as summer turned to fall and his legion failed to form, Brown grew impatient and decided to take action. God was on his side. Once word spread of his rebellion, Brown believed, slaves would flock to the arsenal and take up arms with him.

Shortly before midnight on October 16, Brown and his "army" of 21 men left the farm and traveled to Harpers Ferry under the cover of darkness. As they approached the railway station, the baggage master, a free black man named Haywood Shepherd, came out to see what was going on. When he tried to stop their wagons, a shot rang out and the baggage master was killed. Ironically, a black man had become the first victim of Brown's rebellion to free the slaves.

Brown and his men took over several buildings in town and captured a number of hostages. One of them was the great-grand-nephew of George Washington, who was forced to give Brown a sword that had been a gift to Washington from Frederick the Great of Prussia. Brown strapped it on for the battle ahead. They overwhelmed a small force of defenders at the arsenal, and after setting up their headquarters in the brick engine-house, they waited for the slaves to rise up from the surrounding countryside and rush to Harpers Ferry.

But the slaves never came. Instead, Brown and his followers were attacked by the angry white residents of the town. They laid siege to the arsenal and Brown retreated to the stoutly built fire hall as the mob shot at anyone who dared to show himself. One of Brown's men, a free black man named Dangerfield Newby, was shot and killed as he tried to escape. Members of the mob cut off his ears as souvenirs and then flung his corpse into a hog pen in a nearby alley. The frightened animals ripped it apart.

Before Brown's "great work" was done, nine more of his men – including two of his sons – would die.

On Tuesday morning, October 17, the citizen's militia was joined by a detachment of U.S. Marines under the command of Lieutenant Colonel Robert E. Lee. Brown refused to surrender and Lee ordered an assault. The Marines stormed the building and within three minutes, the rebellion was over.

The U.S. Marine's attack on Brown's position in the federal arsenal.

Brown and his surviving followers were placed on trial and while the verdict of treason was a foregone conclusion, Brown turned the trial into a platform for his abolitionist beliefs. Bound to a stretcher throughout the proceedings because of his wounds, Brown refused to address the matter of his treason, choosing instead to put slavery – and all of America – on trial. Brown declared, "I believe that to have interfered as I have done, as I have always freely admitted I have done, in behalf of His despised poor, was no wrong but right. Now, if it is deemed necessary that I should forfeit my life for the furtherance of the ends of justice, and mingle my blood further with the blood of my children and with the blood of millions in this slave country, whose rights are disregarded by the wicked, cruel and unjust enactments, I submit. So let it be done!"

Brown, a failure in business and battle, managed to triumph through the power of his words and in his bravery when it came to facing death. He "will make the gallows glorious like the cross," Ralph Waldo Emerson stated five days after Brown was sentenced to death. Henry David Thoreau and others echoed this praise. But as Virginia Governor Henry Wise drily noted, if Brown was mad, so were the thousands of "like maniacs" in the North who came to regard him as a hero and martyr.

White Southerners were unhinged by John Brown. In the aftermath of Harpers Ferry, they saw abolitionist conspiracies everywhere, threatening their homes, property and way of life. Their paranoia led to the arrest and occasional lynching of Yankee peddlers and anyone else deemed to be spreading slave discontent. In Congress, Mississippi Senator Jefferson Davis warned of "a thousand John Browns" invading the South, and stated that if Southern sovereignty and property were no longer secure within the Union, "we will dissever the ties that bind us together, even if it rushes us into a sea of blood."

Of course, this is exactly what happened. The doomed raid at Harpers Ferry was devised by a man whose military savvy was as faulty as his business judgment but the attack exposed – and greatly worsened – the angry divide between the North and the South that led to secession and the Civil War.

John Brown might have believed that this result meant his raid was a success, even though at the time he went to the gallows, he could not have foreseen what was to come in the years that followed. To Brown, the rebellion was only the first step of many that he was destined to make – ending in a sea of blood that would ultimately free the American slaves. He had much more to accomplish during his time on Earth and left this world with much in the way of unfinished business still waiting to be carried out. Leaving such things unresolved is the most likely reason for a spirit to be bound to the Earth. And the most likely place for discontented spirits to linger is the place where they suffered the most intense trauma before death.

And so it is with Harpers Ferry, the scene of Brown's greatest glory and his most heartbreaking defeat. Over the years, there have been many ghost sightings in Harpers Ferry but one of the most vivid occurred in 1974. Throughout that summer, visitors to the town frequently commented on the "John Brown re-enactor" whom they saw putting on a realistic performance at the fire hall of the old armory, the site of Brown's last stand. Apparently, this tall, gaunt figure, dressed in old-fashioned clothing and with wild white hair and straggling beard was a dead ringer for John Brown, looking like he did in photographs taken around the time of the raid. Most assumed that the man had been hired to portray John Brown by the National Park Service, which now owns and operates the site, but they were wrong. National Park Service employees knew nothing about the man. A number of tourists photographed the "re-enactor" but when they developed their photos, they found that everything else turned out fine, but the old man was simply missing. Five or six of these photos were sent to the National Park Service office with a note describing the incident.

In another strange incident, a visitor decided to take a stroll near the old fire hall on the night of October 16, the anniversary of the raid. Hearing voices coming from the building, he went to see what was going on and allegedly came face-to-face with men in 1850s-era clothing who were holding rifles. An older man, with an intense, piercing gaze, began to question the visitor, who turned tail and ran. He nearly collapsed when he heard the sound of gunfire behind him. He didn't stop running until he was back in his hotel room. Was this just a re-enactment of the John Brown raid that was stumbled upon by an unknowing tourist? One might think so, until a check revealed there was nothing going on at the historic site that evening.

If John Brown still lingers at Harpers Ferry, he may not do so alone. He is said to be joined by Dangerfield Newby, the first of his men to be killed during the raid. Newby was a former slave who had joined up with Brown so that he could rescue his wife and children from slavery in Virginia. His family was owned by a planter near Warrenton, who had originally told Newby that he could buy their freedom. Newby saved up the money, but then was turned down. Angry and bitter, he joined up with Brown's crusade.

During the fighting, Newby, wearing baggy pants and an old slouch hat, fled from the arsenal and was killed. Shot in the neck, he bled to death in the street and then his ears were cut off and his body was thrown into a hog pen. The animals tore him apart and devoured his body. The mob saw it happen and did nothing to stop it. According to author Joseph Barry, they did not appear to "be at all squeamish about the flavor or the quality of their pork that winter."

According to newspaper and eyewitness accounts, Dangerfield Newby's ghost has been seen at the scene of his death. In Hog Alley, located between High and Potomac Streets, the apparition of a man in baggy pants and a slouch hat has been seen walking down the alleyway. Witnesses are left with the vivid impression of a torn and bloody throat before he fades from view.

1864: "MURDER & BUTCHERY"
The Fort Pillow Massacre

The battle fought at Fort Pillow on April 12, 1864 was not one of the bloodiest of the Civil War. It would likely be barely remembered today if not for the fact that it ended with the massacre of surrendered black troops who fought for the Union. While it has been called "one of the bleakest, saddest events of American military history," there are many modern historians who insist the battle was not a massacre at all, and that Confederate troops were ordered to stand down as soon as their officers realized the soldiers were on a rampage. But are these explanations enough to wash the blood from the hands of the man who was seen as responsible for the massacre – Major General Nathan Bedford Forrest?

And, more eerily, are they enough to finally put the spirits of the dead to rest?

When asked to name the greatest soldier of the Civil War, Robert E. Lee replied, "A man I have never seen, sir. His name is Forrest."

Nathan Bedford Forrest was an extraordinary man, a hero to many and a demon to others, who stained his reputation because of allegations stemming from his capture of Fort Pillow and his part in creating the original Ku Klux Klan.

General Nathan Bedford Forrest

During the war, Forrest killed 30 men in hand-to-hand combat and had 20 horses shot out from under him. General William T. Sherman said, "Forrest is the devil... I will order them [two of his officers] to make up a force and go out to follow Forrest to the death, if it costs ten thousand lives and breaks the treasury. There will never be peace in Tennessee until Forrest is dead."

To the Federal army, he might have been "that devil Forrest" but to the Confederates in Tennessee and Mississippi, he was a hero. He was the embodiment of the ideal Southern soldier: fearless, enterprising, honor-bound and unstoppable.

Forrest was born in 1821, the son of a blacksmith in Bedford County, Tennessee. Although he had little formal education, he was smart, well-liked, hardworking and a natural leader. When it was rumored that Mexico might invade Texas, Forrest went off to fight. But when that war never happened, he set off to make his fortune in the cattle business with his uncle in Mississippi.

He got his first taste of violence in March 1845 when a planter named Matlock, two Matlock brothers and an overseer started trouble with Forrest's uncle during a business dispute. One of the Matlocks shot at Forrest, missing him and hitting the uncle. Forrest fired back with a two-shot pistol, each shot wounding one of the Matlocks. Out of ammunition, he attacked the other Matlock with a knife as the overseer fled the scene. Although outnumbered – and wounded – he proved that he was not an easy man to take down.

Forrest earned a sterling reputation in the community. He was soft-spoken except when angry, then his furious temper erupted. As a chivalrous Southern gentleman, he treated women with great deference and never tolerated dirty stories or foul language, especially in a woman's presence. He didn't drink and never smoked, although he did enjoy gambling and horse racing. He was exceedingly clean and when his headquarters became dirty during the war, he would often be seen sweeping it himself.

Forrest became a millionaire in the 1850s while involved in the slave trade. Working from Memphis, he was impeccably honest in all of his business dealings, but there was no overlooking the fact that he was trading in human lives. Oddly, Forrest actually freed his own slaves.

When the war came, Forrest, as a wealthy man, had much to lose and he opposed secession. He hoped for a regional compromise but when Tennessee seceded, he followed his loyalty to the South and enlisted as a private (as did his youngest brother and 15-year-old son) in Captain Josiah White's Tennessee Mounted Rifles. But Forrest did not remain in the enlisted ranks for long. Local notables petitioned the governor and he was soon promoted to lieutenant colonel charged with raising his own regiment of mounted rangers. Troopers were asked to bring their own horses, equipment and arms but for those men without, Forrest bought 500 Navy Colt pistols, 100 saddles and other cavalry gear, which he smuggled out of neutral Kentucky.

His first major engagement was at Sacramento, Kentucky. His men raced to attack the enemy, engaging first in skirmish fire, and then in a head-on charge that broke the Federals and sent them reeling back through the town. Forrest led the charge against the retreating Union forces. Fighting with a saber and pistol, he brought down several enlisted men and disabled an officer, who was taken prisoner. Forrest was like a man possessed during the action, earning him respect from his men and fear from his enemy.

Forrest fought next at Fort Donelson, battling against the tightening Federal grip around the besieged fort, which fronted the Cumberland River. The first plan agreed to by the Confederate generals Gideon Pillow, John B. Floyd and Simon B. Buckner was to force their way through the Union right. In the fierce fighting that followed – during which two horses were killed beneath him – Forrest and his men opened a wide hole that would have allowed the Confederate Army to escape to Nashville, but General Pillow recalled the troops to their original lines.

That night, the commanders decided to surrender the fort. Forrest, disgusted, told his superiors that the men had a lot more fight left in them and convinced them to let him bring out his own command if he could. He reportedly told his troops, "Boys, these people are talking about surrendering, and I am going out of this place or bust hell wide open." He rallied his men behind him and on February 16, 1862, they rode out into the frosty night and left Fort Donelson behind.

Forrest and his men fought at Shiloh and when General Beauregard decided to retreat, Forrest was assigned the rear guard, where he battled William T. Sherman at Fallen Timbers. In an engagement of typical Forrest-style fury, he charged the Federals, broke through their ranks and suddenly found himself cut off and surrounded by Union soldiers, all intent in killing him. One of the Federals shoved a rifle barrel into his side and pulled the trigger, firing a bullet that lodged near his spine. But Forrest merely grunted with pain, dragged a Federal soldier up behind him as a shield and shot his way out of the clutch of enemy soldiers. He dropped the bullet-ridden Yankee once he was safe.

Thought to be gravely wounded, Forrest suffered through a painful surgery. The doctors probed the wound but were unable to find the bullet lodged in the small of his back. He was given two month's leave to recover, but he only took three weeks, spending most of that time calling for new recruits with an advertisement that cheerfully read: "Come on boys, if you want a heap of fun and to kill some Yankees!"

After his recovery, Forrest took command of a new cavalry unit made of up Tennesseans and Georgians, leading them on raids all across Tennessee. He developed a new tactic that fit his reputation for fearlessness. After shocking a Federal position by his sudden appearance or with a brief, violent attack, he would demand its unconditional surrender. While the Union troops considered his demand, Forrest would make a show of his riders and artillery by parading the same riders and same artillery past the Federals over and over again, fooling them into thinking that his force was much larger than it was.

He performed variations of this same tactic of demanding surrender, followed by the bluff, throughout the entire war. It was crucial to his success because his troops were usually poorly equipped. To gain an adequate supply of guns and ammunition, his men had to take them from the Federals. He was essentially using the Union Army as his quartermaster.

By late July 1862, Forrest had earned the rank of brigadier general and was continuing to lead his men on raids across the state. However, he was irritated by the treatment that he felt he was receiving from General Braxton Bragg. Forrest was a volatile man and even a perceived slight could make him angry. Bragg tended to think that Forrest was best suited for raids and recruiting and tended not to incorporate his troopers with the rest of the cavalry. He consistently pulled them out and sent them on raids across the countryside. Forrest never minded the action, but he came to resent Bragg's limitation of his role in the war.

Forrest was aggressive but he was also a realist and argued against an attack ordered by one of his friends, General Joseph Wheeler, on a Federal position at Dover, near Fort Donelson, in February 1863. The attack itself was a failure — in part because Forrest charged the Union position when he thought they were retreating; they weren't. Forrest's horse was blown out from under him but he survived. His temper flared after the attack and he wrote Wheeler:

I mean no disrespect to you; you know my personal feelings of friendship for you. You can have my sword if you demand it; but there is one thing that I do want you to put in your report to General Bragg – tell him that I will be in my coffin before I will fight again under your command.

Wheeler assured Forrest of his esteem for him and the moment passed. Forrest would serve under Wheeler again in the future but the incident showed that even Forrest's friends were not safe from his legendary temper.

In April 1863, Forrest and his men pursued a unit of Federal raiders under the command of Colonel Abel D. Streight, who charged across northern Alabama. Forrest remained close behind Streight for miles, but it looked like the Federal colonel had bested him when he escaped over Black Creek and burned the bridge behind him. A local woman (Emma Sansom, who received an official commendation for her service) showed Forrest a nearby crossing and the Confederates continued the chase. Finally, Forrest called upon Streight to surrender his exhausted troops and employed the old strategy of moving around a small number of artillery pieces until Streight was shocked at the number of cannons that had been able to keep up with the chase. He quickly surrendered his 1,466 men – only to find that Forrest had less than 600! The reckless tactic had worked once again.

Forrest was both hated and feared by Union commanders, but his daring had also earned him their grudging respect. Once, seeing a white flag over a Union fortification, he rode up, only to be told by an honorable Federal officer that it was merely a signal flag, not a flag of truce, and that he should return to his men. Forrest saluted the man and galloped back to his lines.

He was less fortunate during a misunderstanding with one of his own officers, Lieutenant A.W. Gould, whom Forrest had rashly and wrongly accused of cowardice and ordered transferred to another unit. Gould met with Forrest at the Masonic Hall in Columbia, Tennessee, to personally protest the order and things became heated. When Forrest refused to reconsider, Gould allegedly pulled a gun on him. The gun misfired, wounding Forrest, who struck back with a folding knife, slamming it into Gould's ribs as he pushed the man's gun hand away.

Gould fled and was taken in by two doctors, who tried to stop the bleeding. Forrest was assisted by another doctor, who told him the gunshot wound in his side might prove fatal. Forrest angrily pushed him aside and stumbled out into the street swearing, "No damned man shall kill me and live!" A man tried to stop him, saying Gould was mortally wounded, but Forrest didn't care. He found a revolver and burst in on Gould as he was being attended to by his doctors. Gould tried to escape, shambling out of the house and collapsing in a patch of weeds. Forrest walked over to him, rolled him over with his boot and, seemingly satisfied that the foe had no fight left in him, casually walked away.

Forrest's wound turned out to not be fatal, but Gould was not so lucky. Once he heard that Gould was likely to die, Forrest became remorseful – or more likely, he had simply cooled off. He paid for Gould's treatment according to most accounts, the two men reconciled before Gould finally died.

Forrest's wound did not keep him down for long. Within two weeks, he was back in action, covering the retreat of Bragg's army. He was wounded again at Chickamauga, with another bullet lodged near his spine. He broke his rule of abstinence by accepting whiskey for the pain, but stayed in the battle – indeed, staying in the battle longer than his commanding general Braxton Bragg did. With the Union forces in retreat, Forrest sent a dispatch through General Leonidas Polk for Bragg, laying out what he saw of the Union evacuation and adding that he believed the Confederates should press forward as rapidly as possible. He followed up this dispatch with a second, urging speed in the attack. His reports were seconded by a Confederate soldier who had been taken prisoner by the Federals, but had escaped. He was sent to Bragg to relay information about the Union retreat but the skeptical Bragg failed to act quickly.

Bragg's advance on the Union retreat was not only, in Forrest's view, lackluster at best, but he redoubled the offense by sending an order to Forrest that his command was being transferred to Wheeler. This set the stage for the greatest conflict in Forrest's career. He rode to Bragg's camp, burst into his tent and shouted a speech of damnation that ended with these words:

I have stood your meanness as long as I intend to. You have played the part of a damned scoundrel, and you are a coward, and if you were any part of a man I would slap your face jaws [sic] and force you to resent it.

You may as well not issue any more orders for me, for I will not obey them. And as I hold you personally responsible for any further indignities you try to inflict on me.

You have threatened to arrest me for not obeying your orders promptly. I dare you to do it, and I say to you that if you ever again try to interfere with me or cross my path, it will be at the peril of your life.

Bragg decided to grant Forrest a transfer out of his command.

In early 1864, Forrest's youngest brother was killed in action. To avenge his death, Forrest personally charged the enemy in such fierce fighting that his men thought he was suicidal. By March 1864, Forrest was seeking to avenge more than just his brother: He was seeking redress for outrages against pro-Confederate Tennesseans at the hands of Union troops and pro-Union militia. The alleged crimes included murder, detention without charge, arson, extortion and the torture, mutilation and murder of one of Forrest's officers, who had been captured while looking for deserters. Forrest sent a letter of protest to the Union commander at Memphis and a dispatch to Confederate General Leonidas Polk, but he also prepared for action, which would lead to the most controversial battle of his career at Fort Pillow, Tennessee.

In March 1864, Forrest launched a month-long cavalry raid into western Tennessee and Kentucky. His object was to capture Union prisoners and supplies and demolish posts and fortifications from Paducah, Kentucky, to Memphis. Forrest's cavalry corps consisted of divisions led by Brigadier Generals James R. Chalmers and Abraham Buford. The first of the two significant engagements during the raid was the Battle of Paducah on March 25, and Forrest's men did considerable damage to the town and its military supplies. Numerous skirmishes occurred throughout the region in late March and early April.

Needing supplies, Forrest planned to attack Fort Pillow with about 1,500 to 2,500 men. He had detached part of his command under Buford to strike Paducah again. He knew there was a small force of men at Fort Pillow and they would have all of the horses and supplies that he needed. He didn't expect much resistance at the fort since the Union garrison consisted of only about 600 men, divided nearly equally between black and white troops. The black soldiers belonged to the 6th U.S. Colored Heavy Artillery and a section of the 2nd U.S. Colored Light Artillery, under the overall command of Major Lionel F. Booth. Many were former slaves and understood the personal consequences of a loss to the Confederates – at best an immediate return to slavery rather than being treated as a prisoner of war. Some Confederates had threatened to kill any Union black troops they encountered. The white soldiers were predominantly new recruits from the 13th Tennessee Cavalry, a Federal regiment from western Tennessee, commanded by Major William F. Bradford. Forrest thought little of the black soldiers and considered the pro-Union Tennesseans to be traitors to the Confederacy.

Forrest didn't think much of Fort Pillow itself, either. Located about 40 miles north of Memphis, the fort was built by Brigadier General Gideon Johnson Pillow in early 1862 and was used by both sides during the war. With the fall of New Madrid and Island No. 10 to Union forces, Confederate troops evacuated Fort Pillow on June 4, in order to avoid being cut off from the rest of the Confederate Army. Union forces occupied Fort Pillow on June 6, and used it to protect the river approach to Memphis. The fort stood on a high bluff and was protected by three lines of trenches arranged in a semi-circle, with a protective parapet that was surrounded by a ditch. During the battle, the parapet would prove to be a disadvantage to the defenders because they couldn't fire upon the approaching enemy without mounting to the top, which subjected them to enemy fire. A Union gunboat, the *USS New Era*, commanded by Captain James Marshall, was also used for the fort's defense.

Forrest arrived at Fort Pillow at 10:00 a.m. on April 12. By this time, Chalmers had already surrounded the fort. A stray bullet struck Forrest's horse and he was slightly injured when it fell. This would be the first of three horses that he lost that day. He deployed sharpshooters around the higher ground that overlooked the fort, bringing many of the occupants into their direct line of fire. Major Booth was killed by a sharpshooter's bullet to the chest and Bradford assumed command. Within the hour, the Confederates has captured two rows of barracks at the southern end of the fort. The Union soldiers had failed to destroy the buildings before the Confederates overran then and this mistake allowed the Confederates to rain murderous fire on the defending garrison.

Rifle and artillery fire continued for the next several hours. According to his usual procedure, Forrest sent a note demanding the fort's surrender, threatening the occupants that if they failed to give up, he would not be responsible for the fate of the Federal command. Major Bradford replied, concealing his identity in the hope that Forrest would not realize that Booth had been killed, and asked for an hour to consider the demand. Forrest, who believed that reinforcing troops would soon arrive by river, replied that he would only allow 20 minutes, and that "If at the expiration of that time the fort is not surrendered, I shall assault it." Bradford's final reply was, "I will not surrender." At that, Forrest ordered his bugler to sound the charge.

An illustration of the "Fort Pillow Massacre"

The Confederate assault was furious. On this rare occasion, Forrest did not lead the charge. He was nursing a sore hip brought upon by his horse falling on top of him. While the sharpshooters continued to fire at the fort, the first wave of attackers entered the ditch and stood while the second wave used their backs as steeping stones. These men then reached down and helped the first wave scramble up the embankment. The attack proceeded flawlessly, with little gunfire, except from the sharpshooters and around the flanks. Their fire on the *USS New Era* forced the sailors to close the gun ports and hold their fire.

The sharpshooters paused in firing on the fort as the men went up and over the embankment. They were now firing for the first time on the massed defenders, who fought briefly, but then broke and ran to the boat landing at the foot of the bluff, where they had been told that the Union gunboat would cover their withdrawal by firing grapeshot and canister rounds. But with the gun ports sealed, the boat never fired a single shot. The fleeing soldiers were subjected to fire both from the rear and from the flank, from the soldiers who had been firing at the gunboat. Many were shot down. Others reached the river only to drown, or be picked off in the water by marksmen on the bluff.

Conflicting reports of what happened in the next few minutes created the controversy of the Fort Pillow Massacre. Union and Confederate sources claimed that even though Union troops surrendered, Forrest's men massacred them in cold blood. Surviving members of the garrison said that most of their men surrendered and threw down their weapons, only to be shot and bayoneted by the attackers, who repeatedly shouted, "No quarter!"

The Joint Committee on the Conduct of the War immediately investigated the incident and concluded that Confederates shot most of the garrison after it had surrendered, but the reports that came in from a variety of sources made the events of the day even more confusing.

Lieutenant Daniel Van Horn of the 6th U.S. Colored Heavy Artillery stated in his official report: "There was never a surrender of the fort, both officers and men declaring that they never would surrender or ask for quarter." However, a Confederate sergeant, in a letter written home shortly after the battle said, "the poor, deluded negroes would run up to our men, fall upon their knees, and with uplifted hand scream for mercy, but were ordered to their feet and then shot down."

Forrest's men insisted that the Federals, although fleeing, held on to their weapons and frequently turned to shoot at them, forcing the Confederates to continue firing in self-defense. This claim is consistent with the discovery of numerous Federal rifles on the bluff near the river. The Union flag was still flying over the fort, which indicated that the garrison had not officially surrendered. A contemporary newspaper account from Jackson, Tennessee, stated that "General Forrest begged them to surrender," but "not the first sign of surrender was ever given." Similar accounts appeared in both Southern and Northern newspapers at the time.

Northerners, though, saw the battle only one way. They read newspapers with inflammatory headlines like "Attack on Fort Pillow – Indiscriminate Slaughter of the Prisoners – Shocking Scenes of Savagery; dispatches from Sherman's army declaring "there is a general gritting of teeth here." Reports from the *Missouri Democrat* told of the "fiendishness" of the Confederates' behavior and editorials in the *Chicago Tribune* accused them of "murder" and "butchery."

The *New York Times* reported (erroneously) on April 24:

The blacks and their officers were shot down, bayoneted and put to the sword in cold blood... Out of four hundred Negro soldiers only about twenty survive! At least three hundred of them were destroyed after the surrender! This is the statement of the rebel General Chalmers himself to our informant.

Later, in his memoirs, Ulysses S. Grant, who was not present at the battle, wrote:

Forrest, however, fell back rapidly, and attacked the troops at Fort Pillow, a station for the protection of the navigation of the Mississippi River. The garrison consisted of a regiment of colored troops, infantry, and a detachment of Tennessee cavalry. These troops fought bravely, but were overpowered. I will leave Forrest in his dispatches to tell what he did with them. "The river was dyed," he [Forrest] says, "with the blood of the slaughtered for two hundred yards. The approximate loss was upward of five hundred killed, but few of the officers escaping. My loss was about twenty killed. It is hoped that these facts will demonstrate to the Northern people that Negro soldiers cannot cope with Southerners." Subsequently, Forrest made a report in which he left out the part which shocks humanity to read.

In 1864, the alleged massacre was investigated by General William T. Sherman. He declined to seek retaliation for the incident even though he had been authorized to do so by General Grant, if the facts justified it. Apparently, Sherman thought they did not. Grant did not question Sherman's decision at the time.

As it turned out, casualty rates during the battle were not even as high as Forrest had estimated. The Confederate casualties were low (14 killed and 86 wounded) and for the Union, of the 585 to 605 men present, 277 to 297 of them were reported as dead. Some historians believe these reports were exaggerated. However, it was obvious that the soldiers' race played a role in determining their fate. Of the black members of the garrison, only 58 were taken prisoner, compared to 168 white prisoners taken. But not all of the soldiers who were shot were black – many claimed that even some of the white men who surrendered, including Major Bradford, were killed.

What really happened that day? Was it the mass slaughter that some accounts claimed? No one who was not present can say with complete authority but it's likely that, in the heat of the battle, things got out of control. Confederate anger at the thought of black men firing guns at them, along with the garrison's initial reluctance to surrender, resulted in tragedy. Forrest and his officers, despite their dislike for the blacks and the traitorous Tennessee Union men, tried to rein in their men as quickly as they could, once they realized that what had started as a battle had turned into a bloody rampage. By then, though, it was too late and one of the most horrific events of the war had already taken place.

The Confederates evacuated Fort Pillow that evening, so little was gained except a temporary disruption of Union operations. When word spread of the "Fort Pillow Massacre," it became a Union rallying cry that cemented their resolve to see the war through to its conclusion.

Forrest continued to fight and in June, fought his greatest independent battle, ambushing Federal forces under General Samuel D. Sturgis at the Battle of Brice's Crossroads, where he sent Sturgis' much larger force into a wild retreat. Forrest not only defeated the Federals but also relieved them of 16 pieces of artillery, 176 wagons and huge stores of arms and ammunition. General Sherman was appalled by Sturgis' retreat, but noted that, "Forrest is the devil, and I think he has got some of our troops under cower... I will order them to make up a force and go out and follow Forrest to the death, if it costs ten thousand lives and breaks up the treasury. There will never be peace in Tennessee until Forrest is dead!"

Unfortunately for the Confederate cause, Forrest was not sent to bedevil Sherman in Tennessee and then in Georgia as he made his march to the sea. Instead, Forrest was kept in Mississippi, where he continued to fight, even though the hard years of the war were starting to take a toll on his health. He was shot again, this time in the foot, at the Battle of Harrisburg, near Tupelo, Mississippi, and his command was shattered. Despite rumors to the contrary, Forrest survived and his return to the field reinvigorated the Confederate cavalry.

He spent the last year of the war conducting his legendary raids and rallying the troops for the failing Confederacy. He raided Memphis in August 1864, captured a Union garrison at Athens, Alabama, in September, destroyed a heavily guarded trestle at Sulphur Springs, and caused so much trouble that Sherman sent 30,000 men after him, hoping to "press Forrest to death." Forrest and his men also captured Federal gunboats and shelled Union transports on the river. At Johnsonville, Tennessee, on the Tennessee River, they inflicted millions of dollars' worth of damage on Federal supply depots in November 1864.

Finally, Forrest was recalled to join in the bloody futility of General John Bell Hood's invasion of Tennessee, in which the Confederate army of the west smashed itself to pieces, and then retreated, protected by Forrest, through ice and snow. Forrest finished the war as a Lieutenant General, continuing to fight battle after battle until there was simply nothing left to fight for.

When it came time to surrender, he dismissed the ideas of other commanders to lead his men to Mexico or retreat to the West and continue the war there. He knew the end had come, although defeat left a bitter taste in his mouth. By his own confession, the war "had pretty well wrecked him." His finances were equally shattered. He sold some of his land and worked to farm the rest and return his sawmill to operation. He employed newly freed blacks – at higher than standard wages, according to the Freedmen's Bureau – and went into partnership with several former Union officers.

Oddly, due to the reputation that he has gained in modern times, Forrest exhibited what a Union officer who worked for the Freedmen's Bureau called "a dangerous leniency" with the free blacks in the area. It was one thing to treat the freedmen well – which Forrest did to an unparalleled degree – but it was another thing to make liberal loans to them and allow them to buy and carry arms, which Forrest also did.

Forrest was a man used to violence, which was one of the symptoms of Reconstruction. Disgruntled Confederate soldiers were stripped of their rights. Federal troops occupied the South, executing the laws that had been passed as punishment by the Radical Republicans who controlled the U.S. Congress. Forrest was indicted for treason, although he was never brought to trial. He tried to live by the advice that he always gave his men – to obey the law – but it was difficult in such volatile times. He applied for a pardon from President Andrew Johnson, spent his time working at a variety of business interests and got involved with the newly former Ku Klux Klan, which he hoped would restore order to the South.

What Forrest did within the Klan is unknown, if for no other reason than he denied ever being a member or having anything other than a general knowledge of its doings, even though he is often considered to have been elected as its first commander, or "Grand Wizard." By his own testimony, he was a not a member, but was in sympathy with the organization and would have cooperated in its fight against Reconstruction radicals.

Forrest openly saw the Klan as a defender of Southern rights and publicly dismissed reports of its crimes as untrue. He believed that it was led by former Confederate officers who were honorable and disciplined and whose purpose was not to spread anarchy or insurgency, but to preserve order and peace.

The view that the U.S. government did not have the interests of the South, or the Constitution, at heart, was widespread among former Confederates. They believed the Radical Republicans were using their power in Congress to try and break the former Confederacy, denying them their political and civil rights and settling up newly freed blacks as uninformed voters to push through the Republican agenda. It was an insult to any honorable man who, like Forrest, was now doing his best to be part of the country that had conquered the Confederacy. And Forrest was not a man to tolerate insults well.

In Forrest's public statements, the Klan was not an anti-black organization – except in its origins, which were, it was said, to

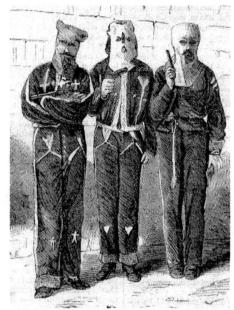

Ku Klux Klan members of the 1860s

defend white women and children from hungry, armed, newly freed blacks looking for food on Southern farms – but an anti-Radical Republican organization. Its primary purpose was to protect Southerners from pro-Reconstruction groups and the only reason that Klan nightriders were threatening blacks was to keep them from coming out to vote in sham elections.

So, whether or not Forrest led the Ku Klux Klan, he did admit to helping to dissolve it as an organization in 1869. By that time, he felt that many of the group's new members could no longer be controlled and that it had merely become a white vigilante organization, something which Forrest publicly opposed.

Nathan Bedford Forrest died in 1877, a complex and complicated man. He was a hero to many and a "devil" to others, but no matter what one might think of him, he always tried to conduct himself with honor, even though he sometimes failed. To the men of the former Confederacy, he was one of the great warriors on the battlefield and covered himself in glory throughout the war. Most Northerners, though, had a different opinion. There is no doubt that his history will always be stained in the minds of many by his connection to the Ku Klux Klan (whatever it may have been) and by the massacre that took place at Fort Pillow.

Today, Fort Pillow is part of a state park in Tennessee's Lauderdale County. Located on the Chickasaw Bluffs, overlooking the Mississippi River, it is a haven for birdwatchers, fishermen and outdoor enthusiasts. Although rich in historic and archaeological significance, there is little remaining today to remind visitors of the horror that occurred there in 1864 – at least on the surface.

In the years since the battle, ghost stories have often been told about the battlefield surrounding the site of the old fort. In 1866, two years after the battle, a cemetery was created for the soldiers on both sides of the conflict who were killed there. In the days after the fighting, they had been hastily buried in a field to the south of the fort. One year later, in 1867, about 250 of the bodies were moved to the National Cemetery in Memphis. Not surprisingly, ghost stories emerged from the disturbance of the graves. According to the stories, the workers on the exhumation crew heard eerie cries, disembodied voices and even claimed to see apparitions of black soldiers walking about in the early morning fog.

And while those stories were told nearly a century and a half ago, strange tales of a haunting at Fort Pillow still continue today. Battlefields are places frequently said to be infested with ghosts, or at least with residual hauntings, those imprints of memory that linger behind at locations where terrible events occurred. There is no question that what happened at Fort Pillow in 1864 was terrible and it seems that memories of it have never left the place. Even now, visitors to the battlefield claim to hear shouts, screams, cries for help, and even a bizarre wailing for which no source seems to exist. Ghost hunters who venture out to the site claim to have recorded bone-chilling sounds and voices that call out for mercy, begging not to be killed.

There is little that is uncomplicated about the history of Fort Pillow and the haunting that seems to exist at the fort today further muddies the waters of the past, so to speak. It is an unsettling pace and one that should be visited by anyone with an interest in the mysteries of the war – and with a penchant for encountering those mysteries first hand.

1873: BLOODY EASTER SUNDAY
The Colfax Massacre

In April 1865, at the Virginia home of Wilmer McLean and his family in the village of Appomattox Court House, General Robert E. Lee surrendered the Confederate Army of Virginia to General Ulysses S. Grant. The two men treated one another with the deference due to old comrades in arms and honored enemies and in a short period of time, they worked out an agreement that would bring an end to the war that had torn apart the country for the last four years.

Ever since that time, history has taught us that the meeting at Appomattox ended the war, and in many ways it did. But in countless other ways, the war between the North and the South raged on. One of the biggest problems that remained was the question of slavery – or at least the question of the former slaves who had been emancipated, but were now without livelihoods and who were stuck in the former Confederacy with their former masters. What would become of them? How were they to survive?

These questions burned with blood and violence for years to come and in 1873, one of the most horrific events in the history of American civil rights took place in a Louisiana county that had been named for Ulysses S. Grant himself. It is an event that is largely forgotten today, but it is one that can be traced back directly to the simmering tensions that were never solved at Appomattox that day in April 1865.

"Reconstruction" simply means "to build again," but there was nothing simple about the period of American history known as Reconstruction after the Civil War. Even while the war was still raging, the Union, under President Abraham Lincoln, debated about how to treat its soon-to-be-defeated enemy. Lincoln, in his second inaugural address, which was given about a month before Appomattox, stated that he was willing to be charitable toward the South, adding the famous words, "With malice toward none, with charity for all…"

But there were others, known as Radical Republicans, who pushed for a much firmer hand when the time came to deal with the defeated Confederate states and with the rights that would be extended to the four million former slaves that lived there. Lincoln wanted to give the freed male slaves the right to vote, but he also wanted to allow the Southern states back into the Union once at least 10 percent of the white voters took an oath of allegiance to the Union and agreed to the emancipation of the slaves. Lincoln also wanted to reimburse the Southerners for the loss of their slaves. As abhorrent as this policy seemed to abolitionists and Radical Republicans, he understood that without their slaves, Southern plantation owners and farmers would be ruined and their resentment would do much to keep the nation from healing.

However, the Radical Republicans rejected the policies of Lincoln and Andrew Johnson, who became president after Lincoln was killed. Johnson, originally from Tennessee, offered a pardon to all Southerners except leading Confederate generals, and authorized them to create new state governments. Freedmen were excluded from the process. Most of the new governments immediately enacted what were called "Black Codes," limiting the ability of the freed slaves to find work off their former plantations. The codes also refused them the right to vote and failed to provide public funds for their education.

Radical Republicans overrode Johnson's vetoes of their legislation, overturned his programs, and came within one vote of impeaching him. They divided the Southern states into five military districts, forced them to repeal the Black Codes, and mandated that each state agree, as a condition for returning to the Union, to give blacks full emancipation, including the right of the men to vote. They were also required to ratify the 14th Amendment to the Constitution, passed in 1866, which guaranteed blacks the same rights of citizenship as whites. But there was a more devious purpose behind what seemed to be the Radical Republicans fair treatment of blacks. They knew that by forcing such laws on the South, and allowed blacks to enter into political office for the first time in history, they would have complete and total control of the black voting blocs in the South. In this manner, they could not only keep an iron grip on the Southern political system, they could also control its wealth, which could be pillaged for personal gain.

Reluctantly, the Southern states complied and soon after began a second bloody and violent period in the South.

Whites, most of them former Confederate soldiers, began forming paramilitary organizations. Chief among them was the Ku Klux Klan, which began in Tennessee in 1865 and evolved, according to many historians, into a terrorist group. The Klan, which called itself the "Invisible Empire of the South," was allegedly led by former Confederate General Nathan Bedford Forrest (although, as noted in the previous chapter, Forrest never publicly admitted to being a member of the Klan). Soon after the end of the war, the Klan began to target blacks and white Republicans, initially by starting riots. In Memphis in 1866, a Klan-inspired riot killed 46 blacks and wounded 70 others. Two months later, in New Orleans, a white mob attacked blacks attending a suffrage convention and killed 37 of them.

In 1868, when Ulysses S. Grant was running for president on the Republican ticket, the Klan tried to keep black voters away from the polling places through violence, murder, intimidation and arson. In spite of their efforts, Grant easily won the election and was instrumental in passing laws that outlawed the Klan. According to Nathan Bedford Forrest, it had been disbanded in 1869 because of the violence associated with the elections.

But the Ku Klux Klan was not the only organization trying to retake control of the Southern states at the time. Other white groups sprang into existence and began fighting against the blacks and the Radical Republicans. By 1870, white Democrats had been returned to power in Alabama, Virginia, Tennessee, North Carolina and Georgia, but nowhere was the power struggle more vicious than in Louisiana.

The Republicans had been more successful hanging onto Louisiana for several reasons. White citizens were vastly outnumbered by blacks, particularly in the more populated parishes (as counties are called in Louisiana). Also, the black population of New Orleans was more powerful and sophisticated than in other southern cities. And finally, New Orleans was controlled directly by its powerful customhouse, where jobs were handed out by political patronage. The chief customs officer at the time was James F. Casey, who was married to the sister of Julia Grant, President's Grants wife. Casey wielded an enormous amount of power for the Republicans, although this power was not always used wisely.

When the Radical Republicans wanted to get Louisiana Governor Henry Clay Warmoth out of office – since he had supported Democrat causes and Grant disliked him personally – they held a state convention and kept

Warmoth from attending using federal troops, armed with rifles and two Gatling guns. In the Louisiana gubernatorial election of 1872, the Radical Republican candidate, an Illinois man brought in for the purpose named William Kellogg, defeated Democrat John McEnery, although the election was tainted with violence and voter fraud, making it hard to tell who actually won. In response, McEnery formed his own state legislature and his own militia, which tried and failed to take control of all of the police stations in New Orleans in March 1873.

The federal government made a few half-hearted attempts to restore order in Louisiana but then backed down, afraid that too strong of a response was liable to enrage white residents even more. So, for months, the state was governed by two governors and two legislatures – one run by the Republicans and one by the all-white Democrat party. Newspapers in New Orleans predicted that "a war of the races" was coming soon.

The unrest in the New Orleans began to spread out to the smaller towns in the region, including a place called Colfax in Grant Parish, along the Red River in northern Louisiana. The parish had been named for President Grant and the town itself was named after Grant's first-term vice-president Schuyler Colfax. It was one of the parishes created after the Civil War to build local support for the Republicans in Washington. Almost all of the land in the parish had originally been part of a large plantation that formerly belonged to the Calhoun family. Colfax was named as the parish seat, although it consisted of a collection of ramshackle old houses, many of which had been slave cabins before the war. The town's population was almost entirely made up of former slaves who now farmed small patches of land owned by white men who owned larger parcels of property in the area. As dismal as this sounds, a few things had changed since the war. The blacks earned a wage, although a small one, and could save a little of their money. A black Union army veteran opened his own general store in town and many of the black men formed political clubs and began voting in the local and national elections, starting in 1868. There were soon black men occupying minor political positions like justice of the peace, constable and county surveyor.

Many of the whites in Grant Parish, greatly outnumbered by their black neighbors, saw Colfax as an example of how Reconstruction was supposed to work and offered support to the community. The white Republican sheriff, Delos White, originally from New York, spoke highly of the blacks from Grant Parish, calling them "sober and industrious." He predicted that, with any favorable chance, they would soon be wealthier than the white men who lived in the area.

But not everyone felt this way. There were plenty of whites in the area who belonged to groups like the White League and the Knights of the White Gardenia, whose purpose, as stated in their bylaws, was "the better preservation of the white race and to see that the white blood was handed down unmixed with the offensive globule of African blood." Some of these men, led by a local Confederate Army veteran named Christopher Columbus Nash, went to Delos White's house on a night in the fall of 1871 and shot him to death when he came to the door.

The captain of the Louisiana state militia company stationed in Colfax at the time was a black war veteran named William Ward. He fearlessly arrested Nash and the others who had been involved the murders and soon after, Ward and members of his 72-man, all-black company exchanged gunfire with hooded nightriders, killing one and capturing others. Whites began claiming that the blacks had instituted a "reign of terror" in Colfax and cheered when a judge dismissed all charges against Nash and his men in November 1871. A year later, as Louisiana was fractured by warring factions, each side part of a different government, two armed forces prepared for battle in Colfax.

By early winter of 1873, violence had broken out across the state between the factions that supported Kellogg and those who backed McEnery. In the elections for sheriff and other officers in Grant Parish in November 1872, both sides claimed victory, but Henry Clay Warmoth, the lame duck governor, declared that the Democrats were the winners – and this included Christopher Columbus Nash, who became the sheriff of Grant Parish, the position formerly held by the man he had murdered.

But in January 1873, when Kellogg was sworn in as governor, he ousted the Democrats and named his own Republican slate. The Democrats refused to leave office and so the Republicans made a daring move. On the night of March 25, a mixed group of white and black men, including William Ward, broke into the Grant Parish courthouse (formerly a stable on the Calhoun plantation) and occupied it. They next day, they swore themselves into office and sent a message with their oaths of office to the secretary of state in Baton Rouge. The secretary filed the oaths and the men who held the courthouse were now officially sworn in. A white Republican named Dan Shaw took over the office of sheriff.

Naturally, though, it was not that easy. Angry Democrats, led by Nash and other former Confederates, gathered and decided that they would retake the courthouse – by force, if necessary. They put out a call for all white men who sympathized with their cause to meet at the courthouse in April. When he heard this, Ward, who had been removed from his position as head of the militia by former Governor Warmoth, managed to find two dozen poorly armed black men to guard the courthouse. Another group of black Republicans were assigned to search the home of a prominent Democrat attorney who lived in Colfax. It was believed that he had stolen a seal from the courthouse before the occupation. While searching, they came upon a small coffin that contained the embalmed body of the man's infant daughter. The tiny child had died six years earlier but he and his wife had kept the body in their home. The search party dumped the corpse out onto the porch, an act of unthinking callousness that enraged the whites who heard about it.

In early April, whites began to assemble in the fields around Colfax and the courthouse. Shots were exchanged with Ward's men. On the evening of April 5, a black supporter of Ward named McKinney was at home about three miles from Colfax, repairing a fence, when a dozen white riders pounded up the road, jumped the fence and surrounded the terrified man. As his wife and son watched from the porch, one of the men leaned down from his saddle and fired two shots into McKinney's head. The man let out a bloodcurdling scream and fell to the ground dead. The riders then had victory celebration around the body, shouting and making their horses prance, and then rode away into the dusk.

As word spread throughout the local population about McKinney's murder, armed black men and their families began to make their way to the Colfax courthouse. By Easter Sunday, April 13, there were 150 black men and about the same number of women and children at the courthouse. There was also a handful of white men among them.

That same morning, a force of 165 white horsemen gathered in a field outside of town. Half of them were former soldiers who had seen a good deal of combat during the war. They brought with them shotguns, muzzle-loading Enfield rifles, pistols and hunting knives. They also had a small cannon, which they moved about on a horse-drawn cart. They were led by Nash and other former Confederate officers, most of whom were members of the outlawed Klan and other white supremacy organizations. One of the more cautious officers, David Paul, gave the men a chance to ride away from the battle ahead, stating that even though it was a fight for the rights of the white man, the government might consider their actions to be treason. Sobered by his words, 25 of the men rode away. The remaining 140 men, led by Nash, rode across the fields to a spot about three-quarters of a mile from the courthouse. At this point, Nash took four of his men and rode under a white flag in the direction of the courthouse and called out for a meeting. Those occupying the courthouse sent out a former slave named Levi Allen to talk with them.

Nash told him that they wanted the courthouse but Allen insisted that they were planning to stay where they were until they received assistance from U.S. troops. Attempting to strike a deal, Nash told him that if the blacks left their weapons behind and abandoned the courthouse, they could leave the village unharmed, but Allen didn't believe him and refused to accept a promise of safe passage from the men outside. Disgusted, Nash gave the defenders 30 minutes to remove the women and children to safety. With nothing else to say, he turned his back and rode away.

The occupiers of the courthouse refused to surrender and sent their women and children fleeing into the woods. They also advised the few whites who stood with them, including Sheriff Dan Shaw, to leave as well, knowing they would be special targets for Nash's men. Then, William Ward took stock of his men. There were 150 of them, but only half (by some accounts, only one-third) had guns. To aid in their defense, they dug a trench in a semi-circle around the courthouse. Sadly though, they only had time to make it only about two feet deep, which offered little protection from a determined attack. They also improvised a homemade cannon from an old steam pipe, but when they tried to fire it, it exploded, injuring two men.

By noon, Nash's men were on the move. They were led by a skirmish line of the men with the best rifles, breech-loading repeaters that could do heavy damage to the defenders. Their military tactics were familiar to all of the veterans among them, using small forces to cover the flanks. When the skirmish line came to within 300 yards of the trench dug by the courthouse defenders, they waited for the cannon to be brought up. Its roar marked the start of the hostilities, followed by the crack of rifle fire that sent bullets flying over the heads of the defenders who crouched in the shallow trench. Fire was returned sporadically as the defenders tried to conserve their ammunition.

For two hours, both sides fought but did little damage to one another. The cannon was too far back to hurt anyone and the attacking whites were out of range of the defender's weapons, which were mostly shotguns. But then Nash's men found a gap in the levee near the Red River and used it to get behind the left flank of the black forces. The cannon was dragged to this spot, loaded with buckshot, and then blasted at the unsuspecting defenders from behind. The shot immediately killed one man. He was flung to the ground in a heap, his entrails torn out. This panicked the defenders, who left the trench and ran for the cover of the courthouse. Nash's men chased after them, firing their guns and shouting. They pulled the cannon along with them until it was 80 yards from the front of the courthouse; then they fired four more thunderous shots as the men struggled to get through the narrow door. Many of them, too terrified to try and get through the jam at the door, fled into the woods where the women and children were hiding. They were pursued by Nash's men, who swarmed among them, killing as many as they could. Some escaped and the whites gave up the chase, turning their attention back to the men who were trapped in the courthouse.

Nash had several choices about what to do next. He could besiege the place, although this would take some time and reinforcements might arrive for the defenders. He could also assault it, but this would certainly cost him many of his men. Or he could burn it down, which was what he decided to do. A burning torch was thrown onto the dry shingles of the roof and it immediately went up in flames. The defenders had no water to extinguish the blaze and so they tried to climb up into the courthouse's rafters and knock out the burning shingles. As they did, they were shot and killed by Nash's men.

With the fire blazing and smoke filling the courthouse, some of the defenders decided to give up. A dozen of them left the building, waving white pieces of paper or handkerchiefs in surrender. As soon as they were outside, Nash's men opened fire, killing several of them at close range. A few managed to escape, running away to hide beneath a nearby warehouse. When they were found, they were dragged out and murdered in the dirt.

By this time, dusk was beginning to fall. The last remaining defenders in the courthouse, who had been crouched under the floorboards for protection from the fire, were told that they would not be harmed if they came out and gave themselves up. With a choice of taking their chances or surely being burned to death, they allowed themselves to be taken prisoner. But they were far from safe. A man named Jim Yawn, whose brother had been killed earlier by William Ward's forces, searched among the prisoners until he found the man whom he thought was responsible. He dragged the man out of the ranks of the prisoners, pulled out his gun and shot him.

Rain began to fall as night came, putting out the smoldering fire on the courthouse roof. Nash's forces had lost one man and two more were mortally wounded. Dead black men littered the field outside the courthouse. By 9:00 p.m., the whites had had enough. They were ready to leave but the question remained of what to do with the remaining 60 or so black prisoners.

Surprisingly, Nash wanted to let them go. He asked the prisoners if he left them go, would they stop "this damn foolishness?" They swore they would and some even promised to kill William Ward, who had escaped, if he ever came back to Colfax. Nash still wanted to be parish sheriff and felt that killing this many people in cold blood – black or not – would hurt his chances. But he was outvoted. Other white men present did not want to let them go, arguing that the freedmen would plot to kill him in revenge. Nash still insisted that they not be killed but he didn't wait around to see if his orders were followed. He quickly got on his horse and rode off up the river.

By this time, it was 10:00 p.m. The blacks were told by a former Confederate officer named Bill Cruikshank that they were to be taken to a jail in the nearby town of Alexandria the next morning, but for the night, they were to be locked up in the sugar house of the old plantation. They were marched in pairs down the road to the sugar house, guarded by pairs of men on horseback. Cruikshank pulled aside two of the prisoners, Levi Nelson and William Williams, and asked them to accompany him. After they had gone a few hundred yards, Cruikshank ordered them to line up one behind the other, and then he pulled out a gun and shot them. He was apparently trying to see if one bullet would kill two men. Nelson only received a minor wound, but pretended to be dead. Williams, shot in the abdomen, began moaning and another white man rode up and shot him six times.

Up and down the line, shots and screams rang out. A former slave named Wash Brannon was shot along with a friend. The friend was killed but Brannon played dead, even when a horse ran over him several times. Another Confederate officer lined up five of the prisoners and attempted to kill them with one shot. Only two of them died, but he went ahead and gunned down the rest. One of the killers later stated that the gunshots sounded "like popcorn in a skillet." Amidst the gunfire, black men fell to the ground and lay scattered up and down the roadway like fallen trees. Soon, silence hung over the field and the carnage was over.

But this was not the final insult of that bloody Easter Sunday. The silence was broken a short time later by the sounds of footsteps and excited voices. Some of the white residents of Grant Parish had come to Colfax to loot the homes of the murdered black men. They returned home with their wagons piled high with bedding and furniture, leading stolen cattle and horses behind them.

Two days later, on April 15, two deputy U.S. marshals heard about the slaughter in Colfax and came to investigate. They were stunned by the sight of bodies lying everywhere, many of them having been partially eaten by dogs, some of them disemboweled and mutilated, beaten beyond recognition. One of the marshals, T.W. DeKlyne, wrote a report about what he saw that day:

The ground was thickly strewn with the dead. We were unable to find the body of a single white man or to ascertain the loss of whites. Many were shot in the back of the head and neck; one man still lay with his hands clasped in supplication; the face of another was completely flattened by the blows of a gun, the broken stock of a double-barreled shotgun being on the ground near him; another had been cut across the stomach with a knife after being shot; and almost all had three to a dozen wounds. Many of them had their brains literally blown out.

The other deputy marshal, William Wright, wrote of "the unusual marks of violence upon the bodies... have been in battle fields after a fight; the wounds in this case were different than those given in a regular fight." Both of the men's reports were used, to little avail, in the trials against those accused of the crimes.

Before the marshals had arrived, women whose husbands lay dead around the courthouse had come out of the woods to try and identify the bodies, only to be harassed by the whites who remained nearby. Nash's men had tried to get some of the local blacks to come and bury the bodies, but they refused. According to accounts, they believed that the ghosts of the dead men were still lingering nearby and they were too frightened to come near the massacre site.

And if ghosts ever had a reason to linger, they were the ghosts of those who had been killed in cold blood that night.

Since the white men refused to bury them, the evidence of the murders was there for the marshals to see. They counted 60 dead men. Five of them were turned over to their families for burial and the rest were eventually interred in a mass grave.

The massacre at Colfax was over, but the repercussions of the bloody event were just beginning. Outrage burned among outspoken blacks and Radical Republicans over the murders and a courageous U.S. attorney in New Orleans, James Beckworth, managed to persuade a federal grand jury to indict 97 of the accused attackers. Because most of the attackers, protected by the local white population, could not be found or brought to justice, only nine men ended up being tried in front of a mixed jury made up of both whites and blacks in 1874. After two trials – the first ended in a hung jury – three of the men were convicted. These included William Cruikshank, who had started the actual massacre. However, none of the men were found guilty of murder, but only of conspiring to violate the civil rights of the black men they had killed, punishable by a sentence of less than 10 years in prison.

Defense attorneys for the three convicted men took their case all the way to the U.S. Supreme Court, which, in 1876, issued a shocking and far-reaching decision in *U.S. v. Cruikshank*. The 5,000-word opinion written by Chief Justice Morrison Waite delivered the unsettling conclusion that federal statutes recently enacted to protect the civil rights of citizens only prohibited the violation of rights of blacks by the states themselves, not by individuals. Because of this, Morrison wrote, the men should not have been tried in federal court but in the Louisiana courts instead. Ignoring the fact that so many black citizens were massacred at Colfax, the decision effectively ended the federal government's efforts to protect black people in the South. Reconstruction was over a year later and the era of Jim Crow laws and segregation began soon after.

The painful story of the Colfax Massacre was not yet over. Well into the twentieth century, the bones of the men killed that Easter Sunday turned up as the result of excavations for various building projects in the area. At one point, bones of the massacre victims were being stored in cardboard boxes in the local newspaper office. No attempt was made to bury them or memorialize those who were slaughtered that day. However, in 1921, a 12-foot obelisk was erected in remembrance of the three white men who died "fighting for White supremacy" in the attack. And in 1951, the state of Louisiana authorized a metal sign to be fixed in concrete just outside of the Colfax courthouse reading, "On this site occurred the Colfax riot in which three white men and 150 Negroes were slain. This event on April 13, 1873 marked the end of carpetbag misrule in the South." Of course, the plaque was wrong in almost every way --- the number of dead was inaccurate and the event had nothing to do with Northern agitators (i.e. carpetbaggers). It was a massacre of American citizens defending their rights that set back the cause of civil rights in the country more than 100 years.

The damage caused by the Supreme Court ruling would not even begin to be undone until 1954, when *Brown v. Board of Education* outlawed school segregation. One has to wonder how different things might have been if the events on that bloody Easter Sunday had never taken place – and how different our country might be today.

1876: BLOOD ON THE GRASS
The Battle of Little Bighorn

The legendary Battle of Little Bighorn, popularly known as "Custer's Last Stand," was the most famous battle of the American Indian Wars of the late nineteenth century. It was a three-part battle, although the most important and well-known part ended with the annihilation of five companies of the U.S. 7th Cavalry and the death of its commander, Lieutenant Colonel George Armstrong Custer.

It also left a terrifying haunting in its wake.

The United States had been at war with the American Indians almost since the first Europeans set foot on the continent. After the Civil War, as the nation began moving west, it became more and more important to move the Native Americans from their traditional lands to make way for American settlement. The events that led to the Battle of Little Big Horn began as the Black Hills wars of the era.

The Cheyenne Indians had migrated west to the Black Hills and Powder River Country before the Lakota and had introduced them to horses as early as 1730. By the late eighteenth century, the growing Lakota tribe had expanded west of the Missouri River. They pushed out the Kiowa and formed an alliance with the Cheyenne and Arapaho to gain control of the buffalo hunting grounds of the northern Great Plains. The Black Hills, located in what is now western South Dakota, became not only a source of game and wood for lodge poles, it also came to be considered sacred by the Lakota.

In 1868, the Lakota and the Northern Cheyenne signed an agreement with the government called the Fort Laramie Treaty, which set aside a large portion of the Lakota territory as the Great Sioux Reservation. It included the Black Hills region, which was designated for their exclusive use. But it was not meant to last...

The growing number of miners and settlers flooding into the Dakota Territory soon nullified the treaty. The U.S. government could not keep the settlers out. By 1872, territorial officials were considering harvesting timber of the Black Hills and were wondering about the possibility of rich mineral resources in the region. When a commission approached the Red Cloud agency about the possibility of the Lakota giving up the Black Hills, Colonel John E. Smith noted that this was "the only portion [of their reservation] worth anything to them." He concluded "nothing short of their annihilation will get it from them."

In 1874, an expedition led by Civil War hero George Armstrong Custer was sent in to explore the Black Hills.

The Lakota were alarmed at this development, but there was little they could do about it. Before Custer and his men had returned to Fort Abraham Lincoln, news that they had discovered gold had been telegraphed across the country. The discovery was confirmed the following year and prospectors began to trickle into the Black Hills, ignoring the treaty that was still in place. The trickle soon became a flood and thousands of prospectors invaded the hills before the gold rush was over.

Initially, the U.S. Army struggled to keep the gold seekers out of the region. In December 1874, for example, a group of miners led by John Gordon from Sioux City, Iowa, managed to evade military patrols and reached the Black Hills. The military ejected them three months later. Such evictions, however, increased political pressure on the Grant administration to secure the Black Hills from the Lakota.

In May 1875, Sioux delegations, led by Spotted Tail, Red Cloud and Lobe Horn, traveled to Washington, D.C. in an attempt to persuade President Ulysses S. Grant to honor the existing treaties and stem the flow of miners into their territories. They met with Grant, Secretary of the Interior Columbus Delano and the Commissioner of Indian Affairs, Edward Smith. The Sioux were told that Congress wanted to pay the tribes $25,000 for the land and relocate them to the Indian Territory (now Oklahoma) but they refused to sign a new treaty under those conditions. The three chiefs went away disappointed, but none of them joined Crazy Horse and Sitting Bull in the war that followed.

Later that fall, a U.S. commission was sent to each of the Indian agencies to hold council with the Lakota. They hoped to gain the people's approval and thereby bring pressure on the Lakota leaders to sign a new treaty. This attempt also failed, which made the Black Hills the center of a growing crisis.

Grant and his administration began to consider alternatives to the failed diplomatic venture. In early November 1875, Major General Philip Sheridan, commander of the Division of the Missouri, and Brigadier General George Crook, commander of the Department of the Platte, were called to Washington, D.C. to meet with Grant and several members of his cabinet to discuss the Black Hills issue. They agreed that the Army should stop evicting trespassers from the reservation, thus opening the way for the Black Hills gold rush. In addition, they discussed initiating military action against the non-treaty bands of Lakota and Northern Cheyenne who had refused to come to the Indian agencies for council. Indian Inspector Erwin C. Watkins supported this option. "The true policy in my judgment," he wrote, "is to send troops against them in the winter, the sooner the better, and whip them into subjection."

Concerned about launching an unprovoked war against the Lakota, the government instructed Indian agents in the region to notify the various non-treaty bands to return to the reservation by January 31, 1876, or face potential military action. This request was impossible to carry out. As noted by the agent at the Standing Rock Agency, the winter weather restricted travel and the distance could not be crossed in such a short amount of time – which, of course, was the point. He asked for an extension of the deadline, but the request was refused.

As the deadline passed, it was decided that Sitting Bull, who had formed the Sun Dance Alliance between the Lakota and the Sioux, was not going to submit. His confederation was seen as hostile, gathering new recruits from reservations throughout the region, and military operations were ordered to commence against him at once. New Secretary of the Interior Zachariah Chandler stated that the Indians "are hereby turned over to the War Department for such action on the part of the Army as you may deem proper under the circumstances." On February 8, 1876, General Philip Sheridan telegraphed Generals Crook and Terry and ordered them to commence their campaigns against the hostiles and the Great Sioux War began.

By May 1876, the Dakota Territory was infested with soldiers. Under General Sheridan's command, the military planned to strike a

Lakota Chief Sitting Bull

(Left to Right): General Phillip Sheridan; George Crooks; John Gibbons; Alfred Terry

decisive blow against the Indians of the Northern Plains. But this was not the Civil War and fighting was much different this time around. Among other things it brought a final and fatal blaze of glory for Sheridan's favorite young officer, an extraordinary cavalryman named George Custer.

While still vastly outnumbered, white soldiers poured into the region. Colonel John Gibbons' column of six companies of the 7th infantry and four companies of the 2nd cavalry had marched east from Fort Ellis in western Montana on March 30 to patrol the Yellowstone River. Brigadier General George Crook's column of ten companies of the 4th infantry, and three companies of the 9th infantry, moved north from Fort Fetterman in the Wyoming Territory on May 29, marching on the Powder River area. Brigadier General Alfred Terry's column, including twelve companies of the 7th Cavalry under the immediate command of Lieutenant Colonel George Armstrong Custer, Companies C and G of the 17th U.S. Infantry, and the Gatling gun detachment of the 20th Infantry, left Fort Abraham Lincoln in the Dakota Territory on May 17. They were accompanied by teamsters and mule drivers with 150 wagons and a large contingent of pack mules, all reinforcing Custer. Companies C, D. and I of the 6th U.S. Infantry moved along the Yellowstone River from Fort Buford on the Missouri River to set up a supply depot. On May 29, they joined Terry at the mouth of the Powder River.

Things began to go wrong on June 17, 1876 when Crook's column was delayed after the Battle of the Rosebud. Surprised by the unusually large number of Indians that fought against him, a defeated Crook was forced to pull back, halt and regroup. Unaware that Crook had been attacked, Gibbon and Terry joined forces near the mouth of the Rosebud River. They reviewed Terry's plan calling for Custer's regiment to proceed south along the Rosebud, while Terry and Gibbon's united forces would move in a westerly direction toward the Bighorn and Little Bighorn rivers. As this was the likely location of Indian encampments, all Army elements were to converge around June 26 or 27 and attempt to overwhelm the Native Americans.

On June 22, Terry ordered the 7th Calvary, composed of 31 officers and 566 enlisted men under Custer, to begin a reconnaissance and pursuit along the Rosebud, with the prerogative to "depart" from orders upon seeing "sufficient reason." Custer had been offered the use of Gatling guns but declined, believing they would slow down their advance.

On the evening of June 24, Terry and Gibbon began marching toward the mouth of the Little Bighorn while Custer's scouts arrived at an overlook known as the Crow's Nest, about 14 miles east of the Little Bighorn River. At sunrise on June 25, Custer's scouts reported seeing a massive herd of ponies and signs of an Indian village about 15 miles from their position. After a long night's march, the tired officer who had accompanied the scouts was unable to see what they were looking at. Custer joined them on the hill and he was also unable to see any signs of an encampment. The bad news for Custer's men was that while they were unable to see the enemy, the enemy could see *them* -- the smoke from their fires had already given away their position.

Finally convinced that the scout's sighting was valid, Custer began making plans for a surprise attack against the Indian encampment to occur early the next morning. In the midst of his planning, though, he received word that the trail left by his troops had been discovered by hostile natives. Assuming that his presence had been exposed, Custer decided to attack the village without delay. On the morning of June 25, he divided his 12 companies into three battalions in anticipation of the battle that was to come. Three companies were placed under the command of Major Marcus Reno; three placed under Captain Frederick Benteen and five would be under Custer's direct command. The final company, under Captain Thomas McDougald, was assigned to protect the pack train, which carried provisions and ammunition.

Unknown to Custer, the group of Native Americans that discovered his trail were actually leaving the encampment on the Bighorn and did not alert anyone in the village. Custer's scouts warned him about the size of the encampment. One of them, Mitch Bouyer, reported, "General, I have been with these Indians for 30 years, and this is the largest village I have ever heard of." But Custer was less concerned with the size of the village and more worried that they might break up and scatter in different directions before he could get to them.

With that thought in mind, Custer began his approach to the Native American village at noon and prepared to attack in full daylight – a frontal attack against an overwhelming and motivated foe.

Custer: "Boy General"

By almost any rational definition, Custer was a dangerous and reckless fool. He was a bad commander and most of his men disliked him, distrusted him and feared him – and did so with good reason. He was personally undisciplined but those who served under him found him to be strict and uncompromising. He had a tremendous ego that had to be constantly fed. He was strangely emotional in that he could kill without flinching, but would break down and weep over a melodrama in a theater. His marriage to the beautiful Elizabeth was a great love story. She adored him with every fiber of her being and spent nearly 60 years of widowhood glorifying his memory. He was a man of many contradictions whose lust for adulation would eventually get him killed.

Custer was the son of an Ohio blacksmith. He managed to talk himself into West Point, where he earned a reputation for slovenliness and a record number of demerits. He graduated 34th in a class of 34, and yet had a flair that caught the attention of powerful men. General George McClellan, Commander of the Army, put Custer on his staff after a chance meeting with the young officer. When McClellan was replaced, Custer returned to the cavalry and promptly made perhaps the most extraordinary series of leaps in rank in the history of the U.S. military. Between July

General George A. Custer

1862 and July 1863, he went first from first lieutenant to brigadier general of volunteers and was given command of a brigade of cavalry. In 1865, when Phil Sheridan held command of all of the Union cavalry, Custer became a major general and took over one of Sheridan's three divisions. He was only 25 years old.

There was no question that Custer cut a dashing figure. He was a natural horseman and athlete who stood just under six feet tall. He had broad shoulders and curly blond hair that he wore to his shoulders. His eyes were a startling, vivid blue, made even more so when his face was tanned by the sun. He wore a black velvet uniform of his own design with puffed sleeves and loops of gold braid. He carried a heavy sword, a trophy that he had taken from a Confederate officer whom he had shot in the back while pursuing him through the woods. In a letter

George and Elizabeth "Libbie" Custer

home, he described the killing as "the most exciting sport I ever engaged in."

Despite his enormous ego and glaring character flaws, there was something about Custer that made men follow him, often to their deaths. When he sighted the enemy, his instinct was immediate and unswerving – he charged. He did not bother to find out how many troops were against him, what reserves they might have, or what problems of tactics or terrain might come against him. He simply charged at full speed.

And rarely did such a charge fail. Once, during the Civil War, he stormed against General James "J.E.B." Stuart's men in the Blue Ridge Mountains, only to find himself surrounded and forced to cut his way out with his sword. But otherwise, his headstrong tactics generally worked and General Sheridan liked them. When Sheridan pillaged the Shenandoah Valley, Custer led the way. When Sheridan blocked Robert E. Lee's final retreat, it was Custer's division that shattered the Confederate cavalry and destroyed Lee's infantry. After Grant and Lee met at Appomattox to end the war, Sheridan paid $20 in gold for the table on which the articles of surrender were signed and presented it to Mrs. Custer with a note that read: "I know of no person more instrumental in bringing about surrender than your most gallant husband."

When the war ended, Custer was dropped to the rank of captain. However, in 1866, partly because he had attracted the attention of President Andrew Johnson, he was given the rank of lieutenant colonel in the 7th Cavalry, which was then being formed at Fort Riley in Kansas. Technically he was second in command, but the regiment's colonel always seemed to be posted elsewhere on staff duties, so Custer effectively became the commander for the rest of his life. Soon, partially because of Custer's ferocious discipline and drilling, the 7th Cavalry became the best – and most famous – horse soldiers on the Plains. But Custer was not out to make a reputation merely as a drillmaster. He wanted to be known as a famous military leader, known to both "present and future generations." In an effort to make himself known, he began to engage in a series of fame-seeking missions that raised serious doubts in the minds of his patrons at headquarters. General Sherman noted in a letter to his brother that Custer had "not too much sense."

Custer adored his wife, Elizabeth, whom he called Libbie. When they were apart, he wrote her long letters every night. They often romped together like children, running through the house, playing tag and shrieking with laughter. When Custer had good news to tell, he became so excited that he charged through the house, knocking over furniture. But despite the laughter at home, Custer tended to be distant with his officers. He rarely had anything to do with them socially. At parties, he would frequently hide in his study, sending his orderly occasionally to invite Libbie to dance with him. He could be petulant, like a child, and was offended by any slight, real or imagined. And yet he found it hard to hold a grudge and quickly forgave his enemies, a gesture that rarely returned.

He was often reckless in the field, a trait that got him into trouble. One morning, deep in Indian country and miles from help, Custer abandoned his marching regiment and galloped off to test his hunting dogs against a herd of antelope. He was completely alone. The chase went on for miles until Custer's attention was diverted by a buffalo, the first he had seen. He followed it as it ran off in another direction. Custer pulled his pistol to shoot the animal, but it suddenly lunged at him, slamming into his horse. Custer's gun went off and the bullet killed his own horse. The animal fell like a stone, throwing its rider to the ground. Custer was now alone and on foot in hostile Indian country, miles from his regiment and without the faintest idea of where he was or in what direction his men might be. Eventually, the dogs chose the direction and their master followed. After walking for miles, he finally saw the regiment's dust on the horizon. When he caught up with them, he learned that no one had any idea that he had been missing.

That kind of reckless behavior was typical of Custer. Whenever he went into the field, he was a fierce driver, setting a demanding pace that he expected everyone to keep up with. He could ride all day with nothing to drink but a cup of tea or coffee at noon, keep his energy up with only a small amount of food, fall to the ground and sleep like a log for an hour or two and then be refreshed and ready to move on. He often pushed his men through the day and then, as they wearily made camp, order a fresh horse and ride off to hunt or scout the trail ahead. While everyone around him slept, he sat in his tent and wrote long letters to Libbie.

The men who did not share his frantic energy found the pace that he set to be cruel, especially when ordered on a whim, but the fact that he never noticed this was just another example of his narcissism. He only looked to his own comfort. His scouts supplied him with fresh game while his men ate moldy bacon and hardtack. Sometimes he even brought along a large iron stove for his tent, as well as a woman to cook for him, neither one of which was much help to a supposedly mobile column that was out on its own in Indian country.

On one occasion, Custer was leading his men on a hot, exhausting summer reconnaissance through Kansas, hoping to engage Kiowa and Comanche warriors in battle. The Indians stayed one step ahead of them and finally Custer ordered a desperate march with no precise military objective beyond a wild hope of possibly running into some Indians along the way. The regiment blundered over 65 miles of alkali flats toward the Platte River without a single break, marching through heat so intense that all of the dogs brought along on the campaign died from exhaustion. At nightfall, they were still miles from the river. Custer summoned a handful of officers and several orderlies and they galloped off, leaving the troops to plod along behind them. His purpose, Custer later wrote, was to find a good camping ground. But without further explanation he added that on reaching the river he had a long, satisfying drink and spread out his blankets to sleep. He slept so soundly that an Indian raid on a stagecoach station less than a mile away never disturbed him. Meanwhile, his regiment eventually struck the river three miles below his camp. It was daybreak before the worn-out, thirsty men finally reached water.

Besides caring little about his men's welfare on the trail, Custer could become murderous toward them when he felt that he had been crossed. The 7th Cavalry always had a high desertion rate, and after that wretched march a number of men quenched their thirst in the river and then simply walked away. Custer was furious. That day, the column halted at noon, well past the Platte, and a dozen men headed back toward the river, five of them on foot. Custer ordered the officer of the day to pursue them and "to bring in none alive." The seven mounted men escaped, but Custer's zealous officer overtook the five men on foot and opened fire on them. One was killed, two were wounded and two survived by pretending to be dead. For the men of the 7th, the incident gave them a chillingly clear indication of what they were worth to their commander.

Days later, the tired and demoralized 7th Cavalry made their way to Fort Wallace in western Kansas. Orders awaited Custer from his commanding officer, General W.S. Hancock, telling him to remain in the field, using Fort Wallace as a base, and to patrol between the Platte and Arkansas rivers. The orders ended explicitly: "The cavalry will be kept constantly engaged."

The commander who had just ordered deserters to be shot proceeded to abandon his own troops. Claiming that Fort Wallace was short on supplies, Custer readied a column of 75 men to travel 150 miles to Fort Hays and 60 more miles to Fort Harker, the nearest supply depot. The column was to return with a wagon train of food and ammunition. But Libbie was at Fort Riley, in eastern Kansas, and Custer wanted to see her so he joined the column and forced it to move at a terrible pace. Some of the men could not keep up and near Downer's Station Indians attacked the rear guard and killed two of the stragglers. The survivors caught up with Custer and told of the attack, but Custer did not attempt to punish the Indians or even pause to recover the bodies of the dead soldiers. He left that chore to the men who occupied Downer's Station.

The column made the 150 miles to Fort Hays in 55 hours, arriving with both men and horses exhausted. Custer rode on to Fort Harker, accompanied by two officers and two orderlies, making 60 more miles in less than 12 hours. When they arrived, he roused the commander from bed and insisted that supplies be sent to the 7th at Fort Wallace, and then rushed off to catch a train to Fort Riley, where Libbie was waiting.

This direct disobedience of Hancock's orders was too much for even Custer's high-placed admirers to overlook. In September, a court-martial convened to try Custer on no less than seven charges, including not only his disregard of orders, but his treatment of the deserters at the Platte River. He was convicted on all counts but his punishment was mild, explaining that his "anxiety to see his family at Fort Riley overcame his appreciation of the paramount necessity to obey orders." The court sentenced him to a year's suspension without pay and yet General Sheridan, wielding his rank to override the court, rescued Custer from even that lenient sentence by calling him back to the 7th for a winter campaign.

During that campaign, Custer's indifference toward his troops had fatal results when, in November 1868, he attacked Chief Black Kettle's village on the Washita River. In the course of the battle, Major Joel Elliott galloped off with 19 men in pursuit of fleeing Indians – and did not return. Twice during the day, a young officer told Custer that he heard heavy firing in the direction Elliott had taken and suggested that the detachment was likely in trouble. Custer paid no heed; he simply gathered his regiment and marched it away without even looking for Elliott.

Weeks later, the bodies of Elliott and his men were found within two miles of the battle site. Evidence around the bodies indicated that the men had held out for most of the day – with plenty of time for Custer to have rescued them, had he been so inclined. He could offer no excuse for his failure to come to Elliott's aid, only saying that he didn't want his men to be attacked. He had brought over 700 men into battle that day and had something that he could point to as a clear-cut victory. Had he risked an Indian counterattack, which chasing after Elliott might have provoked, his victory could have been written off as an indecisive action. Custer chose the road to fame and abandoned Elliott, but he never again had the loyalty of most of his officers. Years later, Captain David Stanley, who headed an expedition in which the 7th Cavalry took part, called Custer a "coldblooded, untruthful and unprincipled man" who was "despised" by most of his officers.

The incident at Washita also emphasized Custer's inadequate tactical skills. During the Civil War, he had fared well with full-frontal attacks, but he was no longer dealing with troop formations and battlefield orders. The fight against the Indians was guerrilla warfare and Custer was poorly equipped to handle it. At Washita, he had divided his force, a gamble that didn't always pay off. If such an attack worked, it could be devastating to the enemy but if it failed, each unit could be surrounded and destroyed. Even more important, Custer had attacked the village without scouting it first. He had never forgotten the success of his blind, smashing attacks during the war but now, because he didn't order a reconnaissance to be done, he did not know that there were other Indian encampments near Black Kettle and had no idea how many warriors were in those camps. He saw the attack as a success and because of this, never bothered to reassess his tactics and thus overcome his tragic shortcomings. It would be a mistake that would soon have fatal consequences.

Over the next two years, the 7th Cavalry saw no action on the plains. Then, in 1873, it joined up with an expedition that was seeking a northern railway route through Dakota and Montana. During this expedition, Custer led his men into battle with Sioux warriors who fled so quickly that Custer began to dangerously underestimate their fighting abilities. Later that year, he also led the reconnaissance into the Black Hills from Fort Abraham Lincoln. One day while the men were at the fort, Sioux raiders drove off a herd of mules and Custer galloped after them with such haste that his troopers were strung out across the prairie for miles. In his haste, he had left the fort completely defenseless. Libbie Custer, who had come to live at the post, never forgot the terror she and the other women felt as the result of being left unprotected at Fort Abraham Lincoln that day.

Late in the fall of 1875, General Sheridan drew up the plans for the climactic campaign against the Indians on the Northern Plains. While these plans were developing, Custer and Libbie, apparently having found Fort Abraham Lincoln during a Dakota winter too dull, traveled to New York City. During the fall of 1875, Custer had taken off on an extended leave and he and Libbie were enjoying the city. They went to parties, dinners and plays and Custer addressed both the Century Society and the New York Historical Society. He also demonstrated his ability at charming important men, like James Gordon Bennett, publisher of the *New York Herald*.

Thanks in part to Bennett, a national scandal was in the works – a scandal in which Custer came to play an important and possibly career-ending role. That fact that 1876 was a presidential election year made the scandal even worse. Democrats charged that W.W. Belknap, Secretary of War to Republican President Ulysses S. Grant, was profiteering from sales at Army posts. According to their stories, the traders at the posts were cheating soldiers and Indians alike and then funneling profits back to Belknap. Even though Belknap quickly resigned as soon as the scandal broke, the Democrats pushed for an impeachment trial before the Senate. Custer himself had experienced trouble with traders at Fort Abraham Lincoln, who imposed outrageous prices on the men of the 7th. When he brought this matter to Belknap's attention, the Secretary had found in favor of the trader and in so doing, earned Custer's permanent hatred. Later, when the scandal broke, Custer helped to fan the flames. He offered to give evidence against Belknap and was probably the author of at least one of the devastating articles that ran in Bennett's newspaper. He was soon summoned to Washington to testify before Congress.

Custer now faced a dilemma. It was now March 1876 and he was supposed to be in Dakota preparing his regiment for the important campaign ahead. That year on the Northern Plains, Custer hoped to regain some of the national fame that he had enjoyed during the Civil War and after the battle at Washita. Anxious to return out West, Custer appeared before the committee and proved himself more righteous than wise. He offered a collection of hearsay evidence against Belknap – evidence that he could not hope to prove – and on equally flimsy grounds, he also accused President Grant's brother, Orville, of influence peddling and receiving pay-offs. This testimony did not earn him the affection of the president.

Custer had blundered into a mess. After the Congressional hearings, he was summoned to testify at the trial. He won release from that duty, but President Grant ordered that another officer lead the Dakota column against the Indians. Custer went to the White House, hat in hand, and sat in the anteroom for hours waiting to plead his cause. Grant refused to see him.

Custer was frantic. The chance of a lifetime was slipping away from him. With a new scandal making the rounds, the Democrats saw the opportunity for their first presidential victory since the end of the Civil War. To pull it off, they needed a popular candidate, strong, well known and perhaps a war hero. While never discussed openly, as is usually the case with politics, Custer may have been led to believe that with a fresh victory behind him, followed by good newspaper coverage, he could be that candidate.

Desperate, he fled Washington without orders. Under instructions from the Commander of the Army, William Sherman, General Sheridan had an aide meet Custer's train at Chicago to place him under arrest. With Sheridan's permission, Custer sent telegrams to Sherman, pleading his case. He never received an answer. Then he turned to General Alfred Terry, who had been named by Sheridan to lead the Dakota column. When he met with Terry in St. Paul, Minnesota, it was said that he got down on his knees to plead with him to intercede on his behalf. Terry did so, perhaps out of pity, perhaps out of decency, or perhaps because Terry had no experience fighting against Indians and felt he needed someone like Custer to come to his own rescue.

With Terry's help, Custer composed a penitent telegram to President Grant asking, as one solider to another, not that he be allowed to lead the expedition, but to be spared the shame of having his men go into battle without him. Terry sent the telegram with a message of his own that stated he would lead the command, but would appreciate having a man with Custer's experience at his side. Sheridan endorsed the plea and Grant relented. Within hours of his reprieve, Custer reportedly told other officers that he would find a way to get free of Terry and run the campaign on his own. Custer also did one other thing. Against Sherman's specific orders, he permitted Mark Kellogg, a reporter for the *New York Herald* to come along with the 7th during the campaign.

By the time Custer returned to the West, the campaign had gone from the planning stages into action and soldiers began pouring into the region, intent on defeating the Native Americans once and for all. Ignorant of everything but the Indians' approximate location, General Terry divided his forces. Custer would take the 7th up the Rosebud to follow a trail that had been discovered by scouts. Terry expected the trail to turn westward from the Rosebud and cross over the divide to the valley of the Little Bighorn. To complete the plan, he and Gibbon would go up the Yellowstone to the mouth of the Bighorn, and up that river to the Little Bighorn. There, the Gibbon and Custer columns would be in a position to trap the Indians between them.

The entire plan was based on the single powerful conviction that the Indians would flee when attacked. They had often done so in the past, fighting mainly in guerilla fashion, running, striking, and running again. For years, these same officers had been repeatedly frustrated by Indians who raided settlers' farms and stagecoach stations and then vanished when the Army arrived.

The Indians would run, both Custer and Terry believed this, and their best escape would be to flee south into the Big Horn Mountains. There, if they split up into two smaller groups, they would be hard to find. Custer was not supposed to attack them, merely block their escape, as Terry instructed him. But those instructions had been purposely vague, issued to an officer that was known for being insubordinate, and whose fame had been created by striking hard and quickly. Terry had to have suspected that Custer would attack the Indians when he found them, without regard to orders. If he didn't, Custer believed his career would be over – a fate that seemed to him to be the equivalent of death. He had become obsessed with the idea that no Indian would ever stand and fight. If they were given the chance to escape, they always would, he thought, but if they could be trapped, he would annihilate them.

It was a belief that would prove to be fatal.

It wasn't only Custer's immense ego that put him and his men at risk. His most fundamental and dangerous weakness was the problem he had with his officers. Even since he had abandoned Major Elliott and his men on the Washita River in 1868, he had been unable to command the loyalty and respect of all of his junior officers. Soon after the Washita incident, one of them had written a letter to a friend angrily accusing Custer of cowardice. The letter was published anonymously in the *Missouri Democrat*, and Custer was enraged. It was obvious that an officer in the regiment had written it. Custer summoned his officers and with the newspaper in one hand and a whip in the other, he promised the thrash the man who had written the letter, if his identity was ever revealed.

Captain Frederick Benteen, the regiment's senior captain with the brevet rank of colonel, six years older than Custer, and a close friend of Elliott's, glanced at the newspaper. He spoke quietly, addressing Custer by the brevet rank that he had held during the Civil War: "If there's to be a whipping, General, you can start in. I wrote that letter."

His bluff called, Custer's face turned crimson. He barked out, "Colonel Benteen, I will see you later, sir." He stormed away but the matter was never mentioned again.

As much as he could, Custer surrounded himself with approving officers and his own family members. His brother, Captain Tom Custer, and his brother-in-law, Lieutenant James Calhoun, were members of the regiment. Another brother, Boston Custer, and a nephew, Armstrong Reed, came along on the campaign as civilian fighters. But Custer was estranged from most of his officers.

While camped along the Rosebud, and before launching the campaign, Custer held a meeting of his officers at which he addressed the subject of loyalty. Some of his officers, he reminded the staff, had gone to headquarters to criticize his conduct. He was willing to hear complaints, he said, but they should be made within the regiment. Now, as never before, he needed the backing of his men. Again, it was Benteen who challenged his commander. He asked Custer if he wanted to be specific as to who was at fault and Custer reddened. "I'm not here to be chastised by you," he snapped. "But for your own information, I will state that none of my remarks have been directed toward you." With that he dismissed the men. It was an inauspicious start to the campaign ahead.

The regiment was on the march by 5:00 a.m. on the morning of June 23. Custer set a terrible pace and as the sun climbed into the sky and the heat grew more intense, the column stretched out with stragglers dropping so far behind that they eventually arrived in camp hours after their leaders. The hard riding had caused blisters to form and then burst on the men's legs and the horses began to suffer from saddle sores. In some parts of the Indian trail they were following, the ground was cut to powder six inches deep. Alkaline dust covered the riders and their mounts, burning their eyes and throats. Swarming buffalo gnats stung them and caused their eyes to swell shut, while deerflies tortured the exhausted horses. It was a brutal day and so far, there had not been an Indian in sight.

The next day was no better. The trail was clear and so rutted by Indian lodge poles and horses that it resembled a plowed field, and was just as difficult to walk and ride on. The grass all around it had been cropped to the roots and the Indian herds had left little fodder for the suffering cavalry horses and mules. As the march continued, the soldiers passed one abandoned campsite after another in quick succession. It seemed to them that individual bands of Indians must have been moving very slowly, a mile or two at a time. But the scouts knew what they were seeing: These were not a series of camps but a single camp made by a group so large that it had stretched for miles. They came to a great camp circle where a framework of lodge poles that were still in place showed that a great sun dance had been held. Custer had no way of knowing it, but at this point three weeks earlier Chief Sitting Bull had experienced a vision of soldiers falling into his camp, signifying that they would attack and be killed.

At first, the droppings that had been left by Indian ponies had been dry, but as the command moved along, the trail became fresher. The men began to notice the remains of fires so recent that ashes still flew in the wind, and roasted buffalo ribs that, while picked clean, had not yet dried in the summer sun.

With their worn-out horses laboring along the trail, the troopers traveled over more than 30 miles of hard terrain on June 23 and about 28 miles on June 24 before stopping at sundown along the upper reaches of Rosebud Creek. They camped under a high bluff where a little grass had been left behind by Indian ponies. The men ate and then went to sleep in their clothes, for they knew that they might be making a night march. Custer had sent three of his Crow Indian scouts ahead to follow the trail. They returned at about 9:00 p.m. to announce that, as expected, the trail turned westward to cross the divide between the Rosebud and the valley of the Little Bighorn.

For the last several days, the scouts, white men as well as Arikara and Crow, had understood the meaning of the trail they were following and had become increasingly cautious. One the first night out, a mixed-race scout named Mitch Bouyer, who had spent more than 30 years in the West, asked a young officer if he had ever fought the Sioux. When the young man confidently replied that the 7th could handle them, Bouyer replied, "Well, I can tell you that we are going to have a damned big fight."

Lonesome Charley Reynolds had scouted the region during the winter and early spring. The Indians had been gathering guns for months, he told Terry and Custer, and he was convinced that they planned to stand and fight. Reynolds had an infected finger that forced him to keep his arm in a sling and he planned to use this as an excuse to avoid the campaign. He asked Terry to relieve him on two occasions, but each time, Terry had shamed him into staying.

The scouts had spent their lives tracking animals and men. They could follow a trail that consisted of little more than broken twigs and a blade of grass that was pressed in the wrong direction, but now they were following a trail that was sometimes as much as one-half mile wide, leaving broken ground and near devastation behind. They knew that this was not the only trail leading in the same direction and that it must involve several tribes of Sioux, as well as Northern Cheyenne. They were certain that the Army was about to face more Indian warriors than anyone had ever seen together at one time.

Custer's favorite scout, an Arikara named Bloody Knife, warned him of the danger in plain language. The Crow and Arikara scouts were commanded by another Custer favorite, Lieutenant Charles Varnum, and they were enemies of the Sioux and eager to help wipe out their traditional foes. The Arikara had been disturbed by bad signs during the campaign – the unusually high water in the streams, a freak snowstorm just three weeks earlier and now, by the terrifying size of the trail they were following. While the regiment was still at the Yellowstone, they had ridden in a somber circle, singing their death songs. At some of the stops along the trail, they had engaged in rites seeking the protection of the spirits. Finally, Bloody Knife approached Custer and solemnly warned him that there were more Sioux ahead of them than there were bullets in the belts of the soldiers.

It was a more accurate prediction than anyone knew, for even the most pessimistic scout did not expect to find more than 2,000 Indian warriors waiting for Custer's 600 men.

Custer had to have known that the Indian force was huge but he rejected Bloody Knife's warnings that the odds against him would be overwhelming. He was more concerned that the enemy might get away from him. He was supremely confident in the capacity of the 7th Cavalry to defeat any Indians that it met and it was likely that the presence of a larger force made him even more eager to fight. The greater the number he defeated, the greater would be the fame of his victory.

With thoughts of glory pulsing in his head, he ordered the troops to march again at 11:00 p.m. He was now officially disobeying orders. Terry had told him to swing well to the south, then double back to prevent any possibility of an Indian escape. Instead, Custer had pushed his troops at such brutal speed that he was far beyond the point that Terry would have expected him to reach. He was now prepared to attack immediately on his own. Waiting for Terry and Gibbon to come up the Little Bighorn from the other side would have meant sharing the victory. Continuing south, as he had been directed to do, would have risked a meeting with Crook's column and that would have reduced Custer to a subordinate and made the victory Crook's.

So Custer started his exhausted men and horses on a night march that extended 10 miles up the divide between the Rosebud and the Little Bighorn. The men noisily clomped along through the darkness, dragging, pushing, cursing and kicking their way along the steep and dusty trail. Their voices, as well as the occasional brays of the thirsty, ill-tempered mules, advertised the presence of a marching army for miles in every direction.

At 2:00 a.m., the head of the column reached a deep, wooded ravine. It took hours before the rest of the regiment caught up to them and stopped. The water in the ravine was too alkaline to drink and the horses wouldn't touch it. Some of the men removed their saddles and rubbed down the lathered mounts with handfuls of dry grass and dust, while others simply lay down on the ground to sleep. Six hours later, they were on the march again.

They continued on for another 10 grueling miles and then stopped at another ravine, just below the crest of the divide. The noise and the clouds of dust that hung over the moving column provided a clear sign of the soldiers' presence but it mattered very little since Sioux scouts had been watching the regiment for some time. The soldiers were somewhat aware of this since their scouts had reported fresh Sioux tracks on several occasions, and one claimed he had been close enough to a Sioux to converse with him in sign language. The only advantage Custer now had was the speed of his movement gained by the night march. Once he had left the Rosebud, orders or not, he was committed to attack. His decision to turn rather than continue south was a crucial moment that led to the battle.

During the previous night, Custer had sent Lieutenant Varnum and a party of scouts to a high knob that later became known as Crow's Nest. Perched high over the divide, it offered a vantage point for the valley of the Little Bighorn, about 15 miles away. Varnum had not slept for nearly 36 hours at this point and during those hours, he had ridden more than 60 miles on constant forays away from the main column. While waiting for the sun to rise, he napped for about 45 minutes and when he awoke, he and his scouts were astonished by what they saw in the emerging light.

The Little Bighorn was a smallish river, running in horseshoe bends through a broad valley. On the eastern side, from which the scouts were looking, the river cut against bluffs 80 to 100 feet high. One the western side was a wide flat plain, sometimes as much as two miles across. In the growing light, while Varnum slept, the scouts began to sense that something about the hills beyond the plain, about 20 miles from their lookout point, looked odd. They soon realized that they were looking at horses. Horses covered the hills like a carpet of brown shrubs and all of the men agreed that it was the largest pony herd they had ever seen. They awakened Varnum and with his eyes blurred with sleep, he was unable to see what they were pointing at. They urged him to look for the horses and though he still couldn't see them, Varnum trusted his scouts. At 5:00 a.m., with the sky growing brighter, he sent word to Custer.

When the message arrived, Custer rode through the camp issuing orders. Soon, the troops moved out at a steady walk, reaching the woods below the Crow's Nest in a little less than an hour. They waited while Custer rode to the lookout point. The sun was climbing higher into the sky and the day promised to be another scorcher.

When Custer reached the observation point, the valley was filled with humid fog. Even with field glasses, he was unable to make out the horses that the scouts had seen in the early morning light with the sun at their backs.

Bouyer told him that it was the largest encampment that he had ever seen in his three decades among the Indians. But it was clear to everyone by now that Custer did not care how big the village was. He might be outnumbered, but he believed that he was more than a match for anything that might come his way. Bloody Knife had warned him of impending doom and the night before, Lonesome Charley Reynolds had given his few possessions to his friends, since he did not expect to survive the day. But Custer was undeterred. He was determined to take the fight to the enemy and even though he could not see them that morning, he knew they were there. Fame and glory awaited him.

Custer returned to the regiment, but Varnum, still at his lookout post, saw something that had a critical effect on the situation. A group on Indians was moving downstream and he assumed they were trying to escape. He sent a runner galloping after Custer to alert him to what was happening. In truth, the group of Indians was actually hurrying to the main camp for safety after seeing the soldiers. Their actions helped to trigger the attack.

Custer put the regiment into motion and at about noon, the command passed over the divide toward the valley of the Little Bighorn. They were still nearly 15 miles from the Indian encampment, but they were moving quickly. The encampment lay on the far side of the river, which ran between banks from five to ten feet high in places and offered a number of convenient crossings. One of the shallow spots was upstream in the direction from which the cavalry was coming. One was near the center of the Indian camp, which was about three miles long. A third ford lay farther downstream, just below the camp.

Near the headwaters of Ash Creek (which would later be named Reno Creek), which ran down to the river at the first ford, Custer stopped the regiment and divided his command. He assigned one entire company and details from each of the others to guarding the slow-moving pack train. He assigned three companies of about 125 men to Benteen and told him to sweep the bluffs well south of the valley, searching them thoroughly for Indians. After Benteen departed, Custer assigned three more companies to Reno and ordered him to go directly down the creek, cross the river and charge the southern end of the Indian camp. Custer, with a five-company main force of about 215 men, would support him. Reno supposed that Custer would be riding behind him, coming in to deal a decisive blow after the initial collision with the Indian forces. But instead of following Reno across the ford, Custer swung to the right, remaining on the other side of the river. Hidden behind the high bluffs, he rode downstream, parallel to the Little Bighorn.

The true motives behind Custer's actions, and his intentions in dividing his force, will forever remain a mystery. However, it's possible that the key lies in Custer's personality. Every victory that he had ever won had come from rushing into an attack. He was a man of intense courage – perhaps too courageous in fact, as once observed by General Sherman – and he likely never felt the same inner stirrings of mortality that warned other men of danger and doom. His confidence in himself, and by extension in his regiment, was boundless and it was a confidence that would kill them all.

Custer's only fear, it seemed, was that the Indians would flee to the south and elude him. It was a fear that he need not have worried about.

The "Last Stand"

Custer's was adamant about the fact that he could not let his enemy escape. He sent Benteen to the west to block them if they broke through and sent Reno to the south in a diversionary attack that would have the effect of holding them in place. Custer would strike them at their heart.

With his command divided, the odds against his five-company force were overwhelming. Bouyer protested against marching into the valley and Custer accused him of cowardice. Bouyer simply shrugged. "If we go in there, we will never come out," he said. Bloody Knife bade farewell to the sun, telling it that he would not "see you go down behind the hills tonight."

On his ride, Reno was joined by Lieutenant Varnum and most of his scouts. Only Bouyer and a few of the others remained with Custer, who watered his horses at a small branch of the Ash Creek before continuing on. At least twice he halted his men and rode up on the bluffs to look down on the river. For the first time, he could see the actual size of the Indian encampment – and he was thrilled by the sight. Because no effort had been made to strike the lodges, Custer apparently believed that he had caught the Indians unprepared. He waved his hat and gleefully yelled to the men, "We've got them this time!" From the bluffs, he sent a sergeant hurrying down to bring up the packs. The sergeant told the men in Benteen's column, which had begun to circle back to the regiment, "We've got 'em, boys!"

Custer's column rode on. Just before turning into Medicine Tail Coulee, which led down to the river at the central crossing, Custer sent back another message, this time to Benteen. Scrawled hastily by an adjutant, Lieutenant W.W. Cooke, it read: "Benteen. Come on. Big village – be quick – bring packs. W.W. Cooke. PS. Bring packs." The message reflected Custer's confidence – it was not so much Benteen's men that he wanted, it was their packs filled with ammunition. There was no indication Custer was worried, either in the message or in the report of the messenger, a trumpeter named Giovanni Martini. But Martini did say that he had paused at the top of the coulee and had looked back and seen Indians rising and firing from the brush on both sides of Custer's position. Martini had been shot at and his horse wounded as he galloped back toward Benteen. Custer's 200 men had ridden down to meet an enemy numbering in the thousands.

Reno had asked no questions when he was ordered to attack the southern end of the camp. His total force amounted to 134 officers and men and 16 scouts, but he assumed that Custer would be right behind him. When that assumption turned out to be wrong, his charge began to fall apart. Although Reno had fared well in the Civil War, he had never fought against Indians. He took his three companies across the river at a trot and then launched his attack on the village, galloping across the valley at a pace that was faster than some of his men had ever ridden a horse.

Indian warriors came out of the village afoot and on horseback to meet them. They sped toward them and then wheeled about, raising a great cloud of dust. As Reno neared them, they seemed to fall back toward the camp so rapidly that Reno suspected a trap. Ahead of him, Reno saw – or thought he saw – a shallow ravine that contained hundreds of warriors. He suddenly ordered his men to halt and dismount. The order caught his men by surprise since, at that point, no shots had been fired, even though several hundred Indians were on the field in front of them. Cavalryman George F. Smith's horse ran away with him, carrying him straight into the Indians. He was knocked from his horse and killed. Then Reno ordered every fourth man to take four horses and retreat to a stand of trees near the river. The remaining men, about 80 in number, formed a thin skirmish line, its right end anchored in the trees. Each man stood about nine feet from the next and many, especially the new recruits, began firing wildly and rapidly, even though most of the Indians were still hundreds of yards away.

Reno's attack was halted almost before it began. Technically, he had disobeyed the order to attack the camp and some believed that he had left Custer without support. Others have argued that he would have been cut down within 500 yards. Whatever the truth of the situation, one fact was clear: In halting and dismounting, Reno had shifted from offense to defense. In addition, he had no chance of holding his position. The mounted Indians soon swept around the end of his line, turning his left flank and putting him in a deadly crossfire. His men reflexively bunched up, making them better targets, and several were hit. As the Sioux turned Reno's flank, they also slipped up the river on his right flank, preparing to take his men and horses in the woods.

Reno began calling for the men on the skirmish line to retreat to the woods, but the men who didn't hear the orders began to collapse from the pressure of the attack. Most of them stopped firing immediately and as the Sioux moved in closer, several more were hit. Defense was easier in the woods, which were heavy with brush and undergrowth, but finding a better position did not help Reno to carry out his orders. He and his men were at least 1,000 yards from the nearest lodge in the encampment and any chance of an attack was gone. At that point, they were thinking in terms of sheer survival.

The Indians set fire to the dry grass along the river bottom and the flames swept through the brush and trees. Warriors slipped in on their bellies under the smoke, rising, shooting and then dropping out of sight. Horses were shot with bullets and arrows, sending them into a panic while the frightened, and now effectively blind soldiers fired wild shots in every direction.

Reno knew that he was in a serious situation, but it was not a desperate one – not yet anyway. He looked upriver, still waiting for Custer's promised support, which, of course, never came. Custer was miles away by this time, heading into the encampment. As more Indians surrounded Reno's position, he ordered a move to the bluffs on the other side of the river. A captain shouted, "Men, to your horses; the Indians are at our rear!" Some of the men were perplexed by the order. One of the other scouts turned to Reynolds and asked, "What damn fool move is this?"

In the commotion, many of the soldiers failed to hear the order. They were still firing when they heard from others that they were getting out. Uncertain, they looked around, searching for their officers, their friends, their horses, anything that looked familiar. As they attempted to scramble to safety, they stopped shooting. In the lull that followed, a group of Sioux suddenly pushed toward them and fired a deadly volley from less than 30 yards. Reno was next to Bloody Knife when an enemy bullet struck the scout between the eyes. His skull shattered, spraying Reno with blood and brains.

That horrifying moment apparently released the panic that had been rising in the inexperienced Reno. Even though he and a number of the soldiers managed to get mounted, Reno lost sight of the immediate plan, which was to leave the woods and escape across the river to safer ground. Shouting maniacally, he ordered the men to dismount and, as they began to do so, to mount up again. He himself swung back into his saddle and his horse leaped out of the timber without being spurred. The other soldiers thundered after him, leaving their wounded behind – which meant certain death for the helpless men. It was a frantic scene of panic, but it was impossible to blame Reno, who was drastically outnumbered. He might not have saved any of his men if he had continued to try and hold that patch of timber. However, his reputation will always be blotched by the fact that he abandoned his wounded and that, as he led his men through a brutal crossfire, he made no attempt to maintain order or to cover the rear. If they had withdrawn in even a somewhat orderly manner the soldiers would have kept up fire as they moved and kept the enemy busy. By running, the Indians were able to pick off scores of them like animals in a hunt. They rode beside them and shot down the soldiers as they fled from the woods.

Reno galloped for more than a mile alongside the river and away from the encampment, making for a high bluff on the far side. At the bank opposite the bluff, the horses were forced to jump four and five feet into the river. As they struggled across, the Indians followed and ran them down, pulling soldiers from their mounts and smashing their heads with clubs. For those who made it across the river, they faced a sheer, eight-foot bank. Varnum's horse threw itself against the bank and managed to reach the top, but others were not so lucky. Many of them toppled backward, crashing back on the men and horses below. The animals thrashed about in the water, fighting the current, frantic with fear and rearing backward as their riders pushed them toward the steep bank.

Meanwhile, Sioux warriors were coming along the bluffs from downstream and shooting down the soldiers as they emerged from the river. Lieutenant Benjamin Hodgson, Reno's adjutant, was hit by a bullet that passed through his leg and killed his horse. A trooper thrust a stirrup at Hodgson and pulled him to the riverbank. He was climbing out of the water when a bullet fired from above split his skull and killed him instantly.

The fight in the woods and the chase across the river had lost Reno about one-third of his men. They straggled to the top of the highest bluff before the Indians could reach it, and lay there, demoralized, exhausted and terrified, fearing another attack at any moment.

Charley Reynolds had died on the way to the river crossing, trying to cover the retreating soldiers. His horse had been shot out from under him and the litter of shells found next to his body showed that he had fought long and hard from the shelter of the animal's body before he had finally been killed. Reynolds had taken his share of enemy lives, and he was not the only one. One of the men had shot an Indian off his horse and came up the bluff with a bloody scalp swinging in his hand.

At the same time, Reno, at least temporarily safe, was already re-writing the history of what had occurred. Told by the company doctor that the men had been demoralized by the rout, Reno snapped at him, "That was a cavalry charge, sir!"

The men set up posts to meet the next attack but by now, except for a few snipers firing from a distance, the Indians were leaving, riding hard downstream toward the center of the encampment. Some of the men heard firing coming from that direction. Custer was giving it to them, the soldiers told one another, grinning and pleased with this small bit of revenge for their own lost men.

They were on the bluff for nearly a half hour when Reno saw Benteen's column approaching his position. He ran out and waved to the captain. "For God's sake, Benteen," he called, "halt your command and help me. I've lost half my men."

Soon after riding off at Custer's order, Benteen had decided that he was on a fool's errand. He moved west as he had been instructed and searched the countryside for hour after hour but after seeing no Indians, he turned back and headed for the Little Bighorn, where he knew he would be needed. He was ahead of the pack train when he received Custer's written order to hurry forward with the packs. The order apparently made no sense to Benteen. If Custer's men were going into a hard fight, they needed his men more than they needed him to herd pack animals. He moved forward at a brisk trot and when he saw Reno, he assumed that he had found the regiment since he had no idea that Custer had further divided his command after sending Benteen away. But Reno had no idea where Custer was. He only knew that he had not received the support that Custer had promised him and he believed that Indians would soon overrun his position.

The two officers were now bogged down with confusion and indecision. Custer's written order to Benteen had obviously come from some position ahead, and Reno and Benteen both knew that a lively battle was taking place there. They could hear the pounding of the guns and the cries of the Sioux warriors. And yet Benteen did not obey the order to swiftly join Custer, nor did either man follow the classic military dictum that, in the absence of orders, one marches toward the sound of the guns. Reno refused to move at all, in fact, until the pack train arrived to resupply his men.

Finally, a junior officer forced their hand. Captain Thomas Weir, who admired Custer as much as Benteen disliked him, set off downstream without his commanders' authority. He and his company reached a high point – known later as Weir Point – from which he could look down on both the Indian camp and the field into which Custer had ridden. By this time, the heavy fire had died down. Weir saw no sign of Custer and his men, but he did see clouds of dust and warriors milling about in the distance.

Meanwhile, Reno and Benteen finally moved the rest of the command in Weir's direction. When they reached the vantage point, Benteen for the first time realized the enormity of the situation. Across the river, he saw at least 1,800 Indian lodges. The air was filled with smoke and dust but he could see the size of the pony herd that was spread across the hills – the same sight that had startled the scouts earlier that morning.

The Indians saw the soldiers on the point and began moving toward them, rushing the slopes and attempting to surround them on two sides. With the position clearly untenable, the soldiers retreated back to the bluff. More men were lost in this second retreat and more wounded soldiers were left to be tortured by the Sioux. Once on the bluff, though, they had a defensible position and were able to hold off the attack for more than three hours. When darkness finally came, the shooting dropped off and the Indians, as usual, broke off the attack for the night. Safe for the time being, the soldiers worked all night to fortify the bluff, using hatchets, knives, tin cups and even their bare hands to dig rough trenches. In the distance, the exhausted men could see great fires burning in the encampment. Figures danced among the flames and the rapid beat of drums could be heard echoing across the fields. No one knew what had become of Custer and his men but at that point, the men could only fear for their own lives.

What exactly happened to Custer that day is still unknown. The messenger Giovanni Martini was the last soldier to see him alive and when Martini rode off with his message to Benteen, he believed that all was well. Soldiers studied the evidence of the battlefield afterward and over the years Indians offered their own accounts – often conflicting ones – of what happened that day. The accounts conflict for several reasons, the most important being that the Indians tended to see the battle from their own point of view. They had no command structure or clear orders, which made it difficult for them to reconstruct what happened in terms of overall battlefield movements. Each warrior recounted what he did and saw from his own perspective. And even then, many of them, fearing retribution, preferred not to talk about what happened at all.

Based on the battlefield evidence and the personal accounts, historians have put together a "best guess" scenario of what happened to Custer during what's been called his "Last Stand" against the Sioux.

Custer led his command to Medicine Tail Coulee, where Martini saw him come under the initial attack. Custer's next move from there would have been to cross the river near the center of the camp and enter the battle against a larger body of Indians. There would have been at least 1,000 warriors facing his 200 men in that area alone. The Indians came across the ford and swarmed up the gullies all around the soldiers. Custer, who

CUSTER'S LAST FIGHT.

ANHEUSER BUSCH BREWING ASSOCIATION.

The famous painting of Custer's Last Stand, which was used by the Anheuser-Busch beer company for many years as advertising in all of its saloons.

never cared about the odds, likely charged against them, despite their superior numbers. Sheer numbers, though, can turn even the fiercest charge. In the midst of flying arrows, a rain of bullets, blue powder smoke, clouds of dust, horses crashing into one another, screams and war cries of the Sioux, Custer's firing, shouting and cursing men surely knew that they were in trouble.

Some of Custer's men may have been turned back at the river crossing, while others likely never reached the river at all. It's likely that some of them were driven to high, open ground downstream, where they hoped to mount a counterattack and hold on until reinforcements arrived – but the Indians were driving them there. What none of them could know was that Crazy Horse, one of the few great battle leaders among the Sioux, was in the camp they were attacking. Although the Indians had no generals in a structured military sense, many of them followed Crazy Horse because the tactics that he suggested always seemed to work. He had fared well in earlier battles, including a recent fight with Crook at the Rosebud, and he now played a leading role in the tactics that destroyed Custer.

Custer moved to high ground and took up an offensive at the front and set up a defensive position at the rear. Then Sioux Chief Gall, leading the attack on Reno, heard the firing downstream and entered the battle. With hundreds of warriors, Gall charged away from the bluffs where Reno's exhausted men had retreated. Crossing the river, these warriors hurled themselves against Custer's rear flank. Custer discovered Company L, commanded by his brother-in-law, Lieutenant Calhoun, and I Company, commanded by Captain Myles Keogh, a battling Irishman who was beloved by the regiment. The men moved backward step by step, firing as they went, covering the rear.

But Crazy Horse, with hundreds of fighters, had gone down through the encampment on the other side of the Little Bighorn, and had crossed the river at the lower ford. He charged toward Custer's position, leading his warriors up the same hill that Custer was climbing from the other side. The Indians topped the final rise, on a high point ahead of Custer's retreating forces, and crashed into Custer and his three forward companies like a battering ram. But Custer rallied once again. He grouped his men back to back for a final stand.

At Custer's rear flank, most of Gall's warriors had dismounted and crawled as close to L Company as they could, picking them off one by one with bows and arrows. A warrior armed with a bow could hug the ground and shoot without making a sound that might reveal his position. He would fire up in the air, the arrow arching high on its trajectory and falling to strike a soldier silently in the back. Many of the soldiers died this way, and lay face down with arrows standing upright in their backs.

Gall's fighters crept closer and finally took L Company by storm. The Indians on the ground rose and fired as one and then mounted warriors leaped over them, falling on the soldiers and beating and hacking them to death. No soldiers broke and ran. They held their position, fighting and dying in place, where they bodies were later found. The Indians moved forward, fighting their way toward Custer.

Custer was still frantically organizing his defense. He remained clear-minded until the very end, as was evident from the strong placement in which the men's bodies were later found. Their positions could not have been better. They fought hard but their carbines eventually failed in the heat. As the metal grew hot, the soft copper shells expanded and the ejectors cut through the cartridge rims and left them jammed in place. When this happened, the men had to work the cartridge out with a knife — while bullets and arrows thudded into the ground around them. The men's eyes burned with sweat and smoke, but they held their places in the line, their pistols ready for the moment when there was no time left to dig out another shell from a fouled carbine. That they were brave was well known — and respected — by the Indians. A year later, Sitting Bull stated, "I tell no lies about dead men. These men who came with 'Long Hair' [Custer] were as good men as ever fought." Another chief, Brave Wolf, said, "It was hard fighting; very hard all the time. I have been in many hard fights, but I never saw such brave men."

The Indians stormed over Company I, just as they had Company L. Again, the soldiers died in place, swinging their rifles as clubs, protecting the rear, emptying their pistols — except for the last shot, which some of the men saved for themselves. A sergeant caught a horse near the end and made a desperate half-mile ride through a rain of gunfire before a bullet finally brought him down. Afterward, an Indian spoke of his courage. There was an officer in a buckskin shirt who rode through unbelievable gunfire. Finally, his horse fell but he managed to catch another and leap into the saddle, riding back and forth, rallying his men and holding his position. The Indians lost sight of him moments later and it was assumed he was killed at that point.

Finally, Crazy Horse, with his warriors behind him, rode over Custer and his men, cutting them down to the ground. The Indians came in a great cloud of dust, which hid the bloody killing that followed. When the dust settled, the soldiers were dead. A handful of white men broke away, running downhill in a panic, but the Indians galloped behind them and killed them as they ran. And then it was over.

The soldiers were all dead, the battlefield suddenly quiet, and the Indians, as they said later, were as surprised as people are when a tornado passes and leaves behind silence after its terrible roar. Custer and one-third of the 7th Cavalry had been wiped out in less than an hour.

The next day, the Indians renewed the siege of Benteen and Reno in hard fighting that lasted until the middle of the afternoon. Then, unexpectedly, the Indians stuck their camp and by sunset were moving south and away from the battlefield. Finally, on June 27, General Terry's troops came up the river from the north. His men counted 197 bodies on the hill. Custer was among them. He had been stripped naked, but he was not scalped or mutilated in any way. He had two clean wounds, one in the temple and one in the heart, either of which could have been fatal. The Indians themselves never knew who had killed Custer or even how or when he had been killed. Many didn't even know that Custer had been on the battlefield that day until much later.

The Battle of Little Bighorn was the U.S. Army's most decisive defeat during the Indian Wars of the late 1800s. It also sealed the fate of the Indians and destroyed whatever chances remained for men of goodwill to bridge the gaps that separated Native Americans from whites. After the death of Custer and his men, the national mood hardened and in Washington and on the battlefields of the West, government officials and military commanders began planning to crush the Native American resistance once and for all. Companies of cavalry were expanded from 64 to 100 and new recruits hurried to join the "Custer Avengers." General Crook took to the field and drove his men to their limit, as if to make up for the foundering campaigns of the spring. Nelson Miles dressed his men in thick buffalo coats and rampaged across the Sioux lands all winter and into 1877. Other columns attacked Indian encampments from all sides, wiping out the Sioux. Their warriors were killed, their villages destroyed, their food supplies burned and their women and children left starving and homeless in the cold. Although fighting flared up periodically for the next decade and a half, but there was never again a real war or even a battle on the scale of what happened at Little Bighorn.

Custer's death marked the end of an era. New railroad lines were built across the West, towns and cities sprang up and settlers spread across the land. And as the country changed, the role of the frontier soldier changed along with it. In time, the frontier forts slowly vanished and the cavalry soldier vanished too. The Indian Wars slowly faded into history, leaving only silent stone markers and designated historic sites behind.

Hauntings at Little Bighorn

The site of Custer's final battle was first preserved as a national cemetery in 1879, to protect the graves of the 7th Cavalry troopers who were buried where they fell. It was re-designated in 1946 as the Custer Battlefield National Monument and later renamed Little Bighorn Battlefield National Monument in 199i. The site is under the care of the National Park Service and many of the staff members as well as visitors at the battlefield are quick to assure you that this is one of the most haunted locations in the West.

Many of those who experience strange things on the battlefield are among the nearly 400,000 visitors who tour the windswept ravines and ridges of the site each year. Standing on the hill where Custer and the last of his men died, they can only imagine the last moments of the soldiers as they met their fate at the hands of the Lakota and Cheyenne. Many of the men lay wounded, helpess and horrified on the bloody grass, their heads filled with the screams and groans of their comrades in arms. When the battle was finished, most of the bodies were mutilated beyond recognition. If there was ever a place where ghosts might linger, it's the Little Bighorn Battlefield.

According to visitors and staff members, the dead are restless at Little Bighorn. Whether all of those who come to the site are believers in ghosts or not, the mysterious happenings on the battlefield are an indeble part of the place. As historian and author Robert Utley wrote, "Stories of the supernatural seem to revolve around legendary spots."

The encounters on the field date back many years. The Crow people were apparently aware of ghostly events at the site long before any others. They called the site superintendent, "ghost herder" because he lowered the flag at dusk, which the Crow believed allowed the

Little Bighorn Battlefield

spirits to rise from their graves and walk amongst the living. When the flag was raised, in the morning, the dead came back to rest.

Robert Utley was a ranger at the battlefield between 1947 and 1952 and reported no ghost sightings during his tenure there, but one experience involving author Charles Kuhlman did take place during that time period. It has been reported that Custer's spirit visited Kulhman. It has also been reported that Kuhlman would visit Last Stand Hill alone, in hopes of making some form of contact with the other world. Utley denies these events happened. However, it could explain Kuhlman's fantastic interpretation of the battle in a book that he wrote about the events at Little Bighorn.

In the later 1950s, visitors began to tell of hearing the sounds of Indian warriors charging on horseback through the cemetery at the site. Others, who walked through the cemetery at night, spoke of cold spots that seemed to spring up from nowhere. A visitor from New Orleans claimed to have been transported back in time to witness the battle. While driving along Battle Ridge, a cab driver from Minneapolis reported witnessing soldiers and Indian warriors fighting to the death. He came shaken and distraught into the visitor's center, where the employees calmed him. Such stories continued to be recounted for years.

One evening in August 1976, a National Park Service law enforcement officer visited Last Stand Hill. He was alone when he felt a sudden drop in temperature go through his body. The cold was accompanied by the soft murmuring of voices. He did not stay long enough to discover whether they were talking to him.

In August 1987, on a moonless night, a psychic from Colorado visited the battlefield. Although she had never been there before, and knew little about the battle, she provided details of the action at Medicine Tail Ford and Nye-Cartwright Ridge. Standing beside the 7th Cavalry Monument and the mass grave of the soldier dead, she felt the presence of restless spirits from the Custer battalion. While visiting the cemetery, the same psychic saw a spirit warrior charge a seasonal employee, then turn and ride past the visitor's center down Cemetery Ridge.

Many other stories come from park employees, who are willing to accept that there is more about the battlefield than first meets the eye. Former Custer Battlefield Park Ranger Mardell Plainfeather had an experience on the battlefield in 1980. Mardell is a member of the Crow tribe and still faithfully practices her people's ceremonies. She and her family regularly visited their sweat lodge that sat quietly in the thick timber along the Little Bighorn River across from the battlefield. Late one evening Mardell and her daughter, Lorena, went to the sweat lodge to make sure the fire was extinguished. While walking across the battlefield after sunset, she saw two Indian warriors on horseback silhouetted upon the bluffs. The warriors were on the battlefield proper within the confines of the fence. They were dressed for war, faces and bodies painted, feathers placed in the long flowing hair of one, while the other wore braids. They carried shields and one had a bow. They were there one moment and then gone the next.

Employees report bizarre stories inside the Stone House, a two-story building that was constructed as a residence for the site superintendent in 1894. It has since been converted into a library, the park historian's office and conference rooms. The lower level was once used to house bodies awaiting burial in the nearby national cemetery. Before being turned into the library, parts of it were used as a summer residence for staff members and was closed up tightly and left empty during the harsh winter months.

While living on the battleground, former ranger Neil Mangum remembered walking home on many winter nights through the cemetery and seeing the lights on in the Stone House's upstairs apartment. He always turned off the lights. Once he couldn't get the front door open. Frustrated, Neil went home, returning an hour later. The door opened easily. He walked up the stairs, and in Neil's usual calm demeanor turned off the lights one more time.

The Stone House can be an unsettling place. A woman's figure has been seen coming down the stairs. Footsteps are heard upstairs when no one is there. During the summer season of 1986, a new battlefield ranger was housed for two nights in the upstairs apartment. He awoke the first night feeling someone sitting at the foot of his bed. He first thought it was his wife, but he remembered she was visiting family overseas, and he was alone. As he reached for the pistol that he kept on his nightstand, he saw a shadowy figure move from the foot of his bed. The ranger distinctly saw a torso of a soldier with the head and legs missing as the apparition disappeared into the other room.

A wooden wall complete with a padlocked door was built to make two bedrooms in the lower level of the Stone House. One night early in the 1989 season, two staff members were sound asleep. One was suddenly awakened by loud bangs on the partition wall. The sound was coming from the opposite side of the wall. The door was locked. The padlock was on the employee's side of the wall. The strong knocks occurred again. The other staff member was awakened, but the sounds had stopped. The only entrance to the other side of the wall is through a window that was securely locked. Neither employee was able to explain the anomalous sounds.

In August 1997, just before the Stone House was converted into the library, four people spent the night there. One man slept in the upstairs apartment bedroom while a father and son shared the sleeper sofa in the apartment's living room. A young woman slept downstairs. She awoke in the middle of the night to the sound of footsteps moving across the floor upstairs. She figured it was one of the fellows heading to the bathroom. The footsteps exited the bedroom, went through the upstairs hall to the bathroom then back again. Then, moments later, more footsteps sounded, but this time they were louder. They became so forceful that she noticed flakes of paint falling from the edge of the downstairs windows. Her first thought was that whoever it was would wake up the whole house. She became very concerned the sounds became louder and more forceful, almost vibrating the entire downstairs. Suddenly, the downstairs kitchen door slammed shut with a loud bang. Startled, the young woman jumped up from her bed. She knew it wasn't a gust of wind because all the windows had been covered with heavy plastic and taped very secure during the renovation. It wasn't wind that slammed shut the door -- it was something else.

She left the house that night and tried to sleep in her car, but spent a very restless night. The next morning she shared this experience with the men who slept upstairs. All were perplexed because none of them heard footsteps banging around the apartment. However, the father who spent the night on the sleeper sofa remembered being awakened by a loud bang from downstairs around 2:30 a.m. It had been the kitchen door as it mysteriously closed on its own!

The visitor's center for the site rests at the bottom of the hill where Custer met his end. Tourists come in to escape the heat of the Montana sun, to browse the bookstore and visit the museum. After they have left for the day and the doors are locked, the spirits sometimes are said to wreak havoc in the building. Voices are heard, footsteps wander the halls and the lights come on by themselves, long after the living have departed.

On a summer's day in 1985, an employee had an odd experience in the museum basement. He had just presented a program to the public and was returning some items to the audio/visual room. Before he reached the inventory storage room, he noticed a figure of a person standing in the dark corner. Although it appeared to him to be a soldier, he thought it was a fellow employee who was trying to play a trick on him. He pretended not to see the soldier and walked past him. As the employee turned left to enter the audio room, he noticed, out of the corner of his eye, the shadowy figure of the soldier moving into the hall. The apparition proceeded to walk through the locked door of the inventory room and disappear.

Recently, a ranger was giving a live presentation to visitors when he was suddenly interrupted by the sensation that something was pulling at his leg and trying to force him to the ground. He looked down to find nothing there. One woman working in the bookstore by herself felt someone tap her on the shoulder. She turned around to find she was alone.

With such tales still being told, it's obvious that Little Bighorn remains a haunted place and that the ghosts of the battle-scarred dead are still restless there. This is a place where history literally remains alive and where the ghosts of the past are still very relevant in the present.

1885: THE ROCK SPRINGS MASSACRE

Trouble had been brewing for a long time. It was hard to say if the rampant anti-Chinese sentiments spreading through the American West in the latter half of the 1800s were spawned by simple hatred and resentment or outright racism. It was probably both, with economic hard times thrown into the mix.

Chinese immigrants were at first welcomed, especially in California where the laborers were badly needed. Many of these immigrants found themselves working alongside whites, although they were never treated as

A Chinese man working on a tunnel for the Central Pacific Railroad.

(Below) Anti-Chinese posters and fliers were distributed throughout Western states, inflaming hatred whenever possible.

equals. Chinese men immigrated to the United States by the thousands for work, leaving their families behind. Most considered themselves "sojourners," or temporary residents of the U.S., planning to eventually return to China. Even with the meager wages offered, they could earn five to ten times at the "Gold Mountain," as they called California, than they could at home in China. Most planned to work for several years in America, saving their wages and living frugally, then return to their families in China with what would amount to a small fortune by Chinese standards. In the end, the reality was that very few of these men ever made it back home and some eventually sent for their families to join them in America.

Records were poorly kept so it's unknown how many Chinese men made the trip across the Pacific but experts estimate that the number must have been between 100,000 and 150,000. Most of them lived and worked in the Western states. Some were able to start their own businesses or work as servants, but a majority took jobs that required hard, physical labor. Regardless of where they went or what they did, they tended to work and live in concentrated groups. White Americans at the time were generally not a tolerant bunch. They tended to be suspicious of foreigners in general and were *especially* suspicious of Asians. They were surely heathens and there was no telling what they might get up to. Whether required to by law or in the interest of mutual protection, the Chinese lived amongst themselves and steered clear of their white co-workers. Since they didn't intend to stay, few learned to speak English other than the few words they needed to do their jobs.

When the Central Pacific Railroad began construction on the transcontinental railroad that would connect the East and West coasts with a single rail line, they needed laborers by the thousands. The railroad tracks would begin in Sacramento and were to head east and over the mountains. Over 12,000 Chinese went to work for the railroad. It was difficult and dangerous work and an estimated 10 percent of them died before its completion.

After years of backbreaking work, the Central Pacific Railroad and the Union Pacific Railroad came together in Utah in 1869. Great celebrations were held across the country to commemorate the completion of the tremendous endeavor. An unfortunate result of this accomplishment was that tens of thousands of men, white and Chinese alike, simultaneously found themselves out of work.

Many people believed that since the railroad was one of the largest employers of Chinese immigrants, and now that the railroad was completed, they would go home. But they didn't leave, and a growing resentment against them was spreading throughout the Western states. Many white workers believed that the Chinese were taking jobs away from them. They also believed that the surplus of Chinese labor was driving wages lower for everyone.

Wages were indeed lower where there were larger numbers of Chinese workers. They had come without their families and had no plans to stay and settle in the U.S, so they were willing to live in rooms with eight to ten other men, sharing the rent. This kept their living expenses down so they were more willing to accept lower wages than their white counterparts who were trying to support families and save to buy homes of their own.

Random outbreaks of violence were seen in growing numbers. In San Francisco in July 1870, a group of white workers started what became a huge street protest against the Chinese workers in the area. In Los Angeles' Chinatown, when a fight broke out between rival Chinese gangs, a mob of whites swept in and killed 23 Chinese. The violence was not limited to California. Chinese workers had been beaten, sometimes fatally, in Arizona and Nevada.

It was becoming all-too apparent to the Chinese that they were not wanted, nor were they safe, anywhere. This did not curb the flow of Chinese immigrants into the U.S. The more who came, the more discontented voices cried out in opposition. After numerous protests, riots, beatings and murders, the federal government finally took action. Instead of cracking down on the violence, the government instead chose to cut off admittance to all Chinese immigrants. The 1882 Chinese Exclusions Act was passed with the intent of suspending the flow of Chinese people into the country for 10 years. This helped appease the white citizens, but only a little. The law did nothing about the Chinese men that were already in the country, so discontent and hatred continued to fester. Nothing had ever been done to quail the anti-Chinese violence. Up until that point, no American had ever been charged with any crime against anyone from China.

With the joining of the two halves of the country, the railroads had a monopoly on transcontinental travel. Train travel rapidly became the most popular mode of transportation for cargo and passengers. No longer did people have to make the trip in slow and dangerous wagon trains or spend days sitting in a stagecoach jolting from town to town. But as train travel increased, so did the need for coal to fire the engines boilers. Coal kept the trains moving -- lots and lots of coal.

The transcontinental rail route through southern Wyoming hadn't been chosen by accident. Wyoming had coal that the railroads needed badly. A Union Pacific Coal Department was created as the railroad went into the mining business. The company set up mining camps all along their rail line, the largest ones in Laramie, Evanston and Rock Springs. The miners hired to dig railroad coal were predominantly white, many of them Irish immigrants who had formerly worked laying track for the railroad.

Coal mining was difficult and dangerous work and the railroad coal bosses were hard taskmasters. The men working in the mines were treated harshly and paid poorly,. To make matters worse, the living conditions in southern Wyoming in winter were brutal. The miners also felt cheated because they were required to buy food, clothing and other supplies at the company stores at inflated prices.

The Union Pacific had spent a fortune getting the transcontinental railroad built and in the early years of its operation, the company found itself in financial trouble. To save expenses, they cut the miners' wages. The miners working the Wyoming mines, and specifically the ones in Rock Springs, were mostly Cornish, Irish, Swedish and Welsh immigrants. They were outraged by the cut in pay and in 1871 they took action by calling a strike and walking out of the mines. Backed by federal troops, the Union Pacific fired the strikers who refused to return to work. Then they brought in Scandinavian miners who agreed to work for the lower wages and promised not to strike, but that situation didn't last long.

By 1875, the Rock Springs miners had become so distressed that they called another strike and again walked out of the mines, refusing to return until their demands were met. They believed that by disrupting the flow of coal needed to keep the trains moving, they would be able to force the railroad to meet their demands for better pay and improved working conditions. Their plan failed. Evidently they had forgotten how they had gotten their jobs when they were brought in as strikebreakers. The Union Pacific simply ignored their protests and hired other miners to replace them.

The Union Pacific didn't have far to look for the workers they needed. Before working on the railroad, many of the Chinese men had worked in the gold mines during the California Gold Rush of 1849. As experienced miners, they were qualified to work in the Union Pacific coal mines in Wyoming, and they were willing to accept the low wages the Scandinavian miners were receiving before their strike. Less than two weeks after the strike began, mining operations resumed when 50 whites and 150 Chinese walked into the mines and went to work. Again, the company was aided in breaking the strike by federal troops. After all, the government had an interest in keeping the trains running.

Eventually the fired strikers who had not left Rock Springs went back to work, but they remained in the minority in comparison to the number of Chinese miners. Wages were at their lowest point ever and the white miners were convinced that the blame lay with the Chinese and their willingness to accept whatever the railroad was willing to pay.

Despite the low pay, the deplorable working conditions and the brutal weather, the Rock Springs mines grew and took on more miners. By 1885, the numbers had become consistent, with 150 white miners and 330 Chinese miners. Though they worked side by side every day, the two groups lived apart and didn't mingle much. The white miners lived with their families in a section of Rock Springs nicknamed "Whiteman's Town." Some of the Chinese workers now had families with them and they lived in company-built huts in an area separated from Rock Springs by the railroad tracks and Bitter Creek called "Chinatown." The two groups continued to work together and live apart amidst growing racial tension and unease.

The white miners became increasingly unhappy and most of them united and formed the Knights of Labor, calling for better working conditions and higher wages. The Knights of Labor became one of the strongest voices against the employment of Chinese workers. Although it is certain that they did what they could to propagate racial tension and hatred, it could never be proven that they instigated the riot and massacre that was to occur in Rock Springs.

Coal miners were paid by the ton; the more coal they dug, the bigger their paychecks. The coal was more plentiful and easier to dig in some areas of the mines called "rooms" than others. If a miner was able to work in a prime room, he could produce more coal and make more money. It was common for fights between white and Chinese miners to break out over the coal in prime rooms. These disputes served to further inflame the whites' anger toward the Chinese.

The Riot and the Massacre

As the work began at 7:00 a.m. on September 2, 1885, a group of 10 white miners walked into a prime room in coal pit Number 6. They found a group of Chinese miners already at work. Angry at the prospect of having to move to a less productive room, they insisted that the Chinese had no right to work there and demanded that they leave. A fight soon broke out when the Chinese men refused. The whites beat one of the men so severely on the head with a pick ax that he died soon after. As they started to beat a second man, a company foreman came in and broke up the fight. That particular day happened to fall on a Chinese holiday and many miners had stayed home to celebrate. They and their families were unaware of what was happening at the mine.

Instead of going back to work, the white miners, all members of the Knights of Labor, stormed out and returned to town. There they raged through the streets, collecting more men and forming a mob as they went. From gathered any weapons they could find: knives, clubs, hatchets and rifles. A few of the men tried to calm things down but were unsuccessful. The mob was becoming increasingly angry. By 10:00 a.m., their number had swelled to over 150. It was at this point that they began their march back toward the mines and Chinatown.

When they got to pit Number 3, they broke up into smaller gangs and positioned themselves around the mine entrance, the mining sheds and the pump house. Another gang moved to block off any routes of escape. Several women who had joined the mob lined up in front of the plank bridge crossing Bitter Creek, cutting off another possible means of escape.

A small group moved forward into Chinatown carrying a warning to the Chinese that they had one hour to pack up and get out or they would be driven out. The Chinese were well aware of the whites' animosity towards them, but they had never taken any precautions or made any preparations to protect themselves. They had left themselves completely vulnerable to the attack that was about to take place.

The mob was far too agitated to wait a full hour and after only 30 minutes, they started randomly firing into the small buildings, shooting two Chinese miners. The groups began again to amass into a large mob and moved toward Chinatown, firing off random shots as they went. The mob was moving in on the Chinese from three directions, from the east and west ends of town and across the wagon road, trapping most of the residents. Not everyone took part in the massacre that followed, but no one tried to stop it.

A Chinese survivor gave an account of what happened next at the Chinese consul in New York: "Whenever the mob met a Chinese they stopped him and, pointing a weapon at him, asked him if he had any revolver, and then approaching him they searched his person, robbing him of his watch or any gold or silver that he might have about him, before letting him go. Some of the rioters would let a Chinese go after depriving him of all his gold and silver, while another Chinese would be beaten with the butt ends of the weapons before being let go. Some of the rioters, when they could not stop a Chinese, would shoot him dead on the spot, and then search and rob him. Some would overtake a Chinese, throw him down and search and rob him before they let him go. Some of the rioters would not fire their weapons, but would only use the butt ends to beat the Chinese with. Some would not beat a Chinese, but rob him of whatever he had and let him go, yelling to him to go quickly. Some, who took no part either in beating or robbing the Chinese, stood by, shouting and laughing and clapping their hands."

As the afternoon wore on, the mob became more violent. Two of the women who were waiting at the plank bridge shot any of the Chinese people who tried to make their escape by heading their direction. The men moved through Chinatown, looting, beating and shooting. Several Chinese were able to sneak out and ran into the surrounding hills, hiding in the high grass to avoid being seen. A few were so badly injured that they died where they were hiding, while their family and friends were being terrorized below. Some of the victims tried to escape by rushing to the creek, and others attempted to cross the railroad bridge. They were either shot to death or left to die of injuries inflicted as they tried to flee.

Some time in the late afternoon, the bloodthirsty mob was no longer satisfied with robbing and brutalizing the Chinese. They were too caught up in their racist frenzy and would only be satisfied with the utter destruction of those they saw as the cause of their woes. Between late afternoon and 9:00 p.m. that night, the mob moved through Chinatown, setting torches to everything that would burn.

Artist's conception of the Rock Springs massacre. No known photos exist.

As the small homes of the Chinese were set ablaze, the mob threw many of their victims' corpses into the flames. Some of the Chinese had hidden in their houses when they heard the attackers coming, too afraid to run away. The rioters ransacked the houses before burning them. If they found anyone hiding inside, they dragged them out, killed them, then threw them back inside to burn along with their homes. If they came upon any sick or disabled people, they left them to be burned alive.

Blood lust had infected the rioters and the murders were becoming exceptionally violent. The riot had started with beating, shooting and burning, and then progressed to mutilation. Many of the injured and dead showed evidence of being scalped or branded; others were decapitated, dismembered or hanged. There was a rumor that one victim's penis and testicles were sliced from his body and displayed in a bar in Whiteman's Town as a trophy.

As the rampage continued, there were certain people who were conspicuously absent: the Union Pacific company bosses. They were there watching from a safe distance, but had not taken any action to halt the violence. Instead, they had positioned themselves around the mine to prevent the fires from spreading to the company buildings. They stood and watched as their Chinese employees were being slaughtered, but little did they know that they themselves were not going to finish the night unscathed.

When all of Chinatown was burning and all the Chinese either had fled, been killed, or left for dead, the mob turned their anger on their bosses, whom they felt were the root cause of their misery. They threatened their lives if they didn't leave town immediately -- which they did as quickly as they could.

As the riot was becoming a massacre, Sweetwater County Sheriff Joseph Young was 14 miles away in Green River. When he heard about the violence, he immediately took a special train to Rock Springs. Before he left, he searched Green River for men willing to form a posse and go with him, but everyone whom he asked refused. Sheriff Young later insisted that there was nothing he could do; he was one man against a violent mob. Instead, he rounded up a few man to replace the company bosses who had left, and protected the Union Pacific buildings from fire.

The mob's rage wilted somewhat as the flames died away. They had burned 75 Chinese homes, leaving only two standing. There were 28 confirmed dead, possibly as many as 50. Fifteen of the Chinese who had been brutalized and left for dead had survived at least through the following day before being carted off to another Chinese mining camp.

Of the dead, four were found mutilated beyond recognition. Nine bodies were completely or partially burned. Victims left to burn inside their homes were found with only the lower or upper parts of the bodies burned, depending on where they had been hiding. In some cases, only a few bones were found: leg bones in a hut near Camp No. 14, the right half of a skull and part of a backbone in another hut, foot bones in a hut near Camp No. 34, an upper torso found in a hut near Camp No. 27, and on and on. Only bone fragments were found from 15 more bodies. Several other bodies were left lying where they died. After the fires burned themselves out, the remaining corpses scattered about the camp, the creek bank, the railroad tracks and the hillside were left where they were, exposed to the elements and hungry animals.

Word of the massacre traveled fast. The other railroad mining towns in southern Wyoming also had large contingents of Chinese miners and the animus toward them was just as vile as it was in Rock Springs. Law enforcement officers at these mines were terrified that the white miners there would follow the example of those in Rock Springs. Evanston was of particular concern as hundreds of Chinese miners lived and worked there, as well as in nearby Almy.

Wyoming's territorial Governor Francis Warren visited Rock Springs the day following the riot. He quickly realized that racial tension was still running high and the area remained unstable. The white miners in Evanston were showing signs that a riot there might be imminent. He quickly telegraphed President Grover Cleveland requesting federal troops. By September 5, just three days after the massacre, one company of infantry was posted in Rock Springs and another in Evanston, with an order for six more companies to be brought up from Utah within the next three days.

Most of the Chinese who had escaped the slaughter were picked up by Union Pacific trains and taken to Evanston, 100 miles west of Rock Springs. By September 5, all the survivors who could be found were clustered in

Evanston's Chinatown. They held their collective breath and waited to see if the pot there would boil over as it had in Rock Springs. Even with the company of soldiers assigned to keep the peace, they knew they were not yet safe as threats of murder, mutilation and torture were hurled at them night and day.

All the white miners working in railroad mines in Wyoming went on strike in response to the riot. They continued to protest the use of Chinese miners. Though there were no corresponding riots at the other mines, they did threaten the Chinese, telling them that if they broke the strike and went to work, they would not leave the mines alive. The Chinese wisely chose to stay home.

The troops collected the Chinese miners from Rock Springs and Almy and moved them all into Evanston's Chinatown. Regardless of their growing numbers, they soon came to believe that they would never be safe in the mines and pleaded to be taken out of Wyoming. The company refused. They then asked to be paid the two months' wages they were owed so they might pay their own way out of Wyoming. Again, their request was refused. In Evanston, 250 white citizens prepared a petition and delivered it to Territorial Governor Warren. They requested that the Chinese be paid enough money to leave the state. Warren refused to interfere with the railroad's decision, claiming it was none of his business. The Chinese miners and their families found themselves trapped in a land where racial hated was so intense that their lives were in constant danger.

Early in the morning on September 9, just one week after the massacre, a special train pulled in to the Evanston station. The train was pulling a long string of empty boxcars. Four companies of infantry provided an armed escort as several hundred Chinese laborers were marched to the train and loaded into the boxcars. The 250 troops then boarded the train. The Chinese were told that they were being taken to San Francisco as they had requested. The soldiers were to travel with them to guarantee their safety until they arrived.

The train moved slowly and eventually arrived at its destination that evening. It must have seemed a horribly cruel trick to these poor, frightened people, for when the doors to the boxcars were rolled aside, they found that they were back in Rock Springs, the stench of burned bodies still heavy in the air. In front of them, they saw the charred remains of the snug little huts that once contained everything they owned. The train had stopped not at

A company of soldiers lined up on Main Street in Rock Springs in 1885, after the massacre.

the station, where a group of angry white miners were waiting, but a little farther down the line where Chinatown once stood.

Some Union Pacific company men had buried a few of the bodies, leaving the rest lying in the dirt. A Chinese miner later reported to a diplomat in New York that the bodies lay: "[M]angled and decomposed, and they were being eaten by dogs and hogs." The Chinese set about the gruesome task of burying what was left of their dead. They then sifted through the ashes of their former homes, searching for more human remains.

Chinatown was gone. There was no place for the Chinese miners to live, so they had to make the boxcars their new homes until the debris could be cleared and new huts built. The white miners lined up across Bitter Creek, an ironically appropriate name for the creek that separated Whiteman's Town from Chinatown, yelling threats and racial slurs. They did the same at each mine entrance.

Again, the Chinese asked for tickets to California or their back wages so they could buy their own tickets. The company refused yet again. There was coal to be dug and there were too few white miners to dig enough to keep the trains running.

The Chinese miners were too terrified to go back to work and the whites refused to work in protest of the return of the Chinese. Union Pacific threatened to permanently fire any miner of any race who was not back at work on Monday, September 21. To further "encourage" the Chinese back into the mines, the company store refused to sell them food and the troops threatened to kick them out of the boxcars and into the cold, unprotected.

Most of the miners saw no alternative and returned to work. One by one, the Chinese miners who were still afraid and bitter left by whatever means they could find on their own.

One month after the mines reopened, all but two companies of troops returned to their original posts in Utah. Two semi-permanent army posts were set up with one company each. Camp Medicine Butte was established in Evanston and Camp Pilot Butte went up in Rock Springs.

There was a token attempt at holding someone responsible for the riot. Sixteen white miners were arrested and jailed in Green River, but they were never tried for their crimes. The Sweetwater County Grand Jury refused to indict them. They were released from jail to a cheering crowd and found themselves treated as conquering heroes. No one was ever charged or held responsible for the murders in Rock Springs.

The vicious brutality of the killings stunned some parts of the country. Eastern newspapers, especially in New York, proclaimed the horrors of the massacre. Not so in southern Wyoming, where local newspapers joined the celebrations, praising the rioters and encouraging white laborers to continue the harassment of the Chinese. Newspapers in nearby states were a bit cooler, not actually praising the rioters but failing to condemn them.

The federal government finally agreed to pay the Chinese miners a small compensate for their losses, but would not go as far as compensate anyone for the murder of a family member. And the government did leave a company of infantry in each of Evanston and Rock Springs for the next 14 years. The racial tension and hatred continued, but the mines of southern Wyoming would never again see an eruption of violence as bad as the massacre in early September of 1885.

The government's attempt at making amends with the Chinese miners was likely done to appease China. American diplomats suggested that the violence experienced by the miners was in partly due to their insistence on living in compact Chinese groups, and their refusal to assimilate into the American culture. In reply to the blame for the murders being shifted to the victims, the governor-general of China's Guangdong region suggested that, "Americans in China might be the target of revenge for the events in Rock Springs." The U.S. government's decision to partially compensate the victims came shortly after China's veiled threat.

A tense peace continued in Rock Springs and Evanston, under the close supervision of the army. The same could not be said for other areas in the West. Many violent outbreaks occurred in Oregon and Washington where angry mobs in small towns drove Chinese workers from their homes and their towns. Anti-Chinese sentiments continued to be expressed as far east as Georgia. Bizarrely, in some parts of the country, the response to the violence against the Chinese workers in Rock Springs was one of approval, fueling the anti-Chinese movement.

Today, Rock Springs maintains a population of around 20,000 citizens. The notable areas associated with the massacre: Whiteman's Town, Chinatown, Camp Pilot Butte and the mines have all lost any resemblance to what they were in the late 1800s. What was left of Camp Pilot Butte was briefly added to the National Register of Historic Places, but as the last of the remaining buildings were razed, the historic designation was removed. An elementary school now sits on a section of what was once Chinatown.

The city has grown over time and has absorbed any of the historic sites that may have remained. Rock Springs citizens with a Chinese heritage now enjoy the same pleasures and respect as every other citizen. The old bitterness and hatred has gone. It is highly unlikely that any of the current Chinese residents have any affiliation with those who suffered through the Rock Springs riot and massacre. As the mines there petered out and the Union Pacific Railroad lost its iron grip on the area's economy, the Chinese miners and their families moved away at their first possible opportunity. Although they had lived in relative peace for many years, painful memories and resentment remained.

Though all the original Chinese families moved away a hundred years ago, some of those who died there so violently may have stayed on. Over the years, several people have reported strange and unexplainable experiences, especially in locations built over the old Chinatown. A common experience is described as having the feeling of being watched, only to turn around and find no one is there. Others have reported seeing the movement of fleeting shapes in their peripheral vision, and the sensation of being lightly tapped or touched. The most common odd experience typically happens out of doors, and especially in one park in particular. Day or night, without any warning, a man-shaped shadow will move out of the shadows and approach the witness, seeming to stare at them, but without any eyes.

Is the increased activity over the old Chinatown just a coincidence or is it an indication that restless spirits linger in the space where they lost their lives so long ago? We will never know, but perhaps someone has remained to make sure that the horrible events of the past are never repeated.

1914: THERE WAS BLOOD
The Ludlow Massacre

On September 23, 1913, some 12,000 coal miners in the thriving town of Ludlow, Colorado, went on strike in an event that started what came to be called the Colorado Coalfield War. As the conflict worsened, miners around Ludlow were driven from their company-owned homes and took up resident in a makeshift tent city. The following spring, on April 20, 1914, armed agents of the coal mine owners attacked the encamped strikers and their families, killing 26 people, including two women and 11 children. The Ludlow Massacre was the deadliest single incident in the southern Colorado coal strikes, but it led to even more bloodshed.

In retaliation for Ludlow, the miners armed themselves and attacked dozens of mines over the next 10 days, destroying property and engaging in several skirmishes with the Colorado National Guard along a 40-mile front from Trinidad to Walsenburg. The entire strike ended up costing between 69 and 199 lives and has been described by some as the deadliest strike in the history of the United States.

Coal deposits had first been discovered in Colorado by William Jackson Palmer in 1867. He was then leading a survey team that was planning the route of the Kansas Pacific Railway. The rapid expansion of the railroads in America made coal a highly valued commodity and it was rapidly commercialized in Colorado by a handful of huge companies. The largest company, Colorado Fuel & Iron, was the largest operator in the West, as well as one of the nation's most powerful corporations. It was purchased by John D. Rockefeller in 1902 and nine years later, he turned his controlling interest over to his son, John D. Rockefeller, Jr., who managed the company from his office in New York.

Life in the American coal fields has never been easy, but conditions in the mines of Colorado proved more deadly and exhausting than in many other mines in the late 1800s and early 1900s. Between 1884 and 1912, more than 1,700 miners died in Colorado, more than twice the national average. It was dangerous and difficult work and miners in Colorado were at constant risk for explosion, suffocation and collapsing mine walls. Miners were generally paid according to the tonnage of coal produced, while those who did so-called "dead work" that involved safety measures such as shoring up unstable roofs, were usually unpaid. The tonnage system drove many miners to gamble with their lives by neglecting precautions and taking on risk, with consequences that were often fatal. The men had to feed their families, but in many cases, they failed to provide a good living and created widows and orphans instead.

No matter how bad the working conditions were, the miners had no way to air their grievances. Most miners resided in company towns in which all land, homes and stores were owned by the mine operators and which were designed to force loyalty from the workers and to silence any dissent. The company had complete power over the workers since rents, groceries and any other amenities were deducted from the miners' wages. The laws in town were company rules, enforced by company guards who often refused to admit any "suspicious" stranger (which usually meant anyone who seemed to be a union organizer) into town. Miners who raised the ire of the company were liable to find themselves and their families evicted from their homes.

Frustrated by working conditions they felt were unsafe and unjust, miners increasingly turned to the unions. Colorado miners had repeatedly attempted to unionize since the state's first coal mines were started in 1883. The Western Federation of Miners primarily organized hard rock miners in the gold and silver camps during the 1890s. Beginning in 1900, the United Mine Workers of America (UMWA) began organizing coal miners in the Western states, including southern Colorado. The UMWA decided to focus on Colorado Fuel & Iron because of the company's harsh management tactics by the distant Rockefellers and other investors. To break or prevent strikes, the coal companies hired strikebreakers, mainly from Mexico and southern and eastern Europe.

Union activity was constantly suppressed in the Colorado. Mine organizers were driven out of town and miners who joined unions were summarily fired. In spite of this, secret organizing by the UMWA continued in the years leading up to 1913. Eventually, the union presented a list of demands on behalf of the miners asking, among other things, for recognition of the union, an increase in wages, enforcement of an eight-hour work day, payment for "dead work," the right to choose their own boarding houses and doctors, and a strict enforcement of Colorado safety laws.

The major coal companies rejected the demands and in September 1913, the UMWA called for a strike across the Trinidad Coalfield of southwestern Colorado. The operations affected by the strike --- Rocky Mountain Fuel Company, Victor-American Fuel Company and the Rockefeller-owned Colorado Fuel & Iron — essentially controlled the industry in the region. The miners who went on strike were promptly evicted from their company homes, threatened and beaten, and tarred and feathered by company thugs.

With nowhere to live, the miners and their families moved into tent villages that had been set up by the union. The tents were

The Ludlow tent colony before the massacre.

Armed union strikers at the Ludlow camp

built on wooden platforms and heated by cast iron stoves on land that had been leased by the union in preparation for a strike. When they had leased the sites, the union had strategically selected locations near the mouths of the canyons that led into the coal camps. In this way, they could monitor the traffic that went into the mines and harass the replacement workers that were brought in. Confrontations between striking miners and working miners (referred to as "scabs" by the union) often resulted in violence and occasionally, in death.

As the strike continued through the fall and winter and coal production fell, the mine owners took drastic steps to try and break the strike. Under the guidance of Colorado Fuel & Iron, the mine owners hired the infamous Baldwin-Felts Detective Agency, a notorious anti-labor firm that was known for its hostile treatment of striking workers. These mercenaries arrived with rifles and Gatling guns, all financed by the Rockefeller family.

Throughout the months of the strike, Baldwin-Felts men raided the tent village in the middle of the night. They lit up the tents with searchlights and fired randomly into them, occasionally killing and injuring people. Men, women and children died from gunshots or under the hooves of horses that were stampeded through the camp. They also used an improvised armored car, mounted with a machine gun, that the union called the "Death Special," to patrol the camp's perimeters. The steel-covered car was built in the Colorado Fuel & Iron plant in Pueblo, Colorado, from the chassis of a large touring sedan. Agents from the detective agency often raced it through the camp, its machine gun ripping apart the tents with a rain of bullets. It got so bad that the miners dug sleeping pits beneath the tents so they

One of the so-called "Death Special" armored cars, mounted with a machine gun, which was used to patrol the camp by detectives hired by the mining company.

Militia soldiers called in to help control the violence added to the chaos instead.

and their families could be better protected at night.

As strike-related violence grew worse, Governor Elias M. Ammons called in the state militia on October 28. At first, the presence of the militia calmed the situation but it soon became clear that the sympathies of militia leaders lay with company managements. Guard Adjutant-General John Chase, who had served during a violent strike at Cripple Creek 10 years earlier, allowed the harsh treatment of the miners to continue. On March 10, 1914, the body of a replacement miner was found on the railroad tracks near Forbes, Colorado. Militia officers stated that the man had been murdered by strikers. In retaliation, Chase ordered the tent camp at Forbes to be burned to the ground. The attack was carried out while the inhabitants were attending a funeral for infants who had died a few days earlier.

The strike continued into the spring of 1914. By then, the state was unable to continue funding the militia and they were recalled. The governor and the mining companies, fearing a breakdown in order, left only two militia units in southern Colorado and allowed the coal companies to finance their own militia, which largely consisted of Colorado Fuel & Iron guards in militia uniforms.

On Monday morning, April 20, three militia members appeared at the camp near Ludlow and ordered the release of a man they claimed was being held against his will. Louis Tikas, one of the leaders of the striking miners, went to meet with the militia commander, Lieutenant Karl Linderfelt, at the train station, which was less than one-half mile from the camp. While the meeting was taking place, two companies of militia installed a machine gun on a ridge near the camp and took a position along the rail route that ran past the town. Anticipating trouble, Tikas ran back to the camp and sounded the alarm. The miners, fearing for the safety of the families, went into Ludlow and took their own position behind a small rise created by the railroad tracks. Some of the men also attempted to flank militia position and a firefight soon broke out.

The rattling machine gun blasts and rifle fire lasted for the entire day. The miners were dug in and kept up the return fire, even after the militia was reinforced by non-uniformed company guards later in the afternoon. At dusk, a passing freight train stopped on the tracks in front of the militia's machine gun placements and the miners and their families used this opportunity to flee into the hills to the east.

By 7:00 p.m., the camp was in flames. The militia set the tents on fire and then began looting and searching the camp. Louis Tikas was still there when the fire was started and he and two other men were captured by the militia. Tikas and militia commander Linderfelt had confronted each other several times in the previous months. While two militiamen held Tikas, Linderfelt broke a rifle butt over his head. Tikas and the other two captured miners were later found shot dead. Their bodies lay along the Colorado and Southern Railroad tracks for three days in full view of passing

Ruins of the Ludlow camp

trains. The militia officers refused to allow them to be moved until a local of a railway union demanded they be taken away for burial.

As the smoke cleared on the morning of April 21, strikers and their families returned to the camp to make a grisly discovery. During the battle, four women and 11children had been hiding in a pit beneath one of the tents and had been trapped when the tent above them was set on fire. Two of the women and all of the children suffocated. The smallest victim, Frank Petrucci, was only four months old. These deaths became a rallying cry for the union, who called the incident the "Ludlow Massacre."

In response to the events at Ludlow, the leaders of organized labor in Colorado issued a call to arms, urging union members to acquire "all the arms and ammunition legally available," and a large-scale guerrilla war broke out. Open warfare between striking miners and agents of the coal companies lasted for the next eight months. As many as 199 people, including those at Ludlow, were killed during the Colorado Coalfield War. The fighting finally ended when President Woodrow Wilson sent in federal troops. The troops, who reported directly to Washington and had no ties to the mining companies, disarmed both sides, displacing and often arresting the militia in the process.

The UMWA finally ran out of money, and called off the strike on December 10, 1914. In the end, the strikers failed to obtain their demands, the union did not obtain recognition, and many striking workers were replaced by new workers. Over 400 strikers were arrested, 332 of whom were indicted for murder. Only one man, John Lawson was convicted of murder, and that verdict was eventually overturned by the Colorado Supreme Court. There were 22 state militiamen, including 10 officers, who were court-martialed. All were acquitted, except Lieutenant Linderfelt, who was found guilty of assault for his attack on Louis Tikas. However, he was given only a light reprimand.

Although the UMWA failed to win recognition by the company, the strike had a lasting impact both on conditions at the Colorado mines and on labor relations nationally. John D. Rockefeller, Jr. engaged labor relations experts and future Canadian Prime Minister W. L. Mackenzie King to help him develop reforms for the mines and towns, which included paved roads and recreational facilities, as well as worker representation on committees dealing with working conditions, safety, health, and recreation. There was to be no discrimination against workers who had belonged to unions, and the establishment of a company union. The miners voted to accept the Rockefeller plan.

The Ludlow Massacre inspired the book *King Coal* by Upton Sinclair, who loosely based the novel on what happened at Ludlow. Several popular songs have been written and recorded about the events at Ludlow, including "Ludlow Massacre" by Woody Guthrie.

The UMWA eventually bought the site of the Ludlow tent colony in 1916. Two years later, they erected the Ludlow Monument to commemorate those who had died during the strike. The site has since been declared a U.S. National Historic Landmark, but this did not save the nearby community from death. As the coal mines played out, Ludlow eventually faded and vanished on its own.

The town of Ludlow today, about 12 miles northwest of Trinidad, is now a ghost town, a collection of abandoned, ramshackle houses and stores. A dusty dirt road runs though the center of what used to be the town, not far from a desolate stretch of railroad tracks. Is that lonesome sound in the distance that of an oncoming train, or is it the cry of the dead, still calling out for justice after all of these years?

Ludlow is a western "ghost town" that has gained a reputation for its actual ghosts. Many believe the place to be truly haunted, tainted forever by what happened there in 1914. Those who find themselves far off the beaten track and go in search of the monument that was placed at the site of the old tent colony years ago occasionally find themselves coming face to face with the past. It is not uncommon for visitors to report the sounds of mournful cries near the mouth of the canyon, especially cries that seem to be those of children.

A number of years ago, while working on a book about outdoor ghost stories, author Troy Taylor interviewed a hiker who was passing through the ruins of Ludlow one summer evening. It was near dusk when she arrived and started looking for a place to camp for the night. She only had a bedroll with her and planned to sleep out under the stars. She found a place that was not far from the memorial that had been erected by the UMWA and after a sandwich and a bottle of water, lay down to try and get some sleep. She woke up less than an hour later, puzzled as to why her sleep had been disturbed – and then she heard it. Out in the darkness was the clear, piercing sound of a crying infant. The cry was very close by and she quickly turned on her flashlight to look around, half-convinced that it was an injured animal, but there was nothing to be seen – no animals, no babies, nothing. She hurriedly packed her gear and got back on the road.

Whatever was out there in the dark, it had unnerved her so badly that she wanted no part of Ludlow. Even though she was an avid hiker and loved exploring old ghost towns, she never went back to the forgotten town with the terrible history again.

1922: GHOSTS OF HARRISON WOODS
Memories of the Herrin Massacre

One of the most shameful events to ever occur in American history happened in the small southern Illinois town of Herrin in the summer of 1922. It would be a horrific massacre that would garner national outrage and would forever stain the area with blood. It would also leave behind a fearful haunting that would linger in a place outside of town called Harrison Woods for more than three decades after the carnage occurred.

The small town of Herrin was located in the heart of what was once considered coal country. In the surrounding area, rich veins of coal were discovered in the late 1800s. For a time, coal became the chief source of wealth and industry in the region, overshadowing the farms that once dominated the economy.

Despite the prosperity that coal brought, conditions for the miners were less than adequate. The lives and health of their employees were of little concern to the mine owners. Men worked in water up to their knees, in gas-filled rooms, and in unventilated mines, where the air was filthy and filled with toxins. There was no compensation for the accidents that frequently occurred, and the average daily wage was usually less than $2. Then, around 1900, the mineworkers began to organize and form unions to combat the low pay and horrible working conditions. New laws were implemented and wages doubled, tripled, and then rose as high as $15. The standard of living finally began to rise and small towns like Herrin began to prosper.

None of these changes came easy. There were many struggles between the unions and the mine owners, frequently leading to strikes and violence. The workers wanted fair treatment and good pay and the mine owners were interested solely in profits. The two sides often clashed in bloody incidents that sometimes led to murder. But nothing could compare to what happened in Herrin in 1922.

By the early 1920s, the mineworkers' unions were secure in southern Illinois. Around this same time, strip mining came into practice. In this method, large shovels and draglines were used to strip the earth above coal deposits that were close to the surface. In September 1921, William Lester of the Southern Illinois Coal Company opened a new strip mine about halfway between Herrin and Marion. The mine employed fifty workers, all members of the United Mine Workers of America.

On April 1, 1922, the United Mine Workers went on a strike across the country, ceasing all coal-mining operations. Lester, who was deeply in debt with his new operation, was in fear of losing his company, so he negotiated with the local union and they agreed to let him continue taking coal from the ground, as long as he did not try to ship it out. With this stockpile in place, Lester would be able to ship the coal as soon as the strike ended.

By June, the union workers had dredged almost 60,000 tons of coal. The price for the product had risen considerably, thanks to the strike, and the chance for making a big profit was a temptation too great for Lester to resist. He fired all of his union miners and hired fifty strikebreakers and mine guards from Chicago. On June 16, he shipped out sixteen railroad cars of coal, effectively breaking the agreement he had made at the start of the strike.

Word soon got out about what Lester was doing and officials from the United Mine Workers, the state of Illinois, and the Illinois National Guard tried to convince him to stop shipping the coal and honor the arrangement that he had made with the union. Local miners were outraged and began to rally. They knew that if Lester got away with what he was attempting to do, other mine owners would follow suit. If this happened, everything the union had fought for would be lost.

In the days that followed, many people tried to reason with Lester, but he refused to listen. He was contacted repeatedly by Colonel Samuel Hunter of the Illinois National Guard, who warned him that the situation he was causing could be very dangerous. Lester ignored him, as he did the local sheriff, Melvin Thaxton, who also urged him to stop shipping out the coal. Instead of heeding the warning, Hunter advised the sheriff to deputize additional men in case of problems.

Rumbling continued among the local miners. On June 21, a truck carrying eleven armed guards and strikebreakers was ambushed east of Carbondale, at a bridge over the Big Muddy River. A contingent of union workers sprayed the truck with gunfire. Three men were wounded and six others escaped by jumping into the water below the bridge. Newspapers later reported that none of the six men were accounted for.

Later that same day, several hundred miners gathered at the Herrin Cemetery and then marched into town. They looted the local hardware store and gathered up all of the firearms and ammunition they could find. With no law enforcement officers in sight, the mob moved on to the mine. The union men began shooting and gunfire was exchanged with the frightened strikebreakers who were huddling inside the mine complex. Three of the union men were fatally shot.

Throughout the rest of the day, a number of attempts were made to try and defuse the situation. The union men were noncommittal and continued to carry out their siege of the mine. Late in the day, Colonel Hunter received a telephone call from C.K. McDowell, the mine's superintendent. He explained that the mine had been surrounded and shots were being fired. He had been unable to locate Sheriff Thaxton and he begged Hunter to send National Guard troops as soon as possible. Orders were sent down from Hunter's officer and National Guardsmen were initially dispatched to stop the attack and disperse the miners. Before they could leave Carbondale, the troops were recalled when Colonel Hunter received word that the mine operators and workers had worked out a truce. The promise of a truce turned out to be premature.

By evening, more union supporters had arrived at the mine. Colonel Hunter, concerned over the situation and worried about the truce, tried to telephone the mine office, but found that the lines had been cut. Strangely, in spite of the fact that he still could not reach the sheriff, he did not dispatch any soldiers.

The terms of the possible truce had called for the strikebreakers to be safely escorted out of the county. The men inside the mine complex were ready to surrender and somehow, Sheriff Thaxton was finally reached. He reluctantly agreed to check with the mineworkers and see if they would still honor the truce. Then, he decided that the hour was too late. He was tired, and he decided that the situation could wait until morning. He agreed that he would meet with Colonel Hunter and officials from the Carbondale National Guard unit the following morning.

Meanwhile, Hugh Willis, a spokesman for the United Mine Workers of America, arrived in Herrin to take stock of the situation. He addressed the local men and, if anything, made matters even worse. He told them, "God damn them, they ought to have known better than to come down here; but now that they're here, let them take what's coming to them." As far as he was concerned, the strikebreakers deserved whatever they got.

All through the night, mine guards and workmen huddled inside the complex, cowering under empty coal cars and behind piles of railroad ties. Gunshots rang out of the darkness and union miners who slipped into the complex used dynamite to blow up buildings, machinery, and the mine's water plant. Bullets bounced off the steel sides of the rail cars and splintered the wooden ties. The men inside were safe for the time being, but they were trapped with no way out.

At dawn, John E. Shoemaker, the assistant superintendent, and Robert Officer, the mine's timekeeper, ran from the barricade to the office to telephone for help. The line was dead. While they were working on the telephone, bullets ripped into the side of the building where they were hiding. The heavily armed miners had created large piles of dirt in a circle around the mine complex and opened fire from this protected position. The men huddling inside the complex were terrified and begged the superintendent to surrender. McDowell finally agreed.

Bernard Jones, a mine guard, tied a cook's apron to a pole and cautiously came out from behind the barricade where he had been hiding. He asked to speak to the mineworkers' leader, stating that the men inside would surrender with a promise that they could come out of the mine unmolested.

He received a curt reply, "Come on out and we'll get you out of the county."

The guards and workmen behind the barricade threw down their weapons and walked out with their hands raised above their heads. They walked along the railroad tracks and emerged where the spur line entered the mine. The besiegers, consisting of some 500 striking miners and their sympathizers, surged toward them. They searched the prisoners and lined them up two abreast. One of the captives near the end of the line went back to the bunk car and grabbed his satchel. A striker took it from him, telling him that he wouldn't need it where he was going.

The procession started along the railroad line toward Herrin, five miles to the northwest. After a short distance, the prisoners were ordered to lower their hands and take off their hats. The mob began to grow ugly. Some of the strikers fired their guns into the air and swore at the strikebreakers.

At Crenshaw Crossing, a scattering of houses about a half-mile from the mine, they were approached by an armed group of men who threatened to kill the strike-breakers. Cooler heads apparently prevailed and the procession continued on – but things were getting more heated by the minute. Some of the strikers began beatng the prisoners with pistol butts. The union men were angry and were determined not to let the strikebreakers and hated guards get off without some sort of punishment. The workers particularly despised mine superintendent C.K. McDowell, who had previously treated the union men with arrogance and bragged that the mine would stay open whether there was a strike or not. On his forced march, McDowell was repeatedly struck and badly bloodied. His wooden leg made it difficult for him to keep pace, further infuriating his captors. When he reached Moake Crossing, he collapsed and declared that he couldn't go any farther. Two men grabbed McDowell by the arms and pulled him off to one side of the rail line. A few moments later, the captives heard two shots fired. It was later learned that McDowell was shot twice in the chest. One newspaper also reported that he had been beaten with rocks after being shot.

When the procession reached a powerhouse for the Coal Belt Electric Railroad, which connected Herrin, Marion, and Carterville, it came to a halt. The leader of the column announced that the prisoners were going to be systematically executed in groups of four. However, at that moment, an automobile drove up and a man got out. Several of the prisoners would later remember that he was referred to as "Hugh Willis" and "the president."

According to these survivors' accounts, he told the miners not to kill the strikebreakers on the public road. He was reported to have said, "There are too many women and children around to do that. Take them over in the woods and give it to them. Kill all you can." After that, he got back into his car and drove away.

The prisoners were then marched to a cluster of trees known as Harrison Woods, located across the tracks and to the north of the powerhouse. Less than 300 yards into the trees, they came to a fence strung with four strands of barbed wire. A big bearded man in overalls called out, "Here's where you run the gauntlet! Now, damn you, let's see how fast you run between here and Chicago, you damned gutter-bums!"

He fired his gun and an instant later, the woods rang with the sound of rifle and pistol cracks. Several of the terrified strikebreakers fell on the spot. The others began to run. Many of them never even made it to the fence. Others scrambled up and over it or became trapped in the wire, then blasted apart with bullets. The strikebreakers, unfamiliar with the area, plunged into Harrison Woods or ran towards Herrin. The miners tracked them through the trees and continued to slay them, one by one.

Sherman Holman, a guard at the mine, fell during the first volley of gunfire. As he dropped, he fell across the arm of assistant superintendent Shoemaker, who was wounded and unconscious. One of the miners came over and kicked Shoemaker's body. When he realized the man was still breathing, he leaned over and fired his revolver at Shoemaker's head.

William Cairns, another guard, managed to almost make it through the fence before his shirt caught in the barbed wire. He was shot twice as he struggled to free himself. He fell but was still alive and was able to see what was happening around him. Not far away, a strikebreaker, covered in blood, was leaning against a tree, screaming. Each time he screamed, someone shot him. Finally, one of the miners placed a pistol to his head and blew out the back of his skull.

Another guard, Edward Rose, made it through the fence, but fell down on the other side. With the attackers close behind, he tried to lie still and pretend to be dead. One of the union men was not fooled and shot Rose in the back. The wounded man stayed conscious and saw boots stomping on bodies nearby and heard the sound of gunshots, both close and far away, as the mob continued to fire on the fleeing captives. Screams could be heard for a time and then, eventually, they died away.

About 8:30 a.m., a local farmer named Harrison, for whom the woods were named, and his son were working in their barn when they heard a barrage of gunfire to the southeast. As they looked in that direction, they saw a man running toward them, with fifteen or twenty men in pursuit. Several of the pursuers stopped and fired and the first man tumbled to the ground. The Harrisons watched as several of his pursuers dragged the man into the nearby timber. A few minutes later, another group arrived with two prisoners at gunpoint. They walked into the trees and the sound of gunshots followed. After a safe amount of time had passed, the Harrisons walked to the spot where the men had entered the woods. There, they found a body hanging from a tree. Three other bodies were splayed out beneath the dead man's feet.

One of the men who managed to make it over the fence was a mine guard, Patrick O'Rourke, from Chicago. In the woods, he was shot twice, but was still able to move. He hid in the underbrush for a time and his pursuers missed him. When they were gone, he started up the road towards Herrin, when, coming around a bend, a car caught him by surprise. He ran to a nearby farmhouse and hid in the cellar, but his pursuers found him. O'Rourke was pulled from his hiding place and clubbed over the head with a pistol butt. He was dragged to a car and by this time, other cars had stopped. A small crowd gathered and they argued about whether to shoot O'Rourke or hang him. During the argument, one of the new arrivals reported that five other captives had been taken and were being held prisoner at the schoolhouse in Herrin. O'Rourke's captors decided to take him there.

In the schoolyard, the six prisoners were forced to take off their shoes. One of the union men forced a captive who was a World War I veteran to remove his Army shirt. The prisoners were then ordered to crawl on their hands and knees for fifty or sixty feet, and then they were allowed to walk again, but without their shoes. About 200 people had gathered by this time, including many women and children. The prisoners were then marched to the Herrin Cemetery. The crowd was vicious as the men stumbled along the road. They were kicked and beaten as children screamed curses and called them "scabs."

At the cemetery, the march stopped. As the prisoners stood along the road bordering the burial ground, several members of the mob came up with a rope and tied them together. Once more, they were forced to march, but had only gone a short distance when word spread through the mob that the sheriff was on his way. An angry taunt came from the crowd, "God damn you, if you've never prayed before, you'd better do it now!"

Several shots were fired. O'Rourke was hit again and he fell, pulling the other five men to the ground with him. Shots continued to ring out and bullets pounded into the bodies of the fallen men. After they had fallen quiet, one of the union men filled the magazine of his pistol and methodically fired into each man. When a few of the men moved about and showed signs of life, one of the bystanders took a large knife from his pocket and slashed the throats of those who still lived. It was a scene of unbelievable horror.

A little while later, Don Ewing, a Chicago newspaper reporter, arrived at the cemetery. O'Rourke and a man named Hoffman, both partially conscious, were calling for water. Ewing found a small pail, filled it from a nearby hose, and started to give Hoffman a drink. A bystander appeared, pointed a rifle at the reporter, and forced him away. A young woman holding a baby taunted the dying man, telling him that she would see him in hell before he got any water. As she spoke, she casually pressed her foot down on the man's body. Blood bubbled out of his wounds and he moaned in agony.

Another man emerged from the crowd, offering to give the men a drink. He opened his pants and began to urinate into the faces of the victims.

During all of this, Sheriff Thaxton was noticeably absent. When he failed to meet Colonel Hunter and Major Davis, they went looking for him. The three men soon arrived at the mine to find the operation in flames. They were able to follow the footsteps of the mob and found a trail of bodies left behind. Those who had not died were taken to Herrin Hospital. The dead (eighteen of them on the first day and one more who was found on the next) were taken to a vacant storeroom downtown. They were stripped, washed, laid on pine boxes and covered with sheets. Then the doors were opened and, for hours, men and women, some carrying babies in their arms, filed past; many of them spit on the dead men. The dead were buried in a common grave in the Herrin Cemetery. Their identities remain unknown to this day.

Word quickly spread across the country about the terrible events. Newspapers and officials cried for justice. Editorials railed against the viciousness of the attack, congressman took the opportunity to attack the unions and President Warren G. Harding denounced it as "butchery ... wrought in madness."

Area miners remained stoic and remorseless. When a newspaper reporter asked a miner how many men had been killed, he replied, "No one was killed at all. We didn't kill them. They just dropped dead of fright when we surrounded the mine." A woman from the area told the same reporter, "One of these days, people will realize that it doesn't pay to break a strike in Williamson County."

The coroner's reports on the massacre ruled that the strikebreakers were killed by "unknown individuals" and declared that the deaths had been caused by the actions of the Southern Illinois Coal Company and not the striking miners. These findings further outraged some factions of the public and several months later, pressure forced a grand jury to indict six men for the murder of one of the strikebreakers. The prosecutor used eyewitness testimony from surviving workers to present his case, but the defense managed to justify the mob's actions. A jury acquitted all six of the defendants.

The press and public officials outside of the area were again infuriated and called for a new trial, which took place in 1923. By this time, public interest in the case had waned, but the prosecutor again tried the same six defendants, although this time for the murder of another strikebreaker. Reliable testimony was once again presented, but once more, the defense attorney justified the mob's actions. The jury was convinced and the defendants were again set free.

Still not satisfied, the Illinois House of Representatives launched its own investigation of the incident on April 11, 1923. The committee drilled the military, police officers, and former sheriff Melvin Thaxton, who was now the county treasurer. All of them claimed that they could do nothing to stop the massacre and were unable to find out who was responsible. Jake Jones, a Herrin policeman admitted knowing about the massacre but claimed that he was unable to stop it. Committee members remarked that he ought to have been indicted for complicity in the murders of the slain men.

The members of the committee soon ran out of patience with the witnesses. Chairman Frank A. McCarthy put into record the statement that he had been practicing law for eighteen years and had never seen more reluctant witnesses. All told, some sixty witnesses appeared before the investigating committee. Mine owner William Lester refused to testify, Hugh Willis left the state and could not be called, and one deputy sheriff and two Herrin policemen moved out of the area after appearing. But what testimony they did obtain was enough for the committee to be able to reach some conclusions about the incident.

After the hearings, the committee drew up a report that became a comprehensive account of what occurred on June 22 and the days surrounding the massacre. It assigned blame to a number of people and entities. The Illinois Adjutant General, Carlos E. Black, was blamed for not taking personal charge before the massacre and ordering out troops. He had been on vacation at the time and had left matters in the hands of Colonel Hunter, who was heavily blamed by the committee. In the words of the committee, Hunter was "absolutely incompetent, unreliable, and unworthy to perform the duties assigned to him." Sheriff Thaxton and his deputies were "criminally negligent" and all of the local police officers were "absolutely derelict in their duty." Hugh Willis, they believed, should have been convicted of murder. If he, and other union officials, "had been prompted by high and lofty motives," the disaster could have easily been prevented. Lester, on the other hand, was not absolved from blame. His greed and foolhardiness were sharply condemned.

The report was filed, but nothing was ever done about it. Union sympathizers in the Illinois House and Senate managed to torpedo the investigation, which infuriated the committee. They had only one last bitter comment to make, stating that they hoped the lawmakers who sabotaged their work would "be replaced by men of high moral stamina and courage, who will think more of the protection of the fair name of the state of Illinois than their own selfish political ambitions."

And the Herrin Massacre simply became another blood-soaked page in the history of Illinois.

Perhaps because no one was ever brought to justice for their role in the massacre, legend states that many of the victims of the day's events have refused to rest in peace. The horrific violence of their deaths, combined with the fact that many were never identified and were buried in unmarked, common graves, apparently left unsettled spirits behind for many years.

For more than thirty years after the massacre, travelers and nearby residents who passed by Harrison Woods at night claimed to see the shadowy figures of the murder victims moving among the dark trees. Their screams, cries and moans, often accompanied by mysterious gunshots were also heard on occasion. During this time, locals avoided the woods, likely both because of their fear of the angry spirits and their own guilt about the events that had occurred.

The stories continued until the 1950s, when they began to die out. Stories of ghosts were replaced with a macabre ritual that occurred every Halloween night, when local boys would hoist dummies into the trees in a sort of twisted homage to the massacre. Today, Harrison Woods has been replaced by a subdivision and homes now stand where men once bled and died.

And the spirits of the past seem to have finally crossed over to another time and place.

1927: HELL CAME TO MICHIGAN
The Horror of the Bath School Massacre

It has been said that in life, only two things are certain: death and taxes. In the case of the horror that befell a Michigan town one spring morning in 1927, it was a deranged man's fury over taxes that resulted in the deaths of 45 people.

On May 18, 1927, hell came to the village of Bath, Michigan.

The community was forever changed when a bomb went off in the basement of the local consolidated school, followed by a car bomb blast. The explosions killed 38 school children, two teachers, four other adults and the bomber himself. The deaths, which occurred two days prior to Charles Lindberg's historic flight across the Atlantic, still constitute the deadliest act of mass murder in a school in American history.

The perpetrator was a farmer named Andrew P. Kehoe who was upset over a property tax that had been levied to build the consolidated school. He ran for and was elected to the board of education, where he tried unsuccessfully to get the school portion of his property taxes reduced. Soon the higher taxes, coupled with his wife's medical expenses, caused him to lose his farm. It was too much for Kehoe to take and he started plotting revenge.

With the recent concern over school violence in our country, we yearn for "the old days," when small-town life was peaceful and schoolchildren were safe from harm. The story of the Bath School Massacre serves as a bitter reminder that the good old days were not always good.

Andrew Kehoe and his wife, Nellie

Andrew Kehoe was born in Tecumseh, Michigan, on February 1, 1872. One of 13 children, he had a troubled life. His mother passed away when he was very young and while his father later remarried, Kehoe and his stepmother never got along. One day, when Kehoe was 14, his stepmother attempted to light an oil stove in the kitchen. The stove exploded and set her on fire. Kehoe simply stood and watched her burn. After a few minutes, he doused her with a bucket of water, which put out the fire. Gravely injured, she later died. It would later be speculated that Kehoe had something to do with the malfunction of the stove.

He attended Tecumseh High School and went on to Michigan State College in East Lansing, where he met his future wife, Nellie Price. He later moved out West for a few years and spent some time in St. Louis, where he suffered a severe head injury as the result of a fall in 1911. He was attending electrical school at the time of the accident. Kehoe was in a coma for two months. Whether this injury contributed to Kehoe's madness will never be known, but it certainly seems possible. His behavior became more and more erratic after the fall, even though he physically recovered.

When Kehoe returned to Michigan, he married Nellie. She came from a rather wealthy family, which owned several pieces of property in Clinton Township. Eventually, Andrew and Nellie bought 185 acres from an uncle's estate. The property was located just outside of the unincorporated village of Bath. Kehoe quickly gained a reputation for his intelligence, cleanliness and rather odd behavior. He was quick to help people, but equally quick to be critical when he didn't get his own way. He was intelligent able to easily articulate his views, but had little patience for ideas that did not agree with his own. He was habitually neat and often changed his shirt twice a day. He liked to tinker with machinery, especially with electrical gadgets. He seemed happiest when repairing or adjusting the machinery on his farm. New ways of carrying out familiar chores intrigued him and he was constantly looking for ways to improve the farm. But there were troubling reports from some of his neighbors that Kehoe was cruel to his farm animals and once beat a horse to death.

Kehoe also gained a reputation for being tight with a dollar, a trait that helped him get elected to the school board in 1926. One the board, Kehoe constantly campaigned for lower taxes because he claimed the current taxes were causing him financial hardship. His creditors tried to work out a payment plan with him, but were unsuccessful. Soon, he stopped paying his mortgage and homeowner's insurance premiums. To complicate matters, Nellie Kehoe was chronically ill with tuberculosis. She required frequent hospital stays, which wiped out what little savings they had left. Kehoe was sure that they would

Bath Consolidated School, which Kehoe inexplicably blamed for all of his financial troubles.

lose the farm and plunge even deeper into debt. In his mind, high property taxes were the source of all of his financial woes. He saw nothing good come from the taxes and believed that many of the town's expenditures were wasteful and pointless. But above all, without any valid reason, he blamed the five-year-old Bath Consolidated School for his troubles.

Throughout the country during this era, most of the one-room schools, where different grades shared the same classroom and teacher, were starting to close down. There was beginning to be a widespread belief that children would receive a better education if all the students from a region could instead be educated at a single facility, with the students divided by age into grades. After years of debate and planning, the local district built a new school called the Bath Consolidated School. A school tax was levied to pay for the project and as a result, property owners like Andrew Kehoe had to pay.

Kehoe argued against the new school and complained constantly about the increase in taxes, stating that they were illegal and unfair. He considered at least one of his fellow school board members to be his bitter enemy – board president Emory E. Huyck. Kehoe claimed that Huyck was influencing the other members of the board to vote for higher taxes. Kehoe became obsessed with school board politics, Emory Huyck and the injustice of property taxes, which he believed were ruining his life.

No one knows for sure when Kehoe conceived the idea for the bombing, but based on the activity at the school and the purchase of explosives, his plan had probably been underway for at least a year. He probably started working things out in the winter of 1926, when the board asked him to perform maintenance inside the school building. Regarded as a talented handyman, he was known to be especially good at installing electrical wiring. As a board member appointed to conduct repairs, he had free access to the building and his presence was never questioned.

At some point that summer, Kehoe began purchasing large quantities of pyrotol, an incendiary explosive that was first used during World War I. Farmers often used it for excavation, so Kehoe's purchases of small amounts of the surplus explosive at different stores on different dates did not raise any suspicions. Neighbors reported hearing explosions on Kehoe's farm, which he explained by saying he was removing tree stumps. No one thought this was odd and no one questioned it when he drove to Lansing in November 1926 and bought two boxes of dynamite at a sporting goods store.

Throughout the spring of 1927, Kehoe began to transport the pyrotol into Bath School. He did so in small

The Kehoe farmhouse before it was set on fire.

(Below) A sign that Kehoe left in the fence at the farm, discovered by investigators after the explosion.

increments and no one noticed anything out of the ordinary. He calculated exactly what he needed each day and brought just that amount. He had volunteered to fix the wiring in the school's basement and what a wiring job he did! He wired the explosives throughout the basement, connecting various charges of explosives beneath the floors and in the basement rafters. He slithered into the sub-floors and crawlspaces beneath the school, hiding large amounts of pyrotol behind pipes and beams. Over time, he managed to run thousands of feet of wire throughout the building. Under the feet of unsuspecting children, Kehoe placed over 1,000 pounds of dynamite.

The horrific project was completed in early May. Kehoe set the charges and waited. During this time, he also wired his home in the same manner. In every structure on the farm, he rigged a series of firebombs – crude devices made from containers filled with gasoline and wired with automobile spark plugs attached to a car battery.

On May 17, he drove his car over to the front of his barn and loaded the back seat with metal debris. He threw in nails, old tools, pieces of farm machinery and anything else capable of creating shrapnel in an explosion. When the back seat was filled with bits and pieces of metal, Kehoe packed dozens of wrapped sticks of dynamite under the front seat and placed a loaded rifle on the passenger's seat next to him.

After he completed this grim task, he set out on another, bloodier one. Records at Lansing's St. Lawrence Hospital revealed that Nellie Kehoe had been discharged on May 16. On the afternoon of the following day, Kehoe killed his wife by hitting her over the head with a blunt object. The exact nature of the object was never determined, because the ever-thorough Kehoe burned his house, barn and outbuildings to the ground. After killing his wife (doubtlessly making a mental checkmark as he did so) Kehoe dumped her body into a wheelbarrow and pushed it over to the back of the chicken coop. Piled around her on the cart were silverware, jewelry and a metal cash box containing the ashes of burned bank notes. After abandoning his wife's body, Kehoe completed wiring the farm to explode. He had placed one of his homemade firebombs in every building and if all went according to plan, his property would simultaneously explode and burn to the ground before help could arrive.

The house, barn, outbuildings and even the farm animals that had been tied in their enclosures would be destroyed. There would be nothing left for the bank to foreclose on.

On the morning of May 18, the children began arriving at the consolidated school at about 8:00 a.m. To the students, it was a day like any other. They laughed and talked, pushed and shoved in the hallways and hurried to their classrooms. They had no way of knowing that – just inches beneath their feet – more than 1,000 pounds of dynamite waited for an electrical current that would start a chain reaction that would change their lives forever.

Meanwhile, about two miles from the school, Kehoe took the next step in his dance of death. At approximately 8:45 a.m., he detonated the firebombs on the farm. The place exploded into flames, sending smoke, fire and debris into the air. Burning streamers of flame fell from the sky, raining down on the farm across the road. The neighbors, hearing the explosion, ran to Kehoe's farm to offer assistance but as they hurried down the driveway, Kehoe was already behind the wheel of his car. He calmly looked at them through the open window and said, "Boys, you are my friends. You better get out of here. You better go down to the school." Kehoe roared away, leaving his confused neighbors and a farm completely engulfed in flames, behind him.

As Kehoe drove away, another tremendous explosion, much larger than the first, was heard in the distance. The sound, it was later said, was heard for 10 miles in every direction. The Bath Consolidated School had been blown up. O.H. Buck, who had run to the Kehoe farm after the first series of blasts, heard the massive explosion of the school. He later told reporters, "I began to feel as if the world was coming to an end."

And for many, it was.

Before the dust from the explosion had been able to settle, townspeople were already digging through the rubble of the school. The sound of children screaming and moaning could be heard coming from the ruins. Fully half the building, the northwest wing, was gone. The walls were destroyed and the roof lay on the ground. Bodies of children could be seen protruding from the bricks and stone, little arms and legs only partially visible. Faces covered with blood and dust peered through the broken windows and from between splintered beams of wood.

Frantic mothers ran screaming to the scene, for almost every family in town had at least one child enrolled at the school. The sobbing of trapped children could be heard as some of the mothers fought with rescuers to pull their children from the wreckage. Men worked feverishly in the mountain of rubble, tossing aside bricks and pushing twisted metal as they searched for survivors.

Monty Ellsworth, a neighbor of the Kehoe, recounted, "There was a pile of children of about five or six under the roof and some of them had arms sticking out, some had legs, and some just their heads sticking out. They were unrecognizable because they were covered with dust, plaster, and blood. There were not enough of us to move the roof." Ellsworth volunteered to drive back to his farm and

The remains of Kehoe's car, which he had also caused to explode outside of the school.

retrieve the heavy rope that was needed to pull the structure off the children's bodies. On his way back to the farm, Ellsworth reported seeing a cheery-looking Kehoe driving into town toward the school. Ellsworth said, "He grinned and waved his hand; when he grinned, I could see both rows of his teeth."

Less than 30 minutes after the explosion, Kehoe arrived on the scene. No one knew that his car had been loaded with dynamite and metal debris. He got out of his car and saw his nemesis, board president Emory Huyck. Kehoe waved and called him over to the car. As he approached, Kehoe picked up the rifle from the seat next to him, aimed it at the dynamite and fired. Another terrible explosion rocked the town. A huge ball of flame shot upwards and shrapnel was sent flying in every direction, ripping apart trees, splintering houses, shattering windows and cutting down everything in its path. Emory Huyck and town postmaster Glen Smith were instantly killed. Kehoe was almost totally obliterated. An eight-year-old student named Cleo Clayton, still dazed from the first blast, was walking along the street when the second explosion occurred. He was struck in the stomach by a large piece of metal from the blast. He died a few hours later.

The people working at the rubble of the school were panicked and confused. No one understood what had happened, most imagining that they were under some sort of military attack. Rumors swept through the crowd about more explosions to come. In the distance, Kehoe's farm was still burning, sending a column of black smoke high into the air. Smaller explosions could still be heard from the farm as Kehoe's leftover pyrotol continued to explode. Across the street from the school, trees, houses and parked cars were on fire from the original blast. Pieces of bodies were strewn on the grass and in the bushes and many people had fainted or had become hysterical. Over 100 people had been injured and more injuries were being found every minute. At that point, no one had any idea just how many had been killed.

Minutes after Kehoe's car exploded, the Lansing fire and police departments arrived on the scene. They were followed by the Michigan State Police and representatives of the state department of public safety, but nothing could have prepared these hardened veterans for what they saw: wrecked and burning cars, downed trees, a collapsed school building that was filled with screaming children, fires everywhere. It was like a battle scene from some distant war – or a taste of hell.

Local physician Dr. J.A. Crum and his wife, a nurse, had both served in World War I, and had returned to Bath to open a pharmacy. After the explosion the Crums turned their drugstore into a triage center. Private citizens were enlisted to use their automobiles as additional ambulances to take survivors and family members to area hospitals.

A short distance away from Kehoe's destroyed car, Mrs. Frank Smith stood in front of her home watching in horror as the events took place before her eyes. In the corner of her garden, amidst the flowers and shrubs, she saw a crumpled mass of bloody clothing. As she looked closer, she saw that it was part of a human body, mangled almost beyond recognition. Protruding from a rear pocket of the clothing, she saw some papers and carefully removed them. When she looked over the papers, she saw that part of it was a bankbook from the Lilley State Bank of Tecumseh. Andrew Kehoe's name was on it. Mrs. Smith ran over to a police officer who was directing rescue efforts at the school, and he brought over some of Kehoe's neighbors to view the body. A positive identification was made. They finally understood Kehoe's odd words to them as he drove away from his burning farm. He had urged them to go to the school. They could have never imagined what he had planned there.

Hundreds of people climbed through the wreckage that day in an effort to rescue the children pinned underneath. Area contractors had sent all their men to assist, and many ordinary people came to the scene in response to the pleas for help. The injured and dying were transported to Sparrow Hospital and St. Lawrence Hospital in Lansing. Michigan Governor Fred Green arrived during the afternoon of the disaster and assisted in the relief work, carting bricks away from the scene. The Lawrence Baking Company of Lansing sent a truck filled with pies and sandwiches, which were served to rescuers in the township's community hall.

As policeman, firefighters and volunteers searched through the rubble, desperately looking for survivors, a chilling discovery was made in the midst of the ruined basement: a huge cache of unexploded dynamite. State Police officers who emerged from the basement of the school with a bushel basket filled with dynamite informed everyone that there was even more still inside, still attached to a battery and a clock. The rescue efforts suddenly came to a halt as the area around the school was cleared. Working frantically in the broken beams and shattered concrete, fearing they could be blown up at any moment, police officers carefully dismantled what remained of Kehoe's mad plan. They carried out 504 pounds of dynamite, along with wires and detonating devices. The pyrotol had been divided up into eight different bombs which were hidden in various spots on the south end of the school. Experts later theorized that the first blast had caused some sort of short circuit, which made the additional bombs malfunction. If the rest of the dynamite had gone off, the school would have been completely demolished and the death toll would have surely been in the hundreds.

Slowly, the bodies of the dead were carried out of the ruins of the Bath Consolidated School. They were placed in neat rows on the scorched grass and hastily covered up. A short distance from this grim scene, Mrs. Eugene Hart sat in the street, with her two little dead girls, one in each

The unexploded dynamite that was found inside of the school after the initial blast. If it had gone off, there may have been no survivors of the massacre.

arm, and her son lying dead in her lap. One of the police officers at the scene later told newspapers, "There were sights that I hope no one will ever have to look at again."

The bodies of the children were taken one by one to the township hall, which served as a temporary morgue. Dazed parents were brought in to identify the remains of children, some of whom were horribly burned and disfigured by the blast.

The following day, police and fire officials gathered at the Kehoe farm to investigate the fires. On May 19, the body of Nellie Kehoe was found. Her body was so disfigured that she first went unnoticed by everyone who walked past her. She had been burned almost beyond recognition. Her left arm and her right leg were both missing. Only the axle and wheels remained of the cart on which her corpse had been placed. All of the Kehoe farm building had been destroyed and all of the animals that had been trapped in the barns were dead. The amount of unused equipment and materials on the property reportedly could have easily paid off the mortgage – but Kehoe had been too obsessed with the "unfair" taxes for him to realize it.

As officials searched the property for clues to the devastation, they found a hand-lettered wooden sign that Kehoe had wired to a fence that bore the short message that he likely imagined would explain his actions: "Criminals are made, not born."

All over the world, newspaper headlines announced the shocking tragedy in Bath. The press struggled to find reasons for Kehoe's rampage, but of course, there were none. The Bath community was devastated and the loss could not be measured in simply the number of children that had been killed. There was no one in the community that had not been touched by the tragedy. Everyone had lost a relative, a friend, a classmate or a teacher. In addition to the human toll, Bath faced financial catastrophe. A new school would have to be built. The future now looked bleak.

The American Red Cross, which set up operations at the Crum pharmacy, did what it could to provide aid and comfort for the victims. The Lansing Red Cross headquarters stayed open until 11:30 on the night of the disaster to answer telephone calls, update the list of the dead and injured and provide information. The Red Cross also managed donations that were sent to pay for both the medical expenses of the injured and the burial costs of the dead.

The ruins of the Bath Consolidated School after the explosion. This horrific event is considered to be one of the worst school massacres in American history.

Over the next few days, there was an endless wave of funerals in Bath, with 18 of them being held on Saturday, May 22. The last funeral was held on Sunday, May 23, the same day that Charles Lindbergh completed the first solo transatlantic flight to Paris. This event shared newspaper space with news of the tragedy in Michigan. Over 100, 000 automobiles passed through Bath that weekend, a staggering amount of traffic for the small village. Some Bath citizens regarded this armada as an unwarranted intrusion into their time of grief, but most accepted it as a show of sympathy and support from surrounding communities. Unfortunately, as with any other tragedy, heartless curiosity-seekers also made their way to town, as did the headline-seekers like the Ku Klux Klan, who proclaimed that the actions of Kehoe, a Roman Catholic, were the result of his adherence to the stance of the Catholic Church against what they considered "Protestant or godless schools."

A coroner's inquest was held the following week. The coroner had arrived at Bath on the day of the disaster and had sworn in six community leaders to serve as the investigative jury. The Clinton County prosecutor conducted the examination and dozens of Bath citizens and law enforcement personnel testified before the jury. Although there was never a doubt that Andrew Kehoe had carried out the bombing, the jury was asked to determine if the school board or any of its employees were guilty of criminal negligence.

The testimony lasted for more than a week and in the end, the jury exonerated the school board and its employees. In the verdict, the jury concluded that Kehoe "conducted himself sanely and so concealed his operations that there was no cause to suspect any of his actions; and we further find that the school board, and Frank Smith, janitor of the school building, were not negligent in and about their duties, and were not guilty of any negligence in not discovering Kehoe's plan."

It was determined that Kehoe had murdered Emory Huyck on the morning of May 18. They also found that the school was destroyed as part of a plan that was carried out by Kehoe alone, without the aid of conspirators, and that he had willfully caused the death of 44 people, including his wife, Nellie. On August 22, some three months after the bombing, fourth-grader Beatrice Gibbs died following hip surgery. It was the final death attributed to the Bath School Massacre.

The jury returned a judgment of suicide as the cause of Andrew Kehoe's death. His body was eventually claimed by his sister. Without any ceremony, he was buried in an unmarked grave in an initially unnamed cemetery. Later, it was revealed that Kehoe was buried in the pauper's section of Mount Rest Cemetery in St. Johns, Michigan. Nellie Kehoe was buried in Mount Hope Cemetery in Lansing by her family. Her tombstone bears her maiden name of Price.

The people of Bath were left with no other choice but to move on. Governor Fred Green created the Bath Relief Fund with the money supplied by donors, the state and local governments. Scores of people from all over the country donated to the fund, which eventually allowed for the demolition of the damaged portion of the school and the construction of a new wing with the donated funds.

School resumed on September 5, 1927 and for the first school year, classes were held in the community hall, the township hall and two retail buildings. Most of the students returned. An architect from Lansing, Warren Holmes, donated plans for a new school and the school board approved contracts for a new building on September 14. On September 15, Michigan's Republican U.S. Senator James J. Couzens presented a personal check for $75,000 to the Bath construction fund and the school's new wing was named in his honor.

In 1928, artist Carlton W. Angell presented the board with a statue called "Girl with a Cat". The statute currently rests in the Bath School Museum, which is located in the school district's middle school, adjacent to the bombing site. Angell's inscription on the piece stated that it was dedicated to the courage and determination of the people of Bath. The sculpture was funded by donated pennies from students all over Michigan. According to legend, the pennies were melted down and used to cast the statue.

In 1975, the new school was also torn down and a small park was created, dedicated to the victims of the tragedy. At the center of the park is the cupola of the original building, the only part that has been preserved. At the entrance to the park is a bronze plaque that contains the names of all of the children who were killed on that terrible day.

The parents of those children survived the massacre, but their lives were never the same again. Some of them moved away from Bath in the years that followed, but it's unlikely they ever really escaped their horrible memories. For those who stayed behind, the bloody history of that day was always present and to many people, the community remains a place where death came calling on what should have been a beautiful spring day. Instead, it became the day when the twisted obsessions of a dangerous man claimed the lives of dozens of innocent people and forever stained the landscape of rural Michigan.

With a horrific event such as the Bath School Massacre, it's no surprise that ghostly tales and legends have sprung up around the scene of the disaster. According to stories, people claim to have had many experiences at the park where the two schools once stood. Voices are heard, as well as cries for help, and recordings have been obtained that allegedly contain the eerie voices of the lost, still seeking help after decades have passed. Unexplained cold spots are also felt -- as well as the strange touch of unseen hands, as if they are reaching out from beyond the grave.

And, according to first-hand accounts, the massacre site is not the only place in Bath that is haunted. A funeral home on Main Street, where many of the bodies of the victims were prepared for burial, was turned into an apartment house many years after the massacre. A tenant who moved into the place in 2000 began to experience odd happenings in the house, starting almost from the night she moved in. As she climbed into bed that night, she felt the unsettling stare of someone watching her -- and things were never the same after that.

She began hearing footsteps going up and down stairs that had been removed years before and voices coming from the basement. Toilets flushed by themselves, water faucets turned on and off and she claimed to hear the sobbing and crying of children. When she heard the sound of breaking glass one night, she called the police. Officers came to search the house but when she unlocked the basement door, both men refused to go down and look around. When the landlord came to her the following day and blamed her for damage that had been done in the basement, she showed him the police report and he was as puzzled by the disturbance as she had been.

A short time later, she began seeing the ghosts.

The first victim she saw said that his name was George Hall and that he had been eight years old when he died at the school. According to the witness, George's ghost had no legs. The spirit, she claimed, was a prankster and loved the tenant's cat, along with other animals. There was also a little girl, who was missing a hand and wanted the tenant to look for it. The spirit told her that she had been wearing a ring that was special to her when she died at the school and the ring was still on one of her missing fingers.

During the time she lived in the house, the tenant stated that the ghostly occupants were always nearby and seemed to need something from her -- something that she seemed to be unable to give. They wanted help, she said, but she didn't know how to help them. For reasons that she couldn't understand, the children were unable to rest.

And one has to wonder if they still linger there, unable to find peace after their terrible deaths, still searching for solace and understanding of the bitter crime that took them from this earth.

BIBLIOGRAPHY
& RECOMMENDED READING

A Report on Explosions and the Causes of Explosions, With Suggestions for Their Prevention. For the Citizens of Cincinnati. Alexander Flash. 1838

Akin, Wallace – *The Forgotten Storm;* 1992

Allen, James B. – *The Company Town in the American West;* 1966

Andrews, Thomas G. -- *Killing for Coal: America's Deadliest Labor War,* 2008

Angle, Paul M. – *Bloody Williamson;* 1975

Bachelder, P.D. & Smith, P. S. (2003) Four Short Blasts: The Gale of 1898 and the Loss of the Steamer Portland.

Baillod, Brendan – *Lady Elgin;* 2008

Bellamy, John Stark III – *The Corpse in the Cellar;* 1999

--------------------------- - *They Died Crawling;* 1995

--------------------------- - *The Killer in the Attic;* 2002

Bernstein, Arnie – *Bath Massacre: America's First School Bombing;* 2009

Bourdain, Anthony – *Typhoid Mary: An Urban Historical;* 2001

Boyer, Paul – *Legend of John Brown;* 1973

Brown, Alan. (2008). Haunted Texas: Ghosts and Strange Phenomena of the Lone Star State.

Brown, Daniel James – *The Indifferent Stars Above;* 2009

Brust, Beth Wagner – *The Great Molasses Flood;* 1998

Burns, Cherie – *The Great Hurricane: 1938;* 2005

Campbell, Ballard C. – *American Disasters;* 2008

Carr, Stephen – *Historical Guide to Utah Ghost Towns;* 1972

Christian, Reece – *Ghosts of Atlanta,* 2008

Coleman, Christopher K. – *Ghosts & Haunts of the Civil War;* 1999

Country Beautiful, Editors – *Great Fires of America;* 1973

Crocker, H.W., III – *Politically Incorrect Guide to the Civil War;* 2008

Cudahy, Brian -- *The Malbone Street Wreck;* 1999

Cummins, Joseph – *World's Bloodiest History;* 2010

Davis, Kenneth – *Don't Know Much About History;* 1993

Ellsworth, M.J. – *The Bath School Disaster;* 1927

Emanuel, Kerry – *Divine Wind;* 2005

Fitzhugh, Pat. (2009). Ghostly Cries from Dixie.

Fliege, Stu – *Tales & Trails of Illinois;* 2002

Fuchs, Richard L. – *An Unerring Fire: Massacre at Fort Pillow;* 2002

Funk, N.R. (1913). A Pictorial History of the Great Dayton Flood: March 25, 26, 27, 1913. Dayton, OH

Gado, Mark – *Hell Comes to Bath;* 2008

Genzmer, Herbert, Sybille Kershner, Christian Schultz – *Great Disasters in History,* 2007

Gero, David. (2006). Aviation Disasters: The World's Major Civil Airliner Crashes Since 1950.

Haine, Edgar A. (2000). Disaster in the Air.

Hartley, Robert E. and David Kenney – *Death Underground;* 2006

Horwitz, Tony – *John Brown's Legacy / American History;* 2011

Howe, Henry. (1888) Historical Collections of OHIO in Two Volumes.

Hunt, Joan & Winn Wendell – *Winter Quarters Mine Explosion;* 2000

Hurd, D. Hamilton. (1888). History of Essex County, Massachusetts: With Biographical Sketches of Many of its Pioneers and Prominent Men. Volume 1.

Kent, Donna – *Ghosts & Legends of Eastern Connecticut;* 2007

Krakauer, John – *Under the Banner of Heaven;* 2003

Lankford, Andrea – *Haunted Hikes;* 2006

Laskin, David – *The Children's Blizzard;* 2004

Leavitt, Judith Walzer -- *Typhoid Mary;* 1996

Lloyd, James. (1856) Steamboat Directory and Disasters on the Western Waters.

Long, Priscilla -- *Where the Sun Never Shines;* 1991

Marcher, B & Marcher, F. (2004). The Great Sea Island Storm of 1893.

Martelle, Scott -- *Blood Passion;* 2007

Metts, Craig G. (2012). The Great Sea Islands Hurricane & Tidal Wave.

Mulligan, T. P. August 2001. Happy Land Fire: Have We Learned the Lessons? Fire Engineering (Pg. 89-98)

Munn, Debra – *Montana Ghost Stories;* 1991

Nash, Jay Robert – *Darkest Hours;* 1976

Oates, Stephen – *To Purge this Land with Blood;* 1970

Oickle, Alvin F. (2008). The Pemberton Casualties.

Online Blog: Wreck of the Broker: The Book Project. Blogger: Gordon Bond.

Parker, Grant -- *Mayday, History of a Village Holocaust;* 1992

Pisacretta, Sharon – *Doomed by the Lake;* 2011

Pletcher, Larry – *Massachusetts Disasters;* 2006

Rarick, Ethan – *Desperate Passage;* 2008

Rea, Tom – *Thunder Under the House;* 2010

Reece, Bob – *Visitors of Another Kind;* 1991

Reed, Robert C. – *Train Wrecks;* 1978

Rosenberg, Jennifer – *Typhoid Mary,* 2011

Satter, Geoffrey -- *The Grim Reaper's Visits to Oklahoma's Coal Mines;* 2000

Schultz-Williams, Docia. Ghosts Along the Texas Coast

Scotti, R.A. – *Sudden Sea: The Great Hurricane of 1938;* 2004

Spegnesi, Stephen J. – *100 Greatest Disasters of All Time;* 2002

Strub, Sherry – *Milwaukee Ghosts;* 2008

Taylor, Troy – *Down in the Darkness*; 2003
-------------- - *Into the Shadows;* 2002
--------------- - *Out Past the Campfire Light;* 2004
--------------- - *Spirits of the Civil War;* 1999
Thompson, George – *Some Dreams Die: Utah's Ghost Towns & Lost Treasures;* 2006
Thurber, James – *My Life and hard Times;* 1933
Vogel, Charity – *The Angola Train Wreck*, American History; 2007
Ward, Andrew – *River Run Red: The Fort Pillow Massacre in the American Civil War;* 2005
Williams, J; West, S & Taylor, J. 1969. *The Redeemed Captive Returning to Zion, or, The Captivity and Deliverance of Rev. John Williams of Deerfield.* 1969 Reprint of 1908 edition of Williams' narrative.

Personal Interviews & Correspondence

Newspapers & Periodicals
American Heritage Magazine
Billings Gazette (Montana)
Boston Almanac and Business Directory (1962)
Boston Globe
Brockton Enterprise (Massachusetts)
Chicago Tribune
Cleveland Plain-Dealer
Cleveland Press
Dayton Daily News Archive of Past Articles / A Day of Horror
Dunkirk Evening Observer
Huntingdon Daily News
Joplin News Herald (Missouri)
London Times
Long Beach Independent (California)
Natchez Democrat (Mississippi)
New York Times
Norwich Sun. (New Jersey)
Oakland Tribune (California)
Ogden Standard Examiner (Utah)
Ohio Journal
Popular Mechanics – The Tri-State Tornado (June 2007)
Portland Evening Express Archives
Scribner's Magazine
Sun-Advocate (Price, Utah)
The Post Standard (Syracuse, New York)
The San Antonio Express News (Texas)
Utah Historic Quarterly

Special Thanks: to:
Jill Hand - Editor
Michael Schwab -- Cover Design
April Slaughter
Elyse Horath
Rachael Horath
Bethany Horath
Allison Jornlin
Mike Chapman
Orrin Taylor

Haven & Helayna Taylor 🐢

ABOUT THE AUTHORS

Troy Taylor is an occultist, crime buff, supernatural historian and the author of almost 90 books on ghosts, hauntings, history, crime and the unexplained in America.

He is also the founder of the American Ghost Society and the owner of the American Hauntings Tour company.

Taylor shares a birthday with one of his favorite authors, F. Scott Fitzgerald, but instead of living in New York and Paris like Fitzgerald, Taylor grew up in Illinois. Raised on the prairies of the state, he developed an interest in "things that go bump in the night" at an early age and as a young man, began developing ghost tours and writing about hauntings and crime in Chicago and Central Illinois. His writings have now taken him all over the country and into some of the most far-flung corners of the world.

He began his first book in 1989, which delved into the history and hauntings of his hometown of Decatur, Illinois, and in 1994, it spawned the Haunted Decatur Tour -- and eventually led to the founding of his Illinois Hauntings Tours (with current tours in Alton, Chicago, Decatur, Lebanon, Springfield & Jacksonville) and the American Hauntings Tours, which travel all over the country in search of haunted places. He is also one of the owners of the haunted Avon Theater in Decatur, Illinois.

Along with writing about the unusual and hosting tours, Taylor has also presented on the subjects of ghosts, hauntings and crime for public and private groups. He has also appeared in scores of newspaper and magazine articles about these subjects and in hundreds of radio and television broadcasts about the supernatural. Taylor has appeared in a number of documentary films, several television series and in one feature film about the paranormal.

When not traveling to the far-flung reaches of the country, Troy resides in Decatur, Illinois.

Rene' Kruse has lived in small towns in the Midwest and Texas but has lived in southwestern Pennsylvania for the past 20 years. She holds a PhD from Texas A&M and teaches Applied Engineering and Technology at California University of Pennsylvania when she is not watching over her 4 children and 2 grandchildren.

Rene' has been fascinated in ghosts and all things haunted for as long as she can remember and has been actively investigating haunted sites for over 30 years. Since her first investigation in 1976, she has been involved in nearly 250 investigations in 23 states. She has had the opportunity to meet and work with some of the most respected paranormal investigators from around the country.

Whitechapel Productions Press is a division of Dark Haven Entertainment and a small press publisher, specializing in books about ghosts and hauntings. Since 1993, the company has been one of America's leading publishers of supernatural books and has produced such best-selling titles as *Haunted Illinois, The Ghost Hunter's Guidebook, Ghosts on Film, Confessions of a Ghost Hunter, The Haunting of America, Sex & the Supernatural* the *Dead Men Do Tell Tales* crime series and many others.

With more than a dozen different authors producing high quality books on all aspects of ghosts, hauntings and the paranormal, Whitechapel Press has made its mark with America's ghost enthusiasts.

You can visit Whitechapel Productions Press online and browse through our selection of ghostly titles, plus get information on ghosts and hauntings, haunted history, spirit photographs, information on ghost hunting and much more. by visiting the internet website at:

WWW.WHITECHAPELPRESS.COM

Founded in 1994 by author Troy Taylor, the American Hauntings Tour Company (which includes the Illinois Hauntings Tours) is America's oldest and most experienced tour company that takes ghost enthusiasts around the country for excursions and overnight stays at some of America's most haunted places.

In addition to our tours of America's haunted places, we also offer tours of Illinois' most haunted cities, including Chicago, Alton, Decatur, Lebanon and Jacksonville. These award-winning ghost tours run all year around, with seasonal tours only in some cities.

AMERICAN HAUNTINGS TOURS

Find out more about tours, and make reservations online, by visiting the internet website at:

WWW.AMERICAN HAUNTINGS.ORG

CPSIA information can be obtained at www.ICGtesting.com
Printed in the USA
LVOW050007260512

283387LV00004B/1/P